The Capitalist Self

In this radical reinterpretation of the financial revolution, Craig Muldrew redefines our understanding of capitalism as a socially constructed set of institutions and beliefs. Financial institutions, including the Bank of England and the stock market, were just one piece of the puzzle. Institutional developments, changes in local credit networks involving better accounting, paper notes, and increased mortgaging were even more important. Muldrew argues that, before a society can become capitalist, most of its members have to have some engagement with 'capital' as a thing – a form of stored intangible financial value. He shows how previous oral interpersonal credit was transformed into capital through the use of accounting and circulating paper currency, socially supported by changing ideas about the self that stressed individual savings and responsibility. It was only through changes throughout society that the framework for a concept like capitalism could exist and make sense.

Craig Muldrew is Professor of Early Modern Social and Economic History at the University of Cambridge. He is the author of *The Economy of Obligation*, which transformed the way we think of the relation of local credit to society.

The Capitalist Self

The Social Origins of Financial Capitalism in Early Modern England

Craig Muldrew

University of Cambridge

CAMBRIDGE
UNIVERSITY PRESS

CAMBRIDGE
UNIVERSITY PRESS

Shaftesbury Road, Cambridge CB2 8EA, United Kingdom

One Liberty Plaza, 20th Floor, New York, NY 10006, USA

477 Williamstown Road, Port Melbourne, VIC 3207, Australia

314–321, 3rd Floor, Plot 3, Splendor Forum, Jasola District Centre,
New Delhi – 110025, India

103 Penang Road, #05-06/07, Visioncrest Commercial, Singapore 238467

Cambridge University Press is part of Cambridge University Press & Assessment, a department of the University of Cambridge.

We share the University's mission to contribute to society through the pursuit of education, learning and research at the highest international levels of excellence.

www.cambridge.org
Information on this title: www.cambridge.org/9781009644471

DOI: 10.1017/9781009644488

When citing this work, please include a reference to the DOI 10.1017/9781009644488

First published 2025

Printed in the United Kingdom by CPI Group Ltd, Croydon CR0 4YY

A catalogue record for this publication is available from the British Library

A Cataloging-in-Publication data record for this book is available from the Library of Congress

ISBN 978-1-009-64447-1 Hardback

To Keith Wrightson, teacher and friend.

Contents

Figures

Tables

Acknowledgements

This book has been a long time in the making. In many ways it is a continuation of my first book, *The Economy of Obligation*, published in 1998, and readers of that book will see some of the suggestions of what happened next worked out here. However, further research by others and myself has led me to very different places than where I thought I might end up all those years ago. Of course I haven't been working on credit for the whole time since 1998. But it has always been my intention to take the story of local credit markets forward, and over the past eight years or so I have published a number of articles dealing with many of the issues in this book. While some small passages have been replicated here, the issues raised in these articles have been woven into the grand narrative of this book. In almost every case these articles deal with issues raised in this book in much more detail, and I have indicated where this is so in the footnotes for any readers who might wish to follow them up.

Since I wrote *The Economy of Obligation*, the perspective of history has also become much more global. My own methodology has always been research that digs down deeply into the workings of local society in England, which I know best, while placing it in the context of ideas and events that were often international. Indeed, this is essential in the time period covered by this book, when England became Britain and pursued a path of global expansion. Since writing *The Economy of Obligation* I have had the good fortune to come into contact with scholars from all over the globe working on matters of credit and money. Thus, my *modus operandi* in this book has been to use comparative history as a contextual framework, to put my deep history of England in perspective. Thus there are many references to developments in continental Europe and the American colonies. I also intended to include a comparative chapter on developments concerning paper currency in other parts of the globe, but this had to be dropped to shorten an already very long narrative, but which I intend to publish elsewhere.

The book could not have been completed without the very generous support of the Leverhulme Trust, who awarded me a Senior Research Fellowship (MRF-2018-018 New Abstract Financial Value and Society in the Early Eighteenth Century) for the years 2019–2021, which allowed me to finish writing the bulk of my manuscript. The British Academy (SRG18R1\181392) also awarded me a grant that allowed me to visit the many record repositories in which the research for this book was carried out in 2018. The Queens' College Fellows Research Fund also helped in this regard. I would additionally like to thank all of the archivists in those places I visited for their always friendly assistance in locating documents. I would especially like to thank the Dorset History Centre, the Hampshire Archives, and the Royal Bank of Scotland Archives for allowing me to reproduce the images of documents in their possession used here.

I would like to acknowledge the help of numerous people. First, as always, is Janine Maegraith, with whom I am in constant conversation and who has read many drafts of work. I have been inspired by many conversations with Roberto Scazzieri on political economy and Italian economic and intellectual history. As will be apparent, I have learned much from the work of Carl Wennerlind, as well, from our many conversations. Keith Wrightson has continued to help me to place economic change in its social context, especially in terms of inequality and class. Throughout my career I've been incredibly influenced by the legal scholar, and great friend, Chris Brooks, who died much too young in 2014. Others who died during the genesis of this book who were helpful are Aaron Graham, Carlo Poni, Peter Spufford, and Sir Tony Wrigley. The following have also been especially helpful and influential: Kuroda Akinoba, Martin Daunton, Laurence Fontaine, Joanna Innes, Paul Slack, and John Styles. Others I would like to thank are: Martin Allen, Gareth Austin, Sir John Baker, Chris Briggs, Ivano Cardinale, D'Maris Coffman, Elise Dermineur, Christine Desan, Jan de Vries, Amy Erickson, Margo Finn, Henry French, Oscar Gelderblom, Harumi Goto, Pat Hudson, Margaret Hunt, Just Junker, Sebastain Keibeck, Lawrence Klein, Paul Kosmetatos, Simon Middleton, Anne Murphy, Larry Neal, Tawny Paul, Carlo Poni, Emma Rothschild, James Shaw, Alexandra Shepard, Hiroki Shin, Richard Smith, Judith Spicksley, Songtao Yang, David Sugarman, Simon Szreter, Naomi Tadmor, Moto Takahashi, Hillary Taylor, Leigh Shaw Taylor, Joris van den Tol, David Waddilove, Alex Wakelam, Paul Warde, Jane Whittle, and Phil Withington. Finally, but certainly not least, I have had the good fortune to supervise many students whose MPhil and PhD dissertations have helped to formulate and alter my thinking. Foremost is my first PhD student, Hank McCurdy, who did research into legal records and showed the importance of paper money, which put me on the right track, and Leslie Chang, Raffaele Danna, Alexandra Digby, David Filtness, Ellen Nye, Stephen Pierpoint, Zack Rauwald, Richard Senior, Ken Sneath, Imogen Webb, and Chris Whittle. Maddy Wright helped to compose the index.

Introduction: Capitalism and Dependence

Any book that claims in its title to be about the origins of capitalism might well seem hostage to the accusation of either arrogance or rhetorical abandon. It is hardly a small subject – it refers to a whole economic system. The use of the term capitalism is so pervasive today that trying to define what it means in practice seems as impossible as, say, defining Christian, Muslim, or Buddhist society. However, I will argue that England, Scotland, and some of the American Colonies, between roughly 1680 and 1760, became the first economies in which the use of capital spread widely enough *throughout society* to change not just economic practice, but culture and society as well. I will, though, primarily focus on England as it was by far the largest of these economies, as well as being the centre of an Atlantic economic system. It was also where the intellectual impetus for change originated in an outpouring of printed works. But this will certainly not be a nationalist history. The institutions of merchant capital all evolved – and were used throughout – Europe and other parts of the globe, and capital as paper money first became socially embedded in the Italian Renaissance cities, most notably Florence and Naples, and certain forms were also then used in Antwerp and the Dutch Republic. But unless further research throws up new evidence, it seems that it was in England and Scotland between *c.*1680 and 1750 that the practices, morals, and institutions of capital formation and maintenance spread *throughout* a national and imperial economic system.

My second aim here will be to create a transformational shift in the way we understand the concept of the financial revolution. This is usually understood as the successful establishment of the Bank of England as an institution that could, for the first time, successfully manage government debt by attracting private investment. It did so as a joint stock company, and, as such, was also part of the development of the London stock market, which expanded at the same time (see 'Government Paper Instruments' in Chapter 2). However, this was only one part of a much broader creation of financial investment capital. While merchant capital had existed for some time, and had long been involved with banking and state finance, the creation of capital in the countryside and other towns and cites in Britan and the Atlantic colonies was just as crucial and should equally be seen as comprising a much broader revolution in finance. I will present a new history of the origins of capital that will move the focus away from London to provide a more comprehensive perspective.

In doing so I will also provide a chronological continuation of my previous study of the culture of credit in early modern England.[1] Capital is first and foremost a financial concept. But many recent histories of capitalism look at social systems, forms of production, or business organisation without reference to the role of capital as a *thing* – that is as a socially constructed form of value. In Chapter 1 I will present a critical analysis of how historians have used the concept of capitalism. Here I argue that the financial history of capital needs to be integrated more fully into the histories of all social relations if we want to use history to refine a 'presentist' concept about financial power and its effect on society and political choice. It is a contention of what has been termed the 'new history of capitalism' that financial history is often too narrowly institutional in that it focuses primarily on economic growth and not the social effects of financialisation on broader society.[2] Finance, in these histories, when socialised, is generally presented as having a negative role on broader social relations. However, it will be a central contention of this book that capital was created institutionally through relations of interdependence first, and then, once created, was used by those who accumulated great amounts of it to become more powerful.

Marx, of course, placed capital at the centre of his theory of class exploitation, but talked of the 'capitalist system', not capitalism. Capitalism, after 1900, was eventually used as a term to refer to the opposite of socialism, and this inevitably meant that it became a broad and politically charged concept, rather than an analytical one. It is often now defined reductively by the degree of free market activity and individual property rights. For many, such as Milton Friedman, this is linked to the freedom of the individual to be able to choose and own what they want. This is claimed to be the best way of increasing economic growth and collective wealth, by incentivising energetic and imaginative people to come up with new services and technological advances through the profit motive. But, like many 'isms', it took form in the late nineteenth

1 Craig Muldrew, *The Economy of Obligation: The Culture of Credit and Social Relations in Early Modern England* (London, 1998).
2 Sven Beckert and Christine Desan, *American Capitalism: New Histories* (New York, 2018), pp. 1–31.

century as a conceptual definition of a competitive economic organisation of society to counter socialist ideals of cooperation. However, it is no accident that the root 'capital' was used, and this derivation points us not towards market freedom, but rather towards an embodiment of abstract value, supported by an institutional structure to preserve financial value over time. Crucially, this process also allowed this value to be turned into paper currency to increase liquidity.

Here, I offer a deeply researched argument for the centrality of the institution of financial capital as a *social* phenomenon. Before it could significantly affect ways of doing business and relations of production, capital needed to progress beyond the high levels of the economy of merchants into wider society. This transformation took place successfully in Britain from roughly 1680 to 1760. This period is crucial because of a number of institutional changes, as well as a significant shift in the cultural history of morals and emotions. The 'financial revolution', which saw the creation of the Bank of England and the stock market, has been well studied, but changes in local credit networks involving better accounting, paper notes, and increased mortgaging were arguably even more important. Equally significant was the evolution of the idea of self-control, which came to supplant the institutional mediation of local law courts. I argue that this was a move that allowed the idea and practice of savings to move from taking the form of a debt owed to becoming interest-bearing capital.

Capital in this study will also be taken to be what Adam Smith called 'circulating capital' as opposed to 'fixed capital'. Fixed capital consists of material things such as land, buildings, and machines. In this sense, capital has existed since the beginnings of the history of agriculture, and in one sense the history of property is a history of how such capital was used and divided for people's livelihoods.[3] Ancient states could mobilise resources to increase agricultural production through irrigation, and markets certainly existed. However, extractive institutions to build religious and political monuments, and to pay for the lifestyles of the elites who governed them, was also a socially important way of using such productive capital. Circulating capital, however, was much rarer. Most market transactions were done with precious metals or some other form of physical currency, or through local interpersonal credit transactions.[4] Trade and merchants have also existed for millennia in both the east and

[3] Such a broad definition is adopted in Larry Neal and Jeffrey G. Williamson, *The Cambridge History of Capitalism. Volume I, The Rise of Capitalism: From Ancient Origins to 1848* (Cambridge, 2014).

[4] David Graeber, *Debt: The First 5,000 Years* (New York, 2011), chs. 3, 5.

the west, and they created ways of exchanging value without forms of metallic or other physical currency, but in ancient societies their activity was small compared to the state and agriculture. But before the early modern period the only sustained effort to create circulating capital to supplement coins, which could be used throughout society, took place during the Song dynasty (960–1279) in China, which created an official state-issued paper currency.[5]

I have chosen to focus on financial capital as forming the basis of capitalism because, in contrast to fixed capital, it is ephemeral. It needs to be socially created by institutions. Its value might be signified by numbers written on various forms of paper, and it might be legally secured by attachment to some material object, but its value is like the thoughts that become books. It is abstract but exists through time in a *written* form. Of course, land, together with other more tangible assets such as buildings, bodies, and goods, have remained central to the capitalist system as forms of collateral. Capital is also supported by an institutional structure involving the production of paper instruments of credit that keep their value over time, such as bonds, bills, and mortgages. It is my intention in this book to examine capital as a 'thing', as it existed in notes and shares, as well as money in an account book. The approach will be to provide a contextual rather than a linear economic history, which tests whether money or capital worked efficiently, or whether certain institutions or cultural practices worked 'better' than other factors, to promote economic growth. The theoretical philosophy of the book is a narrative explanation focusing on exploring the interconnectedness of events, or what we might want to call narrative causation of historical change.[6]

The formative period that will be the subject of this study saw a confluence of a number of factors in England, including an acceleration in the volume of overseas trade, the creation of joint stock companies by projectors to attract investment in speculative projects, and the massive expansion and formalisation of government borrowing, made possible by the creation of the Bank of England in 1695. The development of the legal concept of the 'equity of redemption', which made mortgaging property easier, was also crucial. Other legal changes made the use of informal paper bills and notes of hand valid negotiable instruments. Less

[5] Richard von Glahn, *Fountain of Fortune: Money and Monetary Policy in China, 1000–1700* (Berkeley, 2019), pp. 7–8, 43–8, 51–6, 247–8.

[6] For an excellent discussion of how economic historians and economists should deal with this question, see Sheilagh Ogilvie, '"Whatever Is, Is Right"? Economic Institutions in Pre-industrial Europe', *The Economic History Review* 60, no. 4 (2007), pp. 649–84.

formal, but equally important, social changes also occurred. The concept of interest gained social currency, and the interest rate became not just tolerated but normative and foundational. In the realm of theology and philosophy, the idea of the emotional and thinking self was enormously developed in works such as John Locke's *Theory of Human Understanding* and Richard Cumberland's *Laws of Nature*. This led to the evolution of the idea of self-control, which came to supplant the institutional mediation of local law courts. All of these factors worked to create a financial system embedded within society, which was firmly in place by the time Adam Smith was writing *The Wealth of Nations*, published in 1776. By this time, the mainland British economy, as well as some American Colonies, was cemented by a system of country banks and the Banks of England and Scotland, all connected by a bill system that moved through London.

This study takes a significantly different approach from those that argue that Britain had better and more 'representative' institutions, which made financial capital more secure. Instead, it argues that it was legal flexibility that permitted local credit markets to be transformed through the use of new forms of savings and currency in an *evolutionary* way. Institutional flexibility was, in fact, more crucial than security. The creation of trust in new forms of capital was the decisive factor, and no new institution created trust on its own. This was a complex process that involved changes in theology, ethics, and politics. As I argued in my monograph *The Economy of Obligation*, the early modern market between 1550 and 1700 was characterised more by trust than competition because of the prevalence of oral contracts. In that study I examined how the nature of such trust affected social organisation and the legalisation of society. What I defined before as a culture of credit was changed into something new and more protean: a culture of capital. During the period studied here, capital certainly changed social relations for many people, even if it was not until the 1820s that the first socialists would focus on it as dangerous to society itself.[7] The crux of the argument in my previous study of credit was that financial credit and social reputation were one and the same thing, and this naturally affected how people dealt with each other and wrote about their society. The use of capital increased gradually and did not change this overnight, and much has been written about how credit and reputation remained important. One

[7] Ali Digby, *Political Economy, the Labour Theory of Value, & the Chartist Movement* (PhD Thesis, Cambridge University, 2017).

only has to look at the writings of Daniel Defoe to see that this was certainly the case in the early eighteenth century.[8]

But by the late seventeenth century, England had developed a comparatively well-integrated national economy centred on London, which over the course of the eighteenth century would expand to include Scotland, Ireland, and some American Colonies in an Atlantic system. This allowed changes adopted there to become more embedded, and thus to have a more lasting effect. England managed to transform its relatively informal system of credit into one that combined informal flexibility with institutional accountability at a local level. This was done through a process of public debate about the role of money and credit in the economy in the late seventeenth century, and allowed the formation and use of capital to spread beyond merchants and through the whole national economy. At almost the same time, Scotland and a number of American Colonies pursued the same goals but followed a different path within different legal systems. My method here will be to understand how institutional change took place by noting when people came to *collectively* accept that they could trust such practices and therefore they could trust each other using such practices.

The current book also focuses more on local towns and rural society to add to what we know about the middling sort in London. The premise behind this approach is that the practices of a great part of the inhabitants of the society needed to have changed if the argument is to be made that this was a move towards 'capitalism' as a social practice. It uncovers the ways in which credit transactions changed, and when and where these changes happened or did not happen. I have already made the argument that the concept of saving was a crucial lynchpin of Adam Smith's economic morality, and here I show how prevalent the practice was in both England and Scotland before Smith wrote.[9]

Before the rise of abstract financial capital, the type of wealth that held a steady value over time took the form of land. Aristocrats and other elite members of society were *rentiers* in the sense that they had property rights in land. An often-overlooked aspect of Marx's formulation of historical change is that once 'capital' emerges it represents a different and socially less embedded form of rent. But in its early manifestations capital was not as disembodied as it would become in the classic period of the

8 Julian Hoppit, *Risk and Failure in English Business 1700–1800* (Cambridge, 1987), pp. 162–7.

9 Craig Muldrew, 'Self-Control and Savings: Adam Smith and the Creation of Modern Capital', in Simon Middleton and James Shaw (eds.), *Market Ethics and Practices, c.1300–1850* (London, 2018), pp. 63–86.

nineteenth century. Once 'capital' began to be created, then wealth could become abstracted away from the tenants who paid rent or purchasers owing money to tradesmen and merchants, and placed in the matrix of institutions needed to keep the value of a portfolio of stocks, annuities and other government debt, earning interest bonds, mortgages, and circulating bills of hand. This process was sufficiently developed by the nineteenth century for the first wave of radical socialist thinkers in England to begin to talk about the interests of 'capital' against labour and to argue that the value of labour was the ultimate source of saved capital owned by its wealthy possessors. This was followed, of course, by Karl Marx's massive investigation into both the historical and contemporary processes by which capital accumulated in the possession of certain groups, and how this related to social and political power. How social power was altered in the eighteenth century is also part of my investigation.

Since the publication of Thomas Piketty's book *Capital in the Twenty-First Century*, the question that occupied Marx, of how the formation of capital contributes to inequality, has returned to prominence. Piketty focused on the rates of return to financial capital, arguing that a system that provided steady income through a reasonably high interest rate is often more attractive than risky investment in innovation. This leads to increasing inequality over time, as entrepreneurs inevitably become rentiers and use their increasingly accumulating wealth to intervene in politics to protect their interests.[10] This part of the book has been most controversial with economists who point to the continuity of innovation in generating stock market returns. However, in subsequent work Piketty has moved to deal more with the social effects of inequality.[11] But, as an economic history, *Capital in the Twenty-First Century* offered an empirical investigation of changes in the ownership of capital of all sorts over time, and demonstrated how warfare and taxation in the twentieth century acted to erode the wealth of elites and then how governments of many different political views used taxation in the wake of the devastation of the Second World War to achieve an unprecedented degree of redistribution of wealth.[12]

However, this consensus broke down in the 1970s and financial markets were increasingly deregulated, marginal rates of taxation lowered for wealthier taxpayers and businesses, and laws passed to make

[10] Thomas Piketty, *Capital in the Twenty-first Century* (Cambridge, MA, 2014), pp. 52–5, 199–220, 571–2.
[11] Thomas Piketty, *Capital and Ideology* (Cambridge, MA, 2020).
[12] Piketty, *Capital in the Twenty-first Century*, pp. 140–64.

unions less powerful. Such policies, unsurprisingly, reversed the trend of post-war moves to greater equality, and now in the twenty-first century most western societies are returning to late nineteenth-century rates of inequality. Overwhelmingly it is financial capital that has fuelled this process. While the real wages of workers and the lower- and middle-middle classes have roughly stagnated, the wealth of elites has risen in multiples of ten, twenty, or much more, held in the form of shares. This is the so-called 1 per cent that own most of our societies' non-government wealth. The 2008 financial crisis also demonstrated how much power the managers and beneficiaries of this system of capital production have, when taxpayers bailed out the banks and inequality continued to grow. The economist Joseph Stiglitz has termed this system shareholder capitalism, in which remuneration of elite shareholders has become the primary focus of American companies.[13]

In the early modern period there were certainly large-scale, powerful, and often cavalier owners of capital, such as the Medici family, or large merchants such as Robert Patterson, who earned wealth lending to governments to pay for expensive wars, or by producing cloth or importing expensive commodities such as pepper in the ever-developing global trade after 1495. However, the development of the system of capital formation I will discuss here was initially the idea of radical utopian social reformers of the Hartlieb circle during the period of the English Civil War and Commonwealth. Their primary aim was to alleviate poverty by creating more employment through industrialisation. To do this, they proposed a programme of what modern economists term liquidity creation, much more than capital formation. Basically, they said if the informal credit that existed in England at that time could be turned into paper credit that was as readily transferable as gold and silver coins, then this would allow consumers to purchase more things and for employers to pay more wages, thus kickstarting economic growth. Also, the profits from business or market-oriented farming could be lent out as interest, and then this type of capital could be used to create paper credit. Thus, the early history of capital as it spread away from merchants and government debt was not primarily one of inequality, but rather the formation of new forms of trust that would allow circulating paper instruments to maintain their value beyond only the use of a small elite group of merchants and bankers. Also, most inequality in any early modern society before 1600, apart from major trading

[13] Joseph Stiglitz, *People, Power, and Profits: Progressive Capitalism for an Age of Discontent* (New York, 2020), pp. xiii, 102.

cities, was primarily the result of the unequal inheritance of land as a result of feudal warfare, not market competition.

Perhaps it is ironic, or simply inevitable, that the incredible success of the Commonwealth radicals would come to be used to create new inequalities and forms of power, but capital still needs good governance and adherence to certain social norms to keep its value in the face of ever-emerging new contingencies such as war, climate change, and resource shortages. Inequality fundamentally weakens the social solidarity needed to achieve this. The question of how and why society, social thought, and politics changed, creating the framework by which a concept like capital could come to exist and make sense, is thus more relevant than ever. Capitalism, as I shall argue here, is in fact not about liberty but about social dependence and prudence, and it still depends on institutions that maintain the value of savings that create capital. As even Milton Friedman has pointed out, the market is a system of mutual interdependence.[14]

The argument of this book will weave together five major themes, those of *institutions*, *ethics*, *beliefs*, *social relations*, and *practice*. Although these themes will always be present in one form or another, the book is organised into almost a sonata form with an introduction, thematic material, a development, a recapitulation, and finally a coda. The first two chapters are the introduction, and then Chapters 3 and 4 the thematic material. Chapters 5 and 6 on ethics are the development, while Chapters 7 and 8 offer a recapitulation of how the themes of institutional change presented in Chapters 3 and 4 affected society. There is finally an extended coda in Chapters 9 and 10 to end. As I've already indicated, the great majority of the deep history of social change will be about England, with Chapter 9 placing these changes in a broader context. The sources used vary widely from receipts in family estate collections, institutional records of towns, banks, and the post office, to pamphlets, philosophical texts, and sermons, but throughout I will rely heavily on ego documents, especially those of John Cannon, to provide evidence of practice. This is vital, since it is one of my major claims that it does not make sense to talk of capitalism until capital was used extensively *in practice*. As the title indicates, it is also very much a history of how the nature of the 'self' evolved in philosophy, theory, and everyday practice in a way that aligned with institutional change to make capital feasible beyond the confines of a wealthy elite group of merchants. The role of wealthier women as investors in state debt in the late seventeenth and eighteenth

14 Milton Friedman, with the assistance of Rose D. Friedman, *Capitalism and Freedom* (Chicago, 1962), pp. 4–5, 12–13, ch. 1.

centuries has recently received attention, and I will certainly be considering the role of women as practitioners in this and as users of paper currencies in England.[15] It will also be argued that the development of mortgaging to secure new capital was only possible after legal changes that dealt with the entailments created by women's property rights. But, because of the difficult nature of the records of the English law of real property, the full effect of this change will require much more work than offered here.

I will begin in Chapter 1 with an analysis of how historians of the early modern period have used the concept of capital. Chapter 2 will move on to outlining the history of previous institutions that created forms of capital in Europe, including land, dowries, banks, bills of exchange, and government debt. This part of the book consists largely of an assessment of the existing literature. For those who wish to move directly to the new research, this begins in Chapter 3, but the section on the pamphlet debate over currency in Chapter 2 is important for my reinterpretation of the financial revolution. This section examines the reasons why the system of informal oral credit, as it had developed over the previous 100-odd years, began to be criticised during the Commonwealth period. Many authors claimed that it was both inefficient and an obstacle to economic growth. Many pamphlets were published containing proposals for different sorts of banks, which would issue paper currency to speed up circulation. Some of these were based on previous European examples. The nature of these proposals is examined, together with a summary of how they related to the creation of the Bank of England. Its establishment is normally seen as the successful outcome of this debate, but in fact it was not primarily created as an institution to expand the supply of credit, but to help fund the government debt. The increasing cost of the War of Spanish Succession did, however, result in the issue of things like Exchequer or Treasury Bills, as well as South Sea and Bank stock to fund the war. The last part of the chapter will focus on the significant effect these multiple forms of paper currency had on liquidity within London.

In Chapter 3, I will examine in detail an entirely new source: collections of bundles of loose receipts, notes, and bills in local record offices to demonstrate how older forms of oral credit were augmented by the use of informal local forms of paper currency to add liquidity to local transactions. This is linked to the changing legal status of paper bills and notes. I will also look at the continuing shortage of silver coins and how the

[15] See Chapter 4, fn. 48.

increasing minting of guineas was used to make the circulation of local notes work by providing enough coins to make notes over one pound in value redeemable for cash amounts. This chapter also uses the evidence provided by the extraordinary *Chronicles* of John Cannon as a sort of micro-history within my argument. This is a 500,000-word set of memoirs, diary entries, and record of his scrivening activities from *c.* 1720 to 1742. I examine in detail his diary entries of the bills and notes he wrote for people in his community. His descriptions of how they were accepted and trusted provide an almost unique window into the world of emerging local paper credit. In other chapters I will also use Cannon's memoirs as a sort of running micro-history that, with its huge detail, is able to illuminate much of how local paper instruments and mortgages, for example, worked, and what disputes and emotions they gave rise to. Here I will also examine how the increasing provision of education in mathematics and accounting was necessary for this change to occur.

Finally, there will be a section on the increasing use of inland bills of exchange and their relation to local notes of hand by examining the diary of the mid-eighteenth-century Sussex shopkeeper Thomas Turner, as well as the letters of local tradesmen such as the mercer Joseph Symson of Kendal. This discussion will reinforce the argument made some time ago by Eric Kerridge on the rise of the use of the inland bill. I will use the records of the Royal Mail to show just how developed the national bill market was by the early eighteenth century, as the transfer of such paper instruments was a major part of its growing business.

Chapter 4 focuses on the change in the law known as the equity of redemption, which took form in the late seventeenth century and made the title to mortgaged land more secure through the provision that rents could be sequestered to pay off a loan after the due date, to avoid the title to the property reverting to the lender. This legal change led to a rapid expansion of mortgaging and associated conveyancing. Again, an in-depth study of the *Chronicles* of the scrivener John Cannon will demonstrate the potential scale of capital formation in the early eighteenth century as a result of mortgaging. It also demonstrates how interest-bearing loans, based on the security of property, became a source of both income and, more importantly, stable abstract value that could be used to increase the money supply by underpinning the creation of local notes and bills. Mortgage income could also smooth credit flows by providing capital when outgoings were greater than incomings. In the past this would have triggered the need to litigate to increase incoming income, but now money could be borrowed. This chapter will also examine savings held in the form of bonds.

Chapter 5 moves from examining institutional changes to the cultural history of morals and emotions by examining how the evolution of the idea of the self came to supplant the institutional mediation of local law courts. It traces how three concepts – self-love, happiness, and interest – were developed and disseminated as religious and interpersonal ethics, all related to the development of the self within the singular mind. I argue that this was a crucial move that allowed the idea and practice of savings to move from taking the form of a debt owed, to the interest-bearing capital described above. It also validated the crucial concept of interest within religion, and this was related to the increasing moral acceptance of the interest rate. Although a legal interest rate had existed from the Elizabethan Act of 1571, interest rates are difficult to find mentioned explicitly in the seventeenth century. By the eighteenth, however, they had become commonplace.

Chapter 6 examines how the theological ideas discussed in Chapter 5 were successfully disseminated throughout English society. To do this, it examines the religious split between the established Church of England and Non-Conformity. The development of the theology of self-love, happiness, and interest is examined in the writings of the enormously influential philosopher and theologian Richard Cumberland. I then discuss how this evolved into Latitudinarianism, and use an examination of printed sermons as they commented on these ethical concepts, as well as on consumption and worldly goods. I also look at how diary writers commented on sermons they heard. The writings of the Anglican ministers Joseph Butler and Josiah Tucker are examined to show how these ideas became directly linked to economic thought. The concurrent development of Non-Conformist theology relating to the same concepts is traced through the writings of John Locke on the mind, and the diary of the student lawyer Dudley Ryder. Here I argue that Locke's idea of the penal self, in which misbehaviour was seen to cause mental pain through feelings of guilt, meant that Non-Conformists placed an extra premium on honest behaviour. The Third Earl of Shaftesbury and his theory of polite sociability is also investigated to show how it provided a less austere means to disseminate Locke's psychology of the mind. Central to this investigation will be the process by which individual selves were able to become comfortable with trusting new institutions by using the concept of interest as a form of commitment.

Chapter 7 moves back to institutions to deal with the general decline in litigation over failed credit, which began around 1690, and argues it came about largely because of changes in credit networks. It demonstrates how attorneys' businesses moved away from litigation to conveyancing, and how they profited by becoming local creditors.

It also looks at the increasing use of local summary justice in the Courts of Requests in London, Bristol, and Newcastle to enforce the small debts of poor consumers, as well as the growing use of arrest and imprisonment in the common law courts. While the use of paper currency provided greater liquidity in credit markets and reduced the overall level of litigation massively, those debtors who went broke began to be treated in a much harsher fashion.

In Chapter 8 I argue that this eventually began to crystallise into an ideology of middle-class behaviour based on the ability to save and to maintain enough capital to prevent a cash flow crisis that would result in being arrested or imprisoned. This led to a new type of class-based thinking about society that was closely linked to the security that new forms of capital provided to successful savers. Such individuals were those who were able to accumulate large amounts of capital through entrepreneurship or inheritance, and not dissipate it through overspending. This was a small elite group who gradually came to be termed the middle class, to differentiate themselves from the middling sort of smaller traders. Crucially, this new class had capital worth tens of thousands of pounds – enough to be protected from the vicissitudes of supply and demand and business misfortune. The middling sort, on the other hand, continued to be faced with the prospect of insolvency, and were even more vulnerable to imprisonment for debt due to the changes in the law described in Chapter 7. Because of this, the middle class began to think of themselves as being morally better than the middling sort. They also increasingly thought of their capital as a form of property created out of righteousness, and that the role of the law was to protect it from those who were less able. Poverty was also no longer a just reason for not paying back a contracted debt. This was also the beginning of the legal doctrine of 'freedom of contract'.

Chapter 9 will examine the different trajectory that Scotland adopted to the problems it faced in the 1690s. After suffering a terrible famine in the middle of that decade, which England avoided, Scotland's leaders embarked on a plan to create a modern economy. Since Scotland suffered an even more acute shortage of specie than England, but did not need to bankroll foreign wars, it was decided to create the Bank of Scotland as an institution designed primarily to create specie substitute paper currency. This was done successfully by the mid-eighteenth century, when many local private note-issuing banks existed and Scotland was able to support a flourishing new linen industry. In addition to Scotland, many of the British Thirteen Colonies also issued paper currencies to meet demand for money in the face of even more acute specie shortages than Scotland. By doing so they were able to increase their consumption of British-produced goods. France also attempted to create a system of paper currency under the influence of the exiled Scot John Law, who had previously written pamphlets arguing for the link between currency, liquidity, and economic growth. However, for the French government the conversion of the huge debts it had built up fighting the War of Spanish Succession into currency was more important, and the result was over-issue, inflation, and collapse.

Finally, Chapter 10 will move to examine how the local issue of notes, wage payments, and the brokerage of bills of exchange over longer distances came together in the form of county banks after 1760. Certain tradesmen and industrialists moved from financing their own businesses to providing finance on a more exclusive basis to their communities in the form of institutions they then decided to call banks. This chapter will show how this took place, and how they became a part of local society. They emerged out of local practice, and did not generally copy London institutions such as Child's or Hoare's banks. It will also examine just how important the payment of industrial wage labour was in the formation of county banking. The chapter will end by placing Adam Smith's advocacy of banking and his discussion of capital in the context of the developments described in this book. It was Smith's contention that the value of labour converted into abstract capital was the wealth of a nation, and here I will look at how he drew on the developments in both England and Scotland. His was a 'capitalism' based on the ethics needed to create the conditions to make capital keep its value.

1 Early Modern Capitalism: A Concept Too Big to Fail?

I am hardly the first historian to attempt to empirically investigate the origins of capitalism in the early modern period. There is, of course, a massive historiography, and it is absolutely necessary to place my investigation in the context of what has been done previously. For many historians, and for Karl Marx, it is the early modern period when capitalism is first seen to have taken form. But before doing this we need to start with the origins of the term, since we cannot avoid the hermeneutical weight of the concept. What I mean by this is similar to what deconstructionists suggest: that the connotative meaning of such key words is so vast that they are *always* political and ethical. There are few words currently that have more possibilities than capitalism. There are many things we might term 'capitalist', but just as many exceptions and different ways of putting parts of the economy under state control, regulating them, or leaving them within familial structures. Yet, understanding capitalism is undeniably crucial to the way we think about individual choice and collective action, and is as crucial as democracy or freedom when we think about values in the contemporary world.

Origin of the Term Capitalism

The word *capital* is based on the Latin word for *head* and was first used to refer to any stock of merchandise or money in twelfth-century Italy. By the thirteenth century it had come to be more specifically defined in Italian accounting manuals as an equivalent term for stock or money in an account.[1] It continued to be used in this pragmatic way until the advent of political economy in the eighteenth century. In his compendium of trade and money, the *Lex Mercatoria* (*Law Merchant*) of 1622, Gerard de Malynes explained that a merchant

[1] Fernand Braudel, *Civilization and Capitalism, 15th–18th Century. Vol. II, The Wheels of Commerce* (London, 1982), pp. 232–3.

findeth that he hath one hundreth Clothes, two hundreth Kersies, or any other commodities left him by his father or friends, and moreouer some thousand pounds in readie money, and fiue hundreth pounds in debts owing by seuerall persons, payable at some time to come, besides some hundreth pounds yearely in Lands or Leases: out of all these he maketh a Stocke or Capitall, which he doth enter into a Book called a Iournall.[2]

In pamphlets published in English in the seventeenth century, *capital* used in this way was almost always described in terms of merchants. However, in the later years of the century it came to be used equally commonly to refer to the collective assets of a joint stock company, and was used in many pamphlets advocating various forms of banks from that time. As we will see in Chapter 2, this move to a description of collective corporate wealth was a key development in its popularity as a term to describe financial assets.[3]

However, it was not until the advent of political economy in France that it came to be theorised as something that was an integral part of an economic system. This was first done by the Irish/French writer Richard Cantillon in his *Essai sur la Nature du Commerce en Général* (*Essay on the Nature of Trade in General*), written in 1730 but not published until 1755. He tended to use the word 'fond' to describe savings, but he used the word capital in the following passages in a chapter on hard money:

Mais les gens industrieux qui sont attentifs à amasser du bien n'augmenteront pas d'abord leur dépense; ils attendront jusqu'à ce qu'ils aient amassé une bonne somme, dont ils puissent tirer un intérêt certain, indépendamment de leur commerce. Lorsqu'un grand nombre d'habitants auront acquis des fortunes considérables, de cet argent ... Quoique cette cherté les entraîne dans une plus grande dépense qu'ils ne s'étaient d'abord proposé de faire, ils ne laisseront pas pour la plupart de continuer tant qu'il leur restera de capital.[4]

But undoubtedly the most influential and important work, which more than any other made the concept of capital central to thinking about the economy, was Anne-Robert Jacques Turgot's *Réflexions sur la Formation et la Distribution des Richesses* (*Reflections on the Formation and Distribution*

[2] Gerald de Malynes, *Consuetudo vel lex Mercatoria* (London, 1622), p. 363.

[3] It was used in 68 pamphlets in this way between 1680 and 1720. Based on a search of texts in the *Early English Books Online* database (ProQuest).

[4] Richard Cantillon, *Essai sur la Nature du Commerce en General* (Paris, 2011), p. 51. '...the industrious who are eager to acquire property will not at first increase their expense: they will wait till they have accumulated a large sum from which they can draw a secure interest income, independently of their trade. Though this dearness involves them in a greater expense than they at first contemplated they will for the most part continue so long as their capital lasts.' Richard Cantillon, *Essay on the Nature of Trade in General*, ed. Henry Higgs (London, 1959), II, ch. 6, p. 69.

of Riches) of 1766. In a relatively brief book, he used the term capital 71 times. He defined capital as

> Quiconque, soit par le revenu de sa terre, soit par les salaires de son travail ou de son industrie, reçoit chaque année plus de valeurs qu'il n'a besoin d'en dépenser, peut mettre en réserve ce superflu et l'accumuler: ces valeurs accumulées sont ce qu'on appelle *un capital.* (Whoever, either by the revenue of his land, or by the salary of his labour or industry, receives every year a higher income than he needs to spend, may lay up the residue and accumulate it: these accumulated values are what we name a capital.)[5]

He also used the terms *épargnent* or *l'économie* often to describe how savings became investment capital.

Sir James Steuart, who discussed money and banking extensively in his *Inquiry into the Principles of Political Economy* of 1767, used the term capital often when describing the organisation and function of banking. He did not theorise very much about it; however, he did claim:

> By funds, here, I understand the capital wealth already made, in opposition to the produce of industry, which may be considered as the materials of which such funds are composed. The fund therefore is the accumulation of savings, which, not having been spent by the industrious, form a capital of a nature to produce an income, either from land, or from any other valuable thing.[6]

Following soon after Turgot, and probably influenced by him, Adam Smith made capital central to his description of the economy. Although Smith famously began with labour and its organisation, he moved on to explain how the market value of commodities and work became expressed in monetary terms. He further explained how this value was accumulated in stock and capital, before moving on to how systems of political economy could encourage the productive use of capital.[7] No previous writer had described the nature of capital with such analytical perspicuity.[8] Capital, Smith argued, was primarily created through

[5] Anne-Robert Turgot, *Réflexions sur la Formation et la Distribution des Richesses* (Paris, 1766), ch. 58, also see chs. 79 and 100. Translation from Anne-Robert Turgot, *Reflections on the Formation and the Distribution of Riches*, trans. William J. Ashley (New York, 1898), p. 50.

[6] Sir James Steuart, *An Inquiry into the Principles of Political Economy Being an Essay on the Science of Domestic Policy in Free Nations in Which Are Particularly Considered Population, Agriculture, Trade, Industry, Money, Coin, Interest, Circulation, Banks, Exchange, public Credit, and Taxes* (London, 1767), II, pp. 586–7.

[7] Adam Smith, *An Inquiry into the Nature and Causes of the Wealth of Nations*, ed. R. H. Campbell, A. S. Skinner, and W. B. Todd (Oxford, 1976), I–II. Hereafter WN.

[8] Istvan Hont, *Jealousy of Trade: International Competition and the Nation-State in Historical Perspective* (Cambridge, MA, 2005), pp. 49–50.

savings, which could then be used as investment capital in new enterprise. An increase in capital would then also increase

> the real quantity of industry, the number of productive hands, and consequently the exchangeable value of the annual produce of the land and labour of the country, the real wealth and revenue of all its inhabitants.[9]

This led to the formation of various forms of stock, including fixed capital in machines and property, stock in trade, the value of talent, and, most importantly, circulating capital, which allowed the market to function and without which no other capital could be profitably put to use:

> Every fixed capital is both originally derived from, and requires to be continually supported by a circulating capital. All useful machines and instruments of trade are originally derived from a circulating capital.[10]

This led to the production of cheaper goods through the division of labour, or more efficient trade for foreign goods, resulting in what Smith called the 'progress of opulence'.[11]

Smith famously focused on small producers, and the system through which the products of labour could be converted into value, as capital, through savings and banking. He was notably critical of overseas merchants and their attempts to use mercantile regulation for their own interests over those of consumers, but he did not discuss possible repercussions of their accumulation of capital.[12] In fact, his discussion of the social distribution of capital was more anecdotal than analytical. His examples focused on the products and consumption of labour rather than skilled artisans or middling sort traders, such as mercers or apothecaries, and he did not discuss the accumulation of profits by those engaged in large-scale industrial production, such as clothiers or mine owners.[13]

But, by the first half of the nineteenth century, the fortunes of industrial capitalists had increased tremendously, to be worth hundreds of thousands of pounds.[14] As this occurred, inequality between labour and the owners and investors in capital spread, and this concentration of

9 Smith, WN, II, p. 337. 10 Ibid., II, p. 283. 11 Ibid., III, pp. 376–80.

12 Ibid., I, pp. 115, 144, II, pp. 266–7, IV, pp. 462, 493; Nicholas Phillipson, *Adam Smith: An Enlightened Life* (London, 2010), pp. 28–9.

13 Smith, WN, I, pp. 22–3.

14 The son of the inventor and cotton manufacturer Richard Arkwright was one of the first people to be worth over £1 million. A. McConnell, 'Arkwright, Richard (1755–1843), cotton manufacturer and landowner'. *Oxford Dictionary of National Biography*. www-oxforddnb-com.ezp.lib.cam.ac.uk/view/10.1093/ref:odnb/9780198614128.001.0001/odnb-9780198614128-e-646, accessed 22 April 2025.

capital in the hands of owners was fundamentally challenged by the rise of socialism. In newspaper and pamphlet debates about the social effects of new industrial capital accumulation, the term *capitalist* was used to describe an owner of capital or a 'moneyed man', and the term *capitalism* was used on rare occasions – but the term most commonly used was *capital*. Further, most of these early debates were not about the nature of capital itself, but how it came into being. They centred around Smith's labour theory of value, and many socialists began to argue that wage labourers should be able to retain more of the value of their work, which went to their employers, who turned it into capital.[15] They did not argue that capital itself was bad, but that its concentration in the hands of a few individuals was. Socialists proposed that it could be accumulated in cooperative banks or similar institutions.[16]

Marx, of course, went further to argue that the whole system of capital accumulation was both morally and structurally wrong. In developing these ideas, Marx, who was a careful reader of *The Wealth of Nations*, took Smith's political economy as a fundamental starting place for his critique of the bourgeois foundations of surplus value.[17] In Marx, and most of the subsequent nineteenth-century debate, there were capitalists who owned the means of production and existed as a class opposed to labour, but society was not defined as capitalist. However, the role of *capital* was absolutely central. The *Communist Manifesto* points to the central role of the bourgeois in the historical change that brought about the creation of capital as a form of abstract value – they tore up 'motley feudal ties' and replaced them with self-interest and cash payments for workers. The section on historical change ends with the claim that the very existence of the bourgeoisie was due to the formation and augmentation of capital, the creation of which was taken from wage labour.[18] Capital gave too much power to those who controlled the means of exchange, and in this sense I think we need to take the title of Marx's great work very seriously. Much of *Capital* can be read as a massive attempt to understand this transformation of individually produced value through the exchange of private property into the value represented by bank money.[19] As Marx and

15 Ali Digby, *Political Economy, the Labour Theory of Value, & the Chartist Movement* (PhD Thesis, Cambridge University, 2017), chs. 2–4.

16 Ibid., pp. 50–2, 63–4, 83–8.

17 Spencer J. Pack, 'Adam Smith and Marx', in Christopher J. Berry, Maria Pia Paganelli, and Craig Smith (eds.), *The Oxford Handbook of Adam Smith* (Oxford, 2013), pp. 523–37.

18 Karl Marx and Friedrich Engels, *The Communist Manifesto*, ed. Gareth Stedman Jones (London, 2002), pp. 222–3, 233.

19 Karl Marx, *Capital, I–III*, trans. Ben Fowkes (New York, 1977), I, pp. 188–339, 725–61; III, pp. 379–636.

Engels had put it earlier in the *Communist Manifesto*, money was a form in which the 'social activity, by means of which the products of man mutually complement each other, is *estranged* and becomes the property of a *material thing* external to man'. This was the means of resolving 'personal worth into exchange value' and drowning the 'heavenly ecstasies of religious fervour, of chivalrous enthusiasm, of Philistine sentimentalism in the icy water of egotistical calculation'. It is also how sold metallic money melted into the abstract air of financial value.[20]

Looking at Marx's *Capital*, it is clear that it was capital accumulation that he made the basis of his analysis and the title of his investigation. He begins with a development of Smith's discussion of labour and value by examining the thing produced by labour – the commodity (*Warenform*) and the difference between use value and market value, or what he calls the money form. He then has a general chapter on money, which he terms a commodity to represent the value of other commodities. After this he goes on in an abstract section to describe how money is transformed into capital, suggesting it was a process that started with merchant capital in the sixteenth century.[21] However, at this point he rejects the need for historical specificity, and instead focuses on how the process of circulation for financial purposes created an abstraction that had what could be termed a psychological effect on the capitalist, or the person engaged in such circulation:

> The circulation of money as capital is, on the contrary, an end in itself, for the expansion of value takes place only within this constantly renewed movement. The circulation of capital has therefore no limits.
>
> As the conscious representative of this movement, the possessor of money becomes a capitalist. His person, or rather his pocket, is the point from which the money starts and to which it returns. The expansion of value ... becomes his subjective aim, and it is only in so far as the appropriation of ever more and more wealth in the abstract becomes the sole motive of his operations, that he functions as a capitalist, that is, as capital personified and endowed with consciousness and a will. Use-values must therefore never be looked upon as the real aim of the capitalist; neither must the profit on any single transaction. The restless never-ending process of profit-making alone is what he aims.[22]

It is only after establishing this nature of capital that he goes on to discuss labour, the factory system, and how surplus value was extracted from the productive system and converted into capital, before moving on

[20] Marx and Engels, *Communist Manifesto*, pp. 9–10.
[21] Marx, *Capital*, I, pp. 125–244.
[22] Ibid., I, pp. 253–4.

to the law of capitalist accumulation.[23] Later he would elaborate somewhat more on the early modern period, which he characterised as one of primitive accumulation:

> The discovery of gold and silver in America, the extirpation, enslavement and entombment in mines of the aboriginal population, the beginning of the conquest and looting of the East Indies, the turning of Africa into a warren for the commercial hunting of black-skins, signalled the rosy dawn of the era of capitalist production. These idyllic proceedings are the chief moments of primitive accumulation. On their heels treads the commercial war of the European nations, with the globe for a theatre ... they all employ the power of the state, the concentrated and organized force of society, to hasten, hot-house fashion, the process of transformation of the feudal mode of production into the capitalist mode, and to shorten the transition. Force is the midwife of every old society pregnant with a new one. It is itself an economic power.[24]

Here, crucially, he distinguishes force from capital, and shows how force uses capital to create economic power – a theme which will be explored in Chapter 8.

However, in *Capital* Marx never used the term capitalism. He discussed the concept of capital extensively, the mode of capitalist production, capitalists, and capital accumulation, but only rarely talked of capitalist society.[25] By the early twentieth century, trade union-based democratic socialist parties had become politically powerful in industrial countries – for instance, the Labour Party in Britain or the SDP in the new Germany. But it was the successful Bolshevik revolution in Russia, the attempted revolutions in the immediate post-war period in Germany, and the rise of politically popular and strong communist parties in France, Germany, and Austria (in Vienna) that led the so-called Austrian school of economists to argue that what they now called 'capitalism' as an economic system was both morally and productively better than socialism. It was the adoption of the term by a set of thinkers who wanted to advocate an economic system in order to reject socialism that has had the most profound impact on how we currently think about capitalism.[26]

[23] Volume II goes into the nature of capital and circulation in more detail, while volume III discusses such things as profit, rent, and interest. Both of these volumes were assembled by Engels after Marx's death.

[24] Marx, *Capital*, I, ch. 31.

[25] Stedman Jones, 'Introduction to Marx and Engles', in *Communist Manifesto*, pp. 27–38.

[26] The concept was notably picked up by Max Weber in his *Protestant Ethic and the Spirit of Capitalism* and by R. H. Tawney, who used it to mean justifying profit against older moral prohibitions by the Catholic church.

But they did not invent the term. This was done by Werner Sombart, a practitioner of the German historical school of philosophy and economics, who first used the word to refer to an entire social system that developed historically, in his still not fully translated *Der moderne Kapitalismus (Historisch-systematische Darstellung des gesamteuropäischen Wirtschaftslebens von seinen Anfängen bis zur Gegenwart)*, or *Modern Capitalism: A Historical Investigation of Pan-European Economic Life from its beginnings to the Present*. published in three volumes between 1902 and 1927.[27] Sombart was a socialist who, heavily influenced by Marx, attempted to present a much more purely chronological history of economic change and social relations. In this work he described the foundations of modern capitalism in terms of the state, religion, population, and the transformation of the market through such things as accounting and profit, which changed practices and ways of thinking. He also popularised terms such as the *Geist* or spirt of capitalism, as well as rationalisation and creative destruction, all concepts that would be further developed by Max Weber and Joseph Schumpeter.

Histories of Capitalism in the Early Modern World

For clarity I will examine major texts in thematic sections as follows: (1) how merchant capital evolved through the history of bookkeeping; (2) the agrarian transition from feudalism to capitalism; (3) entrepreneurialism; and (4) the nature of capital as property. Most of this literature also focuses on developments in Europe. As we shall see, Europe's global expansion is often seen as a crucial development, but specifically as an extension of developments within that continent. More recently, histories of capitalism have focused on the effects of capitalism in the world outside of Europe.[28] However, apart from the slave trade, most of this literature focuses on the nineteenth and twentieth centuries.

The History of Merchant Bookkeeping and the Nature of Capital

The role of merchants and accounting has been associated with the rise of capitalism since Sombart emphasised it in *Der Moderne*

[27] Although only the first two volumes have been recently translated into English, the main ideas have been summarised and developed by Frederick L. Nussbaum, *A History of the Economic Institutions of Modern Europe* (New York, 1933).

[28] Most notable of these is Sven Beckert, *Empire of Cotton: A New History of Global Capitalism* (London, 2016); Gareth Austin, 'The Return of Capitalism as a Concept', in Gareth Austin, Marcel van der Linden, and Jürgen Kocka (eds.), *Capitalism* (London, 2016), pp. 207–34.

Kapitalismus.[29] Marx, of course, had discussed merchant capital as the first type of capital formation, but Sombart spent much more time elaborating a more detailed chronological historical narrative. His first volume dealt with the transition from feudalism to capitalism. Subsequently he published a second volume covering the industrial revolution, and in 1927 he published a final volume that dealt with the twentieth century. He termed the industrial revolution *Hochkapitalismus*, or high capitalism, and the early twentieth century *Spätkapitalismus*, or late capitalism. Curiously, this term is still in critical use 100 years later.[30] As mentioned earlier, it was this work that, more than any other, popularised the use of the term capitalism. However, since it was not published in English, most of the substantive nature of the text has remained much more influential in Germany. Sombart very much emphasised economic practice as being associated with religion and nationalism. He had whole sections on *Wesen* (essence) and *Geist* (spirit) to describe the historical evolution of practices, and he wrote a whole book on how the Jewish religion evolved through persecution as well as its own nature to create the 'essence' of capitalism. Socialism, in contrast, he saw as something German.[31] Although he was not a National Socialist, and praised what he saw as Jewish achievements as much as he criticised them, he hoped German socialism would replace what he characterised as Jewish and English capitalism. His discussion of race and his association of economic practices with religious and national cultures is undoubtedly one reason why he has had limited impact in English.[32]

However, when the term capitalism was adopted into English, it was Sombart's stress on accounting that became associated with his name, not religion or culture. He claimed that the invention of double-entry bookkeeping transformed the world. For him, this was not just a technological achievement that allowed the creation of abstract value, but an activity that led to alienated profit-seeking activity. He stated: 'the

[29] Werner Sombart, *Der Moderne Kapitalismus (Historisch-systematische Darstellung des gesamteuropäischen Wirtschaftslebens von seinen Anfängen bis zur Gegenwart)*, vols. I–III (München, 1928).

[30] See, for instance, Frederic Jameson, *Postmodernism, or, the Cultural Logic of Late Capitalism* (London, 1992).

[31] The later book was translated into English: Werner Sombart, *The Jews and Modern Capitalism* (London, 1913).

[32] For more information on Sombart, see the essays in Jürgen G. Backhaus (ed.), *Werner Sombart (1863–1941): Social Scientist* (Marburg, 1996), especially vol. I: Bernhard vom Brocke, 'Werner Sombart 1863–1941: Capitalism – Socialism. His Life, Works and Influence'; Lawrence A. Scaff, 'Sombart's Politics'; Fritz Reheis, 'Return to the Grace of God: Werner Sombart's Compromise with National Socialism'; Rolf Riess, 'Werner Sombart under National Socialism: A First Approximation'; and Heinz Ludwig, 'Sombart and the Jews'.

merchant using double entry bookkeeping necessarily has only one objective, namely to increase value comprehended only quantitatively. When he looks at his accounts, he does not see boots or ship's cargoes, nor flour or cotton, but exclusively money amounts that increase or decrease.'[33] In an intriguing article, Eve Chiapetto has argued that Marx's theory of capital was, in fact, influenced by contemporary instruction manuals on accounting and double-entry bookkeeping.[34]

But, Sombart's thesis has come under sustained criticism from historians who have pointed out that double-entry bookkeeping was a very specific and difficult technique, and ordinary accounts that only tracked expenditure and earnings were enough to promote economic growth.[35] Also, even such basic account-keeping was never very widespread before the eighteenth century, outside of some northern Italian cities, let alone double-entry bookkeeping. But, if double-entry bookkeeping did not revolutionise the world in as dramatic a way as Sombart thought, he was right to think that without bookkeeping, financial – or circulating – capital, as opposed to land and fixed capital, could not have existed. As Mary Poovey has succinctly put it, accounting created a 'fact' out of a relationship of exchange. The value left over after accounts were balanced was something removed from the relationship between any two people engaged in exchange, and could be moved around and used by anyone else who also practised accounting.[36] Besides Poovey, there are many scholars who continue to emphasise the importance of the development of accounting for both economic and social history, even if they do not accept Sombart's thesis.[37] The importance and evolution of accounting in England and Scotland will be explored in Chapters 2 and 9.

Sombart had a great effect on his younger colleague and friend Max Weber. Weber would develop the role of accounting further, arguing that it was the mainspring of a transformation to a 'rational' way of

[33] This translation is taken from B. S. Yamey, 'The Historical Significance of Double-Entry Bookkeeping: Some Non-Sombartian Claims', *Accounting, Business & Financial History* 15, no. 1 (2005), p. 85; Sombart, *Der Moderne Kapitalismus*, II, pp. 119–20.

[34] Eve Chiapello, 'Accounting and the Birth of the Notion of Capitalism', *Critical Perspectives on Accounting* 18 (2007), pp. 276–93.

[35] Yamey, 'Historical Significance', pp. 77–88.

[36] Mary Poovey, *A History of the Modern Fact: Problems of Knowledge in the Sciences of Wealth and Society* (Chicago, 1998), pp. 29–61.

[37] The most succinct summary of this has been presented by Jacob Soll, *The Reckoning: Financial Accountability and the Making and Breaking of Nations* (London, 2014). The scholarship on accounting and its relationship to capitalism has been summarised by Eve Chiapello. There are a number of active journals dealing with the subject, including the *Journal of Accounting Research* and *Critical Perspectives on Accounting*.

ordering the world.[38] Weber also took up Sombart's emphasis on the importance of religious beliefs and practices for economic change in his shorter book, *The Protestant Ethic and the Spirt of Capitalism*, published in 1905 only a few years after the first volume of Sombart's *Der Moderne Kapitalismus*. Here he argued that Protestantism was responsible for the idea that making money through discipline and thrift was morally good, rather than a sign of individual greed. This worked through a process whereby, as he saw it, faith and anxiety about predestination had led to the internalisation of the virtues of hard work as evidence of election, thus making possible the radical changes in belief and behaviour needed to become oriented towards the utility of the counting board and account book, rather than the unity of community or neighbourhood. The ascetic worldview was one of *capitalism* in this sense precisely because it was directed towards 'capital' and the rational accumulation of capital for its own sake.

He went on to link the reason for its eventual development, not to social forces, but to the spiritual content of religion and the spread of 'worldly asceticism' in Protestant thought, which promoted the disenchantment of the world through work discipline and the forgoing of pleasure. This led to rational calculation and accounting, and then to the capitalist organisation of labour, because the same asceticism that frowned on pleasure also frowned on the luxury that provided pleasure. Savings were the result of this process, as Puritans controlled their desire to enjoy material items, while at the same time continuing to work hard. This, in turn, became investment capital, which was used to create rational institutions in the pursuit of more profit.[39] Thus, a moderate increase in consumption and desire for goods eventually led to the creation of a world in which the social organisation of capital through savings permitted development of large-scale institutions, which enabled the production of goods on a massive scale, allowing consumption, saving, and capital to go on increasing. This, in turn, created a world of rationalised alienated work and atomised competitive self-fulfilment in work and material consumption. It was work in which the commensality of community had been lost – a world he termed the 'iron cage'.[40]

[38] Max Weber, *Economy and Society: An Outline of Interpretive Sociology*, ed. Guenther Roth and Claus Wittich (New York, 1968), I, pp. 63–107; III, pp. 958–1002.

[39] Soll, *The Reckoning*, pp. 156–9, 163, 167–8, 173–5. The link between Puritanism and work discipline had in fact already been made by Matthew Arnold in 1869. Matthew Arnold, *Culture and Anarchy* (Cambridge, 1966), pp. 132, 140–4.

[40] Craig Muldrew, 'From a "Light Cloak" to the "Iron Cage": An Essay on Historical Changes in the Relationship between Community and Individualism', in Alexandra Shepard and Philip Withington (eds.), *Communities in Early Modern England* (Manchester, 2000), pp. 159–60; Weber, *Protestant Ethic and the Spirit of Capitalism* (New York, 1904) pp. 172, 240–2. Charles Taylor has also offered a critique of what he

Although Weber's *Protestant Ethic* was not translated into English until 1930, by Talcott Parsons, it was read by the English socialist historian R. H. Tawney, who developed Weber's ideas in one of the first great works of English social history, *Religion and the Rise of Capitalism*, published in 1926. Weber's work had been an essay drawing on historical examples from German and English Protestant writings, but especially those of Richard Baxter. Tawney's work was a much more nuanced chronological history that examined how he thought Puritan ideas changed attitudes to profit. Since he had already devoted a major work to enclosure and the transformation of agriculture to more capitalist practices, he was able to show how religious writings were adopted by profit-making farmers to morally justify their profits. In doing so, he also placed a great deal of emphasis on changing religious attitudes to usury and interest rates on loans. The Catholic Church, following the ethics of Aristotle, had banned usury as an illegitimate practice of making money out of already existing wealth, although the charging of interest was allowed in certain, mostly charitable circumstances. Interest was made legal in England by a statute in 1586, and Tawney argued that this was an important step in the Protestant validation of profit-making in England.[41]

In general, there has also been a great debate not so much about the degree to which Protestantism was favourable to capitalism, but about the degree to which Weber thought Catholicism was not, because of its different attitude towards poverty, festivities, and holidays, and of course monastic institutions.[42] Since Weber and Tawney, there has also been a large, and continuing, debate about the role of scholastic thought and usury in the Italian Renaissance and how it affected the economy.[43] In *The Economy of Obligation*, I also dealt with the importance of religion, but there looked at it in relation to how people thought about credit and debt. But, as we will see in Chapters 5 and 6, religion was also crucial to how capital formation was justified.

After Tawney, most British early modern historians who theorised about capitalism focused on agrarian society rather than religion or bookkeeping and merchant capital. At the same time, the many historians who wrote about the rise of Italian banking, and the international

sees as the spiritually alienating 'search for pure subjective expressive fulfilment' in modern society. Charles Taylor, *Sources of the Self* (Cambridge, 1989), pp. 495–521.

41 R. H. Tawney, *Religion and the Rise of Capitalism* (Harmondsworth, 1926), pp. 179–251.

42 Anthony Giddens, 'Introduction' to Weber, *Protestant Ethic*, pp. xix–xxvi.

43 See, for instance, John T. Noonan, *The Scholastic Analysis of Usury* (Cambridge, MA, 1957); Giacomo Todeschini and Gian Maria Varanini, *Credito e Usura Fra Teologia, Diritto e Amministrazione: Linguaggi a Confronto, Sec. XII–XVI* (Rome, 2005).

economic success of the northern Italian cities, conceptualised their analysis with economic concepts such as institutions, growth, and trade rather than capital.[44] A similar point could be made of historians of the next economic success story, the Flemish Lowlands and the Dutch Republic.[45] It was not until Fernand Braudel's massive three-volume history of the global economy was published in 1979 that an attempt was made to analyse capitalism on the same scale as Sombart. In *Civilisation and Capitalism: 15th–18th Century*, he made an argument for a roughly tripartite division of world economic history into material life, or the 'production at home' of basic foods and material necessities; the market economy, or production away from home of more complex manufactured produce; and capitalism, which was the economy of international merchants trading in luxuries from Asia, and then colonial products from the Americas. The first volume on material life was published twelve years earlier than the other two, in 1967, and as he worked through the literature on trade he came to realise that a history of capitalism had to be a global history because it was merchants who developed capital, and from it the social attributes of capitalism at the top. These merchants created circulating value out of the production and material life described in his first two volumes, and moved it around the globe;

> I have already indicated that capitalism in the past (as distinct from capitalism today) only occupied a narrow platform of economic life. How could one possibly take it to mean a 'system' extending over the whole of society? It was nevertheless a world apart, different from and indeed foreign to the social and economic context surrounding it ... In fact capitalism was what it was in relation to a *non-capitalism* of immense proportions. And to refuse to admit this dichotomy within the economy of the past, on the pretext that 'true' capitalism dates only from the nineteenth century, means abandoning the effort to understand [its] significance.[46]

As a result of this limitation, he debated whether he should actually use the word, and in doing so noted numerous early modern economic historians who had rejected it. But in the end he decided that since it was of undisputed importance to the world of 1979, it was important to the past: 'Personally, after a long struggle, I gave up trying to get rid of this troublesome intruder ... To the historian, understanding the past and understanding the present are the same thing.'[47]

44 Raymond de Roover, *The Rise and Decline of the Medici Bank, 1397–1494* (Cambridge, MA, 1963); Eric Kerridge, *Usury, Interest and the Reformation* (Aldershot, 2002).
45 For instance, the work of Nicolaas Wilhelmus Posthumus on the Netherlands: http://resources.huygens.knaw.nl/bwn1880-2000/lemmata/bwn1/posthumus.
46 Here he was arguing against Lucian Febvre, who had wanted to drop the term. Braudel, *Wheels of Commerce*, pp. 238–9.
47 Ibid., p. 231.

Braudel accepted the importance of bookkeeping and company organisations, but for him it was the *social* difference of the merchant class to other parts of society that made capitalism something different.[48] Because they could create capital, merchants had a freedom to move, and to move themselves *and their wealth*, which those embedded within rural communities could not. Capitalism was thus, for him, definitely not something that originated in the countryside or even in industry. It evolved out of long-distance trade, where there was a high rate of investment and capital formation.[49] Capitalism, for Braudel, was not a system extending over the whole of society as Sombart had postulated, but rather a world apart, 'foreign to the social and economic context surrounding it'.[50] For Braudel, his task was to

> find out why that sector of the society of the past which I would not hesitate to call capitalist, should have lived as if in a bell-jar, cut from the rest; why was it not able to expand and conquer the whole of society? … in yesterday's societies a significant rate of capital formation was possible only in certain sectors and not in the whole market economy of the time. Capital which was adventurously invested outside this favoured zone bore little fruit, when it was simply swallowed without trace.[51]

His answer, which he went on to explore in the final volume of the series, was that capitalism only existed where there was significant long-distance trade, arguing that it 'would have been impossible without the special and as it were liberating action of world trade'.[52]

Braudel's emphasis on globalism was taken up by the sociologist Immanuel Wallerstein, who developed a world-systems theory, in which he theorised that there were different forms of capitalism in core and periphery regions, and explored how the core region in Europe expanded over time. Wallerstein developed Braudel's division of the economy between market exchange and elite merchant capitalism. Like Braudel, he saw the European mercantile expansion into the global economy as crucial to this process. Thus, for him, like Braudel, capitalism depended on the world economy.[53] He did, however, argue that the class relations that characterised capitalism grew out of agrarian relations in late medieval Europe, but that profit-oriented elites moved into towns to make more profit through trade.[54] As he states in his semi-autobiographical

48 Ibid., p. 233. 49 Ibid., pp. 231–3. 50 Ibid., p. 239.
51 Ibid., p. 248; also see pp. 239, 577.
52 Ibid., p. 600; also see Fernand Braudel, *The Perspective of the World* (London, 1984).
53 Immanuel Wallerstein, *World-Systems Analysis: An Introduction* (Durham, 2004), pp. 18–20, 24–6.
54 Immanuel Wallerstein, *The Modern World-System. Vol. I, Capitalist Agriculture and the Origins of the European World-Economy in the Sixteenth Century* (Berkeley, 2011), pp. 14–131.

introduction to world-systems analysis, the main impetus for the core–periphery concept was taken from a school of development economics that focused on South America, and was termed *dependency theory*. Roughly, this theory argued that 'core' US capitalist institutions such as industry and finance used their financial power in tandem with the American state to exploit periphery states in Latin America as producers of raw materials for US industry and consumption.[55] Wallerstein took this idea and, in a series of four detailed volumes, argued that this process developed first in sixteenth- and seventeenth-century Europe. There is not the space here to even begin to do justice to such an elaborate argument, but as empirical examples Wallerstein used the exploitation of eastern European grain as much as Indonesian spice production and Brazilian sugar, whereby distant production was organised around coercive relations of labour to achieve profit.

However, it was not such labour relations that primarily characterised capitalism for Wallerstein, but profit. Although labour was crucial, as he put it, 'we are in a capitalist system only when the system gives priority to the *endless* accumulation of capital'.[56] In order to achieve this, capitalism needed both the world and monopoly. Wallerstein rejected Marxist transition debate history which focused on agrarian history within the nation state. Instead he argued that by operating globally, merchant capitalists could avoid the monetary rapacity of political units and any regulation that might impede their need for a division of labour to manufacture or grow the products they marketed for profit. By operating globally they were able to use states who might be competing with each other for dynastic or religious reasons. Since such monopoly-totalising capitalists first originated in Europe, it was Europe that became the core in the early modern period, and the rest of the world gradually became its periphery.[57]

Since the 1990s, though, a substantial number of historians of Asian and African early modern economies have argued that before the nineteenth century European capitalists did not have the power to fundamentally challenge the autonomy of other economic areas. In this view, the European conquest of the Americas and Caribbean with their demographic collapse caused by the exchange of diseases was quite different to the experience elsewhere. In the rest of the world, apart from the Spice Islands, the Cape, and small parts of India, Europeans, despite using extreme violence, were not able to create colonies before the mid-

[55] Wallerstein, *World-Systems Analysis*, pp. 10–12. [56] Ibid., p. 24.
[57] However, he does not address the question of legal institutions and their role in securing capital, which in Europe were mostly provided by states.

eighteenth century.[58] Historians such as Prasannan Parthasarathi and Kenneth Pomeranz have also argued that standards of living and production in China and India before 1900 were not that different to those in Europe taken as a whole.[59] A large debate has grown around whether this is true or not, which involves attempts to measure the real wages of labourers by various means.[60] But finding good data has been difficult, and the debate continues.

What is more important for our purposes here is what role the formation of capital might have had in such different economies, and here we can note the argument of Bin Wong in his book *China Transformed*.[61] China was by far the largest Asian state economy, and Wong argues against interpreting its economic development through an interpretive framework of Smithian market development and a progression towards capitalism. Instead, he argues that China, because of a completely different relationship between agrarian society and the state, followed a different path. Peasant farms remained relatively small because of partible inheritance, but since holdings, as in Europe, could be rebuilt through active land markets, what was more important was the role of the paternalistic moral Confucian state, which saw the well-being of its subjects as a moral obligation.[62] This was done through grain transfers to prevent dearth, but also by managing levels of inequality by limiting the development of merchants and middleman traders.[63] As a result of this policy, the division of labour did not develop to the same extent as in Europe outside of some very specialised cloth and porcelain production zones, such as the lower Yangtze and Jingdezhen. Most industrial production remained very local and tied to family farms, and class divisions did not emerge as strongly as in Europe. In addition, and more importantly for our subject here, long-distance trade of specialised goods – both internally and overseas – remained limited, which restricted the formation of merchant capital. Thus, the Chinese economy remained more

58 John K. Thornton, *Africa and Africans in the Making of the Atlantic World, 1400–1800* (Cambridge, 1998), pp. 112–25.

59 Kenneth Pomeranz, *The Great Divergence: China, Europe, and the Making of the Modern World Economy* (Princeton, 2009); Prasannan Parthasarathi, *Why Europe Grew Rich and Asia Did Not: Global Economic Divergence, 1600–1850* (Cambridge, 2011).

60 For a summary of this debate, see Craig Muldrew, *Food, Energy and the Creation of Industriousness: Work and Material Culture in Agrarian England, 1550–1780* (Cambridge, 2011), p. 10, n. 30.

61 Roy Bin Wong, *China Transformed: Historical Change and the Limits of European Experience* (Ithaca, 1997).

62 Ibid., pp. 43–50.

63 Roy Bin Wong and William Pierre-Etienne, *Nourish the People: The State Civilian Granary System in China, 1650–1850* (Ann Arbor, 2020).

equal and had very active local markets, but not enough profit and freedom for a 'capitalist' middle class to develop, as we shall see it did in England.[64] In Japan, however, an industrious revolution took place in which intensification was achieved more through labour than the use of machinery.[65]

In a recent essay, 'Return of Capitalism as a Concept', Gareth Austin has argued how the concept is useful in understanding the progress and consequences of nineteenth-century European colonialism.[66] One recent, celebrated history in the same vein is Sven Beckert's *Empire of Cotton: A New History of Global Capitalism*. Although it focuses largely on the nineteenth century, when British and American capitalists undoubtedly used their financial wealth to dominate trade and take over markets around the world in a competitive way, he does postulate that this process began earlier in the eighteenth century. This, he states, began through a process he terms 'war capitalism', through which the British state and private corporations such as the East India Company used force to lower the cost of labour. But nowhere is capitalism defined, and little evidence is actually used to analytically demonstrate how this concept worked in practice.[67] As Robin Blackburn has noted in an excellent review, the concept seems to represent what Marx called primitive accumulation, but this is oddly never mentioned. As a result, 'war capitalism' remains rhetorical rather than analytical.[68] However, Beckert's book does show that once the cotton gin was perfected, slave labour became integral to the capitalist system of cotton production and manufacturing. In a much earlier work, which predates Braudel, the eminent Marxist historian of the Caribbean, Eric Williams, was clearer in his understanding of capital. In his book *Slavery and Capitalism*, written in the 1930s and published in 1944, he provided the first wide-ranging history of the role of African slavery in the development of the British Atlantic economy. Although it was a broad economic history of the African trade and slavery, in particular it was 'an economic study of the role of Negro slavery and the slave trade in providing the capital which financed the Industrial Revolution in England'.[69] To do this, he focused on actual profits from the Liverpool and Lancaster slave trade that were turned

64 Bin Wong, *China Transformed*, pp. 50–2, 146–51; Akinobu Kuroda, *A Global History of Money* (London, 2020), pp. 119–28.

65 Akira Hayami, *Japan's Industrious Revolution: Economic and Social Transformations in the Early Modern Period* (Tokyo, 2015); Osamu Saito, *Pre-modern Economic Growth Revisited: Japan and the West* (London, 2005).

66 Austin, 'Return of Capitalism'.

67 Beckert, *Empire of Cotton*, pp. xv–xvi, 29–48.

68 Robin Blackburn. 'White Gold, Black Labour', *New Left Review* 95 (2015), pp. 151–60.

69 Eric Williams, *Capitalism and Slavery* (London, 2022), p. xi.

into investment capital, which was crucial in the establishment of industry in Lancashire.[70] His thesis has been criticised on empirical grounds by historians who have noted that such capital, while important, was only one relatively small part of overall investment, which was largely drawn from local sources.[71]

However, in a more recent book, with access to a much wider range of sources, Joseph Inikori has detailed the role that Africans played in the eighteenth-century industrial revolution.[72] We can conclude from his work that it is undoubtedly the case that without the labour supply provided by the African slave trade, given the demographic trends in eighteenth-century Europe, the Atlantic economy could not have developed as it did from *c.*1650 onwards. But this expansion was more important in the way it created multiple consumer markets, which could then generate more profits that could become capital. New markets were created, most prominently among colonial settlers, who were relatively wealthy in comparison to Europeans, but also for food and clothing for their slaves. Markets were created in Africa for goods traded for slaves, and in Europe for the sugar, tobacco, gold, silver, indigo, etc. produced in the Americas.[73] Capital, of course, was vital in the creation of the trade. Transatlantic African slavery was possible because it could use merchants' capital and skills to provide ships capable of long-distance voyages, as well as goods that the African slave traders of West African states – such as Dahomey – wanted enough to be continually at war to capture slaves in the interior. As John Thornton argued, the limits of European technology and susceptibility to tropical disease made early modern colonial activity in Sub-Saharan Africa (apart for the Cape) impossible, so they had to rely on indigenous slave traders.[74] Of course, once bought, coercion and extreme violence began, and without question the development of the Atlantic economy depended on cruelly coerced labour. In addition, the gruesome and inhumane ways to save on the expenses of transport were a result of pure abstract profit and loss calculations between the cost of keeping captives alive and the potential profits from their sale.

[70] Ibid., pp. 58–79.

[71] C. Knick Harley, 'Trade: Discovery, Mercantilism and Technology', in Roderick Floud and Paul Johnson (eds.), *The Cambridge Economic History of Modern Britain* (Cambridge, 2003), pp. 196–7; Pat Hudson, 'Slavery, the Slave Trade and Economic Growth: A Contribution to the Debate', in Keith McClelland, Nicholas Draper, and Catherine Hall (eds.), *Emancipation and the Remaking of the British Imperial World* (Baltimore, 2017), pp. 36–59.

[72] Joseph E. Inikori, *Africans and the Industrial Revolution in England: A Study in International Trade and Economic Development* (Cambridge, 2002), pp. 6–8, chs. 4, 9.

[73] Ibid., *Africans*, pp. 405–72.

[74] Thornton, *Africa and Africans*, pp. 112–25.

Capital was also required for the organisation of the slave trade, which required the building of forts as well as ships, and Caribbean plantation agriculture also required large merchant capital to pay for expensive machinery.[75] However, as Paul Lovejoy has shown, the 'other' slave trade in eastern Africa, to provide slaves for Muslim societies north of the Sahara, probably involved the export of 2.3 million people between 1600 and 1800. Although dwarfed by the over 8.4 million Sub-Saharan Africans traded across the Atlantic, this is still a substantial number, and was done without the need for any capital.[76]

But, of course, in Marx's definition, slave labour is explicitly *not* capitalist since its form of exploitation is based on force, not wage dependency and competition. Slavery, as a form of coercion, dominance, and exploitation is also much older than capital. Although Beckert makes great claims for the origin of slave-produced cotton as a force creating global capitalism, slavery was first employed for sugar production in the Maghreb in a non-capitalist way, but was then adapted, first by Portuguese merchants who used merchant capital to buy slaves from North Africa to work plantations on Madeira and then in Bahia in northern Brazil.[77] This process was copied by the British about 100 years later on Barbados and Jamaica, when the supply of British indentured servants declined and thus rose in cost.[78] In this sense, the enslaved became part of a commodity market rather than a labour market.

Another example of how the power of merchant capital contributed to a massive increase in coerced labour is outlined by Braudel. In his second volume he describes how the urban growth of the Lowlands, first to support cloth production and then trade in the Dutch Republic, was supported by grain imports from the Baltic. The small size of the United Provinces meant they could not grow enough grain to support their urban populations, and as a result sought supply from North Sea markets. This was facilitated by the Hanse and Dutch merchants through Danzig. Eastern European seigniors took advantage of the system to maximise their profits by keeping the institution of serfdom, and forcing peasants to produce grain through labour service, which the landlords

[75] Braudel, *Perspective of the World*, p. 272.

[76] Paul Lovejoy, *Transformations in Slavery: A History of Slavery in Africa* (Cambridge, 2009), pp. 60–5, 65–73, 88–92. For items used as money in the trade, see pp. 104–7.

[77] Stuart B. Schwartz, *Sugar Plantations in the Formation of Brazilian Society Bahia, 1550–1835* (Cambridge, 1985).

[78] Hilary Beckles, 'Plantation Production and White "Proto-Slavery": White Indentured Servants and the Colonisation of the English West Indies, 1624–1645', *The Americas*, 41 (1984), pp. 21–45; Hilary Beckles, 'Black Men in White Skins: The Formation of a White Proletariat in West Indian Slave Society', *The Journal of Imperial and Commonwealth History* 15 (1986), pp. 225–47.

could sell on international markets to facilitate their own luxury consumption. At the same time, this suppressed internal market demand in much of the east European countryside by denying peasants much profit.[79] Braudel goes so far as to call eastern Europe a type of colony.[80] This was a system in which capital was used to supply food to an economy in the Lowlands. The latter was market-oriented, had wage labour, and developed many new forms of capital in towns. But in order to do this, freedom was suppressed elsewhere to gain control of a greater proportion of the limited capacity of labour-intensive pre-mechanised production.

This raises the important point that unless population growth is sufficient to produce more workers than needed, it is very difficult to exploit workers in a capitalist way, since demand for scarce labour should raise its remuneration. As a result, labour needs to be sought using force as a means of violent coercion. In terms of slavery, such force is obvious. But gender historians have also pointed out that legal inequality in the household, combined with legal violence, is coercive. In this way, it was used – and continues to be used – to keep down the price of housework and childcare. Much household work was also done by servants hired by families able to afford them. Service was paid mostly with bed and board and remuneration was not very market-oriented. Such cultural coercion cannot be said to have been caused by the advent of capital, but when mothers and children enter the labour market – or today when cleaners or childcare workers are hired – it can certainly be argued that it lowers the effective rate of remuneration in the labour market. This seems to indicate that demography has to be favourable for the labour theory of capitalist exploitation to work as described. Thus, Beckert is on to something in describing how the power of capital is much more effective than feudal relations at coercing labour over long distances, but war capitalism is a poor descriptive term. Perhaps *coercive capitalism* is a better term to describe how the power provided by capital can be used to purchase, ship, and police coerced labour, or to purchase goods from sellers who use and enforce coerced labour, such as the grain purchases from eastern European estate owners using the second serfdom.[81] Coerced labour can certainly exist within a legal regime with protection of the person and property, and it has the advantage of *not needing* a system of circulating currency, which is a necessary precondition of

[79] Much the same can be said about the development of the Italian sharecropping system.
[80] Braudel, *Wheels of Commerce*, pp. 265–71.
[81] On the question of law and forms of labour, see Douglas Hay and Paul Craven, *Masters, Servants, and Magistrates in Britain and the Empire, 1562–1955* (Chapel Hill, 2004).

large-scale wage labour. Different types of capital can produce different social results.

The examples of slavery and the second serfdom both point to another aspect of how capital, when employed in long-distance trade, will often lead to a disjunction between ethics and laws applied in the home market and those used in the place of production. This was recognised very early, as can be seen in the following passage:

> all the world choppeth and changeth, runneth & raveth after Marts, Markets, and Merchandising, so that all thinges come into Commerce, and passe into traffique ... this man maketh merchandise of the workes of his owne handes, this man of another man labour, one selleth words, another maketh traffike of the skins & bloud of other men, yea there are some found so subtill and cunning merchants, that they perswade and induce men to suffer themselves to bee bought and sold, and we have seene in our own time enowe, and too many which have made merchadise of mens soules.[82]

This was taken, unacknowledged, by John Wheeler, the secretary to the Merchant Adventurers Company, from a French publication, and published in his *Treatise on Commerce* of 1601. The majority of the pamphlet was concerned with the sociability of commerce and how it mostly brought people together and made them dependent on each other, but in this passage he shows how the temptation to profit could easily overcome the ethics of religion and civility.[83]

In terms of warfare – from Elizabeth's wars in Ireland, to Cromwell's capture of Jamaica, the Anglo-Dutch wars, King Billy's war in New England, and the many subsequent wars in the eighteenth century – the violent development of the British colonial trading system certainly had a dramatic impact on the path of British political and economic history. But, in terms of the *novelty* of the processes by which capital came to be created and used, the empire did not play a formative role. New plantations created new markets, and commodities were traded with Britain, and this required credit, which was supplied by a system of bills of exchange.[84] But this used practices already established. The Liverpool bill market was vibrant and active after *c.*1740, but, as we will see, a national market in bills of exchange and the use of local paper currency were well developed fifty years earlier. In fact, the Atlantic colonies were often treated cavalierly by the London government in

[82] This translation is taken from John Wheeler's *Treatise on Commerce* (London, 1601), reprinted and edited by G.B. Hotchkiss, (New York, 1931), pp. 316–17, who translated it verbatim from a French work by Louis de Turgot Mayerne.
[83] Craig Muldrew, *Economy of Obligation* (London, 1998) pp. 137–40.
[84] Inikori, *Africans and the Industrial Revolution*, pp. 318ff.

terms of money supply.[85] Also, the system of government borrowing and taxation, which evolved to pay for all of this violence, became an important part of how capital came to circulate in Britain in the eighteenth century, but it would be foolish to say that taxation was introduced to achieve this. As we shall see in Chapter 10, it evolved within a system of capital creation.

Labour as a Commodity: The Transition from Feudalism to Capitalism

Since merchants did not engage in any part of the means of production – they only transported the finished goods – Marx and many subsequent historians have looked more for the origins of capitalism in the countryside, the very place where Braudel claimed it was swallowed without a trace. All over the late medieval and early modern world the main form of production was agricultural.[86] In 1500, even in the most urbanised trading centres of Europe – northern Italy and the Lowlands – only 12–15 per cent of the population lived in cities. In less developed countries such as England, in 1550 only about 5 per cent did so, and in Europe as a whole only 5.6 per cent did.[87] However, agricultural land has always also been a form of capital, and in terms of value it dwarfed all others. But it was fixed, and also bound up tightly by laws of inheritance that governed gendered property in marriage. Mortgages were used everywhere in western Europe to create financial capital out of land, and in England the rules of coverture played an important part in this process, but apart from Amy Erickson few historians have discussed coverture in terms of capitalism. It is a central theme of my book that this is a vast omission, because productive land was the most secure form of collateral for the formation of circulating capital.[88] Although some government debt eventually became almost as secure, it never had the fixedness of a piece of real estate.[89]

Instead, the history of agrarian capitalism has focused on labour. Marx spent a fair amount of space in volume I of *Capital* examining how and

[85] Geoffrey Parker, *Global Crisis: War, Climate Change and Catastrophe in the Seventeenth Century* (New Haven, 2013), pp. 446–56.

[86] The most industrialised areas in the fourteenth to the sixteenth centuries were northern Italy and the Lowlands, where European cloth production was concentrated.

[87] Jan De Vries, *European Urbanization, 1500–1800* (Cambridge, MA, 1984), p. 39.

[88] Amy Louise Erickson, 'Coverture and Capitalism', *History Workshop Journal* 59, no. 1 (2005), pp. 1–16.

[89] Craig Muldrew, 'Mortgages as Mediation between Kin and Capital', in Chris Briggs and C. J. Zuijderduijn (eds.), *Land and Credit: Mortgages in the Medieval and Early Modern European Countryside* (London, 2018), pp. 309–26.

when the feudal mode of agricultural production, based on coercive labour service and organised through political force, became a capitalist mode of production organised around market-based profit and competition.[90] This has become known as the transition debate, and it very much focuses on England because of its specific legal development whereby land tenure and practices of inheritance became much freer from customary local obligations than elsewhere in Europe. As a result, in English historiography, agrarian history has unquestionably been where the term capitalism has been most used and debated. It might be thought that the Netherlands would be equally important when considering this transition since its commercialisation predated that of England. But, as the two historians who used the term 'the first modern economy' to describe this process have claimed, the development of the Netherlands cannot be put into the context of a transition from feudalism to capitalism, since feudal institutions had never fully developed. Also, in comparison to other European states, Dutch agriculture never dominated the economy because of its small geographical area, and towns already relied heavily on grain imports from the Baltic.[91]

Jane Whittle has very usefully analysed how medieval and early modern historians of England, influenced by both Adam Smith and Karl Marx, have employed the term capitalism. Smith described economic history in terms of stages, from hunter-gatherer to agricultural, and then commercial society – to describe the eighteenth century he was living in. He put great emphasis on the division of labour and the function of the market as an essential feature of commercial society, and many historians have followed suit when tracing the transition from feudal society to capitalism. Marx also stressed the importance of markets and profits as the primary means of accumulating capital, but more important, in terms of his discussions of historical progression, was the change in labour relations from serfdom to market-based wage labour. This gave the owners of capital the power to take the labourers' surplus value in terms of profit when selling farm produce on the market.[92]

In an important and much debated intervention, the historian Robert Brenner, in an article entitled 'Agrarian Class Structure and Economic Development in Pre-industrial Europe', argued that England underwent a transformation to a predominantly capitalist form of agriculture, while

[90] Ellen Meiksins Wood, *Origin of Capitalism* (Cambridge, 2016), pp. 35–7.
[91] Jan de Vries and Ad van der Woude, *The First Modern Economy: Success, Failure, and Perseverance of the Dutch Economy, 1500–1815* (Cambridge, 1997), pp. 195–210.
[92] Jane Whittle, *The Development of Agrarian Capitalism: Land and Labour in Norfolk, 1440–1580* (Oxford, 2000), pp. 5–10, 16–17.

other areas of Europe did not.[93] He sought to argue against historians who saw commercialisation as already prevalent and developing along Smithian lines as the main cause of proletarianisation. He also disagreed with demographic historians, who argued that a general rise in population from the late fifteenth century caused agrarian class relations to change. Instead, he argued that class relations changed in England due to its different path of legal development. In England, the law of real property developed differently than civil law jurisdictions. The common law remained tied to the evolution of local manorial customs developed under feudalism. The ability to freely alienate the land was also restricted by such customs according to kinship and marriage. As a result, many rental values of land failed to keep up with the inflation of basic grain prices, which rose by about seven times between 1500 and 1640. This gave those yeomen farmers who rented fields from the land-owning gentry and aristocracy a much greater slice of the increasing profits made by selling on the market during this period.[94] Brenner argued that this was a specific form of class conflict that fostered market relations, as landlords had an interest in the success of larger tenants to make a profit on the market so they could attempt to raise their rents.[95]

Such a grand theory has naturally come in for a barrage of empirical caveats and temporal qualifications. What we can say, as a summary of the work that has been done, is that larger so-called yeoman farmers with 50 acres or more were in a very good position by the sixteenth century to be able to sell food on the market to towns and local artisans, and to make a profit. This was because the growing population and the inflation of food prices caused by this rising demand outstripped the productive capacity of the land. If the rents they owed to their aristocratic landlords were fixed by custom, this meant they became even wealthier. On the other hand, poorer smallholders with only a few acres found it harder to pay for fuel, ploughing, etc., and had to go into debt and eventually sell their lands to make ends meet. This land was bought by the yeomen, who further enriched themselves. Successful artisans also grew wealthy selling yeomen more manufactured goods. This, in turn, opened up more opportunities for employment in local manufacturing trades such as carpentry, joinery, and many others. This growing cycle of demand

[93] Robert Brenner, 'Agrarian Class Structure and Economic Development in Pre-industrial Europe', reprinted in C. H. E Philpin and T. H. Aston, *The Brenner Debate* (Cambridge, 1987), pp. 10–63.

[94] This is the theme of Lawrence Stone, *The Crisis of the Aristocracy, 1558–1641* (Oxford, 1966); Mildred Campbell, *The English Yeoman under Elizabeth and the Early Stuarts* (London, 1960).

[95] The debate has been summarised by Meiksins Wood, *Origin of Capitalism*, pp. 50–64.

became a positive feedback loop as successful artisans in towns also expanded in number, further increasing the demand for food. They also sold to each other, and other urban services such as taverns and ale houses proliferated.

At the same time, the aristocratic and gentry landlords spent much of the sixteenth century spending huge sums on lawyers to fight against custom. To increase their rents when prevented from doing so by manorial custom, landlords had to find ways of challenging custom. This was done in the Court of Chancery. Using expensive lawyers, landlords were eventually successful in most, although certainly not all, cases, using the doctrine that productivity was a more powerful use right and basis for value than simple historical precedent. With this success, as Brenner suggested, they became well integrated into a system of agrarian production for the market. Once the value of their rent became tied to the productive capacity of the estate, it was in their interest to support that land's improvement to increase yields.[96]

In addition to this, a focus on the value of land as a financial investment was also undoubtedly aided by the process through which Henry VIII sold off the land of the dissolved monastic institutions beginning in 1536. Before this there were 840 religious houses in England and Wales, who owned 25 per cent of the nation's land, which had supported 12,000 monks, friars, and nuns before this date. In order to fund his wars in France, many confiscated estates were granted to wealthy individuals for a cash value in the early 1540s, so that by the end of his reign over half of the monastic land had been alienated. The rest was eventually sold off during Edward's and Elizabeth's reigns. This process has been described as the greatest revolution in landholding since the Norman Conquest.[97] Although the original form of transfer – after the Crown had confiscated the land – was a grant in fee through the newly established Court of Augmentations to those close to the court, sales on the market rapidly expanded throughout the country.[98] To do this, the Crown relied on agents and speculators to arrange the grants in London for local purchasers.[99] Initially the land was sold at only ten times its rental value, which later rose to twenty times, and finally thirty times annual value, which became standard.[100] Much of the land was then sold on by the agents to interested purchasers. Although the land market had already been accelerating before 1540 due to population growth, which had

[96] This is discussed in the introduction to R. W. Hoyle (ed.), *Custom, Improvement and the Landscape in Early Modern Britain* (London, 2017), pp. 9–27, 37–8.

[97] Joyce A. Youings, *The Dissolution of the Monasteries* (London, 1971), p. 15.

[98] Ibid., p. 115. [99] Ibid., p. 127. [100] Ibid., p. 120.

reached just over three million by 1551, the rapid introduction of so much undervalued new land onto the market undoubtedly accelerated it.[101]

More importantly, as the rising valuations indicate, it prioritised business and monetary value over any sense of religion. It also increased the number of new, often absentee, landlords with no social attachment to the tenants in their new estates. A good example of this is the London 'adventurer' Jerome Shelton. He came from a family of London merchants and began a career of speculation by purchasing an interest in the estates of Waltham Abbey through an agent, and then later the smaller religious house and manor of Flitcham near King's Lynn for twenty years' rent at £55 per annum in 1540. He proceeded to sublet it to a local farmer for twice that amount: £111. This proved far too high, and the farmer was forced to leave the property early. Shelton continued to make other speculative investments aimed at making steep profits, but almost always failed. We know this because they inevitably led to much ligation over the debts he ended up owing.[102]

Such litigation was far from uncommon in the sixteenth century. There were many conflicts between elite families aimed at bolstering their wealth, involving not just land, but marriage and appointments to profitable government offices. But it would be wrong to think that such conflict had anything to do with capitalism. It had evolved out of bastard feudalism, and resulted in very fierce competition between great families for political prominence and status at court. This led to many fights through lawsuits, which cannot be characterised as in any way bound by the morals of civil society or good neighbourhood.[103] Normally such conflicts took place at a level above the paternalistic relationship of lords and tenants, but the opening up of the land market to so much speculation undoubtedly helped introduce a model of competitive behaviour that could be adopted by those pursuing profit.

Whatever the degree of sharp practice in pursuit of profits versus more conservative paternalistic responsible behaviour towards tenants, it is clear that the late sixteenth century saw the beginning of a decline of independent poor smallholders, who lost their land and had to become either wage labourers or servants, and the rise of larger profit-oriented

[101] Ibid., pp. 18, 128–9. E. A. Wrigley, R. S. Davies, J. E. Oeppen, and R. S. Schofield, *English Population History from Family Reconstitution, 1580–1837* (Cambridge, 1997), p. 614.

[102] James Alsop, 'The Financial Enterprises of Jerome Shelton, a Mid-Tudor London Adventurer', *Guildhall Studies in London History* 4 (1979), pp. 33–50.

[103] Andy Wood, *Faith, Hope and Charity: English Neighbourhoods, 1500–1640* (Cambridge, 2020).

commercial farms.[104] But there has been much debate about when this occurred and to what extent. Braudel set a very high bar for farming to be considered capitalist, but his definition nicely summarises the various elements that are relevant:

For a capitalist system of management and economic rationalization of the land to come into being, many pre-conditions would have been necessary: the seigniorial regime would have had to be if not abolished, certainly reduced or modified; ... peasant liberties would have had to be if not suppressed, at least contained and outmanoeuvred (the sensitive question of common lands came under this heading); the whole undertaking would have to be connected to an active long-distance commodity trade: ... some form of 'rational' management would have to be introduced; ... tried and tested techniques would have to govern investment and the installation of fixed capital; and lastly, the system would have to be based on a wage-earning proletariat.

Unless all these conditions were fulfilled, the enterprise might be on the way to being capitalist, but it was not capitalist in the proper sense.[105]

Most commonly, the search for such change has been traced by using surveys that provide farm sizes, and then labelling a farm of a certain size capitalist, with the argument being that it would need to be independently organised and not based on the use of common fields. It would also need to hire wage labour to be farmed effectively to generate enough profit to sell on distant markets of some scale. For instance, Robert Allen used a size of 100 acres.[106] Such profit could be used to invest in improvement, which would be an obvious use of 'capital'. Recently, Leigh Shaw-Taylor has used the employment of labour as a way to measure capitalist agriculture in the early modern period.[107] Using occupational information from different regions, he argued that if the ratio of the number of farm owners to employed farm workers was less than one then small family farming must have been dominant. When the same ratio was more than two to one, he took this as evidence of a domination of capitalist agriculture, arguing that the amount of land being farmed by hired labour, assuming a similar output per worker, must have been higher than that farmed by only one nuclear family. Using this measure,

[104] Margaret Spufford, *Contrasting Communities: English Villagers in the Sixteenth and Seventeenth Centuries* (Cambridge, 1974), pp. 46–57, 65–72, 144–59; Keith Wrightson and David Levine, *Poverty and Piety in an English Village, Terling 1525–1700* (New York, 1979), p. 28.

[105] Braudel, *Wheels of Commerce*, p. 251.

[106] Allen was also very judicious in precisely defining what he meant by the term *capital*, which involved investment and the possession of fixed capital. Robert C. Allen, *Enclosure and the Yeoman* (Oxford, 1992), pp. 74–5, 191–9.

[107] Leigh Shaw-Taylor, 'The Rise of Agrarian Capitalism and the Decline of Family Farming in England', *The Economic History Review* 65, no. 1 (2012), pp. 26–60.

it was evident that by 1700 capitalist farms were dominant in south-east England, but that family farming still characterised the north.[108]

Certainly, a farm employing labour would almost definitely be selling agricultural produce for a profit, unless it was the demesne farm of a gentry household, and in doing so would be aimed at making a profit by selling to middlemen supplying urban markets. Since much of this market was accounted for by London (in 1600, London accounted for 62 per cent of the urban population of England as defined by towns of over 5,000 people).[109] However, there were different forms of hiring labour. Some were hired as live-in servants with board, hired for a year, and some as day labourers with or without food. To be fully proletarianised, a labourer and their family would have to depend entirely on wages. To pay such wages, a farm would have to be connected to the market to obtain at least some cash to pay workers. But as I have written about at length elsewhere, payment of day wages was a well-acknowledged problem in the sixteenth and seventeenth centuries because the farmers in many cases lacked circulating capital that could be used to pay wages.

This is very important, because none of these studies of capitalist farming, as far as I am aware, also look at the means by which 'capitalist' farmers turned profits into capital as a form I wish to define here, as savings or circulating capital to pay wages. Accumulating 'capital' over time for investment in the improvement of the land's productive capacity was difficult. The farmer either had to try to save coins or he could take out sealed bonds. In the next chapter I will show how the development of new forms of circulating capital were envisioned by the same innovators who promoted agricultural improvements. In this vein, it makes more sense to talk of farms that hired more labour and were connected to the market as *profit-oriented agriculture*, which then morphed into capitalist farming as the financial system evolved into one based on capital as much as informal credit.

Given this, is capitalism the right term to use to describe what was happening in the countryside in the period before the eighteenth century? If it is, then capital should properly be said to have played at least as important a role as the market and profit. Merchant capital was formed of

[108] Ibid., pp. 51–8; also see Joseph Barker's PhD thesis, which uses different evidence of farm size and also concludes that in southern England already by 1650 capitalist farming was dominant, and that in eastern England there was much capitalist farming already in 1600. Joseph Barker, 'Geographical Variation in Patterns of Landholding and Agrarian Social Relations *c.*1800' (PhD Thesis, Cambridge University, 2007).

[109] E. A. Wrigley, 'Urban Growth and Agricultural Change: England and the Continent in the Early Modern Period', in E. A. Wrigley, *People, Cities and Wealth* (Chichester, 1988), pp. 133–56.

balances of money of account kept in account books, but few yeomen farmers in the sixteenth or early seventeenth centuries in England kept account books. Large parts of the wages of their workers were paid without money ever changing hands through the provision of food, lodging, and clothing, even when the value of such things might have been bargained for on the market.

Such farmers possessed land, of course, which is – and remains – a form of capital if it has value through some resource present on it such as crops, pasture, trees, and minerals. In urban areas, land also has a 'space' value based on people's desire to live close to one another.[110] However, while land, since it cannot move, is perhaps the most secure form of value, it is also the most illiquid. It is fixed, rather than financial capital, as this passage from Braudel nicely illustrates:

> Land could be a way of investing money safely: land never tells lies, as they used to say and as merchants well knew. Luca del Sera wrote from Florence on 23 April 1408 to Francesco Datini, the merchant of Prato: 'I advised you to buy some estates and I do so again even more pressingly if possible. Land has at least the virtue of not being exposed to the risk of the sea, or an unscrupulous factor, or a merchant company or a bankruptcy ... The trouble for the merchant was that an estate could all the same not be bought and sold as easily as a share on the Stock Exchange. When the Tiepolo Pisani bank failed in Venice in 1584, the estates which had stood guarantee for it were sold only slowly and at a loss'.[111]

As I detailed in my previous book, *Economy of Obligation*, instead of using circulating capital the financial system of this period below the level of merchants was fundamentally based on interpersonal trust embedded in chains of credit. Account-keeping was the exception, and as a result value within this system was fluid and negotiable. A household's wealth would consist of its material possessions combined with a balance of debts and credits that changed all the time through reckonings. Thus, what we would today call financial wealth was mostly an estimation of value, both by the subjects possessing it within the household and those who they bought from. This social credit was so pervasive that society was in many ways a culture of credit. It was a market society that accepted that most prices of goods traded on the market would be set by supply and demand, but where the formation of wealth was still fragile. In this sense, farmers, before the creation of more liquid financial capital in the late seventeenth century, were not capitalist farmers.

Early modern historians have also often used the term 'capitalist behaviour' as another way of saying 'profit-oriented individualism',

[110] Muldrew, 'Mortgages as Mediation', pp. 309–11.
[111] Braudel, *Wheels of Commerce*, p. 249.

which is usually contrasted with 'older' communal obligations. As Tawney pointed out, there were certainly individuals who aggressively pursued great gains through exploitation of rack rents or money lending. But these actions attracted contemporary odium and could not yet be justified by any terms of individual freedom. They had to be cloaked in the legitimacy of improvement and the increase in national wealth. The concept of 'profit' was legitimised in discourse that did not stress the individual, but rather the nuclear family, town, and nation state over older communal relations such as the commons, while other obligations such as neighbourhood and charity continued to be stressed. In this sense, it might be best to think of the period up to the late seventeenth century as one less characterised by capital than by a legitimation of profit-based improvement, in which wealth consisted of the obligation of credit.[112]

But this still leaves the question of how to deal with labour markets. It has been argued by Ellen Meiksins Wood that, in the early modern period, the involvement of merchants or farmers selling on the market itself should *not* be taken as a marker of the evolution towards capitalism. As she notes, throughout history there have been a great many towns and a great deal of trade that never gave rise to capitalism, and she is in agreement with Braudel that it is possible to have a very advanced market economy with profit-oriented trade and not have capital formation.[113] However, she disagrees with Braudel that capitalism originated among merchants, since for her the key aspect of capitalism is labour relations, rather than the existence of capital. She argues that in the specific cases of both Renaissance Florence and the Dutch Republic in the seventeenth century, the great amounts of riches created by merchant capital did not lead to investment in labour efficiency or new productive machinery. Most investment was in long-distance trade, or even non-economic factors such as buildings, art, and even rent-seeking government officeholding.

For Meiksins Wood, the key element that was missing in the early modern commercial market was internal price competition between producers of the same product. She argues it was this process that drove the need to look for more efficiency in the cost of production, thus keeping wages as low as possible.[114] This, she argues, was an inevitable result of Brenner's theory of a competitive land market that led to the more financially 'efficient' use of labour, by hiring more day workers and fewer servants hired by the year, as a way of reducing the cost of production. Since this was combined with the decline of the smallholder,

[112] Muldrew, *Economy of Obligation*, pp. 95–118.
[113] Meiksins Wood, *Origin of Capitalism*, p. 75.
[114] Ibid., pp. 7, 56–7, 85, 100, 135ff.

it also led to a much larger percentage of the rural population becoming dependent on wage labour.

I have discussed many of these issues in my book *Food, Energy and the Creation of Industriousness*, in which I placed more emphasis on the role of population growth as a causal factor of changes in labourers' employment and work patterns.[115] Meiksins Wood acknowledges the importance of population growth during the period, but, following Brenner, wants to subordinate it as a causal factor in the creation of capitalism in relation to social relations. However, it seems undeniable that without population growth putting pressure on food supply and causing rising prices, the opportunity for profit on the part of the yeomen farmers would have been much less. It also led to a surplus of agricultural labour, which kept down the wages of labour. Further, the advocacy and implementation of improvement was not only about increasing profit for producers; it was as much about increasing the food supply and providing work for labourers. This process was eventually successful by the late seventeenth century, although it was aided by a colonial project that encouraged the emigration of about half a million men.[116] Labour markets were also quite local, and before the developments I will discuss here, the pure money wage was anything but universal – most wages were a combination of cash, credit, and exchange in kind. In addition, even by the 1760s over half of the agricultural labour force consisted of servants, given the age structure of the pre-modern population.[117]

However, the question that concerns us here is how such changes were related to the creation of capital. I believe it is more than simply pedantic to suggest that for something to be called capitalist it should be uniquely affected by the employers' possession of something we can call capital. And, what is important here is circulating capital, which could be used to pay wages or pay for improvement. How the value of land came to be turned into circulating capital in England will be one of the major themes of this book. Also, as Meiksins Wood notes, there were many pre-capitalist forms of surplus labour extraction by violent, political, and juridical means, most notably serfdom and slavery.[118] Meiksins Wood is someone who accepts the Sombartian exegesis on Marx that capitalism is a *system*. But Marx was very much focusing on the *power* that capital gave its owners in the nineteenth century, to treat labour as a commodity. Since the changes in labour relations began in the sixteenth century, before there was much capital formation in the countryside, in Chapter 8, I will investigate the degree to which the creation of such

[115] Muldrew, *Food, Energy*, pp. 2–3, 307–8. [116] Ibid., pp. 284–5, 304–7.
[117] Ibid., p. 223. [118] Meiksins Wood, *Origin of Capitalism*, pp. 7, 55.

capital might have begun to change social relations. However, since labour relations before this were not primarily affected by the presence or absence of capital, such agriculture is probably better described as 'large-scale profit-based farming', rather than capitalist. In fact, it could be argued that it was the very *lack* of capital that made it necessary to increase profits and keep wages lower to avoid cash flow problems. As we shall see in Chapter 3, capital actually made wages easier to pay, not harder.

Finally, it remains to be noted that these discussions tend to assume that first Dutch and then English agriculture was precociously progressive, which is often linked to capitalist organisation and profit-seeking.[119] While it is undoubtedly true that English inheritance laws became much freer than most continental areas governed by Roman law, the idea that partible inheritance led to numerous inefficient small farms has been challenged by many historians.[120] Active land markets could be used to rebuild family farms, and Phillip Hoffman has argued that French agricultural production was actually quite dynamic in the eighteenth century.[121] Also, the use of land as capital through mortgages in most continental countries long predated its use in England.[122] Thus, the reasons for more productive agriculture are more complex than investment capital.

Entrepreneurialism

For the early modern period, most writing about entrepreneurialism is about what causes innovation, and what social and cultural factors either discourage or promote it. For Marx and Engels it was capital that provided the economic power to achieve innovation, and the social power to change laws, religious belief, concepts of honour, and much else: 'in the same proportion the bourgeoisie developed, increased its capital, and pushed into the background every class handed down from the Middle Ages'.[123]

[119] de Vries and van der Woude, *The First Modern Economy*, pp. 195–234.

[120] See, for instance, David Warren Sabean, *Property, Production, and Family in Neckarhausen, 1700–1870* (Cambridge, 1997), pp. 13–17, 44–6, 247–56; Imogen Wedd, 'Gavelkind on the Ground, 1550–1700', *Archaeologia Cantiana* 142 (2021), pp. 1–30; Johannes Kaska, 'Equal but Not Identical: Modes of Partible Inheritance in Early-Modern Schlanders (South Tyrol) and Medieval Lambach (Upper Austria) Compared', *The History of the Family* 27, no. 1 (2022), pp. 100–24.

[121] Philip T. Hoffman, *Growth in a Traditional Society: The French Countryside, 1450–1815* (Princeton, 2018).

[122] Briggs and Zuijderduijn, *Land and Credit*, pp. 1–16.

[123] Marx and Engels, *Communist Manifesto*, p. 15.

However, the role of entrepreneurialism is most associated with the work of the economist Joseph Schumpeter. In his theory of business cycles, he investigated the role of innovation historically, and in contrast to Marx he divorced entrepreneurialism and the use of capital:

> We have to define that word which good economists try to avoid: capitalism is that form of private property economy in which innovations are caried out by means of borrowed money, which in general, though not by logical necessity, implies credit creation.[124]

By 'credit creation' he meant things like company stock or bills of exchange. For Schumpeter this was key, as he believed the entrepreneurial function could be found in others forms of society, including tribal and socialist forms.[125] However, it was investment that enabled innovations to spread and outcompete older, more costly ways of doing things in a profit-based market economy.[126] However, it can also be argued that capital itself was an innovation, but of a different sort. Capital requires security, while innovation requires risk.[127] This is a theme he would re-emphasise in *Capitalism, Socialism and Democracy*.

Another recent attempt to explain capitalism by way of innovation is the economist Deirdre McCloskey's ongoing multi-volume exploration of what she terms *The Bourgeois Virtues*, also the title of the first volume.[128] This wide-ranging but historically based rhapsodic argument in favour of 'natural liberty' is mostly about the achievements of economic growth. Historically, it investigates how this started after many millennia of relative stasis, and why it happened in north-western Europe, while at the same time being an argument for non-governmental initiatives in today's world. McCloskey tries to steer a course between the left and the right by arguing that the bourgeois virtues encompass much more than just profit-making, or the drive to endless accumulation. She argues they encompass the Enlightenment ideas of progress, altruism, charity, and sociability, among others. But the key virtue that allowed growth was the freedom to innovate, not just economically, but politically, and perhaps more than anything else socially. This allowed customary hierarchies and inequalities to be surmounted. For McCloskey,

124 Joseph A. Schumpeter, *Business Cycles: A Theoretical and Statistical Analysis of the Capitalist Process* (New York, 1939), I, p. 223.

125 Ibid., I, p. 223.

126 Ibid., I, pp. 228–30.

127 Joseph A. Schumpeter, *Capitalism, Socialism and Democracy* (New York, 2008), pp. 156–63.

128 Deirdre McCloskey, *The Bourgeois Virtues: Ethics for an Age of Commerce* (Chicago, 2006). The other volumes so far are: *Bourgeois Dignity: Why Economics can't Explain the Modern World* (Chicago, 2010); *Bourgeois Equality: How Ideas, not Capital or Institutions, Enriched the World* (Chicago, 2016).

capitalism is very loosely described as 'merely private property and free labour without central planning, regulated by the rule of law and by an ethical consensus'.[129] Under this definition she admits that such features existed before, and in other places than seventeenth-century north-western Europe, but this is when and where 'modern' capitalism appeared, and then spread to the British North American colonies. She states that her work is intended to be a full-scale defence of capitalism in its American form,[130] although later in the second volume, *Bourgeois Dignity*, she modifies this slightly to become a defence of 'our modern form of innovation – universally if misleadingly called "capitalism"'.[131]

McCloskey also downplays the relationship of slavery to capitalism. She obviously condemns it as an immoral affront to liberty, but argues that it did not contribute much to economic growth, and was not a major part of capitalism.[132] But one could argue that the Atlantic plantation system based on African slavery was indeed an innovation, not based on any bourgeois virtues, but obviously on the desire to make a profit by coercing labour, and which used forms of capital. In the same vein, the system of indentured service developed in England was also extremely entrepreneurial. This involved agents in Bristol and London paying for the cost of shipping labour to the tobacco farms in Virginia from the 1620s. However, in this case little capital was involved, and much payment was done in the form of barter, such as using tobacco as money.[133]

Joel Mokyr is another historian who has been influenced by Schumpeter. He has spent much of his career arguing for the importance of innovation as the prime mover in early modern growth and industrialisation. In a series of books he has focused especially on the relationship between science and growth, and on the Enlightenment. His most recent book, *A Culture of Growth*, is based on the Joseph Schumpeter Lectures he presented. Here, he goes further to examine what sort of social changes in education and attitudes occurred in Europe before innovation became, not just accepted, but lauded as a force for good rather than a cause of dangerous social instability. But, sensibly, to my mind, he eschews the use of the term capitalism and instead focuses on a culture of growth, or innovation, and talks of cultural entrepreneurs rather than capitalists.[134]

129 McCloskey, *Bourgeois Virtues*, p. 14.
130 Ibid., p. 1.
131 McCloskey, *Bourgeois Dignity*, p. 40.
132 Ibid., pp. 229–38.
133 Alison Games, *Migration and the Origins of the English Atlantic World* (Cambridge, MA, 1999), pp. 13–41, 102–31.
134 Joel Mokyr, *A Culture of Growth: The Origins of the Modern Economy – The Graz Schumpeter Lectures* (Princeton, 2017). See, for instance, pp. 59–66 for the use of the term.

Finally, we should mention a fairly recent book that also stresses the role of innovation, by a pioneer who wrote one of the best books on economic thought in early modern England, Joyce Appleby. In *The Relentless Revolution: A History of Capitalism*, she defines capitalism as 'a system based on individual investments in the production of marketable goods'. This book looks at how the capitalist 'system' churned up 'practices, values, and ideals that had long prevailed within the cocoon of custom', and argues, like McCloskey and Mokyr, that capitalism was more a cultural than an economic system.[135]

The most recent book dealing with the relationship between entrepreneurship and capitalism is Koji Yamamoto's *Taming Capitalism before its Triumph: Public Service, Distrust and 'Projecting' in Early Modern England*.[136] This is a much more contextually detailed argument about the role of entrepreneurs in sixteenth- and seventeenth-century England. The strength of his book is that Yamamoto does not only look at rhetoric, ideas, or successful inventors, but at the actual practical problems of innovation in his study of what, in seventeenth-century England, came to be known as projectors. A projector was an individual who wanted to become wealthy by proposing new schemes for producing things. Projection came into England through alchemy and mineralogical theories in the sixteenth century, as the Crown sought new sources of gold and silver to expand its money supply.[137] To try to gain from this situation, they sought royal patents granting exclusive rights to any success, and to pay for costly experiments and digging prospective mines. However, this soon changed into a very different situation in which projectors morphed into rent-seekers rather than risk-takers by applying for patents of monopoly for already-established methods of production, such as making playing cards, music paper, or soap.[138] Since the Crown usually lacked funds, it became much more common to grant monopolies for a price, whereby the Crown actually made money and the projectors received state-backed market domination. As economic theory would suggest, this was no incentive to innovation, but rather the opposite, as any outsider with a new method was excluded from making a profit. This situation

135 Joyce Appleby, *The Relentless Revolution: A History of Capitalism* (London, 2011), pp. 3–4, 6–7, 14–16, 24, 26.

136 Koji Yamamoto, *Taming Capitalism before its Triumph: Public Service, Distrust, and 'Projecting' in Early Modern England* (Oxford, 2018).

137 Jennifer Bishop, 'Currency, Conversation, and Control: Political Discourse and the Coinage in Mid-Tudor England', *The English Historical Review* 131, no. 551 (2016), pp. 763–92.

138 Joan Thirsk, *Economic Policy and Projects: The Development of a Consumer Society in Early Modern England* (Oxford, 1978), pp. 96–101.

was fiercely opposed in Parliament, which forced the Crown to promise not to grant rent-seeking monopolies.[139] As Yamamoto shows, this created an aura of distrust towards projectors through much of the seventeenth century, which was difficult to shake off.

Paul Slack has also shown, in his book *The Invention of Improvement*, how the idea of improvement of the productive capacity of agriculture and industry came to have a very positive cultural value from the 1640s onwards.[140] Most of the new agricultural innovations, such as drainage, liming, marling, and new crop rotations, were undertaken privately by farmers. But larger-scale projects such as fen drainage and river widening needed investment. To do this, projectors needed to seek funds from private investors, and Yamamoto shows how persuasion and elements of trust, and what was understood at the time as science, were mobilised to attract investment. One very enlightening case study concerns Andrew Yarrington and his schemes in the 1660s to improve navigation on the river Stour, which ran from the Severn through the heart of the West Country woollen industry. Yamamoto goes into the financial detail very carefully, and from this we can see how difficult it was to finance such projects within the interpersonal credit system that existed at the time.[141]

However, by the 1690s investment had been reorganised by the creation of joint stock companies, which used an already very old Italian organisational innovation to create capital for investment in a plethora of projects. Many new companies were created, which took out patents for new schemes such as supplying water to London or salvaging treasure wrecks.[142] In this way, projecting can be linked to the many proposals for the creation of credit currencies and banking institutions, which will be examined in the next chapter. These came from the same progressively minded people, and also sought to make a profit for their creators and interested investors.

For the early modern period, it is also worth pondering Schumpeter's original much more economic arguments about the link between credit, capital, and innovation. Product competition and innovation certainly increased in the eighteenth century *after* capital expanded into society

[139] Craig Muldrew, 'Politics and Economics of Markets', in Roberto Scazzieri and Ivano Cardinale (eds.), *The Palgrave Handbook of Political Economy* (London, 2018), pp. 91–132.

[140] Paul Slack, *The Invention of Improvement: Information and Material Progress in Seventeenth-Century England* (Oxford, 2015), pp. 91–128.

[141] Yamamoto, *Taming Capitalism*, pp. 132–73.

[142] Christine Macleod, 'The 1690s Patents Boom: Invention or Stock-Jobbing?', *The Economic History Review* 39, no. 4 (1986), pp. 549–71; W. R. Scott, *The Constitution and Finance of English, Scottish and Irish Joint-Stock Companies to 1720*, vol. III (Cambridge, 1912).

beyond the realms of foreign trade, where it had been used to cultivate new consumer goods such as tobacco and sugar.[143] Entrepreneurs could use its institutions to provide enough security to store their profits, and this safe store of value was an incentive to increase the profit motive. In the older world of interpersonal credit, more time needed to be spent maintaining relations of trust than in making profits. Both were always essential, but for a small but hugely significant number of successful businessmen who became the new middle class the order of importance was reversed – profits took precedence over trust.

Finally, it would be a great wrong in any discussion of the historiography of early modern capitalism to omit the work of Christopher Hill. As a Marxist, he argued that the English Revolution was a bourgeois revolution. He continued Tawney's investigation of how new notions of freedom arose out of anti-episcopalian Protestant radicalism. Under the Commonwealth and Protectorate, the feudal system of tenancy was challenged, and taxation and other forms of administration were reformed. New ideas about education, science, and poverty all benefited from the collapse of censorship, and although the Restoration obviously restored political hierarchy, the administrative revolution continued. Vital to this process was the fact that freedom of the press from censorship proved already too engrained to be rolled back. Long before Mokyr and McCloskey, he identified Bacon and Samuel Hartlib, and their advocacy of experiment and improvement, as a cause of economic growth in the latter part of the seventeenth century.[144]

Property, the Glorious Revolution, and Politics

There is a large literature that deals with what has come to be termed the financial revolution, including the work of Peter Dickson, Larry Neal, Ann Carlos, Christine Macleod, and Anne Murphy.[145] Since capital markets are self-evidently about capitalism on their own terms, we do not need to deal with this literature here, as this will be done in the next chapter. There is, however, one aspect of the historiography of the

[143] Charles Singer, A. R. Hall, E. J. Holmyard, and T. I. Williams, *A History of Technology. Vol. IV, The Industrial Revolution, Cc.1750 to Cc.1850* (Oxford, 1958).

[144] Interestingly, although he discussed capital accumulation, Hill rarely used the term *capitalism*, preferring to stress the cultural effects of religion on a wide variety of behaviour and social forms. See, for instance, Christopher Hill, *Reformation to Industrial Revolution: 1530–1780* (London, 1967), pp. 76–8, 160–1, 180–1; Christopher Hill, *The Century of Revolution, 1603–1714* (Edinburgh, 1962), chs. 3, 9, 13, 17.

[145] Macleod, 'Patents Boom', pp. 594–71.

financial revolution that has been relevant to broader discussions about the rise of capitalism. This is the so-called credible commitment hypothesis put forward in a famous article by Douglass North and Barry Weingast.[146] This thesis argues two basic things: first, that secure property rights are crucial to the development of capitalism because they protect profits and wealth in various forms; and second, that investment in interest-earning government debt only became secure when some kind of democratic accountability existed to protect such investment from confiscation by monarchs or other government officials. As one pamphlet by Hugh Chamberlain, a Tory supporter of the Stuart monarchy, put it, the Whigs

> assured us, that we must never think of setling Banks in England without a Common-wealth: And this Notion became so universal, that it was a matter of derision, for any one to seem to be of a contrary opinion. [Their] main Objection against them in England to be, the danger of Violence from the Prince, they therefore invented certain imaginary Banks and Funds, which they designed to settle far enough from the Prince's reach.[147]

It is this second point that North and Weingast called credible commitment. In this story, England was able to establish continual economic growth because of the Glorious Revolution, which secured the regular election of members of the House of Commons by propertied voters to oversee taxation. This thesis has come under criticism for a number of reasons. These include, in no particular order, that property rights were already well protected before 1688, that reforms of taxation had actually begun during the Commonwealth, and not least that the party politics within Parliament actually created political instability up until the end of the South Sea Bubble. Many states before England, both republics and monarchies, had also issued popular long-term debt, which had been taken up with varying degrees of security.[148] Even in England most of the reforms were initiated first during the Commonwealth and Cromwell's Protectorate.[149]

It has, however, been very influential on subsequent exponents of institutional economics, such as Darron Acemoglu and James

[146] Douglass C. North and Barry R. Weingast, 'Constitutions and Commitment: The Evolution of Institutions Governing Public Choice in Seventeenth-Century England', *The Journal of Economic History* 49, no. 4 (1989), pp. 803–32.

[147] Hugh Chamberlain, *A Brief Account of the Intended Bank of England* (London, 1694), pp. 2–3.

[148] See 'The History of merchant Accounts and European Banking' in Chapter 2.

[149] These are all discussed in D'Maris Coffman, Adrian Leonard, and Larry Neal (eds.), *Questioning Credible Commitment: Perspectives on the Rise of Financial Capitalism* (Cambridge, 2013).

Robinson, as well as modern followers of Milton Friedman, who believe capitalism can only flourish under an electoral democracy. Acemoglu and Robinson argue for the importance of inclusive economic institutions, which are defined as those that allow participation by the great mass of people in economic activities that make the best use of their talents, and must feature secure private property, an unbiased system of law, and public services that provide a level playing field for exchange and contract. They also argue that there is a strong synergy between inclusive economic institutions and inclusive political ones. Extractive institutions, on the other hand, are ones whereby an elite uses undemocratic political power backed up by violence to charge a rent off of economic activity to enrich themselves. They also argue that inclusive institutions promote both economic and political competition, which results in Schumpeterian innovation, as well as creative destruction with winners and losers.[150]

Aristocratic rent and monopolies are early modern examples of extractive institutions. The latter were successfully politically challenged in Parliament long before the Glorious Revolution, while the former were eroded by a combination of inflation and property law that protected customary levels of rent. This, indeed, allowed some farmers to profit and invest in innovation, but customary rents also protected smaller farmers who did not. But, as the Marxist Robert Brenner pointed out, large estate holders went to the law to raise their rents precisely to raise their level of extraction to capture some of the profits of successful farmers. It was this that led them to support improvement, and thus to the establishment of a land market based on competitive rents. As a number of historians have pointed out, the relationship of property law to capital formation *cannot* be reduced to just the simple protection of property. If this was the case, then customary rents, as a well-established form of secure property, would have prevented the rise of market-based rents, but instead they were replaced. While this might well have prevented aristocratic extraction, it would also have stifled the more economically efficient rental market in sub-tenancies and profit-oriented farming.[151]

What was actually needed was what the American legal historian Morton J. Horwitz called an instrumental conception of law, which prioritised economic growth.[152] This was the same ideology which Meiksins Wood and James Tully have shown motivated John Locke's

[150] Daron Acemoglu and James A. Robinson, *Why Nations Fail: The Origins of Power, Prosperity, and Poverty* (London, 2013), pp. 73–85.

[151] Stephen Hipkin, 'Tenant Farming and Short-Term Leasing on Romney Marsh, 1587–1705', *The Economic History Review* 4 (2000), pp. 646–76.

[152] Morton J. Horwitz, *The Transformation of American Law, 1780–1860* (Cambridge, MA, 1977), pp. 1–47.

theory of property. Property in this sense is based on productive labour, not possession.[153] Julian Hoppitt, in an important recent article, has also pointed to other instances in eighteenth-century England where property rights were altered by parliamentary statute in the pursuit of economic growth.[154] One aspect of the institutional economics argument that has proven more robust is the development in the eighteenth century of the patent system in England. This provided legal protection to the intellectual property of entrepreneurs because it promoted economic growth.[155] In this latter case, the law protected profits that could be turned into capital. As we will see, the law was crucial to the creation of new forms of capital but, as might be expected, it was more linked to security than risk-taking.

The Culture of Capital

After this long – but even so by no means exhaustive – survey of how capitalism has been conceptually employed, I wish to propose a radical restructuring of the debate. It is evident by now that the concept of capitalism has become like an unwieldy and bloated monopoly, and as such it needs to be broken up for the good of the academic economy. In order to achieve more conceptual clarity, I propose using the following six concepts instead:

- profit-oriented market activity;
- entrepreneurship;
- competitive employment;
- capital formation and property;[156]
- currency creation
- the self and class relations.

I have chosen these categories because each can exist independently of the others, or they can work together in different ways. For instance, it is possible to have a great deal of innovation without believing in Benthamite individualism. As Braudel and Meiksins Wood pointed out, profit-oriented markets can exist without capital, and it seems to me that it does not make any sense to talk about something being capitalist if it does not use capital. For this reason, for the early modern

[153] Meiksins Wood, *Origin of Capitalism*, pp. 110–15, 157–60.
[154] Hoppit, 'Property Rights', pp. 93–128.
[155] Sean Bottomley, *The British Patent System and the Industrial Revolution, 1700–1852: From Privilege to Property* (Cambridge, 2014).
[156] I have not put property in a separate category for the reasons given above.

period, I think it is incorrect to talk about capitalism in a *systematic* way, unless capital is involved, and this book will very much focus on the last three categories rather than the pursuit of profits and labour relations. I realise that for some people this might seem like it is missing the point, since wage exploitation is such a large feature of capitalism today. But it will be my argument here that this was *not* the reason why capital was created, but rather a *result*, and by understanding this we will then also gain a better understanding of the positive and negative aspects of capital.

Certainly there were early modern merchants who created capital by investing in and profiting by trade, as did joint stock companies created by entrepreneurs. However, their numbers were small. As mentioned in the Introduction, I will argue here that most capital was created for the purposes of expanding the money supply through more liquidity, with paper currencies backed up by collateral rather than for investment purposes. By *c.*1700, people began turning the value of both land and profit into circuiting capital that could be used by many more poorer individuals in their communities. This involved practices that spread throughout society, so it might be argued that this was a system of capitalism, but since capital did not yet transform relations of power in society, it might be better to label the period as one that saw the birth of a *culture of capital* as a better description than capitalism, since *capital* as a word was introduced and became fairly common by the end of the eighteenth century.

It was not until the nineteenth century that capital came to be used to invest in entrepreneurialism on a much larger scale and to transform labour relations, both in Britain and around the globe, as was proposed by Marx and demonstrated by Beckert and other recent historians of capitalism.[157] It could then be plausibly argued that this was becoming a *capitalist system*. Capitalism as a term thus refers better to the social system that emerged in the nineteenth century with factory labour, the hiring of which needed large accumulations of industrial capital. Also, the politics associated with capitalism are those of the nineteenth-century struggle of capital against labour. But, in addition to this, I think what characterises capitalism beyond such systemisation is the power it provided those who possessed a lot of it. My purpose here will be to focus mostly on how capital as a thing came into being in early modern Europe, and then to show how it took specific forms and spread through society in England and Scotland after *c.*1680. I will then examine how it affected

157 Donald Sassoon, *The Anxious Triumph: A Global History of Capitalism, 1880–1914* (London, 2019); Jonathan Levy, *Freaks of Fortune: The Emerging World of Capitalism and Risk in America* (Cambridge, MA, 2012).

wage payments and individual and collective ethics as it developed *before* the nineteenth century.

It will be the central contention of my argument that the key to the development of capital was the establishment of trust in its security over time. Only this could have allowed capital to spread throughout society. Here, property relations are obviously important, as are other aspects of the law such as contract. But in this book, I believe the evidence will convincingly show that capital must be maintained by a whole complex, historically constructed set of institutions that participants accept to some degree. This involves government, the self, and other institutions working together to produce secure capital. Central to this investigation will be the process by which individual selves were able to become comfortable with trusting institutions and also how they dealt with problems of others they did not know who abused such trust. This is very much related to the dynamic between risk and security that is at the heart of the motivation for saving. The social security provided for capital went far beyond just the institutions of property – it was related to the beliefs and behaviours of the people who used it. New forms of capital also conferred new social power on those who operated the institutions that produced it, and this is something I will investigate. My investigation of the development of the early modern self will also elaborate a very different sort of individualism than Benthamite reductionism. It will be an individualism dependent on the institutional reproduction of capital, not an individual born with a natural right of autonomy. But before doing this, we need to understand how merchant capital and state finance were developed.

2 Value in Motion: The Inheritance of Merchant Capital and Debates over Credit

> Domestick Trade depends on the Money. A greater Quantity employes more People than a lesser Quantity. A limited Sum can only set a number of People to Work proportion'd to it, and 'tis with little success Laws are made, for Employing the Poor or Idle in Countries where Money is scarce; Good Laws may bring the Money to the full Circulation 'tis capable of, and force it to those Employments that are most profitable to the Country: But no Laws can make it go further, nor can more People be set to Work, without more Money to circulate so, as to pay the Wages of a greater number. They may be brought to Work on Credit, and that is not practicable, unless the Credit have a Circulation, so as to supply the Workman with necessaries; If that's suppos'd, then that Credit is Money, and will have the same effects, on Home, and Forreign Trade.
>
> (John Law, *Money and Trade Considered*, p. 13)

Before beginning my history of how the use of capital spread beyond the confines of merchants' trade, state finance, and banking, it is first necessary to understand how institutions through which such elevated circulating capital was created and stored were created and worked. This was done in medieval Italy and other European cities. In terms of the development of financial and banking services, England was a very late developer. This happened in the years of the Commonwealth and Restoration, and these developments were built on the practices of English and other international merchants, as well as foreign banks already in existence long before that date. As was noted in Chapter 1, most histories of capital and finance focus on these developments, and in English terms how they were related to the eventual formation of the Bank of England and the stock market, which is termed the *financial revolution*. But during the Commonwealth period, radical thinkers centred around the so-called Hartlib circle began to argue that banks should be set up to create paper currencies that could be used by the whole population.[1] It was such

[1] Carl Wennerlind, *Casualties of Credit: The English Financial Revolution, 1620–1720* (Cambridge, MA, 2011), pp. 95–122.

proposals that created the impetus for change from the practice of transactions based mostly on oral credit to more liquid circulating capital. This chapter will deal with how and why this literature emerged, but in order to do this we need to briefly outline the development of merchant banking and state finance that originally developed in medieval Italy.

The word *capital* came from early thirteenth-century Italian accounting manuals as an equivalent term for stock, and it is undoubtedly the case that circulating capital could not have existed without accounting. Forms of numerical valuation had existed for many centuries in order to *measure* the exchange of things. In Europe, the most popular system of measurement was derived from the *livre*, which was established by Charlemagne as a unit of account equal to 1 lb of silver. It was subdivided into 20 sous of 12 deniers each. In England this was adapted as pounds, shillings, and pence. Under this system, the multiple of ten was used in the first instance because it was more convenient for measuring larger payments, while twelve could be easily divided by both two and three, which could be more easily done for small-scale transactions. It is often assumed by those who are not historians of money that these measurements took the form of coins that were exchanged for goods. Quite often this was indeed the case, but money of measurement – or what came to be known as money of account once accounting started to be used more frequently – existed independently of coins and was used to facilitate the majority of exchange that was done on credit.[2]

Most coins, apart from the very smallest denominations, consisted of silver and gold alloys. This was the case because these were scarce metals, whose scarcity gave them a significantly higher market value than what were termed base metals, such as lead, copper, or iron. Theoretically, an original shilling would have had one-twentieth the amount of silver as a pound. Also, since gold was much more valuable than silver, a gold pound would be smaller. In addition, the market value of gold and silver fluctuated *independently*, but both their values fell continually over the medieval and early modern periods due to price inflation. To further complicate matters, state mints often devalued their coins by reducing the precious metal content of the alloys. This needed to be done because of inflation, but it became an increasing practice for monarchs to devalue their coins to create more money when they could not collect enough taxes to pay for wars.[3] As a result, many coins were

2 Peter Spufford, *Money and its Use in Medieval Europe* (Cambridge, 1988), pp. 33–5, 77, 222–4, 284–7.

3 John Day, *Money and Finance in the Age of Merchant Capitalism* (Oxford, 1999), pp. 43–109.

minted that did not match money of account. Also, since there were a great number of mints operating in Europe, there were countless coins of different values circulating and moving between economies.

To give one example from England, after receiving a loan of £20 on bond in 1612, Richard Cholmeley, a Yorkshire estate owner, gave his 'ould gould' for security, which consisted of, '7 Spur-Ryalls, 3 Elizabeth xxs. peces, 1 angell, 1 half angell, ii duble ducketts, and one single duckett, 1 other strange single duckett, 1 Henrye peese of xxs., 5 Henry xs. peeces, 1 Edward pollard xs. pees, 2 crosse dagger angells, and 1 of vs., and ii Kinge Jeames xxs. peeces'.[4] The ducat was originally minted by Venice and became extremely popular because of its fineness and stability, so was copied by many other countries, but not England. The angel was an English silver coin that varied between 8 and 11 shillings value. The spur-royal was a rare English coin worth 15s. or 16s. 6d. This is important to understand because it means that for the most part prices were remembered or written down in pounds, shillings, and pence independently of the coinage, mostly for the purposes of trading on credit. For most exchange in the medieval and early modern world this was done informally without accounts. The relationship between debts and credits was deeply embedded in cultural practices, and the balance between the two was not measured mathematically but negotiated. In many societies, debt became a social relationship of dependence and subordination.[5] Alternatively, in market societies as diverse as China and England to be in credit was a sign of the personal moral accomplishment of honesty.[6] When coins were used, they would need to be assembled, as in the example above, in such a way to match the price in money of account.

The History of Merchant Accounts and European Banking

An account book overcame this problem by turning money of account into a physical record that also provided a technical way of tracing all of one person's exchanges in the form of credits and debts over time. As was discussed in Chapter 1, accounting created a 'fact' out of a relationship of exchange. The value left over after accounts were balanced was

[4] Richard Cholmeley, *The Memorandum Book of Richard Cholmeley of Brandsby 1602–1623*, North Yorkshire County Record Office Publications, lxiv (1988), 59; C. E. Challis, *The Tudor Coinage* (Manchester, 1978), pp. 214–19.

[5] Graeber, *Debt: The First 5,000 Years* (New York, 2011), pp. 73–88, 137–44.

[6] Craig Muldrew, *Economy of Obligation* (London, 1998), pp. 125–7, 148–56. This is the Chinese concept of xìnyòng.

something removed from the relationship between any two people engaged in exchange, and could be moved around and used by anyone else who also practised accounting. But even such basic account-keeping was never very widespread before the eighteenth century, outside of some northern Italian cities. In the medieval period, great feudal estates and monastic properties hired trained accountants, and large-scale merchants and notaries had to keep accounts. But most of society participated in exchange without them.[7] Even in sixteenth- and seventeenth-century England, keeping accounts was exceptional, and most tradesmen and farmers who managed to learn to keep them only kept lists of expenditures and some earnings, and this did not prevent economic growth. As one advice manual put it, English accounts were 'grosely, obscurely and lewdely kept', and most surviving accounts are simple lists of purchases and sales, intended to be a record of transactions so that the indebtedness or credit of the accountant could be known.[8] Attempting to calculate a value for profit was rarely a concern.[9]

But Werner Sombart was right to suggest that the technology of the account, with both debits and credits (not necessarily double-entry bookkeeping though), created a new sort of value. It might not have immediately changed societies, but it certainly expanded the possibilities of long-distance trade by freeing it from being based either on barter or purchases made with precious metals. It also created an expansion of money of account, which certainly had a significant effect on the economy and society of many Italian cities. But most of all, and crucial to the argument of this book, it allowed value to be stored into the future in a non-physical form instead of land or gold, and this value could be used for liquidity and savings.

The practice of accounting in medieval Europe was developed most extensively in the trading cities of northern Italy, especially Florence. Fibonacci's manuscript text *Liber Abaci*, which introduced Hindu-Arabic numerals, was written in 1202. After this, many manuscripts were composed that dealt with the commercial application of mathematics, of which accounting and exchange were a major part.[10] The availability of

[7] M. T. Clanchy, *From Memory to Written Record: England, 1066–1307*, 2nd ed. (Oxford, 1993), pp. 122. 145–53.

[8] Muldrew, *Economy of Obligation*, pp. 60–9.

[9] The yeoman Robert Loader was one such exception. Craig Muldrew, *Food, Energy and the Creation of Industriousness: Work and Material Culture in Agrarian England, 1550–1780* (Cambridge, 2011), pp. 59, 130, 146–7.

[10] Raffaele Danna, *The Spread of Hindu-Arabic Numerals in the European Tradition of Practical Arithmetic: A Socio-Economic Perspective (13th–16th Centuries)* (PhD Thesis, Cambridge University, 2020).

such manuals meant that schools were able to develop a curriculum that taught commercial mathematics on a wide basis. Renaissance Florence has been the most well studied, but in other cities – such as Venice, Prato, and Genoa – there is evidence that mathematical education was also quite widespread.[11] Once the practice of keeping detailed accounts became common within such cities, merchants could simply transfer value through money of account, with a purchaser entering a payment in the seller's account book and a debit in his own, rather than having to use actual currency or oral credit arrangements.[12] From this practice it was an easy step for certain merchants and tradesmen to branch out into supplementing this activity by offering pure banking activities, such as taking deposits, transferring funds for third parties, and making loans.

They became known as banks from the Italian word for bench. Originally, specialists in the exchange of the peninsula's many different gold and silver currencies sat outside their houses on benches where the exchange would take place. Banking activities combined currency exchange with bookkeeping actions of transferability. Although taking interest was prohibited by the Church on most purely commercial transactions (it was allowed for many charitable institutions and governments), this could be disguised as a type of purchase or hidden in an exchange using different monies of account.[13] It has been estimated that in the years 1300–1350, Florence had eighty such local bankers.[14] In the same period, Venetians learned from the Florentine bankers who set up on the Rialto to process currency exchanges, and by 1322 there is evidence of overdrafts and interbank transfers.[15] In Prato, by the end of the fourteenth century, smaller tradesmen began to turn to merchants offering banking services to facilitate wholesale purchases from more distant places where they themselves lacked contacts.[16] Local bankers could also assist in the transfer of payments within Prato by allowing tradesmen to keep accounts with overdrafts.[17]

Because Florence was the centre of mathematical education and local banking activity, Florentine merchants were the first to employ their expertise in the realm of international trade, both within the Italian

[11] Richard Goldthwaite, 'The Practice and Culture of Accounting in Renaissance Florence', *Enterprise & Society* 16, no. 3 (2015), pp. 611–47.

[12] Richard K. Marshall, *The Local Merchants of Prato: Small Entrepreneurs in the Late Medieval Economy* (Baltimore, 1999), pp. 63–89.

[13] Raymond de Roover, *The Rise and Decline of the Medici Bank, 1397–1494* (Cambridge, MA, 1963), pp. 11–12, 100–21.

[14] Reinhold C. Mueller, *The Venetian Money Market: Banks, Panics, and the Public Debt, 1200–1500* (Baltimore, 2019), p. 7.

[15] Ibid., pp. 16–29.

[16] Marshall, *The Local Merchants of Prato*, pp. 103–5.

[17] Ibid., pp. 106–10.

peninsula and in the wool and cloth trade with northern Europe through Flanders. From the 1320s onwards, English wool was exported and shipped to Florence, where the first large-scale cloth industry developed, the products of which were shipped back to northern Europe.[18] Raymond de Roover has described how this trade evolved from being done at the Champagne fairs to becoming based around settled Italian merchant traders living in Flanders, especially Bruges in the 1280s.[19] They were able to dominate trade through the use of debit and credit accounting, and also, crucially, the introduction of the bill of exchange.[20] This allowed merchants to have their headquarters based in Sienna and Florence and work through agents in Flanders. It was through this trade that the so-called super companies such as the Bardi and Peruzi or Datini became established, with branches throughout Europe.[21] The Peruzzi had at least fifteen branches. These companies evolved in the thirteenth century as centralised joint stock companies in which family members held the largest number of shares.[22]

The whole system relied on the international bill of exchange, and this is worth describing in some detail since they would become crucial to the development of liquidity all over Europe in the eighteenth century. This instrument developed in Italy in the fourteenth century as the *lettera di cambio*.[23] The direct translation of the Italian would be 'letter of exchange', but the translation 'bill of exchange' was adopted in English. This translation first appeared in print in pamphlets about usury only in the 1570s.[24] The English word *bill* comes from the Latin *bulla* or *stud*, which became the medieval word for a wax seal pressed with a ring worn on a finger to keep documents 'sealed' and private, and in a much larger version to grant authority by being attached to the bottom of a deed or statute with string. Presumably the English translation was influenced by the fact that sealed bonds already existed as a means of assigning value from one person to another. But a bond created a debt, which was legally different than a bill of exchange. But, whatever the reason behind its initial usage, the word bill evolved to mean something

18 Richard A. Goldthwaite, *The Economy of Renaissance Florence* (Baltimore, 2009), pp. 217ff.
19 Raymond de Roover, *Money, Banking and Credit in Medieval Bruges: Italian Merchant Bankers, Lombards and Money-Changers: A Study in the Origins of Banking* (Cambridge, MA, 1948), pp. 10–11.
20 Ibid., p. 11
21 Edwin S. Hunt, *The Medieval Super-Companies: A Study of Peruzzi Company of Florence* (Cambridge, 1994), pp. 1–10, 38–75.
22 Ibid., pp. 55, 79–94.
23 de Roover, *Money, Banking and Credit*, p. 53.
24 Nicholas Sander, *A briefe treatise of vsurie, made by Nicolas Sander D. of Diuinitie* (Leuven, 1568), p. 7.

that was almost the opposite of its original link to the concept of personal property or authority. It signified a form of transferable paper value. In America, a 'bill' is still used to refer to a banknote, and everywhere in English usage it still refers to the receipt for goods sold and services done.

Bills of exchange provided the necessary liquidity to keep credit functional, given the lengthy time lags of months or years in international exchange, and worked by making payment assignable to a third party in the same town or city where the goods were bought, which could then be cancelled against past or future debts.[25] Their form was very simple, stating the day it was drawn up and the amount and the party in the destination city from whom the purchase was made, as well as the time allowed for acceptance in days. For example, in their early use Italian bankers in England might draw up a bill on one of their compatriots in Florence to purchase wool, which would then be sent to Florence, where it could be accepted by a merchant who needed payment for Florentine luxury goods such as silks, daggers, or glassware for shipment to London. It was in this way that the Italian companies transferred value to buy the wool they needed from England and to sell the finished cloth. The northern Italian cities also bought grain from the south in this way, and bills of exchange enabled the Papacy to collect revenues from all over Europe and remit them to Rome, eliminating the need to move cash over a long distance.[26] Without them, long-distance exchange would have remained painfully slow. It was also impossible to predict how long it would take to sell the cargoes of outward voyages, and to buy and load the goods for the return journey, as well as to account for the vagaries of the weather.[27]

As European long-distance commerce expanded in the early modern period, the bill of exchange became the primary means by which payments could be made, overcoming limits on stocks of metallic currency. In order for liquidity based on the bill of exchange to increase, the

[25] Bills could be paid, either at sight or more normally a period of a number of months might be given for payment, allowing time for the bill to arrive, and then to be negotiated at the most convenient time for the seller and the third party. This was termed usance. Much has been written on the use of bills of exchange and exchange rates. See, Henry Roseveare, *Markets and Merchants of the Late Seventeenth Century: The Marescoe–David Letters 1668–1680* (Oxford, 1987), pp. 592–3; Raymond de Roover (ed.), *Gresham on Foreign Exchange: An Essay on Early English Mercantilism with the Text of Sir Thomas Gresham's Memorandum – For the Understanding of the Exchange* (Cambridge, MA, 1949), pp. 109ff; Gerald de Malynes, *Consuetudo vel lex Mercatoria* (London, 1622), pp. 391–2.

[26] Hunt, *Medieval Super-Companies*, pp. 49–52, 163–7; De Roover, *Rise and Decline*, pp. 194–224, 317–37.

[27] Roseveare, *Markets and Merchants*, pp. 19–20.

potential number of acceptors also needed to increase. This led to the rise of what Peter Spufford has termed financial centres, which were also entrepôts of trade, such as, first, Florence, Venice, Naples and Genoa, Barcelona, and Seville, and then in the north Bruges, Hamburg, Antwerp, Amsterdam, Pairs, Lyon, and London.[28] This was because the more exchange was concentrated, the greater the options for finding mutual debts and credits for cancellation. Through this system, such cities actually became conglomerates of individual capital on each merchant's account books. There was always some excess capital to ensure liquidity. Larger merchants could even write bills to enhance liquidity.[29] But, since bills of exchange were always in motion, they were generally neither a form of savings nor a currency, but a means of exchange within a limited and defined group of individuals.

Although it was possible to sue over the non-payment of a bill of exchange under a body of law known as the custom of merchants, bills of exchange relied more heavily on the personal credit and reputation of the merchant than ordinary credit, since waging law in a foreign state was inevitably more difficult. Thus, the non-payment of bills of exchange was much more serious than with other debts.[30] Daniel Defoe claimed that, while in the case of informal credit not one tradesman in twenty kept to his time, bills of exchange, in contrast, had to be paid 'without hesitation of any kind whatsoever' if the tradesman expected to keep his credit for long. Another seventeenth-century English merchant wrote in a letter that 'if a man pay them not at the day, you know his credit is clouded'.[31]

Antwerp became northern Europe's entrepôt of international payments in the late fifteenth and sixteenth centuries using bills of exchange. Because of this, it was able to build up enough liquidity in the bill market through its many merchants, such that bills of exchange became assignable through endorsement before their due date.[32] They could also be bought, or discounted, thus acting as a form of paper currency in

[28] Peter Spufford, 'From Antwerp and Amsterdam to London: The Decline of Financial Centres in Europe', *De Economist* (Netherlands) 154, no. 2 (2006): pp. 143–75.

[29] James Steven Rogers, *Early History of the Law of Bills and Notes* (Cambridge, 2009), pp. 107–12; Eric Kerridge, *Trade and Banking in Early Modern England* (Manchester, 1988), pp. 77–82.

[30] Most of the correspondence to the London merchants Charles Marescoe and Jacob David was concerned in part with the negotiation of payment by bills of exchange and the time to be allowed for the acceptance. Roseveare, *Markets and Merchants*, pp. 226–7, 231, 233, 236, 238, 246, 251, 260, 263, 268.

[31] Daniel Defoe, *The Complete English Tradesman in Familiar Letters* (London, 1727), pp. 349–53, 363–4; George F. Steckley (ed.), *The Letters of John Paige, London Merchant, 1648–1658* (London, 1984), pp. 69; Roseveare, *Markets and Merchants*, pp. 30–1.

[32] Spufford, 'From Antwerp and Amsterdam', pp. 12–18.

Antwerp. After the city was sacked during the war with Spain, bringing its ascendancy to an end, these practices were brought to places such as Amsterdam with the diaspora of Protestant merchants from Antwerp. They set themselves up as *kassiers* to broker bills of exchange. But the government of Amsterdam looked on their activity with scepticism, and after trying to reduce this activity with regulation created the Wisselbank to replace them.[33]

In addition to this form of capital investment based on fluctuating short-term trading and exchange profits, what we now call long-term investment grew up by way of government finance. This took some time to develop as bankers such as the Peruzzi or Medici saw loans to princes as highly risky investments, given their propensity to default after spending more than they could collect in revenue. Certainly the Medici Bank tried to avoid them. But given the power of princes over the ability to do business, this was not always possible, and lending to governments remained an undesirable but necessary practice when expensive wars broke out.[34] As is well known, a large number of banks collapsed in the 1340s – before the Black Death hit Europe – for various reasons, including loans to monarchs who defaulted and a general slowdown in trade caused by war with the Ottomans.[35]

But beginning in the thirteenth century, Italian city states began issuing long-term debt sold to investors at interest pegged to future taxes. Perhaps the most famous example was the Genoese *compera* issued to build galleys and to pay other military costs. Eventually investors pooled these to form the famous Bank of San Giorgio, which came to function as a syndicate of merchant investors in the city's debt. Florence and Venice preferred a type of forced loan to issue their debt, but they also came to be administered by city institutions.[36] In Flanders, something similar was introduced, but here they were called *rentes* in reference to the already-existing instrument used to borrow money on the security of land. Such shares in government debt could be bought and sold on secondary markets, although there is little information on how active such selling was. Very long-term debt, in the form of annuities for lives, was also eventually introduced by governments in the early sixteenth century. But losing an expensive war often led to a suspension of interest rates and a

[33] Jan de Vries and Ad van der Woude, *The First Modern Economy: Success, Failure, and Perseverance of the Dutch Economy, 1500–1815* (Cambridge, 1997), pp. 130–1.
[34] Ibid., p. 141.
[35] Hunt, *Medieval Super-Companies*, pp. 212–29; de Roover, *Rise and Decline*.
[36] James D. Tracy, *A Financial Revolution in the Habsburg Netherlands: Renten and Renteniers in the County of Holland, 1515–1565* (Berkeley, 1985), pp. 9–12; Mueller, *The Venetian Money Market*, pp. 453–87.

lowering of the price at which shares in government debt could be sold. For instance, after a disastrous war with Lucca, Florence suspended payments in 1433, and its debt only traded at 15 per cent of par.[37] James Tracy has compared a number of different governments during the fifteenth century, and the Papacy and Holland come out as the most reliable borrowers, while France was the most unreliable.[38]

Because of the uncertainty of both private banks and government debt, by the end of the sixteenth century a number of cities had also created public banks as a service to merchants.[39] As noted above, the private banking model was a profit-based enterprise that sought investments from depositors that they then used to invest in trade. But since trade was susceptible to disruptions by wars or epidemics, private banks suffered runs on their capital by their depositors, which inevitably led to bankruptcy.[40] But these same institutions were also vital to merchants, who used them as a means of payment by transferring money of account from one bank account to another. Private bankruptcies obviously greatly disrupted payment liquidity in this way. The first Italian public bank was set up by two Acts of the Venetian Senate in 1584 and 1587. In a speech by Tommaso Contarini outlining the reasons why a public bank was needed, it was claimed that out of 103 private bankers in Venice over the past two centuries, 96 had failed. But, he went on to argue, without banking the trade of the city was impossible.[41] Thus, the public Banco di Rialto was created as a non-profit institution run by the city solely to provide the banking services of account transfer, specie deposits, and the discounting of bills of exchange. It did not provide leverage by providing paper credit currency and did not make loans. It was a non-profit organisation that only charged enough to pay its costs. Other public banks were set up in cities such as Seville and Hamburg, but the most famous imitator of the Banco di Rialto was Amsterdam's Wisselbank, established in 1609. The question has been raised as to why Amsterdam adopted what has been termed the conservative Venetian model of banking rather than following the practices that had evolved in Antwerp.[42]

Why the government was sceptical of this practice is unclear, but there might also have been a danger of bankruptcy involved. Whatever the reason, the Bank of Amsterdam became an undoubted success in the

[37] Tracy, *Financial Revolution*, p. 12 [38] Ibid., pp. 18–27.

[39] This has been explored by Jacopo Sartori, 'The Diffusion of Public Banking Initiatives in Europe, 1500–1650' (PhD Thesis, Cambridge University, 2023).

[40] Charles F. Dunbar, 'The Bank of Venice', *The Quarterly Journal of Economics* 7, no. 2 (1893), p. 321.

[41] Ibid., pp. 309, 312. [42] de Vries and van der Woude, *First Modern Economy*, p. 132.

transfer service it provided for merchants, and it was copied in other Dutch cities such as Delft and Middleburg.[43] In social terms, however, the accessibility of the service it provided was relatively limited, with only 2,000–3,000 depositors using it. It also became exceptionally successful as a centre for international money transfers by foreign merchants.[44] But, since this was of limited use to smaller tradesmen and shopkeepers in the city, the *kassiers* returned after 1621, and issued 'receipts, for cash deposits which could circulate in the city as a paper currency'.[45] Although little is known about the activity of the *kassiers* since they were not officially recognised, it seems they only dealt in larger-scale paper notes, and not ones that circulated through the whole economy.[46] It might seem odd that where there were so many successful innovations in high finance, including – besides the Wisselbank – the world's first stock market, the Dutch Republic did not develop more popular smaller value paper currency. But because of warfare, coins were more abundant in the Low Countries, so perhaps there was less pressure on wage payment. But it could also be the case that the paper currency I will describe in the next chapter has so far gone unnoticed.

If the Venetian and northern public banks can be called conservative in the sense that they limited liquidity to merchant accounting transfers, the public banks established in Naples were anything but. Between 1584 and 1600, seven public banks were created out of local charitable institutions that were already engaged in regulated pawnbroking. These banks expanded the principle of exchanging monies of account to the issuing of a type of receipt for a deposit, in cash, or transferred from an account called a *fede di credito*.[47] These were then assignable and able to circulate as paper money, albeit with one major restriction. Every transfer had to be recorded in a ledger at one of the banks. Because there were seven banks in a relatively small area, this was not too onerous, but it produced

[43] Ibid., pp. 132–4.

[44] Ibid., p. 136; J. G. van Dillen, 'The Bank of Amsterdam', in J. G. van Dillen (ed.), *History of the Principal Public Banks: Accompanied by Extensive Bibliographies of the History of Banking and Credit in Eleven European Countries* (The Hague, 1934), pp. 105–7.

[45] de Vries and van der Woude, *First Modern Economy*, p. 132.

[46] Oscar Gelderbolm and Just Jonker, 'Enter the Ghost: Cashless Payments in the Early Modern Low Countries, 1500–1800', in R. J. van der Spek and Bas van Leeuwen (eds.), *Currency and Crisis: In Search of Trust, 2000 BC to AD 2000* (London, 2018), pp. 224–47; Christiaan van Bochove and Heleen Kole, 'Uncovering Private Credit Markets: Amsterdam', *Tijdschrift voor Sociale en Economische Geschiedenis* 11, no. 3 (2014), pp. 39–72.

[47] Heinrich Sieveking, 'Das Bankwessen in Genua und die Bank von S. Giorgio', in J. G. Van Dillen (ed.), *History of the Principal Public Banks: Accompanied by Extensive Bibliographies of the History of Banking and Credit in Eleven European Countries* (The Hague, 1934), pp. 17–18, 24.

enough documentation to fill 300 rooms with many millions of notes that still survive in the bank's archives.[48] These banks created the first widespread form of paper currency in the world since the Song dynasty in twelfth-century China.[49] It has been estimated that about 52 per cent of households in Naples had accounts, including unskilled workers. Circulation was also quite rapid. One example of a *fede di credito* for 100 ducats issued on 5 May 1706 passed through seven hands before being returned to the bank on 14 July of the same year, which is one transfer every ten days, on average.[50] Trust in the banks was generated because they were charitable organisations backed by the state, but most importantly because they were based on skilled accountancy and kept a detailed record of all transactions, which could be checked.

The banks were also supposed to be safe from risk since they were only in the business of transferring money that was already in existence. The accounts of some of the banks also show that they were, however, engaged in creating new money through a type of loan in which *fede di credito* were issued without a matching deposit. This went against government policy, but because of the requirement to record every transaction with extensive bookkeeping, the money supply was not overly inflated. The banks' money of account was even more valuable than the state silver currency, which was subject to clipping. The only crisis the banks suffered in their early history was not their fault, but actually that of the Neapolitan king, who decided to revalue the silver coinage in 1622 by almost 20 per cent. But apart from this, Naples provided an example of how capital could be liquefied and expanded into serving a wide social milieu.[51]

Most of these early banks and different forms of government debt created two basic forms of capital. The first took the form of a surplus of exchange in the continual drawing and acceptance of short-term bills of exchange within financial centres like Antwerp or Florence. In order to

48 Luigi de Rosa, 'The Beginnings of Paper Money Circulation: The Neapolitan Public Banks (1540–1650)', *The Journal of European Economic History* 36, no. 2–3 (2007), pp. 261–81.

49 But by 1400 paper had ceased functioning as viable currency and by the eighteenth century China relied on silver and copper coins. Richard Von Glahn, *An Economic History of China: From Antiquity to the Nineteenth Century* (Cambridge, 2015), pp. 262–87, 365–70.

50 Sieveking, 'Das Bankwessen', p. 24.

51 Lilia Costabile and Eduardo Nappi, 'The Public Banks of Naples between Financial Innovation and Crisis', in Lilia Costabile and Larry Neal (eds.), *Financial Innovation and Resilience: The Outstanding Achievements of the Public Banks of Naples (1462–1808)* (London, 2018), pp. 17–53.

ensure that the bills of exchange would find acceptors within the normal 1–2-month acceptance periods, a certain amount of extra value needed to be kept in merchants' accounts to ensure there was enough liquidity to maintain the individual trust upon which the system was based. Such capital was not used for consumption, and could play a part in paying for some aspects of investment since it was short term. But it is best theorised as *liquidity capital* – an extra value kept in accounts to keep exchange functioning.

The other type of capital we can term *spending capital*, since it was created for princes, states, and chartered companies to spend on warfare and fixed capital. Soldiers' wages, uniforms, and food – as well as ships, guns, walls, and forts – all involved more expense than could be immediately provided and so required borrowing at interest. As we saw, states gradually moved from borrowing on more expensive short-term loans from individual financiers to establishing long-term types of capital secured by taxation, on which they paid lower interest rates. Since collecting taxes on variable income, apart from rent, was difficult both practically and politically, most of the taxation for these debts became some form of consumption tax.[52] Thus, in an indirect way, states needed to encourage popular consumption in order to retain credible commitment by paying the interest on their debts. Since states found it much easier to levy customs and excise than taxation on personal wealth, widespread social consumption of taxed goods was always a necessary part of capital based on state spending. However, only in Naples does it seem that banks created smaller liquid capital for everyday spending.[53]

Of course, merchants and smaller traders could create much smaller forms of capital when they issued personal interest-bearing sealed bonds for payment at a future date. In the Roman law system, eventually adopted in most continental jurisdictions but not in England, such lending had to be organised by public officials known as notaries. Again the practice originated and evolved in the Italian city-states in the thirteenth century and spread to other countries.[54] Everywhere under Roman law it was also normal to raise some form of capital on the security of land, but its use was very much tied to rules of inheritance,

[52] In Venice, indirect taxes already constituted 80 per cent of taxation in 1550. Guido Alfani and Matteo Di Tullio, *The Lion's Share: Inequality and the Rise of the Fiscal State in Preindustrial Europe* (Cambridge, 2019), pp. 150–65; John Brewer, *The Sinews of Power: War, Money and the English State, 1688–1783* (London, 1994), pp. 95–114.

[53] It is also possible that Monte di Pieta might have issued tickets against the goods they held on pawn rather than issuing cash, but so far this has not been investigated.

[54] François Menant and Odile Redon, *Notaires et Crédit dans L'Occident Méditerranéen Médiéval* (Rome, 2004), pp. 3–95.

and women's marital property rights.[55] This was also possible in common law England, but it was much more risky for the borrower before the late seventeenth century.[56] After this, mortgages became common and played a crucial part in underpinning the creation of local circulating capital; their role will be discussed in detail in Chapter 4.

But, whether value was created through production, trade, or land, it was indeed account-keeping that allowed it to become liquid, or what Adam Smith, in the eighteenth century would term circulating capital. A mortgage could create capital based on the productive capacity or location of a piece of land, and a bond or investment in state debt could store the value of a tradesman's profits well enough over time, but moving that value around with confidence and accuracy required enough people keeping accounts so that it could be used to increase the number of financial transactions in the economy. Of course, double-entry bookkeeping was the best way to keep track of value in motion, but simple cash accounts could work as well.

It is certainly pertinent to ask why the development of capital and its investment in the silk and woollen industries in Italy in the fourteenth century did not keep developing into a society that sought to increase capital as a form of continual reinvestment in industry for popular consumption and export, as was the case in England after 1650. As Richard Goldthwaite has emphasised, wealth remained enmeshed in the social relations of hierarchical display and taste; in art, charity, feasting, architecture, and fashion.[57] Many historians have also argued for the role of exogenous factors in bringing developments to a halt. These include: the movement of Asian trade to the Atlantic, the development of American colonial trade, the devastating effects of the plague on Florence and other Italian cites, the huge disruptions caused by war with the Ottoman Empire, and the effects of the Counter-Reformation.[58] In addition, since much happened before the printing press, there was

[55] Chris Briggs and C. J. Zuijderduijn (eds.), *Land and Credit: Mortgages in the Medieval and Early Modern European Countryside* (London, 2018), pp. 1–16; Amy Louise Erickson, 'Coverture and Capitalism', *History Workshop Journal* 59, no. 1 (2005), pp. 1–16.

[56] Chris Briggs, 'Mortgages and the English Peasantry c.1250-c.1350', in Chris Briggs and C. J. Zuijderduijn (eds.), *Land and Credit: Mortgages in the Medieval and Early Modern European Countryside* (London, 2018), pp. 17–80.

[57] Goldthwaite, 'Practice and Culture of Accounting', pp. 639–43.

[58] Darren Acemoglu, S. Johnson, and S. J. Robinson, 'The Rise of Europe: Atlantic Trade, Institutional Change, and Economic Growth', *The American Economic review* 95, no. 3 (2005), pp. 546–79; Guido Alfani, 'Plague in Seventeenth-Century Europe and the Decline of Italy: An Epidemiological Hypothesis', *European Review of Economic History* 17, no. 4 (2013), pp. 408–30; Paul Grendler, *Schooling in Renaissance Italy: Literacy and Learning, 1300–1600* (Baltimore, 1991), chs. 12–13.

no concurrent public discourse on economic practice and how it was related to politics and society more generally – what came to be known as political economy in the eighteenth century. Rather, the techniques of double-entry bookkeeping were guarded as an advantageous technology with which Italian bankers like the Medici were able to dominate channels of exchange in northern Europe. One result of this was that the international credit payment system was still underdeveloped compared to what would be the case by the late seventeenth century, something that contributed to the many failures of Italian banks before 1600. What is now termed 'market depth' is when the number of potential buyers and sellers of potential debt is large enough to reduce the possibility of business failure. Outside of places like Florence, Prato, Genoa, Venice, Naples, and Antwerp before *c.*1700, banking and sophisticated bookkeeping were largely confined to merchants, and cannot be said to have changed older social practices.

Credit and Finance in England before 1680

During the late sixteenth century, the English economy had also grown rapidly, and benefited from the great rise in demand for woollen cloth sent to Antwerp, and then to the United Provinces after 1576, to be finished with dying and other processes. At this time, both northern Italy and the Lowlands were significantly more industrialised than England. But England, uniquely, as both an island and a unified political kingdom at peace with Scotland, rapidly developed a unified national market centred on London. Almost all urban growth in England before 1650 took place in London, which grew from 60,000 people in 1525 to 200,000 in 1600 and 400,000 by 1650. At the latter date the next largest town, Norwich, had a population of only 30,000.[59] Because England is a fairly narrow island, a coastal trading system developed along the east and south coasts, in which London acted as an entrepôt. Goods produced in London and those imported from abroad were shipped first to its warehouses and then re-shipped to other towns. This produced an efficiency of scale that was economically advantageous.

But financially neither London nor the rest of the country could match the sophistication of the Lowlands or northern Italy. This was alleviated to some degree by the merchant Thomas Gresham. He spent most of his

[59] E. A. Wrigley, 'Urban Growth and Agricultural Change: England and the Continent in the Early Modern Period' in E. A. Wrigley (ed.), *People, Cities and Wealth* (Chichester, 1988), pp. 158–67.

early career in Antwerp before 1567, where he acted as the 'King's Merchant'. He saw the need to expand the use of bills of exchange in London and to that end built the Royal Exchange at his own personal expense between 1566 and 1570 in Cornhill. But, in terms of state finance, the English system of borrowing continued to rely heavily on short-term loans from individual merchants, and by the 1620s its tax system was so inadequate as to create a series of political crises that were only resolved with the Civil War.[60] There were no banks to speak of, and few notaries, but borrowing on bond was common. Very wealthy London moneylenders, such as Jerome Shelton or Thomas Sutton and the alderman Sir Paul Bayning, lent large amounts. The latter two, respectively, had £45,000 and £136,700 lent out on interest in 1629.[61] The wealthy widow Joyce Jefferies had £5,890 out on loan in 1639, on which she earned hundreds of pounds in income from interest.[62] There was also much investment in joint stock companies worth hundreds of thousands of pounds. The East India Company had been created in 1600 following others, such as the Levant Company, but most of this investment was international mercantile credit.[63]

England in this period was also to some degree different to most continental European economies, in that it relied on a much more informal credit system to propel its advanced marketing system. It was a system based on oral sales credit for everyday goods. Long-distance trade might rely more heavily on the use of account books, but even here oral agreements were the norm, and they were also the basis of contract in English law. In contrast, other European economies, while reliant on sales credit at the bottom of the economy, relied much more on notarial

[60] Robert Ashton, *The Crown and the Money Market, 1603–1640* (Oxford, 1960); Conrad Russell, 'Parliament and the King's Finances', in C. Russell (ed.), *The Origins of the English Civil War* (London, 1973), pp. 91–116.

[61] James Alsop, 'The Financial Enterprises of Jerome Shelton, a Mid-Tudor London Adventurer', *Guildhall Studies in London History* 4 (1979), pp. 43–4; Lawrence Stone, *The Crisis of the Aristocracy, 1558–1641* (Oxford, 1965), pp. 534–5.

[62] B. A. Holderness, 'Widows in Pre-Industrial Society: An Essay upon their Economic Functions', in Richard M. Smith (ed.), *Land, Kinship and Life Cycle* (Cambridge, 1984), pp. 435–42; Robert Tittler, 'Money-Lending in the West Midlands: The Activities of Joyce Jeffries, 1638–49', *Historical Research* 67 (1994), pp. 249–63; Barbara Todd, 'Freebench and Free Enterprise: Widows and their Property in two Berkshire Villages', in John Chartres and David Hey (eds.), *English Rural Society 1500–1800: Essays in Honour of Joan Thirsk* (Cambridge, 1990), pp. 196–200.

[63] de Roover, *Gresham on Foreign Exchange*; Ashton, *Crown and the Money Market*, pp. 1–30, 113–31; Robert Brenner, *Merchants and Revolutionaries: Commercial Change, Political Conflict and London's Overseas Traders 1550–1653* (Cambridge, 1993), pp. 51–112; Theodore K. Rabb, *Enterprise and Empire: Merchant and Gentry Investment in the Expansion of England*, 1575–1630 (Cambridge, MA, 1967).

lending at interest to provide cash or written obligations for more substantial trade and purchases.[64]

England also never relied on its coinage for much of its economic activity. It had no mines and the only way to attract precious metals was through trade. In this sense, England was fortunate to have a product – wool – which was in constant demand elsewhere. But luxury imports also had to be paid for, and as these increased in the late sixteenth and early seventeenth centuries, while wool and cloth exports stagnated, trade deficits led to a decline in the amount of coins.[65] In addition, the destruction of monastic institutions that accompanied the English Reformation also reduced the level of numeracy in the country. The great medieval estates kept accounts that were detailed and sophisticated enough that historians of agriculture have been able to use them to establish production figures, but after the 1530s nothing in comparable numbers is available until the mid-eighteenth century. Thus, what developed in the fifteenth century and expanded in the sixteenth and seventeenth centuries was a very informal system of credit that maximised flexibility at the expense of security and accuracy. Numeracy skills were low, accounts were rare, and notarial records were not required.[66] Instead, local courts enforced contract in a public way if oral agreements were not met. Most ordinary farmers or small artisans operated without accounts, and liquidity depended for the most part on a system of oral credit. As a result, the period from 1550 to around 1700 saw what the legal historian Chris Brooks has termed hyper-litigation as a means of contract enforcement.[67] But this system was able to both foster significant economic growth and accommodate the highly capital-intensive development of some sectors which did require accounts, such as the north-east coal industry.[68]

Both banking and more sophisticated means of taxation and state finance were products of the Commonwealth period as Cromwell's republican government sought to pay for war debts and a continuing

[64] Phillip Hoffman, Gilles Postel-Vinay, and Jean-Laurent Rosenthal, *Priceless Markets: The Political Economy of Credit in Paris, 1660–1870* (Chicago, 2000), pp. 25–49.

[65] J. R. Wordie, 'Deflationary Factors in the Tudor Price Rise', *Past and Present*, 154 (1997), pp. 32–70.

[66] Muldrew, *Economy of Obligation*, pp. 60–9.

[67] Ibid., pp. 212–40; C. W. Brooks, 'Litigation and Society in England, 1200–1830', in C. W. Brooks (ed.), *Lawyers, Litigation and English Society Since 1450* (London, 1998), pp. 63–128.

[68] John Hatcher, *The History of the British Coal Industry before 1700* (Oxford, 1984), pp. 323–43; David Levine and Keith Wrightson, *The Making of an Industrial Society: Whickham, 1560–1765* (Oxford, 1991), pp. 106–34.

military presence. It also engaged on a programme of advancing trade into the Atlantic – his so-called Western Design. The old land tax – the subsidy – was abolished and replaced with a more accurate means of valuing land based on rent, and new excise taxes were introduced for the first time.[69] To facilitate new government borrowing, certain goldsmiths came to play an increasingly important role in the capital's money market by acting as brokers and lenders to individuals, and eventually, after the Civil War, as actual deposit bankers who took in small amounts of money on note, and re-lent it on bond for interest, and shared the profit with the depositors. There were ninety-three goldsmith bankers in the period 1670–1700, and probably an equally large number of scriveners who acted as bankers.[70] The earliest records that exist are the accounts of the scrivener Francis Webb, from 1633 to 1636, which record 1,278 country-dwellers who brought money to London to be deposited. The apprentice who kept these accounts was one Robert Abbot, who would develop his own scrivening banking business though the war years by offering credit and deposit facilities to royalists. By the time of the Commonwealth he recorded receiving £1,137,646 in the three years 1653–1656. Eventually he joined up with Robert Clayton, and in partnership they became two of the most successful bankers of the Restoration period.[71] Some of these men were extremely wealthy, such as Edward Backwell, who borrowed money from other goldsmiths to lend to the government, and once provided forty-six carts to carry £350,000 in silver to the mint. The goldsmith Francis Child operated a bank with assets of between £100,000 and £190,000 in the 1680s and 1690s. Sir Robert Clayton, the greatest scrivener-banker in London of the period, had over one million pounds on deposit in some years.[72] Goldsmith bankers were also involved in lending to the government of Charles II, which needed coins to make payments abroad, and many failed when interest payments were stopped for a time in 1672. When the interest payments were resumed, new bankers took the place of those who had been bankrupted, because their

[69] D'Maris Coffman, Excise *Taxation and the Origins of Public Debt* (London, 2013).

[70] See Chapter 3.

[71] Frank T. Melton, *Sir Robert Clayton and the Origins of English Deposit Banking 1658–1685* (Cambridge, 1986), pp. 2–6.

[72] Ibid., pp. 16–39, 228–32; Peter Earle, *The Making of the English Middle Class* (London, 1989), pp. 48–50, esp. n. 111; S. W. Shelton, 'The Goldsmith Banker', in A. C. Littleton and B. S. Yamey (eds.), *Studies in the History of Accounting* (London, 1956), pp. 247–54; P. G. Stein, R. H. Helmholz, and C. W. Brooks, *Notaries Public in England Since the Reformation* (Norwich, 1991), pp. 69–75, 107–11; Richard Grassby, *The Business Community of Seventeenth Century England* (Cambridge, 1995), pp. 252–3.

services were needed to keep trade going, just as had been the case in Venice in the 1590s.[73]

The Pamphlet Debate over Currency

In his book *Casualties of Credit*, Carl Wennerlind has shown how there was a whole body of economic writing that originated in the period of the English Civil War and made explicit the fact that England's informal system of credit was a barrier to economic growth.[74] Earlier writers such as Gerard de Malynes, Thomas Mun, and Edward Misselden all noted that there was a shortage in the supply of gold and silver coins in England at the time. However, they held a neo-Aristotelian notion that saw the role of money as both a measure and a means of lubricating exchange. For Aristotle, money was a means of commensurability, and he famously provided the moral argument against profit being made from money itself, since a person lending money was not engaging in a productive activity.[75] It was from his thinking that the Catholic Church developed its prohibition on usury. However, England had adopted a legal interest rate for lending in the 1580s. This was based on the concept of property; that is, a lender should be recompensed for what he lent since it was no longer available to be invested in his own work. However, in the 1620s there still existed a moral ambiguity surrounding the charging of interest. It was seen as inevitable and necessary, but people who were professional lenders were often caricatured as misers or greedy profiteers.[76] Money was still considered more in terms of social harmony than liquidity.[77] As we will see in Chapter 5, the social normalisation and acceptance of the practice of interest rates was one of the fundamental shifts allowing the formation of capital at the turn of the next century. Although these writers acknowledged that trade could increase through overseas exploration and colonisation, they did not take the view that money could be used to kickstart new production and trade.[78]

[73] J. Keith Horsefield, 'The "Stop of the Exchequer" Revisited', *The Economic History Review* 35, no. 4 (1982), pp. 511–28.

[74] Wennerlind, *Casualties of Credit*, pp. 95–122; also see Barry Supple, *Commercial Crisis and Change in England, 1600–1642: A Study in the Instability of a Mercantile Economy* (Cambridge, 1959), pp. 73–98, 163–96.

[75] Aristotle, *Nicomachean Ethics*, translated by Robert C. Bartlett and Susan D. Collins (Chicago, 2011), IV, 1–3.

[76] For instance, see Ben Johnson's 'Volpone, or the Fox', in Ben Johnson, *Three Comedies*, ed. Michael Jamieson (Harmondsworth, 1966), pp. 51–3.

[77] Craig Muldrew, '"Hard Food for Midas", Cash and its Social Value in Early Modern England', *Past and Present* 170 (2001), pp. 113–18.

[78] Thomas Mun, *England's Treasure by Forraign Trade* (London, 1664), reprinted in J. R. McCulloch, *Early English Tracts on Commerce* (Cambridge, 1954), pp. 115–209; Perry

The writers who challenged this conception were members of what has come to be called the Hartlib circle, after Samuel Hartlib. Hartlib is a fascinating figure who was born in the Baltic town of Ebbing, to a father who was a factor for the English Eastland Company. After being educated in Germany, he spent the early 1620s at Cambridge University as a protégé of John Preston, before returning to Germany. Preston was master of Emmanuel College, but had originally been a divine at Queens' College, and was popular with puritans who sent their sons to the college. These two colleges would become the home of the Cambridge Platonists in the next decade, who will be discussed in Chapter 5. Hartlib moved permanently to London in 1628 to escape the Thirty Years War. Influenced by Baconian ideas of questioning and reforming accepted practices, he communicated with other scholars in Europe and advocated the setting up of an 'Office of Address' where investigations from all over Europe could be shared by letter.[79] Although this never materialised in the form intended, he did gather around him a group of likeminded thinkers who wrote manuscripts to one another and published many pamphlets.

Because of their interest in the new science, they were also interested in alchemical investigations into the material world based on the qualities of sulphur and mercury, and their relation to other metals in the earth. As one of the members, Sir Cheney Culpeper, argued, the purpose of natural philosophy was to discover 'hidden and inwarde motion'. Political instability ('motion'), like chemical change, involved releasing human energies from the 'gross matter' of 'custome' and the 'dark corners of prescription'. Ecclesiastical monopoly, the aristocratic interest, and even the tyranny of kings had to be cast down in order to release the light of human reason.[80] One aspect of alchemy was, of course, experiments involving the transformation of base metal into gold. In popular print this was often satirised as a selfish desire to get rich quickly and was equated with miserliness.[81] However, for those interested in the problems created by the limited amount of gold and silver

Gauci, 'Malynes, Gerard (*fl.* 1585–1641)', *Oxford Dictionary of National Biography*, www.oxforddnb.com/view/article/17912, accessed 17 January 2017.

79 Mark Greengrass, 'Hartlib, Samuel (c. 1600–1662), Educational Reformer and Writer', *Oxford Dictionary of National Biography*, www-oxforddnb-com.ezp.lib.cam.ac.uk/view/10.1093/ref:odnb/9780198614128.001.0001/odnb-9780198614128-e-12500, accessed 21 July 2022.

80 Mark Greengrass, 'Culpeper, Sir Cheney, Advocate of Political Reform and Technological Innovation', *Oxford Dictionary of National Biography*, www-oxforddnb-com.ezp.lib.cam.ac.uk/view/10.1093/ref:odnb/9780198614128.001.0001/odnb-9780198614128-e-50336, accessed 21 July 2022.

81 This, for instance, is satirised in Ben Jonson's comedy *The Alchemist.*

currency in circulation, the creation of more gold was seen as a potential solution.[82]

This was the genesis for what Wennerlind has termed proposals for 'credit currency' by members of the Hartlib circle as a means of solving not just the shortage of coins, but a whole range of other social problems. Pamphlets advocating some form of new paper money based on credit continued to be published through to the end of the century, but they were first put forward in one of the earliest of the circle's publications in a pamphlet entitled *The Key of Wealth Or a New Way of Improving Trade*, by William Potter in 1650.[83] The only other member of the circle who had published earlier was the well-known writer on agricultural improvement, Walter Blith, in 1649. With the ending of the civil wars, the execution of the king, and the establishment of the Republic, the time seemed auspicious for the implementation of programmes for social and institutional reform.

That the question of money and credit should figure so prominently right away is interesting. From 1632, the shortage of silver coin had begun to be somewhat alleviated by an agreement between England and Spain to use Dover as a point of transshipment of Spanish silver from the New World to pay her armies fighting the Dutch in the Netherlands. The reason Charles agreed to help England's Catholic enemy was an agreement that allowed much of this silver to remain in England, with its value transferred to Flanders through bills of exchange. During the Civil War, Parliament also continued with the agreement. All in all, between 1632 and 1647, £8,360,750 worth of silver coins were minted at the Tower Mint. In these fifteen years, more silver was minted than in all the years between 1550 and 1632 combined![84] This shows how religious divisions were accommodated in the realities of commerce, but also that there were more coins available in England from the mid-1630s. But despite this, the expense of paying for armies during the civil wars, at the same time as fighting disrupted trade, was a large problem for both sides, and the arrears of pay in the New Model Army were still a pressing problem in 1650.[85]

Potter began *The Key of Wealth* as a project for improvement, necessary for the 'future preservation of earthly enjoyments' through increased trade. He went on to describe the nature of money as a 'publique

[82] Wennerlind, *Casualties of Credit*, pp. 44–54; Supple, *Commercial Crisis*, chs. 3–6.
[83] Wennerlind, *Casualties of Credit*, pp. 68, 70–3.
[84] Nicholas Mayhew, *Sterling, the History of a Currency* (New York, 2000), pp. 70–2; C. D. Challis (ed.), *A New History of the Royal Mint* (Cambridge, 1992), pp. 316–24.
[85] Henry Reece, *The Army in Cromwellian England, 1649–1660* (Oxford, 2013), pp. 88–96.

Obligation' that provided security to drive trade. He made a crucial argument that defined the nature of money as liquidity, and further that if the money supply was increased this would create economic growth by creating demand and enabling tradesmen to sell more things, unleashing what he felt was an underutilised productive capacity in the economy.[86] While he did mention that the civil wars had caused people to hoard money, rather than addressing immediate practical problems, his main point was theoretical. An alchemical influence can be seen in his rather utopian argument that a ten-fold increase in money would result in 100-fold economic growth, without then dealing with how agriculture could expand to feed such massive industrial production.[87] He was, however, on more empirical grounds when he rejected the then commonly held view that the great inflation of the sixteenth century had been caused by an increased quantity of money arriving after the conquest of the silver mines in South America. He pointed out that for this quantity theory of money to be true, all prices of all goods would have had to rise in proportion to the increase in the amount of money, which had not been the case.[88]

Despite beginning with this example, Potter did not go on to discuss the use of gold and silver forms of money, marking a break from previous writers in English, such as Thomas Mun and Edward Misselden.[89] In fact, he adopted a rhetorical strategy of discussing the workings of a gold mine in a theoretical country rather than real gold as a means of showing how a fiat form of money could perform exactly the same function, if it was trusted as much. The reason he did this was to point out that only a country with its own gold mines could reasonably govern its own money supply, and since very few countries had gold mines, it would make sense to try to create some other kind of money supply to stimulate production and make 'a poor people rich'.[90] As he put it:

> Seeing for that we cannot increase money at pleasure to any quantity needfull; we have no feasible means whereby to quicken Trade, (as I said before) but by multiplying a firme and knowne credit amongst Tradesmen, fit to transmit from hand to hand.
>
> That there is nothing can be named wherein *credit* comes short of *money*, but in one of the three respects before insisted on; *viz.* That the *security* it gives, is either

[86] Potter, *The Key of Wealth or A new Way for Improving of Trade* (London, 1650), p. 7.
[87] Ibid., pp. 8, 10. [88] Ibid., pp. 13–15.
[89] Craig Muldrew, 'Politics and Economics of Markets', in Roberto Scazzieri and Ivano Cardinale (eds.), *The Palgrave Handbook of Political Economy* (London, 2018), pp. 105–6.
[90] Ibid., pp. 13, 21ff.

not so good, or not so well known, or not so easie to be transmitted to others, all which by the use of such *Bills*, as are before mentioned, will be prevented.[91]

He also noted that 'the greatest part of mens returns in most places of the World, are either upon the Credit of particular persons, as here in England, or else, by means of some Brass or Copper money, made current by a Law'.[92] He went on to claim that, despite the ubiquity of oral credit in day-to-day transactions, it had a number of problems. First, he noted that while interest was not charged on the multitude of small transactions, the risk of non-payment existed. Tradesmen had to accept this risk to avoid losing business in a competitive market. As a result, prices had to be higher to pay for this risk, which he estimated to be about 8 per cent.[93] But, for individual tradesmen who suffered the non-payment of desperate debts, losses could be much higher. He also noted the increasing problem of liquidity being impeded by weak links in chains of credit, which had led to a great rise in litigation in the 100 years before he wrote.[94]

To overcome these problems he proposed a scheme whereby oral credit could be transformed into paper money to increase liquidity. His proposal was to have already-trusted prosperous tradesmen issue paper bills of credit that would act as gold and silver coins did. He believed that these bills could maintain their value as long as all recipients trusted that they could be cashed for goods. Initially this would work because large merchants and traders would have enough business to be able to discount bills brought back to them, and also because people would trust them for the honesty they had gained through their success.[95] From these beginnings, the acceptance of notes could be expanded as new money stimulated new production by more successful tradesmen, leading to new goods that could be bought with the new currency. This would succeed due to what he thought would become a virtuous circle of increasing production and trust. Regulations were also proposed to deal with those who inevitably abused trust through fraud, and bad business practices would be reduced by more education in mathematical skills.[96]

Unfortunately, nothing is known about Potter's life and how he might have become interested in credit and paper currency. He does, however,

[91] Ibid., p. 41.
[92] Ibid., p. 39. For the use of small-scale informal credit in England, see Muldrew, *Economy of Obligation*, pp. 95–120.
[93] Potter, *The Key of Wealth*, p. 33.
[94] Ibid., pp. 40–1; Muldrew, *Economy of Obligation*, pp. 199–254.
[95] On business success and this type of social credit, see Muldrew, *Economy of Obligation*, pp. 152–7.
[96] Potter, *The Key of Wealth*, pp. 45–7.

refer to the discussion by Gerard de Malynes in his *Lex Mercatoria* of 1622 on the practice of using assignable bills of exchange in Flanders (which Malynes calls 'bills obligatory'). There, according to Potter, Malynes claimed that a man who had accepted a bill, before the time of its payment, could

> go to another man and buy other commoditys therewith, as if it were with ready *money* the time onely considered; nay more, if he will have ready *money* for these *Bills*, he may sell them to other Merchants that are monyed men, and abating for the *Interest* for the time, and commonly one moneth over, according to the rate as they can agree, and as money is plentifull, they shall have *money* at all times to imploy in *Commodities*, or to deliver by exchange, or to pay *debts* withall, or to carry *home* in specie, or for any other purpose at their pleasure.[97]

However, another pamphlet advocating paper currency published by the Hartlib circle in 1655, *Description of an Office of Credit*, which was possibly written by the physician Hugh Chamberlain (who went on to write many pamphlets advocating land banks), makes reference to the public banks in Naples and Venice.[98] Certainly, the sophistication and detail of Potter's proposal shows a sound knowledge of the practice of English credit and of banking practices that were already existent in other parts of Europe.

Potter's initial exposition would be the basic platform of many of the credit currency schemes that followed in the next fifty years. The arguments would not only be about liquidity creation, by making existing credit more easily transferable, but about security.[99] How could the fiat value of the paper bills be maintained at least as well as the market value of gold and silver coins? Many authors argued that eventually fiat money should actually be better, since all national coinages were subject to damage, devaluation, and international bullion flows determined by the gap between mint and market prices of the two precious metals. These proposals were thoroughly analysed some time ago by Keith Horsefield in his book *British Monetary Experiments, 1650–1710*. He collected 616 pamphlets, broadsheets, publications of Parliamentary proceedings, and manuscripts on the topic of money during those sixty years.[100] His analysis was textual and economic, focusing on the arguments and many debates between various authors as to the practical merits and disadvantages of

[97] Ibid., p. 79; Malynes, *Lex Mercatoria*, p. 99.
[98] *A Description of the Office of Credit by the Use of Which None Can Possibly Sustain Loss, But Every Man May Certainly Receive Great Gain and Wealth* (London, 1665), f.A2.
[99] See discussion in Wennerlind, *Casualties of Credit*, pp. 68–74.
[100] Keith J. Horsefield, *British Monetary Experiments, 1650–1710* (Cambridge, MA, 1960), pp. 273–338. These pamphlets were found by Horsefield through the Wing Short Title Catalogue.

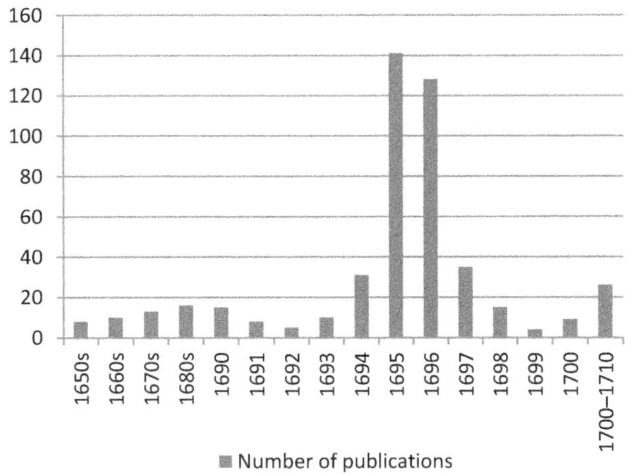

Figure 2.1 Publications on money and bank proposals by date, 1650–1710.

the schemes proposed. In Figure 2.1 I have counted only published material by year listed in his bibliography, which amounts to 474 publications. What is most striking about Figure 2.1 is just how many of these works were published in the two years 1695–1696. Fifty-seven per cent (269) of all relevant publications occurred in this period. By comparison, about 214 sermons, 105 ballads, and 64 almanacs were published in the same period.[101]

These years saw the undertaking of the great recoinage, and the number of pamphlets on money are a testament to the crisis of these years caused by the huge expenditure required to fight the Nine Years War. This rose from £2 million per year in 1689 to £6 million by 1693 and £8 million in 1696.[102] Revenue also rose, but only to around £4 million per year. The crisis was created because of the need to collect much more money through taxation from a supply of coins that was insufficient and much debased through clipping. Charles Davenant calculated the amount of silver money in the country in the 1680s to have been about £8 million, of which almost five million was clipped.[103]

[101] This is based on the categorisation done by *Early English Books Online.*

[102] Brewer, *Sinews of Power*, p. 74.

[103] William Davenant, 'A Memorial Concerning the Coyn of England', in Abbott Payson Usher (ed.), *Two Manuscripts by Charles Davenant*, (Baltimore, 1942), pp. 34–6; William Davenant, 'Memoriall Concerning Creditt', in Abbott Payson Usher (ed.), *Two Manuscripts by Charles Davenant*, (Baltimore, 1942), pp. 67–9. Gregory King made a similar estimate of £8.5 million in silver money: Gregory King, *Natural and Political*

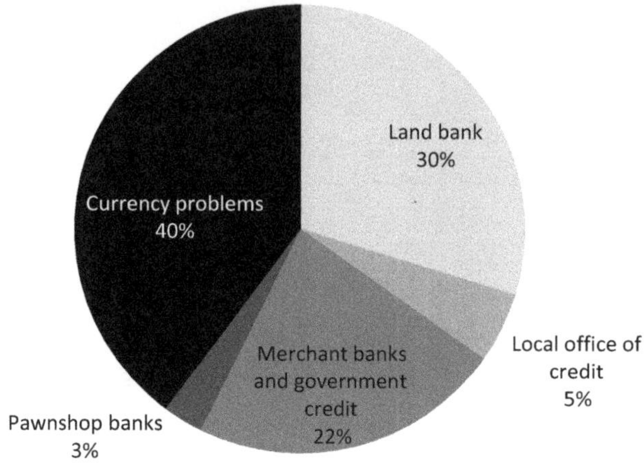

Figure 2.2 Publications on money and bank proposals by subject, 1650–1710.

A rate of taxation of £4 million per year was obviously problematic since much had to be collected in coins. As a result, the issue of currency became a problem that required a quick solution if England was to keep fighting. In Figure 2.2 I have grouped these proposals by their principle subject according to Horsefield's discussion of each. As can be seen, most of the pamphlets dealt specifically with the issue of the metallic currency, but almost as many, 38 per cent, proposed expanding the money supply using land banks, pawnshop banks, or local offices of credit. These were all variations on the original ideas that the Hartlib circle had advocated in the Commonwealth. Another 22 per cent advocated setting up some form of public merchant bank that could lend to the government on the security of taxation. In the following discussion, I will deal with these latter proposals first, since the Bank of England – one such proposal – was established very quickly. I will then go on to look at debates about the metallic currency and finally the most prominent of the credit currency proposals: those involving land banks.

Given the problems with taxation and coinage, paying for the war needed to be done primarily through government borrowing. This became the most pressing problem in the early years of the decade, and pamphlets were written advocating the issuance of paper credit on the

Observations and Conclusions upon the State and Condition of England, printed in George F. Barnett (ed.), *Two Tracts by Gregory King* (Baltimore, 1936), p. 34. D. W. Jones, *War and Economy in the Age of William III and Marlborough* (Oxford, 1988), pp. 15–16.

basis of capitalised national taxation, most notably by the Scottish-born West Indies merchant William Patterson. His original emphasis was, indeed, on the need for England to facilitate 'the circulation of Money', but he strongly believed that any notes issued needed to be backed up by reserves of gold and silver in the same way as the goldsmith bankers had operated. The function of government lending was advocated as a means of earning a profit for the company to further support its note issuance.[104] Patterson was supported by Charles Montaqu, the Chancellor of the Exchequer, and Michael Godfrey, a merchant, who saw in his scheme a way of using a bank to tap capital in London and fund the government's deficit. Thus, the Bank of England was founded on 27 July 1694, without much debate. This was in a year in which there were only 31 publications on money and banks. While it did engage in note issuance, in Horsefield's words it was much more like an investment trust than a note-issuing bank.[105] It was mainly a joint stock company that issued shares to investors and then lent to the government on the security of taxes voted in Parliament.

The Bank distinguished between 'sealed bills' and 'running cash notes' from its inception.[106] The former were primarily used to transfer capital to the government to pay for the loan, and as the name implied were sealed shut. They were intended for high-value payments. They earned interest at 2d. per day per £100 (3 per cent per year) and were used by the government to pay for goods and services. The latter, in contrast, were a form of credit currency. They were initially issued as printed forms with blanks for names and amounts. Initially many were filled in for precise amounts as required by the recipient, but eventually they were all done for multiples of £5 or £10 pounds.[107] In March 1696, the Bank recorded having issued £1,240,000 worth of sealed bills and £887,000 of running cash notes. However, by the summer of 1696 the Bank instructed cashiers not to issue any new notes for less than £50 and to pay off all notes for £5.[108]

There has been much written about the security of such Parliamentary taxation, as we saw in Chapter 1. This was actually put forward as an argument for the establishment of the institution against competing claims. In a pamphlet entitled *A Short Account of the Bank of England*, Godfrey, who was elected the first deputy-governor of the bank, argued

[104] Horsefield, *Monetary Experiments*, pp. 125ff; Wennerlind, *Casualties of Credit*, pp. 110–13.

[105] Horsefield, *Monetary Experiments*, p. 128. [106] Ibid., pp. 129–30.

[107] John Clapham, *The Bank of England: A History. Vol. 1: 1694–1797* (Cambridge, 1944), pp. 22, 144ff.

[108] Ibid., pp. 41–2.

that loans secured on future taxation were much more credible in republics than absolute monarchies, where repayment was based on the word of only the person rather than a public assembly with a stake in the nation's economy and well-being.[109] This was an important argument since the bank was competing with other proposals for institutions that were arguing that security was best offered by goods or land, rather than the volatility of politically based taxation. Godfrey thus needed to focus on why loans to the government were equally secure, and certainly the Bank's notes were supported by the success of its subscriptions to fund the government's deficits. However, as Horsefield stressed, the success of the bank's circulating notes was also due to the fact that they were issued with a legal promise of immediate convertibility to gold. Convertibility was important for merchants and tradesmen because if someone needed to pay a pressing debt in a chain of credit, gold or silver was the most reliable way of doing so because it's value was instant. Of course, this was only true where undebased coins were concerned, and many good coins were hoarded by merchants.

This crisis was exacerbated by the poor state of the silver coinage, which was seriously underweight because of clipping. While the political problems of taxation are well known, the structural problems created by the shortage of specie have not been investigated to the same degree. Taxes could not simply be levied from the nation's stock of wealth; they needed to be collected in coin. Taxation involved the collection of hundreds of thousands of small payments of amounts as small as a shilling every year, whether in the form of excise, customs, hearth, or land taxes.[110] The problems this created are amply illustrated by the comments made a decade earlier by the Sheriff of Monmouthshire when collecting ship money in 1639. Although there were perhaps more silver coins in circulation in the 1630s than any other decade before the recoinage of 1696, he complained that he had been paid in

> such ragged pieces as broken groats, quarter-pieces of thirteen-pence half-pennies, ten-pence half-pennies, harpers, and four-pence half-pennies, that I have had much labour to number the same, the which I intend to change into good money or gold and to send up the same way speedily into the office.[111]

[109] Michael Godfrey, *A Short Account of the Bank of England* (London, 1695), p. 10.

[110] A good description of the nature and difficulties of such collection, which remained just as prevalent in the late eighteenth century, is provided in the diaries of James Oakes of Bury St. Edmunds. Jane Fiske (ed.), *The Oakes Diaries: Business, Politics and the Family in Bury St. Edmunds 1778–1827* (Martlesham, 1990), I, pp. 55–65.

[111] A. E. Feavearyear, *The Pound Sterling: A History of English Money* (Oxford, 1931), p. 84.

Although inland bills of exchange began to be used to transfer some tax revenue from the provinces to London, considerable sums were still having to be remitted as cash by convoys of packhorses or wagons in the late 1680s.[112] This method was slow; the journey from Bedford, though only fifty miles, took five days, and from Somerset twenty-six. The Worcester convoy was twice robbed on the London road. An adequate guard was also expensive. The Herefordshire receiver calculated that every journey to London cost him £55. Treasury papers also note that when currency was scarce, local communities were extremely hostile to specie leaving the district. But, for many years, receivers remitted in this way for lack of any alternative.[113]

The huge amounts of taxes needed in the 1690s made the problem of clipping even worse, as the practice acted as a sort of ad-hoc devaluation to expand the money supply, and the clipped silver coins were of necessity increasingly accepted at face value.[114] But, by the middle of the decade the government decided the heavily underweight silver coinage needed to be reformed because fewer tradesmen were accepting coins at face value, and as a result the price of the gold guinea, which was a new coin with milled edges, had soared from 22s. to 30s., making the problem dangerously acute. On 1 January 1696 the 'Act for remedying the ill state of the coin' was passed to bring in and recoin the silver currency. It provided that receivers of state revenue should take all payments of rates and taxes in clipped coins at face value, and also that loans of clipped money to the Exchequer would be repaid at face value with new milled currency. In the end, the recoinage was successfully carried out by the end of 1697, producing £6.8 million of new silver currency.[115] But more important to the survival of the financial system in England was the signing of the Peace of Ryswick. This was concluded on October of the same year and ended the need for continued high levels of borrowing

[112] As we shall see below, once the use of inland bills of exchange became more developed, collections at the county level could be transferred to London, leaving the cash in the localities.

[113] W. Reginald Ward, *The English Land Tax in the Eighteenth Century* (London, 1953), pp. 46–7; Michael Braddick, *Parliamentary Taxation in Seventeenth-Century England: Local Administration and Response* (Woodbridge, 1994), p. 162.

[114] Davenant, 'A Memorial Concerning the Coyn of England', pp. 31–2; Feavearyear, *Pound Sterling*, pp. 111, 129; Stephen Quinn, 'Gold, Silver, and the Glorious Revolution: Arbitrage between Bills of Exchange and Bullion', *Economic History Review* 49 (1996), 480–1, n. 31; Jones, *War and Economy*, pp. 30–9, 95–126, 228–48; Brewer, *Sinews of Power*, pp. 30; Joyce Appleby, *Economic Thought and Ideology in Seventeenth-Century England* (Princeton, 1978), pp. 221–2, 228–9.

[115] Ming-Hsun Li, *The Great Recoinage of 1696 to 1699* (London, 1963), pp. 135–48.

and taxation. Without this peace, the country might well have required extra currency in some form.

It was in the year before the recoinage, and during it, that the most pamphlets were written, as can be seen in Figure 2.1. Most were about the state of the coinage and the relative merits and problems of devaluation of silver coins. With the coinage, the question was about whether devaluation was advisable, with arguments for and against. Since the coinage had been devalued for all practical purposes by clipping, many – most notably William Lowndes, the master of the Mint – argued that the recoinage should recognise that fact and more coins should be minted with less silver in them. He pointed to the fact that clipped money often circulated at face value, as did copper coins used extensively on the continent. He further noted that if people had been using the clipped coins at face value they were accepting it, so why could they not continue to do so?[116] In a recent book, the legal historian Christine Desan has also shown that from a contemporary legal point of view, money was given its value by the monarch, not by the amount of metal in a coin.[117]

In terms of the coinage, those in favour of devaluation focused on the need expressed by the Hartlib circle to expand the amount of money in everyday transactions. Others, including most famously John Locke, argued that the coinage should be returned to its original ratio, which was what the government finally decided on. Fiscal conservatives, like Locke, based their arguments on the fact that in international trade the exchange rate of a national coinage was based on the value of silver and gold in the coins. Anti-devaluationists pointed out how often devaluations failed. Merchants and tradesmen simply raised their prices based on the amount of the devaluation to ensure they obtained enough precious metal, since foreign exchange was measured in the price of bullion. The last debasement in England by Henry VIII in the 1540s had led to rapid price inflation and economic confusion as outstanding debts became worth about 20 per cent less.[118] Debasements in other European states inevitably had the same effect, which was well known among merchants.[119] Thus, for them, stability in value was desired.

But, whatever the merits of the devaluation thesis in terms of how 'money' was actually used in the years before the recoinage, the fact that the Bank of England was created by merchants meant the conservative

116 Horsefield, *Monetary Experiments*, pp. 49–50.

117 Christine Desan, *Making Money: Coin, Currency, and the Coming of Capitalism* (Oxford, 2014), pp. 8–9, 268–94.

118 Muldrew, 'Hard Food', p. 89.

119 John Day, *Money and Finance in the Age of Merchant Capitalism* (Oxford, 1999), pp. 59–109; Horsefield, *Monetary Experiments*, pp. 26–36.

view of the metallic currency would cast a long shadow over the coming century, and more. Merchants wanted a reliable coinage fit for international trade and finance. The devaluationists had wanted a coinage more widely available for smaller day-to-day transactions. The Bank based trust in its issue of notes on the legal fact that they could always be converted into gold and silver at the Bank. This would evolve into what has come to be known as the gold standard, since gold became the dominant of the two coinage metals in the eighteenth century.[120]

Schemes for Paper Currency

Although the recoinage was the most debated subject in the years 1694–1696, proposals for credit currency schemes continued to be put forward in great numbers. Some of these were developments of Potter's scheme, such as proposals for local credit offices based on the reputation of important merchants and tradesmen, so that their paper notes would have a more limited and traceable circulation. Also, the merchant's reputation would be more known locally, as opposed to trying to create a national circulation based on London. A small number also proposed storehouse banks. These were a variation of the Monti di Pieta found in Italy and France. Such institutions were public pawnshops that issued credit to poor people at a reasonable interest rate upon deposit of household goods such as clothes, linen, or jewellery.[121] In these proposals, merchants would deposit physical goods in a warehouse as security upon which notes would be issued. However, the later proposals faced an obvious problem of how the collateral could be maintained when merchants obviously needed to have the goods available for trade.[122]

By far the largest number of pamphlets concerned much more realistic suggestions for so-called land banks, with 124 pamphlets produced on this subject. Land banks had not featured much before the 1690s, although again they had first been proposed by Potter in an essay published by Hartlib in a 1655 omnibus.[123] The popularity of land bank schemes owes much to the physician Hugh Chamberlain, who through

[120] Angela Redish, 'The Evolution of the Gold Standard in England', *The Journal of Economic History* 50, no. 4 (1990), pp. 789–805.

[121] Maria Giuseppina Muzzarelli, 'From the Closet to the Wallet: Pawning Clothes in Renaissance Italy', *Renaissance and Reformation/Renaissance et Réforme* 35, no. 3 (2012), pp. 22–38; Mauro Carboni, 'Converting Goods into Cash: An Ethical Approach to Pawnbroking in Early Modern Bologna', *Renaissance and Reformation Renaissance et Réforme*, 35, no. 3 (2012), pp. 63–84.

[122] Horsefield, *Monetary Experiments*, pp. 104–13.

[123] Wennerlind, *Casualties of Credit*, pp. 67–9, n. 133.

his father had ties to Hartlib, and who came up with the most detailed proposals. The nature of his and other land bank proposals has been described in detail by Horsefield and also summarised by Wennerlind. They were based on the idea that, since most land in England had a yearly value in rent that changed only slowly, this could be used as security to issue credit currency. To do this, land would need to be mortgaged and publicly registered. The land bank itself would be a joint stock company set up – like the Bank of England – to hire accountants and other officers to print the notes that would then be issued to those providing the land as security.[124]

The idea of land banks became popular with Tories in the intensifying party politics of the years after the Glorious Revolution. The founders of the Bank of England had been mostly Whig dissenters in support of the Dutch King William's war against France. In the 1690s, most of the security provided to pay interest on the loans came from land taxes, so Tory politicians were able to argue that the landed interest in the country was being used to make London investors wealthier.[125] In this light, a land bank, whereby country gentlemen could use their land to create new money, was an obvious attraction. By 1696, three other projectors – John Briscoe, John Asgill, and Nicholas Barbon – became involved in proposing land bank schemes. Barbon is perhaps the most well known of these figures for his writings in favour of popular consumption as a driver of economic growth.[126] He also had links to the Commonwealth as he was the son of Praisegod Barebones, after whom the most religiously radical Parliament of the Commonwealth was named. However, he shared little of his father's earnestness, and had a reputation as a quite ruthless property developer in London. Given that the government was still in desperate need of money, Asgill and Barbon together, and Biscoe independently, proposed schemes that would combine lending landowners £500,000 at 3.5 per cent for 7 years on mortgages with – at the same time – raising over £2 million in specie through a subscription like the Bank of England's, and lending the same amount to the government, but with £895,000 of it in its own bank notes just as the Bank of England had used its own sealed bills. The cash remaining would then act as a reserve to support the liquidity of its running cash notes by offering convertibility

[124] Ibid., pp. 73–5; Horsefield, *Monetary Experiments*, pp. 156–217.

[125] Bruce G. Carruthers, *City of Capital: Politics and Markets in the English Financial Revolution* (Princeton, 1999), pp. 41–50.

[126] Horsefield, *Monetary Experiments*, pp. 201–8; Paul Slack, *The Invention of Improvement* (Oxford, 2014), pp. 143–7, 183–4.

to gold and silver coins.[127] As Horsefield emphasised, this was crucial since land is the most illiquid of securities, with only one-quarter of the rental value being available in cash every three months when rents were collected.[128]

In April 1696 the National Land Bank was created by Act of Parliament. Since this was at the height of the recoinage, there was almost no specie available for investment and it was an immediate failure, attracting only £2,100.[129] At the same time, the politicians in the Whig Junto (ministers supporting William's war policy) actively attacked the company in print. The historian Nathan Rubini has argued that the Junto was largely responsible for the National Land Bank's failure, since it was they who organised the lethargic recoinage that removed the cash needed to start the land bank. As a result, the nation was deprived of much-needed paper money during a period of crisis only resolved by the Peace of Ryswick.[130] Land bank schemes have generally been treated by historians of the financial revolution as failures because none were established after this failure. But, as we shall see in Chapter 4, this is not quite true, as currency was created based on the security of land through private mortgages instead.

Government Paper Instruments

England, however, was not bereft of forms of non-metallic currency apart from Bank of England notes in the 1690s. Between 1688 and 1697 the Exchequer borrowed £32 million on short-term Exchequer tallies at 7–8 per cent interest.[131] Tallies were medieval instruments still being produced in the same way in the seventeenth century. They were sticks notched with monetary amounts, with the lender's name written on two sides and then split in half lengthways to create a unique stock for the lender, and a foil kept by the Exchequer. They were charged upon current or immediately upcoming taxes, usually within about a year. Because there were many different taxes in the 1690s, there might have been anywhere between £6 million and £9 million worth of tallies in circulation in the decade. Most of this short-term debt was loaned by, and circulated among, larger London tradesmen and merchants. For instance, a loan organised by the city of London for £100,000 on a poll

[127] Horsefield, *Monetary Experiments*, pp. 202–5; Dennis Rubini, 'Politics and the Battle for the Banks, 1688–1697', *The English Historical Review* 85, no. 337 (1970), pp. 699–700.
[128] Horsefield, *Monetary Experiments*, pp. 204–5. [129] Ibid., pp. 189–95.
[130] Rubini, 'Battle for the Banks', pp. 693–714.
[131] P. G. M. Dickson, *The Financial Revolution in England 1688–1756* (London, 1967), p. 343.

tax of 1678 was lent to the Exchequer by 653 contributions and paid back 3–11 months later.[132] This equals an average of £153 each.

There was also a secondary market for tallies, which, although they had no intrinsic value, still circulated.[133] This negotiability was given a boost in 1688, when they were issued together with a printed 'order of payment' that was numbered in order of payment and, crucially, could be endorsed by third parties, making the tallies more easily assignable and thus more liquid.[134] However, by the spring of 1697 there was a deficiency of short-term taxes to fund the tallies, of over £5 million, and they were only being accepted as payment for army supplies at a discount of about 25–35 per cent.[135] As a result, the Bank of England bought up a lot of the tallies to convert them to long-term debt. With the Peace of Ryswick in 1697, the use of short-term debt was much reduced, but with the beginning of the War of Spanish Succession in 1701 short-term borrowing again expanded, with over £2 million worth of tallies being issued every year.[136]

From 1696, the Exchequer was also turned into a sort of bank with the issue of Exchequer Bills. Indeed, a number of pamphlets proposed this as a means of creating credit currency directly linked to the security of individual taxes.[137] These were fully transferable printed instruments, and numbered with a marked counterfoil to prevent forgery. In 1697, Parliament stipulated that the circulation was not to reach over £2 million worth of bills at any one time. That is, old bills had to be cashed in at the Exchequer before new ones could be issued above this amount. Crucially, they were assignable, so could circulate like bank notes. They were issued in denominations of £25, £50, and £100, plus a few for £12 10s., but after 1713 £100 became the standard denomination.[138] For most years the number of bills outstanding every year was below the Parliamentary limit, but after 1709, with the cost of the War of Spanish Succession rapidly rising beyond £10 million per year, the Bank of England was given the ability to cash Exchequer Bills in addition to its own notes. After this their circulation rose to around £4 million until peace was signed.[139] In addition, the Treasurer of the Navy also issued Navy and Victualling Bills directly in specific amounts as payment for goods. The volume of these outstanding every year rose from under £500,000 in 1697 to £3–4 million by 1707–1710. Finally, the East

[132] Ibid. [133] Desan, *Making Money*, pp. 171–89.
[134] Dickson, *The Financial Revolution in England*, pp. 350–1; Desan, *Making Money*, pp. 247–54.
[135] Dickson, *The Financial Revolution in England*, pp. 347–52. [136] Ibid., pp. 526–7.
[137] Horsfield, *Monetary Experiments*, pp. 96, 122–4.
[138] Dickson, *The Financial Revolution in England*, p. 376. [139] Ibid., pp. 374–6, 526–7.

India Company also borrowed a large amount of capital using short-term interest-bearing bonds of about £100 each, which were also transferable. This practice had developed during the late seventeenth century, but after 1695 the value in circulation rose from about £500,000 to £3 million by 1709.[140]

At roughly the same time as these various forms of paper currencies were being floated, the London stock market also emerged in the 1690s as a place where paper shares in various joint stock companies were traded with greatly increased liquidity. The first stock market boom was a phenomenon of the early 1690s, when eighty-five patents were taken out for new processes and inventions, many of which sought investment capital by incorporating themselves, joining the already-existing East India Company (1600), Royal Africa Company (1672), and Hudson's Bay Company (1676). Between 1689 and 1695, the number of joint stock companies in England rose from 11 to about 100, and in the early 1690s it was said that the equivalent of the whole stock of the East India Company was changing hands every two years.[141] Whereas the number of transactions in East India Company shares had been only 44 in 1661, and 655 in 1688, by 1691 this had reached over 3,000.[142] With the addition of Bank of England shares from 1694, this added 1,000–3,000 transactions. Share trading fluctuated by year, but in 1698, for which there are figures for share transfers involving four companies, the total number was 4,375.[143] Thus, there was a very active and liquid market in shares facilitated by investors and stock jobbers, and Anne Murphy has argued that it was, in fact, this liquidity that enabled the Bank of England's survival during the years of the recoinage, when its share price fell by half (along with the other publicly traded companies) and it had to fund increased government borrowing with little access to gold or silver.[144]

However, most holdings of stock were for large amounts. In 1696, about 50 per cent of investors in the East India Company held amounts of £500 or more, and the same figure for the Bank of England was 64 per cent. Still, there were over 400 investors in both who invested less than £100. The total value of the shares issued in these two companies at that time was £2,774,608.[145] In addition, there were numerous other companies such as the Albion Flour Mill, New River, and the Bedford Level

[140] Ibid., pp. 526–7, 407ff.
[141] K. G. Davies, 'Joint-Stock Investment in the Later Seventeenth Century', *Economic History Review*, 2nd ser., 4 (1952), pp. 285, 287–95.
[142] Anne L. Murphy, *The Origins of English Financial Markets: Investment and Speculation before the South Sea Bubble* (Cambridge, 2012), pp. 16, 23.
[143] Ibid., p. 225. [144] Ibid., pp. 58–65, appendix 2. [145] Ibid., pp. 149–51.

Table 2.1 *Value of different classes of paper instruments (£)*

	*c.*1696	*c.*1710
Bank of England notes	1,200,000	2,000,000
Tallies	7,000,000	5,000,000
Exchequer Bills	0	3,000,000
Naval Bills	400,000	3,500,000
East India Bonds	600,000	3,000,000
Stocks	3,000,000	5,000,000[146]
Goldsmiths' notes	2,000,000	2,000,000[147]
Total	14,200,000	23,500,000

Company, whose stock was not traded very often, but, based on figures of some share issues provided by W. R. Scott, I have estimated these to be worth about £3 million in 1695.[148] Private goldsmith and scrivener-bankers had also started issuing their own circulating notes of hand from the late 1650s onwards. These will be described in the next chapter, but Horsefield has estimated that there might have been about £2–2.4 million worth circulating in the 1690s.[149]

All of this has been compiled in Table 2.1 for the two years of greatest wartime expenditure. As can be seen, there was a considerable amount of different forms of liquid currency substitutes around. However, apart from some of the goldsmiths' notes and the early Bank of England notes and early Exchequer Bills, most of these instruments were for large amounts in the hundreds of pounds. They often also sold at a discount, and very few of the people using them came from outside London and its immediate surroundings – only 14 per cent.[150] Murphy has estimated that the number of investors in the public funds and joint stock companies in the 1690s was 4,000–5,000 people. Most of the investors in government debt were from the very wealthy London middle class, and this dominance only increased as the eighteenth century progressed.[151] That does not mean they were ineffective in adding liquidity to the market in London, as they could be used to pay for large orders of goods

[146] The rise in the value of shares is taken from Larry Neal, *The Rise of Financial Capitalism: International Capital Markets in the Age of Reason* (Cambridge, 1993), pp. 47–8.

[147] I have not found information on private bankers' note issue in the early eighteenth century.

[148] Scott, *Joint-Stock Companies*, p. 481.

[149] Horsefield, *Monetary Experiments*, p. 12.

[150] Murphy, *The Origins of English Financial Markets*, p. 152. Exchequer bills, though, were sometimes used outside of London by receivers of taxes in the counties. Dickson, *The Financial Revolution in England*, p. 389; Ward, *The English Land Tax*, p. 45.

[151] Dickson, *The Financial Revolution in England*, pp. 256, 290, 297.

for the navy and army, and presumably also by any other wholesalers selling in larger amounts in the capital.

The Failure of the South Sea Company and its Effect on Government Debt

After the end of the War of Spanish Succession the government still needed to fund the £98 million spent during the conflict.[152] During this period, the Whig chancellor of the Exchequer, Godolphin, had largely funded the increased expenditure with much more short-term debt, as indicated in Table 2.1, and also by issuing long-term annuities for ninety-nine years.[153] The Bank of England had issued more shares, but was unable to absorb so much new debt. So, when the Tories came to power in 1711, the South Sea Company was created as a rival to the Bank of England. Its initial aim was to absorb about £9 million of short-term debt with company shares. This debt was trading at only 65 per cent of its value. The company also had a commercial aspect, having been granted the assiento for shipping slaves to the Spanish Empire in 1713, to entice shareholders with the prospect of trading profits. But while the company transported thousands of slaves, it is unclear how much profit was made.[154] It was mostly a holding company for investment in short-term government debt whose income was based on interest on that debt, and the company's shares were traded from 1711, but took some time before they reached par.[155]

The story of the South Sea Bubble has been told often, and it has become probably the most well-known event in financial history after the Wall Street Crash of 1929. Because of this I will not dwell on it in detail, but it is relevant because it demonstrates a central problem of any form of circulating paper capital: overissue based on overvaluation of the underlying security. In the South Sea Company's case this was trade, but this overvaluation was undertaken with the complicity of the Tory government of the time, with the aim of reducing the potentially crippling interest rate on the long-term annuities sold by Godolphin's Whig government a decade or so earlier. As Dickson noted, it happened because, by 1719, the government was paying higher interest on the annuities that had been sold in the first decade of the century. Long annuities due to expire after 1792 earned 7 per cent per year until then, and shorter

[152] Four per cent was on military spending. Brewer, *Sinews of Power*, p. 40.
[153] Dickson, *The Financial Revolution in England*, p. 58.
[154] Wennerlind, *Casualties of Credit*, pp. 216–34.
[155] Neal, *Rise of Financial Capitalism*, pp. 232–4.

annuities earned 9 per cent until 1742.[156] But these contracts could not be altered without the annuitants' consent. Thus, the directors of the South Sea Company, in coordination with the government, offered to buy these for issues of current stock in the company. In order to be convinced to exchange their annuities voluntarily for South Sea stock, the value of the stock needed to rise enough to compensate them for the loss of a long period of future income.[157]

In the end, the operation of the scheme came to include other forms of government debt, and the share subscriptions based on it were not always issued in logical, and certainly not prudent, fashion. Subscribers were also allowed to pay for calls (the option to buy the underlying stock at a predetermined price) on credit. This, which came to be called scrip (from subscription), could also be used as credit towards the purchase of future subscriptions of stock, thus multiplying the amount of paper in share trading.[158] In doing so, the company lent £11 million on the security of its stock, and the price of shares rose from about £125 to £1,000 in 1720. To protect the high price, the company also worked to have what has come to be known as the Bubble Act passed in Parliament to prevent other joint stock companies from issuing shares to compete with it. It then took the English Copper Company, the Lustering Company, and the York Buildings Company to court to enforce the Act. This, however, had the effect of making investors aware that the price was unsustainable, and it quickly collapsed.

The Bubble had an immediate social and cultural impact on the nation, in which it was presented as a disaster caused by reckless and greedy speculation.[159] However, the government's aim of reducing its debt and the interest paid on it through the conversion of it to South Sea stock was achieved. But the Tory Party's association with the Bubble and the culpability of some of the companies' directors, who fled the country to avoid prosecution, put an end to their ministry.[160] Robert Walpole was appointed as a Whig chancellor and, working together with the Bank of England, he was able to keep the South Sea Company solvent as a holding company for government debt by letting shareholders take a loss. As a result, many who had initially converted their annuities into South Sea shares when the price was rising, and held on to them, lost a lot of potential income.[161] But, since this was not an immediate loss in the

[156] Dickson, *The Financial Revolution in England*, pp. 91–2.
[157] Ibid., pp. 93, 125, 134, 232. [158] Ibid., p. 144.
[159] Helen J. Paul, *The South Sea Bubble: An Economic History of its Origins and Consequences* (London, 2011).
[160] John Carswell, *The South Sea Bubble* (Stanford, 1960), pp. 179–206.
[161] Dickson, *The Financial Revolution in England*, pp. 153–6.

same way as those who had bought shares when they were highly valued, it did not feature as largely in the popular condemnation of the Bubble after its bursting.[162]

One influential theory that has come to be known as the 'credible commitment' hypothesis has followed Michael Godfrey's contemporary argument (see 'Property, the Glorious Revolution, and Politics' in Chapter 1) that trust was ultimately maintained in these early English financial markets because taxation was controlled by Parliament and not the monarch. As a result, the merchants and tradesmen lenders had more confidence that their loans would not be repudiated in the manner of previous French monarchs. Such trust gave people more confidence that their property rights would be protected, which made investment in economic growth more likely.[163] As noted in Chapter 1, this has been criticised in a number of ways. However, in a very real sense, the story of the financial revolution in London is not one of how parliaments were more reliable than monarchies, but about how the enormous cost of warfare could be *managed* as interest-paying debt that did not lose its value. In this sense, party politics was to serve England well in avoiding a technical government default and discounting of its debt after the South Sea Bubble, in that one party – the Tories – could be blamed for the failure of the South Sea scheme. This allowed the Whigs to place themselves as the party of financial competence once they had restructured the national debt in its aftermath. But it is important to remember that this was made much easier because Godolphin's expensive long-term annuities had been converted by their holders to South Sea stock. The creditable commitment hypothesis asserts that this was a form of democratic strength because property was not violated, since those who converted to South Sea stock did so voluntarily. In principle, it is correct that this was not a forced repudiation of the government's obligations. However, the fact that much of the blame for the Bubble was placed on the incompetence, and in some cases duplicity, of its directors masked the fact that the initial scheme had been passed by Parliament as a means of debt reduction through speculation.

As Dickson noted, war had created identical problems in France and the United Provinces, and in those countries similar types of schemes

162 Ann M. Carlos, Erin K. Fletcher, Larry Neal, and Kirsten Wandschneider, 'Financing and Refinancing the War of the Spanish Succession, and then Refinancing the South Sea Company', in D'Maris Coffman, Adrian Leonard, and Larry Neal (eds.), *Questioning Credible Commitment* (Cambridge, 2013), pp. 147–68.

163 Douglass C. North and Barry R. Weingast, 'Constitutions and Commitment: The Evolution of Institutions Governing Public Choice in Seventeenth-Century England', *The Journal of Economic History* 49, no. 4 (1989), pp. 816–19, 824–8.

were also floated at the same time, and all collapsed at around the same time. As we will see in Chapter 9, in France, John Law's scheme also attempted to create an actual credit currency secured on annuities and other government debts. But too many banknotes were issued, as well as shares in his Mississippi Company, and both rapidly lost most of their value. However, in contrast to the collapse of the South Sea Bubble, the whole French economy was affected and the government had to repudiate £500 million worth of its debt, which dwarfed the losses of the government creditors in England.[164]

The losses in England were much more limited, and Walpole's skilful reconstruction of the South Sea Company's finances and the consolidation of the Bank of England as the sole future institution to provide long-term funding for government debt – together with twenty years of relative peace – restored trust in debt-based paper instruments, which survived for the rest of the century. But this was the period of the Whig oligarchy, so it was not Parliamentary scrutiny that was primarily responsible for this trust. It was much more to do with financial skill, which the South Sea directors had lacked, despite many coming from commercial backgrounds.[165]

But, in terms of the pattern of the expansion of paper money in this period, the Bubble is significant because it shows the difficulty of basing the value and amount of paper in circulation on a security whose value was speculative and based on potential economic growth. Such growth could only have been viewed very optimistically in the case of the South Sea Company, for the reasons given above. The improvement of land productivity in the case of a mortgage, or trade in the case of the great trading companies, or indeed the national economy as a whole in the case of tax revenue, were more predictable. But their value could still be raised too much on misplaced hopes about future economic activity – pushed up by the psychology of the market, where the fear of being left out of a profitable investment reduces prudence. The Bubble also highlights an aspect of paper debt instruments issued by governments. Their value fluctuated on the market, and often traded at a discount, depending on the collective buyers' assessment of the credit of the government.[166]

This was quite different to how the value of individual merchants, or even poorer consumers' credit, had been judged in the seventeenth century. A merchant with too many debts might have to pay a higher interest rate to borrow money, but once their bills of exchange started to be rejected or began trading at a discount they could soon be excluded

164 Dickson, *The Financial Revolution in England*, pp. 153–5, 176.
165 Ibid., pp. 157–76. 166 Ibid., p. 144.

from the exchange, which worked on very high levels of trust.[167] A poorer consumer might also have to pay a higher price for purchases done with oral credit. But both relied on reputation more than numerical valuation. Yet with the development of the stock market and secondary markets in government debt, trust in these paper instruments was now set *collectively*. As we will see, bills of exchange came to be discounted on secondary markets as well by the mid-eighteenth century. The value of different gold and silver currencies had always been set through international exchange based mostly on any changes in the amount of metal in coins, together with rates of inflation and mint pricing to some extent. But any widespread use of a paper currency would be subject to a fluctuating market value based on the amount of trust in the security behind its issue.

This is an important consideration in the development of the idea of capital. It required that people using it in the form of currency needed to think about the probability of its value changing in the future. In terms of government debt, it also meant that the economic growth of the nation became crucial. All of the different schemes for the creation of a paper credit currency, from Potter to John Law's *Money and Trade Considered*, had argued that economic growth was the *raison d'etre* for paper currency, and also the process by which they would become successful. The main reason for this advocacy, however, had been to use the currency to pay wages to create more employment through the production of consumer goods.[168] However, a number of writers also remarked that growth would make the state stronger by enabling it to collect more taxes. As regards to the large value currency instruments created by the financing of government debt, the relationship became a lasting circular one. Initially, Walpole, and most political opinion, regarded the reduction of the national debt as something necessary, and various sinking funds were set up to achieve this.[169] But with the outbreak of further wars in 1740 and 1756, the debt continued to increase, and so did the consumption taxes needed to fund the interest on it. Although improved agricultural rents supported the land tax established in 1693, from 1715 excise taxes on beer and spirits and duties on colonial tea, tobacco, and sugar increasingly contributed the majority of the tax burden that paid for the military.[170] The very same merchants who made money from these trades invested some of their profits in government debt.

167 Muldrew, *Economy of Obligation*, p. 192.
168 John Law, *Money and Trade Considered with a Proposal for Supplying the Nation with Money* (Edinburgh, 1705), pp. 13–14, 17, 98–117.
169 Dickson, *The Financial Revolution in England*, pp. 199–215.
170 Brewer, *Sinews of Power*, pp. 96–8.

After 1712, about 75–80 per cent of all government revenues came from customs and excise consumption taxes. As a result, economic growth was needed to fund future taxation. Previously, city-states such as Florence and Venice had funded public debts through heavy consumption taxes, and certainly Venice had to fight many wars to try to protect its trading privileges. But the English colonial trade-based system of political economy directed by an interventionist Parliament was of a whole different scale, both in terms of the amounts of government debt contracted and expended on warfare, and in terms of the growth of colonial populations to over two million consumers by *c.* 1750.[171]

Thus, this initial form of large-scale circulating merchant capital was created in London first by war and then sustained by a political economy of trade. The case of England is arguably the first time a nation state had created a form of paper value based on a programme of political economy created in the public sphere of published pamphlets. However, the fact that it became based on a protected imperial trade with colonies in North America and the Caribbean had more to do with the geopolitics of religious war than with any policy of employment or currency creation. Once the Whigs decided to force England's Catholic King James II to leave the country and bring in the Dutch King William, it became embroiled in opposition to Louis IV's Catholic aggression, which would last until the Peace of Utrecht in 1714.

It was through this political economy, which advocated economic growth through more consumption, and imperial bilateral exchange that London's development as a financial centre was supported. By 1709, there were probably about 11,000 national creditors holding large amounts of government debt.[172] Despite the huge losses incurred by the collapse of the South Sea Company, the numbers of these rose to 25,000 by 1737, and by the time of the outbreak of the Seven Years War there were 60,000 holders of public funds in Bank, East India, and South Sea stock, together with annuities, which Dickson has estimated to have been worth £77,000,000.[173]

These are impressive figures, but given that the idealists of the Hartlib circle had proposed spreading circulation much more broadly throughout England, the achievement was still quite limited. All of the paper forms of credit apart from the goldsmiths' notes were created because of

[171] François Velde, 'Neapolitan Banks in the Context of Early Modern Public Banks', in Lilia Costabile and Larry Neal (eds.), *Financial Innovation and Resilience* (London, 2018), p. 211; John J. McCusker and Russell R. Menard, *The Economy of British America, 1607–1789* (Chapell Hill, 1991), p. 218.

[172] Dickson, *The Financial Revolution in England*, pp. 72–3.

[173] Ibid., pp. 250, 260.

government expediency, not specifically to increase liquidity.[174] No independent land bank or pawn-based bank was ever successfully set up, and apart from lottery tickets no small denomination paper currency was created. The reasons for this were undoubtedly the problem of achieving a leap from no circulation to a situation where circulation was wide and efficient enough to generate trust to maintain the value of the paper. In any form of commerce there are risks associated with credit and trust. Plague, war, piracy, and embezzlement could damage circulation and trust in any form of credit, which is of course why all of the schemes for credit currency were based on some form of collateral with redeemable value. The proposals for centralised land banks remained problematic in England because of the lack of official land registries to supply information.

As a result of these various factors, developments in England did not follow a centralised route of currency-issuing 'banks' being set up on already established models. What happened instead was that a series of legal changes allowed local forms of capital and currency to develop. Informal individual promissory notes developed out of oral credit, and these operated like local currency. Many farmers were also able to raise capital on mortgages much more securely than previously after the strengthening of the equity of redemption in the 1680s. In this way, they were able to provide the very security at an individual level for their own informal notes of hand that the promoters of land banks had advocated. At the same time, larger tradesmen around England increasingly used what has been called the inland bill of exchange, mostly drawn on London to do long-distance business. Eventually these two functions were combined by those tradesmen and industrialists who set up the first self-styled county banks in the 1750s and 1760s.

In contrast, at the same time, Scotland (the Bank of Scotland was founded on 17 July 1695) was able to follow the prescriptions of the advocates of credit currency, and purposely and successfully created a liquidity-producing banking system because it had a different legal system. The ideas of its native son John Law proved much more successful there. Scotland was a much smaller country than France or England, and it had an even smaller economy, the effects of which had been laid bare in the famine of 1696 when possibly 15 per cent of the population died, while England saw very little mortality. As a result, the creation of a credit currency formed part of an economic policy of growth that we will

[174] Although Bank of England notes did serve this function, they were created to help support the survival of the bank, whose main purpose was to fund government debt.

examine more closely in Chapter 9. But continuing our examination of England, we now need to look at the country outside of London. First, in Chapter 3, to see how paper currency and inland bills of exchange were created and then circulated, and then, in Chapter 4, to see how this circulation was secured with capital in the form of mortgages and bonds.

3 The Financial Revolution in English Localities

In the countryside, the development of paper credit currency took a very different path than what happened in London. This, I will argue, should be seen as equally part of what we call the financial revolution, but it was not instigated by banks or joint stock companies. County banking did not emerge until after 1750. What occurred instead was a transformation of previous interpersonal – *not* institutional – oral credit into paper promises. These then developed into very local credit currencies. As I have argued previously, England never relied on its coinage for much of its economic activity. In the sixteenth and seventeenth centuries, a very informal system existed that maximised flexibility at the expense of security and accuracy. Numeracy skills were low, accounts were rare, and notarial records were not required. Instead, the system depended fundamentally on interpersonal trust. A reputation for good credit meant you had a good record of paying obligations promptly. This system was secured not by any legally pledged collateral of goods or land, but rather depended on local courts to enforce contract in a public way if oral agreements were not met.[1]

However, with the rapid expansion of market transactions involving credit in the late sixteenth century, disputes began to explode simply because of the pace at which market transactions increased. This was not because people had suddenly become less trustworthy, but because bottlenecks created liquidity problems for individuals. This led them to sue to recover their own debts, which had a domino effect on others. As chains of obligation grew longer, late payment became more of a problem and creditors turned to litigation to try to force payment when they needed liquidity. As a result, there was a dramatic increase in the amount of debt and contractual litigation that came before the courts in all parts of England. The majority of the increase in suits was a result of

[1] Craig Muldrew, *The Economy of Obligation: The Culture of Credit and Social Relations in Early Modern England* (London 1998), pp. 60–9.

the expansion of the market economy, where about 90 per cent of transactions were done on largely oral sales credit.[2]

Although this system of informal credit up front, with enforcement later, was sufficient to achieve very impressive economic growth in the sixteenth century, by the 1630s indirect evidence suggests it had slowed.[3] As we saw in the previous chapter, this was the opinion of William Potter and others, who argued specifically that it was insufficient if growth was to continue, and that is why the country needed credit currencies.[4] Potter also noted that it had led to a lot of litigation, and evidence that local paper currency was beginning to be used is found in the fact that from about 1670 to 1690 the credit litigation that so dominated the previous century and a half began to decline. This transformation in legal culture will be investigated in detail in Chapter 7, but if litigation declined, the most likely reason was that fewer debts were problematic enough to take to court. If more informal local trusted *written* obligations were being accepted as currency and used in addition to oral credit, it would stand to reason that fewer cases would need to be taken to court as a result. In this chapter I will investigate what evidence there is to show when such informal notes became more commonly used and how, and to what extent, they became embedded in local credit networks, and how they were linked to a national system of paper credit based on inland bills of exchange.

As this occurred, a general lack of small coins for transactions remained a continuous problem. Although the Great Recoinage of 1696 produced almost £9 million in silver coins and some £4 million in gold coins, the undervaluing of the mint price of silver in England by Sir Isaac Newton meant that most of this new good-quality silver left the country by 1720. Subsequently, in most years before 1750 less than £5,000 was minted.[5] The recoinage in 1774 produced only about £800,000 in silver. At that time this would only have amounted to about 12 shillings per household. In contrast, estimates of the number of gold coins in circulation indicate a rise from probably around £1,000,000 in 1700 to £17,000,000 after 1750, and by the 1774 recoinage £18.2 million worth of gold coins were minted.[6] This happened because of

[2] Ibid., pp. 203–6.

[3] Barry Supple, *Commercial Crisis and Change in England, 1600–1642: A Study in the Instability of a Mercantile Economy* (Cambridge, 1959), pp. 120–5.

[4] See 'Schemes for Paper Currency' in Chapter 2.

[5] C. D. Challis (ed.), *A New History of the Royal Mint* (Cambridge, 1992), pp. 434, 691–3.

[6] A. E. Feavearyear, *The Pound Sterling: A History of English Money* (Oxford, 1931), pp. 153–4; Nicholas Mayhew, *Sterling, the History of a Currency* (New York, 2000), pp. 106–7; Nuno Palma, 'Reconstruction of Money Supply over the Long-Run: The Case of England, 1270–1870', *The Economic History Review* 71, no. 2 (2018), pp. 373–92. For the English undervaluation of silver to gold compared to their prices in the rest of

the Methuen Treaty with Portugal, signed in 1703, which gave the English cloth industry duty-free access to the Portuguese empire, much of which was paid for with gold from new mines discovered in Brazil. Although, as Angela Redish has argued, England did not formally adopt a gold standard for its coinage until 1816 (when silver coins became fiat or 'token' currency, like copper, freed from the value of the precious metal), the eighteenth century was a period when gold dominated trade so much it was almost a de-facto standard. What silver there was continued to be used in small-scale transactions but did not play much of a role in long-distance and overseas trade.[7]

Attempting to find out just when people made payments in cash or used credit is notoriously difficult. Diarists often just noted that they made a payment, and in account books the terms cash and credit were interchangeable, simply meaning an addition to the accounts rather than a deduction. Evidence from the records of the criminal court of London shows that in London there was a marked predominance of the use of guineas mentioned in trial reports before the mid-century.[8] Other sources are rare, but there are some exceptions. The diarist Thomas Turner, who we will examine below, mentioned sending cash he collected from his customers to someone acting as a local banker, and 94 per cent of the value of these were gold.

Another example is that of the attorney John Plumbe of Wavertree Hall, just outside Liverpool, whose accounts from the 1720s to the 1750s survive. While Plumbe earned fees from the practice of the law as an attorney in Liverpool, representing clients in lawsuits, his business activities were founded on land ownership. Through the purchase of estates and other pieces of land, rent became his chief source of income. At the start of his career he continued to be involved in farming to some extent as well, but over time he became more involved in lending – both on his own account and for others – to individuals from a wide range of society.[9]

Europe, see Thomas Sargent and François R. Velde, *The Big Problem of Small Change* (Princeton, 2003), pp. 296–8.

7 Challis, *A New History of the Royal Mint*, p. 433; Angela Redish, 'The Evolution of the Gold Standard in England', *The Journal of Economic History* 50, no. 4 (1990), pp. 789–805.

8 Craig Muldrew, 'Money and the Everyday', in Christine Desan (ed.), *A Cultural History of Money in the Age of Enlightenment* (London, 2019), pp. 95–120.

9 B. L. Anderson, 'Provincial Aspects of the Financial Revolution of the Eighteenth Century', *Business History* 11 (1960), pp. 11–22; B. L. Anderson, 'Money and the Structure of Credit in the Eighteenth Century', *Business History* 12 (1970), pp. 85–101; B. L. Anderson, 'The Attorney and the Early Capital Market in Lancashire', in F. Crouzet (ed.), *Capital Formation and the Industrial Revolution* (London, 1972), pp. 223–55.

In terms of quantity, the majority of his activity was done using long-term lending on bonds, the use of which also increased in the eighteenth century.[10] His business was secured by a number of larger mortgages, which were worth £318 in 1732. But by 1757 the value of his mortgage lending had risen to £2,990, still only for four mortgages, but now with one for £2,190 on an entire estate. At the same date, his lending on bonds was worth slightly less at £2,700.[11]

In the 1730s and 1740s Plumbe's annual spending was in the region of £300–400, and his investments produced small annual profits of £38–160 over expenditure.[12] But because he was lending money out on bond, he also kept a large amount of cash on hand. For instance, at the end of 1737 he added up his receipts, which amounted to £409 13s. 7d. compared to disbursements of £336 16s. 9d., producing a profit of £72 16s. 10d. On the same page, he noted that he had £154 17s. worth of bonds and notes outstanding, of which £21 were doubtful. But he also noted that he possessed £369 in cash, consisting of 260 'guineas in my Budore' and six in his pocket, as well as some Portuguese gold coins, and £70 of silver also in his boudoir, together with 12s. in his pocket, £8 in a bag, and £4 7s. for 'market money'. Thus, he was in possession of much more cash than he had lent out. Examining the accounts, we can see that he was using his cash not only as a reserve, but to save to buy up land as a rent-earning investment. By the end of 1750, he listed property worth about £755. It seems that his business strategy was to become a renter with the profits of his lending activity.

For the years 1748–1749, in order to keep track of the financing of the purchase of a piece of property, he decided to list his coins by number and value at the beginning of each month (Table 3.1). Obviously, as a broker and moneylender he is anything but representative of average cash holdings, but his precise listings do give us an idea of the proportions of different sorts of coins he possessed at the beginning of each month. What is immediately evident is the dominance of guineas. In almost every year, they formed the majority of his cash. However, the presence of large Portuguese coins is also quite striking – they comprised around 20–25 per cent of his cash, showing the importance of the treaty with Portugal.

Silver coins, although more numerous, formed a much smaller proportion by value. Still, the number he had was considerable, and they were probably collected from rental and interest payments to him. The

[10] See 'Bonds as a Form of Capital' in Chapter 4.
[11] Anderson, 'The Attorney and the Early Capital Market', pp. 236–40.
[12] Ibid., p. 241.

Table 3.1 *John Plumbe's cash on hand each month in 1748–1749*[a]

Date	Guineas (#)	Value (£)	Joan (#)	Value (£)	Moidore (#)	Value (£)	Silver[b] (est. # of shillings)	Value (£)	Percentage of total value in silver	Total value (£)
2 January 1748	103.5	108.7	12.25	45.85	12.25	17.85	1,315	65.75	28	235.5
1 March 1748	103.5	108.7	12	43.4	12	16.4	1,000	50	23	219.75
1 June 1748	169.5	178	16.5	37.8	14	18.9	529	26.45	10	261.15
1 July 1748	188.5	197.9	10.5	37.8	15	19.05	380	19	7	275
1 August 1748	185	194.25	11.5	41.4	17	22.95	480	24	8	284.4
1 September 1748	238.5	250.4	14.5	53.1	24	31.7	166	8.3	2	343.6
1 October 1748	286.5	300	18.5	67.5	25	34.4	760	38	9	440.9
1 November 1748	287.5	301.9	20.25	72.8	25.5	34.4	740	37	8	446.2
1 December 1748	96.5	101.3	1	11.4	0.5	0.7	186	9.3	8	116.7
1 January 1749	152.5	160.1	13	47.5	24.5	33.1	477	23.85	9	264.3
1 March 1749	188	197.9	14.5	54	32	43.85	18	0.9	0	296.7
1 June 1749	240.5	252.5	19.5	58	12	16.2	354	17.7	1	345.2
1 July 1749	281	274	20.5	74.7	13	17.55	916	45.8	11	412.1
1 August 1749	280	293.5	22.5	81	16	21.6	856	42.8	10	439.9
1 September 1749	304	319.2	22.5	81	16	21.6	800	40	9	461.8
1 October 1749	304	319.2	22.5	81	16	21.6	700	35	8	459.3
1 November 1749	291.5	289	23	82.8	16	21.6	800	40	10	410.9
1 December 1749	76.5	80	18.5	11.45	3.5	4.7	1,898	94.9	49	191.9

[a] Liverpool Archives, 920, PLU 9.

[b] Silver coins were minted in crowns worth 5s., half-crowns, shillings, and 6d., 4d., 3d., 2d., and 1d. coins. Thomas Turner recorded using all of these denominations, but the majority he used were shillings and halfpence. Plumbe does not give the types of silver coins he possessed, but for the purposes of illustration I have assumed they were shillings. Challis, *A New History of the Royal Mint*, p. 750.

number of silver coins fluctuated the most, from almost nothing to £95 in the last month, which indicates that they had a fairly high velocity of circulation. In contrast, his holdings of gold coins always went up until he made payment for purchases of land, demonstrating that he was collecting them for that purpose. His use of coins to buy land can be seen in November 1748, when he paid £400 in various coins, which he listed, to one Mr William Eccleston to purchase 'half of low hill hall', and then in November of the following year when his son was instructed to pay Miss Clayton £298 16s. 10d. for the remainder. The number of Portuguese coins fluctuated the least, indicating they were a form of saving. In November 1749 he noted that £44 worth of his gold was underweight, but he does not say by how much. In the same month he also noted that he used £21 worth of gold to get a bill for one of his tenants to take to Cambridge. On two other occasions he noted that he carried 15s. and £2 4s. 6d. in his pocket in silver. He only once mentioned copper, in January 1757, when he noted that Betty (probably his wife) counted the money, which included 13d. in 'brass'.

The small amount of copper coins was typical of the situation in England. The mint only intermittently issued copper coins of very small denominations, such as farthings (one-quarter of a penny) or halfpence. In 1705, the Treasury decided that in the future all issues of copper coinage would be met by the mint and banned private issues of copper and brass tokens by shopkeepers and others. The lack of regal copper change, for the reasons described above, continued to plague the daily economy for the majority of the eighteenth century. The next issue was only in 1717, and then next in 1729. Between that date and 1754, copper coinage was issued with an average output of 7,000 lb of copper coins a year, of which all but 6 per cent was made into halfpennies.[13] Working by weight this would be about 290,500 halfpennies, worth only £614.

In addition, another problem with copper was that its market value as a metal was not high enough for a small coin to be minted in which the value of copper was as great as the value of the amount of money of account stamped on the face of the coin. This made counterfeiting a great temptation, and the value of the coinage then had to be protected by criminal law. Other countries, especially the Netherlands and France, were more successful in producing copper coins that remained in circulation, but in England counterfeiting base metals such as copper was only legally designated a misdemeanour, in contrast to the coining of precious metal coins and counterfeiting, which was awarded the highest

[13] Challis, *A New History of the Royal Mint*, pp. 435, 692–3.

punishment possible: treason.[14] This was why copper coinage was only intermittently used by the English Mint, as it always led to a glut of false coins developing.[15] Also, because of the high costs of distribution, it seems that this royal copper coinage together with a large number of counterfeits flooded the market in London to the extent that the butchers, bakers, and grocers of London petitioned the government to stop issuing copper coinage and withdraw the coinage in circulation in 1754. They claimed that the copper halfpence had supplemented gold and silver coinage in retail, as all salaries of the poor were paid in copper halfpence. The petitioners were burdened with copper coin they could not use in large transactions, for payment of taxes and excise, nor could they be used to purchase bills of exchange. Issues were resumed once again in 1762–1763, but only on a small scale.[16]

One potential solution was for private tradesmen to issue their own local currencies, called tokens, again made of a base metal such as copper or lead, which could be quickly withdrawn if counterfeiting began.[17] However, such private money was at the mercy of government regulation, as minting was part of the monarch's prerogative, and for most of the eighteenth century before 1787 the issuance of such tokens was prohibited. Thus, as was the case in the seventeenth century, there was a shortage of small change, but it was actually considerably worse. Silver currency fell from about £8 million in the 1680s to less than £1 million, and private copper, lead, and brass tokens – which had been allowed in the seventeenth century – were prohibited for most of the eighteenth century. Halfpennies were only intermittently and poorly supplied.[18] However, the total value of the currency rose considerably in the form of gold coins, but this amount was not enough to deal with the payment of wages. In Yorkshire, where the cloth industry had expanded tremendously by the mid-eighteenth century, there was an active trade in the counterfeiting of gold coins, despite it being a capital crime. As John

14 John Styles, '"Our Traitorous Moneymakers": The Yorkshire Coiners and the Law, 1760–83', in John Brewer and John Styles (eds.), *An Ungovernable People: The English and Their Law in the Seventeenth and Eighteenth Centuries* (New Brunswick, 1980), pp. 182–3.

15 Craig Muldrew, '"Hard Food for Midas", Cash and its Social Value in Early Modern England', *Past and Present* 170 (2001), pp. 102–3.

16 Idit Ben Or, *Non-governmental Monies in Early Modern England: A Social, Political and Material Culture Analysis* (PhD Thesis, Hebrew University of Jerusalem, 2021), pp. 141–2.

17 Peter Mathias, 'The People's Money: Trade Tokens in the Eighteenth Century – The Royal Mint, Trade Tokens and the Economy', in Peter Mathias (ed.), *The Transformation of England* (London, 1979); T. S. Willan, *The Inland Trade* (Manchester, 1976), pp. 76–106.

18 Muldrew, 'Hard Food for Midas', p. 97.

Styles has shown, the demand for coins was so great that the profits derived from counterfeiting outweighed the risk of execution.[19] But when used by the middling sort in transactions with each other, this gold, together with the security of land, helped to provide collateral used to create local paper currencies. This could then supplement the oral credit that had always been used in tandem with cash, and such paper currency could then be used to pay wages.[20]

Local Paper Currencies

In his 2007 PhD Thesis, *Social Incidence and Economic Significance of the Growth of transferable Paper Instruments in Seventeenth Century England*, Hank McCurdy argued that informal written bills and notes were taking the place of unwritten obligations from the 1670s onwards. There were undoubtedly some earlier instances of their use, but they were not common. Gerald de Malynes, in his description from 1622 of how merchants in the Lowlands and Hamburg used assignable bills of debt between themselves as a limited form of paper currency, specifically claimed that 'this laudable custome … is not practiced in England'.[21] But by the end of the seventeenth century this was certainly no longer the case, and informal notes of hand and receipts similar to the bills of debt mentioned by Malynes were being used and accepted, not only by merchants, but by tradesmen and farmers as well.[22]

The fact that they were being used is clear from the evidence presented in a series of legal decisions that legitimised their use. The first type of negotiable instrument to gain legal recognition after the Restoration was the inland bill of exchange. Since the use of bills of exchange *within* England – rather than internationally between those legally defined as merchants – was new, it was imperative that the law recognise them as a legally valid instrument. An inland bill worked in the same way as overseas bills of exchange. For example, if a grocer in Cambridge bought 20 lb of Virginia tobacco from a London merchant and sent a bill of exchange for £4 to him in London as payment, the London merchant could use it to pay the tax bill that a Cambridgeshire farmer owed the Exchequer, as long as the Cambridge grocer owed the farm £4. As in international exchanges, this depended on each party keeping detailed

[19] Styles, 'Our Traitorous Moneymakers', pp. 172–7, 234–8, 246–8.
[20] For a discussion of this, see Ibid., pp. 77–120.
[21] Gerald de Malynes, *Consuetudo vel lex Mercatoria* (London, 1622), p. 99.
[22] Hank McCurdy, *Social Incidence and Economic Significance of the Growth of Transferable Paper Instruments in Seventeenth Century England* (PhD Thesis, Cambridge University, 2007), pp. 70, 76, 83, 128, 161.

and accurate account books that clearly showed the amount each customer owed to the accountant, or vice versa, so that when a bill was presented to them they could add or cancel that value.[23]

But since inland bills were being issued and sent to other towns all under the legal writ of the common law, they had to be reconciled with a well-established body of contract law that already existed. However, the foundation of English contract law was based on the concept of consideration. Consideration is basically the promise to give something for something else – usually an amount of money for goods or services between two legal bodies. This was crucial because English contract was based on an oral agreement that could be demonstrated by witnesses. Any writing was only one piece of evidence like any other. But a bill of exchange had no consideration – it was essentially a call to cancel another person's debt to the same amount.[24]

As a result of this, the law of inland bills developed out of the Law Merchant incorporating some aspects of the common law. This was based not on an oral promise with consideration, but on the actual writing of the bill itself, and its recording in an account book. It was also no longer legally confined to only those tradesmen styled as merchants.[25] Early forms of pleading recited the custom of the Law Merchant, but this disappeared before the end of the seventeenth century, and the form of pleading simply came to be known as the law of bills, and was different to the vast number of suits on contract and debt that were still being heard in English courts in the 1680s. The other aspect of bills that had been noted by Gerard de Malynes as being present in the Lowlands, and which became common in England by the end of the century, was circulation by endorsement. Typically, an inland bill of exchange would be issued on a certain day, with 30 days or more before its final day of acceptance, after which, if it was not accepted, it could be sued over. But during this time it could circulate as a form of currency by endorsement.[26]

Case law developed to recognise this practice, making an endorsement to a bill an enforceable legal obligation. As a result, the last endorser

[23] Eric Kerridge, *Trade and Banking in Early Modern England* (Manchester, 1988), p. 47.

[24] Muldrew, *Economy of Obligation*, pp. 206–9; David Ibbetson, 'Assumpsit and Debt in the Early Sixteenth Century: The Origins of the Indebitatus Count', *Cambridge Law Journal* 41 (1982), pp. 153–4.

[25] James Steven Rogers, *The Early History of the Law of Bills and Notes: A Study of the Origins of Anglo-American Commercial Law* (Cambridge, 2004), pp. 144–9; McCurdy, *Social Incidence*, p. 108.

[26] There is little evidence as to the volume of such circulation, but in 1826 one bill came to court which had been endorsed fifty times on an attached piece of paper. Rogers, *Law of Bills and Notes*, pp. 112–13.

became legally responsible for meeting the amount of the bill in case the original issuer did not have the means to pay, usually because of bankruptcy.[27] One public notary writing on the use of bills of exchange in 1651 clearly indicated that inland bills worked in the same way as international bills.[28] By the time John Scarlet came to write the *Stile of Exchanges* in 1684, he included a section on how,

> In the Redrawing of a Bill, the Redrawer Is looked upon, as the absolute and first Drawer, and the Remitter considered as the first Remitter; so that the Endorser of a Bill is as strictly obliged as the first Drawer and Maker of it, and the Possessor thereof hath as much Right and Law against him, as against the first Drawer.
>
> VIII. The Redrawer or the Negotiator of a Bill, does not make a new Bill, but endorseth the old, in suchlike words as these, Pay this for me to A. A. (or to his order) the value hereof in my own hands (or from B. B. or, &c.) C. C.
>
> IX. By this Endorsement, he to whom the Bill is sent, is the true and right Possessor of it ... he to whom it is endorsed as payable, may again endorse it, and so may as often be endorsed as there is room on the Bill for Endorsements.
>
> XI. The Acceptant himself, as well as any other, may freely negotiate those Bills of Exchange that are by him accepted for his own account, ... yet all this time the first Endorsers shall be never the less obliged.[29]

However, at this time there was little legal discussion of more informal bills or promissory notes. In addition to the bill of exchange, a bond was often referred to as a bill obligatory. The legal manual *Symboleographia*, which had been published at regular intervals since the late sixteenth century, but which stopped publication in 1647, described a bill obligatory as a type of bond, a much more formal instrument than notes.[30] There are numerous copies of bills obligatory written in the declarations in cases of debt from the Borough Court of King's Lynn, where they are clearly a type of bond with a penalty and two witnesses, although there is no way of knowing if the originals had been sealed.[31] Many probate documents also continued to list bills obligatory into the beginning of the eighteenth century.[32] But a bill obligatory, being clearly a bond, could be sued over in the law of debt.[33]

The word bill was also used in English before the late sixteenth century to refer to various other things. There were bills of complaint in the common law, bills introduced in Parliament to create and amend laws, and hand bills with announcements. The term bill of sale was also used

[27] Ibid., pp. 147–9. [28] McCurdy, *Social Incidence*, p. 131.
[29] John Scarlet, *Stile of Exchanges* (London, 1684), pp. 54–5.
[30] McCurdy, *Social Incidence*, pp. 81ff. [31] Norfolk Record Office, KLC/C25/17-18.
[32] McCurdy, *Social Incidence*, pp. 78, 83. [33] Muldrew, *Economy of Obligation*, p. 207.

before the seventeenth century, but its use became much more common after the Restoration since it could also be turned into a negotiable instrument once payment was recorded on it and it became a receipt. Bills for goods sold or work done appear as debts in inventories in the early seventeenth century, but did not become commonly transferable until after 1660.[34] The term note of hand, promissory note, or just note seems to have been a development of the Restoration period, but notes were often listed together with bills, such as in one pamphlet, where it was claimed that 'Notes or Bills are lyable to be Counterfeit, Burnt, or Lost'.[35]

The number of cases concerning informal bills or notes that came to be entered in law reports was much smaller than for inland bills of exchange. This is despite the fact that, as McCurdy demonstrated, they were certainly in use during the second half of the seventeenth century. There are enough reported legal cases, though, to establish that promissory notes were being treated in law as if they were bills of exchange that were endorsable, but these decisions did not become a doctrine initially because of the powerful figure of Chief Justice Holt. He was concerned that if the law of bills was to be extended to much smaller debts, it could potentially undermine the entire law of contract based on consideration. He expressed this concern in two famous judgments against an obligation being created by a promissory note.[36] However, since most informal notes or bills arose out of sales contracts, it was in fact possible to plead under the existent form of pleading known as *indebitatus assumpset.* This simply stated that unspecified 'goods sold and delivered' had not been paid for.[37] Once brought into court, the case would be decided in the same manner as an ordinary case of trespass with consideration, but based on an undetermined transaction.[38]

However, this still left open the question of who was responsible if the note was endorsed and passed on as currency. As a result, in the Parliament of 1704, a statute was passed to specifically give them the same legal status as bills of exchange under the custom of merchants, stating that plaintiffs could sue for damages and costs under *Capias facias*

[34] McCurdy, *Social Incidence*, p. 77.
[35] L. R., *A Proposal for Supplying His Majesty with Twelve Hundred Thousand Pounds by Mending the Coin, and Yet Preserve the Ancient Standard of the Kingdom* (London, 1695), p. 15.
[36] Rogers, *Law of Bills and Notes*, pp. 177–86. [37] McCurdy, *Social Incidence*, pp. 163–9.
[38] The rise of the action of *assumpsit*, which over time developed into modern contract law, has been one of the most discussed aspects of legal history. For a summary of this work, see Muldrew, *Economy of Obligation*, pp. 207–8, nn. 52, 53.

(a writ of arrest) or *Eligit* (a writ for distraint of goods).[39] At this time, it was unusual to use a statutory instrument to define contractual doctrine, which had mostly developed through precedents, and the statute stated its purpose was to 'encourage trade and commerce'. This has been interpreted by legal historians as a way of clearly stating the law in favour of notes of hand after Holt's decisions against their negotiability, but it is probably not insignificant that it was passed at a time when government borrowing was on the rise due to the War of Spanish Succession.[40]

Although both inland bills of exchange and informal bills and notes of hand played equally important roles as paper currencies, inland bills of exchange were almost exclusively used by tradesmen and tax collectors, while notes of hand were widely used throughout the entire population. Thus, I will deal with the latter's use first, and then bills of exchange.

London Beginnings

Although we have looked at public finance in the capital, since notes were probably used as currency first by tradesmen in London we need to step back and also examine the origins of private banking there. Some examples exist in the records of the bankers John Morris and Robert Clayton, discussed in the previous chapter. They began actively issuing different forms of paper banker's notes that could circulate as currency in London. The first type of note to be issued was an equivalent of what we know today as a cheque. This was a piece of paper written by the depositor of money with Clayton, ordering a sum to be paid to a third party by deducting it from their account with the bankers. These were not really circulating instruments, but they could be used to pay someone else the payee owed money to.[41] The word cheque was not used at this time (it comes from counterfoils used by the Exchequer); they were instead termed vouchers (the Anglo-Norman word vouch refers to a promise of security) or orders to pay. However, a voucher issued directly from someone promising a payment out of his own account books, not by a banker, was something that could be transferred from person to person in the form of a piece of currency.[42] A receipt was similar, except that it was signed by the recipient of the payment, but it could then also circulate as

[39] *Statutes of the Realm*, 3 and 4 Anne c.8.

[40] Rogers, *Law of Bills and Notes*, pp. 181–4; McCurdy, *Social Incidence*, p. 143.

[41] See the example drawn by Sit John Wolstenholme, pictured in McCurdy, *Social Incidence*, p. 102.

[42] See description of notes issued by Morris and Clayton in Frank T. Melton, *Sir Robert Clayton and the Origins of English Deposit Banking 1658–1685* (Cambridge, 2002), pp. 99–105.

a money substitute.[43] Often a voucher and a note of hand were the same thing. Officially, a promissory note from a banker to someone else was a promise to pay an amount upon demand in the future with a set interest rate, but the term was also used in a more informal sense to refer to a note of hand.

It is clear from the accounts of Morris and Clayton that they issued notes and vouchers to others beyond their own reserves, thus increasing the money supply in the capital in the same way as was done earlier by Italian bankers.[44] In 1677, a London trade directory listed fifty-eight goldsmiths, of whom forty-four offered banking services.[45] This business was London-centred, but they were also involved in offering transfer services to tradesmen outside the capital. After the Stop of the Exchequer in 1672, Parliament authorised selected goldsmiths to offer assignments of long-term annuitised debt to lenders who had used those goldsmiths as a means of resuming payments at a more feasible level. These records include a joiner from Bristol and a saddler from Norwich, among other tradesmen outside of London. They also show that they provided the same service as the scriveners to country gentry. We know about their note issue because a collection of them has survived as evidence from a Court of Chancery case involving the goldsmith Thomas Fowle. These survive as threaded bundles, together with a daily pocketbook of transactions between 1672 and 1696. The notes in this collection include tradesmen's bills, receipts for tax payments, and notes for simple amounts of money.[46] In 1696, the partnership of Moore and Pyne bought eighty-nine bank bills in standard denominations from Fowle.[47] The issuing of such notes evolved as part of the account book transfer, and the notes were given security because the bankers' account books remained open for any potential acceptor of a note to check to make sure the funds were available.[48] Potential acceptors also placed a great deal of emphasis on checking the signature on a note to make sure it matched that of the banker.[49]

London tradesmen began using notes of hand at the same time as the scriveners and goldsmiths.[50] McCurdy has found early evidence from London in the 1670s and 1680s whereby tradesmen could transform their invoices into circulating bills by endorsing them to third parties and then drawing on the credit they accrued with customers. In one example,

[43] Ibid., pp. 107–8. [44] Ibid., pp. 95, 108. [45] McCurdy, *Social Incidence*, p. 248.
[46] David Mitchell, '"Mr Fowle Pray Pay the Washerwoman": the Trade of a London Goldsmith-Banker, 1660–92', *Business and Economic History*, 23 (1994), pp. 33–5.
[47] McCurdy, *Social Incidence*, pp. 249–50. [48] Rogers, *Law of Bills and Notes*, p. 197.
[49] Melton, Sir *Robert Clayton*, p. 108.
[50] See 'Credit and Finance in England before 1680' in Chapter 2.

the grocer Robert Hollowell endorsed a billing statement of £6 13s. 1d. owed by the merchant William Attwood, to a Thomas Blagrand who eventually presented it after a time to Attwood for final payment. Another bill was transferred three months after it was made to another person. Richard Fifield, an ironmonger, probably from London, records being paid with bills in 1685–1687.[51]

There is also evidence of London tradesmen using bills of exchange as currency. The accounts of the London draper Henry Sturmy from 1691 to 1693 contain a list of 'bills and other notes for money' he had received from Cary Boucher, a silkman of Dorset, which consisted primarily of seventeen bills of exchange worth about £497, of which fourteen were listed as having been used as payments to other parties.[52] Here we see bills of exchange working as liquid specie substitutes, although it is impossible to track the velocity of circulation. In contrast, scriveners did not use bills of exchange very often as they needed to be linked to trade channels, and they dealt mostly with gentry rentiers.

A source that provides a great deal of descriptive and contextual evidence of how notes of hand and bills were used in London is the trial records of criminal prosecutions in the London Old Bailey. Although these suits are not about credit or debt, many cases concerned forgery or alterations of notes of hand, and others the theft of notes. Proceedings of the trials held at the court included the plaintiffs' and defendants' statements, as well as witnesses' examinations, and were published in the *Proceedings of the Sessions of the Peace for the City of London and the County of Middlesex.* The first published collection of trials at the Old Bailey dates from 1674, and from 1678 accounts of the trials at each session (meeting of the court) were regularly published at an inexpensive price, and were targeted initially at a popular audience.[53] Although there are some gaps in the early years, since the publication was validated by the mayor of London it is assumed by historians of crime that they contain accurate reports of the great majority of trials, of which there were about 78,000 before 1820. However, the descriptions of the trials are not, and were not intended to be, an official transcript, so the level of detail varies. But in many cases the level of detail contained in witnesses' descriptions

[51] McCurdy, *Social Incidence*, pp. 239–40, 243, 250–1.

[52] The account only listed the last endorser, indicating there must have been others before. Ibid., pp. 70–2.

[53] These have all been digitalised and are available at the Old Baily Online. Tim Hitchcock, Robert Shoemaker, Clive Emsley, *et al.*, *The Old Bailey Proceedings Online, 1674–1913*, www.oldbaileyonline.org, version 7.0, accessed 24 March 2012, hereafter referred to as PBO.

of the events relevant to the crime in question provide accounts of quotidian life simply unavailable in such numbers elsewhere.

It is also the case that when dealing with examples of the use of cash or forms of credit currency, criminal trials are in no way a neutral source from which any kind of accurate statistical pattern of monetary use can be determined. Over 80 per cent of suits concerned property theft. Thieves undoubtedly targeted people and premises that were likely to possess or contain valuable items worth stealing, of which money was the easiest to dispose of. Further, by far the great majority of cases originated in the heavily built-up urban environment of metropolitan London, with a population of over 600,000 by 1750. In order to examine some cases about notes, I have searched from 1720 – when the recording of cases became fuller – to 1740 – the period in which their use had become quite common in rural sources.[54] This search produced 160 cases that mention bills, bank notes, bills of exchange, and notes of hand for various amounts, although in a few cases value is not given. These cases include 110 cases of theft, including pickpocketing (21) and highway robbery (21), and 50 of deception, including forgery (41). In comparison, a search for the word *guinea* produced 604 cases. This much larger figure is unsurprising, as it would be expected that coins featured much more often in cases of theft because of pickpocketing.

It was common to carry money around the body in more than one place. People took the precaution of securing the cash they carried around with them in different pockets, purses, or fobs. Bills and notes were kept in bill books of about 4–6 inches in size, which were flat and often kept inside clothes, from where they were much harder to steal. Also, notes were obviously much harder to dispose of since they had signatures that could be checked. So we cannot take this evidence as reflecting the extent of their use, but the fact that they appear often shows they were certainly common.[55]

There are 118 examples of different notes where the value is given. I have included forgeries in the sample since they seemed authentic enough to have been passed or discounted before arousing enough suspicion to take the case to court. Over half of all the notes mentioned were for £20 or less; of these, 40 per cent were worth £10 10s. or less, and 23 per cent £5 or less. Such values would have been used in everyday trade rather than high-level finance, although there were certainly many

[54] For a comparison of mentions of notes compared to other forms of currency over a much longer period until 1820, see Muldrew, 'Money and the Everyday', pp. 95–120.

[55] Everyday use shows that in comparison to guineas and other coins their use went up dramatically at the end of the eighteenth century.

larger sums used as well. Thirty-two per cent of the notes mentioned were over £50, and 15 per cent £110 or more. The three highest amounts, £1,260, £800, and £6,400, came from a series of forgeries by one man.

These cases offer a lot of incidental information, especially those concerning forged signatures or endorsements, where witnesses' evidence shows the process by which notes were authenticated through the verification of signatures. One such trial from April 1722 involved John Francis and his wife Elizabeth, who were indicted for forging a note for £25 in the name of Ann Lockyer, with an intent to defraud Richard Hemmings.[56] Hemming deposed that John Francis approached him, telling him he needed £25, and Hemming offered to lend it on good security, for which Francis offered the note. Hemming gave him the money, but when he went to Madam Lockyer she denied ever writing 'the bill'. Francis then tried to claim that Lockyer often lent his wife money and that he wrote the note for Elizabeth to obtain Lockyer's signature, which his wife forged in his ignorance. Both were found guilty of a misdemeanour. The witness in the trial record used the terms note and bill interchangeably.

Another case from 1722 concerning mail robbery provides incidental information of the evidence of the validity of how a note was written, and shows which notes were valuable to steal. One of the highwaymen accused related that he and his fellow thieves had waited at around 1–2 a.m. for the Bristol mail rider outside of Hounslow, and after robbing the rider had returned to London, eventually ending up at

> the Cock and George in the Minories, at which House they went into a Room by themselves; and the better to take off suspicion, they call'd for a Candle, Wax, Paper, Pen and Ink: then lockt the door and examined their Prize: and reserving only the Bank bills, they burnt all the other Notes and Letters with the Candle, which they set in the Chimney. They had Three 20 l. Bills, One of 25 l. half a 50 l. Bill, and 2 halves of 25 l. each; which they equally divided.[57]

They could not have used any of the personal bills drawn on people in the West Country, having returned to London, so they destroyed them and kept only the Bank of England bills, which were easier to use in payment before their numbers could be circulated as being stolen. They provided incidental information on another unrelated bill, however, when Hawkins – one of the other highwaymen – attempted to provide himself with an alibi by summoning an innkeeper to depose that he,

[56] PBO, April 1722, trial of John Francis and Elizabeth, his wife (t17220404-39).
[57] PBO, May 1722, trial of John Hawkins and George Simpson (t17220510-3).

Hawkins, had used a note to pay for his room on the night of the robbery, to prove he was not involved. The innkeeper was summoned as a witness and produced the note,

> which was read in Court, viz. April the 10th, 1722. Receiv'd of John Hawkins, the Sum of 1 l. 10 s. in full of all Accounts, by me William Fuller. He then depos'd that Hawkins paid him the Money on the Day mentioned in the Receipt. That Hawkins wrote the Body of the Note in his sight; and that he (Fuller) sign'd it at the same time, and with the same Ink. ... That he had likewise taken an Account of the same Money in his Book, which he had unluckily forgot to bring with him; and reading an Advertisement in the Gazette, concerning the Mail's being robb'd, he compar'd his Book and the Note together, and they exactly agreed. But the Note being examin'd in Court, it was apparent that it was not sign'd with the same Ink as the Body of it was wrote withal.[58]

The most spectacular attempt at forgery in this period has been described in detail by Randall McGowen. This was an infamous series of cases that generated a great deal of publicity because it involved large sums of money – one note was worth £6,400 – and involved as victims Thomas Gibson, a banker who handled some of Sir Robert Walpole's investments, and an MP. The perpetrator of the forgeries, William Hales, was a goldsmith banker who had gone bankrupt in 1721. Since then he had continued to do business but had never received a certificate that he had satisfied the creditors in the bankruptcy.[59] This case involved altering someone's handwritten amounts on franked covers, or sheets of paper marked with prepaid postage that could be folded and used as envelopes, to be sent to someone in Bristol. Gibson, as a member of Parliament, could do this. As the case notes stated:

> between the f and r an o was crowded in, and the two ee's being rubb'd out, the Word *Free* as it was wrote by Mr. *Gibson*, was made *for*, to which was immediately added, *myself and Partners*.

Although it was stated that someone familiar with Gibson's notes would have noticed this change, it was

> not observ'd by the Gentleman who gave his Notes in exchange for it at the Time of his receiving it, [although] the Piece of Paper on which this Note was drawn, appeared to have been cut or torn to serve the Design, and it seem'd ridiculous, to think Mr. Gibson should draw a Note of such Consequence upon such a diminutive scrap of Paper; besides, the Note seemed to have been folded as a Letter.[60]

58 Ibid.
59 Randall McGowen, 'From Pillory to Gallows: The Punishment of Forgery in the Age of the Financial Revolution', *Past and Present* 165 (1999), pp. 112–14.
60 PBO, December 1728, trial of William Hales (t17281204-63).

Deception was also employed to get the forged note cashed. On 7 September, Hales trained a seaman to act as a ticket porter (an early modern courier of documents and letters), who he ordered to go to a banker with the £6,400 note together with three other notes – one worth £40 and another two of £25 each. Significantly, he bought him a pocketbook to carry, evidence of the importance of accounts in this line of work.[61] These he was ordered to have changed for notes payable to Lady Harriet Elliot for £4,300, Sir John Hind Cotton for £2,100, and James Moreton for £70. The first attempt failed as the banker's clerk was suspicious. But the altered note was cashed at Hoare's bank. The next day these notes were sent to be exchanged into South Sea and East India Company bonds, which were then converted into Bank of England notes. However, by this time the suspicious cashier had alerted the Bank and the notes were stopped.[62]

The evidence provided in all three of these cases shows clearly how common it was to be constantly changing notes, bills, bank notes, bonds, and stocks for both large and smaller amounts of money in London at this time. It also shows how government paper and bills of exchange were used as currency together with notes of hand. Another example is a case in which a man asked a tavernkeeper if he could change a Bank of England note for £70 to pay for a dinner. The tavernkeeper offered him a £50 bank bill together with £10 cash, and a note of demand for the remaining £10. Unfortunately for the tavernkeeper, the £70 note was a counterfeit, but the willingness of the tavernkeeper to make such an exchange with a stranger is another telling example of how common an activity it must have been.[63]

Gibson's case, as well as others, shows it was common to use licensed porters to take notes to be cashed or exchanged, presumably because many traders were too busy to do all their financial business on their own.[64] To obtain notes of an amount needed to settle a current transaction, individuals of both genders would go to either friends and associates or professional brokers and bankers to make exchanges. As McGowen has noted, what made Hales' fraud initially successful was the trustworthiness of his signature as an endorsement. 'The endorsement', one judge suggested, 'is complete authority to impower the person in whose possession the note is, to receive the money, and likewise to charge the person that so endorsed it with the reimbursement of the

61 McGowen, 'From Pillory to Gallows', pp. 118–19.
62 PBO, December 1728, trial of William Hales (t17281204-63).
63 PBO, February 1725, trial of Francis Kite, alias Brooks (t17250224-51).
64 PBO, October 1730, trial of Thomas Hassel (t17301016-1).

money.'[65] Although handwriting was checked, a careful fraud like Hales' could not always be spotted, and his forged notes were cashed and passed on. Again the system relied on enough people being able to recognise a fraud encountering the note at some point in its circulation.[66]

Another case from 1735 involving the forgery of an endorsement demonstrates how the system of brokering bills worked, and how it was vulnerable. Thomas Devenish, a backmaker (a maker of iron goods) was indicted for forging an endorsement on the back of a promissory note (dated 25 May 1735). This note was written by Devenish, and was a promise to pay one William Morris, on order, 'One Hundred Pounds'. Devenish then forged an endorsement purported to be the writing of Morris to pay one Thomas Green, on order, dated 29 May 1735. Witness statements give a good sense of how people used local knowledge to assess the validity of endorsements if there was some reason for doubt. James Graham, a pawnbroker, deposed that

> This Note was brought to me first by James Northall a Scrivener. He desired me to get Money for it. I told him I would try. It was then indors'd [by] William Morris. I enquir'd who Morris was, and Northall answer'd, that Morris was a Smith at the lower End of Broad-Street. Northall came several Times about it, and at last he said he was employ'd by Devenish to whom the Note belonged, and to whom I must pay the Money. After this, [Devenish] came himself, and said it was his Note, and that the Name at Bottom was his own Hand.

Graham then stated that he asked Devenish who Morris was, and how he came to owe him such a considerable sum. Devenish answered that the money was owing for nails and other things in the backmaking trade, and that the sum was not considerable for the trade. Graham accepted this and applied to Mr Conran, and he to Mr Green, a jeweller, who offered to give rose diamonds at a market price for the note. He also claimed that he had agreed to do this as: 'It's Part of my Business, as a Broker, to get Notes discounted. The Brokers don't usually enquire after the Indorsers; though it's what we ought to do, but we leave that to the Person who discounts the Notes.' He also noted that Devenish came five or six times to see if it had been done. The jeweller, Green, further deposed that before accepting the bill for diamonds he asked his glazier, who lived near Morris,

> if he knew Morris, and if he was a Man of Worth. He said he did not think he was worth Twenty Pounds; upon which I returned the Note. Mr. Conran came the

65 McGowen, 'From Pillory to Gallows', pp. 116–17.

66 Another case that involved the checking and tracing of notes by their handwriting is: PBO, January 1724, trial of Isaak Yewel (t17240117–68).

next Day to know the Reason of it; I told him it was but a coined Note at best. We went to Morris and shew'd him the Note. He said the Name was none of his Writing, and he wrote his Name before us, and it was not at all like the Indorsement.[67]

This case indicates that in London, by this date, pawnbrokers were commonly discounting paper notes, which must have been done on a large scale if it was not common to check the endorsement before accepting the note. It also shows how many middlemen were involved in passing on the note. But while this was the case, the knowledge of the maker of the note was also passed on to assess his worth and honesty.[68] In the many witness statements, the words note and bill seem to be completely interchangeable – as much as in modern usage. These criminal cases demonstrate in detail how bills and notes were used and passed from hand to hand, and also the various ways people attempted to balance increased liquidity with a necessary amount of trust, by making sure they could trace the path of a note's transmission back to its original maker.

It is also important to consider what sorts of verdicts and punishments were given by the juries in cases of forgery as a deterrent. As Carl Wennerlind has argued, one of the main means by which the Bank of England safeguarded trust in their bank notes was by convincing the government to make forgery of its notes a capital crime in 1696. Under Isaac Newton's mastership of the Mint, prosecutions against coining offences were pursued with great rigour to ensure that those convicted were actually executed, and over seventy people were sentenced to death.[69] Attempts at forging Bank of England notes and other government paper, which carried the death penalty, were much rarer because – unlike anonymous coins – notes had signatures and other writing and so could be traced in the ways described above. Only four people were sentenced to death for this between 1695 and 1725, including two from the sample discussed above: one for forging a Bank note and another for a South Sea Company share. In contrast, cases involving the forgery of private notes and bills remained misdemeanours until 1729. Of the cases of forgery discussed above, nine received punishments involving various

[67] PBO, October 1730, trial of John Dawson (t17301014-75).

[68] For other cases see, PBO, April 1730, trial of Hugh Horton, alias Norton (t17300408-66); June 1720, trial of John Gambol (t17200602-7); May 1723, trial of Philip Hurst (t17230530-24); December 1725, trial of Thomas Warwick (t17251208-54); March 1726, trial of Benjamin Jones (t17260302-26); September 1720, trial of Samuel Bonnet and Mary, his wife (t17200907-15).

[69] Carl Wennerlind, *Casualties of Credit: The English Financial Revolution, 1620–1720* (Cambridge, MA, 2011), pp. 146–52.

combinations of standing at the pillory, fines, and imprisonment. For instance, in the case of John and Elizabeth Francis, who were convicted of forging the note for £25 in the name of Ann Lockyer, John was fined £25 and both were given prison sentences of six months.[70] William Hales and Thomas Kinnersley, who were involved in the forgery of notes for much larger sums, were fined 50 marks (a coin worth two-thirds of a pound) and £200, respectively, prison sentences of five and two years each, and then made to sign bonds for good behaviour for seven and two years. Both were also ordered to stand at the pillory.[71]

The publicity surrounding the Hales case led to a change in the law, and in 1729 an Act of Parliament was passed making it a capital crime to forge or counterfeit 'any deed, will, testament, bond, writing obligatory, bill of exchange, promissory note for payment of money, indorsement or assignment of any bill of exchange, or promissory note for payment of money, or acquittance or receipt, either for money or goods'.[72] As McGowen has stressed, the momentum for this change in making punishment much harsher came not from the tradesmen using notes and bills, but from judges and others, such as clergymen. This was because they were also using bills in their everyday transactions by this time, but had much less experience of detecting fraud. As one of the judges noted, the crime, 'if not suppressed, must tend to hinder all commerce by bills and paper-credit. If this be suffered to increase, none can take such a note, unless he goeth to the person himself. It will render it insecure to carry on commerce by notes or bills.'[73] Between the passing of this Act and 1740, eleven people were sentenced to death for forging private notes, and ten for coining offences.

Provincial Use of Bills and Notes

Most physical bills used by tradesmen, like their account books, have not survived. Hank McCurdy found a few isolated examples, mostly between pages in late seventeenth-century account books.[74] However, many thousands, or possibly even tens of thousands of bills, receipts, and vouchers have survived unnoticed by historians until now in the archives of larger rural estates, as well as the records of town administrations. They have survived in archives where space was not an issue and it

[70] PBO, April 1722, punishment summary (s17220404-1).
[71] PBO, January 1729, punishment summary (s17290116-1).
[72] McGowen, 'From Pillory to Gallows', pp. 127–8. [73] Ibid., p. 130.
[74] McCurdy, *Social Incidence*, pp. 240–9, 257–62.

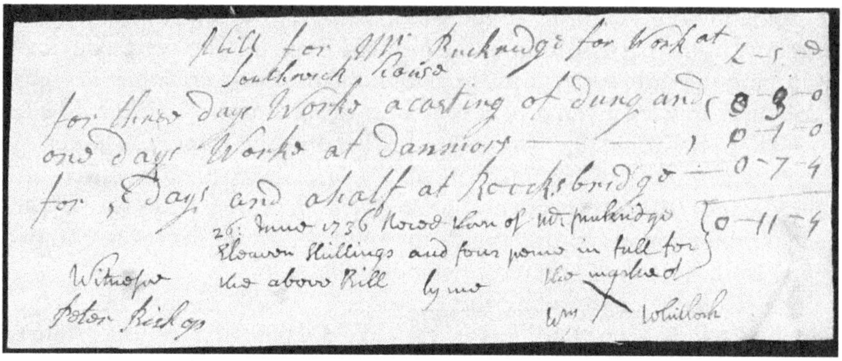

Figure 3.1 The bill of William Whitlock of Hampshire.

was not thought expedient or necessary to cull the archive to save space.[75] They have been catalogued, but since they are called receipts or vouchers, it is not immediately obvious that they have any relevance to questions of currency. Most of them were small slips of paper recording payments to servants and labourers, which could be used as payment in the community instead of cash. Because so many survive, they can be used to examine when their use became common in places where relevant estate and town records survive outside of London. A typical example of a small bill, pictured in Figure 3.1, is that of William Whitlock for three days' work casting dung and one day of other work for 11s. 4d., witnessed by Peter Bishop and receipted by an attorney, Thomas Puckridge, who worked for the Jervoise family of Hampshire.[76]

The collection of the Jervoise family estates in the Hampshire Record Office can be used to track the rise in the use of bills in rural society. The Jervoise family had been prominent Parliamentarians who had married into the Paulet family in Hampshire. Their main lands were there, as well as in Buckinghamshire, Wiltshire, Nottinghamshire, Shropshire, and Worcestershire. The estate papers of Capt. Thomas Jervoise (1616–1693) and Thomas Jervoise III (1667–1743) contain various household, estate, and personal account books, as well as many bundles of 'bills, receipts and accounts'. Those of the elder Thomas contain a few examples of bills from the 1650s and 1660s, and then over 100 from the

[75] One of the most egregious examples of this was the decision of London to burn huge amounts of court and business-related records in the late nineteenth century, leaving historians with less economic data for England's most vibrant economy.

[76] Hampshire Archives, 5M50/1054/14, 17.

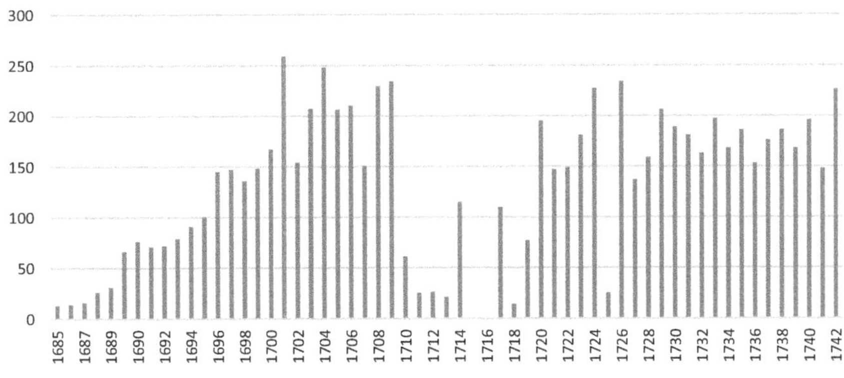

Figure 3.2 Bills and Receipts in the archives of the Jervoise family of Herriard, Hampshire, 1685–1742.

1670s, but beginning in 1680 between fifty and seventy survive each year.[77] However, many more survive for the younger Thomas, beginning in 1685 when he was eighteen. The numbers of these in each bundle can be counted, and these amounts are presented in Figure 3.2. Here we can see a dramatic rise from about 15 per year in 1685, to over 150 annually by the beginning of the eighteenth century.[78] There are gaps in survival after 1710, but in most of the century over 150 survive from each year.

A similar pattern can be seen in the collections of bills and receipts for work done and goods purchased by Queen Elizabeth's Free Grammar School in Wimborne Minster, Dorset.[79] Figure 3.3 lists the numbers in a series of surviving bundles, and again we find a few instances from before the 1680s, but many more after that.

If we look at borough records where bundles of bills and receipts have survived among town chamberlains' records, we see the same pattern. In Lyme Regis, from the beginning of the seventeenth century until 1661, there are ten bundles of bills in total, but thereafter there are ten bundles kept for each decade. The bundles here also get progressively bulkier, and after 1680 they contain hundreds of small bills mixed with larger accounts, which can be seen in Figure 3.4.[80] The borough records from Faversham in Kent contain five bills and a few receipts from the

[77] Hampshire Archives, 44M69/E7/41–44M69/E7/52.

[78] The bundles do not survive individually by year in each case. Often there are some covering a number of years, or more than one for each year, so these yearly numbers are averages in most years, but indicate the general trend. Hampshire Archives, 44M69/E8/7/3–44M69/E8/7/115.

[79] Dorset History Centre, PE-WM/GN/5/1-PE-WM/GN/5/6.

[80] Dorset History Centre, DC-LR/G/9/11-120.

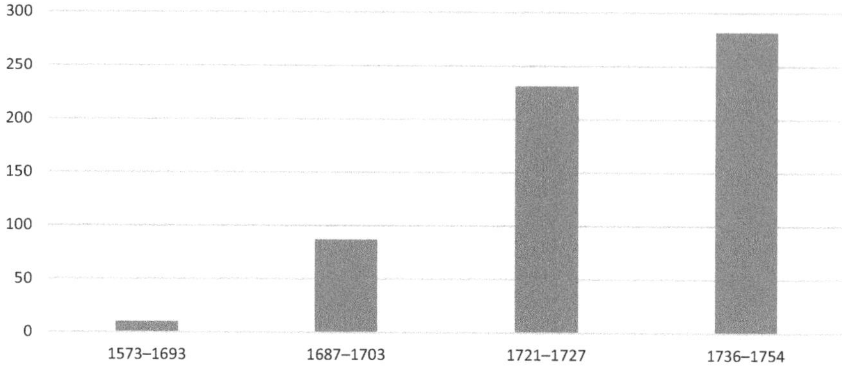

Figure 3.3 Dorset Queen Elizabeth Free Grammar School bills and receipts.

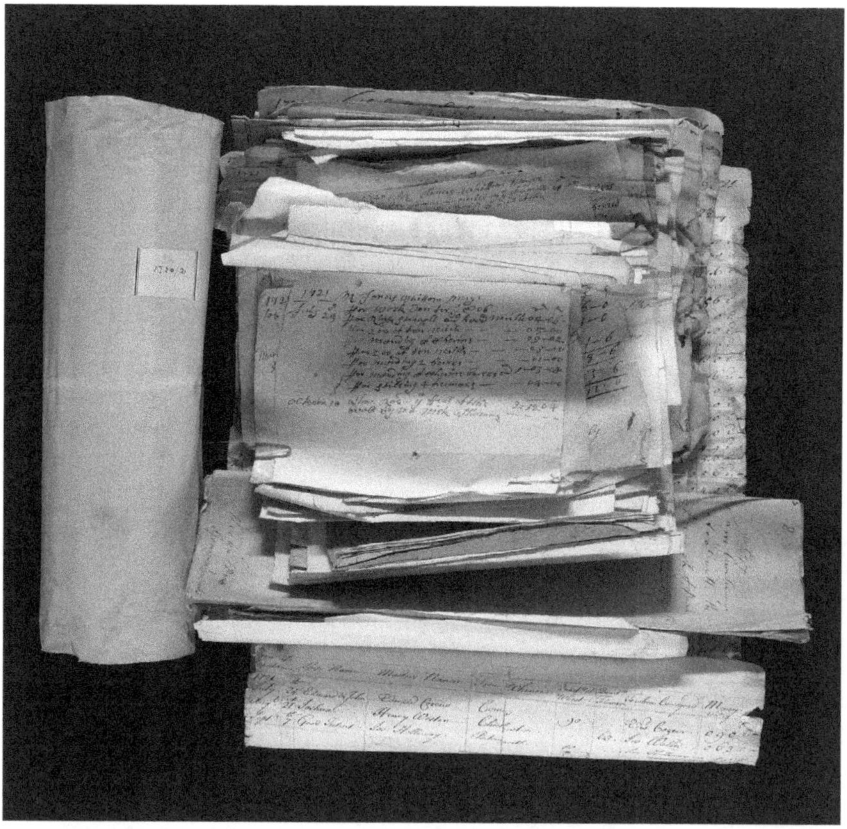

Figure 3.4 Bundle of bills from Lyme Regis *c.*1720.

Civil War period, but after 1660 there are between nine and eleven bundles for each decade, and then fifteen bundles for the first decade of the eighteenth century, and an average of twenty per decade after 1720.[81]

The same pattern is evident in collections of other large estates around England, albeit with variations in the time period during which the use of bills became more common. For the Bradford Stott-Stanhope family of Eccleshill Park, Yorkshire, from the 1690s onward a large number of bills, promissory notes, and receipts begin appearing in the archive.[82] For the Spencer Standhope family of Horsforth, also in Yorkshire, there are a number of earlier receipts listed, but mostly for rent together with some lists of debts; bills and receipts start being commonly used after 1700, and the surviving numbers really expand in the 1730s.[83] The Barrington family of Essex seems to have started using bills somewhat earlier than many others, during the Civil War, but still the number surviving in the archives goes up considerably after 1660, from 47 between 1650 and 1659 to 294 between 1660 and 1685.[84] The very detailed accounts and records of the rebuilding of St. Paul's Cathedral also contain boxes of vouchers, bills, and receipts generated by the great expenditure this activity involved.[85]

The great increase in the numbers surviving in so many different places after *c.*1670 indicates that these bills were not simply kept as a result of chance: it indicates that something more was happening. Just as the numbers of surviving account books goes up for the eighteenth century, so do receipts and bills.[86] The use of receipts and bills as forms of currency evolved by using documents that were already in existence as proof of payment in the case of receipted payments and tradesmen's bills, and a promise to pay in the case of vouchers, although these latter forms were much less common before the late seventeenth

81 Kent Archives Centre, Fa/FV17-195.

82 West Yorkshire Archive Service, ST/ST/3/1-90.

83 West Yorkshire Archive Service, SpSt/5/4/3/1-68, 1701–1713, 3 bundles; 1732–1740, 10 bundles; 1742–1750, 19 bundles; 1751–1760, 21 bundles. The records of the members of the Radcliffe family of Hitchin Priory, who lived in the seventeenth century, contain no entries for bills, but starting in 1704 with Edward Radcliffe (1683–1739) there are receipts and bills. Hertfordshire Archives DE/R/F75/1.

84 Essex Record Office, D/DBa A30-101.

85 London Metropolitan Archives, CLC/313/I/B/032/MS25575/001-5. The cathedral also kept a series of records called Acquittance Books, containing signed receipts that were crossed out when cancelled: CLC/313/I/B/012/MS 25481/003-5; James Campbell, *Building St Paul's* (London, 2007), pp. 45ff.

86 For a discussion of surviving farm accounts in the eighteenth century, see M. E. Turner, J. V. Beckett, and B. Afton, *Farm Production in England 1700–1914* (Oxford, 2001), pp. 25–65, 231.

century.[87] Previously, for example, a labourer cutting wood for a few days might have had to wait until cash was available to be paid for their work, relying on their own credit to purchase food or other necessities in the meantime. But once a properly signed receipt could be accepted as possessing the value of the work done, it could be used by the labourer to pay his baker for bread, who could then use it in payment for something else. There are some examples of tradesmen's invoices being endorsed into specie substitutes by a signature before the 1680s, but very few.[88]

The paper would keep its value until the capital it represented was entered into another account book, whereupon it could be destroyed or taken out of circulation. In this whole system the keeping of accounts was crucial, as explained in Chapter 2. The value of the receipts and vouchers in circulation was created by debiting it from one set of accounts, and eventually adding it to the accounts of some other institution, thus clearing the amount. A voucher would work the same way, except as a promise to pay, as it was a value that would eventually be deducted from the accounts of the promisor. This was exactly the way a bill of exchange was circulated before being discounted, but in the case of these much more informal less valuable pieces of paper the time they remained in circulation could be much longer.

Although account books have not always survived that cover the same time period for which we have surviving receipts, they have done so in enough instances that we can see that each receipted payment or debited bill payment was also itemised in an account book. The fact that these pieces of paper were itemised is clear evidence that they were intended to be currency, since the account book would be a much more definitive and formal source of proof than a rough bit of paper. The clearest example comes from the papers of the estate of the Honour of Clitheroe, where the surviving vouchers are each numbered and listed as disbursements in a corresponding account book from the early 1740s.[89] The vouchers for the Armytage family of Kirklees Hall in Calderdale, Yorkshire also have a series of account books in which many payments by bill and notes of hand are listed.[90]

The way these notes were used can be seen in the following examples. The records of the Armytage family of Kirklees Hall contain bundles of bills surviving from the 1740s onwards each year. In one example,

[87] For examples of some early receipts from Dorset from the 1620s, see Dorset History Centre, DC/SYB/F/1/1/2. They look the same as later receipts.

[88] McCurdy found some payments listed as being by bills in farm accounts, where they seem to have been used as a specie substitute from before 1660. McCurdy, *Social Incidence*, pp. 257, 260.

[89] Lancashire Archives, DDHCL/15/1/3-4, DDHCL/15/2/4.

[90] West Yorkshire Archive Service, Calderdale, KMA/727, 1743–1747.

George Drake sold Armytage some soap from Castile worth 6s. 5d. on 24 January 1745, when this bill of sale was issued. It was then returned on 30 August 1748, stating it was 'received then at the hands of G Ramsden the contents in full', and signed by Drake, thus cancelling the value outstanding, which Drake would have been using as a type of currency in the intervening 3.5 years.[91] But, of course, bills were not always returned by the person to whom they were originally issued as payment. In the same collection there is a bill of John Mason's for the sale of a pair of boy's oiled breeches worth 5s. 6d. on 3 January 1746, which was returned by one Robert Lee on 7 October 1748.[92] Most often the final receipt is in a different hand and different ink. In this, as in all other collections, there are also a good number of bills that consist of work done at various times and added up before being presented and receipted.[93] In such cases the bills would still be folded up into rectangular size, similar to smaller bills.

The examples of bills from the Jervoise estate demonstrate a somewhat different practice. In this collection, the bills were generally written out in a less formal way. Sometimes a bill and its receipted payment would be written out entirely by the same person, as in an example of a bill for medicine by John White, although it is clear that the bill was receipted sometime after it was written out.[94] Others were written out by the worker or tradesman, and then the receipt added in different writing by an estate clerk. Sometimes the payment is stated to be from Thomas Jervoise, and sometimes by Mr Thomas Puckridge, an attorney from Romsey who left a number of personal daybooks and notebooks in the collection of the Norman Court estate.[95] Another receipt, of the carrier Thomas Sylvester for bricks and sand, was very interestingly signed with the mark of his wife, Alice, with the name Thomas crossed out and Alice written instead, and the signature of one other witness (Figure 3.5).[96] Under the rules of coverture, a wife could not contractually assume a debt on her own behalf, but since the bill was only a representation of the original contract, in which the consideration was Thomas' work done, then strictly speaking in this case it was considered more important that the actual recipient of the bill should be listed in order that its

[91] West Yorkshire Archive Service, Calderdale, KMA/732/1.
[92] West Yorkshire Archive Service, KMA/732/1.
[93] Hampshire Archives, 5M50/1054/34, 5M50/1054/38; Lancashire Archives, DDHC/15/2/4, Bill of William Hardman, 30/03/1743; Sheffield City Archives, LD1156/1/3, Bills of John Brown for the Thomas Hollis Charity Hospital, 1730–1731.
[94] Hampshire Archives, 44M69/E7/59.
[95] Hampshire Archives, 5M50/2110-2125. Romsey is about 30 miles from Herriard.
[96] Hampshire Archives, 5M50/1054/40.

1736 Mr Puckridge His Bill for carridge to winchester Castel

For 2 Load of Sand to the Castle 0-10-0

for 6 Hundred of Bricks to the Casel 0-6-0

for 2 thousand of Bricks to the Casel 1-4-0

2: [illegible] 1736 Recd then of Mr Puckridge two pounds in full of the above Bill in full for Work & carriage on Southwick Estate by my Husband thomas 2-0-0

Witness Sylvester Peter Bishop [illegible] the Marke of Alice Sylvester

Figure 3.5 Receipt of Thomas and Alice Sylvester.

authenticity could be traced if needed. However, most bills, receipts, and notes were signed by men or single women. Presumably, though, they could be circulated by women free from the legal constrictions of coverture.

The use of witnesses, especially if someone was signing with a mark, was common, as in the example of William Whitlock for casting dung and other work, which was witnessed by Peter Bishop, who also had his own bills receipted by Puckridge.[97] In the picture of John Marsk's bill (Figure 3.6), we can see that the receipt for the money owed for carting faggots, as well as the location of the work, were written in a different hand, probably at a later date.[98] In these cases, interestingly the bills are stated to be *for* Mr Puckridge, not *by* the tradesman. Here, it is possible that the bills might have circulated before being receipted as evidence of promised payment, but without the writing or signature of the attorney or his clerk they would have been acceptable to fewer people and thus less liquid. It was much more common that they only circulated after receipt.

However, since so few were endorsed, it is impossible to say how many hands they might have gone through before being cashed against an account book.[99] One example of a bill for £7 4s. 6d. signed by

97 Hampshire Archives, 5M50/1054/14, 5M50/1054/17.
98 Hampshire Archives, 5M50/1054/26.
99 Lord Mansfield noted that promissory notes circulated without being endorsed. Melton, *Sir Robert Clayton*, p. 218.

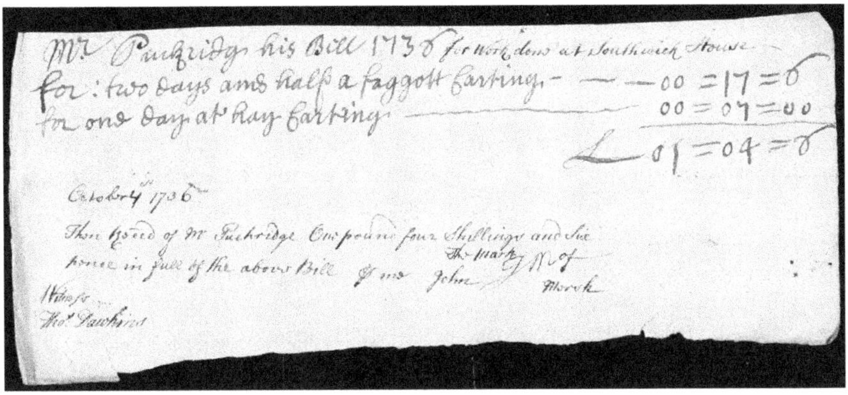
Mr Puckridge his Bill 1736 for work done at Southwick House
for: two days and half a faggott carting — — 00 = 17 = 6
for one day at hay carting 00 = 07 = 00
£ 01 = 04 = 6

Figure 3.6 John Marsk's bill for carriage.

Mr Puckridge for the Jervoise family was used at a later date to pay part of a land tax.[100] The attorney John Howarth of Ripponden near Halifax recorded entering into a promissory note together with William Sutcliffe and Thomas Calverley, made out to one John Preistley and Mr Watson, a curate, for £5 on 30 September 1754, which was not to be repaid until 30 September 1758. In the end it was not credited back into Howarth's account book until 18 March 1760.[101] Thus, it would have been circulating for six years. He also recorded signing a note of indemnity as security, which was given up upon final repayment. Howarth recorded numerous entries into the creditor side of his accounts as being by bills he previously issued for his legal work to individuals whom he promised to pay, with folio references to his bill book where he first recorded them.[102]

The bills and receipts were issued for a wide variety of payments. In Lyme Regis these included 2 lb of candles, coal, cloth, and buttons, twenty-one sacks of lime, the axle for the little brass gun, claret, Rhenish and Malaga wine, land tax payments, clerks' salaries, and labour of various sorts. In a series from a school in Sheffield there were bills receipted for children's clothing, teacher's wages, wine, tobacco, building repairs, mending the scholar's seats, and carrying rubbish.[103] The

100 Hampshire Archives, 5M50/1054/36.

101 M. Miles, 'The Money Market in the Early Industrial Revolution: The Evidence from Two West Riding Attorneys, c.1750–1800', *Business History* 23 (1981), p. 129. West Yorkshire Archive Service, Calderdale, HAS/327, Ledger of John Howarth, f. 80 has a good example of a promissory note being issued from 4 September to 9 October 1762.

102 West Yorkshire Archive Service, Calderdale, HAS/327, f. 137.

103 Sheffield City Archives, LD 1156/1/3.

Clitheroe bills were mostly for building work, including one for sixteen stone of hair for plastering, but there were also bills for wine and tea. In all of these collections, while there are bills and receipts for large amounts for work or goods itemised over longer periods of time, most were intended to replace payments for relatively small sums paid to labourers and other craftsmen. In general it seems the small bills became more common over time.[104] This is not surprising, given that the amount of gold coins was increasing in this period, while the amount of silver was decreasing. Many of these slips of paper would have been used by the poor to purchase necessities.

In twenty-four notes, receipts, and bills from the Lyme Regis collection from 1712 to 1713, 30 per cent are for less than £1, and none is worth more than £10. In twenty-seven notes, receipts, and bills from 1761 to 1762, in comparison, 48 per cent are for less than £1, and only two are for more than £10. In a sample of forty vouchers issued as payment by the school in Sheffield ranging in date from 1728 to 1735, 18 (45 per cent) were worth less than £1 and only seven were worth £10 or more. In eighty-six vouchers from the estate of the Honour of Clitheroe for 1743, 36 per cent were written for sums of less than £1, and 28 per cent were worth between £1 and £2 19s.[105]

It is difficult to know how commonly bills and notes might have been used as a form of credit currency in comparison to oral credit, account book debts, or actual cash. However, by examining some account books, examples of their use can be gleaned. A good source for doing this is the daybooks of the attorney John Plumbe from Waventree Hall, whose cash holdings we examined at the start of this chapter. Some ledgers with daily receipts and disbursements survive from 1697 to 1714, and a series of rough daybooks survive for most years between 1727 and 1757.[106] These were records of transactions that could be written down as they happened, to be entered into a daybook later. They can be used to count the number of times payment was received or made by a bill or note. In 1700, they were used fairly infrequently, usually only 1–3 times per month for a total of 24 out of 373 transactions (6 per cent). By 1729 their usage had increased substantially, to about 20 per cent of transactions.

Interestingly, for these rough daybooks, Plumbe used specially printed pocketbooks called *The British Merlin*. As the title indicates, such publications evolved out of earlier printed almanacs that provided astrological

[104] Hampshire Archives, 5M50/1054/10, 13, 17, 20, 23 are all bills for 7 shillings or less.
[105] Lancashire Archives, DDHC/15/2/4; Sheffield City Archives, LD 1156/1/3; Dorset History Centre, DC/LR/G9/11.
[106] Liverpool Record Office, PLU6, PLU9.

predictions together with practical information such as directions and dates of fairs, law terms, tables of interest, and other things.[107] As astrology became less credible during the course of the eighteenth century, published almanacs were transformed into convenient pocketbooks that contained a variety of advice loosely based on astrology, together with entertaining stories, historical dates, and practical matter. A number of such pocketbooks were also printed specifically for women, of which used examples have survived, including a copy of the *Ladies Complete Pocketbook* in which its female owner recorded delivering some bills in 1771.[108]

The reason why some bills have survived also has to do with accounting practices. It seems most likely they were kept because it was a common practice to keep track of transactions before they were put in a more formal stage of accounting. This could be done in a pocketbook usually called a daybook or waste book, or copies could be made as evidence of issuance. In this way, the accountant would have signed evidence to hand so they could check when entering their transactions into the daybook or cash book, and then to the journal or ledger if these were kept. But they also served a double function, in that they could be kept as a type of counterfoil that was evidence that the bill in circulation was valid. They were kept as a form of protection against fraud. Unlike a Bank of England note, which had elaborately printed counterfoils and numbers that could be checked at the Bank, receipted notes relied on the handwriting and signature of the clerk who issued them as proof of their validity. As we saw in the London examples, it was essentially the handwriting of a clerk trained in penmanship that validated these pieces of paper as currency, as it was this that could be checked most easily, and the recipient of a note could ask who the payer had received it from as a means of establishing trust in it. Although superficially easy to forge, if someone in the same local context attempted to pass a forged note and was discovered, they would ruin their credit immediately. This would be much worse than not paying an oral debt, because it was premeditated fraud, which could be excused by necessity. It would also have been difficult for outside professional fraudsters to gain the knowledge of local

[107] Bernard Capp, *Astrology and the Popular Press: English Almanacs 1500–1800* (London, 1979).

[108] Leeds University Archives, Marriner 184. For more on print and account-keeping, see Natasha Glaisyer, 'Calculating Credibility: Print Culture, Trust and Economic Figures in Early Eighteenth-Century England', *The Economic History Review* 60, no. 4 (2007), pp. 685–711; Brian Maidment, 'Re-arranging the Year: The Almanac, the Day Book and the Year Book as Popular Literary Forms, 1789–1860', in Juliet John and Alice Jenkins (eds.), *Rethinking Victorian Culture* (Basingstoke, 2000), pp. 92–114.

circumstances to write convincing notes and use them before leaving the area. Also, unlike counterfeit coins, they were not something that could be made and sold on to be used. Thus, it is probable that the signed receipts surviving in the archives were kept as a form of proof.

This is corroborated by the fact that in a number of archive collections, there are bound volumes, sometimes actually called bill books, in which the receipt copies are simply written sequentially down each page in exactly the same way as if it had been done on a slip of paper.[109] In the collection of the many bundles of bills in the archives of Lyme Regis, there is a slim volume used for this purpose.[110] In such cases we can imagine the clerk of the estate steward writing in the book as the receipted bills were issued as payment, just as others would have written out individual copies. In some cases there is evidence that the loose bills were kept on a string, just as were the tax receipts in the painting by Bruegel the Younger on the cover of this book, but by the eighteenth century most were not kept this way.[111]

A Provincial Shopkeeper: Thomas Turner

Perhaps the most detailed set of day journals to survive are those of the small shopkeeper Thomas Turner from the parish of East Hoathly in Sussex, dating from 1754 to 1765. These consist of 111 volumes of about 90–100 pages each, covering twelve years from 1754 to 1765. These have become well known in a published format as *Thomas Turner's Diary*.[112] However, as the editor, David Vaisey, noted, in order to make the material manageable over 330,000 words had to be reduced to about 130,000, so most of the financial dealings, his listing of what food he ate, and his evening reading of sermons was left out of the published version, with only some representative passages left in.[113] Thus, the published version retains the many descriptions of his neighbours and their characters, as well as his activity as an overseer of the poor, but this has the unintended consequence of disguising its original purpose as a record of his financial dealings.[114] His entries each day start in the morning, and continue exactly chronologically until the evening. He usually states

[109] West Yorkshire Archive Service, Halifax, John Howard Bill Book, HAS 759.
[110] Dorset History Centre, DC-LR G9/72.
[111] Goldsmiths' notes were also kept this way. Mitchell, 'Pay the Washerwoman', p. 35, n. 7.
[112] David Vaisey (ed.), *The Diary of Thomas Turner* (Oxford, 1985). [113] Ibid., p. vi.
[114] References not included in Vaisey are from the original manuscript of the diary and are referred to by date as *Turner Diary*. Yale University Library, Thomas Turner Papers, Manuscripts and Archives: The Diary of Thomas Turner, 1754–1765.

things happening in the morning, forenoon, afternoon, and evening, and when he is travelling he often writes down times of arrival, sometimes to five-minute intervals, so he must have carried a pocket watch. But, like Samuel Pepys 100 years before him, he also filled the books with reflections on the character and morals of his neighbours, as well as his own behaviour concerning the moral formation of himself. How the development of such reflection was linked to financial dealings will be dealt with in Chapter 6, but here the detailed description of his financial dealings can be used to get a sense of how often he was using bills and notes. Unfortunately, even with this amount of detail, none of Turner's actual account books have survived, and it is clear that he did not use his rough day journals to record most of his shop sales. He often notes that he cast up his daybooks in the evening, which would have been kept in his shop, and anything sold would have been immediately written down there. The day journals do record many purchases from his suppliers, but by no means all of them. Thus, we cannot reconstruct a full picture of Turner's use of different mediums of payment, but since the day journals contain many hundreds of transactions each year we can get a sense of how his financial transactions worked.

The financial information in the diary indicates that Turner's retail trade was small and local, and his profit limited. His wife had to work hop-picking to make extra money, and he continually worried about his financial stability. In August 1756 he fretted about the precariousness of trade in his small country town of East Hoathly and estimated that, while previously his trade had been worth £15–30 per week, it had dropped to £5–10 in 1756. If this weekly estimate was roughly the same over the whole course of the year, this represents average sales of £1,170 in a good year, which at a rate of profit of 10 per cent would have yielded Turner an annual income of about £117. However, in 1756 his sales would only have been £390, providing a profit of £39.[115] In the ten months between October 1757 and July 1758 he recorded using fifty-three inland bills of exchange to pay various wholesale suppliers, mostly in London. In total they were worth £621 or about £15 per week. Given that he also sold some local produce such as wool, this perhaps indicates that 1756 was a bad year.

In the nine months from October 1757 to June 1758 he recorded about 530 transactions on his own account where a monetary value was given (there were a few others on behalf of the parish). He used a variety of different terms to record them. The most common phrases he used

[115] Ibid., pp. 31, 61, 137, 169; Richard Grassby, *The Business Community of Seventeenth-Century England* (Cambridge, 1995), pp. 162, 258.

were 'received from' or 'paid' as in 'received 2 bushels malt 0,,9,,9,,' (meaning £0 9s. 9d.) or 'paid Joseph Fuller 4.5d in full for mutton'.[116] At other times he qualified this to say paid or received 'in cash'. When he was paid with or used a bill of his own, he noted this, as in the following:

Oct 26:
Rec of Mr Patterson on acct of the exec of Henry Pelham, in cash 2,,8,,0 viz
To a bill of nails 0,,16,,6
To the audit bill 1,,11,,6[117]

He also recorded when he used a note of hand. Although he did not distinguish between bills of sale and inland bills of exchange, calling them both simply bills, the use of the latter is always clear as they are always given a sequential number with the person or partnership they were to be drawn on. The term money was also used around fifty times to refer generally to all types of currency.

The number of times he used these terms is compared in Figure 3.7. Here we can see that bills of all sorts were used in 29 per cent of the transactions, while cash was mentioned in 31 per cent, and the ambiguous terms *paid* and *received* in 32 per cent. The remainder were transfers on account. While the use of the terms *bill*, *note*, and *on account* clearly indicate what was being used, the term *cash* unfortunately does not. This is because in the terms of account keeping used in Turner's time, a cash book was a synonymous term for a daybook that documented each financial transaction – all receipts and disbursements, whether cash or credit, were listed together. Entries in the cash book would then have been posted into journals, which were used to balance accounts with different individuals, and could be double-entry. For larger operations than Turner's, the final stage of the accounting process was the general ledger, which provided account information needed to account for assets, liabilities, revenues, and expenses.

Because the daybook was called a cash book, Turner sometimes referred to a payment recorded in the cash book as being by cash. This is clearly stated in this example:

Jan 17

I balanced my cash acct with Mr Collinson there was due to me 20,,11,,8 which was carried to the account of goods I paid him in cash 21,,1,,6 which left more due to him and credited the sum of 10,,0,,0 besides the money due on Mr Sam Virgos account

116 *Turner Diary*, 13 and 29 November 1757.
117 It was Turner's practice to divide pounds, shillings, and pence with two commas.

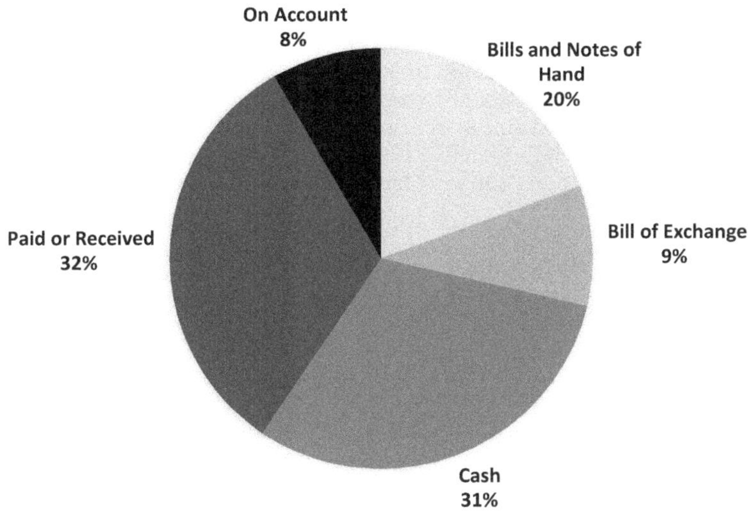

Figure 3.7 Thomas Turner's day journal transactions from October 1757 to June 1758.

I gave him my order after I balanced accts and I paid him in cash 7,,0,,0 which was placed to the credit of my new cash acct.[118]

Quite often Turner simply wrote a series of related transactions out as debits and credits to make them easier to put into his cash book. When he did this, the term cash could be used to mean coins, but it could equally be simply used to note values in the accounts being transferred from one person to another. This can be seen in the following example, in which Turner recorded balancing accounts with his mother in double-entry fashion with debits and credits matching. This involved notes and bills, and he also received £6 3s. 4.5d. in coins from his mother. But, at the same time, he also noted that his mother was a debtor to him for 'cash' and 'money' he had received on his account from Francis Smith and Mr Madgwick, but where no coins were transferred:

Nov 17
I balanced Acct. with my Mother. I Reced of her in Cash £6,,3,,4$^{1/2}$
The Balance on the Other Side Viz
My mother Dr.
My bill of goods 7,,17,,3$^{1/4}$
Paid Beckett the Carriage of a Truss 0,,6,,0

[118] *Turner Diary*, 17 January 1758.

the carriage of wool 1,,0,,0
Paid for 3 pounds of Hop baging and carriage 2,,16,,3
To one years interest on the Bond Val £130 due the 14th Oct. 1757 5,,4,,0
To Cash my Mother Reced of Francis Smith on my Acct 2,,2,,9
To a Ballance left 21st April last 10,,2,,8
To Money paid Mr Madgwick in full on My Mothers Acct 1,,6,,0
But I had of my Mother's in my Hands 6s. for the 4th instant
Total 31,,1,,11.75
Per Contra Cr.
To my Mothers Bill of goods on me 3,,18,,7 1/4
Reced in Cash to Day 6,,3,,4 1/2
To Ballance now remaining 21,,0,,0
Total 31,, 1,, 11 3/4 [119]

There are numerous other instances where cash is simply used to mean an account balance debited or credited.[120] In the period under consideration here he recorded paying out about £196 that he called cash, while receiving only £121.

He obviously also used coins. Sometimes their use is clear, as on 7 November when he borrowed a guinea from the widow Marchant because she did not have enough silver coins to give change for a Spanish doubloon worth 36s., but it is impossible to know how often he used actual metallic currency as opposed to paper or credit.[121] As a shopkeeper, he was in a position to collect money in payment for some of the goods he sold, and we can tell this is the case because he often recorded sending large amounts of coins to Joseph Durrant, a mercer in Lewes, who Turner then instructed to issue a bill of exchange payable to Turner for the same amount, which he used to pay his London suppliers. Turner's dealings in bills of exchange will be considered in more detail below, but he most commonly dealt directly with Messrs Margesson and Collinson, grocers in Southwark, or Sir Joseph Hanke and partners. He wrote out thirty-four bills to be drawn on Margesson and Collinson during the nineten months sampled here, and he did not record sending them any coins. Turner eventually became a collector of the land and window taxes, but not until 1760–1766.[122] Most likely,

[119] *Turner Diary*, 17 November 1757.
[120] *Turner Diary*. On 10 October, £5 was credited to his mother's account to pay for some nails. On 26 October, Turner received of Mr Patterson on account of the executors of Henry Pelham, in cash, 2, 8, 0. On 25 November, he stated 'Cash paid to me for Messrs Margesson and Collinson which was placed to the credit of my mothers acct in full for her wool money see the 17th £10,,0,,0.' Other examples can be found on 19 and 29 December and 12 January.
[121] *Turner Diary*. The example on 11 October is clearly money taken to London.
[122] Vaisey, *The Diary of Thomas Turner*, p. xxii.

Durrant was acting as a local banker, collecting cash from shopkeepers like Turner and redistributing it to others who needed coins to pay workers. The amounts sent were almost always round values, and the different coins sent to make up these values are listed in Table 3.2. It can be seen that 94 per cent of the value was composed of gold coins, most of which were Spanish and Portuguese. Only £10 15s. of silver crowns, shillings, and pence were sent by Turner to make up the round amounts. Turner often complained about the lack of small silver coins, and these amounts strongly suggest that payments involving coins would normally be above 21s., the value of the guinea. He never mentioned using farthings or trade tokens, and pennies were only mentioned when the poor were relieved every 21 December with a penny each under a benefaction, or when playing cards.[123] He also twice used counterfeit coins at face value: paying someone in part 'which with 4d. in bad copper which he allowed' and paying with '2 brass or bad shillings for things'.[124]

Turner mentioned using thirty-seven distinct bills of sale with amounts given during the nine-month period here.[125] The value of these instruments was similar to what has survived in the collections already discussed above. All but two were for values of less than £10, ten for less than £1, and ten for £1–2. Most, unsurprisingly, were for shop goods such as spices or nails, but others were for carriage, work done, and schooling. In contrast, when he noted using notes of hand they were always for larger amounts of money above £5 (only five were below this amount). Many were for the exact sum of £20, and the largest was for £60. Both bills and notes were used in conjunction with cash and/or money of account, as in the following example:

Oct 13

Paid john Cayley in cash 3,,17,,5 and by a bill of goods delivered 26th Aug of 1,,7,,10.5 which together makes the sum of 5,,5,,0 and is in full for the note of hand I gave him 27 sept last in lieu of a draft on Mr Simkin for the same value and which I now tore up.[126]

Quite often bills could be destroyed and an equivalent note of hand created, or vice versa. Where Turner mentions when he issued a note or bill he is taking back, the period of circulation seems to have been about one month.[127]

The diary also gives a very good sense of how and when such bills and notes were written up. Most of the bills he made up and received were

[123] Ibid., pp. 163, 184. [124] *Turner Diary*, 31 January 1759; 9 July 1758.

[125] There are other bills he simply mentioned writing out, and some he mentioned using more than once.

[126] *Turner Diary*, 17 October 1757. [127] *Turner Diary*, 4 December 1757; 4 June 1758.

Table 3.2 *Thomas Turner's cash sent to Joseph Durrant in Lewes*

Date	Amount	Doubloons 36s.	Moidores 27s.	Guineas 21s.	Half-guineas.	Pistoles 18s	Pieces of eight 4s. 6d.	Crowns 5s.	Half-crowns 2.5s.	Shillings	Six pence	Pence
23 January 1758	£17	4	1	3	10					1	25	12
6 April 1758	£40	12	1	16						5		
22 April 1758	£24	4	1	11	2			7.25				
29 May 1758	£26	5	7	8	6		1		11	43	14	
19 June 1758	£28	11		4	1	1			13	31	26	
10 July 1758	£20	3		11	3	1.25				7		
Number		39	10	53	22	2.25	1	7.25	24	87	65	12
Value in £	£155	70.2	13.5	55.65	11.55	2.5	0.25	1.8	2.7	4.35	1.6	0.05

done when he was at home in his shop. Many times he recorded people coming to visit him. There was also a great deal of sociability expected when making and receiving bills, as on 5 December when Turner recorded that he 'received of Mr Sam Gibbs £1,,3,,9 in full. When Mr Gibbs paid me his bill, Mr French and Mr Thomas Fuller was in company with him so that common civility obliged me to ask them to walk.' Quite often the person visiting the house would join the Turners for a meal as well.

He was also constantly sending and receiving various sums from his mother and brother. Most often he recorded his brother coming to his shop in the morning with instructions from his mother, or Turner would send some form of currency for his mother through his brother. But sometimes he walked the four miles to his mother's in Framfield to have dinner and balance accounts. But he also did accounts elsewhere. On 17 January, he was called in the evening to Mrs Virgoe, a widow, where he discovered she wanted him to balance her accounts. He did this, but was then called home to do another set of accounts with Mr Collinson, who had come from London for that purpose. In the morning, both Turner and Collinson walked to Framfield. There they breakfasted with his mother and he paid Collinson some money before the latter left at 10:10 a.m. Turner dined with his mother and came home at 5:10 p.m. When trade was slow he often posted entries in his daybook, and this is also when he usually complained about debts. He very rarely did any business on Sunday, and if so only a little, mostly in the evening.

Turner's diary gives us a sense of how a local shopkeeper used notes in conjunction with different forms of cash, as well as continuing to sell on informal credit to his customers. It also shows, as will be seen below, how this very local circulation of notes was integrated into a larger national system of bills of exchange. Referring back to Figure 3.7, we see that bills of sale and notes were used in at least 20 per cent of his transactions. But, even so, given that over 60 per cent of transactions were simply listed as being for cash paid or received, it seems likely that a lot of his transactions were recorded in his accounts and done on credit without notes. Certainly some of the poorer families he had to chase for their unpaid debts probably did not have enough access to notes to use them in such cases where they were behind on their payments.[128] The diary also shows that gold coins played an important role in local circulation, and although Turner does not explicitly mention directly converting any notes for gold, there seems to have been enough present to do so.

[128] Muldrew, *Economy of Obligation*, p. 181.

What is also evident from Turner's diary is that by the mid-eighteenth century the use of bills of sale and notes was so commonplace that it was not problematic. Turner was a good accountant, and was also in a good position to know whose bills to trust. But it is surprising that he did not mention having any problems, although a study of the full ten years of the diary might reveal some. In order to explore how trust in local bills and notes was created, we need to turn to another even more detailed business/diary from about thirty years earlier – that of John Cannon.

A Local Scrivener: John Cannon

Cannon was a poor Somerset husbandman's son who became an excise man and then a local schoolteacher and scrivener for the less wealthy of the small town of Glastonbury. His ego-document is one of the most comprehensive memoirs we have for the early modern period. In total length it runs to many hundreds of very full pages and cover his life from his birth in 1684 until 1742, ending with no explanation, and there is no evidence of what might have happened to Cannon after this.[129] Although he termed it a 'Memoir' on the title page, this really only applies to the first part of his text until 1735. In January 1737 he began a new fair copy, at which time he decided to only summarise much earlier material before 1635.[130] His description of events is interspersed with local histories, as well as commonplace book entries taken from his voluminous reading on themes such as virtue, riches, the lives of great men and local families, and descriptions of local towns and places.[131] Because of this, the editor John Money has chosen to call it a *Chronicle*, although I will also refer to the daily entries as a diary. Although he was clearly concerned with morality, he was not a puritan. It seems likely, however, that he became more moral as he grew older. He went to church increasingly regularly and took the sermons seriously and

[129] John Money (ed.), *The Chronicles of John Cannon Excise Officer and Writing Master, vols. I–II* (Oxford, 2010). Because of the great length of the manuscript, this edition has had to summarise some of the material. Here, all references to the *Chronicles* are to Cannon's original pagination (provided in the published version) apart from references to Money's introduction, which refer to the published version only. Where quotations are given they have been taken from Money's transcription where available, and from the original manuscript where Money has only been able to provide a summary. The manuscript is in the Somerset Record Office DD/SAS/1193/4: *John Cannon's Chronicles*. John Money, 'Reading John Cannon's Chronicles', in John Money (ed.), *The Chronicles of John Cannon Excise Officer and Writing Master* (Oxford, 2010), pp. cxlv–cxlvi.

[130] Ibid., p. cxxiv.

[131] For a full description of the diary, see, Money, 'Reading John Cannon's Chronicles', pp. cxxiiiff.

expressed guilt at his premarital sex, and some of his gambling.[132] His motivation for writing, however, was not puritan self-examination, but his learning and participation in the expanding world of letters, or public sphere, through his reading. In many ways he was like a much poorer Richard Gough, eager to display his local knowledge combined with a much wider range of assorted learning.[133]

His *Chronicles* are an excellent source to trace the transformation of a very rural credit market far away from the stocks and shares of metropolitan finance, and we will return to them again. Cannon lists over 800 transactions involving bills, notes, bonds, and mortgages, sometimes of great complexity, although only a tiny minority were done for significant amounts of money.[134] Cannon moved to Glastonbury in 1731 – where he spent the rest of his life – and almost all of the mortgages, bills, and notes of hand he wrote up were done after this date for parties within a radius of less than four miles of Glastonbury.[135] He also had some dealings with stationers and booksellers in Wells (six miles away), which was the site of the county court and assizes. But when working out the networks of credit in which Cannon participated and did so much to facilitate, we are only dealing with an area of about four miles radius, containing probably fewer than 1,000 households.

Glastonbury and its surrounding parish were largely agricultural in the early seventeenth century, although the area to the west along the River Brue to the Bristol Channel was the wet, low-lying ground of the Somerset Levels, unsuitable for arable agriculture, which was called moorland at the time and used for pasture. In the town itself there were, as a result, a number of tanners. There was also a mercer, a grocer, butchers, and some clothiers and stocking makers.[136] Bridgewater was the nearest port, 20 miles away. But there is little evidence of much long-distance trade that would have drawn cash into this economy, and the latter seems to have been in short supply.

[132] Cannon, *Chronicles*, pp. 41–7.

[133] Richard Gough, *The History of Myddle*, ed. D. Hey (Harmondsworth, 1981).

[134] I have described Cannon's social background and his writing of notes in detail in Craig Muldrew, 'The Social Acceptance of Paper Credit as Currency in Eighteenth Century England: A Case Study of Glastonbury *c.*1720–1742', in Marcella Lorenzini, Cinzia Lorandini, and D'Maris Coffman (eds.), *Financing in Europe: Evolution, Coexistence and Complementarity of Lending Practices from the Middle Ages to Modern Times* (London, 2018), pp. 133–59. What follows here is a summary of that chapter.

[135] Cannon, *Chronicles*, pp. 196–7.

[136] M. C. Siraut, A. T. Thacker, and E. Williamson, 'Glastonbury: Town', in R. W. Dunning (ed.), *A History of the County of Somerset: Volume IX, Glastonbury and Street, the Victoria County History* (London, 2006), pp. 16–43.

Cannon was born in East Lydford in Somerset, just south of Wells, in 1684. He spent the whole course of his life described in the *Chronicles* in the West Country, apart from one trip to London, finally settling in Glastonbury. West Lydford remained the residence of both his extended family and, after 1732, his wife and children. It was about 10 miles distant, so required an overnight journey, but he still visited often. He began his working life learning husbandry on his father's farm, and he worked as an agricultural labourer before becoming an excise officer, but was dismissed from this position for debts he owed to those he had to assess. He attempted to set himself up as a maltster, but went broke and survived by teaching school, doing accounts, writing letters, and doing small legal work in and around Glastonbury. For most of his life he was poor, despite being very literate. His lame father left him with £200 of debts when he died in 1723, forcing him to sell most of his land.[137] The major reason for his poverty was ironically his love of reading and buying books, which continually drove him into debt despite the fact that he was earning £50 per year as an excise man when he was single. When his wealthy uncle died in 1715, he inherited a close of 4 acres called Butmoor (which was later sold to his cousin Elizabeth Pope for £100), but he soon secretly mortgaged part of it for a loan of £30. He only inherited a house and garden from his father's estate in 1723, where his wife and daughters continued to live when he went to work in Glastonbury.[138] He probably earned £50–90 when he was older from his school teaching, scrivening work, and account keeping.[139]

As John Money has shown, Cannon had to learn proper accounting to be employed as a young man by the Excise, and earned part of his living in later life doing accounts for various people who lacked enough skill. It is striking how much attitudes to learning mathematics and accounting changed during the early eighteenth century. Whereas previously the technique of accounting of all but merchants in England had been poor, and account keeping the exception rather than the rule, the eighteenth century saw a sustained rise in local mathematical schools and increase in the number of practitioners.[140]

[137] Cannon, *Chronicles*, I, plate 8, pp. 28, 44, 155–8.

[138] Ibid., pp. 157–8, 185, 197–8, 215.

[139] Unfortunately, it is impossible from the *Chronicles* to work out how much Cannon was earning and spending because the version that has come down to us is the third transcription that Cannon made from rougher versions. It is clear from an incident while he was working as a bailiff for William Peirs in 1726, when he was asked by Peir's wife to produce his accounts, that they were kept with his journal – which was examined and helped to lead to his dismissal. Ibid., p. 175.

[140] R. V. Wallis and P. J. Wallis, *Index of British Mathematicians, Part III 1701–1800* (Newcastle, 1993), pp. vii–xi; John Money, '"Teaching in the Marketplace", or

In her Cambridge Mphil thesis, Leslie Chang looked at advertisements in eighteenth-century newspapers in the Burney Collection for commercial education and found 1,664 advertisements for 213 distinct institutions through the century.[141] Although the numbers of individuals advertising rose after 1740, there were still a significant number doing so in the early part of the century. The most common topics advertised as being taught were double-entry accounting (called 'the Italian method'), writing, arithmetic, and mathematics. Training in accounting and maths dominated quite significantly. There were 195 references to bookkeeping and 186 to maths, compared to 57 for Latin, 54 for French, 38 for navigation, and 15 for fencing.[142] Additionally, judging by the number of survivals in archives around Britain, there were undoubtedly more smaller farmers, tradesmen, and artisans who kept accounts in the late seventeenth and eighteenth centuries than previously.

Certainly, as already stressed, the institutions of the financial revolution required sound and thorough account keeping. The importance of being a good accountant is clearly demonstrated by Cannon. When he was only twenty-three and just beginning his work for the Excise, he mistakenly entered the symbol for a cask of strong beer instead of small beer, which was taxed at a much higher rate. Instead of redoing his account, he rashly

> took out my penknife and razed out the character 'x' and badly made the character 'vi' in the room thereof which when done, it did not please me. Therefore with my knife I endeavoured to amend it but made it much worse and yet not content still went on to write it and made it still worse and worse … At last I took up a resolution to cover all by burning the same with a coal or candle in such a manner as it might be took for an accident and to make it palpable.

Cannon fretted about what his supervisor would do to him, and tried to maintain his story of an accident, but in the end it was obvious to the supervisor what had been done and he made Cannon promise to him in writing, 'Never, never, never, to be guilty of such practices in future.'[143] Cannon took this advice to heart and by 1730 he reported that he was earning enough from scrivening to help support his family, and by 1736 he could boast about his reputation for honest writing:

"Caesar adsum jam forte: Pompey aderat": The Retailing of Knowledge in Provincial England During the Eighteenth Century', in R. Porter and J. Brewer (eds.), *Consumption and the World of Goods* (London, 1994) pp. 340–3.

[141] Leslie Chang, *Accounting Education and the Use of Double-Entry Bookkeeping by Merchants in Eighteenth-Century England* (Mphil Thesis, Cambridge University, 2016), pp. 34–6.

[142] Ibid., pp. 36–8.

[143] Cannon, *Chronicles*, pp. 83–4.

> Mr. Thomas Nicholls … recommended me to His Honour [Sir Abram Elton] for one of the best accountants they had in those parts; that his care and indefatigable pains by his Method of Bookkeeping and the counterpart from his little book was to satisfy every person who was desirous to know or ask him any question in their town affairs … I declared to His Honour that I never in all my life out of fear or for favour wrote any instrument, deed, bond, bill or accounts for any person hitherto that employed me but what was the true meaning or sense of the parties' agreement.[144]

As we shall see, this reputation for honest writing was crucial to the new system of paper credit, and Cannon's internalised desire for approbation displayed in the above quote is indicative of a new set of ethics eventually validated by Adam Smith.

Cannon's *Chronicles* demonstrates the degree to which the use of informal paper bills had come to supplement oral credit in very local transactions. He mentioned either using or writing out and witnessing over 120 notes of hand and over 250 bills. These are also clearly minimum numbers as they are those he wrote down when he thought a record needed to be kept as a witness. On 3 November 1737, for instance, he recorded that over the course of four days, besides other work, he drew up over 200 bills for the widow Swanton, although he did declare it was the 'most intricate business I ever took in hand'. Unfortunately he does not say how much he charged for drawing a note of hand, but the simplicity would suggest less than a shilling. In contrast, over the whole course of the *Chronicles* he mentioned only about fifteen transactions involving guineas and eleven with shillings. Copper coins or tokens were not mentioned at all, and neither were bills of exchange, even though there were mercers, grocers, and maltsters in the vicinity mentioned in the diary. But perhaps they wrote out their own bills of exchange, which also would have only circulated between other towns such as Wells and Bristol.[145]

It is obvious from reading Cannon's *Chronicles* that the circulation of thousands of such bills was becoming an accepted form of evidence of a transaction that in most cases precluded going to court to establish the nature of an obligation. That they served as a type of local currency is demonstrated by the following examples. On 19 November 1740, Cannon recorded that he 'Received a bill of goods of David Bell, value

[144] Ibid., pp. 188, 239.

[145] The very extensive use of bills of exchange drawn on London and other north-east towns by the wealthy mercer Joseph Symson of Kendal between 1711 and 1720, including 33.9 per cent of local bills with endorsements, has been well documented and discussed by S. D. Smith. *The Letter Book of Joseph Symson of Kendal 1711–1720* (London, 2001), pp. lxvi–lxxii, 787–88.

£3 1s 1/2d for which I gave a note payable the 1st December next and took up and cancelled a former note.'[146] On 10 August 1737, he helped an attorney of Sherborne collect the rent for an inn he owned in Glastonbury, which was paid in the form of '£1 8s 9p in cash and by bills of disbursement onto the said inn in one year £3 1s 3p which is one year's rent for the said inn ending last Michelmas'.[147] On another occasion he noted that it was also important that in some cases the making up of notes were witnessed to bolster their veracity:

> drew a note of hand value £4 4s on demand from Edward Martin to Thomas King, and for further security the said Martin assigned another note value £14 5s given the 21st of April last to William Pearl by John Paget and Mr. George Stibbens, and witnessed William Nicholls only; Witnesses to Martin's note Richard Grinsted and myself.[148]

Having someone like Cannon as a signatory or witness to the making of notes and bills significantly reduced the risk of forgery.

We will never know how many self-trained individuals there were like Cannon around at the time, but his level of education for someone poor must have been fairly rare. However, there would have been an increasing number of clerks working for attorneys, towns, and tradesmen who also had writing and numerical skills, as John Money has argued. Just within 20 miles or so of Glastonbury, Cannon mentioned thirty-three different local attorneys in villages as small as Queen's Camel, Catcutt, and West Lydford, although many are mentioned only a few times.[149] Wells and Shepton Mallet were also places where Cannon had dealings with other attorneys. If all or even some of these individuals performed similar services as Cannon, we can see how local paper credit/currency could have expanded to involve tens of thousands of bills and notes of hand. The attorneys whom Cannon mentioned by far the most were Thomas and William Nicholls, brothers resident in Glastonbury, and much of the work he mentions was done for these two men. Interestingly, his relationship with Thomas seems to have been good, as the latter recommended him to Sir Abraham Elton, a Bristol merchant and local commissioner of sewers who had estates in the levels near Glastonbury. However, although he did more work for William, who remained one of his chief employers throughout the diary, on more than one occasion Cannon complained of his 'treacherous and foul practice in the law'.[150]

146 Ibid., p. 588. Bell was a mercer or tailor. 147 Ibid., p. 301. 148 Ibid., pp. 582–3.
149 Money, *Chronicles*, pp. 699–700 (the index).
150 Cannon, *Chronicles*, p. 557. Cannon also accused him of making up a mortgage 'full of gross blunders and erasures' in 1729 (p. 618).

The remarkable aspect of Cannon's role in writing notes and bills is that he himself was constantly in debt and was sued on a number of occasions. This meant that his credit in terms of reputation for punctual payment was quite bad, and rumours circulated that he haunted alehouses, and, on one occasion, that he kept a stolen coat he had allegedly found on a road.[151] But it seems that people were willing to accept that he could have a good reputation for honest writing that was quite separate from his own spending habits. Cannon had lost his reputation when he went bankrupt after first losing his position at the Excise and then taking on debts trying to become a maltster and then having his father die heavily indebted at the worst time. This meant that his credit was gone, and he was arrested a number of times. He was able to regain his credit through saving, but he never managed to curb his book buying, and this continued to dog him. He did, however, note how important the concept of savings had become by the 1730s:

> had I only saved but six shillings a week, the amount thereof would have risen to a fine sum which laid out in Land would have procured a pretty income for a Support in Old Age. I humbly caution all young people when in profitable places to be careful, frugal and take the example of the industrious Ant or laborious Bee. Treasure up in the summer as they might not want in the winter.[152]

Saving, of course, is a crucial process by which profits, wages, and other earnings are turned into capital.

Once Cannon was able to earn enough from his scrivening and support himself and his family, his debts seem to have mattered less than his skills and trustworthiness to write and witness writing honestly. He went to enormous lengths to create and defend a reputation not as a prudent consumer, but as an honest writer. Previously, local credit was extended orally, and a reputation for thrift and probity were the chief guarantee that someone could be trusted, since overspending built up debts. But once debts began to be written down, trust shifted to the veracity of the writing. Cannon went to great lengths of self-justification both privately and publicly to show why he was more suited than his neighbours to undertake such work and he detailed his many efforts to fashion trust in his accuracy in writing things down and doing proper calculations.[153]

The process by which Cannon had to establish and defend his trustworthiness as a person of 'honest writing' was not easy. He had to defend himself against what he claimed were untruthful accusations of falseness by his quarrelsome and illiterate wealthier neighbours:

[151] Ibid., pp. 259, 673, 682. [152] Ibid., p. 189. [153] Ibid., p. 577.

> [I] found some prejudiced people murmuring against me about my bookkeeping and parish accounts and contradicting some bills which I had drawn for my own labour and several other matters and things to my prejudice.[154]

This can be seen to great effect in the dispute he had with John Roach of Pennard. This dispute concerned a debt on a bill owed to Cannon by Roach's deceased brother-in-law (for whom he was acting as administrator) for some scrivening work and also for a number of prints cut out of a book on the kings of England, which Cannon had sold him to frame for his house.[155] Soon after the death, Cannon had presented Roach with his 'full bill, all the labour and all included, being 2 pounds, 3 shillings and 6 pence'. Roach refused to pay because he had heard from a third party, a Mr Slade, that the debt amounted to 7–8 shillings. However, this was only for the scrivening, which Cannon had mentioned to Slade. Slade proceeded to blame Cannon for not informing him of the full debt, which Cannon claimed 'nettled me as his arraigning my reputation for honesty and Christian virtues to my discredit, who hitherto had passed my life without being the least suspected of any fraud or knavery'.[156] The dispute dragged on without resolution over a year until Roach died and his widow returned the prints to Cannon and agreed to pay his debts.[157] That the dispute arose because he left the transaction open rather than creating a new debt for the remaining prints was a familiar way of doing things in the system of circulating oral credit, but as Cannon found out, was dangerous in a system of writing. He even once recorded a dream he had reflecting his anxiety over his bookkeeping.[158] Thus, reputation remained as important as before, but now it could be focused on specific credit brokers such as Cannon and local attorneys who could profit from their numerical skills combined with honesty.

One other aspect of the circulation of bills in Glastonbury that the Roach example illustrates is the importance of women in local credit networks. Here the affair was finally settled by Roach's widow. Although most of the bills Cannon mentions were done for men, he wrote out bills for over thirty women, including 200 bills for the widow Swanton. Also the main supporter, and sometimes rescuer, of his reputation was his cousin, Elizabeth Pope. As a wealthy widow she maintained the role of a mediator and reconciler between Cannon and others, whereas Cannon was much more self-righteous and unyielding in his relations with others in the community. In the *Chronicles*, she is one of the few people who

[154] Ibid., pp. 289–90, 667.
[155] Ibid., p. 237. This dispute is described in full in Muldrew, 'Social Acceptance'.
[156] Cannon, *Chronicles*, p. 237. [157] Ibid., pp. 237, 260, 263, 266, 277–8.
[158] Ibid., pp. 343–4.

escapes criticism, and it is probably the case that he could not have been as successful as he was in obtaining business without her support.[159]

From the detailed information provided by Cannon, we can see how the continued usage of the bills accustomed people to accepting that they represented a value that could be moved about over short distances between even poorer people such as labourers who received bills for their work. In practice, the organisation of this system simply mirrored what had been developing for some time in the transfer of inland bills of exchange between larger tradesmen. Trust was based on creditworthiness being traced back through the endorsements. Since the last endorser was responsible for meeting the obligation, it was a way of trusting each link in the chain, and in the world of such informal notes and bills it was the local context that made this possible. It was not possible to anonymously receive a bill, as could happen with a note issued by the Bank of England, Bank of Scotland, or any other local private bank. In many ways, such instruments were another exemplar of Mary Poovey's idea of the 'modern fact', based on education and skill, as opposed to what I describe as the culture of reconciliation, where social peace was more important than getting things 'right'.[160] With this move, the veracity of the writing became crucial, and the honesty of the writer paramount. These arrangements required a lot of local knowledge, and it is clear that quite a lot of detailed knowledge of the familial and financial circumstances, as well as land tenure, was needed to keep disputes to a minimum. In many ways, Cannon's *Chronicles* are a compendium of such knowledge. The lynchpins of this system were small scriveners and attorneys, like the poor quarrelsome Cannon, rather than wealthy London bankers.

The Use of Inland Bills of Exchange

As we saw in the first section of this chapter, inland bills of exchange increasingly came to be used as a paper instrument of liquidity, and certainly by 1684 John Scarlet wrote about their use as a normal practice.[161] However, their use was primarily based on long-distance transactions between traders in different towns and London. Thus, what developed was a two-tier system in which notes, small bills, and receipts circulated within local areas, and bills of exchange were used for longer

159 Ibid., p. 450.

160 Mary Poovey, *A History of the Modern Fact: Problems of Knowledge in the Sciences of Wealth and Society* (Chicago, 1998), ch.3.

161 McCurdy, *Social Incidence*, p. 131.

distances. In this system, tradesmen and shopkeepers like Thomas Turner played a crucial role in converting local paper into long-distance paper in the form of bills of exchange.

The rise of the use of bills of exchange within England has been traced by Eric Kerridge.[162] Searching through a great number of documents, he found individual examples going back to the early seventeenth century, but little evidence of any sustained use before the 1660s. Some bills could be found being used by country gentlemen and London goldsmiths in 1615, and in the 1630s some tax collectors paid the money collected into the hands of local clothiers, who had the ability to transfer those sums to London by bill.[163] There is also evidence from the accounts of a partnership of Lancashire cloth merchants of sustained use of bills of exchange in the 1640s. Between 1644 and 1650 they sent 5,119 cloths to London. These were sold for a total of £18,667, much of which seems to have been paid through bills of exchange.[164]

Moving forward in time, an example from the 1660s implies, however, that outside the cloth industry the system of inland exchange was not yet well developed. The letters of the Derbyshire iron manufacturer George Sitwell allow us to glean much more detailed information on the use of bills of exchange. Sitwell was one of the leading figures in the iron industry of the East Midlands in the first half of the seventeenth century, and although he produced his own iron and owned his own forges and woods, he also engaged in the wholesaling of his product both locally and on the London market through the grocer Ralph Francis, who arranged sales with customers in the capital.[165] His letters record only a few problems concerning the organisation of production, and are instead almost entirely concerned with the business of trade: debt collection, marketing, disputes, and litigation.[166] They demonstrate that most of Sitwell's business was done on long-term credit rather than by bill, and over and over they show Sitwell's concern with honesty and his own credit. He once claimed he would do 'any just thinge to keep my credditt'.[167] However, Sitwell did use some bills of exchange drawn on London, but most were drawn on other people in the iron trade. They do not give an indication of connection to a wider pool of inland traders beyond his own business. Many of the bills were written with only a

162 Kerridge, *Trade and Banking*, pp. 45–84. 163 Ibid., pp. 53–5.

164 T. S. Willan, *The Inland Trade: Studies in English Internal Trade in the Sixteenth and Seventeenth Centuries* (Manchester, 1976), pp. 109–13.

165 Philip Riden (ed.), *George Sitwell's Letterbook, 1662–66* (Chesterfield, 1985), p. xviii.

166 Ibid., p. xii.

167 Ibid., p. 59. This is discussed at more length in Muldrew, *Economy of Obligation*, pp. 186–7.

seven-day acceptance period, and some of the letters show it was often difficult to find an acceptor in time. One letter also shows how the arrival of the plague could bring the bill market to a halt. The following two letters give a sense of how such problems affected the bill market:

For Mr Copley

Sir: I have yours of this date wherin was this inclosed bill, which I send you back, for I have none occasion for mony at London, but have some there which would gett returned for my more then ordinary occasions at present for mony here, yf you please to lett your servants looke about they may finde returnes; I must needs have it this weeke or the next at furthest, in which time you may gett returnes: you speake of November and December payments, wherin you are mistaken, for it was all due the first of November noe more but that you must needs help me, in confidence.

February 1°1663

Cosen Franceys

The 10th of September next being this day fortnight John Finch the Ironmonger will be with you, and hath faithfully promised to pay six hundred pounds to you, for Iron which he bought of me; I have contrived it soe that it will be noe trouble to you, but onely to goe into Paules Churchyard to one Mr Joseph Sheldon who lives att the Golden Kay there, and tell him you have an order from me to see soe much paid to him for my Cosen Mr Roger Allestreys use; I intreat you will take a line or two for the receipt of the money when it is paid, and I further intreat you will give John Finch acquittance for so much received for me.[168]

In contrast to the iron industry, an example of a cloth merchant from twenty years later suggests the use of inland bills in the cloth industry was much more common, and thus less challenging. The wool merchant Abraham Bayly of Great Yarmouth recorded many examples from the 1680s in which bills of exchange were issued by his retail customers to pay his wholesale suppliers in London.[169] The clothier Thomas Marsden of Bolton was a putting-out master who then organised the sale of his finished cloth in London. To do this, he maintained a London house with a factor where he sent his finished cloth. From this trade, by the 1680s, he had developed into a discounter in inland bills of exchange and, not coincidentally, was also a collector of taxation in the county of Lancaster, which he returned to London by way of inland bill. In the three years 1685–1688, Marsden's total trade to London was worth £53,741, of which £51,736 was done with bills. He also sent some cash to London hidden in his packs of cloth, but we do not know how much. More significantly, he also acted as a broker for other local traders,

[168] Riden, *Sitwell's Letterbook*, pp. 95, 125. [169] McCurdy, *Social Incidence*, p. 245.

lending to them on return for their bills in London at 1.6 per cent for short-term bills and 0.25 per cent for bills with terms of 4–6 weeks. But the fact that we know of these details from a series of lawsuits shows that even for someone operating on such a scale there were problems getting bills discounted in time. When the dealers he lent to in the north failed to pay on time for bills, he took assignment of their goods at Liverpool or other promissory notes. The lawsuits Marsden was engaged in were the result of a dispute he had with two chapmen in London over their bills that had not been met. It turned out that the factor whom Marsden had been relying on to keep his accounts in London had been negligent in paying and accounting for Marsden's bills.[170]

By 1710 it is clear that the Kendal mercer and clothier Joseph Symson was able to do almost all of his long-distance trading using a very well developed national market for bills of exchange. The evidence for this is his letter book, which contains copies of all of the business letters he sent between 1711 and 1720. These amount to 2,141 – over 200 letters per year. A letter book was a common business practice, and necessary for dealing with a large number of bills of exchange. Such a book contained copies of all the letters and bills of exchange sent out in case any were lost, and also as a record of what bills were sent in case of any challenge. It was as much a part of record keeping as accounts, and indeed Symson's letters make clear that he also kept a full set of waste books, journals, and ledgers, though these have not survived.[171]

He was born in 1650, and his main business was the marketing of Kendal's cotton and linsey-woolsey cloths. Cottons were woollens with a raised nap, usually used for duffle jackets for labourers. Linsey-woolseys were stuffs with a linen warp and a woollen weft. Symson worked by taking orders from clients for specific colours and sorts of cloth and then buying or placing orders with weavers for unfinished cloth and then arranging the dying and finishing himself. His customers included merchants from around the major centres of the north, but the majority were from London. He organised shipments by packhorse all the way by road to London and through Newcastle on returning colliers. During the time period of the letter book, demand generally was greater than supply, so the weavers had considerable power and preferred to produce the finer sort of cloth for more profit.[172] The weavers could also use the situation

[170] This case is described in more detail in Alfred P. Wadsworth and Julia De Lacy Mann, *The Cotton Trade and Industrial Lancashire, 1600–1780* (Manchester, 1965), pp. 83–5, 92–5.

[171] Smith, *Joseph Symson*, p. xxii.

[172] Ibid., pp. 27–8. Letter 86 clearly refers to weavers seeking the highest price for their work through competition between cloth purchasers.

to demand ready money instead of credit when selling their work.[173] In 1711, Symson claimed in one letter that paying ready money was the usual way for purchasing linseys.[174]

In order to keep cash for payment to weavers, almost all of his long-distance business was done using inland bills of exchange, which was by far his greatest preoccupation. Over the course of nine years there were 824 bills listed in his correspondence, worth £16,966. Of these, 72 per cent (representing 81 per cent of their value) were drawn on London.[175] Already in 1711 the letter book reveals Symson writing many bills on days like 30 August, when he wrote out nine. By this time there was a post road to London, but bills could also be sent with the weekly packhorses. What is noticeable about the bills, in comparison to those found in Sitwell's letter book, is the wide range of people involved in the bill market, and the importance of certain merchants who were able to act as bankers. Fully 54.4 per cent of Symson's London bills of exchange were drawn against just eight merchants, although he directed them to be used to pay hundreds of other people in the capital.[176] The system seems to have worked smoothly by this time. Less than 3 per cent of the bills he mentions were not paid or protested, and many of these had to do with the merchant Thomas Bayly, who was in some trouble.[177] Despite these problems, he continued to draw bills against Bayly throughout the nine years the letters cover.[178] Also, although he wrote about a number of bankruptcies that affected him, and other outstanding business debts, he did not mention them being a problem affecting his bills of exchange.

Although almost three-quarters of the bills of exchange were drawn on London, 240 were drawn on other local individuals, and many were used as cash substitutes, as we can see in the following example from 1717:

> Dear Robert, I received both yours of the 15th and 17th with the book about confirmation cost 9d. postage. Mr. Scrimshire wrote to know if the bill I left you on Mr. Hailes for [£] 10.12.00. be paid, of which let me know per first. He promised to pay it the week after I left you. Cousin Joseph Shaw gave me at Liverpool a Virginia bill for £3 drawn by one Frears on Mr. Clement Nicholson of Whitehaven and only 24th instant I received the value vizt. £3. If you can conveniently pay cousin Shaw that sum I desire you to do it on receipt of this and send me his receipt. If you cannot, let me know that I may do it some other way. I have here sent you James Rigg's note for 30 l. Pray get Mr. Gildart to pay it. I have mentioned it [in] my letter to him this post and that the note is in your hand.
>
> Your affectionate father, Joseph Symson[179]

[173] Ibid., pp. 41, 45, 60, 134. [174] Ibid., pp. 500–1, letter 1616. [175] Ibid., p. lxix.
[176] Ibid., pp. lxxi–lxxii. [177] Ibid., see index entry p. 788. [178] Ibid., p. 751.
[179] Ibid., p. 556.

This letter is particularly interesting as it shows a bill from Virginia being used as currency in Westmoreland! It also demonstrates how separate letters were used to provide instructions on the use of bills for security. The average value of these local bills was much lower (£13.40 each), and 34 per cent of them had endorsements, implying that they were circulating as a specie substitute. Also, in a similar fashion to how Thomas Turner sent specie to Joseph Durrant in exchange for bills of exchange forty years later, local Westmoreland attorneys and landowners sent Symson cash in order to remit funds to London by way of a bill of exchange.[180]

In comparison to Symson, Thomas Turner had a much more modest trade with his small shop, although by the time of his diary the bill system had been evolving for forty years. In the ten-month period between October 1757 and July 1758 he issued and received fifty-three inland bills of exchange worth £621, or about £15 per week. He recorded one almost every 7–10 days, but with some very active periods, such as late November or late January. The longest period in which he did not mention a bill of exchange was three weeks, which occurred twice: 2–23 January and 23 April to 15 May. Well over half were drawn for even sums, of which the most common were £10 or £20. The largest was for £46, and the smallest £3 10s.

The other curious thing is that almost all the inland bills of exchange were *drawn on* Margesson and Collinson and others in London to pay his local debts, such as on 26 December 1757, when he sent 'Mr Robert Plummer [a grocer in Lewes] by the post one bill on Messrs Margesson and Collinson 30 days dated today no. 331 val £40,,15,,0 in full … £23,,10,,6 is on my acct and £17,,4,,6 on my mother's', or on 6 March 1758, when he bought a parcel of Manchester goods from Stephen Fletcher of Lewes, and paid 12 shillings in cash and by a bill of exchange drawn on Margesson and Collinson payable to Mr Sam Riding of Manchester within six weeks worth £22. The fact that Turner used bills of exchange and drew on them so often to pay local debts and purchases shows how interwoven the rural Sussex economy was with London trade and capital. All of the bills Turner used to pay for things would eventually have been used to pay for London goods and services, fifty miles away.

Although this system of using inland bills of exchange was dominated by tradesmen like Turner, anyone with a sufficient income and numerical skills could write and use them. Gentry families used them quite

[180] Ibid., pp. lxvii–lxxi.

extensively for remittances to London and there is evidence from attorneys' account books that by the mid-eighteenth century they were also using inland bills. John Howarth was using a lot of London bills for his expenses by 1760.[181] While we will never have any idea of how many inland bills and their accompanying letters might have been sent with carriers, as was done by Joseph Symson, we can get a sense of at least the minimum scale of the national circulation of bills by examining the records of the Post Office.

The Post Office and Business Mail

The history of the development of the early modern Post Office in Britain has been dominated by its role as a means of expediting government correspondence and disseminating laws and decrees. It has also been studied as a conduit for the private correspondence of individuals through letter writing. Susan Whyman has demonstrated the extent to which both personal and business letter writing developed in tandem with the regularity of daily postal delivery.[182] Investigation of the Post Office's role in facilitating business has been less prominent, which is curious because it stands to reason that such correspondence formed the bulk of its private business. Certainly, as more and more middling sort families became literate they might have wanted to write to each other for information or to their children if they moved away to a different town. But in the late seventeenth century the ability to write a whole letter was quite limited; below the level of the gentry and merchants – who were almost all able to write – it was most prominent among the business community. David Cressy found that by the 1690s, 70–80 per cent of tradesmen and craftsmen could sign their name in Norfolk, Suffolk, and London, while about 60 per cent of weavers and tailors were able to do so in rural England. Yeomen farmers had similar rates of writing literacy, but among husbandmen only 20 per cent signed their name in the documents he studied.[183] As many historians of literacy have noted, while the ability to read was probably quite widespread by this time, most writing was confined to business, commercial farming, and government.

[181] West Yorkshire Archive Service, Calderdale, HAS/327 Ledger of John Howarth; Liverpool Record Office, 920 PLU 6, Account Book of John Plumbe.

[182] Susan E. Whyman, *The Pen and the People: English Letter Writers 1660–1800* (Oxford, 2009), pp. 46–71.

[183] David Cressy, *Literacy and the Social Order: Reading and Writing in Tudor and Stuart England* (Cambridge, 1980), pp. 146–63.

As most writing manuals of the time indicate, by far the most important reason for learning to write was for the business of buying and selling goods over longer distances. The communication of central government laws and orders, as well as local representation to Westminster, were important, but government remained quite small in England.[184] There might have been about 800 justices of the peace by the late seventeenth century and 32 sheriffs, but there were tens of thousands of local tradesmen and merchants wholesaling and buying a huge range of both home-produced and imported goods, as well as even more yeomen farmers selling their produce. Already in the late sixteenth century this trade was growing impressively, and probably involved hundreds of thousands of transactions each year. At that time, most inland trade, without the development of the bill system, had to rely on either cash or the personal cancelling of book debts.[185] With the development of the inland bill all of this could be done by letter and enclosed inland bill.

Postal services in England developed later than on the continent. Although there had been attempts in the late sixteenth century to establish private letter-carrying services, they were suppressed because of government concerns with censorship. Finally, in 1635 a 'letter office' for public use was established in London as a government service. As long as it was controlled by the government, letters could be opened and checked by officials for any seditious material, but the actual running of the service was farmed out. Private letters could still be sent with carriers or drovers, but no other private individuals were allowed to specifically carry letters as a delivery service.[186]

After the Restoration, the Stuart monarchy continued the development of the Post Office as a Royal Monopoly. Up until the mid 1670s most of the service continued to be farmed out for set fees, which were paid to the Crown. In 1663, Charles assigned all of the 'rents, issues and profits' of the Post Office to his brother James, who eventually made himself postmaster general in 1677.[187] From this point on, the profits of the service were used as a source of patronage and given out as pensions to royal favourites. Despite this fairly direct royal oversight, the actual financial and bureaucratic organisation of the service was left alone and allowed to operate independently as a government department. The postal charges set up by Cromwell during the English Republic were

[184] The State Papers Domestic give a sense of the volume of such communication.
[185] Muldrew, *Economy of Obligation*, pp. 60–94.
[186] Whyman, *Pen and People*, pp. 48–50; Duncan Campbell-Smith, *Masters of the Post: The Authorized History of the Royal Mail* (London, 2011), pp. 11–30.
[187] Campbell-Smith, '*Masters of the Post*', p. 39.

retained throughout the Restoration and specific salaries for all employees – including clerks, letter carriers, accountants, and postmasters – were established and paid quarterly.[188]

The service operated from a central space called the Letter Office, located on Threadneedle Street in London. The building accommodated sixty clerks, many of whom had beds there. Letters were taken in at 'The Window' and were stamped with the date of discharge. They were sorted into bags and sent off with their riders for dispatch by 2 a.m. The Western and Bristol Roads were the first to develop a regular daily postal service, and by 1756 there was a daily service by individual horse riders carrying the post in leather bags along roads connecting even quite small provincial towns all over England.[189] The Letter Office, along with most of the service's early records were destroyed in the Great Fire of 1666, and the Letter Office had to make do with temporary accommodations in Bishopsgate until 1678, when they moved into the impressively large former home of Sir Robert Viner, the goldsmith banker on Lombard Street. By then the central office consisted of 75 clerks and porters and 182 deputy postmasters working in locations throughout England, who took in mail from outside of London, and 63 clerks and postmasters working in Ireland.[190]

It is from this date that an almost complete set of very detailed accounts have survived. The sources of income came from payments received from inland letters: window money (postage due on letters handed in by the public to the clerk behind the window of a post office), local postmasters, and letter receivers. Expenditure consisted mainly of payments for salaries of postmasters, letter carriers, sorters, window men, clerks of the roads and of the inland and foreign offices, inspectors, watchmen, and other employees, but also included the costs of letters sent abroad, returned letters, furnishings and equipment, travelling expenses, and other things. The net balance of cash after this accounting was then transferred to the Exchequer, which looked after the payment to the various pensioners of the Crown.[191] The accounts were kept using the charge/discharge system of accounting favoured by the government at this time, just as the accounts of St. Paul's were. These can be easily used to determine the amount of money earned from the fees for postage since both sets of accounts state gross revenues broken down by categories of inland and foreign letters and then a list of all revenues received by each of the local postmasters around the country and in Dublin and Edinburgh.

[188] Ibid., pp. 38–9. [189] Ibid., pp. 56–7, 87–105. [190] Ibid., pp. 49–50.
[191] Catalogue of the Post Office Archives Post 2 and Post 3.

Table 3.3 *Postage rates (d.)*[192]

	1657		1711	
	One page	Two pages	One page	Two pages
Within eighty miles of London	2	4	3	6
Over eighty miles from London	3	6	4	8
Scotland	4	8	6	12
Ireland	6	10	6	12

Since the schedule of fees for sending letters was relatively simple, it is possible to use these revenues to make a range of estimates of how many letters were sent by post. The rates only changed once in our period, in 1711, and are given in Table 3.3.

Given that all of the towns where local postmasters were located are given in the accounts, it would be possible to work out exactly how many were more than eighty miles from London and divide the receipts by counting each separately. But since I am only using approximate amounts here, a simpler way is to use E. A Wrigley's county population estimates for the counties within about eighty miles of London. This accounts for 26 per cent of England's population, while London accounted for another 10 per cent.[193] Since letters sent within London were covered by the penny post, which was accounted separately, this means we can estimate that 74 per cent of the letters sent inland cost 3d. or 6d. each, and 26 per cent cost 2d. or 4d. each. For Scotland and Ireland it is possible to use the actual revenues figures, which are quite easy to extract from the accounts. Unfortunately there are no accounts that distinguish between one- or two-page letters, but almost all of those business letters that have survived in copy books such as that of Joseph Symson, and certainly inland bills, were only one page. Even family letters that contained more information, such as those between the members of the Yorkshire gentry Chaytor family – the husband of which was imprisoned in the Fleet in London for family debts for many years – were able to fit a large amount on one page.[194] Given this, I have

192 Campbell-Smith, *Masters of the Post*, pp. 45, 60, 65; A. D. Smith, *The Development of Rates of Postage: An Historical and Analytical Study* (Salt Lake City, 2010; original 1917), pp. 9–18.

193 E. A. Wrigley, 'Rickman Revisited: The Population Growth Rates of English Counties in the Early Modern Period', *The Economic History Review* 62, no. 3 (2009), p. 721.

194 M. Y. Ashcroft (ed.), *The Papers of Sir William Chaytor of Croft 1639–1721* (Northallerton, 1984); North Yorkshire Record Office, ZQH 9/3/3, 9/5/42, 9/10/9, 9/17/70.

estimated that 15 per cent of letters were two pages and 85 per cent were one page.

It is also important to note that these figures are only for mail going to and from London. This was because before the mid 1690s the Treasury insisted that local letters sent by the postmasters be routed through London on request of government spymasters who wanted to read letters for possible subversion. This meant that someone who wanted to send a letter from Exeter or Plymouth to Bristol would officially have to pay postage twice, and the letter would take much longer. As a result, very few people would have used the post for what came to be called 'cross posting' between country towns. Since it was illegal to set up official posts, this resulted in a large black market in cross posts in the 1680s, together with the use of private servants and carriers. Since this represented a large potential loss of revenue, the issue was resolved by farming out all of the cross posts after 1695, which was legal and allowed official cross postage between country towns.[195] Almost all of the cross posts were eventually taken over by the famous Ralph Allen of Bath, who turned it into a highly successful business that he controlled until the 1740s.[196] In 1695 the farmers were paid £5,255, and Allen's farm was set at £6,000, which remained the same throughout his tenure.[197] The cost of letters was 2d. and 4d., which would account for 660,000 letters per year, but since the profits to the farmers are unknown, the figure would certainly be much higher and would undoubtedly have grown through the period. Thus, I have not included cross posts in my calculations.

The figures provided in Table 3.4 for the total number of letters sent are based on the different rates of postage given in Table 3.3 using the one- and two-page estimates of 85 and 15 per cent, respectively. As we can see, already in 1678 probably close to four million letters were being sent to and from London in England every year.[198] In the next decade this grew quite dramatically by 67 per cent, to almost seven million, which by 1720 had increased again to nine million.[199] Certainly any numbers in the millions seem significant for the early modern period, but these are difficult to judge as there is no equivalent work to make a comparison. Also, we have no way of knowing what percentage of correspondence consisted of business correspondence as opposed to personal letters, but even if, say, 20 per cent were personal letters, the

195 Campbell-Smith, *Masters of the Post*, pp. 64–5.
196 Ibid., pp. 66–72.
197 Post Office Archive, Post 2/1, Post 3/3.
198 Note that the figures have been examined for the intervening years and do not show any major fluctuations. These are representative.
199 Campbell-Smith, *Masters of the Post*, p. 51.

Table 3.4 *Estimate of the numbers of letters sent inland to and from London between 1678 and 1730*[a]

Year	Total inland letter revenue	Number of letters over eighty miles	Number of letters under eighty miles	Total letters sent in England via London	Letters to Scotland	Letters to Ireland	Letters per day
1678	£44,408	2,431,793	1,281,621	3,713,360	£500 27,750	£1,895 71,252	11,902
1689–1690	£74,017	4,053,171	2,136,131	6,189,302	£976 54,168	£4,706 176,946	19,838
1694–1695	£83,538	4,574,541	2,410,907	6,985,448	£2,832 157,176	£5,395 202,852	22,239
1699–1700	£84,947	4,651,698	2,451,570	7,103,268	£4,909 272,450	£7,813 293,769	22,737
1720–1721	£151691	6,229,949	2,918,535	9,148,484	£3,764 208,902	£18,733 704,361	29,322
1729–1730	£163,056	6,696,710	3,137,197	9,833,907	£4,938 274,059	£17,637 663,151	31,519

[a] Post Office Archive, Post 2/1, Post 3/3, 7, 9. The accounting years used are March to March.

Table 3.5 *Hits for letter/occupation search combinations in the National Archives Discovery Catalogue, 1650–1750*[200]

Gentry	110
Yeoman	667
Lawyers	374
Business	4,460

business correspondence would still be very great. We also need to realise that not all business letters contained bills, but almost half (47 per cent) of Symson's 2,141 letters concerned inland bills. A very crude search of the national catalogue collections in the various archives of the UK, which list letters by occupation, gives the following results shown in Table 3.5, of which business letters account for 80 per cent of hits.

Dividing the yearly figures in Table 3.4 by a six-day business week, we get about 12,000 letters sent each day in 1678, rising to over 30,000 by 1730. As we saw earlier, most business correspondence concerned inland bills of exchange, and as advice manuals advocated, it was normal to send a separate letter in the post at the same time as the bill of exchange, describing it as a form of added security. It is possible that about half of business correspondence consisted of bills and notes.[201] To put this in some kind of context, Richard Grassby, in his book on the business community in seventeenth-century England, has estimated that by the end of the century there were about 2,000 large-scale traders in provincial towns who might have been involved in long-distance trade, together with about 8,350 in London.[202] By this estimate, even if we subtract as much as 20 per cent for private correspondence, they would have been sending an average of 2.7 letters per day. This obviously implies that more smaller traders were also sending letters. Joseph Symson often sent more than one letter on a single day, but over the course of a year generally sent less than 312, and averaged 232 per year over the period 1711–1719.[203] Symson, of course, sent most of his

[200] This search did not distinguish between hits that produced a single letter or collections of letters, as archives catalogue letters differently, and some hits are about government 'business' or 'letters patent', but such problems occur in all four search categories, and only visual examination of each of the over 5,000 hits could eliminate them.

[201] Daniel Defoe, *The Complete English Tradesman* (London, 1745), reprinted by Burt Franklin (New York, 1970), vol. I, pp. 11–18, 277–90, vol. II, pp. 58–63.

[202] Grassby, *Business Community*, p. 248.

[203] Smith, *The Letter Book of Joseph Symson*, pp. xlv–xlvi.

correspondence not by the post but by carriers, so we must remember this is a minimum figure for correspondence. Along routes where there were goods being moved by road, as with the cloth produced in Kendal or cattle being driven from Scotland down through the fens to London, a great many letters would have been sent by this method.[204] Of course it would have been slower than by horse rider, but probably cheaper. Certainly Symson found it convenient, since none of his wares could move faster. Also, as the eighteenth century progressed, more and more private stage coach services with regular trips were established. In addition to this figure, we should not forget that there were also many hundreds of thousands of letters being sent within London each year through ticket porters and the penny post. The latter was a service set up by the Post Office in the 1680s whereby for a penny a letter could be given in at the Post Office and delivered the same day within metropolitan London.[205]

What these Post Office figures demonstrate is that England was a very integrated financial market area by 1678. Further, although this was the first year for which complete accounts survive, there are cash books from 1672, and although these are more difficult to extract figures from, there are some that suggest the volume of business was as high in 1674 as in 1678.[206] Further, as we can see in columns six and seven in Table 3.4, the integration of Ireland and Scotland into these market networks grew even more rapidly during this period. There was constant and voluminous communication, and the majority was sent back and forth between London and the provinces.

As Kerridge argued, the inland bill system developed as one centred on a national discounting service based in London, which is further evidence that the post was primarily used to develop a national bill-clearing financial system of the sort Joseph Symson and Thomas Turner were engaged in. Furthermore, the postal service was one almost exclusively consisting of letters carried in leather satchels and bags on horseback, often by boys. Thus it was not convenient for sending payment by coins. Any payment in cash had to be sent by carrier. Payments done by the post would have had to be by inland bills primarily, together with Bank of England notes and private notes and bills. The case of Thomas Hassell, who was indicted for stealing a Bank of England note of £50 in 1730 from the Post Office also shows the efforts both the Bank

[204] Campbell-Smith, *Masters of the Post*, p. 59.
[205] Ibid., pp. 59–61. In the 1690s, the revenue of the penny post was about £1,000 per year, equating to 244,000 letters. Post Office Archive, Post 2/1.
[206] Post Office Archives, Post 94/3, p. 192.

and Post Office made to ensure the safety of their notes through the keeping of records of when and where the notes were cashed or sent by post according to their numbers.[207]

But robbery of the post boys was a constant threat, with 10–50 thefts reported in the *London Gazette* each year in the early eighteenth century.[208] The primary motivation for these thefts was to obtain bank notes and other bills that could be cashed before the loss was publicised. The fact that the Post Office offered rewards of up to £200 is indicative of the financial value of the mail. Eventually, although not until 1782, the Post Office gave advice that people should send one half of each bill in a separate mail as insurance against theft.[209] John Cannon described a robbery of the Western mail post boy, with bags intended for over twenty towns – including Axminster, Taunton, Bridport, Exeter, Totness, Barnstable, and Bodmin – by an armed highwayman between Sherborne and Crewkerne in April 1739:

> he broke open the Western Bags and took out what bank bills, accepted bills and notes of hand he could find which he took with him and made back to Salcomb near Kingsbridge, where he agreed with a master of a sloop to carry him to St. Malo in France for eight guineas. He lodged a bank note of £20 in the master's hand for payment of the same and set sail on Wednesday last but were forced back to Dartmouth by contrary winds, when endeavouring to change the said bank notes which was endorsed by one Follet of Topsham and sent in the same mail for London gave some suspicion (which he suspected) ... The notes and bills he took amounted to near £7,000 which he left with the justice except the £20 bank note.[210]

This is the only reference I have found with any indication of how much a robbery was worth. However, if a single post boy was carrying £7,000 worth of currency on one journey, out of the hundreds taking place each day by this time, there must have been hundreds of thousands – or even millions – of pounds worth in circulation on any given day.

This evidence from the Post Office convincingly demonstrates how rapidly England developed a system of circulating paper currency. Already by the 1690s huge numbers of letters were being sent through the post, and although these numbers would continue to rise until 1730, they did so only gradually by 60 per cent in 40 years. In contrast, the samples of estate and town issuances of paper notes in Figures 3.2 and 3.3 show a slightly later rise of paper in these localities. But it is possible

[207] PBO, October 1730, trial of Thomas Hassel (t17301016-1).
[208] D. G. Haslam and C. Morton, *Post Office Notices Extracted from the London Gazette 1660–1800* (London, 1989).
[209] Campbell-Smith, *Masters of the Post*, pp. 87–8.
[210] Cannon, *Chronicles*, pp. 469, 479.

that businesses and traders adopted the use of small notes earlier. We might not be able to measure local issuance and circulation of small receipts, bills, and notes, but given that provincial traders were issuing so many bills of exchange, it stands to reason that local paper credit must have been equally prodigious to support the trade in inland bills. Certainly some institutional paper such as Exchequer Bills and Bank of England notes found their way into local circulation, but all of the sources consulted in this chapter suggest they played a minor role outside of London.

Conclusion

Significantly, the rise of paper credit described in this chapter was not based on the development of institutions that we might recognise as banks, but on a system of private reissuing of various forms of short-term instruments of credit. Although private bankers certainly existed in London in this period, such as Hoare's and Clayton's banks, and issued many small notes, they did not develop into key players in the market in inland bills on London. Their business remained one of lending to the landed elites as well as facilitating transfers of their estate earnings to London when they took up residence there.[211] Instead, this was done by tradesmen such as Margesson and Collinson, the grocers Turner dealt with. Why did England develop along this path rather than using professional bankers to discount bills, as occurred in France (see 'France' in Chapter 9)? One factor that was undoubtedly important was the division between the law of real property and contractual law in the English legal system. Bankers like Clayton focused on mortgage lending rather than evaluating trust in exchange networks, which tradesmen had always done, and continued to do with inland bills. But, at a local level both areas of law came together and complemented each other. Changes in the land law permitted more mortgaging to take place, and it was this that played a crucial role in providing the initial security for local notes and bills, together with the savings of tradesmen and shopkeepers.

[211] Peter Temin and Hans-Joachim Voth, *Prometheus Shackled: Goldsmith Banks and England's Financial Revolution after 1700* (New York, 2012). Temin and Voth argue that this pattern resulted in a banking system that primarily focused on such lending as well as investment in ever-growing government debt. The argument here is that this could be done through different, more local means, which Patricia Hudson has argued was the way in which the West Riding wool textile industry was financed after 1750. Patricia Hudson, *Genesis of Industrial Capital: A Study of the West Riding Wool Textile Industry c. 1750–1850* (Cambridge, 1986), pp. 209–34.

With the backing of such security it was possible to issue paper notes that had what was probably an almost universal social depth. Although we can never know for sure, the examples we have show they were used to pay manual labourers for a great range of jobs – such as one for 1s. 8d. to Thomas Ferry to mend a channel in Lyme Regis – as much as they were used by customers in Thomas Turner's shop and also by him to pay for other things. They were also used by women such as Betty Pope and Alice Sylvester, or Brigit Buck, who sold alcohol to the Lyme Regis magistrates.[212] But although they could be used by all, they could only be issued by those with sufficient wealth and collateral to make them trustworthy, which is the key social change in the transformation from personal credit to the use of circulating capital. However, those with wealth needed to secure it as a form of capital that people could trust to *keep its value* for as long as their notes were circulating. To do this they used mortgages and bonds, which will now be discussed.

[212] Dorset Record Office, DC-LR: G9/11, 61.

4 Little Land Banks: The Mortgaging Revolution and Savings on Bond

In Chapter 2 we saw how the greatest number of proposals in pamphlets for new ways of creating credit currency involved some type of land bank. All of these proposals advocated using the value of land to provide secure banking in order to create paper money. We also saw that none of these many proposals were successful. Convertibility to gold proved a much more flexible means of backing up the value of paper currency than land registered with a bank. This was because collecting the rents, upon which the security rested, occurred only four times a year at most. But land, because its value rarely decreased over time and it was immobile, was perhaps the oldest form of capital upon which income could be earned by renting it out. Because of this, the basic concept of using its value to support the creation of credit currency was sound; it was only the proposal to link it to centralised institutions that was faulty. This chapter will demonstrate how changes in the land law created a surge in mortgaging at roughly the same time as the debates over land banks were taking place in the 1680s and 1690s. Thus, what happened was that much of the paper currency described in the last chapter was created locally by landowners through borrowing on the value of their land.

Everywhere in Europe, capital in the form of land was ubiquitous in the countryside, but it was bound up with the family and was strictly governed by rules of marriage and inheritance. Since remarriage was common due to death, the rights to rental income and who had the right to use it – and for what purpose – were complicated and often disputed. In setting up a nuclear household upon marriage, women brought dowries to add to whatever estate the husband's parents had provided for him in land, goods, or employment, or if poor what he had earned before marriage (usually after the age of twenty-five in most places). This served as a form of capital primarily intended to provide a source of value that could be accessed to set up a household to start having children.

In poorer households this was necessary to cover the costs of young children before they were old enough to work for themselves. In wealthier households the dowry became a source of capital to invest in either a trade or in buying more agricultural land to increase the wealth and power of a family. In terms of inheritance, such capital was primarily secured by legal regulations and enforced in the courts. However, in England it had long been the practice to dispose of movable goods by will, but during the sixteenth century Parliament passed a number of statutes encouraging people to settle the transfer of landed property by will as well, rather than relying solely on the custom of the manor.[1] As a result of this there was more freedom to concentrate bequests of land on the eldest son, or even in some cases on the most economically competent male heir.

However, wives' and daughters' legacies still needed to be secured. In most continental Roman law jurisdictions, the property the wife brought into the marriage remained hers throughout the marriage to bequeath according to the local inheritance rules. However, in England women became *feme covert* under the English rules of coverture. This meant that as a wife she had no legal personality, which was assumed to have been given to her husband upon marriage. Thus, in theory, she could not own property of her own. Customarily, in order to preserve her right to some maintenance and that of her daughters if the husband died, this was done through dower or freebench (also called the widow's third), which preserved one-third of the estate for a wife upon the husband's death. But in the early modern period, a broad range of wealthier middling sort, gentry, and elite families had lawyers develop extremely complex legal devices such as uses and trusts to protect women's property from the husband's power for the duration of the marriage so that they could be bequeathed to siblings and relatives of the wife's choice.[2] Amy Erickson has argued, in a very important article, that the value of such devices constituted the most important form of financial capital in the seventeenth century. Most of these legal devices were written in such a way as to provide annuities or rent charges as support for female descendants. Even if they were not very liquid, they were a means of turning the value of land into long-term investments.[3]

1 Tom Arkell, 'The Probate Process', in Tom Arkell, Nesta Evans, and Nigel Goose (eds.), *Until Death do us Part: Understanding and Interpreting the Probate Records of Early Modern England* (Oxford, 2000), pp. 3–37; Amy Louise Erickson, *Women and Property* (London, 1993), pp. 24–5.

2 Susan Staves, *Married Women's Separate Property in England, 1660–1833* (Cambridge, MA, 1990), pp. 56–130; Barbara Todd, 'Freebench and Free Enterprise: Widows and Their Property in Two Berkshire Villages', in John Chartres and David Hey (eds.), *English Rural Society 1500–1800: Essays in Honour of Joan Thirsk* (Cambridge, 1990), pp. 196–200; Erickson, *Women and Property*, pp. 102–28; D. E. C. Yale, *Lord Nottingham's Chancery Cases* (London, 1957), introduction.

3 Amy Louise Erickson, 'Coverture and Capitalism', *History Workshop Journal* 59, no. 1 (2005), pp. 3–8, 13.

But such devices were hugely expensive, cumbersome, and unsuitable for creating circulating capital. In order to do this, a more flexible form of raising capital was needed, which was done through mortgaging. To achieve this, the rights of primogeniture or partible inheritance, or the widow's third, needed to be balanced against a creditor's right to foreclose on an unpaid loan and claim either property or rent on land that another member of a family might consider theirs by right in the future.[4] In this way mortgaging allowed profits made by a mercer selling cloth to be lent on interest of around 5 per cent to a landowner on security of his land, who could then use this new capital to hire more labour to improve the quality of his soil. He could also use the capital to create paper receipts to pay his workers, who could use them to pay their debts more reliably, thus increasing the profits of bakers and butchers, who might then buy an extra suit of clothes. In this way the liquidity boost to consumption and production advocated by the pamphleteers following the Hartlib school was achieved.

In continental western Europe, the institutionalised practice of mortgaging was already common in the medieval period using remarkably similar legal forms derived from Roman law principles. These practices were designed to provide capital for the borrower and income for the lender. Roman law allowed different forms of mortgaging with varying degrees of security for the creditor and debtor. Under *Mancipatio cum fiducia*, the creditor was provided with very strong security as it granted them both possession and ownership of the land until the debtor made repayment of the principal. A less stringent form of *fiducia* gave the creditor ownership of the land until payment, but allowed the debtor to remain in occupation of it. Under the rules of *hypotheca*, the debtor retained the most security in their property, giving the creditor only an ability to collect repayment from the rent or produce of the land.[5] In general, the history of mortgaging in the Middle Ages was a movement over time from the prevalence of creditor-friendly mortgages to the prevalence of *hypotheca*-type mortgages.[6]

This happened because, while security was important for the creditor, what was much more important in freeing up the capital value of farmland was protection of the borrower from losing title to the land.

4 Christopher Brooks, 'The Agrarian Problem in Revolutionary England', in Jane Whittle (ed.), *Landlords and Tenants in Britain, 1440–1660* (Woodbridge, 2013), pp. 185–6; L. R. Poos and Lloyd Bonfield (eds.), *Select Cases in Manorial Courts 1250–1550: Property and Family Law* (London, 1998), pp. clix–clxvii.

5 Chris Briggs and C. J. Zuijderduijn (eds.), *Land and Credit: Mortgages in the Medieval and Early Modern European Countryside* (London, 2018), pp. 4–6.

6 Ibid, p. 6.

In essence, what allowed the mortgage market to work in these areas of Europe was not the security of property for the creditor, but for the debtor, which crucially allowed the mortgage to be taken out with much less pressure on the familial rights of inheritance. The key to this happening was a myriad of different forms of achieving the same thing, which was the creation of interest-bearing long-term repayments that were less than the rental value of the land. As long as these obligations could legally be passed on with an inheritance of the property, creditors were satisfied with their security and commercialisation could proceed. Land could thus remain as a primary element of familial continuity *and* release its 'capital' value.

A great deal of work has been done on the system of property rights and the precocious economic growth found in the late medieval Low Countries. This work argues that the legal security of using property was key to freeing up capital so that it could be invested with more confidence in agricultural improvement or industrial development.[7] However, while the institutional security and predictability of the procedure for both mortgagors and mortgagees offered by local courts could certainly be used to provide capital for economic investment, the same legal system could equally be used to provide borrowing primarily used to meet expenditure on recurring demands such as marriage, death, and land amalgamation, and for other reasons unrelated to growth.[8]

Development of the Equity of Redemption

In England the use of mortgages to raise capital happened much later because it followed a different path of legal development to adoption of Roman law principles. Mortgaging remained much rarer in the Middle Ages. England's common law system developed in such a way that the laws of property tenure and inheritance remained separate from the common law of contract, which was not the case with Roman law principles. In England, both lawsuits of debt (restitution of movable property) and contract (tort, a breach of trust) were covered by a different set of laws than the customs of each manor, which governed the

[7] Jaco Zuijderduijn, 'The Other Fundamental Problem of Exchange: Mortgages, Defaults and Debtor Protection in Sixteenth-Century Holland', in Chris Briggs and C. J. Zuijderduijn (eds.), *Land and Credit: Mortgages in the Medieval and Early Modern European Countryside* (London, 2018) p. 283.

[8] Eline Van Onacker, 'Proactive Peasants? The Role of Annuities in a Late Medieval Communal Society – The Campine Area, Low Countries', in Chris Briggs and C. J. Zuijderduijn (eds.), *Land and Credit: Mortgages in the Medieval and Early Modern European Countryside* (London, 2018), pp. 253–80.

nature of rent in relation to the rights of the lord of a manor. As a result, real (landed) property could not be attached (garnished) by a creditor to meet a court-awarded judgment against a debtor in a case involving a debt or broken contract. This separation of the law of real property from contract had profound implications for how credit markets developed in England. A distraint for an unpaid debt or broken contract could only be made upon movable goods, not land. This was one of the reasons why England dealt with the problem of usury in a statutory fashion by providing a maximum state-sanctioned allowable interest rate in 1571.[9] Elsewhere, the idea of a rent charge secured by both fixed and movable property was used to avoid the Catholic Church's doctrine that a bare interest rate, simply designed to earn money from money, was a form of usury. As a result, the mortgage in England was conceived of legally in a completely different jurisdictional and procedural framework, even while many concepts were shared, which was typical of English law at the time.[10]

One result of this, as has been argued by Chris Briggs, is that there was very little mortgaging in medieval England, except for a small number of isolated manors where it was common. For most of England, mortgage law contained too much risk of forfeiture for the borrower, and not enough flexibility for the lender in terms of renegotiation.[11] This legal doctrine only began to change in the sixteenth century with the development of a body of law that became known as the equity of redemption. Equity was an important principle that worked alongside the common law; its objective was mitigation of the harshness of strict legal rules, especially of the sort that Shakespeare used in the *Merchant of Venice*, which concerned mitigation of the penal conditions of a sealed contractual bond in the case of a misfortune, such as the loss of a ship in a storm. To achieve this, the lord chancellor, primarily in the Court of Chancery, developed a complex series of procedures to apply fair discretionary principles. But equity also guided the principles of the law of real property, which were based on the discretionary interpretation of remembered customary rules of each manor in the country concerning land tenure. Thus, equity was not just the individual application of discretion but also operated as a guiding precedent, creating a national form of procedure as doctrine. As David Waddilove has demonstrated,

[9] Norman Jones, *God and the Moneylenders: Usury and the Law in Early Modern England* (Oxford, 1989), pp. 59–65.

[10] J. H. Baker, 'English Law and the Renaissance', *Cambridge Law Journal* 44, no. 1 (1985), pp. 46–61.

[11] Chris Briggs, 'Mortgages and the English Peasantry c.1250–c.1350', in Chris Briggs and C. J. Zuijderduijn (eds.), *Land and Credit: Mortgages in the Medieval and Early Modern European Countryside* (London, 2018), pp. 17–46.

the equity of redemption allowed the mortgagor to remain the true owner of the property despite lacking legal title, while the mortgagee's interest was mere security, and forfeiture had to be declared by a court.[12] This meant mortgages became a convenient way of creating a long-term and legal interest-bearing debt that provided an income for the lender and capital for the borrower. As a result, what has been termed 'the family-land bond' was now not threatened by all but the most extensive over-borrowing. Also, the law now allowed the mortgagor and mortgagee a great deal of freedom to arrange their methods of repayment privately, with the knowledge that if the interest payments came close to exceeding the value of the rent this might lead at some point to foreclosure, though at interest rates of around 5 per cent this required huge amounts of borrowing.[13]

The development of the equity of redemption was a workable solution that allowed older forms of social credit and a massive expansion of new interest-bearing capital to coexist. It provided an evolutionary means by which the latter could expand without an overt and rapid transformation of people's moral standards. Interest-bearing lending on bonds had existed before, and was permitted by the Statute of Usury, but the concept of interest as being central to credit relations was something that only evolved slowly in the period after the Restoration, and will be discussed in depth in Chapters 5 and 6. The fact that mortgaging became common much later than in most of the rest of western Europe was possibly an advantage, because rather than capital from mortgaging land being consumed by family bequests and marriage arrangements, it was done in an intellectual climate of improvement for investment, and much was put directly into currency creation and its use to pay workers for improvement or industry.

Relatively little work has been done to assess the actual level of mortgaging in the sixteenth century, though a study of Devon found that most mortgages were made between the gentry, with around five or six per year enrolled.[14] However, work by Juliet Gayton and Imogen Wedd and Henry French and Richard Hoyle all demonstrate the growth in mortgaging in different manors in England over the course of the seventeenth century, especially in the Restoration period.[15] This is when it is usually

[12] David Waddilove, 'Why the Equity of Redemption?', in Chris Briggs and C. J. Zuijderduijn (eds.), *Land and Credit: Mortgages in the Medieval and Early Modern European Countryside* (London, 2018), pp. 117–48.

[13] Ibid., pp. 123–6, 138–9.

[14] J. E Kew, 'Mortgages in Mid Tudor Devonshire', *Report and Transactions of the Devonshire Association* 99 (1967), pp. 168, 176–8.

[15] Henry French and R. W. Hoyle, 'The Land Market of a Pennine Manor: Slaidburn, 1650–1780', *Continuity and Change* 14, no. 3 (1999), p. 371; Juliet Gayton, 'Mortgages

considered that the doctrine of the equity of redemption became fixed as an established legal norm. Gayton's study of three Hampshire manors demonstrated a rise in the number of mortgages taken out, from about thirty between 1656 and 1665 to almost ninety between 1666 and 1675.[16] In Kent the number of mortgages on the manors studied by Wedd doubled between the periods 1650–1674 and 1675–1699, while the mean value rose from £149 to £402.[17] In Slaidburn, Yorkshire, the mean number of copyhold acres mortgages went up from nine between 1650 and 1670 to 18.6 between 1680 and 1720. Further, by the mid-eighteenth century, although the mean amount mortgaged remained the same, the ratio between the amounts borrowed and the sale value of land was continually over 100 per cent, and then by the 1760s reached the 'absurd' level of 267 per cent.[18] In addition, it was an increase in the number of gentry and aristocratic mortgages that led to the rise of scrivener-bankers in the Restoration, such as Sir Robert Clayton, discussed in the previous two chapters.

The 1670s was also the period when legally the equity of redemption was set as standard legal doctrine. This was through the work of Heneage Finch, Earl of Nottingham, as chancellor, before his death in 1682. Although the first use of it occurred earlier, it only then became fully formulated as accepted and secure precedent.[19] This did not involve Parliamentary legislation, and was most likely driven by landowners who wished to borrow, and facilitated by lawyers bringing cases to the Court of Chancery.[20] Finch came from a Kentish family that had produced many prominent lawyers, and his father was the recorder of London. During the Civil War he remained a convinced royalist, and with the Restoration he was elected to Parliament and undertook the management of much legal business, including the prosecution of the regicides. He married the daughter of a Levant merchant, and also

Raised by Rural English Copyhold', in Chris Briggs and C. J. Zuijderduijn (eds.), *Land and Credit: Mortgages in the Medieval and Early Modern European Countryside* (London, 2018), p. 51; Imogen Wedd, 'Mortgages and the Kentish Yeoman in the Seventeenth Century', in Chris Briggs and C. J. Zuijderduijn (eds.), *Land and Credit: Mortgages in the Medieval and Early Modern European Countryside* (London, 2018), p. 93.

16 Gayton, 'Mortgages Raised', p. 51. Curiously, Gayton shows a decline in the early eighteenth century (ending in 1735), but this might also reflect changes away from copyhold tenure.

17 Wedd, 'Mortgages and the Kentish Yeoman', p. 93.

18 French and Hoyle, 'Pennine Manor', pp. 375, 379.

19 Ibid., p. 371; David Sugarman and Ronnie Warrington, 'Land Law, Citizenship, and the Invention of "Englishness": The Strange Case of the Equity of Redemption', in John Brewer and Susan Staves (eds.), *Early Modern Conceptions of Property* (London, 1995), pp. 111–43.

20 Yale, *Lord Nottingham's Chancery Cases*, pp. 45–74.

involved himself with Parliamentary bills concerning economic regulation and taxation. In 1675 he was made lord chancellor and for the next seven years devoted himself to systemising the principles of equity in the Court of Chancery. He generally attempted to avoid direct advocacy of the party politics that evolved during the Exclusion Crisis of the late 1670s, but his loyalty to the established Church and continual defence of the royal prerogative naturally aligned him with the Tories. Since the equity of redemption was also a way of creating capital on the value of land rather than mercantile profit, it could certainly be interpreted as representing 'country' rather than London interests.

Arguments For and Against Land Registries

The move towards the acceptance of mortgaging should be seen as one reaction to part of the larger debate about the nature of credit in England, discussed in Chapter 2. During the Commonwealth there had been calls for the setting up of registries of deeds so that the value of property could be more easily established by prospective lenders and borrowers or purchasers, and during the Restoration many pamphlets were produced advocating the setting up of land banks based on the Dutch model of registering land to make mortgages more transparent in order to convert landed wealth into transferable credit.[21] By the mid-seventeenth century, Holland had well established and effective public land registers that could be consulted with minimal effort and cost. Numerous English commentators, including law reformers during the Commonwealth period, argued that the creation of such registers in England would indeed free up credit and aid economic growth, which they termed improvement.[22]

But such schemes would have required the 'rationalisation' of landholding to some degree, which was made very difficult by the legal nature of English customary tenure. Each manor had its own customs of inheritance, especially for copyhold land, which generally was the most common form of tenure, and these could also change over time as they were remembered by village elders. In addition, there were numerous legal devices for the secret transference of freehold land, done in order to

[21] Keith J. Horsefield, *British Monetary Experiments, 1650–1710* (Cambridge, MA, 1960), pp. 98–9, 107; C. Van Bochove, H. Deneweth, and J. Zuijderduijn, 'Real Estate and Mortgage Finance in England and the Low Countries, 1300–1800', *Continuity and Change* 30 (2015), pp. 10–11, 28–31.

[22] Van Bochove *et al.*, 'Real Estate and Mortgage Finance', pp. 10–11. On the general subject of improvement see Paul Slack, *The Invention of Improvement: Information and Material Progress in Seventeenth-Century England* (Oxford, 2015), pp. 76–128.

evade the obligations of feudal tenure. The practice of coupling a bargain and sale for a term of years with a release that did not require enrolment was developed and became the ordinary form of conveyance. This secrecy was desired by landowners to give them greater powers of disposition over their property, as it reduced the possibility of challenges in situations where there were complicated series of entailments if they had been available for public scrutiny.

Pamphlets advocating the creation of land registries were actually published before those proposing land banks (see 'The Pamphlet Debate over Currency' in Chapter 2), and although their main argument concerned the expansion of credit, they did not directly advocate any link with banking institutions. Their primary focus was on how mortgaging could be made more secure to encourage people to lend more money, which would advance the trade of the nation. As the unsigned pamphlet *Reasons for a Registry*, published in 1678, put it:

> by this means the Wealth of a Nation is transferred from hand to hand in a peaceable way, and Mens necessary occasions are mutually supplied, without the more in-humane contrivances of rapine and force which always end in Confusion.[23]

The same pamphlet did discuss the advantage of commercial banks, which already existed in other nations, but went on to note that other means could be used to achieve the circulation of credit.[24] It argued that land offered the best security to increase lending of the already increasing profits of trade at the time.[25] However, the author claimed that people with capital were afraid to lend on the security of land because of hidden encumbrances involving trusts and jointures.[26] A registry of deeds, he claimed, would make all incumbrances public, enabling the lender to properly judge risk. Doing so would increase the number who were willing to offer credit, thus employing capital more effectively. Interestingly, almost immediately in the same year a rebuttal, *Reasons Against a Registry of Lands*, was published. It argued the opposite case: capital would not be put to use because a registry would disadvantage the borrower, because if they wished to leverage the productive value of their land by more borrowing for a specific purpose, this could adversely affect their reputational credit in their community. The examples given were the costs of apprenticeship or portions for children rather than anything involving investment. These social examples point to the continuing

23 *Reasons for a Registry* (London, 1678), p. 2.
24 Ibid., pp. 4–7; Horsfield, *Monetary Experiments*, pp. 98–9.
25 *Reasons for a Registry*, p. 17. 26 Ibid., pp. 10–11.

importance of the older notion of the economy of obligation and social credit. The first pamphlet argued for something different. This was a transparent and calculated form of credit: an interest-bearing loan secured by a realistic valuation of the productive and/or rental value of a piece of land, which could be used to pay back both interest and principal.[27] This is what would eventually come to be called 'capital'.

There were numerous attempts to set up a registry. Between 1649 and 1700, over a dozen bills for the establishment of such a registry in England were debated in the House of Commons, but none of them passed. In 1701, the justices of the peace of the West Riding of Yorkshire petitioned the Commons for a local registry there, arguing that the West Riding

> is the principal Place in the North for the Cloth Manufacture; and many that trade therein are Freeholders, and have frequent Occasions to borrow Money; but, for want of a Register, find it difficult to give Security, to the Satisfaction of the Lenders.[28]

This failed, as did a second attempt, but in 1704 a West Riding registry was inaugurated. In 1707, the East Riding followed suit, and in 1708 Middlesex and Ireland successfully established registries. Numerous further petitions continued to be submitted to Parliament throughout the eighteenth century, but only one from the North Riding was successful (in 1735). The desire of landowners to keep the details of their property private, with the support of the legal establishment to profitably assist with this, meant that the resistance to registries remained stronger than any support.

The successful Acts provided that only all deeds made *after* the Acts should be registered. A study made of the Middlesex Registry has judged that failure to register was rare and that the vast majority of registrations took place within about six months of the date of the original deed. Bargains and sales, leases and releases, mortgages, and all leases or assignments for terms of twenty-one years or more had to be registered. Short leases and furnished tenancies (which were numerous in London) were thus excluded. Crucially, however, deeds relating to copyhold land were also excluded, and since copyhold still accounted for a high proportion of tenures in Yorkshire and rural Middlesex, the registries are not

[27] *Reasons Against a Registry of Lands* (London, 1678), pp. 7–10, 18.

[28] Francis Sheppard and Victor Belcher, 'The Deeds Registries of Yorkshire and Middlesex', *Journal of the Society of Archivists* 6, no. 5 (1980), pp. 275–6. There were also a number of pamphlets published in the last years of the century. See Horsfield, *Monetary Experiments*, bibliography pamphlet numbers 414, 429, 436, and 440.

a complete record of land transactions by any means.[29] However, of the transactions that were registered, the number in Middlesex quickly rose from 639 in the first year of operation (1709) to over 2,000 per year ten years later, and remained at over 2,000 into the 1740s. In the West Riding of Yorkshire, 55 deeds were registered in 1704 and had reached 648 by 1709, hovering around 1,000 after 1720. The registry in the East Riding started later, but by the 1720s about 400–500 deeds were being registered every year.[30] However, because of the omission of copyhold land, actually tracking the rise in mortgaging in these areas is impossible without looking at individual manorial courts.

Thus, mortgaging can only be studied at a very local level, as was done by Gayton, Wedd, French, and Hoyle. But even here, generalising to a national picture is difficult. Kent, which Wedd studied, was the only significant area of England to practice partible inheritance or 'gavelkind'. This meant that most land here was freehold, which provided a great deal of freedom to mortgage. Gayton's survey is based on an examination of conditional surrenders of title in a selection of manors from Hampshire, but here only 'copyhold of inheritance' could be mortgaged. Tenures held in so-called copyhold for lives often listed two or even three relatives with stated inheritance rights, and these were not mortgaged. But elsewhere they could be, as was the case with mortgages in the manor of Slaidburn in Yorkshire.[31] Chris Brooks has also argued that, by the seventeenth century, possessors of copyhold were increasingly being given more freedom to devise at will.[32] However, because individual deeds on leasehold to freehold land were private, their survival in many places is fortuitous. Since there were about 9,000 manors in England at the time, clearly only an impression can be gained through such hugely valuable but painstaking individual studies.

John Cannon's Mortgaging Work

Although we have no way of numerically tracking the rise of mortgages nationally, the local studies all show a sustained increase into the eighteenth century. For an individual study that can shed light on the social dynamics as well as the prevalence of mortgaging, we can again turn to

29 The above is a summary of Sheppard and Belcher, 'Deeds Registries', pp. 276–8.
30 Francis Sheppard, Victor Belcher, and Philip Cottrell, 'The Middlesex and Yorkshire Deeds Registries and the Study of Building Fluctuations', *London Journal* 5, no. 2 (1979), pp. 209–10.
31 French and Hoyle, 'Pennine Manor', pp. 352–5.
32 Briggs, 'Mortgages and the English Peasantry', p. 35; Brooks, 'The Agrarian Problem', pp. 195ff.

the *Chronicles* of John Cannon. His diary entries make clear that by the 1730s there was an extremely active mortgage market even for small closes, houses, and stints for grazing on common land. But we can also see in his *Chronicles* how such currency was crucially based on the capital released through mortgaging work he also undertook. In addition to informal notes of hand, Cannon was involved in much conveyancing work (and in the drawing up of interest-bearing bonds, which will be dealt with in Chapter 7). Since conveyancing could involve dealing with accounting for different claims on a piece of land, it was much more complicated than writing notes of hand, which were very simple. Most deeds, even those for very small pieces of land, had to be written in the proper legal language to avoid challenges. They were also expensive, since lawyers charged by length of document and they contain many lengthy repeated clauses to cover all future possibilities for each party.

As we saw earlier, Cannon learned his accounting skills while an Excise man. Immediately after his dismissal in 1721 he attempted to set himself up as a maltster, but when his father died in 1723 he inherited many of his debts. As a result, his business was unsuccessful. To make ends meet, he taught reading and writing informally. But at the same time he also began 'to write and Engross for Mr. Andrew Overton at Wales in the Parish of Queen Camell'.[33] This was a few miles south of Lydford and marked the beginning of his legal scrivening work. At the same time, he also did work for another attorney, Thomas Willis of Castle Cary. It was while working for Overton and Willis that Cannon must have learned how to write deeds and other legal documents, but his opinion of both employers suggests they took advantage of his precarious situation and lack of any formal training.[34]

In 1724, Charles Bull of Compton Pauncefoot, a clerk who had originally helped him to become an Excise man, reached out to help him again to do his work when he was incapacitated by depression ('hyppo' as Cannon termed it). Here, Cannon was to do legal work in a more congenial situation, 'drawing and engrossing Leases, Conveyances and other Matters and also writing copies and teaching accompts'.[35] In 1730 he did the accounts for a large estate, which shows that he was probably able to do double-entry bookkeeping. At the same time, he also 'did many writings' for various attorneys, stating 'so that I soon by this means attained to be a pretty good Solicitor and also a good

[33] John Money (ed.), *The Chronicles of John Cannon Excise Officer and Writing Master, vols. I–II* (Oxford, 2010), p. 161. Hereafter Cannon, *Chronicles*.

[34] Cannon, *Chronicles*, p. 167. [35] Ibid., p. 167.

share of Conveyancing'.[36] In 1732 Cannon started his conveyancing work for Glastonbury's two main attorneys, the Nicholls brothers.[37]

As can be seen in Table 4.1, he mentioned at least sixty different mortgages he drew up himself, as well as others made by different attorneys. He retained descriptions of some of his earlier work, but from 1739 onward the amount of mortgage business he described grew quite dramatically.[38] As with the making of local notes of hand (see Chapter 3), a reputation for honesty and accurate legal form was paramount in establishing credit. On one instance he was asked by Elizabeth Harper, a poor woman who ran an alehouse with her husband, to forge a conveyance by altering the succession:

February 24th This day I was importuned by one Elizabeth Harper to look over some writings, which being not satisfactory to her, she used arguments and persuasions for me to draw an Instrument to convey a tenement she lived in to her own Use contrary to a former settlement made by her late husband, Joseph Lambert; deceased, and when drawn I was to set his name thereto as if it had been his own Act done in his lifetime in her favour, and so to make void his real act and she would procure witnesses to this forged deed. ... This I peremptorily refused to do, and then set forth the odiousness of the fact, and the risque and danger I ran in obliging her, but more particularly the discredit I should reap by such a base Compliance being also one day or other to be called in question for so horrid a forgery, and last of all the scandal I might bring on myself and family. And so immediately I left her to pause on her own hellish contrivance and abominable designs.[39]

The earliest mortgage he described was actually his own. In 1719 he mortgaged a close of four acres called Butmoore – which he had inherited when his wealthy uncle died in 1715 – for £30 to a local mercer. This was a result of his being 'straitened for money occasioned by my Extravagant dealing in books as before related, as also my Chargeable housekeeping and expensive Apparel'. It was also done, as Cannon explicitly stated, 'in the most secret manner as could be' to keep the knowledge from his family. Here we have a perfect example of why land registries were resisted. However, in the summer of 1722 he was arrested by the mercer for the debt because he could not pay the interest. Cannon paid bail and

36 Ibid., p. 188.

37 Unfortunately, it is impossible from the *Chronicles* to work out how much Cannon was earning and spending. It is clear from an incident while he was working as a bailiff for William Peirs in 1726, when he was asked by Peirs' wife to produce his accounts that they were kept with his journal – which was examined and helped to lead to his dismissal. Ibid., p. 175.

38 He also mentions writing other types of deeds, of which seven were before 1637.

39 Ibid., p. 223.

Table 4.1 *Number and value of mortgages mentioned by John Cannon*[40]

Year	Number	Amount (£)
1727	2	76
1736	4	120
1737	4	139 (539)
1738	5	340
1739	10	636
1740	12	945
1741	12	3,390
1742	13	3,930
Total	62	9,976

had to ask his cousin, Elizabeth Pope, together with an attorney, for the money to pay off the debt, which cost him an extra 2 guineas in charges.[41] When his father died, the mortgage was discovered and the close sold to Pope for approximately £100. Later he also 'took up money being six pounds, ten shillings by way of a mortgage on my house and gardens, of one William Brown of Lidford by the instigation of my brother, who was uncle by marriage to the said Brown, and to save charges I made the instrument myself but gave no bond of performance as usual in such cases'.[42]

Table 4.1 provides a list of all the mortgages he worked on. It is possible that some of the increase in mortgaging after 1739 is because of his more detailed entries. But the continued incremental rise in the value of the mortgages he was doing himself (the figure for 1737 includes a mortgage for £400 that he looked over but did not write) also strongly indicates that at the age of forty-five he was gaining more responsibility as his financial circumstances improved. But it cannot be taken as evidence that there was any sudden change in the need for capital in Glastonbury.

Of the sixty mortgages described, twenty-five were for land in or near Glastonbury, while most others were from nearby places such as Lidford, Shapwick, and Meare. Only a few were from places farther away. The

[40] There are some slight differences between this and a previous table published in Craig Muldrew, '"Blunderers and Blotters of the Law"? The Rise of Conveyancing in the Eighteenth Century and Long Term Socio-Legal Change', in Michael Lobban, Joanne Begiato, and Adrian Green (eds.), *Law, Lawyers and Litigants in Early Modern English Society: Essays in Memory of Christopher W. Brooks* (Cambridge, 2019), p. 242. Some additional smaller mortgages have been added, and in 1742 one mortgage was listed twice by Cannon and the second listing has been removed.

[41] Ibid., p. 147. [42] Ibid., pp. 180–1.

smallest was for £5, and there were another nine worth less than £20. The years 1741 and 1742 are notable for two very large mortgages worth over £1,500 each. It was also, in fact, probably owing to one of these that Cannon's manuscript was kept as a record.[43] The mortgages mentioned include those done by demise, lease and release, and assignment. In most cases the names of the lenders are given, and in many cases it is possible to investigate who they were. The most common lender was Thomas King of Edgarley, just outside of Glastonbury. His source of capital was the rents from the lands he held with his brother – in trust for his nephew – and perhaps also the land tax balances he posted every year as a collector.[44] Although Cannon seems to have gotten along with King, and treasured his gift of a tobacco box, he was not a close friend. In 1742, Cannon saw 'fit in this place to draw into a total the whole hitherto of the money by him put out at interest, he being a miserly and monied, man'. The latter comment is odd as Cannon had never been critical of King before, as he certainly was about most other residents of Glastonbury, but since he himself was always in debt and had been treated severely by creditors this was perhaps a general comment of a perpetual debtor.[45] The total came to £791 14s. and included eight mortgages and twenty-six bonds and notes. In total the mortgages were worth £222. Four were for £15 or less, and the most valuable was for £65.[46] One of the other chief creditors in the area was Thomas Taunton, who was the son of a Glastonbury mercer whom Cannon went to school with. Taunton was also a Catholic who had become a wealthy farmer. In July 1741, when Taunton was briefly imprisoned for being Catholic, Cannon described him as 'rich and honest'. He was a mortgagee seven times. Various attorneys, including the Nicholls, were the next most common mortgagees, lending five times.

It is striking how often single women were involved in lending. The importance of widows' and spinsters' interest-earning bequests as a source of lending has been pointed out as a feature of credit across Europe. Their investment in stocks and government debt has also attracted attention.[47] But here we can see that they were also an

[43] Cannon, *Chronicles*, p. xc. [44] Cannon, *Chronicles*, p. lxxxvii.

[45] Cannon's book buying was perhaps an attempt to achieve a status contemporary class relations did not allow him. Craig Muldrew, 'Class and Credit: Social Identity, Wealth and the Life Course in Early Modern England', in Henry French and Jonathan Barry (eds.), *Identity and Agency in England, 1500–1800* (London, 2004), pp. 158–72.

[46] Cannon, *Chronicles*, pp. lxxxviii, 644.

[47] For more on this, see the essays collected in Elise M. Dermineur (ed.), *Women and Credit in Pre-industrial Europe* (Turnhout, 2018); Barbara Todd, 'Fiscal Citizens: Female Investors in Public Finance before the South Sea Bubble', in Melinda S. Zook and Sigrun Haude (eds.), *Challenging Orthodoxies: The Social and Cultural Worlds of Early Modern Women – Essays Presented to Hilda L. Smith* (Aldershot, 2014), pp. 53–76; Amy

important source for the formation of local capital. Cannon drew up fourteen mortgages in which the lenders were women, for a total of £1,775. Most of this was accounted for by £660 from a wealthy spinster in Bath, the Lady Bastard of Hinton St. George, and £300 from Mary Thristle of Lyme Regis. Elizabeth Pope also lent on a number of occasions. However, most of the large amounts of capital borrowed were sourced from tradesmen. As with single women, the largest amounts came from urban areas, including local towns such as Sherbourne and Shepton Mallet, as well as Bath, Bristol, and London. These mortgages involved lending of over £3,000.

All of this lending, of course, begs the question of what it was used for. In Cannon's case the answer is obvious: consumption in the form of books. In another case Cannon noted that a mortgage had been used to improve land to the value of 30s. per acre or more in rent.[48] In the majority of cases, though, we simply don't know as Cannon didn't comment on the reasons for borrowing. In a number of cases, especially that of Henry Scrace, it is clear that some people were borrowing too much, but again we don't know why. But, overall, Cannon's descriptions make mortgaging seem like a very normal part of the business of anyone who held land. Juliet Gayton has provided a very valuable breakdown of the reasons why people borrowed. She shows, interestingly, that mortgaging for investment or business was higher than for marriage or paying legacies, but that a large number of mortgages were to deal with financial difficulties in the years after the Civil War, into 1675.[49]

Since quite a few deeds have survived in the Somerset Archives for the areas where Cannon worked, it was possible to go through the mortgages to see if any could be matched with those Cannon mentioned drawing up.[50] Looking at the survival of mortgage deeds in the archives for Glastonbury in Table 4.2, we can see a clear increase in the numbers that survived after *c.*1680.

Table 4.3 shows the number of mortgages and other deeds that have survived in the main places where Cannon did his work for the years 1720–1743. As can be seen, mortgaging was as common as other forms of conveyancing.[51] However, only a few of these are from the four years

Froide, *Silent Partners: Women as Public Investors during Britain's Financial Revolution, 1690–1750* (Oxford, 2017).

48 Cannon, *Chronicles*, p. 425.

49 Gayton, 'Mortgages Raised', pp. 60–1.

50 Although some court papers have survived, the court rolls have not survived for the relevant years since most of these are for freehold land. Somerset Archives, DD/S/BT/14.

51 There are also some leases and releases listed, although it is not clear if any of these were mortgages.

Table 4.2 *Survival of mortgage deeds in Glastonbury 1640–1759*

1640–1659	8
1660–1679	13
1680–1699	21
1600–1619	33
1720–1739	43
1740–1759	56

Table 4.3 *Conveyancing documents surviving near Glastonbury 1720–1743*

Place	Mortgages	Other deeds
Glastonbury	46	51
Butleigh	44	28
Pennard	32	22
Meare	20	25

when Cannon recorded most of his business, and none could be matched with those mentioned by Cannon in his *Chronicles*. Ironically, the only surviving mortgage which could was his own assignment of the mortgage for Butmoore to Henry Pope in 1723.[52] This confirms that there must have been many more mortgages made than have survived.

Those mortgages in the archive, though, are very similar to those described by Cannon. To take one example, in July 1731 the widow Joan James of Butleigh mortgaged three acres of land there to the yeoman Thomas Brice of Baltonborough for £70 and interest, to be paid back on 9 January next. Interestingly, the deed explicitly states the land was transferred with 'use, possession, benefit and Equity of Redemption'.[53] Joan subsequently mortgaged the same piece of land again to a John Smithfield and Richard Bellman, both yeomen of Wooton, also for £70.[54]

In just the last three years of the diary Cannon facilitated £8,901 worth of credit in an area with probably fewer than 1,000 households. However, he was only one of many other attorneys and solicitors in the region who would have been doing a lot of conveyancing. Table 4.4 lists those

52 Somerset Archives, DD/S/BT/2/20. 53 Somerset Archives, DD/S/BT/8/7/16.
54 Somerset Archives, DD/S/BT/8/7/18. Joan does not appear in Cannon's *Chronicles*; however, various members of the Brice family do.

Table 4.4 *Amount loaned by acre on mortgages in John Cannon's* Chronicles

Amount (£)	Acres	Loan per acre (£)
120	15	8.00
153	18	8.50
30	5	6.00
143.25	5	28.65
80	10	8.00
40	4	10.00
100	18	5.56
1741.4	80	21.77
300	26	11.54
50	2.5	20.00
750	33.5	22.39
60	20	3.00
40	5	8.00
800	88	9.1
26	2	13.00
44	8	5.50
6377.65	340	18.76

mortgages where Cannon recorded the number of acres being mortgaged, and here it can be seen that different people borrowed differing amounts when calculated per acre. The land must have been of differing quality, but this is impossible to know without any rental valuations. With an average value lent of about £18 per acre, there could easily have been over £30,000 of capital released just in the parishes where Cannon did most of his work.

Some of Cannon's descriptions of his mortgages provide a succinct commentary on the complex arrangements that needed to be put in place to transfer mortgaged land through a bequest, as in the following example from 19 November 1740:

Engrossed two large skins for William Nicholls being an assignment of two acres or 15 beast leazes in Churchmoor and three acres of pasture in Southwood, Balstonborough, from Rachael Withers, widow relict and devisee of John Withers, her late deceased husband, of the first part, Joseph Taunton of Lidford of the second part, Elizabeth Pope, administratrix to Thomas Pope, her son deceased of the third part, and Thomas Withers, son of the said Rachael of the fourth part. The said Rachael and Mr. Taunton granted and confirmed to the said Thomas Withers, the said premises for the remainder of a term of 500 years, subsisting on a mortgage rented in the said deeds, to one Hannah Burgess for £61 10s. which was transferred to one William Tucker for the said sum, and afterwards by another assignment lent a further sum which in all made £143 5s., and created thereby a term of one thousand years.

Cannon then made an interesting comment, which combines family emotional bonds with legal language, which is not found in an actual deed: '[the] last term was assigned by Mr. Pope and the said Rachael to her son Thomas, consideration, natural love and affection and 5d apiece from the said Taunton, Mrs. Pope and the said Thomas Withers, only in matter of form and acknowledged to have been received being usual in these cases'.

Some of Cannon's descriptions also show specifically how local bills and notes were secured by a mortgage:

Drew two large bills verbatim for Mr. Nicholls on Mr. Cadby of Shapwick ... one was a charge of 100 guineas for his waiting on Mrs. White (now the said Cadby's wife) and himself in their courtship, to procure which Cadby gave him a note of hand of 100 guineas payable on the day of their marriage, and so in this bill he claimed the same.[55]

This example shows just how much money a country solicitor like William Nicholls could make from conveyancing and testamentary work. Another example from 1741 also shows the interest on mortgage capital being turned directly into notes by Cannon:

Drew for Mr. King principal and interest due from Mr. Stibbens on mortgage, principal £100, 14 years' interest from February the 8th 1726 to February the 8th 1740 at five percent £170; one note date 28th January 1729 at five percent, 8 years' interest and 11 days to February the 8th as the mortgage £7 0s 1d 3f, one note £6 dated February 20th 1732 and 7 years and 353 days' interest to February the 8th 1740 . £8 10s, in all £185 10s 1d 3f.[56]

Other more general evidence from elsewhere in England also points to the ubiquity of mortgaging by the second half of the eighteenth century. Pat Hudson has shown it was such capital, combined with local lending on bond, that was crucial for financing industry in the West Riding of Yorkshire.[57] The national aspect of the market for capital secured by mortgage can also be traced through newspaper advertisements, usually placed by attorneys on behalf of those seeking a place to invest their wealth, or by those wishing to borrow on security of land.[58] In the first part of the century, most newspapers were printed in London, and the

[55] Cannon, *Chronicles*, p. 16. [56] Ibid., p. 597.

[57] Patricia Hudson, *Genesis of Industrial Capital: A Study of the West Riding Wool Textile Industry c. 1750–1850* (Cambridge, 1986), pp. 85–6, 93–104.

[58] M. Miles, 'The Money Market in the Early Industrial Revolution: The Evidence from Two West Riding Attorneys, c.1750–1800', *Business History* 23 (1981), p. 131.

advertisements were for significant amounts of money, such as the gentleman seeking to lend £5,000–10,000 on a good mortgage.[59] But by mid-century such advertisements were also appearing in provincial newspapers.[60]

The dramatic significance of the equity of redemption for expanding less risky borrowing on land can be made with a simple estimate. In 1700 there were approximately twenty-one million acres of arable and pasture in England.[61] At £18 an acre this potentially could represent £378 million worth of new capital. Of course the value of land varied greatly across England, but since much of the land near Glastonbury was low pasture and prone to flooding, good-quality arable land near London would have been more valuable. There are also many examples of urban property and houses being mortgaged.[62] This remains a very broad estimate based on only one small area, but in the study of Slaidburn the value of capital borrowed on land had reached 267 per cent of its value!

In comparison, by the time of the outbreak of the Seven Years' War there were 59,000 holders of public funds in Bank, East India, and South Sea stock together with annuities, which P. G. M. Dickson has estimated to have been worth £77,000,000.[63] Also, the recent volume by Broadberry *et al.* estimates that England's annual nominal GDP in 1700 was about £63.51 million and that in 1759 the British GDP was £105.36 million, of which England probably accounted for about £91 million.[64] Thus, in a more private way the aspirations of the Tory land bank proposals of the late seventeenth century were realised, although they have been overshadowed by the London-based financial revolution.

Although mortgages were an important source of capital for investment in agriculture and industry, they also added capital to the local economy, which would have made indebtedness much less precarious. This type of security could then be converted into bills to circulate through the local economy. Previously, if someone had debts they owed to others called in and were unable to collect their own, then they could easily go broke. But by the 1730s, if that same person held even a few

[59] *Daily Courant*, London, England, 3 January 1721, issue 5991.
[60] *Newcastle Courant*, 7 May 1737.
[61] Mark Overton, *Agricultural Revolution in England: The Transformation of the Agrarian Economy 1500–1850* (Cambridge, 1996), p. 76.
[62] London Metropolitan Archives, Middlesex Deeds Register, MDR1/1-610.
[63] P. G. M Dickson, *The Financial Revolution in England 1688–1756* (London, 1967), p. 284.
[64] Steven Broadberry, Bruce Campbell, Alexander Klein, Mark Overton, and Bas Van Leeuwen. *British Economic Growth, 1270–1870* (Cambridge, 2015), pp. 200–1.

acres of land this could provide them with extra capital of up to £50. Handled carefully, such capital must also have been used to facilitate more consumer spending, thus enabling economic growth. Cannon's *Chronicles* show how much detailed knowledge of the familial and financial circumstances of the land and mortgagor was needed to keep disputes to a minimum.

Before the rise of mortgaging, the credit system in England relied much more heavily on personal trust than on securitised collateral. Certainly, lenders took notice of the property of borrowers, but the law was not organised in a way that provided legal security from the onset of the loan. It could only be obtained through the initiation of a lawsuit.[65] As a result, the development of English mortgaging had to accommodate itself to this existing set of institutional and cultural practices. In continental civil law regimes, while informal credit certainly existed, notaries processed larger loans in most places, and as a number of authors note, mortgaging was integrated into this market for secure credit. But in many places the poor also needed to provide security for loans through the institutions of state-operated public pawn shops, where material goods were deposited for loans at interest.[66] The equity of redemption developed slowly to provide flexibility, and the legal historian Christopher Brooks has argued that what landowners wanted from lawyers in the sixteenth century was not added security but to be able to 'use and enjoy, demise or alienate their lands with as much room for manoeuvre as possible'.[67] The English continued to prefer the normative acceptance of redemption and private negotiable nature of equity rather than the public negotiation that, say, the court officers in the Low Countries offered. It could also be argued that the English system allowed mortgagors to borrow more freely because exposure was not made public, and could even be hidden from family members. This is something that John Cannon did, eventually requiring his wealthy cousin to settle his debts so the land would not be lost from the family, even though it was only four acres. However, as we shall see in Chapter 8, it also made over-borrowing easier to hide and led to possible exploitation on the part of unscrupulous attorneys and other lenders in the pursuit of private wealth.

[65] Alexandra Shepard, *Accounting for Oneself: Worth, Status, and the Social Order in Early Modern England* (Oxford, 2015), pp. 303–13.

[66] This literature is summarised in Janine Maegraith and Craig Muldrew, 'Consumption and Material Life', in Hamish Scott (ed.), *Oxford Handbook of Early Modern European History* (Oxford, 2015), p. 379.

[67] Brooks, 'The Agrarian Problem', p. 194.

Bonds as a Form of Capital

People with savings still needed some means of building up their capital before an attractive mortgaging opportunity that they felt would be safe enough came about. Also, since most mortgages were for quite large amounts of money, it would take any one individual some time to build up the capital from yearly profits to supply the entirety of a single mortgage. As Cannon's *Chronicles* show, quite often borrowers sought more than one lender to make up their requirements for capital to overcome this problem. Of course, lenders could simply build up capital in their account books, like a bank account today, but this would be value that was doing nothing. A much more attractive option was to lend out capital in the form of a penal bond that would earn interest. In doing this, lenders were joining up borrowers who needed capital with those with profits that they wanted to lend in the form of interest-bearing capital.[68]

Bonds had to be written in proper legal form and were drawn up by a lawyer or scrivener, and then signed and sealed by two witnesses.[69] They were almost always worth a few pounds and generally much more, because of the time and expense involved in making them. Bonds possessed the advantage of being accepted by the courts as almost certain evidence of the existence of a debt, because they were sealed in the presence of witnesses, whereas the exact particulars of many informal transactions were widely disputed. This made them very secure, apart from the important exception of when someone went broke and the remainder of their estate could not cover the value of the bond. In such cases a mortgage on land would have been better security. But in other cases it was straightforward to obtain a favourable judgment in a civil court against a debtor, with the court fees.

The wording of bonds usually gave no indication of what the debt was for, only stating it as a sum of money.[70] Many bonds did not state a specific date of payment, nor was there any penalty listed for non-payment. Payment was only stated to be required when the creditor 'should

[68] B. L. Anderson, 'The Attorney and the Early Capital Market in Lancashire', in F. Crouzet (ed.), *Capital Formation and the Industrial Revolution* (London, 1972), pp. 223–55.

[69] For an example of a writing obligatory from King's Lynn, see Norfolk Record Office KL/C25/17, 11/03/52.

[70] For a number of examples of Pepys mentioning his tradesmen's bills, see Robert Latham and William Mathews (eds.), *The Diary of Samuel Pepys* (London, 1970–1983), I, pp. 200, 274; III, pp. 7, 10; IV, 2, 4, 351. On one occasion in 1659, Pepys recorded that a tradesman showed him his outstanding bills, but he 'had not money to pay him', I, p. 64. There were also many conditional bonds written out in which the exact nature of the service or work to be done were written out. J. H. Baker, *An Introduction to English Legal History*, 3rd ed. (London, 1990), pp. 368–9.

demand it'. Although such bonds were a formal means of proof of a transaction, they still left a great deal of room for discretion by leaving the date of repayment negotiable if the debtor could not pay on time. A bond termed a bill obligatory or a penal bond, in contrast, set a date on which payment was required (and often the place where the payment was to be made), and a specified penalty of usually 100 per cent if the debtor failed to pay by the specified date.

The bond was not a new instrument. It had been in existence since the medieval period, but its use had increased greatly over the course of the late sixteenth and seventeenth centuries after the charging of interest had been made legal by the statute of 1571. This is reflected in the increasing number of cases involving bonds in the central courts of the King's Bench and Common Pleas. Suits concerning bonds underwent a five-fold increase between 1560 and 1606, and an almost eight-fold increase by 1640.[71]

Probate accounts also provide evidence of the increasing use of bonds. A probate account was the final step of the probate process. It occurred after an inventory had been made of the deceased's movable assets, including debts owed to the estate. The account added up all of the liabilities of an estate and subtracted them from the total value of the probate inventory. Such liabilities included debts owed by the deceased, and usually they listed whether these were on bond or not. An index of over 30,000 surviving probate accounts from all over England between 1550 and 1800 was made by Peter Spufford. It includes information on debts owed and provides us with a source of valuable longitudinal data.[72]

Spufford showed that the number of bonds in probate accounts rose in the seventeenth century.[73] Using his database, we can explore whether this increase continued into the eighteenth century. Unfortunately, the survival of probate accounts declines significantly for the eighteenth century, just as it does for inventories, but the sample remains large enough to use before 1760. Also, we know that, in general, the survival of accounts is biased towards wealthier individuals, and also towards those who were more heavily in debt because of the greater financial complexity of such cases.[74] Thus, the evidence they provide cannot be

[71] C. W. Brooks, *Pettyfoggers and Vipers of the Commonwealth: The 'Lower Branch' of the Legal Profession in Early Modern England* (Cambridge, 1986), pp. 67–70, 93–7.

[72] Records of the nation say something about the survival rates of accounts compared to inventories.

[73] Peter Spufford, 'Les liens du crédit au village dans l'Angleterre du xvii siècle', *Annales HSS*, November–December (1994), pp. 1363–4.

[74] For a more detailed description of probate accounts and their limitations, see Craig Muldrew, 'From Credit to Savings? An Examination of Debt and Credit in Relation to Increasing Consumption in England, c.1650 to 1770', *Quaderni Storici* 137 (2011), pp. 391–414. For the problem of representativeness, see Ian Mortimer, 'Why Were

considered representative, but as long as these biases did not change, probate accounts can be used to assess change over time. In Table 4.5 we can see, first, that for individuals whose accounts have survived, their assets more than doubled between the late seventeenth and early eighteenth centuries. However, the balance that was left over after the subtraction of debts and any other costs such as a final sickness, funeral, or the maintenance of orphaned children was considerably less and rose only slightly over time. Since the largest amount of such deductions was accounted for by debts, this means the amount of indebtedness rose after 1700. Unfortunately, the amount of debt owed to an estate in the inventory is unknown, but in a sample of inventories from Kent they also rose over the same period.[75]

Table 4.5 certainly seems to show that individuals in the eighteenth century were using bonds more often than in the late seventeenth century. While the percentage of accounts that had debts on bond listed as being owed remained the same at about 35 per cent, the number of bonds went up by over 60 per cent. In addition, the average number of debts owed by the deceased went up dramatically. While the final balance left after all of the debts and other costs had been paid remained about the same (£53 and £59), the average original value of the deceased's movable goods and debts owed to them rose from £195 to £429.[76] But the sample for the later period is smaller because the number of surviving probate accounts and inventories declines quite precipitously after *c.*1700.

However, it has been argued that the fact that the value of inventories and probate accounts goes up so much in the eighteenth century is evidence that what we are seeing is simply the fact that after *c.*1700 fewer accounts were being made for poorer individuals, and as a result we might expect them to have been able to borrow more money on bond.[77] But the number of surviving wills remains relatively constant through the eighteenth century.[78] This could mean that inventories and accounts were actually made, but simply not kept as long since once the movable

Probate Accounts Made? Methodological Issues Surrounding the Historical Use of Administrators' and Executors' Accounts', *Archives* 31 (2006), pp. 2–17.

75 Muldrew, 'From Credit to Savings', pp. 16–17.

76 Other costs included funerals, payments for healthcare during final illness, and the costs of raising any orphaned children. Such costs were in the great majority of cases dwarfed by the deceased's liabilities. For an evaluation of this, see Muldrew, 'From Credit to Savings', pp. 12–13.

77 This has been proposed for the survival of inventories by Greg Clark, 'The Consumer Revolution: Turning Point in Human History, or Statistical Artifact?', University of California, Davis Working Paper (2010).

78 Motoyasu Takahashi, *Village Inheritance in Early Modern England: Kinship Structure, Inheritance Customs and Generation Continuity* (Matsuyama, 2003), p. 95.

Table 4.5 *Bonds in probate accounts*

Period	Total accounts	Average total value of the estate for all accounts	Median total value of the estate for all accounts	Average balance	Number of accounts listing debts	Number of accounts listing debts on bond	Average number of debts on bond per account	Median number of debts on bond per account
1650–1699	9,680	£195	£84	£53	6,491 (67 per cent)	3,314 (34 per cent) (51 per cent of accounts with debts)	9	6
1700–1760	1,340	£429	£167	£59	923 (69 per cent)	475 (35 per cent) (51 per cent of accounts with debts)	15	9

estate had been settled they were no longer needed, whereas a will often contained instructions about real property that could have relevance in inheritance disputes long into the future.[79]

One way this can be tested is using a pioneering process developed by Sebastian Keibeck, who has demonstrated that there is a statistically measurable relationship between the probability of being inventoried and wealth. To do this he calculated the ratio of the practitioners of any one single occupation being probated in parishes where the registers of births contained the father's occupation, which could be matched to surviving inventories from the same parish.[80] Using this data, together with the total value of each inventory, an iterative probability function of leaving an inventory based on wealth was worked out for populations at a county level. Using Cheshire as an example, he found that in the early eighteenth century almost every yeoman was wealthy enough to have left an inventory.[81] Since an account was only made if an inventory had already been drawn up, we can assume that the accounts that survive for yeomen are not biased in terms of wealth.[82] Table 4.6 examines only yeomen's accounts in the database; we can see that the percentage of yeomen who held debts on bond in the years after 1700 is about the same as for the larger sample, which indicates that the survival of post-1700 accounts was not biased towards wealthier individuals with possibly more capital than those before 1700. However, in Table 4.6 almost all the yeomen's accounts between 1650 and 1699 had many more debts held on bonds than the sample of all accounts in Table 4.5, although why this should be so is difficult to know using only this database.[83]

Another way of testing to see if wealth had any effect on whether the use of bonds went up between the two periods is to measure their use for only those accounts between 1650 and 1699 whose average works out to

[79] Craig Muldrew, 'Little to Leave: Labourers' Goods and the Probate Process in Early Modern England', in Margareth Lanzinger, Christina Maegraith, Siglinde Clementi, Ellinor Forster, and Christian Hagen (eds.), *Negotiations of Gender and Property through Legal Regimes (14th–19th Century): Stipulating, Litigating, Mediating* (Leiden, 2021), pp. 311–14.

[80] Sebastian Keibek, 'From Probate Inventories to Households: Correcting the Probate Record for Wealth Bias', Cambridge University Working Paper (2017), pp. 4–5.

[81] Ibid., p. 5.

[82] Using the median value of the accounts from 1700 to 1760 of £167 in Table 4.5 produces a similar result. If we take only those accounts from 1650 to 1699 that had a value of £167 or above, to eliminate the possibility that there were more poorer individuals accounted in the earlier period, the number of debts per account rises from 9.8 to 12, which is still less than the later period.

[83] In the late seventeenth century almost all yeomen's accounts mentioning debts have some on bond. This appears to drop in the eighteenth century, but since the numbers are much lower this cannot be taken as good evidence of a drop.

Table 4.6 *Bonds in yeomen's probate accounts*

Period	Total accounts	Average total value of the estate for all accounts	Median total value of the estate for all accounts	Average balance	Number of accounts listing debts	Number of accounts listing debts on bond	Average number of debts on bond per account	Median number of debts on bond per account
1650–1699	668	£241	£160	£68	464 (69 per cent)	449 (67 per cent) (97 per cent of accounts with debts)	9.4	6
1700–1760	97	£420	£259	£101	62 (64 per cent)	36 (37 per cent) (58 per cent of accounts with debts)	14	11

£429, the same as the average for the period 1700–1760. When we do this, the average number of debts on bond per account is ten and the median six, which is almost the same as the average and median for the whole sample given in Table 4.5.

This increase can be seen in the accounts of John Plumbe, the Lancashire attorney studied by B. L. Anderson, who was involved in lending, both on his own account and for others, to individuals from a wide range of society. Although, as we saw above, his business was secured by a number of larger mortgages, in terms of numbers, the majority of his activity was done using long-term lending on bonds. In 1732 his lending on bond was worth £739 12s. 2d., which had risen to £2,700 by 1757.[84] Michael Miles' studies of John Eagle and John Howarth provide detail on just how local attorneys were able to match borrowers with lenders on bonds. Although the records that have survived for John Eagle come from a slightly later period (1747–1783), the survival of a letter book combined with accounts allowed Miles to explore how this was done. He found that bonds were not used very often in transactions involving strangers from outside the community. As Eagle noted to one of his clients in July 1772: 'The Sum wch you have to pay Mr & Mrs Buckle is £279 4s 3d I can I believe procure you yt or £300 on a morge [mortgage] … but as you are a Stranger in these parts there will be no such thing as procuring it on your Bond.'[85]

Eagle's letters show that it was most often the borrower who wrote to Eagle, noting the form of security they could offer, their financial circumstances, and proposed interest rate. Eagle would then approach regular lenders on his books, and if none of these had any ready capital to lend for the time required, he would ask other attorneys either in writing or in person when they met at the Quarter Session or Assizes, or at local courts. Such searches involved both mortgages and bonds, even though mortgages were favoured for larger amounts. In one case, Eagle arranged for one man of East Bierly, near Bradford, to borrow over £40,000 over 25 years, all on bond for sums of £100–200.[86] In another case in which a lender wanted to find a client for £800 he had spare, Eagle found someone in need of £600 and claimed 'I shall be able to get you a good Morge [mortgage] or Bond for the other two Hundred Pounds' within two months.[87]

The amount John Howarth held on bond for clients held roughly steady over time at £1,000–2,000 per year between 1772 and 1796, while the amount he held on mortgage rose from about £2,000 to around

[84] Anderson, ' The Attorney and the Early Capital Market', pp. 236–40.
[85] Miles, 'Money Market', p. 129. [86] Ibid., p. 133. [87] Ibid., p. 132.

£10,000 per year after 1790.[88] However, an examination of his own personal lending shows almost the opposite picture. Of his personal long-term loans, until 1780 almost all was lent on bond or by note of some kind. In 1790 his lending on bond increased dramatically to £4,000, and over £1,500 almost each year thereafter, and a similar amount on notes. Since most of this lending was made in his own neighbourhood, he undoubtedly had enough knowledge to feel more secure about who he lent to on bond, or even more informally by note. Interestingly, his ledgers reveal that he also made 11–36 small unsecured short-term loans each year, averaging around £20 each. He also kept small pocket cash books of interest-free very small short-term loans that were never entered into his ledgers. These include loans to undoubtedly humble people such as John Jessop, who borrowed 3s. to pay some dues, or his own servant who often borrowed 10s. 6d. Others were tradesmen and clothiers who needed cash to pay spinners and weavers.[89] This activity shows how informal unsecured local credit continued to augment more formal lending even by an attorney such as Howarth as late as the 1690s.

In addition to writing up informal notes of hand, and his conveyancing work, John Cannon also earned fees for drawing up interest-bearing bonds. Cannon recorded drawing up about fifty bonds in the last four years of his diary, worth a total of £1,212 10s., mostly for amounts of about £10–60.[90] Although a few were interest-free, the vast majority followed what was by then the standard practice of issuing a penal bond (that is, for twice the amount lent to be recovered if the conditions were not met) with unspecified interest. The accepted practice was to let the bond remain unpaid beyond the date specified for repayment while earning the legal rate of interest, thus allowing the lender to take legal action for the full amount of the bond if it was felt that interest payments were too much in arrears. However, there is only one example where Cannon explicitly noted a bond being redrawn, from 1740, which tells us how long it had been outstanding:

> Drew a penal bond of £20 condition to pay £10 with interest the 3rd of November last past, being only the renewing of a former bond dated in March 1716 now taken up and cancelled and all interest paid home to the 3rd instant obligors George Ashley maltster and Edward Elirth obligee. Witnesses Ann Wrintmore, her mark thus as usual ... and myself.[91]

[88] Ibid., pp. 136–7. In most years there was less than £100 lending on note.
[89] Ibid., pp. 129, 135.
[90] This can be compared to the sixty-two mortgages he wrote up worth over £9,000.
[91] Cannon, *Chronicles*, p. 589.

As with the mortgages he arranged, we can discover a lot about the market for bonds from the extensive comments he made about them, especially concerning who was in a position to lend. The borrowers were a wide variety of people. In the case of George Lloyd, a mercer and mayor of Glastonbury, Cannon made a rare comment questioning why he wanted to borrow £30 on bond:

> it looked oddly that a man as Mr. Lloyd was in trade and estate should thus borrow money. Either he must [have] been in the declining way or for other mysterious occasions or to blind the world. Only his reason to me was that he had many in his book for goods had, and that would not pay him and because he would not spoil his trade by putting his customers to charge, he chose rather to borrow on security till he could advance the same from his dealers.[92]

On a slightly earlier occasion, Lloyd had also borrowed £40 with interest from the cooper Peter Hunt, of which Cannon commented, 'Not that Mr. Lloyd had occasion but Hunt having the money desired Mr. Lloyd to use it.' Here, clearly Hunt was using Lloyd to save his money. The bond was partially repaid four years later in cash, on which occasion Cannon listed the coins used: '8 pieces of 36s. each, £14 8d., 7 guineas, £7 7s., 5 moidors, £6 15s., 1 piece of 18s., 1 half-guinea, 10s. 6d., and silver, 1s 6d., In all, £30.' The occasion for this repayment in cash was, according to Cannon, the fact that 'Hunt sent a scurrilous letter to Mr. Lloyd pretending want', which presumably meant that in Cannon's opinion he was not really in need of the cash. Hunt often took small items for Cannon's family to East Lydford so he knew him quite well. He does not seem to have been especially wealthy, but Cannon once claimed he was worth £100 pounds.[93]

As with mortgages, the lenders were often tradespeople, including one mercer, a cordwainer, and a maltster. There were also some widows. Interestingly, Cannon does not seem to have written up many bonds for either of the Nicholls brothers, the solicitors who employed him the most. It is hard to imagine they weren't brokers lending on bond, like Howarth above, but perhaps they did it themselves. However, by far the most active lender whom Cannon wrote up bonds for was Thomas King, the wealthy landowning burgess and trustee of an estate for his nephew. All of his lending on bond was done out of this estate, and Cannon thought it significant enough to actually make a summary list of all the mortgages and bonds he wrote out on 21 May 1742:

[92] Ibid., p. 350. [93] Ibid., pp. 274, 283, 597.

I thought it fit in this place to draw into a total the whole hitherto of the money by him put out at interest, he being a miserly and monied, man for the use of his nephew the minor.

John Tinney by note, page 238, cash £7.
John Uphill, mortgage, page 268, £10.
William Cassell, bond, page 284, £30.
Mr. Francis Blake and Mr. Wride, bond, page 294, £30.
Edward Martin, mortgage, page 323, £10.
Mr. George Lloyd, bond, page 350, £20.
Robert Hunt, note, page 355, £20.
Robert and Thomas Grinstead, bond, page 318, £20.
Richard Ball, bond, page 414, £2.
Robert Hunt, bond, page 441, £10.
John Uphill and Thomas Jacklet, bond, page 468, £6.
William Allwood, mortgage, page 480, £25.
Richard Grinstead and Thomas Haime, bond, page 495, £50.
Robert Grinstead, bond, page 495, £15.
Richard Grinstead and Thomas Haime, bonds, page 508, £45.
William Allwood and wife, mortgage, page 533, £15.
William Vale, bond, page 538, £50.
Edward Martin, mortgage, page 539, £10.
Richard and Thomas Bartlett, bond, page 545, £30.
Abraham and Thomas Rowley, mortgage, page 545, £40.
Thomas Gilbert, bond, page 549, £10.
Elizabeth Roach, bond, page 557, £20.
William and Thomas Bartlett, bond, page 578, £15
Edward Martin, note, page 583, £4 4s.
Richard Grinstead, note, page 583, £10 10s.
Matthew Perry, mortgage, page 591, £30.
Richard Bartlett and Thomas Bartlett, bond, page 596, £15.
Mr. George Lloyd, bond, page 597, £30.
Richard Bartlett, mortgage, page 600, £65.
John Mores and William Rood, bond, page 607, £30.
John Cozens and Thomas Bartlett, bond, page 607, £60.
Thomas Bartlett, note, page 607, £30.
John Tucker, bond, page 614, £10.
Elizabeth and Bridget Hill, mortgage, page 625, £17.

Total to this 21st May 1742, £791 14s. This all Mr. Thomas King as trustee for his nephew, Thomas King a minor.[94]

In King's case, the majority of lending was on bond: £498 worth compared to £71 14s. by note and £222 on mortgage. In terms of what Cannon could earn from drawing up a bond, on one occasion he noted he was paid 5s. This can be compared to 5s. for a will and 25s. for a

[94] Ibid., p. 644.

mortgage. As with the Yorkshire attorneys John Eagle and John Howarth, bonds were an important way by which people in Glastonbury turned their earnings into a form of capital that was secure and could be saved over long periods of time, earning a rate of interest of 4–5 per cent. In contrast, Thomas Turner only mentioned money bonds twice in the nine months that were analysed above, which suggests that, unsurprisingly, given that their security was based upon obtaining a rapid decision in a common law court, the market was organised by attorneys and scriveners and not shopkeepers like Turner.

The final point that needs to be emphasised about bonds, just as with mortgages, is the fact that by the eighteenth century the charging of interest in local rural society had become overt and freed from any tinges of usury, as much as the financial markets in London. Cannon shows that interest rates were written on the bonds and the earning of interest was a normal income-generating activity. By the time Cannon came to write his *Chronicles*, although he accused many of covetousness and ill dealings, he tied no opprobrium to the charging of interest. But before this could happen, ethical attitudes had to change as well as practice. The idea of earning income from interest had to overcome a legacy of Christian theological reproach, just as the idea of borrowing to spend more had to overcome the concept of good credit being based fundamentally on thrift. In the next two chapters we will move from institutions and practices to the realm of ethics.

5 An Ethical Fulcrum: From Participation in the Body of Christ to the Happy Self

AS God still pleaseth, when the straightned hand
of want, doth threaten to devoure a Land,
To raise some worthy Persons, to procure
Help, for the crying and the dying poore;
So here, He prompts an Instrument to shew,
a way to live, by which the poore may grow
In Riches, and the Rich may Wealth increase,
and both injoy such Wealth, in settled Peace:
By Rules, which are so Just, so Plain, so True,
as none but must confess, excell they do
All Formes of Trade before: so none shall neede,.

(Preface dedication by William Brown to William Potter's *Key of Wealth*)

Nor is God more honoured among any, than He is among such industrious People, who abhor Vice, on equal Principles of Religion and good Husbandry, Labour being usually a Barrier against Sin.

(John Cary, *A Discourse on Trade, and Other Matters Relative to It*, p. 113)

In the last four chapters we have dealt with how ideas were put forward to change institutional practices. But, as we also saw, the changes that happened evolved in ways other than those envisaged by the writers of pamphlets proposing banks and new forms of credit currency. The reasons for this were that, in order to become accepted and trusted by people, they had to evolve out of already embedded practices in ways that did not immediately generate mistrust. In addition, they needed to not disadvantage those whose power and wealth depended on old practices. No national credit currency was created, but local personalised notes of hand evolved out of the practices of oral credit and trust, and were arbitraged into a national system of bills of exchange by people such as Thomas Turner. For similar reasons, land banks failed because of their need to make property-holding public. In contrast, the equity of redemption was much more readily accepted and brought about a great and rapid change.

In addition, most of the pamphleteers' rationale for their institutional proposals was the improvement of society by increasing employment and national wealth. Those in the Interregnum, like Potter, repeatedly claimed they were motivated to do so by God's will, but by the beginning of the eighteenth century most of the tracts on banks and other aspects of improvement had become much more practical and instrumental in their approach to improvement, and increasingly focused on the nation state.[1] But that doesn't mean society was becoming secular. For most people in society, acting ethically was paramount, and this meant acting as a virtuous Christian.

This matters if we want to understand how people used institutions. At some point in time, it stands to reason, new institutions will become common enough that people will grow up with them and accept their existence as normal. But it is important to understand how people came to accept the institutions when they were new; this involves investigating the ethics, beliefs, and emotions of those who used and administered such institutions. It is fair to say that institutional economics barely considers this issue at all – institutions are simply classed as bad or good, based on the criterion of either hindering or promoting economic growth. Looking back to Chapter 1, Acemoglu and Robinson argued that extractive institutions were bad because they channelled wealth into the hands of unproductive elites, while democratic institutions forced elites to spread wealth into more productive uses by the middle class. But the question as to why, at some point in time, elites in some places but not others set aside their greed and self-interest to set up democratic institutions is unanswered. In their version, the Glorious Revolution is a *deus ex machina* that does all the heavy lifting by forcing the monarch into reliance on Parliament.[2] They even suggest it was responsible for creating the observance of the rule of law![3] But, 'law mindedness' – the social attitude that respects the rule of law independent of self-interest – had

[1] Craig Muldrew, 'Politics and Economics of Markets', in Roberto Scazzieri and Ivano Cardinale (eds.), *The Palgrave Handbook of Political Economy* (London, 2018), pp. 91–132.

[2] See 'Property, the Glorious Revolution and Politics' in Chapter 1 for the criticism of credible commitment.

[3] Daron Acemoglu and James A. Robinson, *Why Nations Fail: The Origins of Power, Prosperity, and Poverty* (London, 2013), pp. 102–16. They do try to account for some differences in colonialism between the British and other European empires, especially the Spanish Empire, but these have been criticized by more contextual historians. Ibid., pp. 218–22; D. Acemoglu, D. S. Johnson, and J. A. Robinson, 'The Colonial Origins of Comparative Development: An Empirical Investigation', *American Economic Review* 91, no. 5 (2001), pp. 1369–401; Gareth Austin, 'The "Reversal of Fortune" Thesis and the Compression of History: Perspectives from African and Comparative Economic History', *Journal of International Development* 20, no. 8 (2008), pp. 996–1027.

long been a feature of English life.[4] Many legal historians would go as far back as the reign of Henry II (*d.* 1189) when tracing the origins of the law as an ideology.[5] Historians of the law and political philosophy have long investigated why powerful people should want to curb their power and create conditions for greater equality, with the main reason being social peace. To protect one's self from the violence of others, one submitted to being penalised for one's own violence or other damaging conflictual behaviour.[6] Historians have written many works detailing how different forms of law and political institutions have evolved to keep the peace and organise social hierarchy, thus protecting communities and nations.[7]

However, the psychological processes by which political and legal institutions overcame conflict between competing views about how law-making, authority, and belief should be organised and become normalised, has been less often pursued. There are notable exceptions, such as Mervyn James' analysis of how the English gentry accepted the tenets of civility and loyalty to the common law and state over lineage in the sixteenth century, or Norbert Elias' analysis of behaviours in court society, or the role of Confucianism in Chinese law.[8] But there are even fewer examples concerning economic institutions.[9] In my first book, *The Economy of Obligation*, I attempted to do this, but without expressly relating it to institutional economics. The procedure I adopted was to examine how religion and social and political theory adapted to economic change, which was fundamentally being driven by population growth and the expansion of market transactions over longer distances.

4 C. W. Brooks, *Law, Politics and Society in Early Modern England* (Cambridge, 2008), pp. 241–77.

5 P. A. Brand, 'Henry II and the Creation of the English Common Law', in C. Harper- Bill and N. C. Vincent (eds.), *Henry II: New Interpretations* (Woodbridge, 2007), pp. 215–41.

6 This is the theme of Thomas Hobbes' *Leviathan*, and central to Max Weber's famous theory of the state having a monopoly on violence. Max Weber, *Weber's Rationalism and Modern Society*, trans. and ed. Tony Waters and Dagmar Waters (New York, 2015), pp. 129–98.

7 This generally comes under the term of state-building, and would obviously be a vast list, but three important works on England are Steve Hindle, *The State and Social Change in Early Modern England, C.1550–1640* (Basingstoke, 2002); Michael Braddick, *State Formation in Early Modern England, C. 1550–1700* (Cambridge, 2000); J. A. Sharpe, *A Fiery & Furious People: A History of Violence in England* (London, 2018).

8 Mervyn James, *Society, Politics and Culture: Studies in Early Modern England* (Cambridge, 1986); Norbert Elias, *The Civilizing Process: The History of Manners and State Formation and Civilization* (Oxford, 1994); Roy Bin Wong, *China Transformed: Historical Change and the Limits of European Experience* (London, 1997), pp. 105–26.

9 Richard Goldthwaite has contextualised the milieu of Renaissance Florence that produced banking institutions, and Sheilagh Ogilvie has argued that one motivation for the creation and organisation of European guilds was to protect the interests of privileged actors. Richard A. Goldthwaite, *The Economy of Renaissance Florence* (Baltimore, 2009); Sheilagh Ogilvie, *The European Guilds: An Economic Analysis* (Princeton, 2019).

To examine this change, I used pamphlet literature, works of political philosophy such as the work of Thomas Hobbes, and letters and diaries to examine the role of individuals as they worked within expanding webs of debt and credit. This was all bundled under the concept of the culture of credit.

People overwhelmingly understood credit relations through the lens of religion and the ethics of Christian virtue. The Lord's Prayer talked about forgiving debts or trespasses, and trusting neighbours to pay back debts was related to trust in God.[10] But, because of the great rise in litigation caused by credit disputes, there also came into being in the late sixteenth and seventeenth centuries what might be termed the *juridical community*, whereby religious ethics and dispute settlement in neighbourhoods was augmented by a set of nationally similar legal institutions.[11] One of the most crucial features of this juridical society was that *public dispute resolution* in civic courts, remained a fundamental practice that expressed its members' desire to live in a state of communal relations with their neighbours to the degree that reciprocal trust, mutual hospitality, and civic duty could be maintained. With the increasing use of the law, contemporaries' view of obligation centred on Christian belief also increasingly came to be underpinned by a strongly legalistic and contractual interpretation of social relationships in order to maintain trust therein. This emphasis led to the creation of a very legalistic language of social description that elevated the legalism of contract to a privileged position.

Such legalism found its logical conclusion in Thomas Hobbes' sociology of contract, where human trust *had* to be enforced by fear of punishment. Hobbes rejected the Aristotelian notion of the existence of an original familial natural sociability. He argued that in the broader arena of society, with innumerable relations between many people, mistrust and fear of other people's potential dishonesty was a much stronger factor than any form of natural affinity between men. As a result, Hobbes attempted to create a system of absolute security in which quarrels and disagreements would be held in check by obedience to the authority of contract.[12]

[10] Craig Muldrew, *The Economy of Obligation: The Culture of Credit and Social Relations in Early Modern England* (London 1998). pp. 130–43.

[11] Muldrew, *Economy of Obligation*, pp. 203–36; Craig Muldrew, 'From a "Light Cloak" to the "Iron Cage": An Essay on Historical Changes in the Relationship between Community and Individualism', in Alexandra Shepard and Philip Withington (eds.), *Communities in Early Modern England* (Manchester, 2000), pp. 156–77.

[12] Thomas Hobbes, *Leviathan or The Matter, Forme and Power of a Commonwealth Ecclesiasticall and Civil* (1651), pp. 99–101, 113–14; Thomas Hobbes, *The Elements of Law*, ed. J. C. A. Gaskin (Oxford, 1994), pp. 48, 53, 78, 88, 92; Muldrew, *Economy of Obligation*, pp. 321–5.

Few contemporaries went as far as Hobbes in their moral scepticism, and among divines and theologians the reaction to Hobbes was often violently hostile.[13] But many thought intensely of how to reject Hobbes using his own logic. In political philosophy it would result in what Jerome Schneewind termed 'The Invention of Autonomy' in the seventeenth and eighteenth centuries. The theme of his magisterial survey was the development of self-control as a central precept of morality. Schneewind argued that the idea of the self developed as a reaction to the strict institutional emphasis of natural law ideas about the exercise of state authority over the individual in the pursuit of social order. His work was very much a history of thought, and the focus of his narrative was restricted to ideas of moral reasoning. It did not consider their relationship with actual institutional and social factors.[14] Intellectual history is obviously necessary in order to understand how conceptual change evolved, but we need to go much further in contextualising ideas before they can be used to explain social change. In its current form the history of ideas too often confines itself to a purely linguistic hermeneutics of texts in relation to one another, without an analysis of how they were actually used in the world. Intellectual historians, like Schneewind, have traced the rise of the self in terms of virtue and as a means of morality, but by focusing on thought alone they have missed the huge turning point in the history of practical morality – away from public dispute settlement, whereby the whole community is involved, to virtuous self-controlled individuals.

Although moral philosophy became bound up with seeking ways to reject Hobbes' authoritarian scepticism about human agency after 1651, the development of the idea of autonomy began much earlier. The main reason moral philosophy became more concerned with the development of the idea of self-control of emotions – or what contemporaries termed the passions – was a reaction to the terrible violence of religious warfare. The religious disputation, social divisions, and wars of religion that resulted from the Reformation led to questioning the validity of external moral standards.[15] By addressing the conflictual effects of the passions, thinkers produced lines of enquiry that would combine with new thinking about natural science to try to determine how the mind and the

[13] Jon Parkin, *Taming the Leviathan: The Reception of the Political and Religious Ideas of Thomas Hobbes in England 1640–1700* (Cambridge, 2010), pp. 1–17, 136–99.

[14] Jerome Schneewind, *The Invention of Autonomy: A History of Modern Moral Philosophy* (Cambridge, 1998), pp. 4ff.

[15] Tuck also stressed the revival of Tacitism, used to justify *raison d'etat* in international relations. Richard Tuck, *Philosophy and Government 1572–1651* (Cambridge, 1993), pp. xiii, xiv, 45–64, 82–89.

passions were connected. One result of this was that self-awareness and self-control became advocated as one means of creating a social order that relied on individual happiness achieved through moral action based on empathy and approbation as a means of generating trust.

The evolution of the thought behind this will be described in the remainder of this chapter. In particular, we will trace how three concepts – self-love, happiness, and interest – were developed and disseminated as religious and interpersonal ethics, all related to the development of the self within the singular mind. Within Protestant theology the key movement was a shift from belief in predestination to what has been termed moralism in religion and volunteerism in philosophy. That is, an emphasis on the will in making moral choices motivated by self-love and the desire for happiness over pain or unease, and such choices' impacts on society. Interest was also crucial in the pivot of religion away from searching for evidence of providence in worldly events, and towards a world of interacting interested moral selves. This also affected an individual's relationship with God. An interest in God and Christ became a religious commonplace. This form of interest involved the mutuality of individuals pursuing their own survival in a material sense, relying on others in a society in which all have interests that are organised through an interest in God's goodness. Charity, forgiveness, and providence certainly remained potent features of social relations that affected the way people regarded their interactions, but the individual undoubtedly became more important.

This development of the voluntarist or autonomously ethical self was part of a much broader change in British and European society that affected all walks of life. It was also linked to the rise of the 'new science', whereby the authority of classical writings on the natural world was increasingly questioned through observation, experiment, and new classification.[16] As Barbara Shapiro has argued, concepts of evidence were developed as much in the law courts and history as in the area of scientific experiment.[17] As we saw in Chapter 1, this resulted in the development of the idea of 'fact', which was related to the trusted evidence of account keeping. But in this and the next chapter we will be concerned with religious ethics and how the natural emotional motivation of all creatures to self-preservation could be reconciled with communal Christian ethics. Crucially, this was done by rejecting the idea that the authority of the

[16] The literature on this is vast, but see, for instance, Michael Hunter, *Establishing the New Science* (Woodbridge, 1989); Larry Stewart, *The Rise of Public Science* (Cambridge, 1992); Charles Webster, *The Great Instauration*, 2nd ed. (London, 2002).

[17] B. J. Shapiro, *A Culture of Fact* (Ithaca, 2000).

Church alone was a sufficient causal explanation for morals. This, of course, impacted upon all aspects of people's lives, and certainly had a major political impact. It could be argued that it was also necessary to create what we now consider democracy, but my concern here will be with economic relations.

Because ethics became much more entwined with philosophical investigation and thus to an extent more theoretical, the approach here will concentrate more on philosophy and sermons to track theological change than the sources I used in *The Economy of Obligation.*[18] This in itself reflects the nature of the ethical change that will be analysed: it was a move from a situation in which public behaviour could be learned both in Church and from advice books such as Henry Wilkinson's *The Debt Book* or *A Caveat for Sureties*, to one in which people thought about their public behaviour in terms of how their conduct towards others contributed to their own private happiness and that of others in their neighbourhood.[19] This was an ethics most successfully developed by Adam Smith with his theory of social approbation and self-control as a means of achieving social harmony.

But, crucially for my purposes here, it was also an ethics that was more instrumental in many ways, as it emphasised that increasing material wealth was vital to increasing individual happiness. Neighbourliness and charity, of course, remained vital concepts, but increasingly ethical writing pointed towards material well-being and happiness as its most important aim. This was especially true in terms of its elevation of interest to an ethical concept that could vie with charity and neighbourliness. In this way, these debates about the passions in relation to self-control eventually had a profound impact on interpersonal social and economic relations.[20] An emphasis on the self as a moral agent seeking happiness by looking after itself in relationships with others was eventually used to redefine how problematic credit could be negotiated privately rather than through public negotiation based on Christian belief, or civil litigation before a court. Although much of this transition was motivated by a desire to resolve religious and political divisions, it stressed achieving

[18] Also, I have not had the time I had when younger and less encumbered by academic obligation to include any meaningful survey of imaginative literature as I did in *The Economy of Obligation*, but I'm sure that such as an investigation would indeed unveil many illuminating points.

[19] Muldrew, *Economy of Obligation*, pp. 160–1.

[20] As Patrick Collinson has argued, the Protestant struggle with the Antichrist was seen by Calvinists to be present as much in local village conflicts and misbehaviour as in Catholic ritual and religious warfare. Patrick Collinson, *The Birthpangs of Protestant England: Religious and Cultural Change in the Sixteenth and Seventeenth Centuries* (London, 1988), esp. ch. 5.

social harmony by preventing interpersonal disputes before they became divisive, as opposed to resolving them after they had happened.

It is not too much of an exaggeration to call the move to the interiority, of what we might want to somewhat clumsily call *self-ethics*, one of the great turning points in European history, and one might even say currently global history. One also might say that its long-term effect was even the creation of the discipline of economics. Some have even argued that it led more immediately to a greater 'individualism' and selfishness in the early modern period. But I will argue here the story is greatly more complex than this might imply, and in some ways is a pre-echo of the confusion and endless debate about Adam Smith's writings on interest and benevolence, which we will return to in the last chapter.

Self-Love and the Passions

In his famous passage stating that is was not from 'the benevolence of the butcher, the brewer, or the baker, that we expect our dinner, but from their regard to their own interest', Adam Smith claimed, 'we address ourselves, not to their humanity but to their self-love'.[21] In this section I will trace how self-love came to be used in this way, and show that it did *not* mean the same as what is now generally understood by the term self-interest. In contemporary discourse up to *c.*1600, self-love was indeed always equated with self-interest, selfishness, and sin. After this date it would be increasingly used by those who wished to adapt Christian ethics to the challenge of the logical force of the natural right to self-preservation, which was the basis of natural law thought. While accepting self-preservation as a natural law, these thinkers argued that this did not necessarily imply competing self-interest and the war of all against all that made an authoritarian original contract and foundational law necessary for sociability to survive, as Hobbes had advocated.[22] Self-love was used to link an individual's concern for self-preservation with the soul's love for God.

The increasing concern with self-preservation, self-government, and reason was the result of increasing recovery and translation of Stoic philosophy into European vernaculars, beginning in Italy in the fifteenth

[21] Adam Smith, *An Inquiry into the Nature and Causes of the Wealth of Nations*, ed. R. H. Campbell, A. S. Skinner, and W. B. Todd (Oxford, 1976), pp. 26–7. Hereafter WN. This idea also appeared in the *Lectures on Jurisprudence* almost exactly. Adam Smith, *Lectures on Jurisprudence*, ed. R. L. Meek, D. D. Raphael, and P. G. Stein (Oxford, 1978), pp. 347–8. Hereafter LJ.

[22] For examples of the negative use of the term self-love in the seventeenth century, see Muldrew, *The Economy of Obligation*, pp. 126–7.

century and England in the sixteenth century. Originally such philosophy was designed to help elite Greek citizens live an ethical life within a defined polity supported economically by slave production in a polytheistic world. It was thus able to focus on the relation of passion and action; of feeling and virtue in outward behaviour more than social inequality or national cultural or gender relations.[23] Some of the main characteristics of the Stoic doctrine were that God and the universe are coextensive with one another and that this universe is a rational totality. The goal of human existence was to live in accordance with nature, which was to live rationally or virtuously. Virtue was sufficient for happiness.[24] To do this, passions needed to be controlled with reason. For the Stoics, self-knowledge achieved through reason could be used to control the passions in order to overcome mental unease.[25]

Self-love was also a concern for the Stoics in relation to self-preservation as a natural impulse. 'An animal's first impulse', wrote Diogenes Laertius, reporting the Stoic view, 'is to self-preservation.' This was interpreted as being directed by the emotion of self-love. The idea of what the Greeks termed *oikeiosis* postulated that it was through love of ourselves that we learned to protect, and then to look after our needs and well-being. But the Stoics also insisted that *oikeiosis* included both the tendency to look after ourselves *and* the tendency to develop concern for the interests and the well-being of others, as we are raised, and pursue provided warmth and are fed by our mothers.'[26]

These ideas were also dealt with by Cicero in his *De finibus bonorum et malorum*, and St. Augustine in his *City of God*. St. Augustine accepted that self-love was natural but criticised it as something that most often led to a rejection or diminishing of a higher charitable love for God. He accused the Stoics of pride for believing that human reason alone could control passionate love.[27] But self-love had also been discussed by Aristotle in a different way in the section of his *Ethics* on friendship, where he made a distinction between the virtuous and those who sought advantages for themselves:

> Should a person love himself more than others? People tend to censure those who love themselves most and it is considered noble to disregard one's own good and act for the sake of one's friend ... When people use the term 'self-lover'

[23] For two different approaches to this literature, see Christopher Gill, *The Structured Self in Hellenistic and Roman Thought* (Oxford, 2006) and Michel Foucault, *The Care of the Self* (New York, 1986), pp. 37–95.

[24] Christopher Brooke, *Philosophic Pride: Stoicism and Political Thought from Lipsius to Rousseau* (Princeton, 2012), pp. xii–xiii.

[25] *Plutarch's Moralia*, trans. W. C. Helmbold (London, 1939), p. 169, 191.

[26] This concept is discussed in Brooke, *Philosophic Pride*, pp. 41–4.

[27] Ibid., pp. 1–11.

reproachfully, they are referring to those who take more for themselves than they should. Such men are aiming to gratify their desires and the nonrational part of their soul ... Yet a genuine self-lover is a person who is virtuous, seeks the genuine good and is ruled by the rational part of the soul ... he will do what is noble for himself and also be beneficial to others.[28]

This sense of self-love was cited and discussed by Aquinas. In his *Summna Theologica*, the *Treatise on the Last End* he discussed the question 'Whether self-love is the source of every sin?' He concluded that 'Well ordered self-love, whereby man desires a fitting good for himself, is right and natural; but it is inordinate self-love leading to contempt of God, that Augustine (De Civ. Dei xiv, 28) reckons to be the cause of sin.'[29] Like St. Augustine, he also stressed that the love of God was more important than even a well-ordered self-love: 'God is loved as the principle of good, on which the love of charity is founded; while man, out of charity, loves himself by reason of his being a partaker of the aforesaid good, and loves his neighbour by reason of his fellowship in that good.'[30] This conception was continued in scholastic philosophy until, as Brian Tierney and Christopher Brooke have pointed out, it was taken up by Hugo Grotius, who returned to Cicero and introduced the concept of *oikeiosis* into modern natural law theory in his discussions of self-preservation.[31]

But, this scholastic genealogy was not as important for the subsequent influence of the concept as was the recovery of Stoic and other Greek philosophical discussions by those who sought to deal with disorder and war through individual control of the passions.[32] After Aquinas, emphasis on self-love decreased in favour of collective ethics under the authority of the Catholic Church. Reason was seen to be embodied in the law, and love in spiritual authority, and virtue was more an aspect of belief and participation in the body of Christ than self-cultivation. With the Reformation, both Luther and Calvin rejected the idea that self-love was a natural feature of self-preservation, and denounced it in vehement terms. It was the combination of religious schism and humanism that was to revitalise the concept.

One person vital to this revival was the English Catholic Thomas Wright, who had travelled around the continent before returning to

28 Aristotle, *Ethics*, Book 9, ch. 8.
29 Aquinas, *Sumna Theologica*, Christian Classics online edition, www.ccel.org/ccel/aquinas/summa.html, p. 2130.
30 Ibid., pp. 2921–3.
31 Brooke, *Philosophic Pride*, pp. 35–41, 48–53; Brian Tierney, *The Idea of Natural Rights: Studies on Natural Rights, Natural Law, and Church Law, 1150–1625* (Atlanta, 1997), pp. 321–4.
32 Hobbes, for instance, did not use the term. See *Leviathan*, pp. 82–3.

England in 1595, and published *The Passions of the Mind in General* in 1600.[33] He examined the nature of different passions in relation to the Christian soul for the individual. His approach was also definitely neo-Stoic, emphasising the importance of reason to control the passions. Passions were 'perturbations' that troubled the soul and corrupted judgement and seduced the will to vice:

> the mortified Christian had need know well his passions, because by brideling them he winnes a great quietnesse of minde, and enableth himself better to the service of God.[34]

However, he went further to try to theorise how reason worked as a mental faculty to direct a person towards some good or virtue that would be 'either commodius to himselfe, or profitable to the common weale', by 'delight[ing] the minde with pleasure'.[35] Thus, passions inhabited the confines of both 'sense and reason', but with the crucial difference that reason was not dependent on any corporal organ, but 'as a Princesse in her throne, considereth the state of her kingdome'.[36] This, crucially, allowed someone to be motivated by pleasure as well as discipline, and allowed a reasonable enjoyment of the sensual pleasures of things such as cookery and clothing.[37]

This was crucial because it allowed for positive interpretations to be constructed around self-love as providing both a reasonable and pleasurable motivation for self-preservation. Wright, following Cicero, now defined self-love as something that

> God … hath printed in every creature, according to his divine providence, an inclination, facultie, or power to conserve it self, procure what it needeth, to resist and impugne whatsoeever hindereth it of that appertaineth unto his good and conservation … Men and beastes with one appetite prosecute the good they desire.[38]

[33] This is expounded at greater length in the following article, some of which is reproduced here. Craig Muldrew, 'Self-Control and Savings: Adam Smith and the Creation of Modern Capital', in Simon Middleton and James Shaw (eds.), *Market Ethics and Practices, c.1300–1850* (London, 2018), pp. 63–86.

[34] Thomas Wright, *The Passions of the Minde in Generall* (London, 1604), pp. 3, 5. He linked this to humoral theory and good health. See, pp. 8–10.

[35] Ibid., p. 1. For a contemporary discussion of the meaning of pleasure, see Montaigne's essay 'On Some Lines of Vergil' in Michel de Montaigne, *The Complete Essays*, trans. and ed. M. A. Screech (Harmondsworth, 1993), pp. 947–1016. In English the word was commonly used in a manner akin to the modern usage of a feeling, but it was also more connected to the word 'please', as in the similarity between the phrase 'as you please' and 'at your pleasure.'

[36] Wright, *The Passions of the Minde*, pp. 8–9.

[37] Ibid., pp. 10–11.

[38] Ibid., pp. 11–12; Tuck, *Philosophy and Government*, pp. xiii, 6–7.

This was an unusual step since, in Protestant England at the time, self-love was portrayed as a profoundly antisocial passion leading to sin.[39] However, Wright stated that God had made it necessary to motivate animals, not only men, to seek food and to protect themselves from danger. In one passage, he certainly allowed that self-interest was reasonable in this sense:

> All looke for interest and private commodities … [men] love best that which profiteth them most: and albeit very often it be but base and vitious, yet guided by reason, and ruled by charitie, it may be good and vertuous.[40]

However, as he stated at the end, self-interest had to be governed by Christian virtue, and he went on to end his treatise with a discussion of sin and virtue, concluding quite positively that love and the means to do good were greater than those to do ill.[41]

Happiness

The key figures who developed the concept of self-love further, linking it to happiness in theology, were a group of theologians teaching and studying at Cambridge from the 1630s through to the beginning of the Restoration.[42] They did this by investigating faith and religious feeling, drawing on the classical tradition of investigations into the relationship of the passions to the mind. Their aim was to provide a theology of faith that did not depend on predestination, by describing exactly how faith functioned in the mind. They further sought to modify the tradition of the self-denial of potentially harmful emotions by stressing instead the pleasurable 'happiness' of doing good. They included Benjamin Whichcote, John Smith, Henry More, Ralph Cudworth, and Anne Conway. In the nineteenth century they were termed the Cambridge Platonists, but they drew on Plato only because he invoked a divine essence. He had argued that the soul or mind was trapped in the material world and was alienated from a universal divine mind. Thus, in contrast to Aristotle or the Stoics, he could be cited as a pagan who believed in the need for divine assistance.[43] The Cambridge Platonists name has been often taken to imply

[39] Muldrew, *Economy of Obligation*, pp. 126–7.
[40] Wright, *The Passions of the Minde*, pp. 204–5. [41] Ibid., pp. 2, 201–7, 345.
[42] The discussion below is elaborated in greater detail in Craig Muldrew, 'Happiness and the Theology of the Self in Late Seventeenth Century England', in Michael Braddick and Joanna Innes (eds.), *Suffering and Happiness in England 1550–1850* (Oxford, 2017), pp. 65–86.
[43] Mark Goldie, 'Cambridge Platonists (*act.* 1630s–1680s)', *Oxford Dictionary of National Biography*, www.oxforddnb.com/view/theme/94274, accessed 7 March 2016]

that they practised a metaphysical spiritualism linked to Plato's theory of forms, but, as Jon Parkin has argued, they might better be termed the Cambridge naturalists because of their interest in mental processes.[44]

They engaged with classical philosophy of the passions to develop a positive notion of love as an experience of the soul's love for God. They were very much engaged with new trends in philosophy, including mathematics, and were much influenced by Rene Descartes.[45] As we shall see, their work provided the basis for the emphasis placed in the Restoration church on reason, and they also had a significant impact on the development of philosophy. Both John Locke and Shaftesbury were stated admirers of Whichcote. Locke attended his sermons, and Shaftesbury edited a collection of his sermons that he published in 1698. One of their main aims was to repudiate the Calvinist theology of predestination, which claimed that salvation and damnation was preordained and stressed biblical revelation over reason. They also took issue with moderate Calvinism because they thought it led to antinomianism – the position that for the saved even the moral laws are irrelevant. Their new theology would have great ramifications since Cambridge was, with Oxford, the main training ground for ministers.

Both Benjamin Whichcote and John Smith's ideas were put forward in sermons that were collected and published only after their deaths. Whichcote was the older of the two and taught Smith at the intensely Puritan Emmanuel College. Like Wright and others, including Spinoza, they stressed that reason and knowledge were motivated by emotion, just as other actions were by unruly passions.[46] They appealed to reason and God's love to hold society together. They associated the Stoic idea of self-knowledge and virtue with seeking knowledge of God, arguing that true knowledge was that of God's love.[47] But, crucially, they further claimed that a love of one's self was a reflection of the love of God as creator of the soul, and was a pleasure experienced when desiring good: 'A right knowledge of God would beget a freedome and liberty of soul

[44] Jon Parkin, *Science, Religion and Natural Law: Richard Cumberland's De legibus naturae* (Woodbridge, 1999), p. 72ff.; Edward Stillingfleet, 'The Advantages of Christianity as the Way to Happiness', in *Fifty Sermons Preached upon Several Occasions By Edward Stillingfleet, Late Lord Bishop of Worcester* (London, 1707), pp. 683–5. For information on the Cambridge Platonists, see the Cambridge Platonism Sourcebook website at www.cambridge-platonism.divinity.cam.ac.uk/texts/introduction, accessed 24 April 2025.

[45] Stephen Gaukroger, *The Emergence of a Scientific Culture: Science and the Shaping of Modernity, 1210–1685* (Oxford, 2006), pp. 400–51.

[46] Susan James, *Passion and Action: The Emotions in Seventeenth-Century Philosophy* (Oxford, 1997), pp. 195–200.

[47] Schneewind, *The Invention of Autonomy*, pp. 194–5.

within us, and not servility.'[48] Whichcote strongly believed morality to be associated with orientation towards the self. Individuals acted in a moral way by thinking about themselves. Self-condemnation for immoral behaviour was a form of hell, while happiness was the state of living morally. The best discharge of government, for Whichcote, was government of ourselves. Moral improvement was also something we should all strive for.[49]

This idea of self-love as positive knowledge of God entailed a key move away from the common concept of self-love as selfishness. Now love of self could be considered as encouraging men to experience love and virtue as passions with a greater strength than mere selfish desires. John Smith, who obtained a position at Queens' College briefly before his early death, claimed:

> *A Good man, one that is actuated by Religion, lives in converse with his own Reason …* He knows how to converse with himself, and to love and value himself.
>
> …when the Soul thus retires into it self, and views its own worth and Excellency, it presently finds a chast and Virgin love stirr'd up within it self towards it self, and is from within the more excited and obliged to mind the preserving of its own dignity and glory … A Good man endeavours to walk by the Eternal and Unchangeable Rules of Reason; Reason in a Good man sits in the Throne and governs all the Powers of his Soul in a sweet harmony and agreement with it self.[50]

Reason, they argued, was a form of revelation from within, and they were willing to see ancient pagan philosophers together with Christ and the saints as moral teachers informing us of the best way to consciously direct our lives in a search for happiness, rather than in a search for signs of grace in the context of self-denial.

The crucial difference between Smith and mainstream early seventeenth-century English Calvinism was his quite striking theological move to describe faith as feeling in the soul:

> *Happiness* is nothing else, as we usually describe it to our selves, but the Enjoyment of some Chief good: and therefore the Deity is so boundlesly Happy, because it is every way one with its own Immense perfection; and every thing so much the more *feelingly* lives upon *Happiness*, by how much the more it comes *to partake of God* and *to be made like to him:* And therefore the *Platonists* well defin'd it to consist *in idea Boni.* And as it is impossible to enjoy *Happiness* without a fruition of God.
>
> … This holy *Assurance* is indeed the budding and blossoming of Felicity in our own Souls; it is the inward sense and feeling of the true life, spirit, sweetness and

[48] John Smith, *Select Discourses* (London, 1660), p. 28. See also pp. 362, 364, 424.
[49] Schneewind, *The Invention of Autonomy*, pp. 196–9.
[50] Smith, *Select Discourses*, pp. 387–8.

beauty of Grace.[51] This stress on self-enjoyment was the key contribution of the Cambridge Platonists in changing the theology of earlier Protestant thinkers who emphasised the sinful nature of fallen men.

Richard Baxter

It is perhaps not entirely surprising that the author of the most famous seventeenth-century autobiography, the Puritan Richard Baxter, was the key figure to articulate and popularise a worked-out theory of how self-love and happiness could be used in a positive way in everyday life by differentiating them from selfish actions. As we shall see in the next section, he also crucially developed these concepts much further by joining them with the concept of interest. He did this first in his *Treatise of Self-Denyall* published in 1659, and then again in his *Christian Directory*, written in the following decade and published in 1673. Although Baxter did not attend university, he was resident in London in the years after the Restoration, as was Benjamin Whichcote, who had been forced out of his provostship of King's College by a royal appointee, and Simon Patrick, a former fellow of Queens' and a student of John Smith.[52] In his autobiography, Baxter, when discussing the events of the Act of Uniformity in 1662, claimed there were three sorts of conformists, the second group of which he termed 'Latitudinarians, who were mostly Cambridge men, Platonists or Cartesians, and many of them Arminians … These were ingenious men and scholars, and of universal principles.' On another occasion he mentioned a sermon by Whichcote, and claimed of the Cambridge men that they were 'laudable preachers and the honour of the conformists'.[53] Although Baxter remained a non-conformist after the Act of Uniformity, he had always sought a middle way throughout the war years and afterwards, as a means of achieving peace. He valued reasonableness, good sense, and moderation. *The Reasons of the Christian Religion* (1667) demonstrates his affinities with the Cambridge Platonists, and was to influence the line of developing rationalism in the established Church. He called himself an 'Episcopal-Presbyterian-Independent' and tried to develop a mean between Calvinism and Arminianism.[54]

[51] Ibid., p. 148.

[52] Jon Parkin, 'Patrick, Simon (1626–1707)', *Oxford Dictionary of National Biography*, www.oxforddnb.com/view/article/21568, accessed 20 June 2014; Sarah Hutton, 'Whichcote, Benjamin (1609–1683)', *Oxford Dictionary of National Biography*, www.oxforddnb.com/view/article/29202, accessed 20 June 2014.

[53] J. M. Lloyd Thomas (ed.), *The Autobiography of Richard Baxter, being the Reliquiae Baxterianae* (London, 1925), pp. 177–8, 227.

[54] N. H. Keeble, 'Baxter, Richard (1615–1691)', *Oxford Dictionary of National Biography*, www.oxforddnb.com/view/article/1734, accessed 20 June 2014.

How much he was influenced by Whichcote or Smith in his *Treatise of Self-Denyall*, which was finished in September 1659 before he moved to London – and before the former's collected works were published – is difficult to say, but certainly he had enough connections to have been aware of their ideas. Here he argued, like Wright and Smith, that there was a natural original self-love directed towards God linked to self-preservation, but that it had been perverted by sin into selfishness, or what he termed *inordinate* self-love:

Though the Creator planted in mans Nature the principle of Natural Self-love, as the spring of his endeavours for Self-preservation, and a notable part of the engine by which he governeth the world ... When *sin* stept in, it broke this order ... and turned him to Himself by an inordinate self-love, which terminateth in *himself*, and principally in his *Carnal-self*, instead of God and the Common good.[55]

He also saw reason as a way to deny this aspect of self-love:

Improve the principle of self-love, to the promoting of the love of God, by considering what he hath done for thee, and what he is, and would be to thee. – I mean not *carnal inordinate self-love* which is the chiefest *enemy* of the love of God: but that rational love of Happiness and self-preservation which God did put into innocent Adam, and hath planted in mans nature as necessary to his Government, This *natural* innocent *self-love* is that remaining principle in the Heart of man ... all men should desire and seek to be happy, and choose and do that which is best for themselves. Or else it were in vain for Ministers to preach to them.

Every one that loveth him*self*, will Love that which he judgeth *Best for himself*: And every *wise man* must know, that he never had, nor can have any good at all, but what he had from God. Nature teacheth all men to love their most entire and necessary friends.[56]

Men, he thought, should also seek to '*satisfie their souls in God's Approbation*'.[57] For Baxter, self-love controlled by reason was almost an equivalent to happiness, and in the *Christian Directory* he even included a section titled, 'That thou hast self-love and a desire to be happy', which stated: 'I suppose thee to have a natural self-love, and a desire of thy own preservation and happiness.'

Baxter also directly made a plea that his version of the individual search for self-love could be a non-institutional way to achieve social peace at a time when it had proved to be so elusive. In the

55 Richard Baxter, *A Treatise of Self-Denyall* (London, 1660), preface, pp. d -r, f(3) -v, g(2) -r.
56 Richard Baxter, *A Christian Directory or a Sum of Protestant Theologie, and Cases of Conscience* (London, 1673), pp. 147, 183, 186, 188–9.
57 Baxter, *Treatise of Self-Denyall*, preface (g)–r.

Treatise on Self-Denyall Baxter was dealing directly with the religious divisions of the 1650s and the failure to reach any accommodation between the established Church, Presbyterians, and non-conformists. Like many Puritans, he saw in interpersonal strife the building blocks of institutional conflict:[58]

> Observe but *how difficult a thing it is to keep Peace (as in families and neighbourhoods) so in Churches and Common-wealths;* and judge by this of mens *self-denial.* Husbands and Wives, brothers and sisters, masters and servants, live at variance, and all through the conflicts that arise between their contrary *self-interests.* Few men are sensible of the *Universal* Interest, because they are captivated to their *own.*[59]

Then, in an important development from Thomas Wright and John Smith, he changed the metaphor of reason on a throne governing the mind to the institution of a public court:

> Keep a Court of Justice in your souls, and call yourselves daily to account, and let no passion scrape without such a censure as is due. If reason and Conscience thus exercise and maintain their authority, and passion to be everyday soundly rebuked, it will wither.[60]

This metaphor was one that would be employed again by subsequent writers, most importantly Adam Smith in his *Theory of Moral Sentiments*.[61]

Baxter also used his emphasis on self-government and denial as a way to challenge the hyper-institutionalism of Hobbes' lawful sovereign. We know that in the 1650s he had recently read Grotius, and must have been aware of the debate over Hobbes' challenge to conventional religious morality.[62] Baxter also set out to challenge Hobbes' moral scepticism about goodness being whatever gave men pleasure, in chapters titled 'Mens great averseness to costly or troublesome Duties' or 'The partiality of mens Judgement in their Own cases', showing how reasonable awareness of self-love would counter selfishness. Baxter is a crucial figure in the dissemination of these new ideas because his writing was not simply aimed at a university-educated elite, but at the much wider audience concerned with the debates about Protestant theology, authority, and behaviour engendered by the English Revolution. Undoubtedly the strictness of the *Treatise of Self-Denyall* would have limited its impact,

58 Collinson, *The Birthpangs of Protestant England*, pp. 139ff.
59 Baxter, *Treatise of Self-Denyall*, preface (g)–r
60 Baxter, *Christian Directory*, p. 328.
61 I have dealt with these themes in Muldrew, 'Self-Control and Savings', pp. 63–86.
62 Lloyd Thomas, *Autobiography of Richard Baxter*, p. 205.

but the same idea was repeated in his *Christian Directory*, which was one of the most popular books of the time.[63]

Interest

When thinking of this concept, it is very important to make a distinction between *interest* used on its own and *self-interest*, which is now inevitably linked to the modern notion of *Homo economicus*, who by thinking of maximising his or her own wants promotes economic growth, which then benefits all.[64] *Homo economicus* is usually traced back to Adam Smith's famous passage from the *Wealth of Nations* about the psychological motivation of people selling on the market:

> It is not from the benevolence of the butcher, the brewer, or the baker, that we expect our dinner, but from their regard to their own interest. We address ourselves, not to their humanity but to their self-love, and never talk to them of our own necessities but of their advantages.[65]

This was developed into the idea of the invisible hand, whereby 'a merchant, by pursuing his own interest … frequently promotes that of the society more effectually than when he really intends to promote it. I have never known much good done by those who affected to trade for the publick good.'[66] Many have written about this passage, and we will return to what Smith meant by it in the final chapter, but here it is sufficient to note that he used the phrase self-love, and never discussed self-interest in the *Wealth of Nations*. Self-love and self-interest cannot be simply equated, and Smith certainly knew this as he had written about both extensively in *The Theory of Moral Sentiments*.[67] Self-love in its classical sense was, as we have seen, a passion that motivated people to preserve their own lives. Self-interest had the same function, but here interest referred to utility in the classical sense, rather than a passion. The Roman concept of *utilitas* meant something that was both useful and beneficial, but not ethical in an immediate interpersonal sense in the same way that honesty, duty, or faith were.[68] It was not, however, a

[63] Muldrew, *Economy of Obligation*, pp. 147ff.
[64] Amartya Sen, 'Rational Fools: A Critique of the Behavioural Foundations of Economic Theory', *Philosophy and Public Affairs* 6, no. 4 (1977), pp. 317–44.
[65] WN, pp. 26–7. [66] Ibid., pp. 455–6.
[67] Craig Muldrew, 'From Commonwealth to Public Opulence: The Redefinition of Wealth and Government in Early Modern Britain', in John Walter, Steve Hindle, and Alexandra Shepard (eds.), *Remaking English Society: Social History and Social Change in Early Modern Society* (Woodbridge, 2013), pp. 317–40; Muldrew, 'Self-Control and Savings', pp. 63–86.
[68] Cicero, *On Duties*, ed. M. T. Griffin and E. M. Atkins (Cambridge, 1991), pp. xliv–xlvi.

calculated usefulness, or sum of goodness in the manner of later utilitarian philosophy.[69] Cicero discussed *utilitas* in Book II of *De Officiis* in relation to the acquisition of wealth and the comforts of life, but it was one of the most important aspects of his argument that for something to possess *utilitas* it also had to be honest, and to make something profitable that was not honest 'was a great danger to man's life'.[70] In *The Economy of Obligation* I discussed how business profit was justified as being moral in this way, and consequently, since profit was used to support the material survival of a person's family, it could also be said to be in his or her interest, and this was certainly just.

However, almost all sixteenth- and early seventeenth-century references to self-interest – as opposed to profit – were negative in character.[71] Interest, in contrast, referred to the mutual advantage, benefit, or profit of two or more parties. This had an important economic meaning, as when Henry Parker claimed that 'traffick' was something that 'every Subject of the Land has an interest in', and he quoted a proverb on the common advantage of interest, to the effect that 'every mans interest is nomans intrest, & that every mans businesse is no man's busines'. In the preface to his *Political Arithmatick*, William Petty also discussed trade in terms of the 'common interest'.[72]

Interest, of course, also came to be used to refer to the charge on a loan of money. A great deal has been written on the contemporary debate over the ethics of interest and usury. In medieval scholastic theory, making a bargain in which a fee was charged for a loan was considered a 'dry exchange'. This meant that the lender was adding an extra price to the gold and silver money being loaned for its 'use', to its price as a commodity in its own right. This is why it became known as 'usury'. Thus, it did not merely represent a 'normal' equitable exchange in which a tangible good or service was exchanged for something of equal value. The moneylender was seen to be taking advantage of inequalities in the system of exchange by charging a fee for its use by those individuals who

[69] Jeremy Bentham, *Introduction to the Principles of Morals and Legislation*, pp. 64–7; John Stuart Mill, *Utilitarianism*, pp. 275–7, 320, both printed in Mary Warnock (ed.), *Utilitarianism* (London, 1962).

[70] For other examples of *utilitas* being translated as profit, see Nicholas Grimalde, *Marcus Tullius Ciceroes the bokes of duties, to Marcus his sonne turned out of latine into englishe by Nicoles Grimalde*, ed. Gerald O'Gorman (Washington, 1990), pp. 63, 112, 150; and Cicero, *De Officiis*, ed. Walter Miller (London, 1975), pp. 32, 168, 278–80.

[71] Muldrew, *Economy of Obligation*, pp. 126–7.

[72] Henry Parker, *Of a Free Trade: A Discourse Seriously Recommending to Our Nation the Wonderful Benefits of Trade* (London, 1648), pp. 1, 7; Josiah Childe, *Discourse about Trade* (London, 1690), reprinted in J. R. McCulloch, *Early English Tracts on Commerce* (Cambridge, 1954), preface, p. v.

lacked money, when it should have been circulating freely and allowing the market to function in a natural way. Also, because lending on a small scale to one's poorer neighbours was a duty of Christian charity and neighbourliness, usury was seen to be a highly antisocial activity. It was also antisocial in the sense that it kept scarce coins out of circulation, in the moneylender's chests, until someone could afford to borrow them. As a result, the charging of any form of usury was officially an offence under the statutes of Henry VII and Edward VI.[73]

But as the economy expanded, the need for borrowed money – and eventually for bonds – increased dramatically. The propensity to hoard good coins as they became more rare meant that the charging of interest was increasingly the only means of ensuring that money returned into circulation. Thus, the scarcity of money meant that demand created a market in which interest was inevitably charged for its use. Such economic interest was a reflection of the market value of cash, because both good money and secured bonds were scarce and valuable commodities much in demand. As long as usury was illegal and there was a social stigma attached to charging for a loan – and while lenders were in danger of being prosecuted – demand far outstripped supply, and like illegal drugs today the price of interest was enormously high when it could be obtained, and such rates were not calculated but depended very much on individual circumstance. In Devon in the 1560s, the rates charged ranged from 25 to 180 per cent, and even a very good risk like the wealthy London merchant John Isham paid 12–16 per cent for short-term money.[74]

For these reasons, new arguments justifying the charging of 'interest' for economic reasons were increasingly made. As Eric Kerridge has argued, the concept of interest was different than that of usury. In medieval Latin, *interesse* differed from *usura* in that it referred to compensation for loss of a debt. The measure of compensation was *id quod interest*, the difference between the creditor's position in consequence of the debtor's losses and what might have been anticipated if the debtor had fulfilled his obligation. At a later period, loss of profit through inability to reinvest was also recognised as giving a claim to *interesse*. The *interesse* was originally a fixed sum specified in the contract, but could be a percentage reckoned periodically, so as to correspond to the creditor's loss.[75]

[73] Norman Jones, *God and the Moneylenders: Usury and the Law in Early Modern England* (Oxford, 1989), p. 76.

[74] Ibid., pp. 73–7; Tawney, 'Introduction', in T. Wilson (ed.), *Discourse upon Usury* (London, 1925), pp. 25, 28–9.

[75] Eric Kerridge, *Trade and Banking in Early Modern England* (Manchester, 1988), pp. 34–5; OED, III, pp. 1099–100. The description of an interest rate was not really used before 1660, and then not very often in publications.

As the market expanded and the potential profitability of businesses and trades grew, in many cases traders who borrowed money or credit on bond profited by doing so. As a result, it was reasonably argued that if the lender was simply another tradesman lending to another, he should be allowed to share in some part of the profit made through the use of his credit. Interest was also useful in other ways: as Francis Bacon argued, 'were it not for this easy borrowing upon interest, [by the 1620s] men's necessities would draw upon them a most sudden undoing, in that they would be forced to sell their means ... far under foot'.[76] Economic interest was increasingly justified on these grounds because in a competitive economy profit was needed for subsistence.

It wasn't until Elizabeth's reign that the charge for lending came to be more generally termed interest. A statute of 1571 tolerated interest rates under 10 per cent for the first time, and subsequently interest rates fell very rapidly as lending on bonds became common without fear of prosecution. By the 1630s, lending on bond had become so normal that interest rates had dropped to 6–7 per cent, and the legal rate was reduced to 6 per cent after 1651.[77] However, even though interest became legal, when applied to direct lending on bond it was not commonly written in the document before the end of the seventeenth century. Interest rates still seem to have retained an element of opprobrium because of the religious association with self-interest rather than charity and neighbourliness. This was the case in all of the examples of bonds sued over in the borough court of King's Lynn, which I examined from the 1650s in *The Economy of Obligation*.[78] Although interest was normally charged on bonds and loans of money, it does not seem to have been recoverable at law in King's Lynn. Since interest was meant to compensate for risk of default, presumably the ability to obtain a judgment for recovery of the debt was an alternative means of being compensated for this risk, and the court probably acted on principles of conscience in not awarding any interest that remained unpaid.[79]

As we saw in Chapter 3, by the eighteenth century the writing of interest rates on documents was unproblematic and publicly recognised. What needed to happen before this became fully normalised as an ethically acceptable commonplace was a change in how it was dealt with

[76] F. Bacon, The *Essays* (London, 1625), p. 184.

[77] Jones, *God and the Moneylenders*, pp. 24–65, 78–90, Lawrence Stone, *The Crisis of the Aristocracy, 1558–1641* (Oxford, 1966), pp. 530–2. Also see Muldrew, *Economy of Obligation*, pp. 114, n. 119

[78] Muldrew, *Economy of Obligation*, 266–7.

[79] W. J. Jones, 'The Exchequer of Chester in the Last Years of Elizabeth I', in A. J. Slavin (ed.), *Tudor Men and Institutions* (Baton Rouge, 1972), pp. 142–3.

by religious ethics. This change was related to the acceptance of self-love. But before we look into how theology changed, it is useful to examine just how much the use of the word interest increased over time. A search in Early English Books Online (EEBO) for the word usury used at least once in printed works before 1700 results in 3,998 books.[80] Usage rose to over 250 publications per decade by 1600, and it was used in 473 publications in the 1650s. Although it is impossible to measure the number of works mentioning interest rates of loans, since the word could be used in so many other ways, we can measure how many works mentioning usury *also* mentioned interest. Not surprisingly, these were very few before 1571, and this number only rose to over 100 in the 1590s. But there was a marked increase in usage in the 1650s. In that decade, the number of works mentioning both usury and interest rose to 370, compared to 195 in the 1640s, and remained above 200 for the rest of the century.

Table 5.1 compares the total number of works using either word in any way from 1550 to 1750 in both EEBO and Eighteenth Century Collections Online.[81] It shows that both words were used in a similar number of publications in the second half of the sixteenth century. But, while works containing the word usury went up by just under three times, those using the word interest went up by an incredible forty-five times by the eighteenth century, to a situation whereby it was used in over half of all publications, about the same number as used the word virtue and ten times as many as used the word politeness!

The popularisation of interest as a concept occurred in tandem with the revival of the classical notion of self-preservation used to justify self-love. Once it was accepted that self-love was a natural passion needed for self-preservation, then it could logically also be accepted that there was a natural form of interest as well, in the sense that preserving one's person was both useful and beneficial. In this way, human actions aimed at material self-preservation could be justified, while at the same time

[80] *Early English Books Online* (EEBO) is a Proquest database that features page images of almost every work printed in the British Isles and North America, as well as works in English printed elsewhere from 1470 to 1700. It is important to note that when multiple editions of a work exist the hits will be counted when repeated by edition. In this way, the popularity of reprinting is picked up. However, in 2009 the comprehensiveness of the database's coverage of *all* editions was questioned, but hundreds of new titles are added every year. https://www.midlandshistoricalreview.com/early-english-books-online-mass-digitization-and-the-archive.

[81] *Eighteenth Century Collections Online* is a database produced by a different publisher – Gale – but which also claims to include all work published after 1700. It too is updated annually. Thus, there could be some difference in compilation between the two different databases, but they both claim comprehensiveness. Mikko Tolonen, Eetu Mäkelä, and Leo Lahti, 'The Anatomy of Eighteenth Century Collections Online', *Eighteenth-Century Studies* 56, no. 1 (2022), pp. 95–123.

Table 5.1 *Publications containing the words usury and interest, 1550–1750*

1550–1600 Usury: 740 (7%) Interest: 807 (8%) Total publications: 9,932	*1650–1700* Usury: 1606 (3%) Interest: 17,467 (27%) Total publications: 65,039
1600–1650 Usury: 1,564 (4%) Interest: 5,921 (14%) (55% from the 1640s) Total publications: 41,669	*1700–1750* Usury: 2,125 (3%) Interest: 36,668 (51%) Total publications: 71,824

excess selfishness could be condemned. An interest in God came to be promoted as a means of allowing the natural law function of self-interest, while at the same time overcoming it with a stronger interest in God.

The concept of believers having an 'interest' in God was not new. The Puritan William Perkins stated in his *Golden Chain*:

> The poore man hath as good interest in Gods kingdome, and may call God father as well as the king. Therfore the weaker sort are to comfort themselues hereby, knowing that God is a father to them as well.[82]

William Bradshaw also used the word interest in a similar way in five sermons. But it can hardly be said that it was a commonplace in the Elizabethan or early Stuart periods.

But unlike the case of self-love, it does not seem to have been the Cambridge Platonists who developed this interpretation. The Cambridge Platonist John Smith only used interest in a positive way once out of twenty-one usages. He did not portray it negatively, but did claim that it distracted men from proper self-love.[83] The popularisation of the word interest came about during the Civil War, as can be seen in Table 5.1. This is hardly surprising, as political divisions meant that what was private interest to some could be public interest to others. Historians of political thought have noted that around the mid-seventeenth century the idea of national interest developed in politics as an extension of reason of state theory. This was done as a way of reducing potential warfare by assuming that all states would predictably follow their own interests

[82] William Perkins, *A Golden Chaine: Or the Description of Theologie Containing the Order of the Causes of Saluation and Damnation, According to Gods Word* (Cambridge, 1600), p. 536.

[83] Smith, *Select Discourses*, pp. xxi, 389.

which, being more transparent, were then more negotiable.[84] However, during the Civil War, with a state broken in half, the concept of interest was not taken up for this reason, but was rather employed by Parliament as a means of justifying their actions and authority as being in the *public interest.* Although Parliament claimed to be acting for the office of the king, this was obviously conceptually problematic. Public interest came to be used by Parliament as a concept that was not republican but had classical roots. Also, as attempts to negotiate with the king failed, especially after the First Civil War, the public interest of Parliament could increasingly be contrasted to the self-interest of Charles I. In 1647, for instance, Marchamount Needham published his *The Case of the Kingdom Stated, According to the Proper Interests of the Severall Parties Ingaged.*

In a very well-known argument, the economist Albert O. Hirschman argued that in the Renaissance and seventeenth century the state took on the task of repressing conflictual passions by force if necessary.[85] However, around the mid-seventeenth century this idea of national interest in politics came to be adopted by Enlightenment writers such as the Jansenists and Hume, who argued that the interest of making a profit came to be seen as a usefully benign passion. In a commercial society all tradesman would recognise that it was in everyone's interest to earn a profit, and thus commerce could proceed peacefully and competition for markets could take the place of bloody competition for glory, honour, or land.[86] In this way, interest tamed the disruptive passions.[87] While the effect of interest I wish to develop here is similar, its genealogy is somewhat different. In my story, interest as a theological concept is more important. It was Christians' interest in God that worked to help people control their passions in the first instance. It was only after this had happened that it could be used in an economic sense without the taint of self-interest.

If the problem of schism was an important motivation for the reconfiguration of the basis for political authority, the same problem was doubly true for religion once Church unity and hierarchy were shattered. The ethics of neighbourliness, love, and charity were all based on faith, and being neighbourly and charitable to someone with whom you disagreed with on fundamental issues of faith was a huge problem. Of course, this problem had existed between Protestants and Catholics since the

[84] Tuck, *Philosophy and Government*, pp. xiii, 31ff; J. A. W. Gunn, 'Interest Will Not Lie: A Seventeenth-Century Political Maxim', *Journal of the History of Ideas* 29 (1968), pp. 551–64.

[85] A. Hirschman, *The Passions and the Interests: Political Arguments for Capitalism before its Triumph* (Princeton, 2013), pp. 15–17.

[86] Ibid., pp. 105–13. [87] Ibid., p. 32ff.

Reformation, but this had resolved itself into a sharp division resulting in confessionalism in most places. It was the potential of religious civil war and unreconcilable division among English and Scottish Protestants that was so frightening to many. Again, interest was a concept that was adopted to avoid just such a confessional schism. Just as national interest developed in politics as a way of reducing potential warfare by assuming that interests were more negotiable, arguing that all Christian *selves* had an interest in God and Christ's sacrifice was a way to make doctrinal differences more compatible. In a sermon preached before the House of Commons, the famous Presbyterian Robert Baillie claimed:

> The ordering of the State and Kingdom, how necessary soever, ought not to precede the setling of the Church; In this, the interest of God, in that, the interest of man is chiefest.[88]

It seems to have been Richard Baxter who adopted the term to emphasise mutual interest over self-interest. This is unsurprising, as Baxter was heavily involved in efforts for comprehension between the Church of England, Presbyterians, and Independents. The stress on interest was a strategy to help bring this about.

As early as 1650, in *The Saints' Everlasting Rest*, he used the word interest in the very first sentence and then fifty times thereafter to develop this theme in a style designed to popularise it:

> IT was not only our interest in God, and actual fruition of him, which was lost in Adams Covenant-breaking fall; but all spiritual knowledge of him, and true disposition towards such a felicity ... as the poor man that would not beleeve that any one man had such a sum as an hundred pound, it was so far above what he possessed: So man will hardly now beleeve, that there is such a Happiness as once he had.[89]

The term was used over 1,000 times in his voluminous writings in the 1650s alone, including one work where it appeared in the title.[90] He advised his listeners and readers to understand that they had an interest in God and Christ's promise, and that this interest should be stronger than any self-interest that inordinate self-love and passion might lead them to prioritise. At the very beginning of his *Treatise of Self-Denyall* he claimed that 'The Eternal God was the Beginning and the End, the

[88] Robert Baillie, *Satan the Leader in Chief to All Who Resist the Reparation of Sion. As It Was Cleared in a Sermon to the Honourable House of Commons at Their Late Solemn Fast, Febr. 28. 1643* (London, 1643), p. A3 verso.

[89] Richard Baxter, *The Saints Everlasting Rest* (London, 1650), p. 1.

[90] *Richard Baxter's Confession of his Faith, Especially Concerning the Interest of Repentance and Sincere Obedience to Christ, in Our Justification & Salvation* (London, 1655). EEBO count.

Interest, the attractive, the confidence, the desire, the delight, the All of man in his upright uncorrupted State.' He argued that '*self-denial* is principally required in the *first Commandment*, that is, The *denying* of *self* as opposite to God, and his Interest. And *self-denial* is required in the Last Commandment; that is, The denying of *self*, as it is an enemy to our neighbours.' Self-denial was the means to overcome inordinate self-love, which was the same as self-interest, which Baxter attacked many times over in his treatise. In contrast,

> Love of God, in *this Degree*, is *sensibly predominant*, and we refer even our *own Salvation* to his *Interest* and *Will*: In this Degree, a Christian is grown more deeply sensible; *he is not his own*, but *his* that made him and redeemed him; and that his principal study must not be for himself, but for God; and that his *own* interest is in it self an inconsiderable thing, in comparison of the interest of the Lord.
>
> ... we are sensible that the Happiness of *Many*, even of *Church* and *Common-wealth* ... is incomparably more excellent and desirable than our own felicity.[91]

He was also quite specific about how he thought the concept of interest could be used to heal religious divisions, as in the quote from the *Treatise of Self-Denyall* where he claimed 'Few men are sensible of the *Universal* Interest'. He developed this further in the same work:

> If I know my heart, I speak not this in any great sense of the loss of my own interest, but in the sense of the lamentable Power and Prevalency of *Self-love*, and *Self-conceitedness* in the world. And while I am bitterly censured by almost every party, how easily could I recover my interest and reputation with any one of them, if I could but be of their mind and side?
>
> Observe but how commonly with men called Christians, the interest of Christ is trodden in the dirt, when it seemeth to cross any interest of their own.[92]

The chapters on self-denial have many examples of how self-interest and selfishness could be denied.

However, by the time he came to write what is often termed his magnum opus, the casuistical *Christian Directory* published in 1673, interest had become a normalised way of dealing with day-to-day problems for people and was not just a salve for religious division.[93] In the *Christian Directory* he uses the word interest an incredible 600 times. It is used more than the words saved, happiness, hell, belief, and passion, but slightly less than honour and dishonour (799). In comparison, faith is used 943 times, grace 922 times, and heart 1,176 times. Many of these usages again delineate the difference between self-interest and interest in God.[94]

[91] Baxter, *Treatise of Self-Denyall*, preface. [92] Ibid. [93] Baxter, *Christian Directory*.
[94] Ibid., p. 213.

But, since many people's ordinary problems involved their economic lives, Baxter often described faith and trust in legalistic language, as when he advised:

crediting the Word or Nature of God ... judging it to be a sufficient ground of our security and expectation: ... We have not only Gods *Nature*, but his *Promise* also to *trust* upon: And this giveth us a *certainty*.[95]

In the same way, he also used the term interest in an economic sense, as a financial interest in someone else's business through some form of investment:

Gods Nature, and *Love* are the sufficient *general* security to the soul [and] ... his *Promise* is the sufficient *particular* security. And that our unfeigned self-dedication to him, is our sufficient evidence of our interest in his love and covenant, which may warrant our special trust and expectations.[96]

Make sure of your saving interest in Christ: get proof of your adoption and peace with God, and right to everlasting life.[97]

In this last sense it is that the Holy Ghost is said to dwell in believers, and to be the ... witness of our right to Christ and life, and Christ's agent and witness in us, to maintain his cause and interest.[98]

... whether he subject all his worldly interest to the will of God, and the interest of his soul? ... and whether he make an impartial, diligent inquiry after the truth, with a desire to receive it at the dearest rates?[99]

Thus, by the beginning of the Restoration, the three concepts of self-love, happiness, and interest had been firmly established in religious thought. Over the course of the next fifty years they became discursive ethical commonplaces, as is shown in Table 5.2.

It is hard to state just how important this change was, not just to ethical thinking but to economic and political thinking too. Grace and well-being had now moved from existing *within* a community of one church believing the same things (albeit with regard to tender consciousness), to a religion of conscious interior selves *coming together* into a religious community. People now could think about *their* passions and how to deal with them to act ethically or virtuously to achieve personal happiness, which could then be taken as a sign of grace. Also, the Christian self was inevitably a self, *interested* in the well-being of others and one's own proper relationship with God. It is not an overstatement to suggest that interest replaced unity as the defining feature of community. It also changed the nature of hierarchy in communities and helped to create a

95 Ibid., pp. 157–9. 96 Ibid., p. 157. 97 Ibid., p. 285. 98 Ibid., p. 190.
99 Ibid., p. 215.

Table 5.2 *Works with sermon in the title containing the words interest, happiness, or self-love*[100]

1630–1639 (655)	*1670–1679 (836)*
Interest 113 (17%)	Interest 365 (44%)
Happiness 186	Happiness 331
Self-love 9	Self-love 67
1640–1649 (1,389)	*1680–1689 (1,254)*
Interest 368 (26%)	Interest 623 (50%)
Happiness 430	Happiness 542
Self-love 61	Self-love 74
1650–1659 (1,047)	*1690–1699 (1,390)*
Interest 432 (41%)	Interest 752 (54%)
Happiness 438	Happiness 697
Self-love 96	Self-love 100
1660–1669 (800)	*1700–1750 (7,240)*
Interest 347 (45%)	Interest 4,431 (61%)
Happiness 326	Happiness 4,490
Self-love 71	Self-love 389

notion of class as a group of families whose wealth made their economic interests coincide. This will be investigated in Chapter 8.

An interest rate was also not seen as making money out of someone else's need, but rather as helping with the economic success of their investment in the improvement of land or the establishment of trade. Needing to borrow because of financial difficulty increasingly came to be seen as a sign of economic failure when applied to the middling sort, and as a sign of excess consumption on the part of the poor. Also, whereas previously lending in such instances of need was stressed as a form of charity, as was the forgiveness of debts, now saving up of capital was stressed as a preventive individual measure to avoid the need to borrow since the legal rate of interest limited the extent to which risk could be priced into the interest rate.

Happiness could justify material possessions, and the interested, controlled self could be used to construct the institutions that would maintain the value of saved financial capital, reducing the need for risky

[100] From EEBO and Eighteenth Century Collections Online. The number in parentheses is the number of titles that contain the word 'sermon', while the other figures are the number of such works with at least one mention of each term.

lending and costly legal procedures for recovery. Another advantage of secure capital savings was that its possession could reduce the propensity for self-interested cheating. Once enough individuals came to believe that it was in their interest to keep honest accounts and use accurate notes because they could accumulate significant amounts of financial wealth as a secure form of property by being scrupulous, then the incentive to cheat became reduced psychologically. It was also reduced in a practical manner by increasing liquidity, thus reducing the incidence of credit squeezes that would much increase the temptation to cheat in order to survive such a financial problem. Here I have traced how these concepts were developed in philosophy and theology. Tracing how self-love, happiness, and interest were disseminated through the population after the Restoration and early eighteenth century, and how they were internalised and acted upon, will be the subject of the next chapter.

These developments would eventually profoundly influence Latitudinarian preaching, and also laid the basis for the Scottish Enlightenment's notion of benevolence and approbation, and the Third Earl of Shaftesbury's conception of polite social self-control in conversational associations. The other main attempt to create a more individualist ethic is more well known, as it formed part of the development in the new science of the seventeenth century, which attempted to logically model the workings of thought as an internal mental process. Descartes famously proposed mathematical reason as a form of mental authority over the passions, and in his *Essay on Human Understanding* John Locke dissected the workings of thought in order to let 'all the light we can … upon our own minds' in order to understand how thinking led to knowledge.[101] Both of these developments were always fundamentally concerned with the idea of self-control, for without it a voluntarist ethic could not meet the challenge of the authoritarian state.

[101] John Locke, *An Essay Concerning Human Understanding*, ed. Roger Woolhouse (Harmondsworth, 1997), p. 55; Rene Descartes, *Discourse on Method*, trans. F. E. Sutcliffe (Harmondsworth, 1968), pp. 49–52.

6 Practical Ethics, the Self, and the Economy in an Era of Religious Dissent

> For pray wherein do the Joys of Heaven consist, but in the Fruition of GOD the Only and All-satisfying Good? and how can we Enjoy Him but by Loving him? And is it not the property of that Passion to think it can never Enjoy enough but still to thirst for more? How then can we Love GOD if we do not Long and Labour for the fullest Enjoyment of him? … He sent us hither to pass our Probation, to Prepare our selves and be Candidates for Eternal Happiness. And how shall this be done but by Labour and Industry?
>
> (Mary Astell, *A Serious Proposal to the Ladies: Wherein a Method Is Offer'd for the Improvement of Their Minds*, pp. 38–9)

Over the course of the end of the seventeenth century and early eighteenth century the theological ideas discussed in the previous chapter were successfully disseminated throughout English society. As Mark Goldie has noted, the success of the Cambridge Platonist's ideas, in essence, meant that Arminianism had become commonplace. Given that opposition to Archbishop Laud's promotion of Arminianism had been one of the causes of the Civil War, this was an astonishing transformation.[1] Calvinist belief in predestination had been dislodged, and 'moralism' became the norm for moderate Dissenters and Anglicans alike. Moralism held that good action in the world was efficacious, and would lead to salvation. In terms of the self, this was undoubtedly crucial, as it meant that a person did not now just look for grace, but could also actively examine and act upon their behaviour.[2] Good behaviour became less about following moral and civil laws and hoping the ability to do so was a sign of grace. It was now more about examining how passions and feelings were related to compassionate actions towards others, and how these could be impeded by anger, lust, greed, and other selfish emotions. The motivation to good action was also now based not on obedience and unity, but interest. All in society were interested in God, and everyone

[1] Mark Goldie, 'Middle Way Religion', in Mark Goldie (ed.), *The Entring Book of Roger Morrice: Roger Morrice and the Puritan Whigs* (Woodbridge, 2007), pp. 257–9.

[2] Alexandra Walsham, *Providence in Early Modern England* (Oxford, 1999).

was interested in promoting good behaviour to achieve social harmony as well as individual happiness. This was developed by the Bishop of Peterborough, Richard Cumberland, as benevolence, a concept that would have a profound influence on the Scottish Enlightenment and ultimately Adam Smith.

This chapter will examine both how the concepts of self-love, happiness, and interest developed in the wake of Richard Cumberland's writing, and most crucially how they were disseminated through print and sermons. By looking at their impact on some representative diarists, I will also examine how these ethics were adopted and impacted social relations and how people now thought of their 'selves' within those relations in their economic lives. As stressed in the Introduction, one of the key arguments of this book is that in order for capital to become a thing that affected all of society, not just mercantile elites, it needed to be both broadly practised institutionally *and* acceptable as a cultural phenomenon. This would not have been possible if it could not have been justified within the basic matrix of Christian ethics that underlay early modern society.

An essential feature of the Restoration was the convergence of Presbyterian dissent with Latitudinarian theology within the Church of England. Both adopted the basic tenets of the Cambridge Platonists, and were also heavily influenced by Richard Baxter, who was an enormous force through his attempts to organise meetings aimed at bringing about comprehension that could accept limited voluntarism within Church government.[3] But such attempts failed to find agreement, and with James II's Declaration of Indulgence, dissent became a permanent reality within English religion. Within this context, the ideas of self-love, interest, and happiness were further developed in both philosophy and theology.

A work that combined all of these factors was Richard Cumberland's *De Legibus Naturae*, published in 1672, attacking the authoritarian conclusions of Hobbes.[4] Like Baxter, Cumberland was motivated to argue for a natural law in which good actions were innate, against Hobbes' reduction of moral and political obligation to self-interest alone. Drawing on the Cambridge Platonists, he sought to develop their use of natural law as an Anglican alternative to Hobbes' account, and to recover a godly

[3] Comprehension is the term used to describe attempts to integrate dissent into the Church of England; voluntarism refers to the belief that faith in God can be achieved by will as opposed to requiring a prior divine gift. Goldie, 'Middle Way', pp. 225–37.

[4] Richard Cumberland, *A Treatise of the Laws of Nature*, trans. John Maxwell (1727), ed. Jon Parkin (Indianapolis, 2005), p. 298; Jon Parkin, *Science, Religion and Natural Law: Richard Cumberland's De legibus naturae* (Woodbridge, 1999), pp. 5–12.

role for natural philosophy.[5] These ideas were subsequently developed by Latitudinarian writers and disseminated through sermons within the Church of England. They were further developed by John Locke in his philosophy as an example of what might be considered a development of an 'independent' voluntarist self, which was subtly different to the post-Baxter Dissenter/Latitudinarian version. This was further developed by Locke's student Anthony Ashley-Cooper, the Third Earl of Shaftesbury.

Richard Cumberland

Cumberland attended Magdalen College, Cambridge from 1649 to 1656, precisely the period in which the Cambridge Platonists were teaching and preaching. At Cambridge he absorbed both the new science and new theology, which he would use to create the basis for his science of morality. After graduating he became a rector and then domestic chaplain to the Lord Keeper Orlando Bridgeman in 1667. In the wake of the Glorious Revolution he was recommended to become the Bishop of Peterborough by his fellow student at Cambridge, John Tillotson, who would soon become the Archbishop of Canterbury.[6]

His major work, *De Legibus Naturae*, was published in 1672 in a difficult Latin, but it had a large and immediate impact both on philosophers such as Locke, Pufendorf, and Shaftesbury, and on the development of what has come to be termed Latitudinarian theology. It was soon translated in adapted forms by Samuel Parker in 1681 and James Tyrrell in 1692.[7] Cumberland was especially influenced by mathematics, and wished to use science to discover proof of natural law and its obligatory character. He cited Descartes more than anyone else.[8] Also, in order to challenge Hobbes, and prove that morality was natural and not relative to individual desire, he adopted a voluntarist theory of discovering God's will through the mind, in reason's relation to the senses and emotions. This had an important impact on John Locke.[9]

To do this, he followed the Cambridge thinkers already discussed, but placed much more emphasis on the classical heritage of Aristotle, Cicero,

[5] Parkin, *Science, Religion and Natural Law*, foreword.

[6] John Parkin, 'Cumberland, Richard (1632–1718), bishop of Peterborough', *Oxford Dictionary of National Biography*, www-oxforddnb-com.ezp.lib.cam.ac.uk/view/10.1093/ref:odnb/9780198614128.001.0001/odnb-9780198614128-e-6887, accessed 11 March 2021.

[7] All the quotations are taken from Parkin's edition of James Maxwell's translation of 1727 where, as Maxwell states in his introduction, he strove to make the Latin sentences more idiomatic to English, and he offered his own summaries at the end of each chapter.

[8] Parkin, *Religion and Natural Law*, pp. 10–11, 115–16, 151–2.

[9] Ibid., pp. 140ff, 205–22; Cumberland, *Laws of Nature*, pp. 293–7.

and the Stoics in linking rationality with morality and good actions. In his text, however, he did not refer to them extensively in order to emphasise the Christian, rather than the pagan, elements of his morality. But, when John Maxwell produced his definitive translation in 1727, he was much more open about the Stoic influence. Maxwell prefaced the work with a long essay on just that subject and inserted many footnotes in order to defend the work against charges of Deism.[10] Maxwell's additions are indicative of the extent to which attitudes changed between 1672 and 1727, and will also be discussed here.

Cumberland was also probably the first philosopher of the seventeenth century to develop the concept of benevolence as an innate feeling that worked both to the common good and individual happiness through expectation. Here he was reacting to Hobbes, who had defined benevolence as something that could easily be frustrated by the failure of the receiver to reciprocate. In contrast to Hobbes' scepticism, Cumberland theorised that people would do good in the expectation that others would also do so, leading to the multiplication of happiness.[11] For Cumberland, the pleasure of benevolence was experienced as individual happiness, linked to God's love through self-love. Maxwell's translation of Cumberland used the word happiness over 600 times, while Maxwell, in his added essays, used it a further 151 times. Cumberland crucially made the claim that self-love could be 'excited to good Actions from *Benefits* already *receiv'd*' from others,' and that this led men to acts of benevolence towards others, motivated by this pleasurable memory:[12]

> The *whole Frame* of Animals, (because it is the necessary Cause of their usual Functions and Actions,) plainly *indicates*, 'That from the *same* internal Causes proceed both *Actions* in order to *Self-preservation*, and *Affections* of so great *Benevolence*, as are sufficient for a friendly Association with other Animals of the same Species'.[13]

Unlike many other writers, however, Cumberland did not dwell on the relationship of selfishness to self-love. Instead he focused on what he termed a limited and regular self-love:

[10] Parkin, *Religion and Natural Law*, p. xix.

[11] Cumberland, *Laws of Nature*, p. 292. Baxter had thought that Benevolence was something less than love, which had to be motivated by the love of God. Richard Baxter, *A Christian Directory or a Sum of Protestant Theologie, and Cases of Conscience* (London, 1673), pp. 194–5. This is discussed at more length in Craig Muldrew, 'Happiness and the Theology of the Self in Late Seventeenth Century England', in Michael Braddick and Joanna Innes (eds.), *Suffering and Happiness in England 1550–1850* (Oxford, 2017), pp. 81–4.

[12] Cumberland, *Laws of Nature*, 274.

[13] Ibid., pp. 404, 415–16.

we hence learn the *Limits* of a laudable *Self-love:* For we must always, in providing for our-selves, 'Abstain from invading another's Property,' and take care, 'That we promote the Publick Good.' This limited Self-love displays it-self chiefly in *temperance, Frugality* and *Modesty.*[14]

This idea of limited self-love became a very important one for divines and preachers who promulgated it into the eighteenth century. By using the concept, they could maintain that happy self-love was a religious state, while continuing to preach warnings against selfish behaviour. In this way, people could worry about immorality caused by inordinate self-love as selfishness, while thinking of their own happiness in terms that could validate good actions towards neighbours and others. At the same time, in economic terms, it could also justify the consumption of material goods, personal savings, and interest as a foundation for a happy self as much as good credit in the community.

The achievement of happiness was also now something that could be thought of in a 'voluntarist' way. That is, people were urged to think of their own happiness with regard to their emotions. In a sense, the practice of the ancients was now being democratised in standard Church of England theology. As Maxwell put it, summing up Cumberland's chapter 5,

The Benevolent are at *Peace* with all Men, and enjoy the Advantages of good-Neighbourhood ... The *Tranquillity of Mind,* which arises from *Self-approbation* is constant and uninterrupted, and disposes the Mind for the Enjoyment of all its other Pleasures ... a Man, who upon sedate Reflexion does not approve of his own Actions, his Pleasures are pursued in a broken, turbulent, and interrupted manner, and as it were by a War within a Man's self; and give Uneasiness, when reflected on.[15]

In order to argue against Hobbes, Cumberland asserted that 'Universal Benevolence is a *more* effectual means of Happiness',[16] and included a section arguing that through the division of labour individual happiness could be vastly augmented by the more lavish provision of material goods:

it is well known by the Experience of all Men, 'That the Powers of any single Person, in respect of that Happiness, of which from without he is both capable

[14] Ibid., p. 679; also see pp. 331, 404, 648 (Maxwell), 678–9, 936. Maxwell, in his second introductory essay, was more ready to acknowledge that unchristian acts of selfishness were a result of self-love:

All the Wickedness that is in the Animal Nature, involveth in it an *inordinate Self-Love,* whence it ariseth. Self-Love is unquestionably innate in all, and a vicious carnal Self-Love is innate in all, *in a degree of prevalent Tendency that Way,* for it is a Root of Bitterness in all Men.

[15] Ibid., pp. 649–50. [16] Ibid., p. 357.

and stands in need, are so *small*, that he wants the *Assistance*, both of many Things and Persons, to lead his Life *happily*; but that *every one* can nevertheless *afford* many Things for the use of *others* which himself does not at all need, and which therefore can be of no use to him.' ... the *divided* use of Things and of human Labour; ... is necessary to the Preservation of the Whole. Such *Division*, which is a kind of *Property*, after things are occupied and applied to uses truly necessary, is very consistent with some *Community*.[17]

Indeed, the concepts of both happiness and interest could be used to argue that the increase in the purchase of consumer goods was more beneficial than excessive. Paul Slack has convincingly argued how ideas about improvement favoured a new emphasis on industrial production, and many writers also saw this as an opportunity to increase domestic consumption in order to create jobs.[18] Here we can see clearly how self-love could ethically encourage consumption as a form of creating happiness. This is crucial, as being virtuous became more than just being about belief and dealing with others. It was now also a virtue to make a 'self' happy with material comfort.

Cumberland also employed the concept of interest as a means to show how individuals were motivated towards acting benevolently for the common good.[19] This was a key part of his strategy of proving Hobbes wrong with the same logic. Hobbes did not place a great deal of emphasis on the concept of interest. He confined its use to that of self-interest, as when describing the 'Passions and Interests of men' as 'different, and mutable'.[20] In contrast to this, Cumberland argued that individual interest, rather than driving men to disagreement and war, actually brought them together, as they would inevitably come to see through experience that an accumulation of good actions was in both the individual's and society's interest:

[17] Ibid., pp. 322–4, 376. The inverted commas and italicization were added by the translator for his own emphasis; p. 6.

[18] Paul Slack, *The Invention of Improvement: Information and Material Progress in Seventeenth-Century England* (Oxford, 2014), ch. 4. Also note that there were some authors who continued to argue that domestic consumption should be limited but foreign exports increased to earn from the balance of trade. Craig Muldrew, 'Politics and Economics of Markets', in Roberto Scazzieri and Ivano Cardinale (eds.), *The Palgrave Handbook of Political Economy* (London, 2018), pp. 91–132; Istvan Hont, 'The Early Enlightenment Debate on Commerce and Luxury', *The Cambridge History of Eighteenth-Century Political Thought* (Cambridge, 2006), pp. 377–418.

[19] Cumberland, *Laws of Nature*, p. 269.

[20] Thomas Hobbes, *Leviathan or The Matter, Forme and Power of a Commonwealth Ecclesiasticall and Civil* (1651), p. 717. Also see William Rushworth, *The Dialogues of William Richworth or The iudgmend* [sic] *of Common Sense in the Choise of Religion* (1640), pp. 87, 88, 93, 213, 393, 395.

> *Every One is oblig'd … to consult his own Interest in the Use of his own Advantages, that they may be of the most Advantage to all Others* … 'When we limit our Love of our-selves, by the Bounds prescrib'd by Universal Justice, which gives to God and Men their several Rights.' This *limited Self-love*, being enjoin'd in this Law of Nature … cannot but be *Just* and *Laudable* … 'The necessity of a Law commanding every one constantly to use his own Things in order to his own Happiness, where that is no way Inconsistent with, or Prejudicial to, the Happiness of the whole Community'; *for* 'The Happiness of the Whole consists in the Happiness of all the Parts' … nor can the Happiness of every One be procured by Others, if they neglect Themselves.[21]

Then, in a passage that has led some modern philosophers to consider him a source of utilitarianism, he went so far as to discusses interest rates in a positive sense:

> 'That the End is to be conceiv'd as the greatest Aggregate, or Sum, of good Effects, most acceptable to God and Men, which can be effected, by the greatest Industry of all our future Actions.' It often *happens*, (and we ought to endeavour that it should happen as often as may be,) 'That the good Effects of our Power increase in a Geometrical Progression'; (as in increase arising from Interest upon Interest, or in Husbandry, or Merchandizing, when every year the increase of the former is added to the main Stock;) *whence* arises a vast increase, both of publick and private Happiness, beyond what can be distinctly foreseen.[22]

As Jon Parkin has put it, Cumberland's most distinctive theoretical move was his argument that it was possible to identify the sanctions attached to the law of nature in the structures of reward and punishment that God had ordained for the observance and dereliction of the law of nature. Punishments take various forms, ranging from the traditional scourges of conscience through to the state of war.[23] But the rewards of happiness were much stronger, and in a desire to experience the pleasure of happiness, self-interest would become a social interest in acting benevolently towards others. In this way, Cumberland's scheme allowed a reconciliation between natural law and the requirements of Protestant theology. This made Cumberland's theory of natural law incredibly influential for other intellectuals who could read it. His immediate influence on Samuel Pufendorf is well known, and it is a testimony to the force of his theory that it was used by both the high royalist divine Samuel Parker to defend the divine authority of the Church, and by John Locke's friend James Tyrrell. The latter published the first abridged translation of *De Legibus Naturae*, and used it to defend his own hyper-rationalist

[21] Cumberland, *Laws of Nature*, pp. 604, 693. [22] Ibid., p. 491.
[23] Parkin, *Laws of Nature*, pp. xiii–xvi.

insistence that morality could be reduced to mathematical propositions, which were in harmony with both natural sociability and with the pattern of the divinely created universe.[24] Cumberland also had a supreme influence on the Scottish Enlightenment through his influence on Francis Hutcheson, both in terms of a voluntarist religious ethics and his idea of ethical sociability achieved through benevolence.[25] The opening sentence of Adam Smith's *Theory of Moral Sentiments* significantly stated:

> How selfish soever man may be supposed, there are evidently some principles in his nature, which interest him in the fortune of others, and render their happiness necessary to him, though he derives nothing from it except the pleasure of seeing it.[26]

The fact that Cumberland was translated again by Maxwell in 1727 in such a full edition together with the latter's commentary and over 400 pages of additional essays interpreting Cumberland in English is evidence of the impact that Cumberland's ideas had on the popular theology of the Church of England by that date.[27] Maxwell's preface makes it clear that his intention was to produce a full translation for the first time for those who could not read Latin, but were interested in the subjects of morality and the laws of nature.

[24] Ibid., pp. xviii–xviv; M. Goldie, 'Tyrrell, James (1642–1718), political theorist and historian', *Oxford Dictionary of National Biography*, www-oxforddnb-com.ezp.lib.cam.ac.uk/view/10.1093/ref:odnb/9780198614128.001.0001/odnb-9780198614128-e-27953, accessed 11 March 2021.

[25] Jerome Schneewind, *The Invention of Autonomy: A History of Modern Moral Philosophy* (Cambridge, 1998), pp. 330–1, 349–53; Knud Haakonssen, 'Moral Philosophy and Natural Law: From the Cambridge Platonists to the Scottish Enlightenment', *Political Science* 40 (1988), pp. 97–110. There is also a passage by Maxwell summing up Cumberland's discussion of the relation of public to private happiness, which Adam Smith must have read:

> '*That publick* and *private Happiness* are so *interwoven*, that the very Actions which promote the private Interest of any particular Person, do in all, at least in all common Cases, necessarily tend to the Advantage of the Publick: *That* our *Possessions* of all Kinds, our Lands, our Houses, our Money, are all *enjoy'd* by many': ... The most ingenious Mechanick would not, perhaps, be able of his own proper Labour, to furnish himself out so much as a commodious Garment. *Who*, that but reflects upon the Number of Hands that one single Garment must pass thro', before it becomes fit for Use, and upon the Number of curious Arts that contribute to its Perfection (a competent Knowledge in none of which can be attained without the Industry of some Years:) *Who*, I say, that yields but the least Attention to these things, can doubt of our *Dependence*, nay, of the *Necessity* of our Dependence, on one another?

Cumberland, *Laws of Nature*, pp. 361–2.

[26] Adam Smith, *The Theory of Moral Sentiments*, ed. D. D. Raphael and A. L. Macfie (Oxford, 1976), part I, ch. I, para. 1.

[27] W. M. Spellman, *The Latitudinarians and the Church of England, 1660–1700* (Athens, GA, 1993).

Sermons and Dissemination

Although Cumberland's work was accessible to only a few before its translation, his ideas and those of other divines were disseminated within sermons during the Restoration and early eighteenth century. Baxter's printed works, as we saw, reached a wide literate middling sort audience able to afford them, and were printed in the tens of thousands of copies. But, as historians like Arnold Hunt have shown, by far the most widespread means through which ideas were disseminated around the country were the sermons preached weekly, and on special occasions in all of the over 9,000 parishes of England, and 950 in Scotland. Of course, the vast majority of these cannot be recovered, but a great deal were printed, as can be seen in Table 5.2. We also do not know what the social composition of the audience was at church services, and there has been much debate over the extent to which poorer members of communities regularly attended services.[28] But through diaries we can access middling sort attitudes on theology and opinions on the sermons they heard, and how they applied them in their economic dealings. Writing notes on sermons in diaries seems to have been almost as common as the motivation for keeping financial notes. Samuel Pepys, Dudley Ryder, John Cannon, and Thomas Turner all included many summaries of sermons, which will be discussed at the end of this chapter.

Important Latitudinarians published volumes of their sermons that influenced many lesser clergy. These were those who had found accommodation with the Interregnum government but were removed from positions in Cambridge after the Act of Uniformity in 1662. Many, such as Whichcote, More, and their students Thomas Tenison, Edward Stillingfleet, and John Tillotson – moved to London to take up ministries.[29] There, they were not restricted from preaching, as were Dissenters, who objected to episcopacy or aspects of the prayer book. It was not until after the Glorious Revolution that the Latitudinarians found themselves in favour with the new king, and Tillotson became Archbishop of Canterbury. All of these clerics preached on the themes of self-love, happiness, and interest as they related to virtue and material life on Earth.

[28] Keith Wrightson, *English Society 1580–1680*, 2nd ed. (London, 1993), pp. 212–15; Margaret Spufford, 'Puritanism and Social Control', in Anthony Fletcher and John Stevenson (eds.), *Order and Disorder in Early Modern England* (Cambridge, 1985), pp. 41–57; John Broad, *Bishop Wake's Summary of Visitation Returns from the Diocese of Lincoln, 1705–1715* (Oxford, 2012), pp. xxxv–xxxix.

[29] Spellman, *Latitudinarians*, pp. 33–40.

Tillotson's style of sermon-giving became incredibly influential after he became Archbishop, to the extent that the subsequent period has been termed the age of Tillotson in regards to sermon-giving. He also became the most published preacher of the late seventeenth and eighteenth centuries, with over 160 items published, whose copyright was worth £2,000.[30] In these published works, the word happiness was used over 1,600 times, and interest over 500 times.[31] He argued that, to achieve happiness, it was in a person's interest to look after one's self both spiritually and in terms of worldly well-being:

> 'Tis to be wise for our selves. There's an expression, Job 22.21. He that is wise is profitable to himself; and Prov. 9.12. If thou be wise, thou shalt be wise for thy self: intimating that wisdom regards a man's own interest and advantage, and that he is not a wise man that doth not take care of himself and his own concernments … As self-preservation is the first principle of Nature, so [is] care of our selves and our own interest.[32]

> The greatest wisdom is to secure the interest of our souls and of eternity though it be with loss and to the prejudice of our temporal and inferior Interests. Therefore Religion directs us rather to secure inward peace than outward ease … In a word, our main interest is to be as happy as we can, and as long as is possible.[33]

As with Baxter and Cumberland, the concept of interest was crucially employed to argue for a world where thinking about one's self could be urged as a way of encouraging virtuous actions rather than the merely selfish.[34]

The question of happiness and material life was directly addressed in a series of sermons delivered by Edward Stillingfleet, who trained at Cambridge and became the Bishop of Worcester in 1689.[35] Happiness, for Stillingfleet, was experienced as tranquillity of mind, and the love of God was needed to achieve this. But he also engaged in a lengthy discussion about how tranquillity entailed reasonable allowance for the 'conveniences of life', to enable men to serve God with cheerfulness and to give them an opportunity to do good freely.[36] He certainly cautioned against too much love of things of the world, but he provided considerable latitude for enjoyment through the senses of the earthly pleasures of

[30] William Gibson, 'The British Sermon 1689–1901', in Keith A. Francis and William Gibson (eds.), *The Oxford Handbook of the British Sermon 1689–1901* (Oxford, 2012), pp. 3, 20.

[31] Word search with Early English Books Online. This is not the total of the times he used the word, as some things were reprinted in collections.

[32] John Tillotson, *Sermons Preach'd Upon Several Occasions by his Grace John Lord Archbishop of Canterbury, vol. I* (London, 1694), p. 15.

[33] Ibid., pp. 17, 176–7. [34] Ibid., pp. 70–3, 88, 194, 206, 219, 223, 249, 349.

[35] Edward Stillingfleet, *Fifty Sermons Preached upon Several Occasions By Edward Stillingfleet, Late Lord Bishop of Worcester* (London, 1707), p. 657.

[36] Ibid., p. 655.

material goods, alongside the spiritual happiness to be found in God. He argued specifically against more puritanical objections that material goods should provide no more than 'use and conveniency', suggesting that our desire for our daily bread was moved by the same passion given by God which impelled us to love our neighbours:

> Because of the Strict Union of Soul and Body here, and that the Comforts of Life depend so much upon the External Objects about us, God hath shewed his Bounty and Goodness to us in affording great variety of them for our Support and the more chearful Service of himself, and ... doing good to one another.[37]

It would be tedious to go through too many other sermons from the period, which reiterate the same concepts, but as Table 5.2 shows, after 1690 both interest and happiness appeared in over half of all texts with the word sermon in their title. Some developments are, however, also worth pointing out. There are examples where we can see the dissemination of sympathy towards others. In one of Whichcote's sermons collected by Shaftesbury and published in 1698, he stated:

> *Now* by Humanity, fair Carriage, and Suitableness of Disposition, a Man doth gain a general Interest; and this is an Argument to a Man's self ... For, there is in Man, a secret Genius to Humanity; a Bias that inclines him to a Regard of all of his own Kind ... there is a secret Sympathy in Human Nature, with Vertue and Honesty; with Fairness and good Behaviour; which gives a Man an Interest even in bad Men.[38]

Similarly, in William Dawes' *Self-Love the Great Cause of Bad Times*, published in 1701, he stated:

> every Man is in Duty bound in the first Place to secure, if he can, the Salvation of his own Soul. And unless a Man has taken care of himself first he is an Instrument very unfit to reform another.
>
> [however] Nature has implanted in us a most tender and compassionate Sense and Fellow-feeling of one another's Miseries, a most ready and prevailing propension and inclination to assist and relieve them.[39]

Adam Smith made such sympathy the lynchpin of his philosophy, and it was a key way in which the well-being of others was made a component of

[37] Ibid., pp. 658–60. Tillotson also preached a positive version of self-love in order to move it from the realm of Puritan asceticism to a much more positive form of worldly enjoyment. John Tillotson, *Of Sincerity and Constancy in the Faith and Profession of the True Religion, in Several Sermons* (London, 1695), p. 418.

[38] Benjamin Whichcote, *Select Sermons of Dr. Whichcot* [sic] *in Two Parts* (London, 1698), p. 381.

[39] William Dawes, *Self-Love the Great Cause of Bad Times: A Sermon Preached before the Society of the Mystery of the Goldsmiths* (London, 1701), pp. 7, 9.

self-love. Thinking well of others, and doing good towards them, contributed to the happiness of each individual self. Neighbourly charity was now not only obliged by scripture, it was innate in a way that could coexist with individual accumulation of material wealth.

The nature of this theology by the 1730s can be examined in the published sermons of Joseph Butler. Butler was born in 1692 and was the son of a cloth merchant from Berkshire. Although he attended a Dissenting academy, where he was introduced to the work of Locke, he conformed to the Church of England in 1714. Subsequently he was appointed preacher at the Rolls Chapel in Chancery Lane and became Bishop of Bristol in 1738. Butler was a popular preacher and the published version of his sermons went through six editions before 1770. He also published a major work, *The Analogy of Religion*, in 1736, which went through ten editions by 1775. Like Cumberland, he influenced figures of the Scottish Enlightenment, including Hume and Smith. He propounded an idea of voluntarism through self-government and the idea of a reflective conscience, and stressed that self-reflection was the key to moral action for Christians:

> He hath the rule of right within: what is wanting is only that he honestly attend to it.[40]

> What is lawful in civil government, [is] applicable to the several principles in the mind of man … to preside and govern, from the very economy and constitution of man, belongs to it.[41]

Virtue was interpreted in terms of pain and pleasure, which would motivate self-government:

> it is manifest, that self-love is in human nature a superior principle to passion … if we will act conformably to the economy of man's nature, reasonable self-love must govern.[42]

> virtue is naturally the interest or happiness, and vice the misery of such a creature … interest in one's own happiness is a manifest obligation.[43]

It was precisely having an interest in self-love that led people to avoid stronger passions. It also led them to acts of benevolence, which he defined as the love of society or friendship, placing him closer to the Stoic concept of *oikeiosis* than Cumberland's theory of multiplied reciprocity. For Butler, self-love and benevolence sprang from the same natural law, but the first was directed inwards and the latter outwards.[44] In a passage of which a definite later echo can be heard in Adam Smith's

[40] Joseph Butler, *The Works of Joseph Butler Containing the Analogy of Religion and Sixteen Celebrated Sermons* (London, 1867), p. 28.
[41] Ibid., p. 24. [42] Ibid., p. 23. [43] Ibid., pp. xv–xvi. [44] Ibid., pp. xix, 3–6.

famous description of the invisible hand, Butler went so far as to suggest that what Cumberland would have termed inordinate private self-love was a form of providence:

> If any or all of these may be considered likewise as private affections, as tending to private good, this does not hinder them from being public affections too … by acting merely from regard (suppose) to reputation, without any consideration of the good of others, men often contribute to public good. In both these instances, they are plainly instruments in the hands of another, in the hands of Providence, to carry on ends, the preservation of the individual and good of society, which they themselves have not in their view or intention.[45]

He made clear that he thought these principles could be used for the self-government of the poorest people, as well as men of education.[46]

Thus, we can see, by this time, the Church was disseminating a way of belief that placed a great deal of emphasis on the importance of individuals in having an interest and obligation in their own happiness and that of others. People were urged to think that doing good for themselves and others was reasonable and virtuous, and the evidence was to be found in happiness rather than a strong Calvinist search for salvation. Also, instead of Baxter's puritan stress on self-denial there was an emphasis on self-cultivation through love of virtue. As we have seen, self-love was used to achieve this. Rather than self-interest leading to selfish behaviour, it was now seen to be a means of leading people to think that their own rational interest was in doing good to be happy rather than primarily following catechisms, commands, or laws. An interest in one's self, multiplied through society, was now seen to create more happiness rather than selfishness. One can see how this, combined with politeness, would have effected how men and women dealt with disputes caused by passions.[47]

More indirectly we can see how the accumulation of interest-bearing capital could be validated as a good promoting happiness, whereas it had previously been seen as either miserliness or as a danger to the economy of reciprocal obligation. People were now living in a world of the serial sociability of selves through an obligation to happiness, rather than a serial sociability of chains of obligations in the form of debts. In fact, now, too many obligations could be seen as harmful to one's well-being.

[45] Ibid., p. 7. [46] Ibid., pp. xiii, 10.

[47] Robert B. Shoemaker, 'The Decline of Public Insult in London 1660–1800', *Past and Present* 169 (2000), pp. 97–31; Hellen Berry, 'Rethinking Politeness in Eighteenth-Century England: Moll King's Coffee House and the Significance of "Flash Talk"', *Transactions of the Royal Historical Society*, 6th ser., 11 (2001), pp. 65–81.

Independents

After Baxter, the moderate Presbyterian wing of non-conformity adopted the concepts we have been discussing in a very similar way to the established Church. Although they were not numerous, those Dissenters, often termed 'independents', remained apart from the official Church, and need to be considered because of their influence on business and philosophy. Groups such as Baptists and Quakers continued to believe in predestination, while others adopted a much more extreme form of voluntarism, such as Socinianism. Quakers were often very successful businessmen in the eighteenth century because the high value they placed on honesty made them very trustworthy.[48] But all forms of Dissenters often organised their own education in Dissenting academies. Although these undertook the education needed to provide ministers (since they were barred from attending either Oxford or Cambridge), for those not intending a clerical career they tended to stress a much more practical business-oriented education than did local grammar schools, including accounting.[49]

But here we will be interested in how such practical matters interacted with moral teachings. In general, the independent wing of dissent placed much more emphasis on individuals who personally controlled themselves rather than the serial sociability of selves obligated to worshipping and loving God within the established Latitudinarian Church. In part, this was because, as their name suggests, they had always supported a strong sense of an individual's personal relationship with God through the exposure to scripture, whether through listening or reading. But also, since they were forced by the Act of Indulgence into worshipping separately, and were banned from public office, this made membership of a Christian community problematic. They certainly felt a strong sense of what we might call Anglo-Scottish Protestantism, fortified by fear of Catholicism and Louis XIV's aggression, but their exclusion from

[48] See, for instance, Nuala Zahedieh, 'Credit, Risk and Reputation in Late-Seventeenth Century Colonial Trade', in Olaf Uwe Janzen (ed.), *Merchant Organization and Maritime Trade in the North Atlantic, 1660–1815* (St. John's, Newfoundland, 1998), pp. 69–74; Lindsay Houpt-Varner, 'Maintaining Moral Integrity: The Cultural and Economic Relationships of Quakers in North-East England, 1653–1700', in Adrian Green and Barbara Crosbie (eds.), *Economy and Culture in North-East England, 1500–1800* (Woodford, 2018), pp. 136–55; James Walvin, *The Quakers: Money and Morals* (London, 1997).

[49] William Ashley Smith, *The Birth of Modern Education: The Contribution of the Dissenting Academies, 1660–1800* (London, 1954), p. 324; F. Robinson and P. J. Wallis, 'Some Early Mathematical Schools in Whitehaven', *Transactions of the Cumberland & Westmorland Antiquarian & Archaeological Society*, ser. 2, 75 (1975), pp. 262–74.

national institutions meant that when not interacting within their own religious community they would be conscious of this exclusion, while at the same time being part of a larger Protestant community.

Given this need to negotiate, it is unsurprising that Dissenters focused on the role of reason, both as used by Cumberland in his system of obligation towards others, and in the control of the passions elucidated by Baxter and those who influenced him. Certainly, this does not mean they neglected the emotional side of worship, but this had, by law, to be confined to their own religious communities. In public it made sense to think of the national Protestant community as held together by the 'reasonableness of Christianity'. This, of course, was the tile of a tract written by John Locke and published in 1695. Here, and in the earlier *Essays on the Law of Nature* (1664), Locke argued that through the use of reason human beings could gain access to and knowledge of basic moral truths, which ultimately arose from a moral order in 'the soil of human nature'.[50] Although Locke never publicly considered himself a non-conformist, and went to some pains to stress the providential truth of scripture, his sympathies were undoubtedly with Protestant toleration and independent thought. There has been a tendency to link dissent to the Enlightenment because of the emphasis on rationality, but as we have seen, Cumberland and the Latitudinarians were heavily committed to the new science and to rationality. In this sense, Locke can be studied as an example of the differences between the independent self and the one thought about by more moderate Dissenters and Latitudinarians.

Although Locke's family had puritan sympathies, as a young man at Oxford he welcomed the return of Charles II and was sceptical of enthusiastic visionary politics. In the early 1660s he wrote a series of disputations on natural law in which he expressed an opinion that was to set him apart from the Latitudinarian developments. Here he argued that natural law is not inscribed on our hearts by God, but is only discoverable through the experiences of our senses.[51] By the late 1660s he had also come to believe in the toleration of all speculative opinions from legal censorship. But he remained sympathetic to Whichcote and Tillotson before his exile in the Netherlands. This exile was necessary because of his friendship and work for the First Earl of Shaftesbury and the exclusionist Whigs after 1679. While in the Netherlands, he wrote the

[50] John Locke, 'Essays on the Law of Nature (1663–1664)', in M. Goldie (ed.), *Locke: Political Essays* (Cambridge, 1997), pp. 79–133.

[51] J. R. Milton, 'Locke, John (1632–1704), philosopher', *Oxford Dictionary of National Biography*, www-oxforddnb-com.ezp.lib.cam.ac.uk/view/10.1093/ref:odnb/9780198614128.001.0001/odnb-9780198614128-e-16885, accessed 11 March 2021.

Second Treatise on Government and also finished the manuscript of his *Essay on Human Understanding*, which was eventually published in 1690 after the Glorious Revolution. Soon after, he also had *A Letter Concerning Toleration* published anonymously and translated by a merchant of Unitarian views. In 1695, he published *The Reasonableness of Christianity*. This, with its simple acknowledgement of Jesus as the Messiah, seemed to some readers to suggest the anti-trinitarianism of the Socinians.[52] In fact, Locke had a large number of Socinian books in his library. But in the *Essay on Human Understanding*, Locke went to some lengths to show how revelation combined with reason worked in his model of the mind to produce virtue, and as a result it was not seen as a challenge to the established Church.[53]

Locke believed in the ability of individual reason to provide objective knowledge to control the passions. But he firmly placed much more of an emphasis on self-control than mutual interest, as is evident in this description of natural law:

> First, the divine law, whereby I mean that law which God has set to the actions of men, whether promulgated to them by the light of nature, or the voice of revelation. That God has given a rule whereby men should govern themselves, I think there is nobody so brutish as to deny. He has a right to do it, we are his creatures: he has goodness and wisdom to direct our actions to that which is best; and he has power to enforce it by rewards and punishments, of infinite weight and duration in another life.[54]

In his *Essay Concerning Human Understanding* he followed Descartes by shifting the locus of epistemology away from the value of social interaction to the construction of the internal mind, which famously began as a 'blank slate'. Such a mind learned about the physical world through certain mechanical processes, and about value through the providence of God's laws and punishments.[55] The philosopher Charles Taylor has termed Locke's project the creation of the 'punctual self', meaning that it was Locke more than anyone else who was responsible for the creation of the philosophical linguistic notion that the 'self' was in an internal

52 Ibid. At this time Unitarian referred to a Transylvanian religious sect, while the doctrine was termed Socinianism after the teachings of the sixteenth-century Italians Lelio Sozzini (Latin: Laelius Socinus) and Fausto Sozzini (Latin: Faustus Socinus).

53 John Locke, *An Essay Concerning Human Understanding*, ed. Roger Woolhouse (Harmondsworth, 1997) (Book I, IV, 17–18), pp. 100–1. However, Locke and Stillingfleet became engaged in a bad-tempered argument over the existence of the Trinity and other aspects of faith, but this argument contained nothing material to the morals under consideration in this chapter.

54 Locke, *Essay Concerning Human Understanding*, p. 317.

55 John Dunn, '"Bright Enough for All Our Purposes": John Locke's Conception of a Civilized Society', *Notes and Records of the Royal Society of London* 43 (1989), pp. 140–1.

space, or point, properly belonging to each autonomous individual.[56] For Locke, development of the self involved 'the great privilege of finite intellectual Beings' to take responsibility for 'our selves' to examine good and evil in order to achieve real happiness.[57] For Locke, happiness came from the self's success in being able to achieve rational understanding and control over passion.[58]

Although Locke had no children of his own, given his theory of the mind, he understandably thought that education of children was important. As a result he published *Some Thoughts Concerning Education*, where he argued that the central purpose of education was education into virtue, and this meant training in self-control: 'The Principle of all Vertue and Excellency lies in a power of denying our selves the satisfaction of our own Desires, where Reason does not authorize them.'[59] The happiness achieved by such self-control was central to Locke's theory of thought and of modes (as he termed them) of pleasure and pain. Happiness, he baldly stated, was the utmost pleasure of the mind. It was something that all desired, and enjoyment constituted happiness:

> the highest perfection of intellectual nature lies in a careful and constant pursuit of true and solid happiness, so the care of ourselves, that we mistake not imaginary for real happiness, is the necessary foundation of our liberty. The stronger ties we have to an unalterable pursuit of happiness in general, which is our greatest good, and which, as such, our desires always follow, the more are we free … from a necessary compliance with our desire … till we have duly examined, whether it has a tendency to, or be inconsistent with our real happiness.[60]

Locke, unsurprisingly, advocated learning to keep accounts of daily expenses as part of his programme of education in order that the 'labour and pains' involved in such 'sober and advantageous reflection' would make young men reflect on the pains involved in earning the money they spent.[61]

Such a view of happiness was very different than the almost ecstatic feeling described by the Cambridge Platonists and their Latitudinarian followers, where happiness was achieved by faith and interest in the faith

[56] Charles Taylor, *Sources of the Self* (Cambridge, 1989), pp. 159–73.
[57] Dunn, 'Bright Enough', p. 136.
[58] Locke, *Essay Concerning Human Understanding*, pp. 224–5; James Tully, 'Governing Conduct', in James Tully, *An Approach to Political Philosophy: Locke in Contexts* (Cambridge, 1993), pp. 214–19; Susan James, *Passion and Action: The Emotions in Seventeenth-Century Philosophy* (Oxford, 1997), pp. 284–8.
[59] John Locke, *Some Thoughts Concerning Education*, ed. John Yolton and Jean Yolton (Oxford, 1989), section 38; Milton, 'Locke, John'.
[60] Locke, *Essay Concerning Human Understanding*, XXI, ch. 51, p. 244.
[61] Locke, *Some Thoughts Concerning Education*, pp. 261–2.

of others. For Locke, the quest to achieve happiness was done by avoiding desires that would contravene God's will.[62] Since Locke remained suspicious of enthusiastic religion and its emotionalism, his view of happiness was expressed as a negative avoidance of punishment. Public forms of discipline to reform manners and attempts to instil habits of work in the able-bodied poor had a long history by the end of the seventeenth century. But previous acts of punishment and institutions such as houses of correction had been instruments of public authority, and what Locke was proposing was something new. His aim was not public punishment, but to use institutions like schools and workhouses to educate private consciences against received customs and replace them with virtuous habits, obedience, and work discipline.[63]

By all accounts, Locke was an unusually self-disciplined man and was quite able to follow his own dictum, and he kept very detailed accounts of his daily expenses. He also took concern with the most intricate details of his estate, lived a very frugal and well-controlled life, and saved enough to die in 1704 worth £15,000–16,000.[64] He had inherited a small estate from his father in Somerset, and although he bought stock in the Bank of England and made some other investments, he earned most of his income from his official salaries. As a member of the Board of Trade he was paid £600 per year.[65] He also kept a journal and pocket memorandum books from 1675 until he died. This link between the keeping of regular accurate accounts and the success of an educated rational self was a crucial development that stood at a remove from more religious

62 Ibid., pp. 242–8.

63 Tully, 'Governing Conduct', pp. 234–9. Also see James Tully 'Rights in Abilities', in James Tully, *An Approach to Political Philosophy: Locke in Contexts* (Cambridge, 1993), pp. 247–61. Tully traces the origins of disciplinary institutions back to the late eighteenth century in England, and compares the houses of correction and workhouses advocated by the framers of the English Poor Laws to the French institutions analysed by Foucault. But, as Paul Slack has shown, such institutions were never very successful in England before the eighteenth century because of their expense, and as a result the able-bodied unemployed poor were more often provided with outdoor relief in the form of cash payments in the same manner as the impotent poor, and were not disciplined. Tully, 'Governing Conduct', pp. 208, 234, 237–8; Paul Slack, *Poverty and Policy in Tudor & Stuart England* (Harlow, 1988), pp. 29, 128, 149–56. For such institutions in the eighteenth century, see Joanna Innes, 'Prisons for the Poor: English Bridewells, 1555–1800', in Francis Snyder and Douglas Hay (eds.), *Labour, Law, and Crime: An Historical Perspective* (London, 1987), pp. 42–122; Margaret R. Hunt, *The Middling Sort: Commerce, Gender, and the Family in England 1680–1780* (Berkeley, 1996), pp. 101–24.

64 Bodleian Library, Oxford: Lovelace Collection, MS Locke c.1 'Ledgers of Accounts, 1671–1704'; MS Locke F.1-10, 'Locke's Journals, 1675–1704'.

65 Patrick Hyde Kelly, 'Introduction: Locke's Finances', in Patrick Hyde Kelly (ed.), *Locke on Money* (Oxford, 1991), I, pp. 100–4.

treatments of the self, although they were by no means incompatible. When we examine some diaries below, we can see how important new ideas about the self were to the social expansion of account keeping.

Locke also wrote about economic matters directly, although not in a systematic way. As Patrick Kelly, the editor of his writings on money, has noted, there was nothing about the atmosphere at Oxford in the time when Locke was there that might kindle an interest in matters of trade or finance.[66] However, this changed once he joined the First Earl of Shaftesbury's household as physician and tutor in 1667. Shaftesbury was chancellor of the Exchequer from 1661 to 1672, and also very interested in trade and colonial policy. This led Locke to become concerned with writing up a constitution for the colony of Carolina. But more importantly, in 1668 a controversy arose over the question of interest rates after the merchant Josiah Childe published a pamphlet calling for the reduction of the legal interest rate, arguing that this would boost trade. Childe, who amassed a fortune as a supplier to the Navy, had become a major stockholder in the East India Company and was a vocal supporter of its monopoly privileges (he became a director in 1677). It was suspected that his pamphlet was an attempt to make it easier for the Company to attract scarce investment after the Second Dutch War. This had come about because of heavy government borrowing in what was still an underdeveloped market for financial capital.[67] As a result of this, a bill to reduce the official interest rate from 6 to 4 per cent was introduced in Parliament, and the new Council of Trade set up that year and headed by the First Earl of Shaftesbury was instructed to look into the question. Locke wrote a manuscript arguing against the proposal, noting that since there was a market for borrowing money, the interest rate represented the balance between supply and demand for money. Any attempt to reduce it by law would be bound to fail, since people would stop lending if they thought the interest rate was insufficient to compensate them for the risk involved.[68] We don't know how influential Locke's opinion was at this time, but the bill was unsuccessful, and as far as Locke's career was concerned the political events of the Exclusion crisis overtook Shaftesbury's and his own work on economic matters when they had to go into exile in 1675.

Locke was unable to return to England until after the Revolution in 1689. While in exile, however, he wrote his *Two Treatises on Government*. These dealt primarily with criticising the divine right of kings and

[66] Ibid. [67] Ibid., pp. 7–9.

[68] Locke, 'The Early Writings on Interest', in Patrick Hyde Kelly (ed.), *Locke on Money* (Oxford, 1991), I, pp. 167–342.

outlining his theory of the basis of legitimate government, but in doing so he also developed a theory of property based on his idea of the personal self and labour, which argued that it was work that created the right to both land and things created with its resources.[69] This is the punctual self working towards the improvement of the material basis of society using his or her discipline to avoid 'fancy'. Although Locke also developed a theory of money in the second *Treatise*, he did not explicitly link it to his writing on interest rates.[70]

Locke was only brought back into debates about the interest rate once he returned to England. This was because the entry of England into the Nine Years' War had led to the need for the government to tap into the London capital market. With the return of the Whigs to power, even though Shaftesbury was dead, Locke was sought out by their now leader, Sir John Somers, who convinced him to revisit the question of interest rates and to publish his opinions. As a result, Locke wrote a tract titled *Some Considerations of Consequence of the Lowering of Interest, and the Raising the Value of Money* in 1691. Here he repeated his argument that interest rates on borrowed money should be set by the market by supply and demand. But he also put forward a quite elaborate account of how money circulated through society, looking at wages, rent, commodity purchases, and to some extent banking. He also continued his scepticism about the ability of government to enforce an artificial interest rate, arguing that it would lead men using higher interest rates to lie about it:

> For where [temptations] are strong, (as they are where Men shall Swear for their own Advantage) there the fear of Penalties to follow will have little Restraint; especially if the Crime be hard to be proved.[71]

He extended this scepticism to the viability of fiat money. While he accepted that paper instruments such as bills of exchange were used commonly by merchants, they could not enter general circulation because of the amount of trust they would require:

> The Necessity therefore of a Proportion of Money to Trade, depends on Money not as Counters, for the Reckoning may be kept, or transferred by Writing; but on Money as a Pledge, which Writing cannot supply the place of: Since the Bill, Bond, or other Note of Debt, I receive from one Man will not be accepted as Security by another, he not knowing that the Bill or Bond is true or legal, or that

[69] John Locke, *Two Treatises of Government*, ed. Peter Laslett (New York, 1963), II, chs. 26–8, 34, 40.

[70] Ibid., chs. 48–51.

[71] John Locke, 'Some Considerations of the Consequences of the Lowering of Interest and the Raising the Value of Money (London, 1692)', in Patrick Hyde Kelly (ed.), *Locke on Money* (Oxford, 1991), II, pp. 212–13.

the Man bound to me is honest or responsible; and so is not valuable enough to become a current Pledge, nor can by publick Authority be well made so, as in the Case of Assigning of Bills. Because a Law cannot give to Bills that intrinsick Value, which the universal Consent of Mankind has annexed to Silver and Gold … they are liable to unavoidable Doubt, Dispute, and Counterfeiting, and require other Proofs to assure us that they are true and good Security.[72]

As a result of this position, Locke became involved in the pamphlet debates over the question of devaluation in the years leading up to the Great Recoinage. Locke was recruited by those Whigs who supported the case for revaluing all of the clipped silver coinage back to its original value. These were mostly merchants who did not want to lose out by having to use devalued coin in foreign exchange. There were also those who supported the idea of the creation of a public bank to create credit currency for merchants and tradesmen based on convertibility to gold or silver for security. This, as was discussed in Chapter 2, was done in opposition to the Tory proposals for a much more socially inclusive form of paper currency. Since Locke had become famous as the author of the *Theory of Human Understanding* (published in 1689), it was felt that his opinion would carry considerable weight. As a result, Locke wrote a number of tracts that carried the day, and the recoinage was done as a revaluation.

Ever since, Locke has been painted as the godfather of monetary conservatism, which seeks to restrict liquidity to protect the value of existing assets rather than aiming for economic growth. However, Patrick Kelly has argued that Locke's main concern was never ideological, but rather was motivated by the practicalities of the recoinage. But, as can be seen in the quote above, his caution over devaluing the currency probably stemmed as much from his belief that a currency with a solid intrinsic value was needed as a touchstone in a world where so many lacked the discipline he thought necessary to maintain trust in a non-intrinsic fiat currency.[73] Overall, Locke seems to have been much more sceptical about trust than were Cumberland or other Latitudinarians, which was possibly linked to his greater stress on the need for discipline.[74]

As both Kelly and the legal historian of money Christine Desan have pointed out, Locke's theory of the state supporting the intrinsic market

[72] Locke, 'Some Considerations', II, p. 234.
[73] Ibid., I, pp. 22–33; II, pp. 226–9, 235; Craig Muldrew, '"Hard Food for Midas": Cash and Its Social Value in Early Modern England', *Past and Present* 170 (2001), pp. 86–7, 94.
[74] John Dunn, 'The Concept of "Trust" in the Politics of John Locke', in Richard Rorty, Jerome B. Schneewind, and Quentin Skinner (eds.), *Philosophy in History* (Cambridge, 1984), pp. 279–302.

value of money was not conservative, but intensely radical, since it overturned the monarch's well-established legal right to set a standard for the coinage.[75] Perhaps this was an extension of his argument against divine right, even if he did not state it as such. But whatever his motivation, the idea of paper currency supported by an immediate right to have it converted into gold or silver, proposed by Locke and adopted by the Bank of England, created a new ideology that would eventually be supported by the Tories in the early nineteenth century as the gold standard.[76]

As we saw in Chapter 2, the tumultuous years of the early eighteenth century saw continual party conflict between the Whigs and Tories over the expenses of continental warfare, which led to the formation of the South Sea Company, the infamous bubble, and subsequent debt restructuring. In these events we can certainly see how the non-conformists, and their Anglican supporters among the Whigs, were able to use a Lockean discipline to make investors trust that government finance was secure. The institutions of the financial revolution required sound and thorough account keeping, but as the collapse of the South Sea Company and the Charitable Corporation demonstrated, it was more prudent to trust directors and accountants who, like Locke, possessed some religious reason to feel internal guilt and mental pain in the face of the temptations of misfeasance. In addition, it was important that the idea of saving be both understood and safe.[77] Individuals had to be able to forgo immediate pleasure for long-term gain, but – more importantly – they had to be able to trust institutions like the Bank of England, the British imperial state, or individuals such as local solicitors, with whom they could safely invest their capital or wages over long periods of time without the anxiety that it would be embezzled or lost through bankruptcy.

In contrast, the Tories became associated with failed institutions and with much less disciplined, more freewheeling, speculative, and to a degree more ambitiously innovative economic activity. But also, with the directors of the South Sea Company, a more mendacious form of activity. But the so-called Bubble Act, passed just before the South Sea Bubble burst, limited the ability to create new joint stock companies, and

75 Christine Desan, *Making Money: Coin, Currency, and the Coming of Capitalism* (Oxford, 2014), pp. 345–53; Kelly, 'Introduction', p. 29.

76 Desan, *Making Money*, pp. 354–53, 404–15; Boyd Hilton, *Corn, Cash and Commerce: The Economic Policies of the Tory Governments 1815–1830* (Oxford, 1977), pp. 31–66.

77 On the fraud of the Charitable Corporation, which ostensibly aimed to help poor debtors, see Beverly Lemire, *The Business of Everyday Life: Gender, Practice and Social Politics in England, C.1600–1900* (Manchester, 2005), pp. 56–81; John Carswell, *The South Sea Bubble* (Stroud, 1993).

thus ended the speculative type of business organisation found in the boom of the 1690s.[78] In addition, the mint continued a policy of monetary conservatism over the eighteenth century in minting very few small silver coins or non-precious tokens. In this sense, one might speak of a Whig policy of conservatism pursued with the aim of securing trust in a small number of joint stock companies that the government relied on to fund warfare through the national debt. This forced those wanting to use capital for economic investment to seek other means, which was achieved as we saw through the nexus of inland bills of exchange and local notes of hand. This, as we will see when we examine some diaries, could also well be achieved within a less stringent Latitudinarian moral framework.

Third Earl of Shaftesbury

Locke's theory of the disciplined self attained a much wider social influence through the writings of his student Anthony Ashley-Cooper, the Third Earl of Shaftesbury. Shaftesbury developed a much less analytic and austere form of happiness than his teacher. Shaftesbury was also influenced by Cumberland, and famously advocated polite conversation as a means of creating sociability. Although his philosophy was not aimed directly at economic practices, he also had a huge influence on eighteenth-century practices of moral self-government and sociability.[79] Shaftesbury, who was a good accountant, did not advocate a penalised thriftiness, but rather moderate polite pleasure through acts of socialised self-expression in the form of wit.[80] His ideas were collected in a series of previously published essays entitled *Characteristics of Men, Manners, Opinions and Times*, published in 1711, which ranged widely over many subjects and examples and often took the literary form of contemporary conversations rather than being presented in the form of deductive analytical philosophy of the mind and human behaviour. Shaftesbury associated with radical Whigs such as John Toland, and his writing

[78] Koji Yamamoto, *Taming Capitalism before its Triumph: Public Service, Distrust, and 'Projecting' in Early Modern England* (Cambridge, 2018); Christine MacLeod, *Inventing the Industrial Revolution: The English Patent System, 1660–1800* (Cambridge, 2002).

[79] Lawrence E. Klein, *Shaftesbury and the Culture of Politeness: Moral Discourse and Cultural Politeness in Early Eighteenth-Century England* (Cambridge, 1994); Lawrence E. Klein, 'Liberty, Manners, and Politeness in Early Eighteenth-Century England', *Historical Journal* 32 (1989), pp. 583–605; Lawrence E. Klein, 'Politeness for Plebs: Consumption and Social Identity in Early Eighteenth-Century England', in Roy Porter and John Brewer (eds.), *Consumption and the World of Goods* (London, 1993), pp. 362–82.

[80] Klein, *Shaftesbury and the Culture of Politeness*, pp. 8, 11–12, 54–5, 71–109; Robert Voitle, *The Third Earl of Shaftesbury 1671–1713* (Baton Rouge, 1984), pp. 164–213, 217.

certainly demonstrates a thoroughgoing familiarity with moral philosophy, but it was not theological. He combined a sense of the interiority of the self, which he undoubtedly learned from his tutor Locke, with pedagogic examples of how this was linked to style of self-performance, which came to be known as politeness.

To achieve the disposition needed to engage in polite conversation, Shaftesbury advocated practising inner conversation, or what he called 'soliloquy'. This was emphatically not a form of puritan self-examination, which he thought would lead to zealotry, of which he was critical:

> Stricter Attention to Self-good, and private Interest; ... must insensibly diminish the Affections towards publick Good, or the Interest of Society; and introduce a certain Narrowness of Spirit, which ... is peculiarly observable in the devout Persons.[81]

However, despite being opposed to Baxter's form of strict self-denial, he also used a similar metaphor of establishing a court within the mind to judge thoughts with what he called his Doctrine of *Two Persons* in one individual *Self*:

> Thoughts can never appear very correct; unless they have been us'd to sound Correction by themselves, and been well form'd and disciplin'd before they are brought into the Field. 'Tis the hardest thing in the world to be a good Thinker, without being a strong Self-Examiner.[82]

> For let Will be ever so free, Humour and Fancy, we see, govern it. ...So that if there be no certain Inspector or Auditor establish'd within us, to take account of these Opinions and Fancys in due form ... we are as little like to continue a Day in the same *Will*...

> As cruel a Court as *the Inquisition* appears; there must, it seems, be full as formidable a one, erected in our-selves; if we wou'd pretend to that Uniformity of Opinion which is necessary to hold us to one Will, and preserve us in the same mind, from one day to another.[83]

He then added a further metaphor of a well-inventoried home, which has an obvious affinity to thrifty household accounting:

> There is no way of estimating Manners, or apprizing the different Humours, Fancys, Passions and Apprehensions of others, without first taking an Inventory of the same kind of Goods within ourselves, and surveying our domestick Fund. A little of this Home-Practice will serve to make great Discoverys.[84]

But the potential severity of this inner economy was tempered, because its aim was not to discipline and deny, but rather to organise thoughts

[81] Anthony Ashley Cooper, Third Earl of Shaftesbury, *Characteristics of Men, Manners, Opinions, Times*, ed. Lawrence Klein (Cambridge, 1999), pp. 184, 188.
[82] Ibid., p. 76. [83] Ibid., pp. 83–4. [84] Ibid., pp. 85, 198.

through the use of reason in inner conversation before engaging in public conversation so as to avoid conflictual public pronouncements.[85]

Once all minds began to engage such organisation of thoughts, they would realise by their effect on others that they could experience greater feelings of pleasure from this polite conversation than from self-interest:

That as we have more or less of this Intelligence or Comprehension of our-selves, we are accordingly more or less truly Men, and either more or less to be depended on, in Friendship, Society, and the Commerce of Life.[86]

Every mind in this sense became a 'spectator or auditor' of other minds:[87]

When we have thorowly search'd into the nature of this contemplative Delight, we shall find it of a kind which relates not in the least to any private Interest of the Creature, nor has for its Object any Self-good or Advantage of the private System. The Admiration, Joy, or Love, turns wholly upon what is exterior, and foreign to our-selves.

... the Exercise of Benignity and Goodness; where, together with the most delightful Affection of the Soul, there is join'd a pleasing Assent and Approbation of the Mind to what is acted in this good Disposition.[88]

However, unlike Cumberland, he was critical of the idea of self-love, believing it would 'insensibly diminish the Affections towards publick Good'.[89] He did not deny that self-love was connected to self-preservation, but argued that it needed to recognise the social importance of honesty as an object of love:

Other Authors there have been ... who have run Changes, and Divisions, without end, upon this Article of Self-Love ... to set forth this Riddle; That 'act as disinterestedly or generously as you please, Self still is at the bottom, and nothing else.'

The answer to this riddle, he stated, should be not

'Who *lov'd* himself, or Who *not*'; but 'Who lov'd and serv'd himself the *rightest*, and after the truest manner.' 'Tis the height of Wisdom, no doubt, to be rightly *selfish*. And to value *Life*, as far as Life is good ... To be without *Honesty*, is, in effect, to be without *natural Affection* or *Sociableness* of any kind.[90]

Shaftesbury also specifically chose to argue against the idea that a balance of interests could be a substitute for natural law

85 Ibid., pp. 84, 144. 86 Ibid., pp. 127–8. 87 Ibid., p. 172.
88 Ibid., p. 203; see also pp. 78, 175, 126, 208, 217.
89 Ibid., p. 188. For more on this theme, see Muldrew, 'Happiness and the Theology', pp. 81–6.
90 Ibid., p. 56.

theorists' emphasis on absolute civic authority.[91] Only sociability could achieve this:

> YOU have heard it (my Friend!) as a common Saying, that *Interest governs the World.* But, I believe, whoever looks narrowly into the Affairs of it, will find, that *Passion, Humour, Caprice, Zeal, Faction,* and a thousand other Springs, which are counter to *Self-Interest,* have as considerable a part in the Movements of this Machine.

He complained that authors who subscribed to this view claimed that 'nothing shou'd be understood to be done *in Kindness*, or *Generosity*' and that

> They wou'd new-frame the human Heart; and have a mighty fancy to reduce all its Motions, Balances and Weights, to that one Principle and Foundation of a cool and deliberate *Selfishnes.*[92]

In this way, Shaftesbury married the older Renaissance tradition of pleasurable civil conversation, motivated by the pleasures of wit, humour, and honesty, with new ideas about the mind and its passions.[93]

Largely through the work of Lawrence Klein, we know how influential Shaftesbury's model of sociable politeness became after being promoted by Addison and Steele in the *Spectator*, named after his model of the sociable mind. Individuals now formed themselves into voluntary associations or met in coffeehouses and taverns to practise the art of conversation. These were perhaps not always as sober and polite as Shaftesbury might have desired, but there were enormous numbers of them where men met to discuss politics and knowledge disseminated through periodical literature.[94] John Brewer has also shown how eighteenth-century clubs and voluntary associations were increasingly used to negotiate creditworthiness.[95]

Bernard Mandeville

Another writer to argue for the effect of self-love on the economy was somewhat of an outsider – Bernard Mandeville. Mandeville was born in

[91] Albert O. Hirschman, *Passions and the Interests* (Princeton, 2013), pp. 31–48.
[92] Shaftesbury, *Characteristics of Men*, pp. 51, 53–4.
[93] Phil Withington, 'Tobacco and the Social Life of Conquest in London, 1580–1625', *The Historical Journal* 65, no. 1 (2022), pp. 30–48.
[94] Peter Clark, *British Clubs and Societies, 1580–1800: The Origins of an Associational World* (Oxford, 2000).
[95] John Brewer, 'Commercialization and Politics', in Neil McKendrick, John Brewer, and J. H. Plumb (eds.), *The Birth of a Consumer Society* (London, 1983), pp. 217–30.

Rotterdam in 1670 and was of Huguenot background. He trained as a physician in Leiden and moved to England at some time in the 1690s. However, probably because of his training in Holland, he developed a much more sceptical view of self-love, one that had evolved in France in the late seventeenth century, and which was quite different from the version developed in England that we have been discussing. There, the Jansenists Pierre Bayle and Pierre Nicole cast doubt on the claim that there was any sort of basic morally good self-love that could be developed separately from what Richard Baxter had termed carnal self-love. For them it was impossible for an observer to distinguish between a true act of benevolence and a secretly egotistical performance of benevolence to obtain a purely selfish desire.

Mandeville's satiric poem and subsequent commentary, *The Fable of the Bees: Or, Private Vices, Publick Benefits*, first published in 1714 with additions in 1723, constructed an entire sociology of consumption based on the egoistic satisfaction of private desires driven by passions. Government, in his argument, was now based neither on virtuous authority nor on an original contract to administer a body of laws. Rather, the authority and respect embodied in governmental offices channelled individual competition for power into beneficial administration, in which virtue was merely a display.[96] Mandeville thought the unbridled consumption of luxury was far more conducive to the promotion of prosperity than government. In the view of moralists, such consumption was 'private vice', but in Mandeville's view it led to public benefits.[97]

In his *Fable of the Bees* he famously abandoned the trope of household thrift to advocate unfettered luxury consumption on the part of elites as part of his argument for how the pursuit of self-interested appetite for pleasure would lead to the social good of employment for the poor in industries producing luxury goods.[98] However, he almost totally disregarded financial probity and indebtedness, and went so far as to criticise the act of saving as being based on the error of frugality.[99] He specifically claimed that saving by labourers and working people would only lead them to work less, and he also thought that in terms of political economy saving would hinder luxury consumption:

Frugality in *Ethicks* is call'd that Virtue from the Principle of which Men abstain from Superfluities, and despising the operose Contrivances of Art to procure

[96] E. G. Hundert, *The Enlightenment's Fable: Bernard Mandeville and the Discovery of Society* (Cambridge, 1994), pp. 62–75. Muldrew, 'Self-Control and Savings,' pp.77–9.
[97] Bernard Mandeville, *The Fable of the Bees*, ed. F. B. Kaye (Oxford, 1924), I, pp. 104–6.
[98] Ibid., I, pp. 104–6, 119–20, 128, 170–3. [99] Ibid., I, pp. 181–3.

either Ease or Pleasure, content themselves with the natural Simplicity of things … As this prudent Oeconomy, which some People call *Saving*, is in private Families the most certain Method to increase an Estate, so some imagine that whether a Country be barren or fruitful, the same Method, if generally pursued (which they think practicable) will have the same Effect upon a whole Nation, and that, for Example, the *English* might be much richer than they are, if they would be as frugal as some of their Neighbours. This, I think, is an Error.[100]

For Mandeville, only unhindered desire for luxury could motivate consumption.

Mandeville also chose to specifically debunk Shaftesbury's notion of sociable happiness. For Mandeville, approbation was nothing but vain glory:

The great Recompence in view, for which the most exalted Minds have with so much Alacrity sacrificed their Quiet, Health, sensual Pleasures, and every Inch of themselves, has never been any thing else but … the Aerial Coin of Praise … it consists in a superlative Felicity which a Man, who is conscious of having perform'd a noble Action, enjoys in Self-love, whilst he is thinking on the Applause he expects of others.[101]

Even though it was presented as a satire, Mandeville's attack on traditional mainstream religious and classical notions of virtue made him notorious and unpopular, and his main popular effect was as someone who could be argued against rather than as someone whose advice was practised.

Josiah Tucker

Latitudinarian ideas of self-love affected economic practice before they were incorporated into political economy. This was eventually done by Josiah Tucker, an Anglican minister who wrote largely on economic matters. He was born in Wales in 1713 and educated in Oxford. He was appointed curate of St. Stephen's, Bristol, in 1737, where he met Joseph Butler, who became a great influence on him, and was appointed Dean of Gloucester Cathedral in 1758. He remained in Bristol until he died in 1799. His first publication was an attack on Methodism, and he published numerous works on religious subjects including a defence of naturalisation for foreigners of different religions, but by the 1740s his main interest had become the burgeoning field that has come to be known as political economy, after the French term that had become current in that decade.[102] In the early eighteenth century, Bristol was Britain's

[100] Ibid., I, pp. 191–3, 182ff. [101] Ibid., I, p. 55.

[102] Muldrew, 'Politics and Economics of Markets', pp. 119–21; G. Shelton, *Dean Tucker and 18th-Century Economics and Political Thought* (New York, 1981), pp. 91–132.

second largest port, and the gateway to the Atlantic colonial and slave trades, which were rapidly expanding at the time. It became a centre outside London and produced writers on economic subjects.

The most famous of these was the merchant John Cary, who traded in the Caribbean and Mediterranean. In 1695 he published a tract entitled *A Discourse on Trade*, which, as Sophus Reinert has shown, became probably the most influential tract on economic matters in the first half of the eighteenth century.[103] Interestingly, Cary became a great friend of Locke, as both were interested in the questions of how policies on trade and the colonies could be used to advance industry and manufacturing to provide employment for the poor and for the national wealth. While there had been a number of writings on similar topics in the late seventeenth century – such as John Houghton's *England's Great Happiness* of 1677, William Petyt's *Britannia Languens* of 1680, and Joshua Child's *Discourse of Trade* of 1690 – Cary's work was the most comprehensive. Although monetary matters were dealt with in such writings, and while many such authors participated in the debates discussed in Chapter 2, they focused more on promoting industry and foreign trade.[104]

These authors also, for the most part, focused much more on providing advice on how to improve the economy rather than giving advice on individual moral behaviour in the form of older advice manuals. This is not to say that such advice disappeared. Daniel Defoe wrote many pamphlets and tracts on economic matters, but one of his most popular works was his *Complete English Tradesman*, first published in 1726, which was written as a series of letters of advice to a young man just starting in business.[105] A number of these letters stressed the behaviours necessary for the formation of capital, such as the importance of keeping good accounts, lending at interest, and writing promissory notes and bills of exchange in an honest way. But, even more, his emphasis was on older behavioural morals such as personal credit, reputation, and living within one's means.[106] It was published when he was sixty-six, only five years before he died, so he was obviously looking back over a long career, and of course personal credit remained vital through the eighteenth century, so this is not surprising. In addition, as a number of authors have discussed, the vast increase in public borrowing discussed in Chapter 2 was publicly debated not so much in terms of what was the correct rate of

[103] Sophus A. Reinert, *Translating Empire: Emulation and the Origins of Political Economy* (Cambridge, MA, 2011), pp. 73–128.
[104] John Cary, *A Discourse on Trade* (London, 1745), pp. 26–32.
[105] Daniel Defoe, *The Complete English Tradesman in Familiar Letters* (London, 1727), chs. 27–33.
[106] Ibid., chs. 8, 10, 17.

interest, but in terms of the risk that the state and monarch would lose their credit if the public debt was too large.[107] The collapse of the South Sea Bubble was also written about more in moral terms of excessive folly than rational investment.[108]

Tucker was the first writer I have discovered who developed a *system* relating the new self to commerce. This was not a common trope; even Locke had not provided a worked-out conceptual link between his *Theory of Human Understanding* and his economic writings, even if he thought about them in private.[109] Tucker theoriseed about the relationship of commerce to society in terms of self-love and interest instead of mutual dependence.[110] In one of his sermons he asked, 'How are the ends both of religion and government to be answered but by the system of universal commerce?' This, he went on to say, employs mankind, 'so as to make self-interest and the social coincide. And in pursuing this plan ... it serves as a cement to connect together the religious and civil interests of mankind.'[111] His ideas were most explicitly stated in what he termed his preliminary discourse to *The Elements of Commerce and Theory of Taxes*, which was intended to be the first part of a much larger work dealing with all aspects of commerce, including population, free trade and monopolies, colonies, money, taxes, and the poor. This was entitled 'The natural Disposition, or inclination of Mankind towards Commerce'. Here he began with a standard Ciceronian assumption about sociability:

> M A N K I N D therefore being thus under the Influence of Social and benevolent Affections ... naturally seek Society in order to gratify these social Instincts.[112]

But he then quickly moved into much more individualistic territory, arguing that although society was the best means for procuring natural

[107] J. G. A. Pocock, *The Machiavellian Moment: Florentine Political Thought and the Atlantic Republican Tradition* (Princeton, 1975), pp. 436–61; Sandra Sherman, *Finance and Fictionality in the Early Eighteenth Century: Accounting for Defoe* (Cambridge, 1996); Natalie Roxburgh, *Representing Public Credit: Credible Commitment, Fiction, and the Rise of the Financial Subject* (Routledge, 2016). Charles Davenant, *Discourses on the Public Revenues*, in Sir Charles Whitworth (ed.), *The Political and Commercial Works of That Celebrated Writer Charles Davenant* (London, 1771), pp. 151–2.

[108] Helen J. Paul, *The South Sea Bubble: An Economic History of its Origins and Consequences* (London, 2011), pp. 109–22.

[109] David Wootton (ed.), *John Locke, Political Writings* (Harmondsworth, 1993), pp. 440–2.

[110] For writings on mutual dependence, see Craig Muldrew, *The Economy of Obligation: The Culture of Credit and Social Relations in Early Modern England* (London 1998), pp. 138–47.

[111] T. W. Hutchison, *Before Adam Smith: The Emergence of Political Economy, 1662–1776* (Oxford, 1988), p. 228.

[112] Josiah Tucker, *The Elements of Commerce and Theory of Taxes* (Bristol, 1755), p. 5.

wants, or necessities, it also gave rise to a 'multitude *of artificial* needs'. These were consumer goods, the desire for which was created by the difference between 'the several Ranks and Stations in Society'. But although emulation and social advancement might have been motivating factors for increasing consumption, they would have no force without the desire for happiness as a result of self-love:

> And as our present *secular* Happiness appears to arise from the Enjoyment of superior Wealth, Power, Honour, Pleasure, or Preferment, SELF-LOVE, the great Mover of created Beings, determines each Individual to aspire after these social Goods, and to use the most probable Means of obtaining them.[113]

Tucker condemned Mandeville's views as absurd, and made a counter-argument that 'virtue alone could make a nation flourish'.[114] This virtue involved using reason in the form of both self- and social governance to direct self-love and self-interest into a useful form:

> For the Love of Self is implanted in Mankind much more Strongly than Love of Benevolence; according to the English Proverb, *Self knows no Fellow.*
>
> THEREFORE REASON and REFLECTION must be called to the Aid of the *social* and *benevolent* Principle. But what is the *office* of Reason? – Not surely to extinguish Self-Love; that is impossible ... Consequently, the main Point to be aimed at, is neither to extinguish nor enfeeble Self-Love, but to give it such a Direction, that it may promote the public Interest by pursuing its own.
>
> ... the Reason or public Wisdom of a State, or Community is particularly called upon to pursue such a Plan. Divert therefore the Pursuits of Self-Love from vicious or improper Objects, to those that are commendable and virtuous ... The Country will be blessed with Plenty, and abound in Commerce, by means of the Industry of its Inhabitants in their respective Callings; And the Subjects of such a State must feel ... happy in each other, because their several pursuits, Interests and Happiness do all coincide.[115]

Such a system would incline people to virtuous industry and greater production, reducing the cost of manufactured goods, which would encourage more general consumption and also frugality and savings, in contradistinction to Mandeville.[116] All of this was so consistent with his view of Christian morality that he was able to conflate utility with faith:

> having so linked our Duty and Interest with that [of] the Community, and prescribed such Regulations for our Conduct and Behaviour, that a Man cannot act the Part of a *good Christian*, without being good and useful, and a public Blessing.[117]

113 Ibid., p. 6. 114 Hutchison, *Before Adam Smith*, p. 229.
115 Tucker, *Elements of Commerce*, p. 7. 116 Hutchison, *Before Adam Smith*, pp. 233–5.
117 Tucker, *Elements of Commerce*, p. 8.

He also condemned monopolies and protective charters as unproductive institutions created as a result of undirected self-love and interest, and supported the naturalisation of productive and industrious foreigners. In subsequent work he praised the natural liberty of the small artisan, and criticised Britain's colonial policy, going so far as to claim 'the love of country has no place in the catalogue of Christian virtues'.[118] Although Tucker is not well known today, in his time he was much admired and translated into French by Turgot. A number of his works were also owned by Adam Smith, and as we will see in the final chapter, there are many similarities to be found in Smith and Tucker, even if the former never cited the latter directly.[119] One reason for Tucker's ensuing disregard is undoubtedly the fact that he never became a coherent philosopher studied by intellectual historians, as did Locke, Hume, or Smith. The fact that he was translated by Turgot is certainly evidence that he can be placed among the Enlightenment republic of letters. Like early French political economists, most of his writings were aimed at practical outcomes rather than system building. In this regard I have dealt with him here because as a sermon-giving member of the Church of England, he undoubtedly had an effect on, and is representative of, the changing moral mentalitié of his time.

Diary-Keeping and the Moralist Self

One aspect of what I think we can confidently call the new 'moralist' psychology of the self was a change in the way people kept journals and diaries, rare though they were. As we saw, moralism meant that people did not now just look for grace, but could also actively examine and act upon their behaviour. In this way, the effect of the dissemination of the theology of personal happiness, and the moral validation of interest and self-love and their effect on economic relations can be traced in ego documents. Good behaviour increasingly involved examining how passions and feelings were related to good or bad actions towards others.

Although the teachings of the Cambridge Platonists questioned strict Calvinism, and they were accused of Arminianism, their emphasis on the self had a corollary in the development of puritan self-examination and the conversion narrative, which developed out of the Protestant prioritisation of consciousness. As a result of this, many chose to write their experiences in diaries and in spiritual autobiographies and conversion

[118] Hutchison, *Before Adam Smith*, pp. 236–8.
[119] Note, however, that Smith rarely cited any of his influences unless to disagree with them.

narratives in which they prioritised their past subjective experience of grace.[120] However, another equally important reason was to keep a record of one's economic activity undertaken within the community. Many diaries from the seventeenth century were pragmatic and spiritual at the same time, and were also used as a means of keeping track of bargains and functioned as informal daybooks. Like formal accounts, they were another means of aiding memory. Such things as debts, money, agreements, disagreements, and sales transactions are all listed in great detail.[121] As formal account keeping became practised by more people, diary-keeping also became modified by moralism and the practice of examining passions and actions. In many cases the two were entwined. The practice of writing accounts generally advocated in accounting manuals was to keep informal daybooks and then transfer information to formal accounts of debtor and creditor at the end of the day or at regular intervals. This became linked to the practice of diary-writing, which also involved rough notes being expanded upon at the end of a day.[122]

It is undoubtedly significant that the first two most detailed diaries in terms of description of a wide variety of personal experience are those of Ralph Josselin and Samuel Pepys, the first started in 1644 until his death in 1683 and the latter from 1660 to 1669.[123] In both cases their diaries were mnemonic devices for their financial dealings, as well as in Josselin's case being about his experience of grace. But the richness of detail that he included moved it beyond the realm of puritan soul searching, in fact creating an 'account' of his day-to-day life that was also a rough financial daybook that would go into the writing of his formal accounts. Such accounts also enabled individuals to make *private* judgements about consumption.[124] In this way they could be used in a Lockean sense to govern appetites by reason and increase private wealth, and therefore in turn reduce the precariousness of tangled webs of interpersonal obligations for the accountant.

Samuel Pepys' case demonstrates this very well. Pepys became a fanatic and very successful accountant, in both his personal life and in

[120] Michael Mascuch, *The Origins of the Individualist Self: Autobiography and Self-Identity in England, 1591–1791* (Chichester, 2013), pp. 51–96.
[121] Muldrew, *Economy of Obligation*, pp. 61, 64–5.
[122] Henry Roseveare, *Markets and Merchants of the Late Seventeenth Century: The Marescoe–David Letters 1668–1680* (Oxford, 1987), pp. 10–16.
[123] Alan Macfarlane, *The Family Life of Ralph Josselin, a Seventeenth Century Clergyman: An Essay in Historical Anthropology* (Cambridge, 1970), p. 33. To these examples could be added the diaries of Thomas Turner, Roger Lowe, and William Stout.
[124] On accounts and public reputation, see Muldrew, *Economy of Obligation*, pp. 128–9, ch. 6.

his employment at the Navy Office. The diary he kept from 1660 to 1669 is full of concerns with his accounting and its terrible difficulty, and was, in fact, a spillover from this practice, as he often wrote it at the same time after doing his personal accounts, alone at night.[125] Even his practice of writing the diary mirrored his account keeping and also formed part of it. Just as a daybook would have been used to make his formal accounts, Pepys composed and organised his diary entries from rough notes, often some days after the events he was describing.[126] It is also probable that much of the financial material included in his diary would have gone into his formal accounts. His obsession with his experience allowed him to strategically measure his pleasure against his need to save and to gain credit, and his obsession with his accounting of finances and experience allowed him to do this successfully. In this way, his diary put an order to his personal experiences just as his accounts created order in his financial dealings that allowed him to become rich.[127]

Pepys does not provide an explanation as to why he started his diary, or any reasons for commenting on what he chose to include. Although Pepys' branch of his family was not wealthy, his cousins included the recorder of Cambridge and the lord chief justice of Ireland. Pepys' father had moved to London in 1601 from an agricultural background in Cottenham, Cambridgeshire to be apprenticed as a tailor. There he married a washer woman.[128] His father was successful enough to give Pepys a very good education at St. Pauls' School and then Magdalen College Cambridge from 1651 to 1654, where he won two scholarships. This put Pepys in a position to take advantage of his familial connections to obtain his position at the Navy Office in 1660.

[125] We can see this with the entries from 10 to 19 April 1668, which were transcribed from three leaves of rough notes, which are inserted in the manuscript. The rough notes were made to serve for a sort of account book, but the amounts paid are often not registered in the fair copy when he came to transcribe his notes into the diary. On Pepys' accounting and rapid financial success, see the discussion in Muldrew, *Economy of Obligation*, pp. 167–71. Robert Latham and William Mathews (eds.), *The Diary of Samuel Pepys* (London, 1970–1983), VII, pp. 65–6, 70, 74, 85–6, 89; VIII, pp. 51, 87, 444. Pepys only gave up writing the diary after worrying that he was losing his eyesight from spending so much time writing by candlelight, but before doing so even experimented with a set of glasses with tubes on to protect his eyes from the candlelight. Ibid., X, 'Companion', pp. 135, 174–5.

[126] Ibid., I, 'Introduction', pp. xxviii, xliv–xlv, xcviii–ciii, cix, cxii.

[127] For a fuller description, see Craig Muldrew, 'Self-Love and the Transformation of Obligation', in Laura Kolb and George Oppitz-Trotman (eds.), *Early Modern Debts* (New York, 2020), pp. 386–7.

[128] Arthur Bryant, *Samuel Pepys: The Man in the Making* (Cambridge, 1933), pp. 3–4, 13, 24–7, 31, 47.

It is clear that Pepys was socially ambitious. Although he was not a freeman of London (since he did not apprentice in a trade), he socialised with many citizens, such as the goldsmith banker and alderman Edward Backwell, the merchant Sir John Banks, and alderman Denis Gauden, who held the contract to victual the Navy. He related his material ambitions to his wife in bed, telling her he would like them to be worth £2,000 so that he could buy a coach to impress others. In the diary he often recorded the progress of his wealth.[129] He was very successful, and the entries in his diary show how he and others, in his appreciation, judged his credit by the standards of his business diligence, and how this dramatically increased his success.

Although he was certainly worried about his personal reputation for credit, taking great care in one instance to hide his being arrested and making rules for himself to curtail his drinking and play-going, he also used accounting to keep track of his wealth, even while he remained uneasy about keeping it as capital. His accounting created financial security based on the knowledge of self-order, and the attempt to achieve this form of *individual security* resulted in keeping a record of his inner experience. It is also obvious that in a sense he gained pleasure simply from the success by which he was able to order his experience every night on his own:

> [I] find myself most happy in the keeping of all my accounts, for that after all the changings and turnings necessary in such an account, I find myself right to a farthing in an account of 127,000l.[130]

He also showed little uneasiness caused by God's pronouncement about adultery, as there should have been in Locke's virtuous model.[131]

Pepys had been a student at Magdalen during the years when the Cambridge Platonists were teaching and preaching, and he might well have been influenced by their emphasis on happiness and pleasure as an expression of God's love, and thinking about the mind and its passions. He possessed books by Henry More and the Latitudinarians Jeremy Taylor and Edward Stillingfleet, and read Descartes. We have little evidence of the nature of Pepys' religious upbringing, but it seems to have contained some elements of the Puritanism so prevalent in the world of London tradesmen in the 1640s and 1650s. Pepys himself, though, made little comment on matters of theology, although he attended many sermons and seems to have been of the moderate rational

129 Pepys, *Diary*, III, p. 125. 130 Ibid., VII, p. 255.

131 Ibid., VII, p. 70; IX, 564–5. Also see the list of 'pleasures' in the index (XI) under the heading of 'Diary'.

Latitudinarian tendency. He found what he termed Presbyterian sermons long-winded and 'dull' or 'lazy', and seems to have preferred a more modern attitude that incorporated the new science. But at the same time, he criticised the puppet show of Bartholomew Fair for its 'stale' satire on Puritans, whom he claimed would be found the wisest in the end.[132]

His diary also discusses his state of mind and feelings about his status and social milieu. He was sometimes vexed in his mind, or mightily pleased, and noted when things like music gave him pleasure. He used the phrase 'my mind' over 700 times to describe his thoughts, and whether they were troubled or whether his mind was at ease, or on occasion 'at mighty ease' or quiet.[133] He also used the word pleasure many times, as in 'So to sleep, every day bringing me a fresh sense of the pleasure of my present life.' Consumption of clothes and household objects was something he often recorded as giving him pleasure.[134] He also commented on his friends, noting their faults or his sympathy towards them. By comparison, Ralph Josselin talked about his emotions entirely in the language of providence and God's immediate effect on his and others' feelings, whereas Pepys talked about his own pleasure and happiness.[135]

In the following passage, Pepys reflected upon the fact that he had been able to purchase his horse and carriage and use it to travel with his servants to visit a lady. Here he directly links consumption of goods to a mental feeling of pleasure, and contemplates how the act of saving is necessary for this:

> [I] do look upon myself at this time in the happiest occasion a man can be, and whereas we take pains in expectation of future comfort and ease, I have taught myself to reflect upon myself at present as happy, and enjoy myself in that consideration, and not only please myself with thoughts of future wealth and forget the pleasure we at present enjoy.[136]

Pepys was certainly concerned with the act of 'saving', even if he did not often use the term. At the end of every year he calculated how much more he was worth in 'money and goods', or in his 'estate', or what he had 'laid up' more than last year. At one point he called himself a 'creditor', but not a saver[137]

Due to his work at the Navy Office, Pepys was intimately involved with the new London bankers and their notes. From 1665 to 1667 he

[132] Ibid., IX, p. 299. [133] Ibid., VII, p. 190.
[134] Janine Maegraith and Craig Muldrew, 'Consumption and Material Life', in Hamish Scott (ed.), *Oxford Handbook of Early Modern European History* (Oxford, 2015), I, pp. 388.
[135] Pepys, *Diary*, VI, pp. 240, 167–71. [136] Ibid., VII, p. 57.
[137] Ibid., V, p. 359; VI, p. 341; VII, p. 426; IV, p. 438.

mentions doing much government business with the goldsmith bankers Sir Robert Viner and John Colville in order to finance purchases for the Navy and to pay its debts. Most of this was done with tallies for £1,000 pounds or more, but he also used bills of exchange drawn on merchants on numerous occasions.[138] However, there are a lot of entries showing he was already writing and using notes, bills, and receipts as currency in the 1660s, both for the Navy and on his own account, as when he used stationer's bills to the Navy to buy some books for himself.[139] On a different occasion he noted that someone brought him their own notes and some good Navy notes for payment. He also 'examined and liked well my notes', and wrote a few notes of hand, but these were all for large amounts.[140]

However, while he did not record having any problem using bills and receipts on his own behalf, he noted that because the Navy was so underfunded their bills were only being accepted at heavy discounts on the Exchange of 10–20 per cent.[141] This resulted in people who had accepted Navy bills as payment 'being forced to sell their bills at 15 per cent loss; and ... they are in a very angry pettish mood at present, and not likely to be better'.[142] The Navy was not helped by the fact that it had yet to develop a reliable and professional bookkeeping system. This was something that Pepys often complained about, such as when he called them 'a company of fools who after they have signed [Mr Creed's] accounts and made bills upon them yet dare not boldly assert to the Treasurer that they are satisfied with his accounts'.[143] He even noted an early case of fraud in the case of one Colonel Appesley, from whom he claimed the Navy had caught 'counterfeiting of bills with all our hands and the officers of the yards, so well counterfeited that I should never have mistrusted them'.[144]

When it came to his savings, though, he was still very cautious and feared that the bankers he dealt with were in danger of bankruptcy since they depended so much on lending to the Crown. He preferred to keep his savings in the form of actual cash in the basement of his house. He was able to collect a great deal of cash collected as taxes by reason of his position at the Navy Office. In August 1665 he reported that he had above 1800*l* in cash, but noted that 'this is very troublesome to have in my house at this time'. He also stored £6,000 of Navy money there. Such

[138] There were about 100 entries for tallies and about 23 for bills of exchange.
[139] Ibid., VII, pp. 197, 217.
[140] Ibid., II, p. 48; VI, p. 325; VII, pp. 308, 382; VIII, pp. 37–8.
[141] Ibid., II, pp. 154, 166. [142] Ibid., IV, p. 103. [143] Ibid., IV, p. 102.
[144] Ibid., III, pp. 43–4.

an arrangement was not very secure, and he worried constantly about theft.[145] Despite such anxieties, he was more worried about the desperate state of government finances at the time: putting his money out at interest with a goldsmith banker could lead to it being lost if the government defaulted, which it did when it delayed payments in 1672. On one occasion he refused 'to put out some money ... into Backwell's hands at 6 per cent interest, which he seldom gives ... being doubtful of trusting any of these great dealers because of their mortality'. But at the same time he also noted the service provided by a bank of 'having one's money, at an houre's call is very great'.[146]

It is interesting to note that at this time earning interest was still considered too risky, as the institutional structure was not robust enough to be trusted. Since he was dealing with government borrowing, he certainly was experienced with the charging of interest rates on loans.[147] He seems to have taken this as normal, which indeed it had been for centuries in relation to government borrowing, although at one point he was concerned that the Crown was losing out by having to pay an interest rate as high as 10 per cent.[148] In terms of theology he also expressed some reservations about the new ideas of interest that were beginning to be preached in the 1660s. After one sermon he noted:

> Mr. Mills preached upon Christ's being offered up for our sins ... speaking again, the Father is now so satisfied by our security for our debt, that we might say at the last day as many of us as have interest in Christ's death: Lord, we owe thee nothing, our debt is paid. We are not beholden to, thee for anything, for thy debt is paid to thee to the full; which methinks were very bold words.[149]

Although Pepys composed his diary roughly twenty years before John Locke wrote his *Essay Concerning Human Understanding*, both men were influenced by similar 'Puritan' ideas. The diary shows that accounting could create a 'punctual' economics to replace chains of interpersonal obligations, which was necessary before savings could develop into secure and mobile investment funds.

Dudley Ryder

Moving forward to the period of the financial revolution, in the diary that the young Dudley Ryder kept between 1715 and 1716 we can see the influence of the Third Earl of Shaftesbury and the effects of the split

[145] Ibid., VII, p. 367; VIII, pp. 262–4, 273, 280–1, 296, 472–4.
[146] Ibid., V, pp. 268–9; VIII, pp. 275–6.
[147] Interest rates are mentioned over thirty times in the diary.
[148] Ibid., VII, pp. 201–2.
[149] Ibid., III, p. 13.

between Dissenters and Latitudinarians within the milieu of the London business world.[150] Ryder was the son of a very successful London linen draper, Benjamin Ryder, who had a shop held with a partner in Cheapside at the corner of Ironmonger's Lane. His grandfather, also called Dudley, had been a Dissenting preacher in Bedworth, Warwickshire and had been ejected from his living at the Act of Uniformity in 1662. Thus, although Dudley would go on to pursue a very successful career in the law, eventually becoming lord chancellor, his roots were in the London business middling sort. Furthermore, he was part of the Dissenting community, which was prominent in trade and finance. The Reverend Dudley's eldest daughter also married a Dissenting preacher from St. Ives, Huntingdonshire, Robert Billio, who by the time of the diary was the minister of a Presbyterian meeting place in Hackney.[151] Ryder's diary provides a very good indication of how close moderate Dissent and Latitudinarian Anglicanism had become, but also shows how Dissent shaped his activity of moral self-criticism. He began the diary a few months after the Whigs had been returned to power in the election of 1715, and after the coronation of George I in the same year. These events had been the cause of many riotous High-Church attacks on Dissenting meeting houses. As a Dissenter, Ryder often expressed unsurprisingly pro-Whig and anti-Tory sentiments.[152]

In contrast to Pepys, Ryder did not keep his diary as an aid to remembering financial transactions and indebtedness.[153] Nor was it a Puritan narrative of grace and search for election, despite his non-conformity and education in Leiden and Edinburgh. It was, rather, a result of the new culture of self-reflection, sensibility, and politeness advocated by Shaftesbury. In June 1715, at the age of twenty-four, he began the diary in the following way:

> Mr. Whatley told me the other day of a method he had taken for some time of keeping a diary. And I now intend to begin the same method and mark down every day whatever occurs to me in the day worth observing. I intend particularly

150 William Mathews, *The Diary of Dudley Ryder 1715–1716* (London, 1939), pp. 2–6. Hereafter, Ryder, *Diary*. This is the published diary he kept between 1715 and 1716. He also wrote a diary from 1746 until his death in 1756, in addition to many notes on legal cases.

151 Richard Grassby, *The Business Community of Seventeenth Century England* (Cambridge, 1995), pp. 272–5.

152 Ryder, *Diary*, pp. 42, 65, 181.

153 Mathews cut out a considerable amount of the original 350,000-word text that he transcribed for the published edition, but none of what he cut out seems to have been financial transactions, simply more examples about his feelings of the type described here. I would like to thank Lucy Morgan of the University of Sheffield for sharing some images of Mathew's original transcription.

to observe my own temper and state of mind as to my fitness and disposition for study or the easiness or satisfaction it finds within itself and the particular cause of that or of the contrary uneasiness that often disturbs my mind. I will also take notice especially of what I read every day … I intend also to observe my own acts as to their goodness or badness. I think there will be many advantages from this way of setting down whatever occurs to me. I shall be able then to review any parts of my life, have the pleasure of it if it be well spent, if otherwise know how to mend it. It will help me to know myself better and give a better judgement of my own ability and what I am best qualified for.[154]

With Ryder there was a very definite process of self-examination of his behaviour, but not in relation to election or desire to explicate sinfulness, but rather to create behaviour that would be pleasing to others and therefore also to himself. We can see him searching for happiness caused by mutual acts of benevolence in society. Although, this had its origins in the moderate Puritanism of people like Richard Baxter, and it became a standard argument of Latitudinarian preaching, Ryder's diary shows it was equally influential for non-conformists. The diary proved an ideal way to help deal with the vicissitudes of life by recording events for future examination and evaluation, whether spiritual, economic, or political, where success had to be earned and maintained, or it would be lost.

When he began the diary, Dudley resided at the Inner Temple and spent his weekends at his father's suburban villa in Hackney. His father's brother had also married Anne Lomax, who had brought the Manor of Westbrook Hay in Hertfordshire and other property into the family, where Dudley spent some time.[155] The Ryders' near neighbours in Hackney included Sir Gilbert Heathcote, one of the founders of the Bank of England; possibly the richest commoner in England, John Gould, a director of the East India Company; and many other successful merchants who participated in the financial revolution.[156] Dudley was friends with the son of the Heathcotes. Dudley was a young man of some leisure, and his law study took up a minority of his time each day in contrast to visiting coffeehouses, clubs, dancing rooms, and other families' houses. Although he stated his father rose by great industry, Dudley rarely had to worry about money as he had an allowance of £80 and clothes from his father's shop.[157] His father's estate is described at the end of the diary as being worth £500 per year income, chiefly from the rent on houses he owned. Much of the profits of his trade must have been put into purchasing real estate as a form of capital to provide a regular income. His father was less sure about the value of his business, which he first valued at £3,000, but two months later reduced to £1,000 after his

[154] Ibid., p. 29. [155] Ibid., pp. 4, 13–14. [156] Ibid., p. 14. [157] Ibid., p. 326.

debts had been paid and Dudley's brother given money to set up and marry. Dudley registered his disappointment at what he would inherit.

Dudley attended the Hackney non-conformist Academy, where he studied mathematics, so he almost certainly would have learned to do accounts.[158] However, in the printed version of the diary Dudley does not write down his own spending. His comments indicate he was careful with money and certainly kept track of his spending, so a separate account book might have existed. He continually worried that his younger brother, William, who had just finished his apprenticeship in the same trade as his father, was spending too much money. This was based on the expense of his clothing, including lace ruffles, and Dudley worried that he was either stealing money from his father's shop or borrowing the same.[159] But the diary does not seem to have been used as a means of immediately recording small debts for purchases and repayments.

Rather, as the quote above succinctly indicates, it was used to evaluate his state of mind according to pleasure or uneasiness in relation to the 'goodness or badness' of his behaviour. In the use of the term uneasiness we can see the influence of Locke, who Ryder often noted.[160] Although he never mentioned reading Shaftesbury, he did read through all of the issues of Adison and Steele's journal the *Spectator*. This had begun publication in 1711. Its title reflected a quote in Shaftesbury's *Characteristics of Men* that 'The Mind, which is Spectator or Auditor of other Minds, cannot be without its Eye and Ear.'[161] It aimed to propagate many of the same ideas, 'to enliven morality with wit, and to temper wit with morality'.[162] Throughout the diary Ryder placed a great deal of emphasis on conversation and wit, and was continually anxious about being overly shy in company. He also kept a book of anecdotes he read to be worked into his conversation.[163]

Two key elements are very prominent in the diary. These are his desire to control antisocial passions, and his concern with mutual approbation. On one occasion, when in his father's shop, he noted that both his parents, then present, expressed kindness and love towards him, but not to each other. According to Dudley they continually argued, using 'a cross and peevish way of talking'. As a result he vowed to 'check every hot rising of my passions if I should be married'.[164] Such concerns were intimately bound up with his religiosity. He attended many sermons, and

[158] Ibid., p. 150. [159] Ibid., pp. 151, 172, 205, 254–5, 293.
[160] Ibid., pp. 29, 75, 155, 156, 194, 295. [161] Shaftesbury, *Characteristics of Men*, p. 172.
[162] *The Spectator*, 12 March 1711, Issue 10. [163] Ryder, *Diary*, p. 286.
[164] Ibid., pp. 38, 49–50; also see p. 214 on a man who has no self-management.

was a member of a Dissenting society of fellow law students. As the editor of the published volume noted regarding reducing the roughly 330,000 shorthand words of the manuscript to half that length for publication, most of what was omitted concerned his religious feelings and tendency to moralise.[165]

But much remains of his comments on published books. These included the classics such as Cicero's *De Legibus*, as well as the *Spectator* already mentioned. But he also read many published sermons, and chief among these were those of Tillotson, who Ryder admired greatly. Ryder was certainly not a strong Calvinist, and could reasonably be described as one of Mark Goldie's middle-way Presbyterians. He used the term Latitudinarian, and once claimed the difference between Dissenters and churchmen like Tillotson was merely one of patience and their speed in rooting out evil habits.[166] Eventually, after being called to the bar to advance his career and to support the Whig cause, he joined the Church of England and became an MP and assistant to Robert Walpole, and then attorney-general in 1733. In the diary he expressed an aversion to what he termed the 'unreasonableness' of an established Church, 'because it laid a bias upon the mind in the search for truth, and a man ought not to have any bias, passion, or interest given to him'.[167] But at the same time he argued with his father against a strict interpretation of predestination, which 'shocked' the latter.[168]

On one Saturday in April 1716 he rose between seven and eight to read a sermon of Tillotson to 'teach me to govern my passions, conquer my unruly inclinations and live by the rules of reason'.[169] At another time 'he prayed to God that he would turn the current of my affections towards himself', and one evening while walking around the Middle Temple he reflected upon external and internal happiness, vowing to make God 'his friend' and to live up to his rules and precepts.[170] One could not hope for a better proof of the link between philosophy, theology, and behaviour than these statements. It is also noteworthy that he rarely talked about sin, but rather about good or bad behaviour, so much had he embraced the moralist theology.[171] With this emphasis on behaviour, it was only a short step to arrive at approbation. He noted that 'the most agreeable state of mind a man can be in is to be pleased with his own performance, or to be praised for what he does'.[172] He was always worried that his reputation would suffer if he behaved or spoke badly. Of course, such

[165] Ibid., p. viii. One lengthy example of religious feeling is given on pp. 303–5.
[166] Ibid., pp. 148, 331. [167] Ibid., p. 210. [168] Ibid., p. 170. [169] Ibid., p. 219.
[170] Ibid., pp. 45, 294. [171] See, for instance, ibid., pp. 303–5.
[172] Ibid., pp. 31–2, 90.

judgement easily led to snobbishness, of which Ryder recorded much among his friends in Hackney.[173] But among those who were more serious, like the melancholy Mr Whatley, who introduced Dudley to diary-keeping, religious feeling meant good behaviour was praised and supported as well.[174]

Despite choosing to follow a career in the law rather than business, at the time of the diary Ryder was still socialising within the circle of trading families known by his father, and various comments of his allow us to see how his morality reflected on business life. He often discussed trade. On one occasion he became interested in questions about money and the national debt. As a result, he read Locke's tract *Some Considerations of the Consequence of the Lowering of Interest, and the Raising the Value of Money*, as well as a pamphlet attempting to refute Locke's arguments. He was careful to live within his allowance, and worried that he had too much desire for material objects and 'external show' over 'solid virtues of the mind and endowments of the understanding'.[175] He was also, as already noted, constantly worried that his brother was stealing from his father's shop or borrowing at extravagant interest to buy expensive clothes.[176] At other times he commented critically on the way in which both estate stewards and judges could use procedure to delay legal proceedings to make more work for themselves in order to earn larger fess, a practice he called 'very dishonest and unjust'.[177]

In this respect, it seems that being a Dissenter added an extra sense of anxiety and guilt over bad behaviour which, of course, included dishonesty and cheating. Like Puritans before him, Ryder worried that people were attending church and listening to sermons, but not altering their behaviour:

> people don't, I believe, generally come to church with a design to grow better, to have their hearts bettered and more disposed to their duty. The general view of most people seems to be either because it would be disreputable not to go to church ... I observe [little care] in mankind to govern their passions and watch over themselves.[178]

He gave off his youthful diary-keeping in 1716, so we don't have his self-reflection as he rose in his profession, but he was very successful financially. But to become so successful he had to join the established Church to serve as attorney-general under Walpole. However, he remained sympathetic to his non-conformist origins, and supported the Whigs without becoming part of the party machinery. He died only two

173 Ibid., p. 143. 174 Ibid., pp. 221–3. 175 Ibid., p. 119.
176 Ibid., pp. 2, 213–14, 252. 177 Ibid., 106–7. 178 Ibid., p. 311.

years after becoming chief justice of King's Bench in 1754, possessed of a great estate, which he had valued in 1752 at about £110,000 in cash, stocks, and securities, and £3,000 per year in land.[179] He retained a reputation for honesty and carefulness, and when he took up diary-writing again after 1746 his penchant for self-evaluation does not seem to have changed that greatly:

> My present character in the world as to ability is, I believe, that I am a good lawyer and some parts. As to the belief that I am thoroughly honest and of great humanity and candour, I am sometimes tempted to attack the enemies of the Administration in a severe manner, but I check myself in that design. I am more fitted to act the part of candour, mildness, sincerity and good nature and reasoning. My own disposition leads me to this. It will give me more credit in the world.[180]

Overall, Ryder serves as a good example of moderate dissent, and demonstrates that it was not that far from moralist Anglicism by that time. Dissent certainly reinforced self-examination, and the presence of such feelings of guilt over honesty were crucial in creating the security of capital against fraud. But there was no significant difference in theology to prevent a devout Anglican from feeling guilty in the same way, as we shall see later when looking at Thomas Turner.

John Cannon

Before moving on to Turner, for the sake of chronological order, we will first move forward in time 20–25 years, and away from the heart of England's trading and legal world, to the distant rural environment of John Cannon's Somerset. Here we encounter a very different world of morality and religion. We have already examined his honesty with regard to the accuracy of his accounts and writing, and noted how often he felt it necessary to justify his own behaviour in comparison to the multiple moral failings of many in his community. But he also felt other aspects of morality deeply. Intriguingly, though, he did not fully accept the theological argument of self-preservation leading to virtue, although he does not explain why:

[179] Ibid., pp. 21–2, 326–7, 369–70; David Lemmings, 'Ryder, Sir Dudley (1691–1756)', *Oxford Dictionary of National Biography*, www.oxforddnb.com/view/article/24394, accessed 25 July 2014.

[180] Harrowby MSS, 22 August 1741, cited in History of Parliament Trust, www.histparl.ac.uk/volume/1715-1754/member/ryder-dudley-1691-1756#family-relations, accessed 28 April 2025.

self-preservation is a principle in Nature never to be deserted. But this will not hold in religion where virtue is at all times to be the guide of our actions.[181]

In his *Chronicles*, Cannon listed attending over 100 sermons, and in many instances included summaries of the subject of the sermon. However, he rarely tried to relate it to his own behaviour in the manor of Ryder. In this regard he seems to have been a passive member of the national Church, and not that interested in theological modes of reasoning.

But this does not mean he was unconcerned with morality. He just thought about it in a different way. His method of thinking about morals was done through the investigation of historical examples gleaned through his vast reading. Almost all of the books he bought concerned history and contemporary politics, exemplified by his subscription to the *Gentleman's Magazine*, which mixed science, trade, and contemporary events with poetry and history:

My chiefest care Amidst all pleasures or recreations, was my books and ingenious persons by which I found vast advantage of improvement by which means I endeavoured to maintaining principles in sound morals and in religion, just virtuous & honest both to my God & also to man, abhorring & detesting all base & sinister ways by which some rak't and scrap't to get together great and perhaps unwarrantable riches.[182]

He certainly knew the *Bible*, and read biblical and classical history, but he does not seem to have bought any books specifically on religion among his many purchases. Whenever he wished to expound upon the effects of poverty or acts of charity, for instance, he would do so by citing examples from what he had read. This implies that he must have kept a commonplace book organised around such topics.

Near the beginning of the *Chronicles*, when briefly summarising the events of 1696, he included a passage on his religious belief which, with its emphasis on happiness, tranquillity, and beauty of the soul, demonstrates some influence of the Cambridge Platonists in rural Somerset:

Let youth carefully shun those dangerous and pernicious powers of vanity & vice … but rather study and apply thyself to right reason in order to procure the never fading but everlasting treasures of virtue, morality and eternal felicity not only in this short and mundane life but also will procure thee unlimited bliss and never dying happiness in the heavenly regions of God and Christ.[183]

181 John Money (ed.), *The Chronicles of John Cannon Excise Officer and Writing Master, vols. I–II* (Oxford, 2010), p. 5. Hereafter, Cannon, *Chronicles*.
182 Ibid., p. 37. 183 Ibid.

> How happy are all those who ... avoid the temptations of the world flesh and the devil & to learn to live vertuously ... in a profound peace, a quiet conscience and perfect tranquility of mind ... beautified with the lively image of God.[184]

Given that he wrote out many bonds and mortgages with explicitly stated interest rates, he also used the concept of interest in a normative way, using the word many times. He often discussed his own and other people's interest; however, he remained continually critical of self-interest.[185]

Because of his downward social mobility, his moral outlook concerning happiness was also overwhelmingly coloured by inequality and class.[186] Because he was poor and depended on those much wealthier than himself for work as scrivener and school teacher, he always felt resentment at the power wealth gave others. But, at the same time, he believed in the ideology that industry, education, and ability should allow one to rise in the world.[187] As a scrivener he portrayed himself as more honest than his main employer, and a better keeper of the parish accounts and school teacher than the men the vestry replaced him with, presumably after tiring of his superior attitude and hearing his criticisms of their inability.[188] In general he was quite relaxed about sex and drink, although on one occasion, after failing to receive debts from a poor man removing his family from the parish, he did complain about 'the vanity and folly of the present age having for several weeks past addicted themselves to horse racing, backsword, cudgels, bull baiting, et cetera'.[189]

In general, he was much more focused on charity, honesty, and good neighbourliness in judging others, and how wealth corrupts virtue. He was much less concerned to analyse his own behaviour in the manner of Dudley Ryder, possibly because there was no 'interest' involved in it. He could not really hope to advance himself in Glastonbury society without property. His interest was in honesty to obtain employment as a scrivener, rather than good conversation in rural terms. His reading meant he could have certainly participated in the sort of educated

184 Ibid., p. 29. 185 Ibid., pp. 60, 66, 367.

186 This is discussed at length in Craig Muldrew, 'Class and Credit: Social Identity, Wealth and the Life Course in Early Modern England', in Henry French and Jonathan Barry (eds.), *Identity and Agency in England, 1500–1800* (London, 2004), pp. 147–77.

187 Cannon, *Chronicles*, pp. 182–3.

188 There is no evidence of this, but given that Canon relates criticising them to others, it is probable that word would have circulated in such a small community.

189 Cannon, *Chronicles*, p. 390.

politeness advocated by Shaftesbury, but this was not what was required among the middling sort of rural Somerset.[190]

As John Money has noted, the Glastonbury of the late 1730s and early 1740s, and its surrounding parishes where Cannon engaged in most of his scrivening work, seems to have been an exceptionally quarrelsome place.[191] When drawing up a bill for a butcher, Cannon described him as 'a man in great trade and circumstances, but very illiterate having three sons being bred up like himself only to cursing, swearing and ill manners'.[192] Although religion played a role, most conflict seems to have originated over wealth and status, but much also seems to have been exacerbated by the great expansion in the mortgaging of land. Families could successfully expand their wealth through borrowing to improve their farms, but since the land was prone to flooding and not the most productive, it was easy to go into debt as well. According to Cannon, many also borrowed and spent unwisely beyond their means. This led to a more avaricious land market. The effects of this on the social structure and the role that mortgaging and new forms of capital had in the class formation of the middling sort will be examined in more detail in Chapter 8. However, in terms of quarrelling, it is relevant because Cannon tried to avoid it, and made explicit claims about the importance of self-control for himself:

> Aristotle says that no excellent soul is exempt from a mixture of folly … for as much as wisdom is a regular Government of ye Soul which is carried on with measure & proportion & while she is responsible to herself. For it's the ruin of men of shallow capacity that they … swallow all that come first to hand without examination.[193]

In 1738 he wrote how self-government could explicitly be used to save up capital, something he had been unable to do as his passion for purchasing books bankrupted him in 1721:

> Having once acquired the art of governing himself and his affairs, there will be no temptation enough strong to induce [a man] to give up the liberty which he thereby possesses … the practice of this virtue enables a man to live upon a little if in spite of all honest precaution he should through the strokes of fortune have but little left. He who by his prudent management has acquired a small bank has it in his power to serve his friends and to do great kindnesses to others with no inconvenience to himself which is one of the highest and most rational pleasures a man can enjoy. …It is no shame to raise a great fortune from a small one provided it be done honestly.[194]

190 Henry French, *The Middle Sort of People in Provincial England 1600–1750* (Oxford, 2007), ch. 4.

191 Ibid., pp. lxxxii. 192 Cannon, *Chronicles*, p. 264. 193 Ibid., p. 29.

194 Ibid., pp. 376–7.

Overall, Cannon certainly seems to have been a failure at such self-control, managing to lose most of his inheritance by quarrelling with his uncle, spending constantly on books, fighting with his wife, and getting involved in other people's quarrels. Also, according to his own comments, his life would have been much worse if he had not been able to rely on his cousin Mrs Pope, who spent much effort to resolve disputes, and was a key player in what I have termed elsewhere the culture of reconciliation.[195] In Glastonbury and West Lydford, public dispute resolution remained important at this informal pre-institutional level. In the end, although Cannon might not have successfully found the tranquillity he aimed for, he does seem to have been successful at being honest and resisting the temptation to be swayed by any faction. The following passage, occasioned by a report of possible perjury at an assize trial, shows the link between religion and his internalised sense of the importance of honesty and dislike of self-interest:

> Divine and humane laws have left men no greater assurance of truth and fidelity than that of an Oath, which should be taken in sincerity and kept inviolably. But since corrupted and depraved nature hath perverted those laws by wilful perjuries skinned over with equivocations, mental reservations and base ends for the service of a faction or some private interest, and have made oaths like to gypsies knots, fast or loose at pleasure ... for he that hath once broken down the bounds of honesty and makes no religion of an Oath where his interest is concerned, his Cauterized Conscience will never scruple to swear falsely upon very advantageous occasions.[196]

It had long been a commonplace in English law that the poor were not to be trusted as honest witnesses because they were vulnerable to bribery on account of their need and bullying on account of their dependence on their betters for employment.[197] Despite being constantly in debt, and, at the end of the *Chronicles*, accused falsely of petty theft, Cannon's earnings from writing bills, bonds, and mortgages was constantly increasing.[198] This indicates that enough people realised that his moral sense of self-worth based on honesty was strong enough to resist temptations. In this sense we can see how one specific example of internal moralism was

[195] Craig Muldrew, 'The Culture of Reconciliation: Community and the Settlement of Economic Disputes in Early Modern England', *Historical Journal* 39, no. 4 (1996), pp. 915–42.

[196] Cannon, *Chronicles*, pp. 245–6.

[197] Alexandra Shepard, *Accounting for Oneself: Worth, Status, and the Social Order in Early Modern England* (Oxford, 2015); Hillary Taylor, 'The Price of the Poor's Words: Social Relations and the Economics of Deposing for One's "Betters" in Early Modern England', *Economic History Review* 72, no. 3 (2019), pp. 828–47.

[198] Cannon, *Chronicles*, p. 690.

judged specifically in the context of the production of trustworthy financial instruments. This worked in a more *targeted* way than overall reputation of creditworthy behaviour. The latter was focused primarily on the prevention of having too many personal oral debts fail, leading to litigation and reduced liquidity, while the former focused on how best to produce trusted paper credit substitutes that lowered the risk of personal debts within the liquidity of local finance. Here we can see how a new model of the mind and self focused on internal self-worth – working between guilt and happiness – was introduced into a system of social credit based on community reputation spread through spoken and written communication. Oral credit did not go away, nor did public dispute settlement, but the economy was no longer so reliant on it.

Thomas Turner

In the mid-eighteenth century, oral credit was still very much a part of Thomas Turner's East Hoathly. Although, as we saw, he played a central role in brokering bills within the local economy, many of his small sales still had to be made on oral credit. As he stated in his diary, 'the greatest part of trade being trust, and doubtless in so many small articles we forget a great many'.[199] When he mentioned the loss of a bad debt worth £40 he claimed he had shown his customer too much indulgence, not knowing enough about his honesty or lifestyle.[200] But at the same time he also never had to worry about his position as a writer and acceptor of small notes and bills. Unlike Cannon, his honesty was taken for granted and he never noted any problems with trust in paper credit as opposed to oral credit. In part this might have been because his diary was written around twenty years later, but it was probably more because of the higher social status he had in his community. While by no means very wealthy, Turner was part of the middling sort and possessed his own shop as fixed capital.[201] But in other ways, Turner was very much like Cannon in that he was also someone who used his diary to evaluate the ethics of his own, and others', behaviour:

> May the God of all mercy and goodness pour into my heart the grace of His Holy Spirit, that as I grow in years so may I increase in goodness and daily be renewed

[199] David Vaisey (ed.), *The Diary of Thomas Turner* (Oxford, 1985), p. 207. Hereafter, Turner, *Diary*.
[200] Ibid., pp. 186–7.
[201] Craig Muldrew, 'The Emergence of the "Middle Sort" of People', in Keith Wrightson (ed.), *The Cambridge Social History of England, c.1500-c.1750* (Cambridge, 2016), pp. 301–4.

in the inner man, and so number my days that I may apply my heart unto wisdom, through the merits and intercession of my blessed Saviour and only Redeemer, Jesus Christ.[202]

Like Cannon, he was also a member of the Church of England and routinely attended sermons, which he used to reflect upon his behaviour. There are about forty-five sermons mentioned and summarised in the edited version of Turner's diary, but probably more in the complete manuscript. Also, like Cannon, he read extensively, and while his reading comprised newspapers and other periodicals such as the *Universal Magazine*, the *Spectator*, plays, poetry, and history, there was definitely a much greater focus on theology than in Cannon's case. He recorded his enthusiasm for reading Tillotson's *Sermons* on numerous occasions, and the influence of the Latitudinarians on the theological turn away from denial to happiness can be clearly seen in the following passages:

Oh, may the Supreme Being give me grace to lead my life in such a manner as my exit may in some respect be like that divine creature's. Oh, how happy must that life be which is spent in virtue.[203]

Oh, that I lived in solitude and had not the occasion to act in trade. But still I hope and think I have done nought but what is consistent with self-preservation and the laws of equity.[204]

Although lack of trade led him to feel unhappy, success was not described as producing happiness. It was still, in his mind, touched with a Calvinist anxiety over worldly success.

As a result, Turner did try to control his behaviour. On the whole, life in East Hoathly seems to have been less factious than that in Glastonbury, although Turner records many social occasions where considerable drinking took place, which could lead to fights breaking out.[205] This led Turner to make continued unsuccessful attempts to limit the amount he drank on such occasions.[206] He specifically construed such attempts in terms of mental control over his actions:

Oh, how unhappy am I that I have no more resolution! How much greater is the glory to have a just command of one's actions than all the knowledge in the world besides. Oh, how frail is mortal beings! How much do we stand in need of the divine assistance of grace.[207]

He complained of coming home in liquor well over fifty times, and each time he bemoaned his sinfulness and inability to control his appetite for

[202] Ibid., p. 207. [203] Ibid., p. 32; also see, for example, pp. 39, 49, 64, 65, 75.
[204] Turner, *Diary*, p. 152. [205] Ibid., pp. 44–5. [206] Ibid., pp. 26–7.
[207] Ibid., p. 162; also see p. 138.

what he interestingly termed a vice rather than a sin. However, as he also noted many times, there was a great social pressure to engage in merry-making with his neighbours, including one occasion where he was woken up at 6:00 in the morning by a drunken group of neighbours, including the Reverend Porter, and forced to drink wine and dance in his wife's petticoats until breakfast.[208]

Like Cannon, he also held honesty to be a chief virtue, and on more than one occasion described his work as honest.[209] Although, being the son of a shopkeeper and most likely educated with other sons of tradesmen in Lewes, he did not feel the need to justify his accounting skills and trustworthiness. While Turner worried that he was too trusting with his poor customers, and never lost his anxiety that he might fail in business, he never recorded anyone doubting his trustworthiness as a writer of bills and notes of hand. But one very telling passage illustrates how anxiety about honesty was felt through religious moralism. It concerned the mortgaging of a £900 estate by the landlord of The King's Head public house to the Reverend Thomas Porter, the partying and acquisitive rector of East Hoathly. Turner obviously felt that Porter, as a man of the cloth, was exploiting his parishioner in the terms of the mortgage, while at the same time realising that as a purely financial transaction it was a legitimate and normal means of raising capital. This caused him to go into great circumlocutions about honesty and interest:

> I was present and witness to a thing my conscience told me not right (as mine undoubtedly did) then undoubtedly I am culpable and to blame in acting contrary to my own conscience and of consequence to the Christian religion, of which I am an unworthy member … Neither do I mention it to condemn Mr. Porter as an over-reaching and unjust person. No, I mention it purely to show how frail, how weak, our nature is, that when self interest is the concern we are always as it were partial in our own favour, even so fond are we of our dear selves as to do things which we would blush at and even condemn as blameworthy in another.[210]

Interest, as a concept, as well as interest rates on the bonds he made, was just as common as it was for Cannon. Also, like Cannon, Turner accepted mutual interest as morally acceptable for a Christian:

> I have always done to the utmost of my power to serve [my friends]. I can with justice to myself and all mankind say I have their interest entirely at heart and never think myself more happy than in serving them; … But oh, let me stop my pen and say, 'May they all be ever happy, and may the Supreme Being crown them all with His blessings.'[211]

[208] Ibid., pp. 138–9. [209] Ibid., pp. 61, 145. [210] Ibid., pp. xxxi–xxxii, 221–2.
[211] Ibid., p. 31.

Some self-interest could also be acceptable, as when he gave 2s. in charity and noted, 'not that I did it so much from principle of charity as self-interest, having formerly bought some brandy of them'.[212] However, it was condemned much more often, as in the following case in which some of the wealthier farmers in the parish attempted to avoid paying their proper Poor Law assessments:

> however great their outward zeal for justice appeared, that cankerworm of self-interest lay so corroding in their hearts that it sullied the outward beauties of their would-be honesty. I say 'would-be' honesty because I look upon that man, be him who will, that endeavours to evade the payment of his just share of taxes to be a-robbing every other member of the community that contributes his quota, and also withholding from the poor what is their just right.[213]

At the same time, though, he enjoyed the pleasure of their hospitality and conversation. This was also a group who, despite such criticism, or possibly due to the very factors Turner was criticising, were commonly trusted with notes and bills of various sorts. The shop debts over which Turner worried so much were mainly owed by outsiders, most of whom were poorer. Probably Turner was trusted to be a nexus of local exchange as a result of his heightened sense of religious morality, but overall a certain sort of class formation centred around the use of paper instruments and the type of trust it entailed seems to have coalesced in East Hoathly, which will be discussed further in Chapter 8.

This chapter has hopefully shown how elevated discourse on ethics and society were linked to social practice through dissemination in sermons and how they affected economic life in the way individual selves experienced happiness through the creation of capital and wealth through interest, honest accounting, and saving. This was supposed to be done with benevolence towards others in mind, and in most cases probably was, but as both Cannon and Turner noted, the line between moderate and selfish self-love was a thin one and could more easily justify acquisitive behaviour. It needs to be reiterated that these new ideas of the self did not totally replace older neighbourly interpersonal reputation-based credit, but gradually augmented it. In addition, certainly not everyone subscribed to or felt comfortable with these new ethics. The middle-class dyer Joseph Ryder (1695–1768), who worked in Leeds and kept a diary, was one such individual. Analysed by Matthew Kadane, his diary demonstrates that he continued to bear the weight of sin and what Kadane has termed his 'watchful' search for grace, which was common among Puritans 100 years before he wrote. How many other non-

[212] Ibid., p. 122. [213] Ibid., p. 268.

conformists there were like him is hard to say, but again – as Kadane has stressed – holding to a fading religion did not prevent him from participating in the middling sort culture of a new industrial town.[214] Examining such matters will give us more opportunity to further explore the wider social implications of the new ethics that have been detailed over these last chapters, but before we do that we need to return to the subject of institutions, and examine in particular the evolution of institutions central to how the culture of credit operated – the law and local courts.

[214] Matthew Kadane, *The Watchful Clothier: The Life of an Eighteenth Century Protestant Capitalist* (New Haven, 2013), pp. 6–8.

7 The Transformation of Legal Culture

Once private happiness for the self and others became central to morality, it stands to reason that self-control and benevolence would eventually become seen as a more prevalent force for creating social order than the authority of the courts and the law. Indeed, the period from around 1680 to 1750 witnessed a continued decline in interpersonal litigation of all sorts, but especially that concerning credit. In this chapter I will examine how changes in institutional practice affected the function of the law – which, of course, remained vital. The new forms of credit currency still relied on trust and this still needed to be backed up by enforceable contract law, but increased liquidity meant that the *threat* of litigation did not need to be issued as often. Also, as we saw in Chapter 3, new forms of credit currency needed to have some sort of legal definition, just as metallic money did. Additionally, the creation of capital through mortgaging was an intensely legal process. But given that credit litigation had been so ubiquitous in supporting trust in previous credit networks, investigating how and why it declined is obviously critical.

In the sixteenth century, one of the most significant results of market transactions involving credit was a dramatic increase in the amount of debt and contractual litigation that came before the courts in all parts of England. The majority of the increase in suits was a result of the expansion of the market economy, where about 90 per cent of transactions were done on largely oral sales credit. Credit caused disputes to explode because of the pace at which market transactions increased. Bottlenecks created liquidity problems for individuals, leading them to recover their own debts, which then had a domino effect on others. As chains of obligation grew longer, late payment became more of a problem and creditors turned to the initiation of litigation to try to force payment when they needed liquidity. In the central courts of King's Bench and Common Pleas the number of suits that reached advanced stages of pleading increased from 5,278 in 1563 to 28,734 by 1640. In addition, there were much greater numbers of suits concerning debts being heard in local courts.[1] Estimates from the town courts of King's Lynn, Bristol, Exeter, Taunton, Carlisle, Great Yarmouth, and Scarborough indicate that there were in the region of 400,000 suits being initiated in urban courts each year by the 1580s. Examples of manorial and hundred courts from Yorkshire, Devon, and Norfolk also suggest that 626,316 private suits were begun in the thousands of rural courts throughout the country, and by countrymen in urban courts.[2]

The Decline of Credit Litigation

The level of litigation remained high for about a century, before beginning to decline around 1670. During the period 1670–1750 the number of cases in advanced stages in the central courts of Common Pleas and King's Bench fell six times, from about 30,000 to 5,000 cases.[3] My study of urban litigation also found a general decline that roughly matched that in the central courts. In King's Lynn, for instance, complaints dropped from 1,500 to about 100 per year between 1650 and 1750, and the situation in Great Yarmouth, Exeter, Newcastle, and Shrewsbury was similar.[4] One reason put forward for this decline was increasing court costs. The overall costs of litigation in the central courts doubled between 1680 and 1750, from less than £10 to £20–30 for the same kind of work.[5] However, the evidence of indictable offences at the Quarter Sessions and Assizes in Essex, Surrey, and Sussex does not indicate any obvious decline in the late seventeenth or early eighteenth centuries.[6] Thus, it seems that the litigation decline was concentrated in

1 This is discussed at more length in Craig Muldrew, *The Economy of Obligation: The Culture of Credit and Social Relations in Early Modern England* (London, 1998), pp. 216–36.
2 Ibid.
3 These figures are based on three-year averages. C. W. Brooks, 'Interpersonal Conflict and Social Tension: Civil Litigation in England, 1640–1830', in C. W. Brooks, *Lawyers, Litigation and English Society Since 1450* (London, 1998), pp. 31–3; C. W. Brooks, *Pettyfoggers and Vipers of the Commonwealth: The 'Lower Branch' of the Legal Profession in Early Modern England* (Cambridge, 1986), pp. 51, 68.
4 Muldrew, *The Economy of Obligation*, pp. 230, 237–42; Brooks, 'Interpersonal Conflict', p. 40. Also see W. A. Champion, 'Litigation in the Boroughs: The Shrewsbury *Curia Parva*, 1480–1730', *Legal History* 15, no. 3 (1994), pp. 208, 216–17.
5 Brooks, 'Interpersonal Conflict', pp. 45–9. W. A. Champion, 'Recourse to the Law and the Meaning of the Great Litigation Decline, 1650–1750: Some Clues from the Shrewsbury Local Courts', in C. W. Brooks and Michael Lobban (eds.), *Communities and Courts: Proceedings of the Twelfth Legal History Conference held in Durham* (London, 1997), pp. 192–3.
6 J. A. Sharpe, *Crime in 17th-Century England: A County Study* (Cambridge, 1983), p. 183; John Beattie, *Crime and the Courts in England 1660–1800* (Oxford, 1986), pp. 182, 202–3.

suits about credit in both senses of its meaning: as obligation and reputation.[7]

When the overall pattern of decline is examined more closely, it seems that the decline really started around 1690.[8] That litigation should begin to decline at this point in time quite strongly suggests that the reason can be linked to changes in the way credit markets worked. Since much of the initial boom in litigation was caused by the very informal oral nature of sales credit and reckonings, it stands to reason that logically, if credit started to become more formal, this would lead to a reduction in litigation. As credit became focused more on good bookkeeping and honest writing of small bills and notes of hand, these could increasingly replace oral credit and its public resolution in the setting of a civil court. Another result of this was that the role of the legal profession in credit networks went from handling litigation, which was used to ensure liquidity in *already existent* chains of oral credit, to creating forms of securitised interest-bearing credit in the form of mortgages which became capital, allowing the creation of local short-term paper credit currency.

Since it was such mortgages that underpinned much of the security of small-scale transfer of notes, as the number of people borrowing on the security of mortgages rose, increasingly more money could be made by what is generally termed 'conveyancing'. Conveyancing refers to the process by which formal rights of property were transferred. This involved investigating any possible entails or other encumbrances and charges on land to help judge that the amount borrowed could be repaid through the rental income of the land while still satisfying other claims on it. In 1670, the year that saw the peak of central court litigation, and when local suits were still extremely numerous, conveyancing was conspicuous by its absence in the standard manual for attorneys, *The Practique Part of the Law*, but by 1724, when William Bohun's *Practicing Attorney* was published, it was discussed as one of four main aspects of an attorney's business. A guide to the professions published in 1747 provided a definition of conveyancing as:

> the drawing of Deeds, Mortgages and Conveyances of Estates. This is the most profitable Branch of the Law; for to that of Drawing Deeds they commonly add the Trade of a Money-Scrivener; that is, they are employed to find out Estates to purchase, or have Money to lay out for some, and borrow for others, and receive

[7] Peter King, *Crime, Justice and Discretion in England: 1740–1820* (Cambridge, 2000), ch. 2.

[8] This is discussed in more detail in Craig Muldrew, '"Blunderers and Blotters of the Law"? The Rise of Conveyancing in the Eighteenth Century and Long Term Socio-Legal Change', in Michael Lobban, Joanne Begiato, and Adrian Green (eds.), *Law, Lawyers and Litigants in Early Modern English Society: Essays in Memory of Christopher W. Brooks* (Cambridge, 2019), pp. 233–4.

Fees from Borrower and Lender; and of course are employed to draw the Securities.[9]

The role of the attorney in arranging mortgages as a source of credit in eighteenth-century society was first identified by the economic historian B. L. Anderson. He used the specific examples of the attorneys Isaac Greene (1679–1749) and John Plumbe (1670–1763) from Lancashire, emphasising their link to investment in new industry and trade through Liverpool.[10] Both of these individuals came from yeomen families. Greene drew most of his clients from landed society, arranging mortgages for them; but with his earnings he also bought land himself and invested in glassmaking.[11] Plumbe, whose accounts of saving cash we already examined in Chapter 3, was more involved in lending, both on his own account and for others, to individuals from a wide range of society (see Chapter 4). At the same date, his lending on bonds was worth slightly less at £2,700.[12] Most importantly, though, Anderson noted that while Plumbe was active in earning fees from representing clients in lawsuits in Liverpool, most of his business activities were founded on land ownership, and through the purchase of estates and other land rent became his chief source of income. As we have already seen, rural estates could be mortgaged for thousands of pounds.[13]

Anderson's findings were confirmed in two important articles published by Michael Miles in the early 1980s on the role of country attorneys and the money market by the mid-eighteenth century.[14] Miles' studies of two West Riding attorneys show that they made 47 and 40 per cent of their profits from conveyancing, in comparison to 25 and 13 per cent, respectively, derived from litigation.[15] In an examination of the securities held by John Howarth on behalf of his clients from 1762 to 1796, the amounts of mortgages were consistently 2–10 times as valuable

[9] M. Miles, '"Eminent Practitioners": The New Visage of Country Attorneys c.1750–1800', in G. R. Rubin and David Sugarman (eds.), *Law, Economy and Society, 1750–1914: Essays in the History of English law* (Abingdon, 1984), p. 475.

[10] B. L. Anderson, 'Provincial Aspects of the Financial Revolution of the Eighteenth Century', *Business History* 11 (1960), pp. 11–22; B. L. Anderson, 'Money and the Structure of Credit in the Eighteenth Century', *Business History* 12 (1970), pp. 85–101; B. L. Anderson, 'The Attorney and the Early Capital Market in Lancashire', in F. Crouzet (ed.), *Capital Formation and the Industrial Revolution* (London, 1972), pp. 223–55.

[11] Anderson, 'The Attorney and the Early Capital Market', pp. 229–30.

[12] Ibid., pp. 236–40.

[13] Anderson, 'Provincial Aspects', pp. 16–19; Anderson, 'Money and the Structure of Credit', pp. 237–9, 245.

[14] M. Miles, 'The Money Market in the Early Industrial Revolution: The Evidence from Two West Riding Attorneys, c.1750–1800', *Business History* 23 (1981), pp. 127–46.

[15] Miles, 'Eminent Practitioners', p. 474.

as those on bonds.[16] In 1789, for instance, John Howarth held £12,800 worth of clients' mortgages and £2,140 on his own behalf. In addition to this, Henry Horwitz and Patrick Polden have found that in the Court of Chancery between 1627 and 1735, suits over debts and bonds fell, while those concerning estate matters and other business contracts rose.[17]

By comparison, the account book of the Hitchin attorney George Draper for the earlier period from 1671 to 1694 shows that most of his earnings still came from litigation. In just one year he was engaged in 1,954 transactions, and in the index to his account book there were 1,286 clients listed from Hitchin and much of the surrounding countryside around the town, who owed amounts as small as a few shillings.[18] Certainly, lawyers had grown very wealthy on such fees, but as the business of conveyancing expanded it offered better opportunities for earning more through fees. In addition, it encouraged lawyers to actively participate in the land market both as lenders and purchasers of land. Lending on mortgage offered opportunities to purchase land from those who were too indebted to become rentiers.[19] Almost all conveyancing was made complicated by the land law, and this could be used to justify high fees.

A good example can be drawn from the *Chronicles of John Cannon*. In 1736 he recorded that he was sent for by Thomas Merriot, a clerk of the solicitor William Nicholls, who was lending £50 (actually the money of his wife) to one William Payne on a mortgage on two acres of meadow. In order to facilitate the transfer, both the deed of transfer to a former mortgagee – one John Giblet (which Cannon had written up) – and a copy of the will of Benjamin Payne of Huntspill from 19 September 1721 – who was the father of William Payne – needed to be consulted. According to Cannon, it was by this will that the title of the meadow was conveyed. Both Cannon and Marriot acted as witnesses to the new deed of transfer, and he noted that Merriot's legal bill was £3 11s. 2d., although he did comment that this 'was looked on as a price extravagant and unreasonable'.[20] But compared to the fees that an

16 Miles, 'Money Market', pp. 136–7.

17 But there was legislation in 1697 that allowed the common law to give the kind of relief on penal bonds that was previously only available in Chancery, so the fall in litigation over such matters was not necessarily indicative of a decline in overall litigation. Henry Horwitz and Patrick Polden, 'Continuity or Change in the Court of Chancery in the Seventeenth and Eighteenth Centuries?', *Journal of British Studies* 35 (1996), p. 35.

18 George Draper's Day Book 1671–1694, Hawkins and Co., 7/8 Portmill Lane Hitchin; Brooks, *Pettyfoggers*, pp. 105, 248.

19 Miles, 'Money Market', p. 137.

20 John Money (ed.), *The Chronicles of John Cannon Excise Officer and Writing Master, vols. I–II* (Oxford, 2010), p. 268. Hereafter Cannon, *Chronicles*.

attorney, as opposed to a mere clerk, could charge it seems quite small. In 1741, Cannon reported drawing up two large bills for William Nicholls, to be paid by one Mr Cadby of Shapwick, in which were noted many days out on business for which he charged 1 guinea per day. In addition, a bill for 100 guineas was made for Nicholl's work in negotiating a marriage contract with Cadby's wife, which involved payment through a mortgage![21]

By the mid-eighteenth century, the court fees that could be earned from litigation were low in comparison to earnings from conveyancing. Even though fees had risen, litigation in local courts might earn an attorney £2–5 for the few cases that went all the way to trial.[22] Fees were greater in the central courts, but suits could take months or years before they could be realised, whereas fees could be charged immediately for conveyancing work.[23] From the point of view of supply and demand, this suggests that lawyers increased their fees for litigation to make the value of the time spent in that activity more closely match the earnings from time spent on conveyancing. Thus, as the number of suits started to fall, poorer clients and smaller suits no longer became worthwhile, and litigation was increasingly engaged in by wealthier plaintiffs who could pay higher fees.[24] Between 1768 and 1780, John Howarth, another West Riding attorney studied by Miles, did conveyancing work for 55 gentry clients, 201 clients from the upper middling sort (such as yeomen clothiers and shopkeepers), 61 clients of the lower middling sort (such as weavers and craftsmen), and only 9 clients from poorer occupations.[25]

Attorneys also played an important role in capital formation in the writing up of formal sealed bonds and administering trusts – both in writing them up and then lending out the money at interest. For wealthy families these were an important part of the maintenance of what is called 'strict settlement', whereby the entailment of land was bequeathed solely through male primogeniture, while all other claims on the estate were dealt with through the formation of uses and trusts to provide a yearly income for the claimants. These could be based on rental income, but were also composed of interest-bearing capital invested in various ways.

[21] Ibid., p. 616.
[22] Champion, 'Recourse to the Law', pp. 184–5; Craig Muldrew, 'Credit, Market Relations, and Debt Litigation in Late Seventeenth Century England, with Particular Reference to King's Lynn' (PhD Thesis, Cambridge University, 1990), pp. 371–84.
[23] Muldrew, 'Blunderers and Blotters', pp. 246–8.
[24] Ibid.; Christopher Brooks, 'Litigation, Participation and Agency in Seventeenth and Eighteenth Century England,' in David Lemmings (ed.), *The British and Their Laws in the Eighteenth Century* (Woodbridge, 2005), pp. 164, 167–8, 180; Champion, 'Recourse to the Law', pp. 184–6, 190.
[25] Miles, 'Eminent Practitioners', pp. 478, 500.

Many less wealthy people, but individuals who had still inherited substantial amounts, also increasingly began to lend out the bulk of their patrimony and live on the interest.[26] Annuities for lifetime incomes also became increasingly common over the course of the eighteenth century.[27] New legal work emerged in the post-1750 period with the administration of Parliamentary enclosure and valuing of lands after the establishment of navigation and turnpike trusts.[28]

Litigation and Local Bills

Even if attorneys spent more time on conveyancing and scrivening activities than litigation, the latter still formed an important role in securing the use of bills as well as, of course, still offering protection to informal credit. However, it is difficult to know if a bill or note of hand was involved in any dispute, since the form of litigation was done as if the transaction was one of normal broken contract sued over in an action of assumpsit. Such a suit was treated as a promise to pay, in which the value of the note was traced back to the initial issuer. To use a hypothetical example, we can take one of the notes issued by the Jervoise family to William Whitlock for casting dung and other work done, discussed in Chapter 3. If it passed through the hands of a number of tradesmen in payment before coming to someone who needed cash to make a payment instead of the note, he would go back to Thomas Puckridge, who issued it, to ask for the cash, and if he was not paid then he could sue him for the amount in an action of trespass on the case. Since all proceedings were oral, the involvement of the bill would only arise if the case went to the stage of declaration, or from private case notes.

Suits brought before the central courts of Common Pleas, King's Bench, and Exchequer have been examined in some detail by Clinton W. Francis for sample years from 1740 to 1840. As noted above, 1740 was the nadir of litigation in the central courts. However, whereas for most of the sixteenth and seventeenth centuries pleading in the central courts had been dominated by suits of debt involving written bonds that were almost unassailable evidence of the validity of the obligation, by 1740 cases of assumpsit had reached about 40 per cent of pleading. By examining cases in the actual plea rolls, Francis was able to show that cases involving bills of exchange and promissory notes

26 Miles, 'Money Market', p. 132.

27 Sybil Campbell, 'Usury and Annuities of the Eighteenth Century', *Law Quarterly Review* 44 (1928), pp. 473–91.

28 See Chapter 8, note 69.

comprised 11.5 per cent of pleas of assumpsit in King's Bench, while notes comprised 7.3 per cent of total cases in Common Pleas. Furthermore, looking at the law notes of Dudley Ryder, he found that there were a number of cases of general assumpsit involving tradesmen's bills, although these were in a minority.[29]

This shows that these instruments were being enforced at law, but the fact that they formed a minority of cases at this time is good evidence that they were less problematic forms of obligation than oral promises. Of course, it might also be argued that this is evidence that they were still being used much less frequently, but the great numbers that remain in those archives where they have been kept suggests that the first explanation is more likely. But to investigate this we can once again turn to the *Chronicles of John Cannon*, where we can see that, of the many hundreds of informal notes he mentions, only a few needed to be litigated over.

Cannon wrote out many notes of hand and receipts, both on his own business and while employed by the town attorneys the Nicholls brothers. At the same time he was continually in debt because of his book buying, and had to settle his father's extensive debts as the eldest son when the former died in 1723. This meant that he was often involved with law in matters concerning debts, both his own and others'. Such involvement demonstrates that despite a much lower aggregate of cases, local courts still played an important role in credit networks, and from them we can see how notes featured. For most of Cannon's later career after his dismissal from the Excise he lived in Bridgewater, West Lydford, and finally Glastonbury. None of these towns had a borough court. The closest towns with their own courts were Taunton and Wells. Since suits initiated in borough courts needed to be based on actions undertaken within the town's liberties, this meant that almost all of the suits Cannon was involved in over this period were undertaken in the local hundred court located in Glastonbury, and the Somerset county court in Wells. However, there were occasions when working for the Nicholls brothers that he wrote documents for much larger suits in the central courts in Westminster, and some suits in Taunton.

Turning first to those lawsuits against Cannon, the first he mentioned actually took place in London in 1714. He had journeyed there on Excise business, but also decided to use the trip to marry his intended bride, Susanna, whom he had met when she was a servant maid on one of his Excise rounds, and whose family came from High Wycombe. After his

[29] Clinton W. Francis, 'Practice, Strategy, and Institution: Debt Collection in the English Common-Law Courts, 1740–1840', *Northwestern University Law Review* 80, no. 4 (1986), pp. 813–15, 912–13.

wedding, when he was preparing to leave London to take up his new Excise outriding of Taunton and Somersetshire, he first went up to Wycombe where he had been staying and

> packed up my Clothes and things in a great Trunk and sent them to London by the carrier to the Inn where the Taunton carrier came … owing some money, I gave Notes who were easy, all except one Henry Hunt, a mercer. I gave him good words and offered a note but he would not accept, and so I parted.[30]

Cannon then left for the short trip to London, but in the meantime Hunt had sent one Thomas Morris ahead to arrest Cannon for the unpaid debt. This Morris, it seems, was able to get a writ of attachment out of the London Sheriff's court and seized Cannon's trunk from the inn where it had been sent. Morris, as Cannon put it, 'feigned great friendship but drawed about from place to place pretending to be my friend in Hunt's affair till at last he brought me into the Comptor'.[31] There, Cannon paid the fees to release the attachment and Morris 'accepted a note of hand for the use of the said Hunt payable at a certain day'. They went back to the inn, where Cannon borrowed money from the landlady to pay Morris an unspecified amount of cash. According to Cannon, this was basically just a way for Morris, 'a lurching notorious rogue', to extract some extra money from him with Hunt's acquiescence.[32] It is impossible to tell from Cannon's account whether or not Hunt had any legitimate reason for rejecting Cannon's note. This was a time – before his father died – when he was earning a good salary as an Excise man, and certainly he was able to pay off his other debts with notes of hand. The fact that Hunt accepted a note in the end, in addition to some cash, indicates that his lawsuit was unnecessary and he was taking advantage of Cannon's lack of ready money in this case. But it nicely illustrates how notes were being used to settle normal debts, here at quite a distance, and were also being used to resolve a legal dispute.

As will be discussed below, arrest had become a much easier process by the early eighteenth century, and Cannon was next arrested in 1717 for an 8 guinea debt arising from the purchase of a horse in 1714. In this case, a bailiff, probably from the borough court in Taunton, where Cannon was based at the time, arrested him in 'private … nobody was ever the wiser or knew his Errand'. This bailiff (John Green) took Cannon to an attorney near Taunton Castle, where Cannon entered 'into a Judgment bond which Green took for the use of the plaintiff'.

30 Cannon, *Chronicles*, p. 119.
31 This was one of the Sheriff of London's debtors prisons.
32 Cannon, *Chronicles*, pp. 115–16.

The bond was for the value of what remained of the original debt. As a judgment bond it enabled the plaintiff to have him incarcerated right away if the plaintiff went unsatisfied when he desired payment. However, shortly after Cannon paid him off, claiming he 'took up the bond, though he was so good as to forgive me the Cost'.[33] After the death of his father in 1723, Cannon was left with over £200 of his debts, while he himself had built up over £60 in debt. For these he reported he was 'arrested in several actions', but claimed: 'Nevertheless I got clear though not with small Cost which also hurted me in my Credit.' To pay all of these he had to sell all of his father's land that was not already given to his other children. In this way he was able to satisfy all the creditors and remain out of prison, but it left him insolvent and in poverty for the next 7–8 years.[34]

After this, although he was threatened with arrest once, and issued with two summonses and one declaration generated by suits in the county court in Wells, he mostly managed to avoid any further entanglements with the law despite his debts.[35] However, on one occasion in 1727, during his years of greatest poverty, he described in detail how a note he had used to pay for an original purchase became questioned in a threatened lawsuit. The debt concerned some barley he had purchased from someone called Jenkins in 1723, during his failed attempt to start up as a maltster in Bridgewater. Although much of this debt had been paid off in 1726, at least one part of the rest had been paid in the form of a note of hand worth 1 guinea.[36] As Cannon described it, he was at a fair in 1727 when he was approached by a 'loose debauched Attorney' to recover the debt:

> This Barber showed me a note which I gave old Jenkins and set me a time to pay it off on, which said note was a receipt for one guinea received by young Jenkins at Bradley. Barber gave me one month or I was to be put to Charge, but times and my Circumstances was so bad and low and my credit quite lost that I did not provide against the promised time, so that Barber came and served me with a copy which yet I suffered till it came to a declaration, and still I refused payment having Queried if Barber's proceedings were regular, for I was informed he was one great villain.

As it turned out, Cannon was owed 30s. for work he had done for Thomas Willis, an attorney of Castle Cary. As a result of this he was able to arrange for him to check on the form of the said Barber's suit, which indeed was found erroneous, and Willis was able to halt it with a demurrer.[37] Presumably the note had lost its value as Cannon's poverty

[33] Ibid., pp. 135–6, 155–6. [34] Ibid., pp. 157–9. [35] Ibid., pp. 180, 292–3, 650.
[36] Ibid., p. 175. [37] Ibid., p. 180.

increased, so Jenkins wanted it cashed. One example Cannon gave clearly shows how the writing of notes could avoid a threatened arrest. On 6 September 1741 he noted that he 'borrowed of John Meaker 9s 4d 1/2d and owed him before 9s 7d 1/2d and 1s, in all 20s and gave him a note payable in four or five days'. He did this to satisfy Meaker's debt, 'by reason I could not get it where due'. Then, ten months later, on 6 July 1742, when opening his door in the morning he saw 'a paper pushed into the entry under the door, and upon view of it I found it a summons against me in County Court at the suit of John Meaker'. Two months later he noted that the same bill had been transferred to Mr Wilcox, a hosier and previous mayor, and drew an order for him to pay Meaker within three months, thus avoiding arrest.[38]

In subsequent years Cannon's work as a scrivener highlights a number of instances where he was involved in drawing up paper instruments to avoid litigation going further after an arrest or summons, as in the following May 1739 case of William Pearl, the landlord of the Rose and Crown in Glastonbury, who was

> arrested at the suit of a Tradesman of Bristol, being an action of debt of £14 3s, and to stop it, I drew a note of hand value £20 on Edward Martin, blacksmith, on condition that he, the said Martin, did procure and see the body of William Pearl the 6th instant to the house of William Everett, a bailiff in Wells, which note Edward Martin signed and witnessed by myself and one Philip Bakehouse.[39]

Earlier that month Cannon had performed an almost identical service for John Thomas, a baker in Wells, who was arrested by a corn jobber for wheat he had sold Thomas. The original debt was £20, of which £16 9s. had been paid. To resolve the suit, Thomas gave 'a note of hand payable to him on his order the 27th of December next which I drew, William Allwood signed and I witnessed it and dated it for the 18th instant', worth £3 12s. to cover the remainder.[40]

On another occasion Cannon noted that Elizabeth Blake had been arrested by her brother on 5 June 1738 for a bill Cannon had drawn up the preceding April for £31 for her room and board for one year and 48 weeks. The arrest seems to have been part of a dispute between the siblings over their inheritance, as it was made up by their uncle, the mayor of Glastonbury, and paid by Elizabeth with household goods, plate, and cash, which formed part of her bequest.[41] In yet another iteration, in 1736 Cannon drew a bill of sale for an edge tool maker, 'of one bed and furniture and all his household goods and working tools and

[38] Ibid., pp. 615, 650, 665. [39] Ibid., p. 467. [40] Ibid.; also see p. 216.
[41] Ibid., pp. 364, 370.

interlined his edge tools ... set back the date to the 30th of March last past and so to continue to the 25th March 1738 or to be redeemed sooner, consideration, 4 pounds'. This was done to prevent an attachment of the same goods in a lawsuit.[42]

One other interesting practice the *Chronicles* shed light on is the use of private penal 'judgment bonds', such as the one issued against Cannon earlier. As Steve Hindle has shown, the use of such bonds by justices of the peace to enforce parish business or to resolve interpersonal conflicts such as fights had become increasingly common from the late seventeenth century onwards and was popularly known as 'binding over'. For instance, if two people got into a fist fight and one was injured, the JPs would issue a bond signed by the injuring party not to have business with the other for some period of time upon a stated financial penalty. If violated, the sealed bond could be presented at a civil court for quite speedy recovery of some amount of damages, although the stated damages in the bond were almost always much higher than what would normally be awarded.[43] But Cannon's *Chronicles* show that it was also quite common for such bonds to be drawn up privately using a scrivener or attorney. In one case, Cannon's landlord, a cordwainer, was arrested for a debt of £15 3s. in March 1740 for leather he had bought. He sent to ask both his own brother and brother-in-law for bail, but they refused. To resolve the suit he instead

> gave him a judgement bond of ... £20 returnable fifteen days after Easter, which he signed and was witnessed by myself and Mr. William Nicholls with a promise from the plaintiff not to file the same, but [except] in the case of the said Allwood's absconding or embezzling of his goods and effects with a design to defraud the said Giblet.

As Cannon recorded, Alwood promised to pay the debt and cost as he could raise it:

> being £18 3s which he did the last being paid and the bond taken up in March 1742, having at several times stripped and sold the best and choicest of his household goods and furniture to do it and pay some other debts.[44]

It is hard to get a sense of how much litigation there was over credit in the area around Glastonbury from just this source, but overall in the six years between 1737 and 1742 Cannon mentioned about forty-two lawsuits, or an average of six per year. In the very last year of the *Chronicles* he became a clerk to Charles Marsh, a victualler who had taken over the

42 Ibid., p. 262.
43 Steve Hindle, *On the Parish? The Micro-politics of Poor Relief in Rural England, c. 1550–1750* (Oxford, 2004), pp. 94–115.
44 Cannon, *Chronicles*, p. 536. Also see pp. 556, 595–6.

Rose and Crown in Glastonbury, and became bailiff for the hundred court there around April 1742. During the next eight months he wrote out over twenty summonses for March to small debtors to appear at the court in cases of assumpsit.[45] Cannon does not always mention the costs of litigation, but when he does it could be quite a lot. When he was arrested for not being able to meet the interest payments on his four acre Butmoor mortgage for £30, the charges cost him two guineas, and he had to get his maternal uncle Thomas Pope to pay it.[46] On another occasion he used William Nichols to sue one John Rood for a debt of 8–9 shillings he owed Cannon to pay for his brother's schooling, but Rood was so indebted he never recovered the debt, but had to pay Nicholls 30s. in fees – three times the value of the debt![47] Again, very late in the *Chronicles* on 19 May 1641, Cannon recorded another instance where fees amounted to more than the small debt, which this time he owed someone else:

> Borrowed 20s of William Chapman and went and paid Cook's debt and costs in his suit against me by Mr. Rook, and took a receipt for the same. … The debt 6s 6d, cost and fees 7s 10d, in all 14s 4d besides about 5s 4d. one Richard Allan, a bailiff fellow, had of me first and last, he pretending to be a friend but proved a great rogue.[48]

Two further examples demonstrate the very high fees charged for litigation around Glastonbury at this time: the cost of drawing up an inventory of goods worth £18 10s., to be sold to pay off a debt amounting to £43, was £12, while a clerk to an attorney in Wells, Mr Goldfinch, charged fees of £1 3s. 6d. for a debt of 11s. 3d. sued in the hundred court of Glastonbury.[49] Such high fees certainly support the evidence that litigation was becoming much more expensive than it had been in the seventeenth century, making it much less attractive to sue over small debts. Cannon's examples also show, however, that such litigation was still undertaken, although the examples he gives must have been unavoidable cases, or those that did not work out according to plan, since they often involved spending more than the debt was worth. These high fees were still much lower than those earned from conveyancing, but they contributed to the realignment of justice, making it much more expensive.

By the 1730s, the country attorney had become a central fixture of local middling sort village life.[50] Although the centre of legal culture

[45] Ibid., pp. 637, 641, 647, 649, 685. [46] Ibid., pp. 155–6. [47] Ibid., pp. 199, 212.
[48] Ibid., p. 605. [49] Ibid., pp. 294, 345.
[50] Craig Muldrew, 'The Emergence of the "Middle Sort" of People', in Keith Wrightson (ed.), *A Social History of England, c.1500–c.1750* (Cambridge, 2016), pp. 301–4; Henry French, *The Middle Sort of People in Provincial England 1600–1750* (Oxford, 2007), ch. 4.

remained the Inns of Court and Westminster, in many other ways there was a shift in the gravity of legal life away from the metropolis and major towns towards the wider nation, including the countryside and small towns like Glastonbury. The two attorneys studied by B. L. Anderson, for instance, were from Wavertree Hall and Childwell Hall in Lancashire. From being litigators centred around borough courts of record doing moneylending on the side, attorneys became sorts of proto-bankers, attracting profits from trade and either lending on bond or leveraging mostly rural land on mortgage to create capital and a larger money supply. Also, in contrast to the previous century, when the poor were quite active in making complaints through attorneys in courts for a fee of 4d. – which would have been done through one of the town attorneys – now an attorney focusing on conveyancing would be more likely only to deal with a poor client through the Poor Law administration, not through litigation or negotiating a mortgage.[51]

Local attorneys stood at the centre of networks through which lenders could seek out borrowers, and as they themselves saved their profits from doing conveyancing they too could begin to lend out on mortgages. But, as we shall see, they could also use their knowledge of the borrowers' state of indebtedness as a sort of 'insider knowledge' to allow over-indebtedness in the hope of being able to foreclose on certain mortgages. In the absence of any public land registries, it was only attorneys who had any wide-scale knowledge and records of the state of borrowing in communities, and this was knowledge they could use to their advantage.

Urban Litigation, Bills, and Notes

But, if there was a shift away from provincial towns such as King's Lynn as centres of legal activity, there was certainly no concurrent shift in economic activity in the early eighteenth century. This was actually a period when the population of provincial towns began to grow at a faster pace than in the 100 years when the growth of London had dominated. This was especially true of provincial ports such as Bristol, Newcastle, and Liverpool, and after *c.*1720 the new northern industrial towns such as Birmingham and Leeds. As we saw in the discussion of evidence from the Old Bailey in London, the use of small notes and other paper instruments was very widespread there, just as in the countryside. The

[51] Gwenda Morgan and Peter Rushton (eds.), *The Justicing Notebook (1759–64) of Edmund Tew, Rector of Boulton* (Durham, 2000); Peter King, 'The Summary Courts and Social Relations in Eighteenth-Century England', *Past and Present* 183 (2004), pp. 125–72.

town government in Lyme Regis certainly used informal notes and bills to pay workers.

Nevertheless, whatever the extent of the use of notes as payment to workmen, it remained the case that their earnings were vulnerable to fluctuations in employment opportunities, and the cost of living was generally higher in towns and significantly higher in London.[52] In addition, their level of remuneration was often very close to their cost of living. Any increase in food prices due to a bad harvest, or the arrival of small children to look after, meant that they still needed to rely on informal credit to buy goods. While the notes they would have been paid with would help to reduce the need for any potential litigation when they were used to purchase something from a shop, the poor lacked security to be able to write up notes for themselves. As a result, they still had to rely on informal credit, and debts they built up needed a form of legal enforcement, as we saw in the case of Cannon after he became impoverished and his creditors lost their trust in him.

As a result, urban tradesmen much preferred efficient, low-cost summary jurisdictions in new courts of requests – also called courts of conscience – to recover small debts, rather than the much more participatory and egalitarian civic courts where decisions had to be made by a jury.[53] This change was part of what C. W. Brooks and William Champion have argued was part of a realignment of an 'old' regulatory regime based on manorial courts, local borough courts, and civic institutions such as guilds. In the old legal regime, all creditors in society had equal access to sue over broken contracts based on equality before the common law and a jury of one's peers. This was increasingly replaced by summary justice based on arbitration forced on poorer debtors by justices of the peace, and what legal historians studying the nineteenth century have called the 'class law' of the courts of requests. In the nineteenth century, county courts were developed based on similar principles.[54]

Courts of requests were for small debts of under 40s., which were decided *summarily* by a commission of town mercantile and legal elites in a very short time and for little cost. Debts were almost always ordered to be repaid according to an extended schedule of weekly payments of small amounts, but if they were not paid the commissioners had the power to

[52] Jeremy Boulton, 'Food Prices and the Standard of Living in London in the "century of Revolution", 1580–1700', *The Economic History Review* 53, no. 3 (2000), pp. 455–92.

[53] Margot C. Finn, *The Character of Credit: Personal Debt in English Culture, 1740–1914* (Cambridge, 2003), pp. 202ff.

[54] Paul Johnson, 'Class Law in Victorian England', *Past and Present* 141, no. 1 (1993), pp. 147–69.

order short-term imprisonment of the body as a punishment, or the distraint of certain non-essential household goods. As Margo Finn has argued, this power to imprison somebody for an unpaid debt for punishment on the basis of a commissioner's discretionary power was a new feature of these institutions.[55]

In doing so, the development of the courts of requests was following a broader move towards summary justice meted out by justices of the peace for certain misdemeanours. Short-term imprisonment as a punishment for vagrancy, prostitution, minor assault, and other offences came to be crucial to this process. This was done in institutions that came to be known as bridewells, after the original institution established in the 1550s, located in the old Bridewell Place in London. These were also called houses of correction, and by the late eighteenth century there were over 170 of these 'prisons for the poor' in the country. Although most inmates were incarcerated for the offence listed above, it was in such spaces that courts of requests debtors were also confined.[56]

The first court of requests was established in London on a permanent basis in 1604.[57] Before 1760, the only others created were in Bristol (1689), Gloucester (1689), Norwich (1701), and Newcastle (1689), and Gloucester's went into decline in the early eighteenth century.[58] Those in Norwich and Gloucester were established upon petition of clothiers who wanted an institution where the small debts of their large workforces could be recovered.[59] After 1660 there were forty attempts made in Parliament to establish new institutions that could deal with small debts in a summary process, and some were supported by John Locke. All, however, were unsuccessful. It was only after 1749 that the numbers of courts of requests expanded rapidly, first in the London suburbs and then in Lincoln, Birmingham, St. Albans, Liverpool, Canterbury, Boston, Sheffield, and Great Yarmouth, all in the 1750s. There were a further eight courts established in the 1760s, eleven in the 1770s, and ten in the 1780s.[60] In this period up to 1810 there were 100 Acts of Parliament to create courts of requests. By the 1820s the courts of requests were hearing some 200,000 cases each year.[61] For most of these cities, the establishment of courts of requests followed rapid urban growth and industrialisation.[62]

[55] Ibid., pp. 150–1.

[56] Robert Shoemaker, *Prosecution and Punishment: Petty Crime and the Law in London and Rural Middlesex, C.1660–1725* (Cambridge, 1991), pp. 166–98; Finn, *Character of Credit*, p. 113.

[57] It had originally been informally established in the reign of Henry VIII, but it is not known how often it sat. Finn, *Character of Credit*, p. 198.

[58] Ibid., p. 202. [59] Ibid., p. 212. [60] Ibid., p. 202. [61] Ibid., p. 236.

[62] P. J. Corfield, *The Impact of English Towns, 1700–1800* (Oxford, 1982), pp. 82–99.

Table 7.1 *Cases in courts of requests before 1750*[63]

Period	Bristol	London	Newcastle
1692–1693	580		
1697–1698			1,826
1700		2,385	
1711–1712			1,789
1729–1730	535		
1734–1735	511		
1739–1740	417		
1743–1744			923
1744–1745	359		
1755–1756		2,246	

For the period we are concerned with, the availability of summary justice was still quite geographically limited. Records survive for three of the five jurisdictions, and those of Bristol are very full and can be analysed. Table 7.1 presents the numbers of cases heard in the courts of Bristol, London, and Newcastle. London, as might be expected, heard the largest number of suits, but the numbers heard in Newcastle were very large as well. At this time, although both Newcastle and Bristol were growing, the latter was generally more populous; however, fewer suits were brought to court there. The most likely reason for this is administrative. In Bristol, the steward of one of the old common law civil courts, the Tolzey Court, had opposed the establishment of the court of requests, and it is likely that it and the other civil court in Bristol, the Mayor's Court, continued to hear suits that might have otherwise gone to the court of requests. The combined total of suits heard in the two borough courts remained at around 3,000 per year. Although this was only about half of the 6,000 suits the courts were entertaining in the late sixteenth and seventeenth centuries, it was still much more than the 1,200 or so cases that were being heard in the two borough courts in Newcastle in the early eighteenth century.[64]

The Bristol court of conscience was held weekly before the mayor, two sheriffs, and a registrar. Normally judgments took the form of set

[63] The years in question are generally Michaelmas to Michaelmas, except for London in 1700, which starts at January and is extrapolated from the four months of cases that survive. Bristol Archives, Z33 04413, 04753, 04754, 04414; LMA, Court of Requests, Ledger Books, CLA/038/02/001-002.

[64] Muldrew, *Economy of Obligation*, pp. 222–5; Brooks, 'Interpersonal Conflict', pp. 40–1; Bristol Archives catalogue, entry of Court of Conscience.

schedules of repayment of all, or part, of the debt in question. These were entered in the court action books beside the plaint. The names of the plaintiffs and defendants, their occupations, and street of residence were also listed. Most cases have the amount of the debt sued for (under 40s.), and about 35–45 per cent contain descriptions of what the debt was for. In 1692, for instance, two widows sued Thomas Browning, a tobacco roller, for a debt of 22s. that was five years overdue. He asked for more time and the court ordered him to repay it at one shilling per week. All kinds of small debts were sued over by every sort of occupation imaginable, including a hairweaver and a frying pan maker, for things as varied as meat and drink, rent for lodging, payment for gate keeping, carriage of hay, butter and eggs, a hat, coffee, hauling stones, bread, poles, children's shoes, fees for teaching a deaf child, dressing wounds, a pistol, work done, and of course much beer and cider.[65] From these entries a vivid impression can be gained of all the odd jobs and sales poor people provided on credit to earn a living.

The occupations of the most active plaintiffs in the court in 1692–1693 were tailors (43 suits), cordwainers (31), victuallers (31), mariners (29), and bakers (21). Interestingly, tailors were also the most sued occupation as defendants (33 suits), followed by tobacco rollers (23), victuallers (16), cordwainers (15), butchers (14), porters (12), hauliers (11), and labourers (10). It is unsurprising that cases involving food and clothing should dominate, as these constituted most of the purchases on credit of poorer families. The fact that tailors, cordwainers, and victuallers were also sued the most suggests that many who supplied the poor were also vulnerable themselves. Bristol was, after London, the main port of entry for American tobacco before 1750, and the presence of so many tobacco rollers suggests this was a common labouring occupation, together with the transport occupations listed. Also, as in the later courts studied by Margo Finn, women, including wives, were quite active in the court. In 1692–1693, 13 per cent of plaintiffs were widows, 4 per cent spinsters and executrixes, and 2 per cent wives. In contrast, only 9 per cent of defendants were women. However, many wives also came to court on behalf of their husbands to either plead or end a suit.

In 1692, where the goods sold were listed, food and drink accounted for 29 per cent of all sales. Debts owed for work and specific small services were always more common than wages. Rent for lodging was

[65] Bristol Archives Office, Z33 14413, 04754. The court records do not list the nature of every suit. In a sample of 257 cases from the King's Lynn Guildhall Court from 1652 to 1654, only four concerned wages. Norfolk Record Office, KL/C25/17-18.

also common.[66] However, there is also evidence that the litigants were using notes of hand and bills for small debts under 40s. In 1692–1693, seven cases specifically stated the unpaid debt was on a note of hand, and two mentioned bills.[67] In comparison, eight cases were for money lent and nineteen only mentioned a debt with no description. By 1739–1740, seventeen cases were about notes of hand.[68] Those cases described generically as 'money lent' had increased to thirty-three, and it is possible that some of these also involved notes. In comparison, twenty-nine cases were about goods sold and fourteen concerned work done. Here we have good evidence that notes of hand were increasingly being used by poorer people to pay for purchases, although oral credit remained more common.

The Rise of Arrest and Imprisonment

It wasn't just the poor who found themselves more vulnerable to summary legal action based on perceived moral failure for not prioritising repayment of their debts before other spending. As two recent books by Tawny Paul and Alexander Wakelam have demonstrated, it became much easier to use imprisonment as a means of punishment within the normal civil law procedure, even though the law did not fundamentally change.[69] In the sixteenth and seventeenth centuries, while levels of litigation were high, most suits were resolved out of court to avoid the expenses of a trial going all the way to judgment, which would require empanelling a jury. Only about 4 per cent reached this stage. The first step in any suit was the entering of a complaint in the local court's records. In most jurisdictions, a summons by a bailiff or sergeant-at-mace for the defendant to appear at the court and answer the plaintiff was the next procedure. A summons was the least imposing for the defendant, but increasingly in the seventeenth century either attachment of goods or an arrest of the debtor's body with a writ of *capias* to secure appearance at the court became more common. Both of these procedures were intended to put much more pressure on the defendant, but while an attachment was considered a civil step, arrest was much more serious as it indicated that the creditor feared the debtor was in trouble and was in

66 Almost fifty years later, in 1739, there were only four cases dealing with wages compared to over forty for goods sold. Bristol Archives Office, Z33 14413.
67 This was out of 217 suits that mentioned the nature of the debt.
68 Out of about 208 cases where the nature of the debt is described.
69 Tawny Paul, *The Poverty of Disaster: Debt and Insecurity in Eighteenth-Century Britain* (Cambridge, 2019); Alexander Wakelam, *Credit and Debt in Eighteenth Century England: An Economic History of Debtors' Prisons* (London, 2020).

danger of absconding. As such, it could lead to other creditors going to court to sue over their debts. For this reason, it was usually done privately and was only used selectively. In Bristol in 1655, for instance, 289 people were arrested because of actions initiated in the mayor's court. This was only 16 per cent of all of the 1,756 actions initiated that year, and in the same city's Tolzey Court, 12 per cent were arrested as a result of actions initiated there. In comparison, another 177 (8 per cent) were attached by goods.[70]

Once arrested, a defendant was usually taken to an alehouse and given time to find two people to bail him or her by entering into a recognisance, which contained a monetary penalty for the defendant's future appearance. But if they could not do this they were put in prison on what was termed mesne process to await trial. In King's Lynn in the 1680s there were on average 224 arrests per year (15 per cent of suits initiated) of about 150 different people. Of those arrested, 87 per cent found bail, which meant that 29 people were imprisoned on mesne process. As a result, 0.67 per cent of the adult household heads or 6–7 out of every 1,000 in King's Lynn, spent some time in prison every year. These individuals who could not find bail had lost their credit, and were in serious financial difficulty. We do not know how long they had to remain in prison before their trial, but only about five or six prisoners per year would have been finally incarcerated by their creditors after a trial verdict. Such numbers were common elsewhere, and such individuals were essentially those imprisoned to prevent them from contracting more debts.[71]

However, from some time around 1700 it became much more common to arrest someone immediately without the issue of a summons, a procedure allowed by one of the chief justices to speed up debt recovery.[72] We do not know how many more arrests there were as a percentage of cases, and how many found bail, but from the work of Paul and Wakelam we know that while the number of cases of debt and contract declined dramatically in London, as elsewhere, the rates of imprisonment remained steady. As Paul has shown, a steady amount of about 550 people per year would have been committed to all of the London prisons between 1710 and 1760, after which the numbers start to rise quickly.[73] This was due to another change in legal practice that allowed

70 Muldrew, *Economy of Obligation*, pp. 280–1. 71 Ibid., pp. 281.
72 Brooks, *Lawyers, Litigation*, pp. 32–3.
73 This is based on the average of 300 commitments per year to the Fleet and King's Bench being 55 per cent of all London prison commitments, and change over time indicated in figure 1.1 in Paul, *Poverty of Disaster*, pp. 44–7.

plaintiffs to keep defendants in prison indefinitely on mesne process by delaying the trial. Theoretically the defendant had the right to apply to be removed from prison by a writ of *supersedeas*, but by making the charge of applying for this writ much higher it effectively barred prisoners from using their legal rights.[74] This meant that over half of debtors remained in prison for over six months and 30 per cent for more than a year.[75]

Paul has estimated that the population of incarcerated debtors in London might have been as high as 9,500 by 1729.[76] Unfortunately we have very limited evidence on the numbers of prisoners in the seventeenth century, so it is impossible to say how much of an increase this was. There is a list of 623 prisoners in the Fleet from 1628, where the average number of years of incarceration was 3.3. Certainly the number of prisoners incarcerated for debt was a problem identified by radicals who wished to enact law reform during the Commonwealth. In December 1649 an Act was passed in Parliament that allowed imprisoned debtors to apply for their discharge if they swore they were worth no more than £5. After this, the creditor had thirty days to deny that the debtor was actually this poor if they had evidence to the contrary. After 1695, Acts were also passed for the relief of poor debtors which allowed them to draw up an inventory of all of their assets for sale and distribution among their creditors.[77] From this point onwards, Parliament regularly passed Acts that allowed the poorest debtors in prison to petition for their release on the grounds of poverty. In the five main London prisons, from May to October 1691, 105 prisoners were released, and 63 from August to October 1696. However, by 1725 almost 3,000 prisoners applied for release, and in later years when Acts were passed, 1,000–2,000 in London applied for relief.[78]

The surviving schedules of the wealth and assets of the prisoners applied for relief under the Relief of Poor Debtors Acts are revealing. On average their assets seem quite substantial, but 55 per cent of this consisted of debts they were owed by others. Also, their liquid assets – such as financial instruments and household goods – were quite similar in value to the debts for which they had been imprisoned, so potentially could have been liquidated to pay their debts.[79] This means they chose to

[74] Paul, *Poverty of Disaster*, p. 42; Wakelam, *Credit and Debt in Eighteenth Century England*, pp. 38–40, 92–5.

[75] Paul, *Poverty of Disaster*, p. 43. [76] Ibid., p. 48. [77] Ibid., p. 42.

[78] Wakelam, *Credit and Debt in Eighteenth Century England*, pp. 61–4, 93. A commitment book for the Fleet has survived from the late 1680s and early 1690s which shows that approximately 140 prisoners were committed per year. National Archives, PRIS 10/157.

[79] Although 44% declared in their schedules that they had no estate at all. Wakelam, *Credit and Debt in Eighteenth Century England*, p. 107.

remain in prison rather than liquidate other forms of assets, which presumably could have been used by other members of their families. Crucially, the debts owed *to* the prisoners were much higher. As Paul has shown, most of the prisoners were shopkeepers and tradesmen, and these were mostly small debts owed by their customers, who were probably also too poor to pay. Those who applied for relief were in prison because of a lack of liquidity.[80]

Another major change in the eighteenth century in comparison to the seventeenth was that it became much more common to arrest and eventually imprison debtors for very small debts. Between 1730 and 1770, 34 per cent of prisoners had been incarcerated for debts on average worth less than £5, and over 50 per cent for average debts of less than £10.[81] Although about 45 per cent of those incarcerated were released in under six months in London, and the majority in under a year in both London and Lancaster, imprisonment was still a harsh use of the law.[82] Wakelam has argued that the debtor's prison was an economic institution that facilitated the expansion of credit by providing creditors with a means of recovering their debts with a cheap and effective punitive threat.[83] So, just as it was argued that the courts of requests needed to be able to threaten the customers of small shopkeepers with imprisonment, the new forms of easier arrest and imprisonment on mesne process were needed by the wholesalers who supplied the shopkeepers with their goods to imprison them when small debts proved unrecoverable.

In the first part of this chapter I argued that the increased use of bills, notes, and other informal credit currency decreased common law debt litigation by making credit networks more liquid. In relation to this, it is vital to understand why the residual use of the law became much harsher. One answer, of course, is that the increased liquidity went along with an ongoing increase in consumption. Debtors schedules from London in 1725 had an average of four people owing them obligations, but this had expanded to thirteen by 1748. In Lancaster there was a similar rise from an average of six people owing debts to the imprisoned debtors, to seventeen by 1755.[84] Credit currency undoubtedly helped to enable this expansion, but it was still credit and could fail. We can see this because some of the debtors schedules list debts owing to them being in the form of notes of hand or bills.[85] Thus, although the use of credit currency

[80] Paul, *Poverty of Disaster*, pp. 76–9. This last point is made on p. 108.
[81] Ibid., pp. 112, 130–1. [82] Ibid., ch. 6.
[83] Wakelam, *Credit and Debt in Eighteenth Century England*, pp. 10, 214–19.
[84] Paul, *Poverty of disaster*, p. 88.
[85] Ibid., pp. 83, 90; Wakelam, *Credit and Debt in Eighteenth Century England*, pp. 18, 25.

made circuits of obligation less vulnerable by reducing the number of times unpaid debts slowed down the velocity of transactions, this increased liquidity and velocity of circulation also meant that creditors needed, or at least wanted, a faster means of dealing with those instances where unpaid debts threated to slow things down too much due to lack of payment. Therefore, judges and lawyers modified existing practices to create a faster means of debt recovery, which gave creditors much more power to act in a coercive way and left the debtor with few legal options to delay repayment.

In this system it was the small shopkeepers dealing with the poor who were most vulnerable to being arrested and imprisoned as small debts built up over time. While bills increased liquidity, these sorts of small shop debts were the same ones that shopkeepers sued over in the courts of requests. And, while some labourers would have been paid with notes, many would have worked for small contractors who did not themselves have enough credit to issue notes. The increasing use of imprisonment clearly shows there was still a need for legal sanction to be used. Many people still had to buy on long-term credit, and shopkeepers had to offer it to stay in business. According to Paul's estimate, in London about 7 per cent of adult men would have experienced incarceration at some point in their life between 1708 and 1780.[86] But since imprisonment went up after 1760, this rate would have been closer to 3 per cent in the early eighteenth century. While certainly an increase on what it was before, it is still a minority of the middling sort, and many fewer than experienced debt litigation previously, which was almost 100 per cent.

In this chapter, and previously when discussing notes and mortgages, we have seen how it was legal change much more than government policy that changed the way credit was transacted. Apart from the Bank of England and the South Sea Company, new institutions of the sort proposed in the hundreds of pamphlets and manuscripts examined in Chapter 2 were not the prime movers of change as it occurred in most of England. Instead, case law regarding the equity of redemption and the validity of transferable paper notes and bills was more important. Further, as we have now seen in this chapter, the existing law concerning arrest on mesne process simply needed to be reinterpreted and court fees raised to instigate a profound change in making it easier to arrest and imprison someone for small debts. This is not to say Parliament was unimportant. It was a statute in 1704 that cemented the legality of transferable notes, and the Statute of Frauds of 1677 made written

[86] Paul, *Poverty of Disaster*, p. 46.

contracts more important as legal evidence. Statutes were also used to make forgery of Bank of England notes and government paper instruments punishable by death, and statute law was needed to create the new courts of requests. But overall, most institutional change is best described as organic, in that people grew accustomed to it as it developed through the modification of existing practices.

The use of the term 'organic' is now usually taken as a hallmark of conservatism. But this would be anachronistic, as land bank schemes and the South Sea Company were quite radical in this sense. It was probably more that with the memory of protectorate legislation still present, people found it easier to adapt to gradual change. Case law was also inherently more *flexible* in that it could adapt to practices that developed before they were made legal. I would argue that it was such flexibility that was important to make changes work. In contrast, a new institution – like the South Sea Company – was dynamic but, as it tuned out, also fatally vulnerable to new forms of speculation that could not be controlled. Some have also argued that the Bubble Act of 1722 might have held back economic growth by preventing the creation of new joint stock companies until the nineteenth century. But even in this case, larger businesses were able to develop through evolution and adaptations of the laws of partnership and those of trusts, thus overcoming this statutory limitation.[87]

Of course, incidental change was also used to protect existing interests, none more than those of attorneys who were able to make even more money as time progressed.[88] But the equity of redemption also protected the family lineages and other private interests of large landholders, which would have been exposed by land registries. As regards to the poor and lower middling sort, however, the result was more ambiguous. The poor lost much of their sense of access to legal equality. Suing someone became too expensive. However, the availability of notes to pay wages meant that it also became less necessary, although the incremental introduction of local paper notes meant they were not always available. Also, the poor were much more exposed to corporal punishment in the form of imprisonment; so, too, were the shopkeepers who relied on them as their main clientele when their wholesalers sued them. I will now turn to a wider discussion of just how legal and ethical changes were used to redefine social relations based on the possession of capital.

[87] Ron Harris, *Industrializing English Law Entrepreneurship and Business Organization, 1720–1844* (Cambridge, 2000), pp. 19–36, 85–198.

[88] Muldrew, 'Blunderers and Blotters', pp. 245–9.

8 The Dark Side of Thrift: Capital and Class Formation – Institutional Stability and Ethical Inequality

In the previous chapter we saw how the law of debt and contract was transformed in the eighteenth century. It moved from a legal system where all were contractually equal and most participated fairly regularly as plaintiffs to recover their debts, to one increasingly used only by wealthier creditors to recover their debts. This change can be interpreted as marking the beginnings of the creation of a new middle class of wealthier, more secure creditors who used the law to protect their capital, which they termed property. This can be most clearly seen in the writings of William Hutton, the Birmingham entrepreneur who wrote about the cases that came before him as a judge in the court of requests there in the 1770s and 1780s, and who became the courts of requests' most passionate advocate. This, of course, covers a period somewhat later than the approximate dates of this study, but it represents the culmination of the changes I have been describing which began earlier, so is certainly worth examining in this light. The changes that led to the basis for a new type of class-based thinking about society were closely linked to the security that new forms of capital provided to successful savers. These were those who were able to accumulate large amounts of capital through entrepreneurship or inheritance, and not dissipate it through overspending, and who protected it against accidental loss with new forms of fire and maritime insurance and diversified investment.[1] In brief, they began to think of themselves as being morally better than their fellows, and their capital as a form of property created out of righteousness. It was the role of the law to protect it from those who were less able, and there were no extenuating circumstances that might justify not paying back a contracted debt. This was the beginning of the legal doctrine of 'freedom of contract', where contracts entered into freely became seen as sacrosanct and inviolable; this doctrine would become dominant by the mid-nineteenth

[1] Robin Pearson, *Insuring the Industrial Revolution: Fire Insurance in Great Britain, 1700–1850* (Aldershot, 2004); Adrian Leonard, *London Marine Insurance 1438–1824: Risk, Trade and the Early Modern State* (Woodbridge, 2022).

century.[2] This was a morality that stood in stark contrast to the biblical concept of forgiveness or equity, in which misfortune, poverty, and even misjudgement about spending could all be interpreted as mitigating circumstances justifying non-payment. Previously, in a world where everyone was so vulnerable to non-payment due to a lack of liquidity, this could be applied universally through religion, and it was still being advocated as a form of charity for creditors in the late seventeenth century.[3]

The Rise of the New Middle Class

Of course, if we want to use the term 'class' we also need to discuss Marx. In the Introduction I examined the essential influence of Marx on how capitalism has been used and conceptualised as a term of analysis. He, of course, argued that classes arose through the definition of common interests based on their ownership of the means of production. Capital was created by the bourgeoise through the expropriation of the difference between the cost of labour they employed and the selling price of the goods they produced in their workshops and factories. He saw the early modern bourgeoisie in conflict with the feudal aristocratic class, who defined themselves by the land they held and by their relationship with the tenants from whom they expropriated labour value in the form of rent. But by the nineteenth century industrialists had gained the upper hand by organising labour into factories, turning their profits into capital. In the rhetorical flourishes of *The Communist Manifesto*, this created a vast new power of destructive modernity that was overwhelming the world.[4]

However, as discussed in Chapter 1, in England there was no strict division between town and country in terms of profit-making. We also saw that it was perfectly possible to make large profits without turning them into capital. Here I wish to argue that the middle class did not create itself through a process of conflict with the landowning aristocracy, in which capital was used as a means of *power* to create new institutions in the first instance. Rather, the origins of the middle class had more to do with making capital, as a thing, stable. In England this occurred in tandem with the landed interest through the legal processes described in Chapter 4, in which the male family lineage – so valued by the

[2] P. S, Atiyah, *The Rise and Fall of Freedom of Contract* (Oxford, 1979), pp. 1–7, 388–418.

[3] Craig Muldrew, *The Economy of Obligation: The Culture of Credit and Social Relations in Early Modern England* (London, 1998), pp. 304–9.

[4] Karl Marx and Friedrich Engels, *The Communist Manifesto*, ed. Gareth Stedman Jones (London, 2002), pp. 222–3.

aristocracy and upper gentry – was protected, while at the same time trading capital gained access to the latter's land as a secure investment through mortgages. Female inheritance was more difficult to accommodate but does not seem to have inhibited the rise of mortgaging. The landed interest and trade came together through the mortgage as an instrument of capital, which allowed primogeniture and strict settlement as well as investment in improvement and local industry such as wool production. In addition, although Marx stressed merchant capital and joint stock companies, the state also created instruments for holding capital in the form of interest-bearing obligations such as annuities or Treasury bills and bonds to pay for war.

Of course, profits were needed to create capital, and any producer or trader of either agricultural or industrial goods could make more profits if they hired labour to increase the scale of their enterprise. Large-scale capitalist farmers were the first to employ wage labour at significant scale. However, the creation of capital was not in any way dependent on the employment of wage labour, and, as we shall see, the morals that came to define the middle class were as much aimed at distinguishing it from the middling sort as from workers. It was only in the nineteenth century that the employment of large workforces commodified labour through the cash nexus, to an extent that made class an alienating force due to social distance. Capital, crucially, made this possible by making middle-class wealth more secure and different than that which workers and smaller traders could achieve. But it was the religious ethics that stressed happiness, self-control, and interest (discussed in Chapters 5 and 6) that made this eventuality possible. The institutional security offered by mortgages, account keeping, and the law enabled circulating capital to spread downwards into society at the local level. But eventually self-control and the ability to save became linked to security of capital as savings, and protecting this security came to define what it meant to be a member of the middle class.

Beginning in the late sixteenth century, profit-making through selling on the market came to characterize what was gradually termed the middling sort.[5] This evolved from older notions of rural hierarchy organised around the lord of the manor. Certainly profit from selling food and other goods had existed long before the sixteenth century, but it was at that time that marketing of all sorts accelerated, and the numbers of people in non-agricultural occupations steadily increased until they

[5] Craig Muldrew, 'The Emergence of the "Middle Sort" of People', in Keith Wrightson (ed.), *The Cambridge Social History of England, c.1500-c.1750* (Cambridge, 2016) pp. 290–309.

comprised half the population by the end of the seventeenth century. As they expanded, the wealth they created through their profits was justified as being good for the commonwealth.[6] However, these profits existed within the insecure webs of credit that led to much litigation. Security in this system primarily depended on reputational credit. The ownership of goods also certainly added to one's creditworthiness and security, since a creditor knew they could be sold to meet an obligation.[7] A creditor still needed to sue at common law and receive a judgment of attachment. Land was also immune from action at common law, and could not be attached to satisfy creditors unless it was mortgaged, which was relatively rare before the 1680s (see 'The Decline of Credit Litigation' in Chapter 7) Overall, the system was characterised by insecurity. The middling sort worried as much about downward mobility and over-indebtedness as they did about rising in the world. Many families rose and others fell.[8]

In the early eighteenth century, reputation for good credit certainly did not go away, especially between those who dealt in bills of exchange, as Defoe pointed out. But as we saw in the case of John Cannon, it was shifting towards good accounting and honest writing. The example of Cannon also shows that insecurity remained a defining experience for many. Cannon termed himself a 'tennis ball of fortune' to describe his various misfortunes.[9] And, as we saw in the previous chapter, poorer middling sort shopkeepers – whose clientele was the labouring poor – had no choice but to continue to extend risky sales credit. But wealth became much more secure for those who could show enough self-control to accumulate capital. As long as an owner of land or urban property did not borrow too much, they could gain money for investment, and the lenders could earn interest based on the landowner's profits. In addition, people could earn interest by investing in company stocks and

[6] Ibid., p. 294; Christopher Dyer, 'The Consumer and the Market in the Later Middle Ages', *Economic History Review*, 2nd. ser., 42, no. 3 (1989), pp. 305–27; Campop, 'The Occupational Structure of Britain c.1379–1911 and the International Comparative History of Occupational Structure: An Overview of Findings and Where to Find Them', www.campop.geog.cam.ac.uk/research/occupations/outputs/preliminary, accessed 28 April 2025.

[7] Alexandra Shepard, *Accounting for Oneself: Worth, Status, and the Social Order in Early Modern England* (Oxford, 2015), pp. 279, 298–313.

[8] Craig Muldrew, 'Class and Credit: Social Identity, Wealth and the Life Course in Early Modern England', in Henry French and Jonathan Barry (eds.), *Identity and Agency in England, 1500–1800* (London, 2004), pp. 147–77; Keith Wrightson, *English Society 1580–1680* (New Brunswick, 1982), pp. 26–30; Michael Mascuch, 'Social Mobility and Middling Self-Identity: The Ethos of British Autobiographers, 1600–1750', *Social History* 20 (1995), pp. 45–61.

[9] Muldrew, 'Class and Credit', p. 160.

government debt. These investments formed a pool of secure savings which could be sold to supply any needed liquidity when debts owed needed to be paid, whereas previously a debtor would have mainly had to try to recover debts owed to them by others. This reduced the chances of going broke by not having funds to meet immediate obligations.

But spending still needed to be controlled to make profits, and to avoid becoming over-mortgaged and having to sell one's land. This is why self-control and saving became emphasised. The old universal dichotomy of thrift versus profligacy was modified to one between consumption based on capital resources – defined by careful accounting – and profligacy, now defined as the lack of ability to save rather than the temptation to submit to appetites. Submitting to appetites was now fine as long as one could afford it.[10] When one couldn't, it was a moral failing. Cannon could have been quite successful by the standards of someone without a business or land, given his earnings, if he had been able to buy fewer books. But because he couldn't, he always remained at the very bottom of the middling sort, on the verge of poverty. The achievement of happiness also came to be employed as a definition of the 'middle class' of people. We can see the link of this to the achievement of happiness and moderation, stressed by the Latitudinarian Anglican Church, in the advice given to Robinson Crusoe by his father early in Defoe's 1719 novel:

> My father, a wise and grave man, gave me serious and excellent counsel … He told me … mine was the middle state, or what might be called the upper station of low life, which he had found, by long experience, was the best state in the world, the most suited to human happiness, not exposed to the miseries and hardships, the labour and sufferings of the mechanic part of mankind, and not embarrassed with the pride, luxury, ambition, and envy of the upper part of mankind.
>
> He bade me observe it, and I should always find that the calamities of life were shared among the upper and lower part of mankind, but that the middle station had the fewest disasters … they were not subjected to so many distempers and uneasinesses, either of body or mind, as those were who, by vicious living, luxury, and extravagances on the one hand, or by hard labour, want of necessaries, and mean or insufficient diet on the other hand … the middle station of life was calculated for all kind of virtue and all kind of enjoyments; that peace and plenty were the handmaids of a middle fortune; that temperance, moderation, quietness, health, society, all agreeable diversions, and all desirable pleasures, were the blessings attending the middle station of life.[11]

[10] Paul Slack, *The Invention of Improvement: Information and Material Progress in Seventeenth-Century England* (Oxford, 2015), pp. 142–56, 215–22.

[11] Daniel Defoe, *Robinson Crusoe*, ed. John Richetti (London, 2001), p. 6.

Of course, Crusoe as a young man ignored his father's advice and went to sea for adventure. After encountering a near-fatal storm he met a helpful captain who introduced him to English trade with Guinea. At this time, Crusoe simply sold English goods for gold, but managed to earn about £260 profit. However, on his next voyage as a captain he was captured by Barbary pirates and made a household slave in present-day Morocco. Eventually, though, he escaped in a small boat and was picked up by a Portuguese ship on its way to Brazil. There he used £200 of the money he had made on his first Guinea voyage to set up farming tobacco with a Brazilian–English neighbour.[12] He lived there for four years and he and his partner were very successful, but as he reported,

> now increasing in business and wealth, my head began to be full of projects and undertakings beyond my reach; such as are, indeed, often the ruin of the best heads in business. Had I continued in the station I was now in, I had room for all the happy things to have yet befallen me for which my father so earnestly recommended a quiet, retired life, and of which he had so sensibly described the middle station of life to be full of; but other things attended me … to pursue a rash and immoderate desire of rising faster than the nature of the thing admitted.[13]

This rash course of action was to join a scheme to ship slaves from Africa to Brazil illegally, outside the strict regulations imposed by the Assiento.[14] It was this voyage that led to his shipwreck and his many shipwrecked years during which he had to learn to live self-sufficiently before meeting Friday. Although this section of the novel understandably receives the most attention, it turned out that when he was finally able to return to Europe, he made his way to Lisbon, where he was able to find the original captain of the ship that rescued him from his North African captors. The captain related that the Brazilian government, together with his former partner, had kept his interest in his plantation current through various forms of trusteeship. As a result, he was able to return to Brazil and sell it for 33,000 pieces of eight (dollars) worth £7,425 sterling in bills of exchange. Thus, through the honesty of his associates and good institutions of the Brazilian government his capital was able to grow. However, the means by which he did so through the exploitation of slave labour is nowhere treated by Defoe in the book as a moral question rather than one about trade.

Defoe's treatment of the morals needed for the formation of capital does not include empathising with the enslaved. Although he described the ship captain's overwhelming kindness in a lengthy scene, the cruelty of the middle passage and plantation slavery in its many forms is absent. This is, perhaps, early evidence of how a focus on profit directed towards

[12] Ibid., pp. 11–29. [13] Ibid., p. 30. [14] Ibid., pp. 32–3.

capital formation could lead to the exclusion of any morality directed at labour, by focusing specifically on empathy within the middle class only. Such a limitation would be rejected by the abolitionists, who argued that empathy should be universally directed against cruelty. This was also Adam Smith's position, but to it he added an economic argument against the whole slave economy.[15]

Although Defoe used the word 'station' here, elsewhere he used class to refer to the same group. As Penelope Corfield has argued, it became increasingly common in the eighteenth century for authors to divide society into classes when describing the social order. This involved a new conceptual framework 'fuelled by Enlightenment rationality', and especially by investigations into the natural world which sought to classify plants and animals according to common characteristics.[16] Although the word 'sort' continued to be employed into the eighteenth century as well as class, a difference arose in what each term referred to. Linguistically, the term sort came from the verb 'to sort' and implied a continual process.[17] The middling sort were sorted by their qualities as they lived their lives. In contrast, new classes were classified according to the character given to them by their property and capital based on self-control. The values of being middle class were also much more socially disconnected than the middling sort. In the seventeenth century, to achieve the status of being termed one of the 'better sort', or to be labelled a gentlemen, success in business was not enough. A family had to demonstrate the virtues of hospitality to a wide range of neighbours and charity towards the sick and poor.[18] But, by the mid-eighteenth century, hospitality for the new middle class had become much more proscribed by wealth, and the operation of the Poor Law more dominant and time consuming than charity.[19] This can already be seen in the diary

[15] J. R. Oldfield, *Popular Politics and British Anti-slavery: The Mobilisation of Public Opinion against the Slave Trade, 1787–1807* (Manchester, 1995); Adam Smith, *An Inquiry into the Nature and Causes of the Wealth of Nations*, ed. R. H. Campbell, A. S. Skinner, and W. B. Todd (Oxford, 1976), I, pp. 388–9; II, pp. 577–90.

[16] P. J. Corfield, 'Class by Name and Number in Eighteenth-Century Britain', *History* 72 (1987), pp. 38–45; Michel Foucault, *The Order of Things: An Archaeology of the Human Sciences* (London, 1970), pp. 125–65.

[17] Keith Wrightson, 'Sorts of People in Tudor and Stuart England', in Jonathan Barry and C. W. Brooks (eds.), *The Middling Sort of People: Culture, Society and Politics in England, 1550–1800* (London, 1994), p. 43.

[18] Andy Wood, *Faith, Hope and Charity: English Neighbourhoods, 1500–1640* (Cambridge, 2020).

[19] This is not to say that charitable giving and causes disappeared. As Steven King has shown for the north of England, charitable giving remained a crucial part of dealing with poverty, as it did for the provision of education. But the sheer scale of Poor Law redistribution and workhouse construction meant that its administration became

of Dudley Ryder, where almost all of his socialising took place with the wealthy merchant families in Hackney rather than with the suppliers or customers of his father's London shop. It then developed through the course of the century into the snobbishness concerning wealth and courtship satirised by Jane Austin.

The transition from middling sort to middle class has been analysed most acutely by John Smail in his book on the cultural creation of an elite middle class in the mid-eighteenth-century cloth town of Halifax.[20] Smail characterises the late seventeenth-century middling sort in Halifax as quite egalitarian among themselves; while they maintained a traditional hierarchical respect for the small numbers of local gentry, for the most part they ignored them in their social interactions.[21] Their wealth came from making kerseys, a coarse narrow cloth used mostly for blankets and work coats for home consumption rather than export.[22] Such production had already begun to make the town prosperous by the time of the hearth tax of 1672: 30 per cent of the houses listed had three or more hearths, while in the rest of the West Riding only 20 per cent of houses had more than two hearths.[23]

During this time, the diarist Oliver Heywood often recorded fraternising with his social inferiors, and all but the very poor participated in events such as cockfighting and horse racing.[24] But this changed beginning in the early eighteenth century as the cloth industry became much more sophisticated and expanded into the production of worsteds aimed at a more luxurious export market. This led to the gradual replacement of home production with the putting out system, whereby larger manufacturers bought raw wool and then washed, dyed, sorted, and combed it centrally before 'putting it out' to spinners and then weavers, and collecting it for finishing processes. Successful clothiers started to employ hundreds of workers, and they could become very much wealthier than others in the community. One giant manufacturer, Samuel Hill, had an annual turnover of £30,000 by 1745.[25]

dominant. Also, as Cannon's *Chronicles* show, much charity was also controlled by local vestries and could be contentious. Steven King, *Poverty and Welfare in England, 1700–1850: A Regional Perspective* (Manchester, 2000), pp. 190–1, 217–18; Paul Slack, *Poverty and Policy in Tudor & Stuart England* (Harlow, 1988), pp. 162–87; John Money (ed.), *The Chronicles of John Cannon Excise Officer and Writing Master, vols. I–II* (Oxford, 2010), pp. 283, 362, 638, 666–7, 672; hereafter, Cannon, *Chronicles*.

[20] John Smail, *The Origins of Middle-Class Culture: Halifax, Yorkshire, 1660–1780* (Ithaca, 1994).

[21] Ibid., pp. 29–30, 137–9. [22] Ibid., pp. 21–2.

[23] Ibid., pp. 24–5; David Hey (ed.), *Yorkshire West Riding Hearth Tax Assessment Lady Day 1672* (London, 2007), p. 8.

[24] Smail, *Middle-Class Culture*, pp. 32–4. [25] Ibid., pp. 56–7.

These great manufacturers also created large amounts of capital. Some had working capitals of over £10,000, and with operations on this scale they hired bookkeepers to keep professional and exact accounts to create it. Many also formed partnerships as a way of increasing investment.[26] They used internal bills and bills of exchange to sell their cloth in London and abroad, and several of them acted as local bankers.[27] A study of their wills also shows that they were increasingly lending out their capital on mortgages, but much more so using interest-bearing bonds.[28] Some advertised in the *Leeds Mercury* to lend out as much as £3,000 on security of land. Undoubtedly most capital was invested in the operations of the business of cloth-making, but much was used to provide security as well, since demand for foreign trade was notoriously elastic and downturns were common even as the market grew over the longer term. It was for this reason that investment in land became increasingly popular.[29] Later in the century, when canal navigation projects were undertaken, they also invested heavily in them.[30]

Manufacturing wealth could now be measured by the amount of such capital rather than simply by the size and turnover of the business. This, according to Smail, led to the creation of an elite group among the middling sort who become the middle class in the decades around 1750. This group consisted of about 60–70 substantial manufacturers and merchants and fifteen professionals, including lawyers. Since the population of Halifax consisted of about 8,400 households in 1764, this represents only 1 per cent of the town's population.[31] They were supported by a further group of about 120 smaller manufacturers, but there would have remained a much larger group of the middling sort, considering that already in 1664 those with three hearths or more – which usually indicates a dwelling larger than those affordable to cloth workers or labourers – comprised 30 per cent of the population taxed.[32] However, it does not seem that language changed at this time. The term class did not replace expressions such as the 'principal inhabitants' or 'gentlemen merchants' of the town, but such expressions did distinguish the elite from the rest of the middling sort.[33]

The middle class also sought to describe themselves as an elite as wealthy as the landed gentry and aristocracy, but with a gentility based on different values.[34] To this end they emphasised thrift, saving,

[26] Ibid., pp. 72–3. [27] Ibid., pp. 85–7. [28] Ibid., pp. 88–9. [29] Ibid., p. 91.
[30] Ibid., pp. 159, 182–3. [31] Ibid., pp. 52, 124, 128. [32] Ibid., p. 25.
[33] Dror Wahrman, *Imagining the Middle Class: The Political Representation of Class in Britain, c. 1780–1840* (Cambridge, 1995), pp. 17–18.
[34] Smail, *Middle-Class Culture*, p. 201.

prudence, and piety as virtues, which by creating capital permitted the enjoyments of peace, plenty, temperance, moderation, and quietness as outlined by Robinson Crusoe's father.[35] They also increasingly voiced opinions on the importance of manufacturing and trade in politics and foreign policy via new newspapers and pamphlets, emphasising the importance of work and wealth creation through industry, scientific investigation, invention, and investment.[36] The creation of stability went hand in hand with the exclusion of those who would threaten that stability. Because self-control was increasingly seen as the key virtue to create savings and form capital without it dissipating, then conversely the lack of self-control became a definition of moral inferiority defining the poor, just as lack of ability to pay debts had in the previous century.[37]

The elite in Halifax divided their places of residence from their workplaces by building large houses in the manner of the country gentry near, but away from, the centre of town. In this way, they came to distance themselves both physically and culturally from the other members of the middling sort. They formed socially exclusive institutions such as the Union Club to support an imperial Protestant foreign policy, and put on expensive subscription events such as dances, musical concerts, and dinners.[38] They also formed a club to raise a subscription to build a new Anglican church in the centre of Halifax. This, of course, was an act of charity, but it was very different from older forms. They used the fact that it was their money that had paid for most of the church to assert their right to control most of the pews, and to exclude many of the poorer middling sort from possessing pews altogether. Pew ownership had always been hierarchical and highly contested, but such contestation was based on family inheritance versus changing family fortunes over

[35] Ibid., pp. 43, 202–65.

[36] John Money, *Experience and Identity: Birmingham and the West Midlands, 1760–1800* (Manchester, 1977), pp. 121–55; Jenny Uglow, *The Lunar Men: The Friends Who Made the Future: 1730–1810* (London, 2002); Joel Mokyr, *The Enlightened Economy: Britain and the Industrial Revolution* (London, 2011), pp. 30–124.

[37] A good example of someone who interpreted his ability to save as the foundation of his success was the bookseller John Lackington. In his autobiography he recounted how despite being born into a very poor family supported by his mother's spinning labour, he was able to eventually open a bookshop in London with a turnover of £4,000 per year. This he claimed was due to his uncommon ability to save from even very small earnings. He also argued that his business success was due to the fact that he decided never to sell on credit to avoid bad debts. James Lackington, *The Memoirs of the Forty-Five First Years of the Life of James Lackington* (London, 1794), pp. xvii, 38–9, 167–74, 208, 212, 220, 442; Michael Mascuch, *Origins of the Individualist Self: Autobiography and Self-Identity in England, 1591–1791* (Cambridge, 1997), pp. 25–52.

[38] Smail, *Middle-Class Culture*, p. 127.

the long term.[39] It had also been a matter for the ecclesiastic courts. Such traditional hierarchical rights were now being challenged by the concept of property based on capital and investment as a mark of ownership.

Peter Borsay, in his book *The English Urban Renaissance*, has also argued that by the mid-eighteenth century there was an increasing cultural split between the very wealthy urban elite and those of more modest trading fortunes. His book was published somewhat earlier than Smail's, and although he does not adopt the terms middling sort and middle class to describe this bifurcation, there are many similarities between his national account and Smail's case study. Borsay also focused much more on cultural practices and how elites used their increased wealth to invest in new buildings. First among these were new purpose-built private residential dwellings separated from shops and workshops, using classical architectural forms. In 1726, John Cossins created a famous map of Leeds that was illustrated with the locations and depictions of the homes of the wealthiest merchants of the day.[40] Increasingly, though, town elites joined together to invest shares in new 'public' buildings such as town halls, assembly rooms where balls could be held, and public gardens and walks. However, these structures were only public in the sense of their outward facades facing the street, where all could partake in their visual message. Otherwise entry was restricted by the high price of tickets, designed to recoup the initial investment and to restrict entry to only the very wealthy. They were also erected for a very specific purpose, which was to provide entertainment in which the urban elite could mix with local gentry during assize sessions, horse races, and other seasonal events.[41] Here marriages could be arranged, as well as other business such as mortgaging. Concerts and other cultural entertainments could also take place in such spaces, as well as in new purpose-built theatres. Although money was also spent on beautifying streets and squares, Borsay argues that the cultural ethos of priced entertainments was a form of elite polite civility that distinguished itself from 'vulgar' plebian sports and drinking.[42]

Such spending, however, was not always as linked to self-control as it was with the non-conformist elite of Halifax. Horse racing and its associated betting, for instance, was a prominent elite activity, but, regardless,

[39] Ibid., pp. 130–8; Christopher Marsh, 'Order and Place in England, 1580–1640: The View from the Pew', *The Journal of British Studies* 44, no. 1 (2005), pp. 3–26. Also see the dispute John Cannon had over his family pew: Cannon, *Chronicles*, pp. cxv, 443–54, 464–6.

[40] Peter Borsay, *The English Urban Renaissance: Culture and Society in the Provincial Town 1660–1770* (Oxford, 1989), pp. 43–4.

[41] Ibid., pp. 150–72. [42] Ibid., pp. 60–79, 284–308.

the ideology of race meetings as well as balls and walks was that they were sites of 'civil' behaviour where the sexes could mix to engage in Shaftesbury's polite conversation without drunken arguments and other 'rude' conduct. This was not only contrasted with riotous lower-class drinking and fairs, but also with the male sociability of intoxication that occurred in taverns, mayors parlours, and other voluntary societies, such as depicted by Hogarth's popular print of *A Midnight Modern Conversation* of 1733.[43]

There had certainly been wealthy merchant families who could dominate town politics in the seventeenth century, and, as Robert Tittler has shown, many new town halls were also built with money lent by the elites of towns.[44] But, in general, there was much less private capital available before the 1720s, and many towns' finances were limited to the upkeep of basic infrastructure such as roads, walls, marketplaces, and most expensively harbours.

But in the earlier period there was also much more social mixing. Although there was a general social divide between taverns or ordinaries – where wine and meals were served that were favoured by elites – and alehouses where the poor met, the distinction was far from absolute.[45] The main social space remained the town marketplace, where all ranks congregated. In the sixteenth and seventeenth centuries, town halls were also generally the site of the civil courts, where the massive amounts of litigation over credit took place and involved litigants from all over the social scale. Finally, most town workshops and warehouses were places where the masters and their families lived and worked together with their journeymen. The move to suburbs such as the Ryder family house in Hackney would lead to much more separation.[46]

However, attaining such elite status remained elusive for most families, and the middle class as opposed to the middling sort remained small. Margaret Hunt has shown that while most of the middling sort avidly learned bookkeeping and adopted the values of prudence, civility, temperance, and especially self-control, most – like John Cannon – failed in one or more aspects, or were simply unlucky or uncompetitive in the

43 Mark Hallett and Christine Riding, *Hogarth* (London, 2007), p. 228; Phil Withington, 'Intoxicants and Society in Early Modern England', *The Historical Journal* 54, no. 3 (2011), pp. 631–57.

44 Robert Tittler, *Architecture and Power: The Town Hall and the English Urban Community c.1500–1640* (Oxford, 1991).

45 Withington, 'Intoxicants and Society', p. 647.

46 Leonore Davidoff and Catherine Hall, *Family Fortunes: Men and Women of the English Middle Class 1780–1850* (London, 2007), ch. 8.

business they chose.[47] These were the same smaller shopkeepers who made their living selling beer, bread, other food, and clothes to poorer customers less likely to pay them back, and who remained vulnerable to imprisonment, as we saw in the previous chapter.[48] As the evidence of probate inventories shows, for any trading occupation there was a wide range of wealth – from the very poor to the very wealthy.[49] Again, we can refer to Thomas Turner, who, despite being fully enmeshed in the world of paper currency, still worried incessantly that the unpaid debts of his poorer customers would lead to his business failure. He once noted how, when he went to dun a debtor, he 'received the comfortable news of his keeping out of sight for debt. Sure I am a most unfortunate man! … I must certainly fail and leave off trade.'[50] But even if most middling sort families did not achieve the level of security of the elite, it remains the case that the decline in litigation over credit is good evidence that the extra liquidity provided made most of them more stable than their ancestors or parents, and as a result wealthier as well.

Bankruptcy and Property

It was wholesalers and larger merchants who dealt mostly with other middling sort customers rather than poorer customers, who benefited most from the use of new forms of capital. Once they had accumulated enough savings they could invest in long-term capital such as property, bonds, and stocks and shares in large enough amounts to earn income from interest. They were also granted another advantage by changes in the law of bankruptcy that were passed in 1706. This statute modified the law from a procedure that was structured solely for the benefit of creditors who had to be overseas merchants, to one that conferred privileges on both creditors and bankrupts. The new law accepted that a certain amount of business failure was inevitable, and that honest bankrupts needed more legal protection.[51] This meant that honest and responsible bankrupts who made a quick and full declaration of their affairs were

[47] Margaret Hunt, *The Middling Sort: Commerce, Gender, and the Family in England, 1680–1780* (Berkeley, 1996), pp. 32–4, 41–62.

[48] Tawny Paul, *The Poverty of Disaster: Debt and Insecurity in Eighteenth-Century Britain* (Cambridge, 2019), p. 50.

[49] Joanne Sear and Ken Sneath, *The Origins of the Consumer Revolution in England: From Brass Pots to Clocks* (London, 2020), p. 262.

[50] David Vaisey (ed.), *The Diary of Thomas Turner* (Oxford, 1985), p. 171. Hereafter, Turner, *Diary*.

[51] Julian Hoppit, *Risk and Failure in English Business 1700–1800* (Cambridge, 1987), pp. 19–23.

given a certificate of discharge from the balance of their debts, and could be accepted back into the business community and given a chance to start over again. In many ways it was a law that for the first time in England separated the concept of a liquidity crisis from the moral failing of overspending or bad business practices.

Before this change in the law, bankruptcy proceedings were generally very expensive, and could often consume much of the remaining estate in fees, as they sought to bring large numbers of creditors into agreement, and to arrange for the sale of goods and land. As a result, the number of actual bankruptcies was small.[52] The changes in the law in 1706 made commissions more effective and cheaper because it became more advantageous for the bankrupt to cooperate with the commission to get a speedy settlement. However, a number of important restrictions remained that limited who could be declared a bankrupt. A bankrupt still had to be considered a 'trader' as defined by the discretion of the court. But, more importantly, a potential bankrupt had to owe at least £100 to a single creditor, and four-fifths or the total number of creditors had to be in agreement before a bankruptcy proceeding could be initiated.[53] What this meant was that, in practice, bankruptcy was only available for traders operating on a large enough scale to be trusted with debts of hundreds of pounds. Thus, the law only considered individuals of a certain level of wealth to be capable of liquidity problems rather undergoing the moral stigma of going broke and probably being imprisoned to recover what was left of an estate.

The average number of annual bankruptcies was generally less than 200 per year between 1710 and 1750.[54] However, the value of the debts of those who became bankrupt seems to have risen enormously throughout the eighteenth century. Unfortunately, very few accessible case papers have survived, and most of those are from 1780–1800. These have been analysed by Julian Hoppit, and in Figure 8.1 we can see that over 50 per cent of cases amounted to over £15,000, and a striking 20 per cent were for more than £50,000, even taking late eighteenth-century inflation into account. These were sums unheard of in the seventeenth

[52] W. J. Jones has estimated that the annual average number of formal bankruptcies in the Elizabethan and Jacobean periods may not have been more than ten per year. Bankruptcy proceedings could only be initiated against a limited number of individuals who could reasonably be considered tradesmen under the fairly strict definitions imposed by legislation. W. J. Jones, 'The Foundations of English Bankruptcy: Statutes and Commissions in the Early Modern Period', *Transactions of the American Philosophical Society* 69 (1979), pp. 18–21, 25–35, 56; Hoppit, *Risk and Failure*, pp. 23–5.

[53] This is described in Alexander Wakelam, *Credit and Debt in Eighteenth Century England: An Economic History of Debtors' Prisons* (London, 2020), pp. 31–5.

[54] Hoppit, *Risk and Failure*, pp. 46. 182–3.

century,[55] when a very large bankruptcy was in the region of £20,000; even in 1714 Hoppit has estimated that failures for more than £10,000 were very rare.[56] This shows the degree to which capital had facilitated an increase in investment credit, as Hoppit has forcefully argued.[57] In the first half of the eighteenth century, London also dominated numbers of bankruptcies: it provided 52 per cent of all bankrupts in the first twenty years of the century. In Hoppit's estimations, around 3 per cent of larger London businesses, numbered at 2,250 in 1740, went bankrupt every year.[58] For an earlier period in the 1710s and 1720s, Earle uses a much larger estimate of the population at risk of about 12,000 households, which gives a bankruptcy rate of 1–2 per cent, but he also calculated that 10–15 per cent of the very wealthiest tradesmen and citizens in London had commissions of bankruptcy sued out against them at some point in their careers.[59] But whatever the rate of bankruptcy before 1750, afterwards it fell by around 22 per cent.[60]

Marx argued that private property was the means for the individual accumulation of capital, and that the establishment of the legal 'rights' of property were one of the chief characteristics of this stage in the

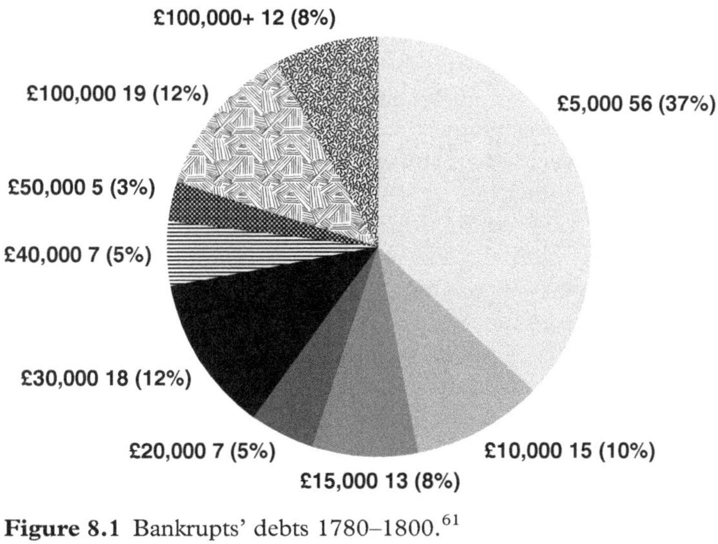

Figure 8.1 Bankrupts' debts 1780–1800.[61]

[55] Jones, 'Bankruptcy', p. 39. [56] Hoppit, *Risk and Failure*, pp. 140–4.
[57] Ibid., pp. 51–5. [58] Ibid., p. 67.
[59] Peter Earle, *The Making of the English Middle Class* (London, 1989), pp. 129–30.
[60] Hoppit, *Risk and Failure*, p. 67. [61] Ibid., pp. 142–3.

transformation to capitalism.[62] In the eighteenth century, capital held in the form of bonds, shares, and other investments was also increasingly considered a form of property based on the Lockean notion that it was the fruit of hard labour and needed protection as much as real estate. The legal historian W. J. Jones has argued that sixteenth-century law did not have a notion of private property, at least in land. Property in this period was considered something held in trust for the community into the future. The word propriety was used interchangeably with property, and mean looking after something. It was only with the arrival of ideas of improvement in the 1630s that personal ownership became a legal concept that could be employed to effect change against a custom-based legal ideology.[63]

The political theorist Lara Brace has also argued that there was a causal relationship between the development of agrarian capitalism in terms of the 'improvement' of land by farmers in order to increase its profitability, and the development of property as a territorially based, 'bounded' geographical unit.[64] To show this she drew upon the large body of literature concerning enclosure and agrarian improvement, which sees farming increasingly becoming organised around the individual household rather than the medieval vill – what might be called 'productive (household) individualism'. She notes that some writers even compared improving husbandry to the original act of creation. This, of course, was most famously employed in the debate over enclosure between moral 'conservatives' who argued that smallholding kept people in work and prevented unemployment, and 'progressives' who argued that population growth made smallholders untenable and instead argued that increased food production would enable industries to expand and provide employment for the poor. Brace examined how this affected notions of property in relation to tithes. If a farmer could increase his production through labour or skill without the help of the Church, why should the extra owed as a tithe go up in proportional terms? This led to a clash of ideas about the nature of tithes in relation to productive property. In her analysis of this debate Brace makes an important argument for the increasing importance of contractual thinking based on a notion of

[62] Karl Marx, *Capital, I–III*, trans. Ben Fowkes (New York, 1977), I, pp. 875–95, 1083–4; III, pp. 917–50.

[63] W. J. Jones, 'A Note on the Demise of Manorial Jurisdiction: The Impact of Chancery', *American Journal of Legal History* 10 (1966), pp. 304–6. Also see Eric Kerridge, *Agrarian Problems in the Sixteenth Century and After* (London, 1969), pp. 65–93.

[64] Laura Brace, *The Idea of Property in Seventeenth-Century England: Tithes and the Individual* (Manchester, 1998); R. W. Hoyle (ed.), *Custom, Improvement and the Landscape in Early Modern Britain* (Farnham, 2011), pp. 1–38.

landed property as something whose value increasingly came from market-based profitability. This came into conflict with older notions of hierarchical obligations; in this case, tithes due for pastoral care.

This debate was central to much of the politics of the Civil War period, but only achieved a theoretical unity in the writings of John Locke on contract and self-ownership. In his *First Treatise of Government*, written in the 1670s when Locke was in exile, he presented a lengthy argument about why people joined into political society on a voluntarist basis as opposed to a natural patriarchy society of monarchical absolutism. They united, 'for the mutual *preservation* of their lives, liberties and estates, which I call by the general name, *property* ... The great and *chief end*, therefore, of men's uniting into common-wealths, and putting themselves under government, *is the preservation of their property*.'[65] Crucially, though, he based the creation of such property in the individual:

> Though the earth, and all inferior creatures, be common to all men, yet every man has a property in his own person: this no body has any right to but himself. The labour of his body, and the work of his hands, we may say, are properly his. Whatsoever then here moves out of the state that nature hath provided, and left it in, he hath mixed his labour with, and joined to it something that is his own, and thereby makes it his property. It being by him removed from the common state nature hath placed it in, it hath by this labour something annexed to it, that excludes the common right of other men: for this labour being the unquestionable property of the labourer, no man but he can have a right to what that is once joined to, at least where there is enough, and as good, left in common for others.[66]

There has been some debate as to whether Locke considered this form of property absolute, or whether others had a right to some of it based on both Christian charity and the natural law of self-preservation – as indicated in the last sentence of this quotation. This could justify the state taxing it for the purposes of redistribution to the poor to keep them alive.[67] He also believed one could contract one's property to another as in the form of a contract of labour service.[68]

Thus, ownership became more personal, but only as long as it was tied to improvement and productivity gain. As Morton Horwitz and Julian Hoppit have shown in different ways, Parliament in the eighteenth

[65] John Locke, *Two Treatises of Government*, ed. Peter Laslett (New York, 1963), ch. 123–5.
[66] Ibid., books 27–8.
[67] James Tully, *A Discourse on Property: John Locke and His Adversaries* (Cambridge, 1980), pp. 131–55.
[68] Jeremy Waldron, 'The Turfs My Servant Has Cut', *Locke Newsletter* 13, no. 13 (1982), pp. 9–20.

century was willing to use statutory legislation to override property rights if they stood in the way of economic growth.[69] This was especially necessary in the case of the building of turnpike roads and canals that needed to go through private property. It was also later employed in the formation of enclosure by Parliamentary Act, which could compel lesser landowners on a manor to comply with an enclosure argument arranged by the principal landowners. Of course, in all of these cases the property owner was provided with compensation for the alteration or use of their property, but in terms of right, they could not decline the change according to their personal desire. Thus, it was not an absolute private right in reality, but compared to the situation described by Jones for the period up until the early seventeenth century, where the laws of real property were conceived as a means of making the manorial community work, this was now a conception of property designed to make economic growth work. Crucially, for the theme of this chapter, it was organised around very large holders of capital. Turnpike and canal trusts were usually set up by wealthy traders and manufacturers to improve the transport infrastructure on which their businesses depended, and to do this they needed to attract investment from other wealthy people in the form of shares.[70]

But the ideology of property went well beyond this dry legal right. As Paul Langford has succinctly put it in his book *Public Life and the Propertied Englishman*, property became what he terms 'the grand enchantress'. It became the overwhelming ideology of the eighteenth century in England. Whether or not it was personal or based on labour did not matter so much as its use to define a national character: 'a world without property was almost inconceivable to 18th-century Englishmen'.[71] Although this was fundamentally based on a belief in protecting the fruits of commercial growth as private wealth, the possession of such wealth became inextricably linked to governance through Parliament. As such, 'liberty and property' became a catchphrase referring to the Revolutionary Settlement in which property could only be

[69] Morton J. Horwitz, *The Transformation of American Law, 1780–1860* (Cambridge, MA, 1977), pp. 63–108; Julian Hoppit, 'Compulsion, Compensation and Property Rights in Britain, 1688–1833', *Past and Present* 210 (2011), pp. 93–128.

[70] Dan Bogart, 'Turnpike Trusts and Property Income: New Evidence on the Effects of Transport Improvements and Legislation in Eighteenth-Century England', *Economic History Review* 62, no. 1 (2009), pp. 128–52; Dan Bogart, 'Did Turnpike Trusts Increase Transportation Investment in Eighteenth-Century England?', *Journal of Economic History* 65, no. 2 (2005), pp. 439–68; J. E. Ginarlis and S. Pollard, 'Roads and Waterways, 1750–1850', in C. H. Feinstein and S. Pollard (eds.), *Studies in Capital Formation in the United Kingdom 1750–1920* (Oxford, 1988), pp. 182–224.

[71] Paul Langford, *Public Life and the Propertied Englishman 1689–1798* (Oxford, 1994), p. 1.

taxed by statute law debated in Parliament. As Langford has argued, although this was based on 'commercial growth and the enthusiasm of the age for "improvement"', commercial society was chronically unstable:

> Clashes of interest and the legal security granted to forms of property which assumed reliance on credit made nonsense of simple appeals to the landed proprietor against the moneyed man. Even where landowners were concerned, the complexity of tenures and the impact of economic expansion made for confusion and conflict.[72]

Thus, it stands to reason that it meant most for those who held enough of it that they could most easily deal with such instabilities – that is, the middle class, *not* the middling sort. They, along with the landed elite, also had the greatest financial means to influence electoral politics in the boroughs where most MPs were elected.[73] However, the ideology of property obscured this by looking outward and claiming that the residents of other countries did not enjoy such rights and freedoms, and in the end the link between liberty and property became a tautology. As one comment put it: 'Pray, what is Liberty – but a Freedom to possess Property, a Liberty to enjoy it, and a Right to defend it.'[74]

William Hutton, Property, and the Birmingham Court of Requests

A source that provides a great deal of evidence about how property was understood in class terms is William Hutton's *Courts of Requests*. In that work he not only provided examples of what was sued over, but discussed his court and its litigants in terms of what he saw as its necessary social function of protecting profits as a form of wealth. The courts of requests, and summary justice, were necessary in his eyes to promote a new type of commercial society based on the ethics of material progress. Late in his life he also wrote an autobiography detailing how he rose from being the son of a poor stocking knitter to a wealthy owner of capital, detailing the values that, in his eyes, made this rise possible in one lifetime.

Hutton lived to the remarkably old age of ninety-two, being born in 1723 and not dying until 1815. Although he did not write his autobiography until 1798, when he was in his seventies, he had been writing other things from an earlier age, starting with a history of Birmingham in 1781. His life shows how someone of a relatively poor background who had

72 Ibid.
73 John A. Phillips, *Electoral Behavior in Unreformed England: Plumpers, Spitters and Straights* (Princeton, 2014).
74 Langford, *Public Life*, pp. 4–5.

internalised the values of thrift and saving could become successful.[75] Although obviously remembered from the distance of many years of financial success, his narrative does not shy from mistakes he made. He was born in Full Street, Derby, and his father was a woolcomber who could read, and who taught his children to read religious books. Hutton attended school in Derby at 5–7 years old before going to work, but according to him, the teacher there beat his head against the wall, and as a result he hated all books and what he learned was rudimentary. His father failed in around 1725, becoming 'distressed' and as a result had to return to working as a journeyman for another woolcomber.[76]

Because of this, Hutton was sent to live with various aunts and uncles, and in 1730, at age seven, he was put to work in a job that was highly unusual at that date, but which would come to characterise the industrial revolution some seventy years later. This was in the first large-scale factory built in England by the Lombe brothers.[77] In an early example of industrial espionage, John Lombe visited one of the large-scale Italian silk-throwing mills in Piedmont in 1716 (machines that had existed in Italy since the fifteenth century), and returned to Derby with the necessary knowledge and a group of Italians, and built a mill of his own design. The building was five stories high to house the large imitations of Italian silk-throwing machines. Hutton claimed that 300 people worked in the mill when he went there. Children were needed in such machines to repair broken thread and bobbins while the mill was in operation. Because of their small size they could work in the small spaces required, although Hutton seems to have been too small at age seven, since he records they had a special raised set of pattens made for him to stand on.[78] Hutton spent the next seven years working in the mill, and his description of its environment is undeniably 'dark and satanic':

> I now had to … submit to the cane whenever convenient to the master; be the constant companion of the most rude and vulgar of the human race, never taught by nature, never willing to be taught. A lad must be … as impudent as they, or be hunted down.[79]

> No friendships are formed there, but such as the parties are willing to break. The attendants are children of nature corrupted by art.[80]

[75] His life is discussed by Susan Whyman, *The Useful Knowledge of William Hutton: Culture and Industry in Eighteenth-Century Birmingham* (Oxford, 2018).

[76] William Hutton, *The Life of William Hutton* (Studley, 1998), pp. 1–5.

[77] William Henry Chaloner, 'Sir Thomas Lombe (1685–1739) and the British Silk Industry', *History Today* 3 (1953), pp. 778–85; Carlo de Angelis and Alberto Guenzi, 'Distribuzione dell'energia nel "cuore industriale" della città in età precapitalistica', in *Bologna El'Invenzione delle Acque: Saperi, arti e produzione tra '500 e '800* (Bologna, 2001), pp. 106–23.

[78] Hutton, *Life*, p. 6. [79] Ibid., p. 6. [80] Ibid., p. 12.

At one point he was caned so badly that his back became infected. This experience as a boy must have had a profound effect on his view of society. In his later works descriptions of industry are usually positive, but here he described it as an alienating 'bear pit' of corrupting violence and ignorance.

After this he began a second seven-year apprenticeship working as a stocking frame knitter for his uncle in Nottingham. At first he did not find working the frame any more satisfying than the mill, as his aunt was tight-fisted with food and the method of renumeration for any spending money was that he had to produce goods worth 5s. 10d. each week, and any profit would be his own, but if he produced less he would go into arrears. For his first three years he was mostly in arrears, and claimed to be envious of other boys who could wear clothes fine enough to impress girls. However, by 1741 he had become skilful enough to make enough by over-working to buy a genteel suit.

However, soon after he ran away as a result of a terrible beating he received from his uncle for being idle during the week of the horse races, in defiance of his uncle's orders to work full-time. He describes leaving his uncle's with two shillings he took from his buffet, a leather bag containing his new suit, a white linen bag containing a sixpenny loaf of coarse bread, some butter wrapped in the leaves of an old copy book, a new Bible worth three shillings, a shirt, stockings, a sundial, and a wig. His excursion as a runaway apprentice only lasted a week before he returned and was accepted back by his uncle, whom he claimed was 'naturally of a good temper, despite the beating'.[81] But during his time on the road, remembering back, Hutton made a point of emphasising how his theft of two shillings actually elevated his reputation by his great frugality in being able to survive on such a small amount for so long. However, his misadventure, as he said, ruined him in point of dress for five years. He also, perhaps surprisingly, claimed it was the first time he got into debt for the work lost and the money taken.

After finishing his apprenticeship he continued to work as a stocking maker, and lived with his sister from 1746. He was not very successful in the trade, but at the same time – encouraged by his sister to read more – he was able to afford to buy cheap, unbound books, which he learned to bind himself.[82] He eventually moved to Birmingham and became a bookbinder, and then gradually moved into the business of bookselling, where he was finally successful after 1751. From this period he was able to save money, and this is an activity he emphasises strongly as part of his

[81] Ibid., pp. 16–25. [82] Ibid., p. 30.

remembered self. He claimed he was 'an economist from my cradle, and the character never forsook me'.[83] By this he meant he was frugal. When he took up bookbinding he recorded how he had to walk 129 miles to London with three guineas sewn into his shirt. In making this journey he spent only 5d. per day, almost collapsing from hunger at the end.[84] When he started to sell books he bought 200 lb worth, the contents of a man's library, and paid by an informal note of hand for £1 7s. He was poor enough at this point that the overseers in his new parish of residence ordered him to procure a settlement certificate from the parish of his birth, fearing he would become a burden on them. However, that parish refused, even though it was technically illegal, leading Hutton to exclaim that this was an example of the 'exultations of power over the defenceless'.[85]

Despite the worry of the overseers, in his first year as a bookseller he survived on 5s. per week and saved £20. By 1755 he had saved £200, and also recorded that he was an exacting accountant. With his savings he first tried to invest in a paper mill, but because of his inexperience he was 'cheated on all sides' and lost about £1,000. He gave this up and instead learned to use his savings to invest in the speculative purchase and resale of property, which he called 'a delight, a study, and a profit'.[86] In 1772 he bought a farm seven miles from Birmingham for £850, which was already mortgaged for £800, so he only paid £50 and took over the mortgage. He then sold its trees for £220, enclosed the commons, and took an allotment of eight acres worth £100, let the farm for £50, and eventually sold the place for £900. He does not say when he sold, but the profit was at least £370.[87]

Although Hutton does not place much emphasis on religion in his *Life*, he came from a strong Dissenting family, and his father and sister appear to have been very religious and remained Calvinist. On one occasion he noted his father and friends had argued over the Trinity for seven years, which Hutton claimed came too close to quarrelling to be compatible with Christian practice.[88] But if theology did not interest him, certainly self-control did. He considered himself 'naturally of a frugal temper', and never recorded drinking or entertaining much, but often noted how his fellow apprentices and workers were given to drunkenness.[89] The ability to overcome the impulses of drink and violence would be key in his

[83] Ibid., p. 18.
[84] Ibid., pp. 33–4. Also claims to have survived on bread, cheese, porridge, and a little ale when setting up his shop, while walking ten miles a day, which could be an exaggeration of memory.
[85] Ibid., pp. 40–1. [86] Ibid., p. 55. [87] Ibid., p. 56. [88] Ibid., pp. 13–14.
[89] Ibid., p. 32.

interpretation of social differences. Certainly in his later portraits he looks very stern.[90] However, he clearly enjoyed material goods, especially clothes, and once he was wealthy enough he built himself a large house at Bennetts Hill.[91]

In 1772 he had become successful enough to be appointed one of the commissioners on the bench of the new Birmingham court of requests. From this date, for nineteen years he attended it two days a week and claimed to have heard more than 100,000 cases, or 50 a day, although some days he said he got through 250! He called the court his 'favourite amusement', and although he took his task to detect fraud seriously, he claimed that with so many cases error was likely.[92] In 1787 he wrote a book about the Birmingham court of requests, describing its practice, together with potted summaries of selected cases he thought were interesting. He wrote this to defend courts of requests in general against an attack that had recently been launched by the most eminent jurist of the time, Sir William Blackstone, on the basis that by denying trial by jury they were an erosion of basic constitutional liberties.[93]

Hutton wrote his book to defend the institution against such charges. To do this he used an economic argument, saying that a trading nation needed a speedy and cheap means of resolving contractual disputes and enforcing debts, and that the benefits arising from the wealth this produced outweighed the loss of liberty. This was especially the case concerning imprisonment. As we saw in the previous chapter, imprisonment had become more common in the eighteenth century, and by the 1770s both the numbers of those incarcerated and their conditions within prison had attracted the criticisms of a humanitarian dissenting voice, that of John Howard. In his recently published *The State of the Prisons* (1777), Howard had made a survey of the numbers of prisoners living in deplorable conditions, and the high rates of mortality this caused.[94] Hutton agreed with Howard's criticism, and advocated prison reform, but still argued that the institution was necessary because, at least in the case of the courts of request, many poor debtors did not possess enough goods to be distrained or so few that they could easily be hidden by friends and relatives. Thus, the threat of incarceration was the only enforcement lenders could use.[95] Hutton argued that if the poor were to continue to be allowed to buy on credit, then imprisonment had to remain.[96]

[90] Whyman, *The Useful Knowledge*, cover, pp. 94, 115, 133. [91] Ibid., p. 54.
[92] Ibid., p. 57. [93] Finn, *Character of Credit*, pp. 220f.
[94] John Howard, *The State of the Prisons in England and Wales: With Preliminary Observations and an Account of Some Foreign Prisons* (Cambridge, 2013).
[95] William Hutton, *Court of Requests* (Birmingham, 1887), pp. 43–4, 63–78.
[96] Finn, *Character of Credit*, pp. 172–89, 315.

The cases presented in *The Court of Requests* are a mine of information about the economy of the poor in Birmingham during the 1770s and 1780s. Most are about debts of one sort or another. A lot concern landlords and tenancies, many cases are about wages, and women feature prominently. Many also concern box clubs, or friendly societies – voluntary savings clubs set up by the poor to help each other out in times of sickness and old age.[97] But equally interesting are Hutton's attitudes to the cause of much indebtedness, and to the weaknesses that he saw as their cause. In his own mind he philanthropically spent two days a week of his own time helping people settle their quarrels. But, as we shall see, this was not the view of those he thought he was helping. In describing the litigants in the court, he uses the concept of character to develop an idea of social class based on conscience and property, which is worth quoting at length:

> Mankind divide themselves into three classes. The first, from conscience, and a rectitude of heart, would not appropriate any property to themselves, but what they have a fair title to. No temptation can lead them from the line of justice. They wish to call property their own, but upon such terms only, as no man can dispute …Another class, and by far the most numerous, have not much to do with conscience, yet: have a natural honesty about them. The principles of the mind tend towards honour. They seek no occasions to take the property of others; and yet, can-not withstand a temptation. Their circumstances determine their character: if they are easy, the man is generally proof against wrong, can support himself without preying upon others, and passes through life without a blot. But if necessity stares him in the face, the ties of honour are forgotten. The Third, the degraded class are such whose lives are a series of mischief. They are distinguished by depredations of plunder, fraud, finesse, &c. founded in idleness, poverty, and baseness of mind, a vile example to the guilty, and pest to the innocent, From the above description of that mischievous animal man, it follows, there is much evil about him, and – this evil demands a cure. Hence originate all our courts of justice.[98]

Here society is broken down into groups based on the capability for self-control. In another passage he also anticipated Malthus in claiming that many of the young workmen in Birmingham, by marrying in their teens, had produced large families that could only survive on credit. Hutton noted that, theoretically, they could be protected from being sued because of their young age, but that the court of requests could override this because such youth 'gain credit by solicitation and distress, on one side, and by self-interest and pity, on the other'. As a result, Hutton explained, the court aided such families by allowing tradesmen recovery

[97] Hutton, *Requests*, pp. 92, 104, 259, 262, 321, 338. [98] Ibid., pp. 4–5.

of their debts; otherwise they would not have been given credit in the first place:

the Bench seldom plead a minority in favour of the defendant, because it would be putting a wicked argument into his mouth, against paying a just debt. The Court are [*sic*] not bound to take notice of his non-age.[99]

Instead, he claimed the court was moderate with the schedules of repayment it ordered, and refused to enforce debts of the poor arising from gambling, tippling, horse hire, and interestingly notes of hand.[100] In doing so, it was indicating that creditors should not encourage the poor to go into debt for unnecessary things. By refusing to enforce notes of hand, the court was in essence saying that the poor had no business writing notes on their own behalf. They could use them, but it was not in their power to write them or to have them written on their own behalf.

In contrast to what Hutton termed these 'infant families', the best were entirely capable of self-control, and here we can see a pointed emphasis on the Lockean self associated with Dissent. The association of this with property also has Lockean overtones, although we don't know if Hutton ever read him. Even if in this passage he does not spell out property's relation to labour, this is how he actually began the work, with a description of the world in a state of nature, and how improvement created property and 'stamped' it with value:

The world we tread is furnished with variety of matter, which is more or less valuable according to the uses to which it can be appropriated … assemblages of people convert matter into property, and stamp that property with value … now the man of nature may lay out his guinea to advantage.[101]

Later in the work he claimed:

Labour is also a duty which a man not only owes to himself, but to others; for if we take away labour, we destroy social benefit. It assumes various names according to the class of people it influences, but is laudable in all.[102]

Compared to Locke, he was more explicit about what he thought was mankind's insatiable desire for more and more property – 'the grand struggle of life is to grasp it'. For Hutton, all men were innately ambitious to have more, which he describes in terms of monetary value.[103] Although he did not use the term capital here, he did elsewhere, and what he was referring to was savings. Thus, for Hutton, the non-payment of a debt owed to a tradesman for goods sold was not about the potential damages of a broken contract as the common law would have it, but a

[99] Ibid., pp. 52–4. [100] Ibid., pp. 53–5. [101] Ibid., pp. 1–2. [102] Ibid., pp. 68–9.
[103] Ibid., pp. 1–3.

potential diminution of the latter's ability to save up his own capital or property. The law, in Hutton's view, was meant to protect this property specifically on behalf of those who had the moral and industrious ability to accumulate it:

> Nothing is so necessary, in the whole system of English jurisprudence, as a concise method of recovering property, and terminating disputes. This is the great hinge upon which the welfare of a nation turns. The more a people encrease their trade, the more they must venture their property; how necessary is it then, to enact such laws as will best secure that property, and, when in danger, point out the easiest method to recover it. To multiply the Courts of Requests, and enlarge their powers, is the likeliest way to attain this end.[104]

Here we see the beginning of what has come to be called class law – the idea that the law protects property, and that the property being protected was created by those of better character, in contrast to those whose 'baseness of mind' inevitably led to dishonesty and crime.[105] Competitive success would be rewarded, and its absence not:

> The manufacturers of Birmingham require an amazing number of people to conduct them, and though their wages are from ten shillings a week to two guineas, yet they are as poor as the common labourer, who earns but eight. Imprudence is the characteristic of this class. The few that are otherwise, soon become masters, and rise to fortune.[106]

This link between law, moral behaviour, and the accumulation of capital considered as property, is a key feature of our story. It stands in a very stark contrast to the much more universalist older concepts justifying the need for laws found in the sixteenth and seventeenth centuries. In this conception, *all* were susceptible to the temptations of sin.[107] In the 1540s, the humanist lawyer Sir John Hales wrote 'if law be gone farewell love, farewell shame, farewell honestie, farewell truthe, farewell faith and all virtue. And in with deceipte, Craftie subtiltie, perjurye, malice, envie, discorde.'[108] The defence of property also certainly featured in sixteenth- and seventeenth-century legal theory, but the emphasis then was on the property of inherited titles and their estates, the protection of which was considered a part of the social order, since those without property had

104 Ibid., p. 9.
105 Paul Johnson, 'Class Law in Victorian England', *Past & Present* 141, no. 1 (1993), pp. 147–69.
106 Hutton, *Requests*, p. 190.
107 Cynthia B. Herrup, 'Law and Morality in Seventeenth-Century England', *Past and Present* 106 (1985), pp. 102–23.
108 C. W. Brooks, 'The Place of Magna Carta and the Ancient Constitution in Sixteenth-Century English Legal Thought', in C. W. Brooks (ed.), *Lawyers, Litigation and English Society Since 1450* (London, 1998), pp. 206–7.

little chance of obtaining it. As Richard Hooker put it, to 'take away all such mutual grievances, injuries, and wrongs' men formed governments and granted authority to them to enforce the rule of *laws*'. Such laws protected rights and prevented men from hurting each other through outright competition.[109]

Here the role of law was meant to curtail competition so men could live in peace with one another. But, by the 1770s, a presumption had evolved that certain types of competition – here economic competition – could be realistically allowed and even promoted without anxiety that they would threaten the social order. This was because chains of interpersonal trust were no longer as vulnerable to competition. In the seventeenth century we know that merchants and traders competed in the sense that they sought to be the first to market to either sell or buy at the best price, but that their reliance on each other to be able to discount bills of exchange or to buy and sell on credit meant that competition was always secondary to this need.[110] Also, the middling sort in the seventeenth century had always been acutely aware of the precariousness of their wealth, as it was tied up in interlocked chains of credit, and downward mobility was always a possibility if loans went bad or customers did not pay.[111]

Hutton rarely talked of trust, and certainly never described the function of his court as an institution designed to maintain it in society. Overwhelmingly what Hutton's *Courts of Requests* shows is how the emergence of capital created a *much* starker difference between those with access to secure credit and those who had not. For him, its role was the restitution of the property of the lender or seller or others – the moral equality of contract found in the common law of contract had vanished:

> It is dangerous to deposit money with the necessitous. It may be trusted with him who *has*, but to trust it with him who has not, is like trusting it to the bottom of the sea. In the commercial world, a rich knave is preferable to a poor honest man, one pays in money, the other in promises. An acquaintance of mine remarked, he would in future endeavour to trade with rascals, for he was almost ruined by trading with honest men. When a man holds the property of another, has nothing of his own, and want becomes urgent, the temptation overpowers the honesty. There are ways to oblige a man of fortune to refund what he ought, but what way is there to oblige *him* to pay money who has none?[112]

Here property has trumped honesty. This can also be seen in his description of the meaning of labour to different classes:

[109] Muldrew, *Economy of Obligation*, pp. 87–96. [110] Ibid., pp. 188–92.
[111] Ibid., pp. 290–312. [112] Hutton, *Requests*, pp. 259–60.

With the opulent it is termed *amusement*; with the independent, *exercise*, and with the inferior ranks, who wish to preserve a character, and enjoy conveniences, *industry*. These last are what we call the prudent poor, and are a people extremely valuable. But when a man possesses no income, and his inclination for indolence surpasses that for labour, many mischiefs ensue.[113]

Since he termed his activity in the court of requests an amusement, we can assume he believed he possessed enough property to engage in a very different sort of labour than he had endured previously when he was industrious. The following passage demonstrates that he took the notions of interest and self-love as commonplace. It also suggests he had read Adam Smith's famous passage about the invisible hand in *The Wealth of Nations* published in 1776 (or read it somewhere second-hand, since Smith's public interest was not political):

Public interest proceeds from private; they are both shoots from self-love. Private interest is the benefit of one, public of many. Take away the first and the second ceases. While we serve ourselves, we serve others. The farmer's dame serves the public while she sells her butter in the market, although her sole view is to serve herself. The man who buys a coat, designs no interest but his own; whereas, from that interest arises an emolument: to every person, from him who first owned the fleece, to him who collects the last rag for a mop. To serve his country, is the patriotic watch-word of the senator, the interpretation of which is, to serve himself.[114]

His belief, however, that his service at the court was philanthropic dispute resolution of quarrels rather than self-interest was brutally shattered during the Church and King riots that occurred in Birmingham on 14–17 July 1791. The riots occurred after a dinner held by James Keir, an industrialist who was a member of the Lunar Society of Birmingham. In attendance were Joseph Priestley and other Dissenting free-thinkers. It was held to celebrate the second anniversary of the storming of the Bastille during the French Revolution, and to promote its ideas of liberty. The rioters were the artisans and industrial workmen of the city, who had probably been stirred up by Anglican members of the middling sort in defence of the monarch and unreformed political institutions. Both Dissenting meeting houses as well as Dissenters' residences were looted and burned down by the rioters.

Hutton was among those targeted because of his role as a commissioner of the court of requests, even though he had not been politically active. Although his friends warned him that his house was to be targeted, he ignored them until it was too late. He attempted to avoid

[113] Ibid., pp. 68–9. [114] Ibid., pp. 153–4.

its destruction by giving the rioters all his ready cash to the last half-penny, 'which one of them had the meanness to take', and then shaking 'a hundred hard black hands' and offering to buy them drink, whereupon he was taken to a nearby public house and within half an hour was faced with an ale-score for 329 gallons.[115] Since he had enforced many debts for ale in his court, this was obviously a form of retaliation. Certainly drink played a large role in fuelling the riots. The wine cellar of the large wine manufacturer, John Ryland, with £300 worth of wine, was raided while the house burned and collapsed around the rioters with the loss of six or seven lives.[116] Hutton claimed the rioters were 'people whom would have sold their King for a jug of ale, and demolished the Church for a bottle of Gin'.[117] Soon after both his house in town and at Bennetts Hill were looted and burned. During the looting of the latter, when his furniture was being thrown out the window, the looters asked who bids for this, while the crowd below exclaimed 'I'll give sixpence and come again next Friday', mimicking Hutton's usual sentence for debt repayment in instalments at the court.[118]

While it is not hard to sympathise with Hutton's revulsion at this destructive attack on progressive ideals, humanitarianism, and learning in general, it has to be acknowledged that there was a class element in the activities of the rioters.[119] Undoubtably Hutton's admonitions against wasting money on drink rankled and led the rioters to the humorous running up of his alehouse score. But Hutton also noted that ten of the houses attacked belonged to 'masters of nearly a million sterling, all arising from the manufactures of the place' and three employed more than 10,000 people between them. In Hutton's eyes the riots had the effect of 'cutting off the bread of the laborious class'. But they might have seen the difference between their wages, which Hutton considered high, and the profits of those each employing thousands of them otherwise.[120] Although the rioters were engaged in a bigoted attack on Dissenters, as Hutton pointed out, because so many were industrialists, this amounted to an attack on much of the wealth of the elite. As such they also show the degree to which the poor resented the summary nature of the court and its inherent division of society into class based on character rather than the older system of legal equality in the realm of contract.

115 Hutton, *Life*, pp. 91–3. 116 Ibid., p. 90. 117 Ibid., p. 85.
118 Finn, *Character of Credit*, pp. 226–7.
119 Hutton opposed cock fighting, stating 'The more people are civilised, the less they are addicted to cruelty.' Hutton, *Requests*, pp. 27–8.
120 Hutton, *Life*, pp. 92, 102.

This can be seen quite starkly in the case of a bricklayer reported by Hutton in his *Courts of Requests*, who lacking employment over the winter when work was slow had to buy necessities from a shopkeeper on credit. In order to do so, his master (Hutton does not say whether the defendant was a journeyman or a usual employee) vouched for the bricklayer, promising to pay the shopkeeper during the summer once the bricklayer started to do work. As it turned out, the master went broke and ran away before paying the shopkeeper, who then sued the bricklayer for the credit he had provided. In a civil court this would have been treated as a case of contract, with the master's promise being the consideration. However, the commissioners on the bench with Hutton in the court of requests treated it as a case of debt over the restitution of property, arguing that the shopkeeper had 'a natural right' to the value of the goods he sold. Rather than applying the rules of equity as in a case of a verbal contract, the court focused on the restitution of property, claiming it would 'destroy any security, which a man holds in defence of his property'.[121] In doing so, the court stressed the inequality between the two parities. In contrast, contractual litigation had offered some small escape for the system of patriarchal hierarchy defined by wealth.[122]

Apart from being a source in which the author's opinions represent a changing view of the role of law and credit in relation to the social order, the potted summaries of ninety-two cases presented in Hutton's *Court of Requests* also provide detail on notes and bills used between 1772 and 1786, which can be added to the discussion of cases from the Bristol court of conscience and the Old Bailey. These examples fall somewhat outside the temporal scope of this study, but are relevant for the detail provided by Hutton's descriptions. On one occasion, Hutton commented on a bill that had passed through his hands and was returned to him for non-payment. Hutton then went to the person from whom he received it initially, who paid him. He then asked Hutton how to recover the money from the individual who originally drew up the bill. Hutton does not supply the value of the bill, but claimed that it would be more expensive than the debt to hire an attorney to recover it, which underlines the importance of having informal bills drawn up by people with property.[123]

There is an interesting case concerning three notes of hand, all of the same value of £1 19s., each signed by three people: Booth, Hall, and Smith. This was the result of an original debt by Booth to one Ethell, the plaintiff of £5 17s. – which was the combined value of the notes of hand

[121] Hutton, *Requests*, pp. 171–6. [122] Muldrew, *Economy of Obligation*, pp. 242–55.
[123] Hutton, *Requests*, pp. 80–2.

and another of 'two or three pounds'. At the time of contracting the debt of £5 17s., Ethell thought it too much value to be trusted to Booth alone and so the other two joined him by making the notes in question. As it transpired, the plaintiff was right to doubt Booth. He could not pay, and had to sell some of his possessions, for which he provided the plaintiff with a bill of sale covering all but £1 5s. of the debt, which Ethell was now suing Hall and Smith for. The court decided that since some of the debt had been repaid, the plaintiff had no claim on Hall and Smith as their bills had been satisfied, but found itself in a dilemma, since they were still valid proof of the part of the debt still owed by Booth, but it worried that if the plaintiff kept them 'he might indorse them to others for the same evil purpose'. In the end it decided that two notes should be destroyed and a memorandum added on the back of the third that it was only valid against Booth for the remaining £1 5s.[124] This example certainly suggests there was a great deal of freedom employed in the use of notes.[125]

Other cases, like some at the Old Bailey, demonstrate that there were brokers for bills who charged for the risk entailed by the impersonal nature of their business. An executor of an estate took a £15 bill in payment for a debt owed to the deceased of £6, but had no cash to make up the difference. He claimed that it would cost half a crown (2.5s.) to discount it, or 0.8 per cent with a broker to obtain the cash. The case revolved around the fact that the debtor plaintiff refused to allow such a fee to be charged, but the defendant executor charged it anyway. The court decided in favour of the debtor claiming: 'A receiver may return a bill, as well as a light guinea, and demand something better in payment, but he cannot sell either, without the consent of the owner.' This case demonstrates that where acceptance was done by a known receiver, no charge was expected, but that there was a market beyond trusted individuals in which certain individuals brokered notes between trusted circuits of use. The fact that the fee was less than 1 per cent implies that such arbitrage had reached quite a sophisticated level in Birmingham.[126]

As we saw in Chapter 2, there are numerous examples of notes and bills being signed by women, some of whom were probably wives. Although under the rules of coverture married women were not granted the legal personality to be responsible for a debt, as Margaret Finn has shown, it was quite common in other courts of requests for wives to be active litigants in the court under the rules of female sole traders.[127] The

[124] Ibid., pp. 114–15. [125] Ibid. [126] Ibid., pp. 102–4.
[127] Margot Finn, 'Women, Consumption and Coverture in England, C. 1760–1860', *The Historical Journal* 39, no. 3 (1996), pp. 703–22.

following case also shows this; however, in his judgment Hutton applied the rules of coverture very strictly, claiming that a wife's note of hand was illegitimate under its rules:

> Upon examination: the note proved to be signed and given by Hunt's wife. The debt may be just, and we believe, it is, for we are too well acquainted with your probity to doubt it but you cannot recover by this note ... few women know their sphere, the full liberty of a female pen is dangerous. Though the laws allow our wives but a narrow latitude, if they were allowed to act of themselves, they might quickly sign away a fortune. The haberdasher and the china-shop would divide the profits of the week and their notes would be negotiated through the hands of milliners and mantua-makers, till there would be no *effects*, and the notes would, like this, be returned, with a protest for non-payment. Our love for the sweet little dears will oblige us to set bounds to their conduct ... we honour them, though we cannot honour their notes.[128]

Hutton, here, is trying to be humorous, and perhaps his contemporaneous male readers might have found it so, but he is wrong as many notes must have gone through the hands of milliners and mantua-makers. But if the quote's condescending tone was how he spoke in court, many must have found it offensive. Hutton himself noted that women were frequent visitors to the court, but he never missed an opportunity to belittle their behaviour.[129]

On some other occasions the court actually had notes drawn on its order to facilitate repayment of old debts, as in the following case: 'it was therefore agreed between the parties, that L. should give his note to pay the debt: without interest, at four instalments, six months between each; two of them were paid, the third became due June I'.[130] In another example an original note for 10 guineas was drawn up to be paid in instalments. Presumably, as such a note was paid, each payment would reduce its value.[131]

New Wealth and Property in the Countryside

Hutton and the examples used by Hunt and Smail are from larger towns where most of the middling sort resided, and also where large mercantile fortunes were made. But since the great increase in the practice of mortgaging involved more agricultural than urban land, this meant there was a constant interaction between the town and the countryside. As we have seen, many urban traders and manufacturers took out adverts in local newspapers seeking mortgages to invest their capital, and

[128] Hutton, *Requests*, pp. 297–9. [129] Ibid., pp. 262–6. [130] Ibid., p. 310.
[131] Ibid., p. 348.

increasingly urban and rural elites mixed socially at balls and other entertainments. A previous body of work from the 1970s and 1980s debated the extent to which large urban merchants purchased land for reasons of emulation.[132] It was postulated that status still resided with the rural aristocracy and greater county gentry, who continued to look down on trade. As a result, merchants, once wealthy enough, abandoned trade and purchased rural estates; they turned themselves into agricultural rentiers and married into country society. Examples have been shown of some who did this, but most remained focused on trade.[133]

In many ways the premise of this debate misses the point of the relationship between urban trading and manufacturing success and landed society. Since the late Elizabethan period, merchants and traders had worked to show that their profit-making was as valuable to the commonwealth as that of gentry estates. They did this by arguing that overseas trade provided profits from exports that could be taxed by the state to pay for its military protection.[134] In addition, the whole discourse and programme of improvement that began in the 1630s focused on improving agricultural production through investment in land to increase crop yields, thereby increasing food for the poor and providing extra employment through the work involved in drainage, marling, liming, and so on. This was accompanied by the argument that increased production of food could also be used to employ many more people in manufacturing.[135] This especially focused on the woollen cloth industry, but also on ironware, glass, and many other commodities. Although the initial arguments focused specifically on increasing exports, by the end of the seventeenth century, as Paul Slack has shown, many people began arguing that increased home consumption could also lead to a virtuous circle of prosperity.[136] This new discourse of political economy drew no or little distinction between the process of investment in agrarian capitalism and urban production. Indeed, as the eighteenth century progressed, many aristocrats began not only urging their tenants to improve their

[132] Nicholas Rogers, 'Money, Marriage, Mobility: The Big Bourgeoisie of Hanoverian London', *Journal of Family History* 24, no. 1 (1999), pp. 19–34; Henry Horwitz, '"The Mess of the Middle Class" Revisited: The Case of the "big Bourgeoisie" of Augustan London', *Continuity and Change* 2, no. 2 (1987), pp. 263–96. Donna T. Andrew, 'Aldermen and Big Bourgeoisie of London Reconsidered', *Social History* 6, no. 3 (1981), pp. 359–64.

[133] Earle, *Middle Class*, pp. 152–7.

[134] Craig Muldrew, 'The Emergence of the "Middle Sort" of People', in Keith Wrightson (ed.), *A Social History of England, c.1500–c.1750* (Cambridge, 2016), pp. 294–5.

[135] Craig Muldrew, *Food, Energy and the Creation of Industriousness: Work and Material Culture in Agrarian England, 1550–1780* (Cambridge, 2011), pp. 304–12.

[136] Slack, *Invention of Improvement*, pp. 142–56, 215–22.

land but also invested themselves in mining, milling, and smelting on their land, and then transport projects.[137]

Some social snobbery between trade and land might have surfaced in assembly room gossip, and a political discourse continued which exaggerated the difference between London-based 'Whig Finance' and a country-based 'Tory landed interest'.[138] But the importance of mortgages to capital creation and spending means that we cannot accept that there was a divide between the worlds of investment and rent. Reality was much more subtle than a subordinate relationship of trade engaged in snobbish emulation of the gentry. The very nature of stable capital required a working interaction between trading and manufacturing profit, and between urban and manorial cultures. An older Marxist formulation saw class conflict between two different interests, but in fact the capital generated from agricultural profits and industrial profits was the same in institutional form, and land was – and still is – the most secure form of capital. Rents, of course, were a different way of earning wealth than relying on profits earned from selling on the market, and ostensibly were more secure than profits based on the vagaries of demand for goods. But rents depended on the profits of the farmers working the land, and were often in arrears. Land was the best security because it was immobile.

In Chapter 4 we saw that in the 1720s and 1730s different forms of capital were invested in the mortgages made up by John Cannon, and once again it is worth returning to the micro-history of rural Glastonbury to investigate how capital used in this way affected class relations there. This will also give us an insight into the rise of possible members of the middle class in a rural setting before the mid-century. Here we can examine the difference between the very wealthy in Glastonbury and a person of the lower middling sort, such as Cannon. In addition, we can trace his relationship with the poor of the parish and show that while he did not consider himself part of the poorer sort, his wealthier neighbours probably did.

Cannon's father was a small husbandman with a copyhold estate, who was at least wealthy enough to have a fairly substantial two-storey house, a maidservant, and to be an overseer of the poor.[139] However, due to an injury caused by a falling hay knife he became lame in 1692, until his

[137] See, for instance, K. Fairclough, 'Egerton, Francis, Third Duke of Bridgewater (1736–1803), Canal Promoter and Colliery Owner', *Oxford Dictionary of National Biography*, www-oxforddnb-com.ezp.lib.cam.ac.uk/view/10.1093/ref:odnb/9780198614128.001.0001/odnb-9780198614128-e-8584, accessed 19 October 2022.

[138] Steven Pincus, *1688: The First Modern Revolution* (New Haven, 2009), pp. 366–99.

[139] Cannon, *Chronicles*, I, plate 8; p. 44.

death in 1723. This meant he accumulated debts, and when he died Cannon had to sell most of the estate to pay them off. Since these amounted to about £250 and he was left with only four acres, this was probably the approximate value of his father's farm.[140] Just before his father's death, Cannon recorded that he had become liable to pay Church and poor rates on his four acre close at Butmoor.[141] In 1722 he had tried to sell to set up in trade as a maltster, but was convinced not to do so by his Father. As a result, he had to borrow money to buy barley, which when combined with his father's debts meant he failed in this trade, leading to a period of severe poverty that lasted about eight years.[142] During this period his family was the recipient of charity from friends, although he never mentions receiving poor relief.[143]

By the early 1730s he was able to earn around £50 per year through his scrivening and teaching. At the same time, his cousin on his mother's side of the family, Elizabeth, became very wealthy through a piece of family fortune. Although she married one Thomas Pope of Butleigh, whom Cannon described as 'a man of Middling fortune but very honest and industrious and prosperous', she became wealthy after inheriting her sister's estate. As a young girl, she had lived together with this sister, Sarah, where they 'followed Women's employment with the Needle or Spinning wheel for some time which gave opportunity for some young men to make addresses to them. Among many that offered was one Robert Walter, a Baker by trade, a very Industrious young man, of an honest and indifferent family'. However indifferent his family might have been, 'they lived lovingly together many years very prosperously and increased in riches, wealth and reputation'. Walter left the bakery trade to become a dairy and grazing husbandman, and in 1705 Cannon went to work for his uncle, as he put it, 'his hynd and servant'. But this ended in a fight with Walter, which caused Cannon to leave off husbandry and join the Excise service, and also led him to become disinherited when Walter died in 1715. According to Cannon, this was on the advice of a woman Walter lived with after his wife died in 1705. Whether it was under her influence or because of their disagreement, the great bulk of Walter's estate was given to Sarah's sister, Elizabeth, who gained full

140 Ibid., pp. 28, 157–8. 141 Ibid., pp. 155–6.

142 Ibid., pp. 157–66, 180–6. Although this was the time when he learned to work as a 'tolerable solicitor' by working for an attorney on Castle Cary and some others (p. 170). It was also broken up by a period when he became estate bailiff and steward to one Colonel William Peirs Esqr. at Bradley between Lydford and Glastonbury in 1726, but owing to disputes over the payment of the colonel's bills he gained little from this employment (pp. 172–5).

143 Ibid., p. 193.

control over it 1731 when she became a widow. This, according to Cannon, was worth £5,000 or £6,000, making her one of the wealthiest individuals in West Lydford.[144] Perhaps to make up for Cannon's lost inheritance, she remained his sympathetic patron for the rest of his life, and he did the accounting and scrivening work for her farm. Thus, we can categorise Cannon as a very precarious member of the lower middling sort, although linked by kinship to two of his father's sisters, Sarah and Elizabeth, who through work and marriage had, with their husbands, practised the virtue of saving to amass a considerable fortune.

However, eight miles away in Glastonbury, where Cannon lived after 1732, he did not have any such connection with the local elite; and as I have written about elsewhere, he felt resentful towards them. He considered himself to be much more learned, literate, and numerate than they were, but powerless in comparison because he lacked wealth.[145] The *Chronicles* abound with stories of the follies of many wealthy and powerful people from history, and, although Cannon was comfortable with the concept of interest, when discussing most of his wealthier neighbours from Glastonbury, their wealth was generally described as being gotten through usury and/or sharp dealing. Interestingly, most of the individuals Cannon described in this way were traders of the town, not farmers. This was especially true of the Glastonbury vestry and town council, whose meetings he had to attend in his role as bookkeeper. When introducing the history and nature of Glastonbury just after he moved there, he provided a potted description of what he thought of the 'better sort' of the town:

> They are naturally given to Conceit and Self Interest especially when in any Office, making then a light and trivial matter to meet at any time and spend 5, 10 or 30 shillings and place it to the whole parish accounts ... That when a Choice is made of one to bear the office of a proctor or Mayor, it happens Sometimes on such who perhaps has Some Small Substance in the World but without Learning, and it is so Notoriously gross that they cannot Read a Warrant nor Sign their name Altho' writ by a Clerk or penman whom they will Imploy as their Clerk (which Sometime have been my fortune) ... in this Grand Office [mayor] comes in their turn other Mechanicks such as Black Smiths, Tanners, Taylors, Chandlers, Woolcombers etc.[146]

In contrast, he was almost always much more respectful towards two of the largest local landholders. The most important of these was his main

[144] Ibid., pp. 19–21, 54, 59–61, 129–30, 192.
[145] Muldrew, 'Class and Credit', pp. 166–9.
[146] Cannon, *Chronicles*, p. 211. Also see pp. 229, 250. On the quarrels of the town elite, see Ibid., introduction, p. lxxxii.

employer, the attorney Thomas Nicholls, and the other was Thomas King, who held a lot of land in trust. We encountered the latter in Chapter 4 as a major source of lending in the area (see 'John Cannon's Mortgaging Work' in Chapter 4).[147] Nicolas also owned the majority of land assessed for the poor rates in St. John's parish in Glastonbury. In a list of the rates charged in 1741, drawn up by Cannon, Nicholls is listed as having 247 acres worth £100 2s. in rents.[148] Cannon never explained how Nicholls obtained the lands, whether by inheritance, purchase, or foreclosure, but got on well with him, in contrast to his brother William, whom he thought rapacious. Nicholls treated Cannon well, recommending him to Sir Abraham Elton as the best accountant around (see 'A Local Scrivener: John Cannon' in Chapter 3) and inviting him to dinner with the steward of the Prince of Wales.[149] Cannon had less contact with King, but treasured the gift of a silver tobacco box from him, drawing a picture of it in the *Chronicles*.[150]

King, Nicholls, and Elizabeth Pope are probably the closest individuals described by Cannon comparable to the emergent middle class of Bradford described by Smail, emerging some decades later. Although we learn little of their cultural interests, we know at least that Cannon did not chastise them for their ignorance and provincialism. More importantly, they represented the qualities of saving and the prudent maintenance of significant amounts of capital. They are also generally described as being honest and possessing the older virtues of hospitality that included poorer individuals like Cannon. His idea of a commendable person of wealth is encapsulated in the following description of an attorney from Sherborne, eighteen miles away:

> Attended one Mr. Stephen Beaton … who also had an estate in Glaston of about £150 per annum who sent for me to breakfast with him on coffee and also obliged me to dine with him and to keep him company which I did till 10 that evening … I obliged this gentleman to a sight of the Church Book and survey of his estate as rated to the Church and poor, with which he was well pleased; and casting his eye on James Courts estate, being surveyed at £8 6s per annum but worth about £24 per annum besides his houses, he was pleased to say that the same was mortgaged to Mr. John Cook of Sherborne, stationer, for £400 in right of his wife. This Mr. Beaton had the report of a very honest good natured man of a forgiving temper to all especially to those who are in any ways indebted to him and when unable to

[147] Ibid., pp. lxxxviii, 401.
[148] Ibid., p. 672. At another point, Cannon stated there were 215 names on a survey of the landowners of St. John's in Glastonbury for a poor rate assessment in 1737, although he did not say if all of these were rate payers, or if this was a survey of all landholders. Given the number, it was most likely the latter (p. 274).
[149] Ibid., p. 566; see also pp. 239–40, 478.
[150] Ibid., p. 171; II, plate 6.

pay accepting his tenants bill unquestionable. In conversation merry, facetious and pleasant, not subject to passion. In short, if a lawyer may be counted just and honest he in that part exceeded many.[151]

Here his honesty is not only commended, but demonstrated by the fact that he pointed out Court's fraudulent under-assessment of his land and its mortgage. In contrast, the middling sort, composed of traders and a number of farmers who mortgaged their lands too steeply, were continually characterised by Cannon as drunken and self-interested spendthrifts with little self-control.[152]

In stark contrast to Hutton, who after raising himself out of the ranks of the poor was highly critical of their behaviour, Cannon was much more sympathetic to the local poor. Although he did not consider himself as one of them as a group, one of the wealthier residents of Glastonbury called him 'a poor lousy shabby dog' on one occasion.[153] He included a long passage on the subject of how central poverty was to social relations, stating that a poor man was nothing but 'a footstool for every man to trample on or a wall to piss against' and that 'the greatest misery in the world is the remembrance of having been happy'.[154] Throughout the *Chronicles* Cannon made many statements in favour of the poor, and often helped individual paupers by writing letters for them to the justices of the peace about the lack of payment by the Glastonbury vestry, as well as other matters.[155] For instance, he helped to defend those who did not want to make the poor wear their badges.[156] He was also a key middleman in the organisation of the town's poor relief, standing between the vestry of rate payers and the recipients of relief. Not only did he attend vestry meetings and keep the overseer's accounts of both ratings and disbursements, he seems to have been responsible for the actual payment of the doles.[157] On one occasion, when writing to arrange a meeting, he wrote 'I must this next Sunday attend the payment of the poor for without me they can do nothing.'[158] Also, when a workhouse was established in Glastonbury in 1634, 'by the advice and direction of Mr. William Goldfinch, an eminent Attorney for the better and more regular management and support of the poor of St. Johns Parish', Cannon noted its detrimental effect on the poor

they soon furnished [it] with all sorts of furniture fit for the reception of the Intended Inhabitants which was scarce one-third of the poor people who before this Establishment had relief or weekly pay. The rest were excluded and no relief.

[151] Ibid., p. 301. [152] Ibid., p. 239. [153] Ibid., p. 490. [154] Ibid., pp. 182–3.
[155] Ibid., pp. 35–6, 54–5, 60, 336, 483, 548. [156] Ibid., p. 239.
[157] Ibid., pp. 212, 234. [158] Ibid., p. 278.

The noise of a work house so terrified most of them that they compared the same no less than a house of Correction. By which means the monthly pay which was before £10, 11, 12 or 16 pounds was now reduced to £5, 6, 7 or 8 pounds ... This occasioned still more writing for me besides attendance but not Increased my salary.[159]

After the workhouse was set up, he noted that out-relief payments were still made, but now done from the workhouse. One of these occasions, fascinatingly, demonstrates that those on relief were using bills from traders and then taking them to the overseers to be discounted against their dole payments:

Attended the payments of the poor at the workhouse, where many poor people crowded in, some for clothes, some for pay, but were all rejected and put off till another vestry, neither would the inspectors sign their bills by reason of a large bill of expenses brought in by John Meaker from Easter last.[160]

John Meaker was the proprietor of the Bell Inn in Glastonbury and one of the overseers, so presumably had been supplying some of the poor with food and brought a bill for it.

Finally, there is considerable evidence in Cannon's *Chronicles* that the increase in borrowing on mortgaged land, while it added stability and liquidity into credit networks and the economy in general, also added a new element of instability to the composition of the middling sort. While those who were most successful and self-controlled rose to the very top to become middle class, within the middling sort new divisions developed between those who had substantial acreages of land of *c.*50 acres or more but who were still tempted to over-mortgage their estates, and those who were not. For small-scale mortgagees like Cannon it was not hard to borrow too much, but as we saw in Chapter 4, it took quite a bit of spending to go into too much debt on a sizeable estate. One person who managed to do so was George Stibbens, who had an estate of 56½ acres worth £48 7s. which he mortgaged for £152 18s. 2½d. to Thomas King, but was unable to pay the interest.[161] Stibbens was described by Cannon as 'very supine and careless' about his own affairs.[162] Cannon noted how his great uncle had lost his substance in the last half of the seventeenth century by committing all his money 'to the hands of one John Hole a neighbour, by some called Broker Hole ... who made it his Sole business to put out other person's moneys on security to himself & in his own name as if really his own making them to give Releases to himself for their

[159] Ibid., p. 201. [160] Ibid., p. 270. [161] Ibid., pp. 572–3. [162] Ibid., p. 260.

own money.' By this indirect practice he gained great substance and ill name, and was odious to all who knew him.[163]

The practice of lending on mortgage led to increasing complaints about lawyers. Complaints about lawyers were nothing new, but previously had been about stirring up vexatious and costly suits to earn more fees, but now became charges of sharp practice concerning mortgaging. Cannon, on more than one occasion, complained of the 'treacherous and foul practice in the law' of the attorney William Nicholls, and also accused him of making up a mortgage 'full of gross blunders and erasures' in 1729.[164]

This bad reputation came to a head in the case of the complicated mortgage of one Henry Scrace. Scrace seems to have been continually in debt; although he had come into possession of quite a large farm of 86 acres, he mortgaged it to various people for increasing amounts from £260 to £1,300 between 1732 and 1742, paying interest of 5 per cent until finally it was foreclosed upon in 1747, after his death.[165] We don't know why Scrace continually borrowed so much. In the very last entries in his *Chronicles*, Cannon reported that William Nicholls had negotiated a bond of £200 to help Scrace out, but had run off without delivering the money, leaving Scrace at the mercy of creditors:

> He has left a strong rumour of many vile practices by him acted of late, especially concerning the affair of Henry Scrace and the Clarks … that he had drawn the said Scrace and one of the Clarks into a bond of £200 to one Mr. Thomas Cooth of Shepton Malet, and to colour the matter made himself a surety in the said bond, and as soon as it was executed swept the money into his hat and kept it for his own use, which act proved of great damage to Scrace. For the mortgagees and his creditors levyed execution on his estate and goods.[166]

At the *Chronicles*' end, Scarce was holed up in

> the house of one Pearl in Glaston who sold spirituous liquors and was also under a cloud; and keeping firearms dared any to attempt the taking them and that the said Nicholls pretended they had a design on his life because in the evening they fired pistols and guns etc. Besides the aforesaid several others loudly exclaimed against him for his unjust dealing.

[163] Cannon noted that 'Hole had his deserved End, for falling from his horse at a gate in the road (since called Hole's Gate) he break his neck … *What is gotten upon the devil's back is spent under his belly*.' Ibid., p. 8.

[164] Ibid., pp. 557, 618. When discussing the parish accounts, Cannon further claimed that 'Mr. William Nicholls had undertook to erase, alter, put out and set in several matters and things (especially his own unjust and extravagant bills, etc.) that had been denied at Easter last and also had blotted and defaced the book in a very shameless matter with tallow grease and dirt.' Ibid., pp. 289–90.

[165] Ibid., index, p. xci. [166] Ibid., p. 695.

They remained here for a number of days, 'living in a riotous manner ... gaming, cheating and shuffling every person that came into their company'.[167] But the *Chronicles* end before we learn how this was resolved.

This example demonstrates that credit secured on mortgage could provide temptation in the form of going further into debt while the security of land was there, and for a lender with capital – especially a sharp attorney like William Nicholls – to encourage more lending until the equity of redemption would no longer hold. Notably, though, William does not seem to have been as successful as his brother. Again, we don't have evidence of his wealth, but he never held an important public office in the town, and as Cannon noted earlier he had been guilty of altering the town's accounts. At the very end of the diary Cannon notes 'a strong rumor of many vile practices by him acted of late'. In this case, the new idea of the self allowed self-interest to flourish and the accumulation of capital, as William Nicholls did through foreclosure, but not without loss of reputation. This is another way a divide was created between the still insecure middling sort and the capital-rich middle class. The latter's lives also became further removed from the experience of the poor apart from arguments within vestries about how much tax they should pay. The actual management of poor relief payments and charities increasingly fell to people like Cannon.[168]

A similar division can be traced twenty or so years later in Thomas Turner's Sussex village of East Hoathly.[169] There too, an elite group of very large landowners – Jeremiah French, William Piper, and the Reverend Thomas Porter – dominated parish business. We know even less about the amount of their wealth, but they clearly dominated vestry politics, and again members of the middling sort like Turner were much less secure. However, Turner, being an independent shopkeeper, was clearly of a higher social status than Cannon, and described many dinners together with various collections of these individuals, with French, Piper, Porter, and the Fullers (a local butcher) being his most common companions. But like Cannon, Turner continually criticised these wealthy individuals. He complained about French's lack of charity because he continually attempted to avoid paying his proper share of the poor rates, and his attempts to remove paupers from the parish without proper regard to their character or circumstances. He also commented on Piper's meanness in offering hospitality, lending to, or doing favours for others, and the land-hungry Porter's acquisitiveness and recycling of old sermons. Although he clearly enjoyed the socialising and especially

[167] Ibid., p. 695. [168] Ibid., pp. 239–40.
[169] This is described in more detail in my 'Emergence of the "Middle Sort" of People'.

drinking with the local middle class, he was more at ease with other tradesmen and became friends with those who were of the lower middling sort and some who were poor. In terms of self-control, Turner does not mention much about the financial affairs of the elite, but they enjoyed partying and drinking. Turner claimed French got through twenty gallons of spirits every year, beside other liquor. He was not in the business of drawing up mortgages like Cannon, but he does mention them occasionally. A mortgage was used to raise some capital to help a poor blacksmith try to earn a living, and the poor widow Virgoe was left with a heavily mortgaged house by her deceased husband. He also described some copyhold land that Mr Porter 'had a deep mortgage thereon'.[170]

Although we can see an incipient divide in terms of security and power between the middling and capital-rich elite in East Hoathly, this does not seem to have resulted in the same violent tension that erupted in Glastonbury. In addition, the elite such as French remained heavily involved in the operation of the Poor Laws, although this was generally to ensure costs were kept down through the removal of paupers and illegitimate children.[171] The land was of a generally better quality in the area than the flood-prone Somerset Levels, and Sussex was one of the wealthiest farming areas of Britain. As a result, farm profits and rents would have been greater, making borrowing easier to pay off regularly.

We cannot tell how many villages and towns were seeing similar developments without more studies, but such over-mortgaging was not unique to Glastonbury, and left many to become the prey of conveyancing attorneys or other lenders who could use their assets to acquire land that might not otherwise come onto the market. The Lancashire attorney John Plumbe was able to use his arrangement of mortgages to gain land as payment for debts. As an example, he lent one Alexander Hesketh of Aughton £2,400 in 1715, and by 1718 had agreed to purchase manorial rights to two estates as payment. At the same time Hesketh mortgaged a number of properties to Plumbe, who was eventually able to foreclose between 1724 and 1744, although only after the former put up a long legal defence. Presumably he must have been so indebted that it was difficult for him to continue annual interest payments.[172]

[170] Turner, *Diary*, pp. 40, 44, 123, 135, 303.
[171] See, for example, the index entries for Jeremiah French.
[172] B. L. Anderson, 'The Attorney and the Early Capital Market in Lancashire', in F. Crouzet (ed.), *Capital Formation and the Industrial Revolution* (London, 1972), pp. 242–3.

Despite such examples, it is probable that most mortgagors were not over-leveraged and benefited from being able to borrow – certainly this is true when compared to the previous century, when the gentry was overburdened to the extent that many failed. In seventeenth-century Lancashire, for example, 278 of the 763 families present in 1600 lost their gentility.[173] After 1760, developments such as the rapid expansion of canal and turnpike trusts, as well as other business trusts and the emergence of formal country banks, meant there was a proliferation of new ways to hold capital outside of London in addition to mortgages and bonds. It was also only then that an ideology of the sort professed by William Hutton came to fruition. How the first country banks evolved out of the system I have been describing will be dealt with in Chapter 10, but before doing that we need to broaden our enquiry to show how the creation of paper currency took a different institutional path in Scotland, France and the American colonies.

[173] B. G. Blackwood, *The Lancashire Gentry and the Great Rebellion 1640–60* (Manchester, 1978), pp. 18–21.

9 The Success of the First 'Modern' Banks: Scotland and the Thirteen Colonies, and Failure in France

Up to this point I have focused on England because it was the most populous and politically and economically most powerful part of the British Isles. But it is a crucial contention of this book that the financial revolution was not only a much broader social phenomenon than has previously been thought, but was also *geographically* wider as well. The pamphlet debate carried out in the public sphere detailed in Chapter 2 did not just influence England, but Scotland, the American colonies, and – through John Law's scheme – France. In all of these areas, paper currency projects were undertaken with the same aim as in England: promoting economic growth through creation of liquidity. However, whereas in England institutions calling themselves banks only began to emerge after *c.*1760, elsewhere in the British Empire formal banking institutions were successfully developed from the 1690s. This chapter will discuss the varied experiences of Scotland, the American colonies, and France in turn, noting the similarities and differences with each other and with the English experience. Fairly extensive historiographies exist for all three areas, but so far they have been written in isolation from one another. While this chapter includes new research on the use and circulation of Scottish bank notes, it consists mostly of a comparative reinterpretation of already excellent, if siloed, literatures.

Scotland

The Bank of Scotland was founded only a year after the Bank of England, in 1695, and was designed as an institution to issue credit currency from its inception.[1] Scotland successfully created a banking system whose primary aim was to initiate economic activity by attracting capital from landed property and merchants to turn it into a circulating currency of

[1] The Bank of England was primarily an institution to fund the government debt, although as discussed in Chapter 2 it did issue large denomination notes into the London economy.

bank notes, including £1 sterling notes. At roughly the same time, various paper currency-issuing institutions were set up in the Thirteen Colonies. In both Scotland and the Colonies the creation of credit currency was a much more central aim than in England.

In the late seventeenth century, Scotland was much poorer than England, and still largely agrarian. Although by 1688 Edinburgh and – to a lesser extent – Glasgow were important trading ports and had wealthy merchant communities, there was, as yet, little industry in Scotland. It also had a less developed state. The two harvest years 1696 and 1697 turned out to be among the worst in the century, and the resulting famine is estimated to have led to the deaths of over 15 per cent of the Scottish population. The localised Scottish transport and Poor Law system was unable to cope with redistribution of what little grain there was.[2] In contrast, England saw little increase in mortality.[3] This disaster led to the Scottish elites being convinced that the economy of the country needed to be improved, and that to do this they would first need to focus on banking.

During the Restoration, trust in Scottish coinage had suffered a great blow from the actions of the then master of the Scottish Mint, Charles Maitland – Lord Hatton – who was the younger brother of John Maitland, the Second Earl of Lauderdale, Charles II's Secretary of State in Scotland. One account claimed he contained 'as much folly, Insolency and bossines as ever met in one breast ... God and nature had made him a mad foole'. Since Lauderdale was politically important to Charles II as a means of supporting the Restoration episcopacy against a Presbyterian majority, he was secure in his position. This allowed him to organise three large-scale coinage frauds: a secret debasement of the Scots silver coin; the production of counterfeit foreign coins; and a huge over-issue of debased copper coinage. He apparently made huge profits from this, earning £56,000 sterling from the copper fraud alone. Obviously having someone in government committing acts that would have been high treason in a commoner was disastrous and made it difficult to use silver coins without scales to know what they were worth.[4] It was not until 1682 that the Scottish nobility felt they could move

[2] Karen J. Cullen, *Famine in Scotland: The 'Ill Years' of the 1690s* (Edinburgh, 2010), p. 2.

[3] E. A. Wrigley and R. S. Schofield, *The Population History of England* (Cambridge, 1989), p. 533.

[4] Richard Saville, *Bank of Scotland: A History, 1695–1995* (Edinburgh, 1996), p. 71; C. Jackson, 'Maitland, Charles, Third Earl of Lauderdale (c. 1620–1691), Politician and Judge', *Oxford Dictionary of National Biography*, www-oxforddnb-com.ezp.lib.cam.ac.uk/view/10.1093/ref:odnb/9780198614128.001.0001/odnb-9780198614128-e-17818, accessed 20 October 2022.

against him, and he was removed from office. The Mint was closed and did not reopen until 1686, when it began to issue proper coins. But when a tax was imposed to help pay for the Nine Years' War, gold and silver were drawn out of circulation, creating problems for the economy.[5]

There are no estimations of the value of the circulating currency in Scotland at this time, but as part of the Act of Union in 1707 all of the coins circulating there were reminted and reduced to the London Mint par of 12 Scots pounds to £1 sterling in 1708. At that time, £142,180 sterling of pre-1673 Scots hammered silver coin was brought in, together with £96,856 of post-1673 silver and £132,080 of foreign coins. This means that before the Act of Union there was probably about £370,000 sterling in circulation for a population of 1.2 million, whereas in England – with a population of just under five million people in the period before the recoinage of 1696 – Charles Davenant calculated the amount of silver money in the country to have been about £8 million, although almost five million of this was clipped.[6]

The Bank of Scotland was created as a joint stock company by an Act of the Scottish Parliament on 17 July 1695, with a monopoly on banking activity in the country for twenty-one years. The nominal capital to be raised was £1,200,000 Scots or £100,000 sterling. Of this sum, £800,000 Scots was raised in Scotland, with about half coming from landholders and the other half from merchants, traders, and professionals. The rest was purposely raised on the London money market in order that the Bank would have access to the much deeper financial markets that existed in the metropolis at this time.[7] The Bank aimed to pay a dividend to the subscribers through the profits of the 'trade of banking', which would be earned by lending on interest and discounting bills of exchange. The primary aim of the Bank was explicitly stated to be liquidity creation. It aimed to establish a circulating paper currency that could be used to replace the scarce coinage and oral credit. Unlike the Bank of England, it was actually explicitly prevented from lending to the Crown by the Act of Parliament. This was because the founders wanted to distance the stability of the bank from any political problems created

[5] Saville, *Bank of Scotland*, pp. xxvii–xxx.

[6] William Davenant, 'A Memorial Concerning the Coyn of England', in *Two Manuscripts by Charles Davenant*, ed. Abbott Payson Usher (Baltimore, 1942), pp. 34–6; William Davenant, 'Memoriall Concerning Creditt', in *Two Manuscripts by Charles Davenant*, ed. Abbott Payson Usher (Baltimore, 1942), pp. 67–9. Gregory King made a similar estimate of £8.5 million in silver money. Gregory King, *Natural and Political Observations and Conclusions upon the State and Condition of England*, in George F. Barnett (ed.), *Two Tracts by Gregory King* (Baltimore, 1936), p. 34; D. W. Jones, *War and Economy in the Age of William III and Marlborough* (Oxford, 1988), pp. 15–16.

[7] Saville, *Bank of Scotland*, pp. 1–3.

by the continued existence of Jacobitism. Its primary business model was to attract investment from shareholders, which would then be lent out at interest in the form of new banknotes printed by the Bank. It could also take money at deposit.

Although the intellectual origins of the structure of the bank are difficult to discern, it is probable that many of the pamphlets published in London discussed in Chapter 2 would have found their way to Scotland, as there was an important community of Scottish merchants in London who organised trade between the capital and Scotland. In fact, William Patterson, one of the proposers of the scheme for the Bank of England, was a Scot. Other Scottish merchants had spent time in Amsterdam and Antwerp, where they would have experienced the use of transferable bills of exchange as currency. But it was explicitly a project not just about mercantile credit, but about the creation of credit currency aimed at improving the local economy through liquidity, as well as making taxes easier to pay. The Scottish Parliament and government at the time was dominated by landowners and important Edinburgh lawyers who certainly took an interest in the economy, but undoubtedly the organisation of the bank must have come from the merchant community. By the 1690s the population of Edinburgh was growing, standing at 20,000–30,000, and its merchants were trading throughout the Baltic. Other towns also had sizeable merchant communities, with Aberdeen having over thirty merchant houses handling foreign shipments. Although Scotland exported goods such as fish, coal, and livestock, most merchant activity involved the import of foreign manufactured goods and luxuries for the growing middling sort and aristocratic and gentry families in the countryside.[8]

Since Scotland was a relatively small country, there was a great deal of interaction between the landed and mercantile communities. Although the structure of the Bank was created by merchants, the social support that the great landlords gave the Bank – both by investing in it and by borrowing from it on the security of their estates – was crucial to its success. Fifty-five of the initial 176 subscribers were merchants and professionals, 7 were women, and 63 were nobles and lairds. The Bank also had crucial links to important Scottish merchants who resided in London, where 36 of the initial subscribers were resident.[9] The importance of the London connection is indicated by the fact that it was a London Scottish merchant, John Holland, who was elected as the Bank's first governor. He had been born in London, the son of a sailor, but

[8] Ibid., pp. 8–10. [9] Ibid., p. 3.

apparently learned Dutch bookkeeping techniques in Holland in the 1670s. He worked as an auditor for the East India Company and was a successful merchant in his own right, and being resident in London he was certainly aware of the pamphlet debates about banking projects. He got involved with other Scottish merchants by supplying Scottish army regiments in Flanders with clothing and food. With the founding of the Bank he moved to Edinburgh, where he was crucial in helping to defend the fledgling Bank of Scotland from the challenge of William Patterson's Scottish Company's (known as the Darain Company) attempt in the summer of 1696 to add note issuing to its various activities, publishing his own pamphlet: *A Short Discourse on the Present Temper of the Nation with Respect to the India and Africa Company, and of the Bank of Scotland; Also of Mr. Patterson's Pretended Fund of Credit* (1696). However, in 1697 he stepped down as governor in favour of the Third Earl of Leven, a professional soldier and governor of Edinburgh Castle who was able to offer political protection in Scotland.

Merchants also dominated the main administrative offices and sat on the General Committee, which met regularly to decide on all matters of governance and to approve larger loans. One of the most important of these was George Watson, who came from a merchant family and had received tuition in Edinburgh in a wide range of bookkeeping techniques, before being sent to the Netherlands where he learned mathematics and further accounting skills, and received training in various legal systems. There was a strong connection between Scotland and the Lowlands, with twenty Scottish merchant apprentices present in the latter learning accounting at any one time. James Marjoribanks, from another merchant family, was appointed treasurer.[10]

The professionalism with which the double-entry accounting was done is evident in the surviving documents. The General Committee also acted as auditors by checking them regularly. Finally, the Bank had an advantage in that the Scots used civil Roman law, which had a straightforward and well-defined law of contract ruled on by the Court of Sessions in Edinburgh. It could also use the Register of Sasines, a Scottish form of land registry where, since 1617, every claim on estates had to be registered.[11] Thus, unlike in England, but like Holland, the Bank's officials could be sure of the security of the land pledged against the loans it made. In this way, it had some elements of the land bank proposals we encountered in Chapter 2, in that its bank notes would be issued and circulated as payment for loans it made based on the security

[10] Ibid., pp. 9–13. [11] Ibid., pp. 2, 27.

of land whose value was overtly public. Loans were also made on personal bonds up to a value of £500 sterling, based on an evaluation of the creditworthiness of the borrower; many were made to tax collectors. But goods such as linen or plate could also be put forward as collateral. An interest rate of 4 per cent was charged on the loans, and in the first four months the treasurer paid out £25,846 in loans.[12] The Bank also dealt with the discounting of inland Scottish bills (bills used here refers only to bills of exchange) and bills of exchange with London as a means of maintaining cash flow, but in its early years this was not the Bank's main business, although subsequently the Bank expanded its bill business as a profitable activity.[13]

The minutes of the court of directors of the Bank reveal that the directors went to London to find a printer for the first issue of notes, since there were printers there with experience of making Bank of England notes, as well as Exchequer bills and other forms of paper currency. They were printed in books of 200 notes each, with a simple promissory clause obliging the Bank to pay the bearer the sum listed in Scots currency, although the account book valuations were done in sterling and a simple multiple of 12× was used for the Scots value (i.e. £10 sterling was £120 Scots). They were then numbered and made payable to the Bank's secretary, David Spence, and signed by the treasurer and accountant. Each note was printed with an identical counterfoil that would have been signed and given the same number, so that when the note was cut from the book it could be later matched up with the stub left as a measure of authenticity, combined with the signatures and printing.[14] The first book of notes was delivered on 25 March 1696 and contained 200 £100 notes. Then, in April, 800 £10, 200 £5, and 200 £20 notes were delivered. By the following June 6,400 notes had been delivered, broken down into the denominations listed in Table 9.1, first by order of issue and then by percentage of different notes.

Thus, the first issue of notes would have increased the circulating currency of the country by 38 per cent, and would have amounted to around 10s. sterling each for the approximately 250,000 households in Scotland. It was therefore a sizeable injection of liquidity in quite a short period of time. Over half of the notes issued were for £5 or £10. The Bank of England only issued notes of £5 or £10 for a short period of time, while the Bank of Scotland increased the issuance of small notes. It is difficult to know how quickly or widely the notes circulated, but they

12 Ibid., pp. 26–7.
13 Bank of Scotland (hereafter BOS), General Ledger NRAS 945/1/94/1.
14 Jonathan Callaway and Dave Murphy, *Paper Money of Scotland* (Sutton, 2018), I, p. 40.

Table 9.1 *(a) Numbers of bills of different denominations in the first banknote issue of the Bank of Scotland in 1696*[15]

Note numbers	Denomination	Quantity
1–200	£100	200
201–1000	£10	800
1001–1200	£20	200
1201–1400	£50	200
1401–1800	£5	400
1801–2000	£20	200
2001–2200	£100	200
2201–2400	£50	200
2401–2600	£5	200
2601–2800	£10	200
2801–3200	£5	400
3201–3800	£10	600
3801–4000	£5	200
4001–4600	£50	600
4601–4800	£20	200
4801–5000	£5	200
5001–5200	£10	200
5201–5400	£20	200
5401–5600	£10	200
5601–6200	£5	600
6201–6400	£20	200

(b) By percentage of different notes

Denomination	Numbers of notes printed	Percentage	Value
£5	2,000	31	£10,000
£10	2,000	32	£20,000
£20	1,000	16	£20,000
£50	1,000	15	£50,000
£100	400	6	£40,000
Total	6,400	100	£140,000

were sent to four branches that had been set up in Glasgow, Aberdeen, Montrose, and Dundee. Most notes were injected into the rural economy as they were used to pay the loans made by landowners.[16] With the lowest value being £5, such notes would not have been very useful for daily necessities, but they would certainly have been effective in freeing up silver coins for smaller transactions.

[15] BOS, NRAS 945/1/94/1 fol.5.
[16] BOS, Minute Book NRAS 945/1/5/3 p. 53; Saville, *Bank of Scotland*, pp. 21, 26.

In 1699, another 4,400 notes were printed, including 1,600 £5 notes and 1,800 £10 notes. This brought the total to 10,800 notes worth £202,000. However, in February 1700 seven £5 notes were discovered to have been altered by Thomas McGee of Prestonpans near Edinburgh by adding a 0 to make them appear to be £50 notes. Although McGee was discovered (he quickly fled to Newcastle and disappeared), the success of this forgery led to much discussion among the directors and resulted in a decision to redesign the notes with printed monetary amounts on them, and to have them printed in Scotland. The Bank's precautions against forgery seem to have worked remarkably well without the need to employ the death penalty as was done by the Bank of England. The next forgery recorded in the minutes did not take place until 1710, when someone tried to alter some £20 notes with a pen. In March 1723 a more serious forgery occurred in which seven fully engraved 20s. notes were discovered, and the notes were repaid but no further action taken. But three years later three more notes appeared that were identical to the first seven. Upon this discovery, a reward of £100 was offered for any information on the forger, and all of the engravers in Edinburgh were searched. The forger was not discovered until 1729: a bookbinder who was apprehended in November, whipped, and banished. In total, £48 worth of his forged notes in circulation had to be refunded by the Bank.[17] The only other forgeries recorded in the minutes occurred in 1730, 1749, and 1787.

As a protection against forgery, as well as to replace worn notes, old banknotes were regularly removed from circulation and burned. By November 1702, £197,265 worth of old bills from the first issues had been recorded as being burned.[18] From May 1700 the Bank ledgers record thirty-seven roughly regular issues of new bills of 200 or more at a time until March 1703, when 9,800 bills had been issued, consisting of 5,400 £5 notes, 2,600 £10 notes, 1,200 £20 notes, 400 £50 notes, and 200 £100 notes.[19] A further 3,200 notes were printed in the second issue.

On 27 March 1704 a separate issue was made of 9,000 £1 notes – or what they called 20s. or £12 Scots notes.[20] Although the directors had discussed issuing small denomination notes in the first issues, it was decided that it would be more prudent to only issue notes of £5 sterling and above. But since the first three issues were enthusiastically taken up and used without depreciation, and with the first attempt at forgery being

[17] BOS, NRAS 9451/11/1 Index under F.; BOS, NRAS 945/1/5/4, p. 84.
[18] BOS, NRAS 945/1/ 4/1 f.26 l. [19] BOS, NRAS 945/1/94/1 f.26 r.
[20] BOS, NRAS 945/1/94/2, f.3.

Table 9.2 *Bank of Scotland note issue in 1705*

Denomination	Numbers of notes printed	Value
£1	11,400	£11,400
£5	4,600	£23,000
£10	2,000	£20,000
£20	1,200	£24,000
£50	400	£20,000
£100	200	£20,000
Total	19,800	£118,000

successfully discovered and promptly dealt with, it was now thought that small notes could be issued to aid with much smaller transactions. As we have discussed in relation to the use of the guinea coin in England, a 20s. note would still be much too large for any daily market purchases, but would have been a great help in reducing the intervals of paying off sales credit extended for basic foodstuffs to 3–4-week cycles instead of a few times per year. In the third set, issued between 1705 and 1707, over half of the notes were for 20s (Table 9.2). Fewer large notes were printed because more of these from the original issues had remained in circulation since they were used only rarely and thus did not wear out nearly as quickly.[21]

After this, 20s. notes continued to be issued until by 1713, by which time over £60,000 of small notes had been released, as can be seen in Table 9.3. As with the main issues of notes, the Bank also kept a book with a strict record of when each numbered note was taken out of circulation and put in bundles of 600 notes each – which was the same number in each book in which they were issued. These bundles were sealed up in the presence of the deputy governor and two or three other bank officials and put in one of the Bank's safes. This was done both to take worn notes out of circulation, since they were printed on relatively thin paper, and to check any attempts at forgery by limiting the time any single numbered note would have been legal tender. By comparing the months at which the notes were taken out of circulation with the months when they were issued, we can get a sense of how long this was. This is shown in Table 9.3, where we can see that most of the first issue of 20s. was removed from circulation after about a year, but that the notes issued after September 1705 mostly remained in circulation for about two years.

However, as would be expected, some notes circulated for longer than others. Of the first 20s. notes issued in 1704, most were taken out of

[21] BOS, NRAS 945/1/94/2, f.16.

Table 9.3 *Issues and removals of Bank of Scotland 20s. notes, 1704–1713*[22]

Month	Issued	Removed
April 1704	2,400	
May 1704	2,400	
June 1704		
July 1704	1,200	
August 1704	1,200	
September 1704	600	
October 1704	600	
November 1704	600	
December 1704	**9,000**	
January 1705		
February 1705		
March 1705		3,600
April 1705		1,200
May 1705		1200
June 1705		600
July 1705		600
August 1705		600
September 1705	600	**7,800**
October 1705		
November 1705	600	
December 1705		
January 1706	600	
February 1706	600	
March 1706		
April 1706	600	
May 1706	600	
June 1706	600	
July 1706		
August 1706		
September 1706	600	
October 1706		
November 1706		
December 1706	600	
January 1707	600	
February 1707		
March 1707	1,200	
April 1707	1,800	
May 1707	600	
June 1707	600	
July 1707	600	
August 1707	600	
September 1707		

[22] Bold figures are totals BOS, NRAS 945/1/248/1.

Table 9.3 (*cont.*)

Month	Issued	Removed
October 1707	1,200	
November 1707		
December 1707	1,200	
January 1708	1,800	
February 1708	1,800	
March 1708	600	
April 1708		
May 1708		
June 1708		
July 1708		
August 1708		3,600
September 1708		1,800
October 1708		600
November 1708	600	1,200
December 1708	600	
January 1709		600
February 1709	600	1,200
March 1709	600	600
April 1709	600	600
May 1709	600	600
June 1709		1,200
July 1709	600	600
August 1709	600	600
September 1709	1,200	600
October 1709		600
November 1709	600	600
December 1709	600	600
January 1710	600	600
February 1710	1,200	
March 1710	1,200	1,200
April 1710	600	600
May 1710	600	600
June 1710	600	
July 1710	1,200	600
August 1710	600	600
September 1710	600	600
October 1710		600
November 1710	600	600
December 1710	600	
January 1711	1,800	1,200
February 1711	600	600
March 1711	600	
April 1711	1,200	600
May 1711	600	600
June 1711	600	600
July 1711	1,200	600

Table 9.3 (*cont.*)

Month	Issued	Removed
August 1711	600	600
September 1711		600
October 1711	1,200	
November 1711	600	600
December 1711	600	600
January 1712	600	600
February 1712	600	600
March 1712	600	
April 1712	1,200	1,200
May 1712	600	**30,600**
June 1712	600	
July 1712	600	
August 1712	1,200	
September 1712		
October 1712	600	
November 1712		
December 1712	600	
January 1713	600	
February 1713	1,200	
March 1713	600	
April 1713	**52,800**	

circulation between 5 March and 27 August 1705, but 2,500 remained in circulation.[23] Once withdrawn, the first fifteen bundles were only burned in January 1710, and the next fifty-three bundles were burned in May 1712, amounting to 40,800 notes.

Remarkably, this issue of notes also seems to have been done with very little cash reserves. At the time of the first note issue of £140,000, coins held by the Bank were only worth £6,666 13s. 4d., and in subsequent years the running cash books and journals of daily transactions rarely mention any holdings of specie. Before the recoinage, the general ledgers did not even have a section for cash reserves.[24] This issue of Scottish circulating notes was much more ambitious than any previous scheme in Europe. A similar scheme had been tried by the Palmsbuch bank in Sweden, which had issued paper banknotes in 1661. Sweden, like Scotland, was an economy on the periphery of European exchange, and thus had similarly low amounts of precious metal in circulation.

[23] BOS, NRAS 945/1/248/1.
[24] BOS, NRAS 945/1/94/1; BOS, NRAS 945/1/134/1A, 1B. BOS, Journal NRAS 954/1/93/1.

However, the Palmsbuch bank soon over-issued its notes, leading to a collapse in their value; in 1668 the bank was nationalised by the Diet and Sweden returned to a currency based on copper.[25] In contrast to the more cumbersome Neapolitan procedure for the *fede di credito*, the Scottish notes were freely transferable, without any need to record the transfer, and were issued for specified rounded amounts.

To achieve this success, the directors of the Bank of Scotland had to overcome numerous exogenous challenges during its early years. Perhaps the most serious of these was William Patterson's scheme for the Darien colony in Panama: The Company of Scotland Trading to Africa and the Indies. Although Patterson had been raised in Scotland, he left when he was seventeen, and after spending time in the Caribbean he made his wealth as a merchant in London engaged in the slave trade, among other ventures. Although one of the founders of the Bank of England, he was a classic projector in that he used publicity to drum up investment in a scheme promising large returns.[26] In this case he used Scottish nationalist sentiment, returning to Edinburgh in 1696 to promote a Scottish colony, which he claimed could be as successful as other European colonies in the Caribbean. This appeal to national pride evidently hit a nerve and he raised £400,000 sterling in a few weeks to outfit an expedition, with 1,317 subscribers from every level of society. It has been roughly estimated that this totalled about one-fifth of the wealth of Scotland.[27] This inevitably put pressure on the Bank of Scotland's cash flow, but the directors wisely decided not to loan money to anyone who was investing in the Darien Company, and this caution proved astute as the two expeditions to found the new colony in 1698 and 1699 failed due to disease and hostility from the English and Spanish governments. This resulted in the loss of most of the investors' capital. If this wasn't enough, the famine of 1696 and 1697 required the export of much gold and silver to pay for imports of grain.[28] Only twelve out of forty-seven Scottish joint stock companies founded since 1690 survived until 1700. All of this meant that the Bank stopped lending for a time in July 1696 and increased their trade in bills, which earned the Bank a profit of £600–800 per year. This retrenchment and caution with lending meant

[25] Saville, *Bank of Scotland*, p. 21.

[26] Koji Yamamoto, *Taming Capitalism before its Triumph: Public Service, Distrust, and 'Projecting' in Early Modern England* (Oxford, 2018), pp. 1–9.

[27] Dennis R. Hidalgo, 'To Get Rich for Our Homeland: The Company of Scotland and the Colonization of the Darién', *Colonial Latin American Historical Review* 10 (2001), pp. 323–4.

[28] Saville, *Bank of Scotland*, p. 39.

the Bank did not grow much during this period, but given the challenges it faced, it is significant that it survived at all.[29]

Undoubtedly, Presbyterianism played an important role in the success of the Bank. Presbyterianism, like Puritanism in England, stressed the Calvinist notion of predestination, and if anything was even more concerned with emphasising self-denial as a means of avoiding sin. It also, as Gordon Marshall has argued, placed great emphasis on the importance of the calling and economic success.[30] There is not the space here to go into theology to the same extent as we did for England, but Presbyterianism also had a large influence in England during and after the Civil War. Richard Baxter was influenced by it, and in the pamphlets published by mid-seventeenth-century Scottish ministers and divines we find an equally important emphasis and discussion of the importance of the self and self-examination as in the work of someone like Baxter. In *An Exposition of All St. Pauls Epistles Together with an Explanation of Those Other Epistles of the Apostles St. James, Peter, John & Jude*, David Dickson (1583–1663), the son of a merchant, who was professor of divinity at both Glasgow and Edinburgh, used the word 'self' at least 556 times in 323 pages. Similarly, in ten of the works of James Durham (1622–1658) the word self is used almost 3,500 times, including one entitled, *The Great Corruption of Subtile Self, Discovered, and Driven from It's Lurking-Places and Starting-Holes and the Contrary Grace, Self-Denyal Commended, as an Indispensably Necessary....*

These authors also discussed interest in Christ as an important guiding principle against passions. For instance, in James Durham's *Heaven Upon Earth*, worldly interest is coupled with credit and inclination as temptations that work against what he terms conscience:

> When Credit, Interest, and inclination in their impulses are thwarted, they storm, they vex and torture the man; ... when the impulse of Conscience is thwarted.[31]

Conscience he defined as a mental disposition to act morally caused by faith:

> when Conscience judgeth it self bound to owne Gods revealed will for its rule, and when it impelleth or pusheth the man to act according to that rule, and withall the more ordinary disposition of his will is to comply with these impulses of his Conscience.[32]

[29] Saville, *Bank of Scotland*, pp. 39–44.

[30] Gordon Marshall, *Presbyteries and Profits: Calvinism and the Development of Capitalism in Scotland, 1560–1707* (Edinburgh, 1992), pp. 70–80, 232–5, 253–62.

[31] James Durham, *Heaven Upon Earth in the Serene Tranquillity and Calm Composure, in the Sweet Peace and Solid Joy of a Good Conscience Sprinkled with the Blood of Jesus* (Edinburgh, 1685), p. 33.

[32] Ibid., Introduction.

But conscience also relied on an interest in Christ to achieve goodness:

> it may be said that the Believer hath a good Conscience and may take it as a mark of his saving interest in Christ.[33]

> ...when Believers think that Gods Interest and their own interest go joyntly together in such and such a thing or practice, though their own interest swayeth more with them then Gods interest, yet they will be ready to alleadge that they care not so much what become of their own interest, but they cannot endure nor admit such ... a prejudice should come to Gods interest.[34]

Another minister, William Guthrie (1620–1665), in *The Christian's Great Interest: In Two Parts* ... specifically used the word rate to refer to this interest:

> Glory be to Christ Jesus, who at so dear a Rate, did Purchase the out-letting of that Love from the fathers Bosome.[35]

In this way, interest was justified in a similar fashion to the English experience, and when combined with the emphasis on hard work and business success the Presbyterian church was easily able to accept interest-bearing investment as a crucial part of banking culture. However, predestination was not challenged by Arminianism or Cambridge Platonism, and remained a potent force. Although happiness was certainly mentioned by the Presbyterian theologians, it does not seem to have played such an important role in the Scottish Church.[36] It was, however, very prominent in the development of Scottish moral philosophy from Hutchinson through Hume, and was central to Adam Smith's *Theory of Moral Sentiments*. There, he very definitely stressed personal enjoyment in contrast to a focus on pain and suffering, even if his emphasis on enjoyment was very much on a moderate bettering of one's material condition and saving.[37]

Although there was some division between rural elites, who tended to be more influenced by Anglicanism, and the bulk of the population, there was nothing like the theological divisions that existed south of the border between conformists and non-conformists. Since the Glorious Revolution, the Church of Scotland had been recognised as unequivocally Presbyterian, and as such was enmeshed in local society through the democratic governance of the kirk sessions, who elected ministers to sit

[33] Ibid., p. 40. [34] Ibid., p. 65.
[35] William Guthrie, *The Christian's Great Interest: in Two Parts* ... (London, 1705), p. 139.
[36] Marshall, *Presbyteries and Profits*, p. 87.
[37] Adam Smith, *The Theory of Moral Sentiments*, ed. D. D. Raphael and A. L. Macfie (Oxford, 1976), editor's introduction, ch. 1, ii, paras. 10–11.

on regional Presbyteries. Importantly, though, the kirk sessions could act as congregational courts to enforce moral discipline among parishioners. This was a function that straddled ecclesiastical and civil jurisdiction, and in this way they kept watch on the probity of important figures in the community.[38]

Since the role of the Church had traditionally always been strongest in Edinburgh, this provided a sort of democratic evaluation of the moral soundness of the merchants and clerks who created and administered the new bank. The Church of Scotland's stress on education and literacy also helped in the provision of numeracy and writing skills. Punishment for breach of contract and non-payment of debts seems to have been stronger than in England. In Edinburgh, the number of imprisoned debtors in the town's Tollbooth Prison was 3–4 times as high as in London. However, very few of these men were imprisoned for more than a year, as there were more effective legal routes to satisfying creditors.[39]

Thus, just as with the influence of Dissenters in the success of London financial institutions, the Calvinist emphasis on self-examination and self-discipline created honest and trustworthy bookkeepers. The minutes of the Bank suggest that the company was run with the utmost probity, and was governed by principles of caution rather than the search for individual profits. Both the merchants and the landowners involved wanted to guide the bank as an institution that could aid other economic endeavours, by which they earned their profits. It was run for the good of the Scottish economy, and this allowed the inner group of managers to keep secret the organisation of the Bank's finances – including the auditing of its books and, most importantly, its cash reserves.[40] By 1725 the circulation of notes totalled £46,625, lending on bond stood at £87,783, and bills at £31,727.[41]

One crucial aspect of the Scottish system, in contrast to the Bank of England, was that it was not based on convertibility to gold, but rather relied almost entirely on the probity and good management of the Bank's directors. The small amount of gold in circulation essentially made convertibility impossible. With the Act of Union, more gold was introduced into the economy as part of the settlement, which included a payment of £398,085 10s. from England to Scotland to pay for the conversion of the coinage and then all other public debts. However, the

[38] Callum G. Brown, *Religion and Society in Scotland since 1707* (Edinburgh, 1997), pp. 18, 69–72.
[39] Tawny Paul, *The Poverty of Disaster: Debt and Insecurity in Eighteenth-Century Britain* (Cambridge, 2019), pp. 42–7.
[40] Saville, *Bank of Scotland*, pp. 24, 52, 92. [41] Ibid., p. 89.

largest part of this was reserved to pay off the £232,840 debt of the Company of Scotland.[42] All of this, including the recoinage, was administered by the Bank of Scotland. But the users of its banknotes were never anxious enough to demand convertibly. They continued to be happy to trust in the management of the Bank, and to allow it to recall debts and curtail lending when needed.[43]

However, political events stemming from the fact that holders of pre-Union Scottish government debt were never fully paid off eventually led to the creation of the rival Royal Bank of Scotland in 1727. These debtors were supposed to have been paid with funds drawn from Scottish customs. However, this always fell short, and when a new malt tax was introduced there were riots in Glasgow. As a result of this, the holders of this old debt were anxious to start a banking operation to compete with the Bank of Scotland, through which they hoped they could transfer their illiquid debt into something more fungible that could earn a profit through note issue. These hopes were dashed by the spectacular failure of the South Sea Company in London, which had aimed to do a similar thing with English debt. But in 1724 they incorporated themselves into the Society of the Equivalent Company, and with the support of the then ascendant London-based Second Duke of Argyll in the Walpole administration, they were able to incorporate themselves as the Royal Bank of Scotland in 1727.[44]

The Royal Bank began business with £111,347 worth of so-called 'equivalent stock' invested by the old government creditors, which earned a 4.5 per cent annual income guaranteed by the British Treasury, and a contract to funnel all of the revenues of the Scottish customs through the Bank to be transferred to London. The political nature of the new Bank's creation is demonstrated in the fact that there were almost no merchants involved in its administration. Most were landowners, lawyers, or politicians who were anxious to compete with the old bank (from this point on, the two companies were colloquially referred to as the 'old' and 'new' banks). To do this they called up a further £20,000 of investment from their subscribers to engage in lending on interest and to issue banknotes specifically to compete with those of the Bank of Scotland.[45] Table 9.4 shows that overwhelmingly they concentrated on issues of 20s. notes for everyday use (Figure 9.1).

[42] Ibid., pp. 57–8, 75–7.
[43] Ibid., p. 89; Sidney Checkland, *Scottish Banking: A History, 1695–1973* (London, 1975), pp. 101–2.
[44] Saville, *Bank of Scotland*, pp. 84–92.
[45] Ibid., pp. 94–6; Checkland, *Scottish Banking*, pp. 59–62.

Table 9.4 *Notes issued by the Royal Bank of Scotland, 1728–1730*[47]

Notes	1728	1729	1730	Total
£1	11,600	13,200	9,200	34,000 (80.5%)
£5	3,600	800	800	5,200 (12%)
£10	1,200	200	1,000	2,400 (6%)
£50	400	0	0	400 (1%)
£100	200	0	0	200 (0.05%)

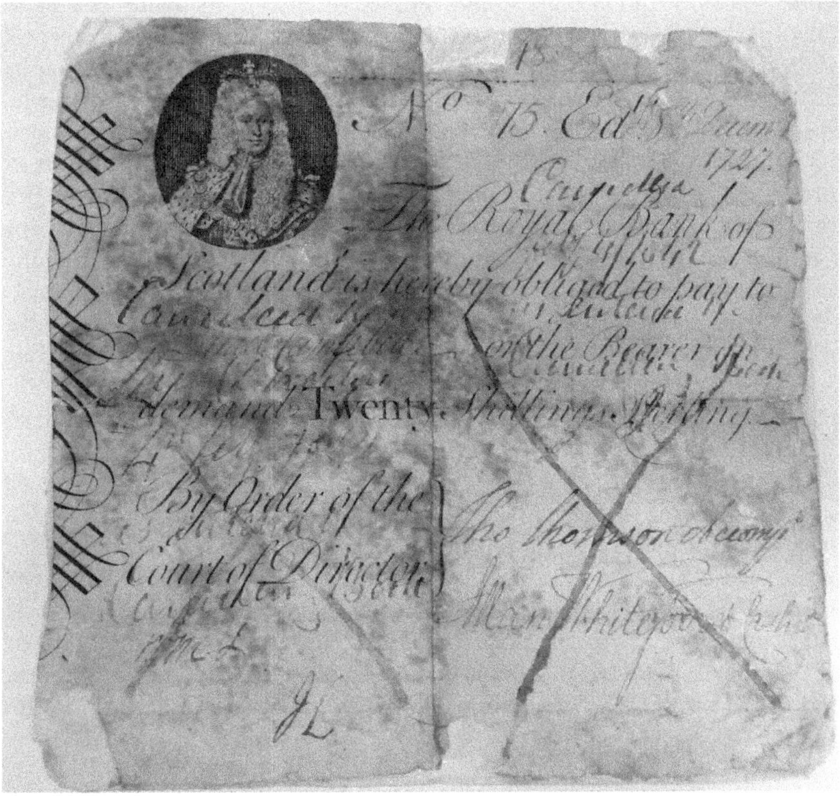

Figure 9.1 Royal Bank of Scotland 20s. banknote from 1727.[46]

The books in which the bank recorded these issues are even more detailed than those of the Bank of Scotland. In large ledgers, each page is given to listing the numbers of notes, with the date of issue at the top and

46 Royal Bank of Scotland Archives (hereafter RBA), RB/252.

47 RBA, RB/175/1.

a remark of when they were withdrawn recorded for every single note. Thus, if one had enough time it would be possible to work out how long every note was in circulation before being withdrawn and burned. In a sample of the first fifty notes issued on 4 January 1728, each note circulated for an average of 535 days, with the shortest time in circulation being 281 days and the longest being 2 years and 284 days.[48]

But the purpose of the Royal Bank in issuing these notes was not simply to try to add to note circulation by expanding liquidity into new areas where there was demand, but to try to aggressively drive the old bank's notes from circulation and replace them with its own new notes. This marked the start of what has been called a 'bank war', which was described by the first historian of the Royal Bank, Neil Munro, in explicitly military terms in which 'the combatants used each other's notes as missiles'.[49] The new bank engaged in a ruthless campaign of harassment by collecting the old bank's notes and keeping them out of circulation to force use of its own.[50] As a result, it is impossible to judge just how many notes were in circulation as opposed to being hoarded in the first years of the new bank's existence. Eventually the war ended and the two banks settled into a tolerable coexistence, although the buying up of each other's notes did not stop. The new notes of the Royal Bank would eventually have increased the total number and value in circulation, but since neither bank sought to move to establish any branch offices outside of Edinburgh, circulation would have been much lower outside of the Lowlands.

During this period, Glasgow had been rapidly expanding its commerce in the Atlantic trade, especially in the commodity of tobacco. By 1730, over 7,000,000 lb were being imported into Glasgow, which would rise to an incredible 47,000,000 lb by 1771. By the 1750s there was more tobacco being imported into Glasgow than all of England.[51] Most of this was re-exported to other European countries, with France being the most important destination. Although the actual tobacco trade in the Atlantic and with France was done using bills of exchange, it meant that, as the

[48] RBA, RB/175/1.

[49] Neil Munro, *The History of the Royal Bank of Scotland, 1727–1927* (Edinburgh, 1928), pp. 50, 55.

[50] Checkland, *Scottish Banking*, pp. 59–61.

[51] T. M. Devine, 'The Modern Economy, Scotland and the Act of Union', in T. M. Devine, C. H. Lee, and G. C. Peden (eds.), *The Transformation of Scotland: The Economy since 1700* (Edinburgh, 2005), pp. 25, 29–30; Robert C. Nash, 'The English and Scottish Tobacco Trades in the Seventeenth and Eighteenth Centuries: Legal and Illegal Trade', *The Economic History Review* 35, no. 3 (1982), pp. 364–6.

wealth and population of Glasgow expanded, so too did its need for currency.[52]

In the 1730s this was mostly achieved by certain Glasgow merchants who acted as local bankers, borrowing and buying notes from the banks in Edinburgh, but mostly from the Royal Bank. These individuals became known as 'exchangers'. But without any branches this still meant that worn notes needed to be collected and taken back to Edinburgh. Thus, by the 1740s there was a demand for actual banks in the western city; however, the events of the 'Forty-Five' slowed any further development in that decade. The occupation of Edinburgh by the Jacobites resulted in both banks burning many of their notes, and the Royal Bank locked many more inside Edinburgh Castle.[53] However, after the defeat of the Jacobites, two new private banks were set up in Glasgow by the beginning of the 1750s, and one much smaller operation in Aberdeen. All of these began to issue their own banknotes to meet local demand. The two Edinburgh banks saw this as a threat to their profits from their notes, so they tried to stop their circulation by buying them up, just as the Royal Bank had done with the Bank of Scotland's notes in 1728–1729. Although the smaller Aberdeen bank was unable to withstand this assault and folded in 1753, the Glasgow banks had support from increasingly wealthy merchants and survived.

As well as the expansion of the Glasgow tobacco industry, by the 1730s and 1740s efforts to create an export-based linen industry in Scotland were beginning to come to fruition. Linen and coarse woollen cloth had long been made for household use throughout the Highlands and Lowlands, but when the Act of Union opened up new markets a concrete effort was made to turn linen production into a Scottish industry that would not have to compete with the already powerful English woollen industry.[54] It was also hoped that the local climate was suitable to grow flax, which could eventually replace imports from Holland and the Baltic.[55] Various societies were set up with the express aim of educating poorer families in the arts of growing flax, heckling, and other preparatory processes, together with spinning and weaving. As a result, production grew from just over 2 million yards of linen in the 1720s to an average of 4 million in the 1730s, 7.8 million by 1748, and over 10 million

[52] Checkland, *Scottish Banking*, pp. 66, 69. T. M Devine, *The Tobacco Lords: A Study of the Tobacco Merchants of Glasgow and Their Trading Activities, c. 1740–90* (Edinburgh, 1990), pp. 55–71.

[53] Checkland, *Scottish Banking*, pp. 71–4.

[54] Alistair Durie, *Linen Industry, The Scottish Linen Industry in the Eighteenth Century* (Edinburgh, 1979), pp. 8–10.

[55] Ibid., pp. 35–7.

after 1760.[56] Like woollen cloth production, the manufacture of linen was labour-intensive.[57]

Figures for the amount of labour required for hand preparation are hard to come by since much was done in the producer's households. It is easier to make an estimate of the amount of spinners needed. Estimates for the weight of yarn needed to make a yard of linen cloth vary from 1.75 yards per pound to 2.5 and even 5 for very coarse cloth, but 2 is probably a good average. Also, estimates of the amount of flax a person could spin in a week range across 1–3 lb, depending on skill and time. Given that the Scottish industry was dependent on cottage production, and was expanding to tap previously unskilled labour, and that there were many complaints about the need for more organised training to improve quality, I have chosen an average rate of 1.5 lb per week for the purposes of calculation.[58] Assuming a 40-week working year, with the missing weeks being occupied with harvests, and other intensive labour in addition to some holidays, this gives us a workforce in the region of 33,000 spinners in the 1730s, and around 70,000 by the 1750s. In addition, some thousands of weavers would have been required, as well as workers involved preparation and in bleaching.[59]

This production developed as an industry using the putting-out system, with merchants buying prepared flax or building lint-mills for its preparation, and then paying spinners and weavers. To make this work, the industry needed currency to pay suppliers and especially workers. For this purpose, the small 20s. banknotes must have been useful. It was reported that by 1750 weavers could earn 9–14s. per week; however, spinners only earned about 16d. to 2s. 6d. per week.[60] As a result, the British Linen Company was set up in 1749 and in 1750 issued small-value banknotes for as little as 10s. for the express purpose of making it easier to pay spinners. This meant there were now five institutions issuing banknotes in Scotland.[61]

The 1750s also saw the beginning of a new phenomenon: the issue of very small-value banknotes by petty tradesmen, in addition to those issued by the chartered banks listed above. The continued shortage of silver specie was becoming even more acute as the rural economy became more commercialised, and as more men and women entered the industrial labour market. These small notes were issued to make up for this. Notes for 10s., 5s., and even 1s. were issued, which looked much like the

[56] Ibid., pp. 22–3. [57] Ibid., pp. 37–8.
[58] Alice Dolan, 'The Fabric of Life', *Home Cultures* 11, no. 3 (2014), pp. 360, 363.
[59] Durie, *Linen Industry*, pp. 43–59. [60] Ibid., pp. 76, 79.
[61] Checkland, *Scottish Banking*, pp. 98–103.

official bank notes, by any individuals who could arrange to get them printed, and who could convince people to accept them. It seems that the success of the official notes had already made people accustomed to trusting paper without too much anxiety, and they were thus willing to use these notes.[62] Such private issue was similar to the system of informal handwritten notes in England, but with the crucial difference that the notes themselves were identical to the institutional notes of the major banks, and thus less embedded in the local transactions of the tradesman who issued them. They also did not have anything like the elaborate system of accounting employed by the older banks to keep track of their notes in circulation. They still, of course, had their name on the note, which could be refused, but users were accustomed to being able to use notes within a system that was, by this time, almost one of a national circulation throughout Scotland. This meant that there was a real possibility that an over-issue of notes could happen, leading to their devaluation.[63]

This was certainly something that the Bank of Scotland and the Royal Bank worried about, especially after Britain entered the Seven Years' War in 1756. The war led to disruptions in trade and international credit flows, as well as increased taxation that required more remittances to be sent to London. They limited which notes they would accept in payment, and the old bank even issued its own 10s. notes in 1760. In addition, the number of 'proper' banks continued to proliferate with the establishment of provincial banking companies in Dundee, Perth, Aberdeen, Ayr, and Dumfries all in the 1760s. This led to even greater anxiety on the part of the larger Edinburgh and Glasgow merchants as well as the landed gentry, who were now genuinely concerned about the stability of the capital they held in the older banks and the two Glasgow banks.

As a result of this, many meetings were held and an enquiry by the Scottish Commissioners of Supply (a type of county governor) was set up. Eventually delegates were sent to London to attempt to have Parliament pass a statute to solve the problem by confining banking to a monopoly of the two old banks and possibly one more in Glasgow. There, a committee of the Privy Council, which included a number of Scots who knew David Hume and Adam Smith, was formed to consider the problem. In the end a bill was passed in 1765 that explicitly rejected any possibility of monopoly banking outright, stating that 'nothing that would have the appearance of an exclusive privilege in favour of the Banks would be listened to by the people of this country'. It also made

[62] Checkland, *Scottish Banking*, pp. 104–6.
[63] Saville, *Bank of Scotland*, pp. 136, 139–40.

the inclusion of option clauses in banknotes illegal. An option clause reserved the issuing bank the right to delay redemption in specie for six months, with interest to be paid in the interval. This, in effect, transferred the English notion of convertibility of notes to precious metal into law in Scotland. But most importantly, in regards to the proliferation of banknotes, it made the issuing of notes under 20s. illegal.[64]

Despite this measure, a crisis still occurred. At its founding the Ayr Bank, as it has come to be known, acted in a dynamically entrepreneurial fashion, setting up seven branches – more than any of the other banks – in order to capture as much market share as it could. Less usefully, and certainly less prudently, it also liberally granted cash credits on its books in order to extend its note issue to the point that it was said that the Ayr Bank notes formed two-thirds of Scotland's circulation. This expansion led to increased speculation by individuals in London, who purchased drafts drawn on the bank's London correspondents in the hope of profiting from the exchange rates for its notes. By 1772 the bank had created £1,120,000 in liabilities, including £200,000 worth of banknotes and £600,000 in the form of drafts on London correspondents. The bank's assets consisted of £409,079 in bills of exchange and £827,963 in loans and advances. It was the drafts and bills on London that led to the bank's downfall.

When one of the London correspondents – the London banking house of Neale, James, Fordyce, and Downe – collapsed (when Fordyce lost £243,000 gambling on the stock exchange), Scottish paper in the form of draft, bills, or notes fell to a heavy discount, placing great demands on the Scottish banks, which all relied to some extent on bill exchange in the London money market. When the news reached Scotland there was an immediate panic, and a demand for notes of all sorts to be redeemed for coin. Since there was nowhere near enough coin, this led most banks to stop trading. The directors of the Ayr Bank made a bad decision when they refused a lifeline of £300,000 offered by the Bank of England, possibly for nationalist reasons.[65] This refusal resulted in their bankruptcy with the loss of £663,397 for the bank's shareholders and depositors, which in turn led to another 114 private bankruptcies. The situation was alleviated to a great degree by the fact that the older banks had shielded themselves from the Ayr Bank's notes and bills by not accepting them. As a result they were in a position to expand their own credit to fill some of the loss of liquidity caused by the many bankruptcies. However, they did not want so much of their liquidity to be tied up

[64] Checkland, *Scottish Banking*, pp. 118–21.
[65] Paul Kosmetatos, *The 1772–73 British Credit Crisis* (Basingstoke, 2018), pp. 188–9.

in such long-term credit as was required to aid those who had lost money in the collapse. With the support of the British Treasury and the Bank of England, Parliament sold £500,000 worth of 5 per cent annuities to cover the value of the outstanding debts.[66] They also negotiated the settlement of the outstanding £200,000 worth of Ayr notes still technically in circulation. Even if they were not being accepted, they were still being held as an asset, and the Bank of Scotland traded them for the new annuities and replaced them with its own notes at a reduced level of circulation.[67]

To put the collapse in perspective, of the 152 English bankruptcies studied by Julian Hoppit, largely drawn from the years 1780–1800, only 12 were for more than £100,000, and one of the largest of these was, in fact, the Fordyce bankruptcy that precipitated the Ayr Bank's collapse. At the time, England's population was roughly five times as big as Scotland's, which means that a £663,000 loss was vast in both absolute terms and even more so in terms of the size of the Scottish economy. But the quick and well-organised programme of transferring the losses into long-term government debt meant that it actually had much less effect on the Scottish banking system and economy than it could have. It did, however, have a salutary effect in bringing to an end the era of note wars and speculative banking ventures, and firmly cemented the role of the two old banks' oversight of note circulation. It also convinced Adam Smith of the need for regulation in banking for the good of the economy.[68]

As a result of the Ayr Bank failure, Smith revised his discussion of banking in the *Wealth of Nations*, and in contrast to the *Lectures on Jurisprudence*, there was an increased stress on the probity of bankers, and a discussion of the proper value of banknotes.[69] He claimed that the Scottish banks originally operated very prudently:

> The banking companies of Scotland, accordingly, were for a long time very careful to require frequent and regular repayments from all their customers, and did not care to deal with any person, whatever might be his fortune or credit, who did not make, what they called, frequent and regular operations

[66] Saville, *Bank of Scotland*, pp. 161–6. [67] Ibid., p. 165.

[68] Craig Muldrew, 'Self-Control and Savings: Adam Smith and the Creation of Modern Capital', in Simon Middleton and James Shaw (eds.), *Market Ethics and Practices, c.1300–1850* (London, 2018), pp. 73–5.

[69] Adam Smith, *An Inquiry into the Nature and Causes of the Wealth of Nations*, ed. R. H. Campbell, A. S. Skinner, and W. B. Todd (Oxford, 1976), I–II, p. 313 (hereafter WN); Saville, *Bank of Scotland*, pp. 156–6; Nicholas Phillipson, *Adam Smith: An Enlightened Life* (London, 2010), pp. 206–8.

with them ... by this attention they were enabled to make some tolerable judgment concerning the thriving or declining circumstances of their debtors.[70]

Again very prophetically, he claimed it was demands by traders for more credit that eventually led to its over-extension beyond what the economy needed.[71]

It is impossible to know just how many banknotes were in circulation during the period after 1740, since no records survive for most of the tradesmen who issued small notes. But estimates can be made for the two main banks. For the Royal Bank of Scotland we actually have very precise figures, since a book has survived, titled *A Record of Royal Bank Notes Struck and Cancelled by the Directors*, which lists the number and amount of notes in circulation each September after subtracting all those cancelled from those issued each year. This information is provided in Table 9.5. From this table we can see that although the numbers and value of the notes in circulation fluctuated between about 45,000 and 77,000 notes worth between £109,000 and £186,000, the average figures were 63,737 and £176,265, respectively. This reflects the fact that in some years more notes were created than others. In total, 22,453 notes were cancelled compared to an average total circulation of 63,256 or 36 per cent of the circulation each year, and £57,253 worth or 32% of the total value in circulation.

The equivalent records of burned notes for the Bank of Scotland unfortunately do not simultaneously record the total number remaining in circulation, but do show that between 1751 and 1763 they burned 12,000 £5 notes, 4,356 £10 notes, 4,435 £20 notes, 434 £50 notes, and 801 £100 notes, or 22,026 in total, worth £294,060.[72] In addition, another £250,000 worth of 20s. notes were taken out of circulation between 1753 and 1761.[73] If we turn these figures into a yearly average, this is 33,086 notes worth £55,755 being destroyed each year in the 1750s. This implies that although the Bank of Scotland had more small notes in circulation, the value was probably similar to that of the Royal Bank since they seem to have been withdrawing notes from circulation at the same rate. We don't know what the note issue of the Glasgow Ship Bank was in 1750, but by 1761 it was £82,331, of which the largest amount was £1 notes. The Linen Bank's note issue is shown in Table 9.6 for these periods.[74]

This results in a total of just over £530,000 worth of notes potentially in circulation, in addition to the abovementioned small private notes, for

[70] WN, p. 305. [71] WN, p. 308. [72] BOS, NRAS/945/248/13.
[73] BOS, NRAS/945/1/248/14.
[74] Callaway and Murphy, *Paper Money of Scotland*, pp. 238–9, 457.

Table 9.5 *Total Royal Bank of Scotland notes in circulation, 1743–1754*

Year	£1 value	£1 cancelled	£5 notes	£5 value	£10 notes	£10 value	£20 notes	£20 value	£50 notes	£50 value	£100 notes	£100 value	Total notes
1743	£49,895	30,000	6,195	£30,975	3,334	£33,340	2,725	£54,500	382	£19,100			62,831
1745	£37,962	16,166	3,910	£19,550	1,913	£19,130	1,090	£21,800	212	£10,600			45,088
1746	£41,562	8,000	4,893	£24,465	2,563	£25,630	1,877	£37,540	657	£3,285			51,552
1748	£46,962	16,800	8,243	£41,215	2,660	£26,600	1,511	£30,220	589	£29,450	89	£8,900	60,054
1749	£52,562	18,800	9,107	£45,535	2,864	£28,640	1,683	£33,660	641	£32,050	67	£6,700	66,924
1750	£55,462	17,900	7,863	£38,315	2,823	£28,230	2,062	£41,240	626	£31,300	143	£14,300	68,979
1751	£58,362	19,500	5,783	£28,915	2,213	£22,130	1,732	£34,640	472	£23,600	91	£9,100	68,653
1753	£47,900	17,650	6,201	£31,005	2,021	£20,210	1,601	£32,020	321	£16,050	111	£11,100	71,617
1754	£60,500	6,400	6,511	£32,555	1,745	£17,450	1,529	£30,580	406	£20,300	182	£18,200	77,935

Table 9.6 *(a) Linen Bank note issue total in 1762*

10s.	38,400
20s.	33.600
£5	4,750
£10	250
£79,050	77,000

(b) Linen Bank total note issue in 1762–1765

10s.	18,600
20s.	63,900
£5	6,850
£107,450	89,350

a population of 1.25 million in 1755.[75] Of course, at any one time a certain percentage of these notes would have been held by the banks, but this still represents a remarkable growth of circulating capital of 400–500 per cent since 1700 for a population that had remained relatively static. There is unfortunately no way to measure the velocity of circulation without any GDP estimates, but there is some partial evidence of economic growth. Most notable, of course, was the growth of the linen industry already discussed. But, in addition, as lowland agriculture became enclosed and productivity increased, this would have created increased need to pay waged farm labour and would also have increased commercialisation as farmers became wealthier.[76]

As far as we can tell, the issuing of all of these paper notes did not lead to inflation. The long-term price trends of oatmeal, wheat, and bear (a type of barley) were relatively steady between 1700 and 1750. After this date there was a long-term upward movement to 1780, when the price of wheat and oats went up by about 40 per cent and barley (or bear) about

[75] T. M. Devine, 'Industrialization', in T. M. Devine, C. H. Lee, and G. C. Peden (eds.), *The Transformation of Scotland: The Economy since 1700* (Edinburgh, 2005), p. 39.

[76] T. M. Devine, 'The Transformation of Agriculture: Cultivation and Clearance', in T. M. Devine, C. H. Lee, and G. C. Peden (eds.), *The Transformation of Scotland: The Economy since 1700* (Edinburgh, 2005), pp. 71–92.

25 per cent.[77] However, in the same period the population also began to grow, from 1.25 million in 1755 to 1.6 million in 1801, or almost 30 per cent.[78] It is possible that the expansion of small notes in the 1750s played some role in this inflation, but the increasing demand from population growth is a much more likely cause, since the rapid contraction in notes after the collapse of the Ayr Bank in 1772 did not have any marked deflationary effect on grain prices in that or the following year.[79]

The success of the Scottish note issue, which functioned as its designers intended – providing liquidity to encourage economic growth – up until the 1760s without significant over-issue is a truly remarkable story. It is one that Adam Smith certainly recognised, and made it the centrepiece of his proposals to increase the wealth of nations. It was the first successful *national* issue of a paper currency since the Chinese Song dynasty issued *huizi* currency in the twelfth century. It, much more than the Bank of England, should be seen as the foundation of modern banking if we take the role of a bank to be the creation of a supply of money for the entirety of the economy, not just investors who can afford to buy public debt. It was able to provide sufficient liquidity to encourage industrial and agricultural transformations over the course of the eighteenth century.[80] However, it was not the only English-speaking territory to attempt to improve its economy through the provision of paper liquidity. The pamphlet debate about credit currencies carried the ideas of the benefits of liquidity creation throughout the English-speaking world in the 1690s and later. Ireland and most of the North American British colonies also attempted similar projects, and France, under the influence of the Scottish exile John Law, attempted to refinance its huge national debt through the issue of a paper bank currency.

Ireland, like Scotland, on the periphery of the European system of exchange, also lacked coins, and adopted different schemes to create paper currency. In Ireland between 1700 and 1721, six private banks were formed mostly as partnerships. Their main function was to facilitate bills of exchange around the country, but they also held money on account and issued some amount of banknotes. However, little work has been done on these early banks and it is unknown how many notes

[77] This is discussed in J. S. Gibson and T. C. Smout, *Prices, Food and Wages in Scotland 1550–1780* (Cambridge, 1995), pp. 173–84.
[78] Devine, 'Industrialization', p. 39.
[79] Gibson and Smout, *Prices, Food and Wages*, p. 185.
[80] Saville, *Bank of Scotland*, p. 168; Checkland, *Scottish Banking*, pp. 211–76.

circulated.[81] By the 1730s the philosopher George Berkley wrote a series of articles in the *Querist* proposing the establishment of a national bank, but this was not established until 1782.[82] Certainly the Irish linen industry expanded probably to an even greater degree than that of Scotland after its Linen Board was set up in 1711, but the degree to which this was helped by note issue remains opaque.[83]

The American Colonies

In stark contrast to Ireland, there is a very sizeable literature and an ongoing debate concerning the paper currencies issued by the American colonies. In no other early modern historiography has the subject of paper money received so much attention, or been the subject of such spirited debate. The subject was first dealt with in a major monograph by Curtis Nettles in 1934, *The Money Supply of the American Colonies before 1720*, and in a more extensively researched PhD thesis from 1941 by Leslie Brock, *The Currency of the American Colonies 1700–1764: A Study in Colonial Finance and Imperial Relations*, which was eventually published in 1975 with some revisions.[84] This seminal work has been followed by numerous articles and chapters in books on colonial economies.

The shortage of metallic specie was even more acute in the American colonies than in Great Britain.[85] This led to the adoption of commodity money such as tobacco or bushels of grain. In Massachusetts, for instance, taxes often had to be collected in bushels of barley, even though

[81] Rowena Dudley, 'The Failure of Burton's Bank and its Aftermath', *Irish Economic and Social History* 40, no. 1 (2013), pp. 1–30. L. M. Cullen and T. C. Smout have claimed that the circulation could have been as high as £400,000 by the 1720s, but they give no evidence, and also greatly underestimate the Scottish circulation in the 1740s. L. M. Cullen and T. C. Smout (eds.), *Comparative Aspects of Scottish and Irish Economic and Social History, 1600–1900* (Edinburgh, 1977), Introduction, pp. 10–11.

[82] Patrick Kelly, 'Berkeley and the Idea of a National Bank', *Eighteenth-Century Ireland* 25, no. 1 (2010), pp. 98–117. Also see Charles Ivar McGrath, 'Banks, Paper Currency and the Fiscal State: The Case of Ireland, Stated, 1660–1783', in Aaron Graham and Patrick Walsh (eds.) *British Fiscal-Military States* (London, 2016), pp. 35–60.

[83] Cullen and Smout, *Comparative Aspects*, Introduction, p. 7; H. D. Gribbon, 'The Irish Linen Board, 1711–1828', in L. M. Cullen and T. C. Smout (eds.), *Comparative Aspects of Scottish and Irish Economic and Social History, 1600–1900* (Edinburgh, 1977), pp. 77–87.

[84] Curtis P. Nettels, *The Money Supply of the American Colonies before 1720* (Madison, 1934); Leslie V. Brock, *The Currency of the American Colonies, 1700–1764: A Study in Colonial Finance and Imperial Relations* (New York, 1975).

[85] Nettles, *Money Supply*, pp. 162–79; Katherine Smoak, 'The Weight of Necessity: Counterfeit Coins in the British Atlantic World, circa 1760–1800', *The William and Mary Quarterly* 74, no. 3 (2017), pp. 467–502.

there was a 33 per cent penalty for not paying in specie.[86] Before the rise of Caribbean sugar plantations, tobacco was by far the largest American agricultural export, and bales of tobacco became the most common currency in Virginia, Maryland, and Pennsylvania. Many account books from the Chesapeake economy included a column for tobacco beside the standard ones of pounds, shillings, and pence.[87] But, as the rise of sugar production in the Caribbean increased at the end of the seventeenth century, so too did trade in agricultural supplies from the middle colonies. These were exported to the Caribbean to feed the growing number of enslaved labourers, and to provide work animals and manure as fertiliser.[88] Following this, the New England colonies expanded their financial services and shipbuilding to facilitate this trade.[89] All of this led to a demand for more money to facilitate a growing number of transactions over longer distances, for which commodity money was clumsy. Since English merchants commonly carried colonial debts for a long time in their books as a cost of doing business there, there was also a demand for cash in this trade when bills of exchange were not in balance.[90] Some Spanish silver coins entered North American commerce and were used by the colonists through a sizeable illicit trade with the Spanish empire, but were not enough.[91]

During the English Republic, the colonial governors had previously attempted to deal with the shortage of currency by minting their own coins. But when Charles II returned to the throne he forced the colonists to close their mints as it was part of the prerogative of the king to have the sole right to mint coins. Given the movement of important Puritans between America and New England in the mid-seventeenth century, it is not surprising that some were influenced by the proposals of credit currency that emanated from the Hartlib circle, discussed in Chapter 2. There is some evidence that as early as the 1660s John Winthrop Jr. suggested a scheme for the creation of a joint stock company to issue bills

86 Dror Goldberg, 'The Massachusetts Paper Money of 1690', *The Journal of Economic History* 69, no. 4 (2009), pp. 1100–1.

87 Mary Schweitzer, *Custom and Contract: Household, Government, and the Economy in Colonial Pennsylvania* (New York, 1987), p. 121. For other, older forms of commodities used as money, see Akinobu Kuroda, *A Global History of Money* (London, 2020), p. 68.

88 John J. McCusker and Russell R. Menard, *The Economy of British America, 1607–1789* (Chapel Hill, 1985), p. 199.

89 Ibid., pp. 189, 195–7.

90 Schweitzer, *Custom and Contract*, pp. 118, 122; Jacob M. Price, *Capital and Credit in British Overseas Trade: The View from the Chesapeake, 1700–1776* (Cambridge, MA, 1980), ch. 6.

91 Smoak, 'Weight of Necessity', pp. 472–6.

of credit backed up by land and goods, and other similar proposals followed.[92] In 1686 there was an attempt by John Blackwell to set up a land bank in Boston. He was the son of an English Puritan merchant who had served in Cromwell's regiment, and who subsequently became co-treasurer responsible for taxation and military expenditure in 1645–1659. He survived being prosecuted during the Restoration, and moved to Boston in 1684. Since land seized by conquest from indigenous tribes was abundant in the Thirteen Colonies, and unencumbered by feudal claims, the concept of creating credit currency lent on the security of real estate was a much more feasible proposition than in England. This early experiment failed, though, because the royal governor of New England voided all land titles in Massachusetts and reverted private property back to the king until 1691 as a part of the dispute between the Crown and the colony.[93]

As it turned out, private order solutions were not to be adopted in America, apart from a few failed attempts, until after the 1776 Revolution.[94] In contrast to England and Scotland, all of the paper currency issues in the Thirteen Colonies would be done by colonial governments. On the face of it, it might seem surprising that the American colonies would chose 'state' institutional solutions to the problem of currency shortage in contrast to England, but there were a number of reasons for this. One of the most important was the need to pay soldiers' wages. This motivated the very first issue of colonial currency by Massachusetts in 1690, to pay soldiers who had been hired by the colony in its failed attempt to conquer French Canada. At that time there was neither enough specie in the colonial treasury, or in circulation, to be collected by taxes. The colony's solution was to issue notes that they called bills of credit to the amount of £7,000 backed up by future taxation – four years before the founding of the Bank of England.[95] These notes were redeemable for goods or specie, and could also be used to pay debts and taxes. In general, the new currency worked quite well, although at one point it fell by 33 per cent in comparison to wheat, but soon recovered.[96]

With the outbreak of fighting in the American theatre of the European War of Spanish Succession in 1702, Massachusetts again found it necessary to issue more bills of credit. Between 1703 and 1713, over £170,000

[92] Nettles, *Money Supply*, p. 252.
[93] Goldberg, 'The Massachusetts Paper Money of 1690', pp. 1094–7.
[94] Edwin J. Perkins, 'Conflicting Views on Fiat Currency: Britain and its North American Colonies in the Eighteenth Century', *Business History* 33, no. 3 (1991), pp. 18–20, 24.
[95] Brock, *Currency of the American Colonies*, pp. 22–3.
[96] Goldberg, 'The Massachusetts Paper Money of 1690', pp. 1102–3.

worth was issued.[97] These issues of colonial currency came to be valued at about £132.75 par to £100 sterling as a unit of account.[98] Apart from Drummer's war with the Wabanaki Confederacy from 1722 to 1725, the colonies were largely at peace after 1714, until the War of Jenkin's Ear broke out in 1739. However, the issuance of bills of credit by Massachusetts continued to expand. In addition, Rhode Island, New Hampshire, and Connecticut all began issuing notes in 1710, and their note issue was quite large by the 1720s. Leslie Brock has estimated that the outstanding amount of bills in circulation in New England rose to £276,859 in 1720, £494,922 in 1730, and £880,261 in 1740.[99] New Jersey also began issuing notes in 1709, although only small amounts were issued before 1724; after this, circulation moved between £11,000 and £37,000 until 1740.[100] New York also issued smaller amounts of notes from 1709.[101]

It was soon realised by all of these colonial governments that the issuing of bills of credit had an economic utility beyond simply paying off war debts, because the colonists found them useful in facilitating their day-to-day transactions. As Daniel Vickers has shown, early America was an extremely numerate society, and the keeping of business and household accounts was much more common than in England by 1710.[102] The transferring of debts between accounts was a common practice, and thus it proved relatively easy to introduce bills and to keep track of them in accounts.[103] America was also a land-rich society, and it was not long before colonial administrators realised that the land bank proposals that had dominated the debates over credit currency in England in the 1690s, would be much easier to implement in a country where the European legal title to the conquered land had no history of encumbrances. In England, as we saw, the land law was much too complex –and the procedure for forfeiture upon default too slow – to allow an institution to use land as security for a bank-issued currency. In contrast, in America,

[97] Brock, *Currency of the American Colonies*, p. 591; Farley Grubb, 'Is Paper Money Just Paper Money? Experimentation and Variation in the Paper Monies Issued by the American Colonies from 1690–1775', *Research in Economic History*, 32 (2016), p. 209.
[98] Grubb, 'Is Paper Money Just Paper Money?', p. 222.
[99] Brock, *Currency of the American Colonies*, pp. 591–2.
[100] Farley Grubb, 'Creating Maryland's Paper Money Economy, 1720–1740: The Confluence of Political Constituencies, Economic Forces, Transatlantic Markets, and Law', *Journal of Early American History* 2019, no. 1 (2019), pp. 33–4.
[101] Brock, *Currency of the American Colonies*, pp. 69–70.
[102] Daniel Vickers, 'Errors Expected: The Culture of Credit in Rural New England, 1750–1800', *The Economic History Review* 63, no. 4 (2010), pp. 1032–57.
[103] Elizabeth E. Dunn, '"Grasping at the Shadow": The Massachusetts Currency Debate, 1690–1751', *The New England Quarterly* 71, no. 1 (1998), p. 60; Schweitzer, *Custom and Contract*, p. 133.

the administrative structure whereby legal title could be made secure and easily proven simply needed to be set up. Thus, in 1713 Massachusetts introduced a land bank where bills of credit were issued as loans against the value of real estate, just as had been done in Scotland, although here the loans made were much smaller and supplied to ordinary farmers.[104] However, since the quality of the security depended on the productive value of the land, which for new land was not always obvious, it was often the case that land was over-leveraged. This was especially true in New England, where land was not generally as good for arable farming as that further south.[105]

This became a problem, because Massachusetts and then Rhode Island began issuing far too many bills of credit. As we saw above, in New England there were £494,922 worth of bills in circulation for a population of 211,100 in 1730. Although the colonial pound was worth less, this still represents about four times as much paper money in circulation than was the case in Scotland in 1755. During King George's war in the 1740s, bill circulation rose to the incredible figure of £4,000,000 compared to a population of about 400,000 in 1748.[106] The result of this was a substantial depreciation in the value of the currency in exchange with London, from £219 Massachusetts to £100 sterling in 1720 to £516 in 1736, and £1,033 in 1750.[107]

Pennsylvania, in contrast to New England, did not establish any banks until the 1720s. This was done after an extensive debate following an economic depression brought on by the effect the South Sea Bubble had on trade with the colony. Here it was successfully argued that a land bank office could engage in liquidity creation to reinvigorate the economy through the stimulation of internal trade. The first bank there was set up in 1723 and was designed from the beginning to be based on loans backed up by landed property. It was called the General Loan Office, and its records show that it made over 3,000 loans between 1724 and 1756 for an average value of £65 13s. Almost all of these were for under £100. The borrower had to show clear title to the land, and the amount lent was usually three times the selling price of the land mortgaged. Interest rates were about 5–6 per cent and any potential default was dealt with by local courts, which had a great deal of discretion to try to avoid

[104] Dunn, 'Massachusetts Currency Debate', pp. 56–7.
[105] Ron Michener, 'Redemption Theories and the Value of American Colonial Paper Money', *Financial History Review* 22, no. 3 (2015), p. 321.
[106] Brock, *Currency of the American Colonies*, pp. 591–3; McCusker and Menard, *Economy of British America*, p. 103.
[107] Schweitzer, *Custom and Contract*, p. 138.

forfeitures.[108] Since the quality of the land was good, it held its value and the currency held its exchange value at around £160 to £100 sterling before 1750.[109]

Benjamin Franklin took a great interest in the Loan Office, and in 1729 published one of his earliest pamphlets, *A Modest Inquiry into the Nature and Necessity of a Paper Currency*, where he claimed that 'Bills issued upon Land are in effect Coined Land'. He also repeated the argument that John Law and others had made previously, that a want of money for wages of labourers and handicraftsmen was an impediment upon economic growth.[110] Later, in 1752, he chaired a committee that reported favourably on the success of the paper currency.[111] Indeed, the capital provided by the Loan Office was used to build mills and other infrastructure. As a result, the population grew at a rate of 4–6 per cent between 1730 and 1760, and Philadelphia rapidly became larger than Boston, and then the second largest city in the British Empire after London.[112] Account books also show that the bills of credit circulated widely and were used by labourers in their transactions.[113]

In London, the Board of Trade remained more responsive to the concerns of English merchants, and would not allow the colonial governments to claim that their currencies were legal tender in the same way that they prevented them from coining their own money – in order to protect the prerogative of the British Crown.[114] Nevertheless, it realised the need for the colonial economies to have something more liquid than book or oral credit, and thus tolerated the de facto legal status of colonial currencies within their borders. The English Treasury also desired to keep gold and silver in England to pay military remittances to the continent, and to help with paper redemption during years of huge tax burdens. The Board of Trade did intervene on some occasions by shipping some Spanish silver to the colonies to help pay for war.[115] But after the huge inflation of currency in New England in the 1740s it had Parliament pass an Act in 1751 outlawing the issuance of any new currencies in New England. The more stable currencies in the middle colonies were excepted until 1764, when the ban was then extended to all

[108] It has been argued that these courts were based more on Quaker meetings than any common law jurisdiction. Schweitzer, *Custom and Contract*, pp. 47–151, 144.
[109] Ibid., p. 137.
[110] Benjamin Franklin, *A Modest Inquiry into the Nature and Necessity of a Paper Currency* (Philadelphia, 1729), pp. 258–9.
[111] Schweitzer, *Custom and Contract*, p. 142. [112] Ibid., pp. 161–7.
[113] Ibid., pp. 133, 141.
[114] Ibid., p. 125; Perkins, 'Fiat Currency', pp. 20–1; Dunn, 'Massachusetts Currency Debate', pp. 58–9.
[115] Perkins, 'Fiat Currency', p. 15.

of the colonies in the Currency Act. But by this time these colonies' economies could not survive without paper currency, and the colonial legislatures continued to issue bills of credit, adding to the tensions that would eventually led to the outbreak of war.[116]

In contrast to the middle and New England colonies, Virginia continued to use tobacco currency throughout the eighteenth century. A positive trade balance also meant that more specie could be imported into the colony, and bills of exchange could be used as currency.[117] Because of the scale of the Virginia tobacco trade with Britain, the merchants there had much more power to block paper currency.[118] When Maryland decided to introduce a paper currency after seeing the benefits of the experience of its northern neighbour, Pennsylvania (by 1770 Baltimore had a population of only 6,000 compared to Philadelphia's 30,000), it took some time before its tobacco currency could be demonetised.[119] The power of British home-based merchants also meant that paper currencies were never successful in Barbados. The planters there were also desperately short of cash and joined together in 1706 with the island's governor and assembly to establish a system of bills of credit that were issued to one-quarter of the value of a planter's land. While some notes were issued, the scheme was immediately opposed by the Royal Africa Company and other merchants in London, and the governor was replaced by the Board of Trade and the paper notes disallowed. All had to be redeemed by 1707.[120] For merchants, trade could be done with bills of exchange to cover the value of slaves the enslaved and commodities imported into the island and sugar exported to England. The island's inhabitants, however, had to use oral credit or sugar as money.[121] Jamaica, because it had a larger export trade with the Spanish colonies, was able to accumulate Spanish dollars, which could be used on the island.[122]

Thus, the American experience varied greatly from colony to colony, with Pennsylvania emulating the Scottish economic success of kickstarting economic growth with new liquidity. In contrast, Massachusetts was burdened by its over-issue of bills and, as a result, Boston lost its role as the mercantile capital of the Thirteen Colonies to New York and Philadelphia. Virginia saw no need for a currency, remaining happy to

[116] Perkins, 'Fiat Currency', pp. 21–3, 26; Grubb, 'Is Paper Money Just Paper Money', Appendix.
[117] Price, *Capital and Credit*, pp. 96–123.
[118] McCusker and Menard, *Economy of British America*, pp. 115, 130, 174, 199.
[119] Ibid., p. 131; Grubb, 'Creating Maryland's Paper Money', pp. 34–58.
[120] Nettles, *Money Supply*, pp. 269–72. [121] Ibid., pp. 203, 208.
[122] Ibid., 203–4, 234–6, 256.

prosper from its tobacco trade.[123] South Carolina, even though it was the second colony to issue paper currency in 1703, badly mismanaged further issues.[124]

In all the colonies the issues were always controlled by the colonial administrations. There was no preference for private order solutions. This was undoubtedly because the most powerful private individuals who had enough existing capital to incorporate were merchants who were generally hostile to paper money. This does not mean there were no attempts to create private banks, but none succeeded.[125] In contrast to Scotland, there was a different dynamic between merchants and landed society. In the former they worked together to make the Bank of Scotland currency work in its early days, but in America those primarily engaged in agriculture or crafts had very different needs from merchants, who were worried about having to store value in a volatile medium that they thought would be less stable than their bills of exchange or gold. This was amplified by the much greater distance to London as a centre of bill discounting, which was months rather than days away, as in the Scottish case.

The experience of the colonies was entirely an outcome of the ideas generated by the pamphlet debate on credit currency, and – like the Scottish experience – it needs to be considered as a part of the financial revolution. We can also say that such local currencies played little *direct* role in facilitating the triangular trade, which was done with barter or bills of exchange. In fact, the overseas merchants involved actually *opposed* local currencies as they did not want to be paid with them. But, undoubtedly, the use of paper currencies did facilitate economic growth and increased consumption of British manufactured goods in mainland America, and much of this growth was linked to supplying goods and services to the slave-based sugar and tobacco plantation export economies.[126]

France

France is the one country outside of British political control where the English discussion about credit currency also had an enormous impact. This is because the government came under the influence of the Scot John Law, one of the more prominent participants in the pamphlet

[123] There exists a vibrant and quite heated debate on the causes of success and failure of the various currencies between Farley Grubb and Ron Michener.
[124] Brock, *Currency of the American Colonies*, pp. 106–8, 114, 116, 122.
[125] Perkins, 'Fiat Currency', pp. 17–20; Dunn, 'Massachusetts Currency Debate', p. 59.
[126] McCusker and Menard, *Economy of British America*, pp. 277–94.

debate, who had been forced to flee Britain after killing an opponent in a duel in London in 1694. The establishment – and eventual failure – of his scheme to undertake a government debt-to-equity swap while at the same time creating a national paper currency is worth examining in brief. It demonstrates the difficulties inherent in creating a national paper currency in an economy much larger than Scotland or any of the American colonies, while being under the influence of a powerful interventionist government.

Even more than was the case for England, the cost of warfare left the French state with enormous burdens. When Louis XIV died in 1715 he left France virtually bankrupt from the cost of the twenty-nine years of war he had initiated in 1672 when he invaded the Dutch Republic. The overall debt of the state was over two billion livres, with interest payments running at 90 million livres per year, and a total state expenditure of 146 million livres. This was the equivalent of about £153,846,154 and £6,923,074, respectively, at contemporary exchange rates.[127] Although France had a large population, it was burdened by an inflexible medieval system of taxation and expenditure. To pay for this, the state could raise about 30 million livres in direct taxes and 60 million livres in indirect taxation, leaving a large deficit. As a result, France had to rely directly on forms of long-term borrowing. This consisted of annuities with an interest rate and the *rentes constituées*. The latter category was formed of loans to the king, whereby the lender received a form of income for life. In the same class as the annuities were the wages of 50,000 public servants that had been sold for immediate sums.[128] In this way, most of the aristocracy, as well as significant numbers of the bourgeoisie, relied on the earnings from this capital to finance a great part of their lifestyle, and thus had no interest in modernisation.

Although most of the French debt was extremely long term, in the midst of continual war, as in England, it was the financing of short-term debt that required immediate attention. One attempt to do this was the issue of paper IOUs, termed *billets de monnie*. These were first issued in 1701 by the French Mint because of a shortage of specie, much of which was being used to pay troops and suppliers in the Lowlands. But financial shortages soon forced the government to expand their issue so that by October 1706 there were 173 million livres worth in circulation, but only

[127] John McCusker, *Money and Exchange in Europe and America, 1600–1775: A Handbook* (Chapel Hill, 1978), p. 95. The exchange however, could be quite volatile.

[128] James Buchan, *John Law: A Scottish Adventurer of the Eighteenth Century* (London, 2018), pp. 119–20; Antoin E. Murphy, *John Law: Economic Theorist and Policy-maker* (Oxford, 1997), p. 133.

of high denomination. These were not the only government paper issued. There was also short-term paper such as bills on the receivers-general, but the *billets* formed the bulk of government paper. Given the state of government finances, they quickly fell to a discount of 50–75 per cent, and were thus not very liquid.[129]

With the death of Louis in 1715, to avoid a default, more serious action was needed. Interest rates on annuities were cut by 1 percentage point, 4,000 offices were suppressed, and the currency was devalued. But to deal with the pressing demands of short-term unpaid debts owed to wartime contractors and suppliers, it has been estimated that another 900 million livres of promissory notes and *billets* were put into circulation – termed the floating debt – that were not linked to any tax revenue.[130] To deal with this, a declaration by the regent reduced 597 million livres of this to 198 million, simply annulling 400 million. A further 250 million livres were converted into a new form of paper state debt, called *billets de état*. This reduction was justified by the creation of the Chamber of Justice to investigate dishonesty and profiteering among the state financiers, and over 8,000 individuals were investigated. These *billets* supposedly carried an interest rate of 4 per cent, but there was no assigned tax revenue to pay this. They were essentially banknotes payable to the bearer and could be used in any payment.[131] However, the *billets de état* fared no better than the *billets de monnie*, and the market marked them down by 50 per cent.[132]

It was against this background that John Law conceptualised a system to deal with the debt. As we saw in Chapter 2, Law, in his *Money and Trade Considered*, was one of the most preceptive writers to have developed William Potter's original idea of the positive relationship between monetary liquidity and economic growth by linking it to the payment of industrial wages.[133] He was also a supporter of the idea that land could be used as security for such new money. However, he saw that the situation in France presented him with an opportunity to establish a similar monopoly institution to the Bank of England, which would fund government debts through share issues based on tax revenue. He proposed this to the regent in 1715 but it was rejected. However, Law was allowed to set up his own private bank to issue notes. In 1716 the General Bank was created and was given a twenty-year monopoly over banknote issue in France. But crucially these notes were to be backed by deposits of specie, not land or taxation. Eventually the bank

[129] Murphy, *John Law*, pp. 116–17. [130] Buchan, *Scottish Adventurer*, p. 120.
[131] Buchan, *Scottish Adventurer*, p. 123. [132] Murphy, *John Law*, pp. 136–8.
[133] See 'The Pamphlet Debate over Currency' in Chapter 2.

was also allowed to issue banknotes against *billets de état* at 50 per cent of their face value. This bank began with a small amount of capital, but by 1718 had issued 148,560,000 livres worth of notes – the equivalent of about £7,400,000. These notes were issued in denominations of 10, 100, and 1,000 ecus (worth three livres each), although no records exist as to how many of each were printed. Thus, the smallest note was roughly equivalent to £1 sterling.

In 1717, Law created the Company of the West, a monopoly trading company based on exclusive privileges to settle and trade with the territory of Louisiana, which had recently been ceded to the Crown in lieu of tax payment by a financier. He did this with the purpose of imitating the intentions of the London South Sea Company as both a profit-making enterprise and an institution designed to absorb government debt through an equity swap scheme by converting it into company shares. However, unlike the South Sea Company, he also planned to integrate his liquidity-issuing bank into the scheme at arm's length, with the theory being that its banknotes could be used to pay for shares to help fund the purchase of government debt and to generate more economic activity to make the size of the government debt less threatening to investors and the economy. Crucially, the success of the system would depend on accurate macro-economic control of the issue of banknotes.

If this had been possible, the scheme might have succeeded, but it was brought down because in order to gain permission to integrate his bank into the Company of the West, he had to sign up to the government priority of debt management over monetary policy, when the priority should have been the other way around. The debt was simply too big.[134] In addition, the issuing of the stock in Law's Company of the West kindled a speculative fever that had been encouraged by projectors of new companies since the 1690s. We have already seen this phenomenon at work earlier in Scotland with the Darien Company, and in England with South Sea Company shares, which occurred at roughly the same time that Law's scheme was attracting investors. People were engaging in the new activity of buying and selling stocks in rapidly changing markets, hoping for an easy gain by playing the market. In 1720 the large amounts of paper government debts in England, France, and Holland provided more fuel for speculation than ever before, and the temptation to play with fire was irresistible.

The chronological events of the progress of the scheme have been described in detail by Antoin Murphy, and more recently by James

[134] Murphy, *John Law*, p. 122.

Buchan, and can only be summarised here in brief.[135] It began when, in January 1719, Law's General Bank was made a Royal Bank and Law became a part of the government's monetary policy decision-making. The Company of the West was merged with the Company of the Indies and China in May 1719, to form the Company of the Indies, which eventually became known popularly as the Mississippi Company. He then began issuing shares and new banknotes. By August he persuaded the regent and *Conseil de Finance* to allow the new company to take over the whole national debt of 1.2 billion livres. The share price rapidly rose from around 2,500 livres to over 9,000 between August and December. It has been estimated that shares purchased for 221,500,000 livres in August had become worth eight billion livres by the end of November, and that the value of banknotes put into circulation was 640,000,000 livres.[136] Estimates of the value of specie circulating at the time vary, but it seems to have been around 500,000,000 livres.[137]

By the end of the year, private dealers were contracting to buy future options for share purchases at prices up to 15,000 livres. Law believed that much of this was being conducted by foreign speculators in Holland and England. Whether true or not, in order to dampen this speculation, which he also thought was increasing the price of the shares too much, Law introduced a type of company option known as *les primes*, by which through the payment of 1,000 livres one bought the option to purchase 10,000 during the next six months. He thought that by destroying the private futures market he would be better able to control the rise of share prices, but the demand for *primes* by a public that expected price rises became enormous and Law issued too many – 300 million worth, entitling the owners to purchase three billion livres worth of shares! This had the immediate effect of causing a fall in the old share issues – termed *filles*, *petite filles* and *cinq cents* – as they were sold to buy the new *primes* and the share price fell in January at one point to just over 7,000 livres.[138] Although the price recovered to above 9,000 livres, it never went above 10,000 again, thus leaving Law in a predicament about what to do to sustain the price of the vast share options he had just issued.

The path he chose proved to be the undoing of the whole system, but was based on the fact that as a government banker he had to focus first on the sustainability of the state debt, and this meant supporting the value of the shares rather than his banknote issue. To do this he decided on the unorthodox solution of encouraging the use of banknotes by first reducing the use of specie, and then banning it altogether! In France the price

[135] See footnote 128. [136] Murphy, *John Law*, pp. 188–211.
[137] Buchan, *Scottish Adventurer*, p. 210 [138] Murphy, *John Law*, pp. 214–17.

of gold and silver, as well as the face value of its coins, could be changed instantly by a government proclamation known as an *arret*. Between the end of January and the beginning of March, *arrets* limited the movement of specie, and then how much could be held by individuals to only 500 livres. The louis d'or and the ecu were also devalued. The effect on actual transactions was, of course, imperfect, but France did have a fairly extensive system of police, whose main function was market regulation, but who could be used for currency enforcement.[139] This stood in sharp contrast to England, where John Locke's argument was that government proclamations setting the value of money were futile in the face of market forces, and the value of banknotes and shares became secured by their ability to always be converted to gold based on its fluctuating market price.[140]

To replace specie, Law began printing more banknotes, and by May it is estimated that there were 2.1 billion banknotes in circulation. Most of these new notes were of high valuations of 1,000 and 10,000 livres since they were meant to be used to buy shares.[141] Thus, the total value of paper money (stocks plus notes) amounted to about four billion livres. In March the system seemed to be working, and the public was content to use the paper notes instead of coins, but Law was worried that there was too much paper in relation to the economy, and on 21 May 1720 issued a new *arret* ordering the devaluation of the price of shares and the value of banknotes by an immediate 20 per cent, together with planned future devaluations of almost 50 per cent. This, unsurprisingly, created a panic and threatened a run on the bank, and it is still debated as to why Law attempted such drastic action. Some have suggested that he was pressured by elements in the government, influenced by a group of financiers who had benefited from the old system and wanted Law's bank to fail. But whatever the case, it cannot be denied that he acted very often too hastily to use the immense legislative power the French *arret* system gave him to change macro-economic policy on a dime.

To stave off further runs on the bank, the *arret* of 21 May had to be repealed on 1 June, and through the summer Law improvised various measures in an attempt to save the system, including offering annuities and creating interest-earning bank accounts to attract potentially 600 million livres of the notes to remove them from circulation. But these efforts failed to stop the decline in the value of the banknotes. By July they had fallen by 46 per cent in relation to silver, and by September 56 per

[139] Murphy, *John Law*, pp. 218–26.
[140] See 'The Pamphlet Debate over Currency' in Chapter 2.
[141] Murphy, *John Law*, pp. 211–29; Buchan, *Scottish Adventurer*, p. 282.

cent.[142] An *arret* of 15 September demonetised 10,000 and 1,000 livre banknotes and ordered them to be publicly burned. An order was then made stating that 10, 50, or 100 livre notes could only be used when 50 per cent of transaction value was made in specie. Most seriously, bank accounts were reduced to one-quarter of their value. This was a partial liquidation of the system by decree. By the end of October banknotes were only worth 22 per cent of silver and by December 12 per cent.[143] The price of Mississippi Company shares likewise fell to below 5,000 livres by the end of June.[144] As a result of the expansion of banknotes to save the share price, both the rise and fall of Mississippi Company shares was not as great as the equivalent rise and fall of South Sea Company shares in England, which occurred a few months later.[145] However, the social effect was much more catastrophic because it affected almost everyone in the economy, who had been using Royal Bank notes, rather than a small section of wealthy investors. But in another way it was similar to the South Sea Bubble, in that the Crown debt was reduced to a fraction of its former level by its conversion into Mississippi Company shares and then into banknotes. In essence, everyone who lost part of their initial investment paid off a fraction of Louis XIV's debt. The size of this loss, which was the equivalent of £500 million sterling, dwarfed the losses of the government creditors in England.[146]

Unfortunately, how people actually used the paper notes of both the General and Royal Bank over the four short years of their existence has been overshadowed by the audacity of Law's scheme and the peregrinations of his increasingly hectic and desperate macro-economic mismanagement. In the end, both Law's scheme and the South Sea Company were necessary to prevent outright state bankruptcies in France and England. However, in England the Bank of England directors managed to keep their private bank at arm's length, and it fortuitously survived and was able to ameliorate the losses of those who converted their state annuities into South Sea stock, whereas the Royal Bank was sacrificed by Law to save the Mississippi Company stock, leading to much deeper economic losses. It also meant a return to the older system of state finance, and a suspicion of forms of paper money.

In 1720, France probably had a population of around twenty million, or about four times the size of England. Estimates of the amount of

142 Murphy, *John Law*, p. 294. 143 Ibid., pp. 294–6, 306. 144 Ibid., pp. 303–4.

145 The high point of share valuation was £1,000 in August 1720, which fell back to £100 by December.

146 P. G. M Dickson, *The Financial Revolution in England 1688–1756* (London, 1967), pp. 153–5, 176.

specie in the country range from the equivalent of £25–50 million, which implies there was more per capita in France. But the Bank of England took a conservative approach by tying its paper to gold convertibility and leaving the creation of small paper instruments to private individuals who largely secured them on land. Their share issues were also secured by a tax system that had already been reformed and was accepted by those paying it.[147] In contrast, Law, who had initially been one of the most vociferous proponents of land banks, ended up creating his paper money with little security apart from the value of the Mississippi Company shares, which were in turn dependent on future trade and reform of the French tax system. He then actively legislated to prevent convertibly of his banknotes to gold or silver.

It has often been said that after the collapse of Law's bank money, France experienced a long-term collapse of confidence in both public and private credit, and that capital markets remained underdeveloped compared to London or Amsterdam. However, Phillip Hoffman, Giles Postel-Vinay, and Jean-Laurent Rosenthal have argued that this view is much exaggerated since France had a vibrant credit market organised through the notarial system. Almost all of the long-term lending was secured by collateral, which mostly took the form of land. This is perhaps one reason why Law did not attempt to issue any currency secured by land, as so much was already mortgaged.[148]

Hoffman, Vinay and Rosenthal have estimated that these notaries were dealing with about 60,000 loans per year in Paris, of which 15,000–30,000 were new contracts each year.[149] The average loan size between 1662 and 1700 varied from 4,000 to 5,000 livres.[150] Although the number of notarial offices was limited in Paris, in France as a whole by the eighteenth century there were tens of thousands of notaries.[151] In the seventeenth and eighteenth centuries, Parisian notaries managed government borrowing, but primarily arranged long-term private loans called *rentes perpétuelles* and the *rente viagère*, which were both types of annuities. With the first, the lender surrendered the principal for an income stream of fixed annual interest payments that would last indefinitely, even through generations, until the borrower decided to pay back the principal in full. The second was similar, but only lasted until one or more individuals specified in the contract died. There was a third type of loan called

[147] C. D Chandaman, *The English Public Revenue, 1660–1688* (Oxford, 1975); Stephen Pierpoint, *The Success of English Land Tax Administration, 1643–1733* (London, 2018).

[148] Philip Hoffman, Gilles Postel-Vinay, and Jean-Laurent Rosenthal, *Priceless Markets: The Political Economy of Credit in Paris, 1660–1870* (Chicago, 2000).

[149] Ibid., pp. 26, 15–17, 32, 45–6, 52. [150] Ibid., p. 52. [151] Ibid., p. 26.

obligations, which were simply recorded promissory notes, but they remained in the minority of recorded loans until after the Revolution.[152] Almost all of the long-term lending was secured by collateral, which mostly took the form of land.[153]

This system was certainly a very stable institutional means of turning savings into capital, and thus it is perhaps not surprising that it was Turgot who first theorised about the relation of saving to capital as a concept.[154] Notaries were also a very successful institution for overcoming informational asymmetries and thus reducing the cost of the risk posed by defaults. But what they certainly did not do was to create liquid circulating capital.[155] We know from the work of Laurence Fontaine, Julie Hardwick, and others that small-scale informal credit issued by shopkeepers and others who sold on the market was common in France, as in England. Much of these debts also ended up in the courts when borrowers were unable to pay, although we don't have as much quantitative evidence as exists for England.[156] However, there is evidence that notaries also wrote obligations for small amounts that did not have to be entered in their official records and were therefore cheaper.[157]

The evidence from court cases also reveals that, besides obligations, there were a variety of notes such as *cedulas*, *memoires*, and *billets*. Such notes could vary from a few livres to around 150.[158] In a sample of probate inventories examined by Daniel Roche for working wage-earning artisans in Paris, of those who left assets of 3,000 livres (*c.*£125) or more, 33 per cent consisted of promissory notes and bonds in the period 1695–1715. This was in comparison to *rentes*, which formed 28 per cent, and other debts worth only 4 per cent. Their household goods were only worth 5 per cent of the value of their assets. Over time, however, this group transferred much of their financial assets to the less liquid *rents*, which formed 64 per cent of their assets by 1775–1790, compared to only 16 per cent in promissory notes. Those who left less than 500 livres (£20) had many fewer assets in both periods, and only 6 per cent consisted of *rentes* and notes. For these poorer individuals, almost all of their wealth

[152] Ibid., pp. 15–17, 46.
[153] The loans of some provincial notaries have been studied by Elise M Dermineur, 'Rethinking Debt: The Evolution of Private Credit Markets in Preindustrial France', *Social Science History* 42, no. 2 (2018), pp. 317–42.
[154] Muldrew, 'Self-Control and Savings', pp. 75–6.
[155] Hoffman *et al.*, *Priceless Markets*, pp. 11–20.
[156] Laurence Fontaine, *History of Peddlers in Europe* (Cambridge, 1996), pp. 121–39; Julie Hardwick, *Family Business: Litigation and the Political Economies of Daily Life in Early Modern France* (Oxford, 2009), pp. 58–74, 132–7.
[157] Hoffman *et al.*, *Priceless Markets*, p. 15.
[158] Hardwick, *Family Business*, pp. 140–1.

consisted of goods. Poorer servants, however, held 15–20 per cent of their assets as promissory notes.[159] From this evidence it appears that informal paper existed in France, but work still needs to be done on how it circulated.

Overall, the failure of Law's scheme offers us a compelling reason why paper note issue failed when it was tied to the hungry demands of servicing state debt instead of land. A similar problem occurred in Massachusetts, and in England with the South Sea Company. However, in the latter case the shares issued were confined to a small segment of the wealthy holders of long-term state debt, and the consequences of their collapse in value could be managed. The overview here has shown that currency creation was at least an Atlantic phenomenon, and we have also seen how the establishment of formal banks aided the development of consumption in the American colonies and thus helped to promote Atlantic trade. In Scotland they also aided in the development of the linen industry. We now need to return to England to examine how informal paper currency issue there morphed into the development of country banks to help industry after 1750, before ending the book with a new examination of Adam Smith's ideas about banking and national wealth.

[159] Daniel Roche, *The People of Paris: An Essay in Popular Culture in the 18th Century* (Leamington Spa, 1987), pp. 80–2.

10 The Emergence of Local Bankers in England: Savings and Adam Smith's 'Capitalism'

Deciding when to end a narrative involving the interplay of a large number of slowly changing social institutions and beliefs can never be clear-cut or tidy. I've chosen 1760 as an approximate date to end this story because it was about this time that various local shopkeepers and traders involved in the issuing of local notes and exchange of inland bills began to call themselves bankers in England. It was also roughly when the middle class, discussed in Chapter 8, began to emerge, and about the time when the British Parliament attempted to ban the issuance of paper currency in the Thirteen Colonies, contributing to the tensions that would lead to the American Revolution. Finally, Adam Smith began to work on the *Wealth of Nations* around 1760, in which he would use the example of the history of Scottish banking as a lynchpin for his theories about the formation of capital. Thus, to conclude my narrative, I will briefly describe how a banking system emerged in England out of the system I have described here, before saying something about how Adam Smith should be seen in the context of the culture of capital as it had developed up until the point of his writing. Then, in a short conclusion, I will outline what I think we can learn about interpreting economic change from the story that has been told here.

In Chapter 3 we saw how central the inland bill was to the development of a national financial system based on local traders, such as the shopkeeper Thomas Turner, who used local notes to run his shop, but then used bills of exchange drawn on London to make his wholesale purchases, and often to obtain coins needed for day-to-day transactions. Large London brokers such as the grocers Margesson and Collinson, whom Turner relied on, were essentially acting as bankers, as well as dealers in material goods. Unfortunately, to date, no records of any such businesses have been identified, let alone studied, and because early tradesmen–brokers did not call themselves bankers it is impossible to know how many there were, or what their level of business was. However, as also discussed in Chapter 3, the business of the Post Office was prodigious. By 1720, over ten million letters were being sent every year, which must have included, probably, millions of bills of exchange. Another thing that hasn't been investigated is the role the Bank of England increasingly played in discounting bills. Systematic data on the Bank's discounting operations do not survive, but John Clapham was able to identify some sporadic reports that indicate a large increase in such activity. For 1699, the data reveal that about £1,000 of bills were being discounted every day. By 1730 the median day's volume was over £10,000, and by 1760 it was common to have days when over £100,000 worth of bills were discounted.[1] If by 1730 the Bank was discounting over £3,000,000 of bills every year, private trade must have been many times higher.[2]

In the early eighteenth century, the term 'banker' to denote the activities we associate now with banking – taking deposits, making loans, issuing notes, discounting bills, or arranging mortgages – seems to have been confined to London. Most of these were the goldsmith and scrivener-bankers discussed in Chapter 2. These included Hoare's, Coutts, and Child's banks.[3] While such institutions inevitably must have discounted some bills for tradesmen, their businesses mainly revolved around investment in government finance and remittances from agricultural landlords.[4] Presumably the linguistic heritage of the word bank from the Italian activity of money changing meant that this is what it referred to, and as a result remained confined to the capital.

When tradesmen and manufacturers who engaged in banking activities, both in London and in the counties, first started to call themselves bankers is very difficult to know, as only scattered references exist. To give one example, Thomas Smith of Nottingham set up business as a mercer in 1658. Although little is known about his mercery business, Nottingham was evolving as the centre of the hosiery trade and stocking knitting industry, and as such required banking activities. Later family letters indicate that Smith began banking activities around 1688 for local stocking frame masters in order to provide them with a means to pay workers, and as a way to remit and receive payments from London.

[1] John Clapham, *The Bank of England: A History* (Cambridge, 1944), I, p. 126.

[2] Using the Bank's year end ledger rather than minutes, which Clapham used, Paul Kosmetatos estimated there were *c.* £1.5–3 million worth of bills discounted by the Bank yearly between 1760 and 1785. Paul Kosmetatos, *The 1772–3 British Credit Crisis* (Basingstoke, 2018) pp. 117–18.

[3] D. M Joslin, 'London Private Bankers, 1720–1785', *The Economic History Review* 7, no. 2 (1954), pp. 167–86.

[4] Peter Temin and Hans-Joachim Voth, *Prometheus Shackled: Goldsmith Banks and England's Financial Revolution after 1700* (New York, 2012), pp. 125–47.

A legal case from 1711 shows how Smith merged his bill remittance business with that of issuing notes. In a deposition, he stated that he

> actes in the nature of a Banker, and returnes great sums of money to London, and from thence and diverse other places in this Kingdom; and also for several years past, and his father many years before him, hath used to take in and receive great sums of money of diverse persons and upon receipt thereof to give notes under his hand for the same, thereby promising to pay the said sums so received to the person authorized in the money, or the Bearer of the note upon demand; and in case any Note so given by this Deponent [Smith] be produced and endorsed only with the name of the person to whom it is payable. Upon delivering the said Note this Deponent pays the same to the Bearer; so that sometimes this Deponent's Notes are paid by endorsement to several persons before the same is demanded of this Deponent.[5]

This example not only shows that he was acting as a banker, but also provides valuable evidence of how at this early date he was already combining local note issue with bill remittance to London. However, it was not until he entered a formal partnership agreement with his brother, who had moved to London and become a goldsmith banker, in 1758 that the business formally became a bank.[6]

When Edmund Burke arrived in England from Ireland in 1750, he claimed that there were not a dozen banking shops outside London. Some of the others we know of besides Smith's were: Praed's of Truro, Fector's of Dover, Wood's of Gloucester, and Gurney's of Norwich. In the court of bankruptcy there were only eight failures of people calling themselves bankers from outside London between 1710 and 1760, compared to many more in London and even more London goldsmiths.[7] However, in a pamphlet written in 1762, advocating the creation of a Bank of Parliament to take over the issue of paper currency, the author made a rough estimate that there were 400–500 individuals around the country acting as bankers.[8] But, for whatever reason, from roughly 1760 onwards, it became increasingly common for individuals and partnerships who had been banking under other occupational titles to abandon any remaining activities related to trade and become solely occupied with banking. This was possibly due to the great increase in government debt created by the Seven Years' War, for in this decade the bill-discounting activity of the Bank of England rose to over £30 million per year. But

[5] J. A. S. L. Leighton-Boyce, *Smiths, the Bankers, 1658–1958* (London, 1958), pp. 7, 16–17.
[6] Ibid., pp. 1, 53–4.
[7] L. S. Pressnell, *County Banking in the Industrial Revolution* (Oxford, 1956), p. 4.
[8] Clapham, *Bank of England*, I, pp. 99, 157; *An Essay on Paper Circulation* (London, 1764).

economic growth almost certainly also played a role. By 1784, Bailey's *British Directory of Trades* listed 119 banks in England.[9]

The very small number of such institutions that have left records have been examined by Leslie Pressnell in his classic survey of the rise of county banking from 1760 to the 1820s. According to him, two main groups predominated in this transition: industrialists and wholesalers.[10] We have already examined how wholesalers like the grocers Margesson and Collinson, and Joseph Symson the Kendal mercer, acted as nodes between localities and London in networks of bill exchange. In Liverpool, ten out of fourteen early banks were formed by merchants and wholesalers, and in Newcastle half were.[11] Various grocers also acted as bankers, such as William Miller, who became a founding partner in the first Bristol bank in 1750.[12]

Overall, the main reason for creating a banking business was not simply the practice of bill exchange. What was just as crucial was its combination with the need to create local paper money for wage payments, which the increasingly rapid industrialisation of the eighteenth century depended on. It was industrialists, or shopkeepers dealing in the products of industry, who found that the sheer scale of the need for making local payments meant that it was more profitable to go into banking on its own rather than combining it with productive activities. The expansion of the cloth industry also meant there were probably 1–1.5 million women and girls spinning wool alone by the 1770s.[13] To this we would need to add cotton spinners and probably over 100,000 weavers, combers, winders, and other cloth-finishing workers. Other industries, such as the Birmingham and Sheffield metal works and mining, were also expanding their workforces. Shopkeepers collected cash from their sales, which they sold on to employers to help pay wages.[14]

A very early, and in many ways pathbreaking, example was Ambrose Crowley, the large-scale iron manufacturer with major works on the Derwent River south of Newcastle. An inventory of 1728 valued his assets at £153,000, but he is most well known for the survival of what is termed his 'law book' – a series of incredibly detailed rules begun

[9] Pressnell, *County Banking*, p. 44. [10] Ibid., pp. 12–14, 47. [11] Ibid., p. 49.
[12] Ibid., p. 46.
[13] Jane Humphries and Benjamin Schneider, 'Spinning the Industrial Revolution', *The Economic History Review* 72, no. 1 (2019) p. 139, n. 59; Craig Muldrew, 'The "Ancient Distaff" and "Whirling Spindle": Measuring the Contribution of Spinning to Household Earnings and the National Economy in England, 1550–1770', *Economic History Review* 65, no. 2 (2012), pp. 518–19.
[14] Pressnell, *County Banking*, p. 45.

around 1700 that attempted to implement a 'modern' type of factory discipline and accountable organisation at a very early date.[15] The law book goes into great detail on how the value of different types of work were to be reckoned on a weekly basis.[16] But in order to reduce the complexity of such reckonings and to make them more amenable to central accounting, he attempted to forbid lending money or equipment to his workmen, which he claimed made them 'negligent, extravagant and delayed their reckonings' and which 'brought disorder upon the Cashier, by answering the workmen's solicitations in lending and correcting payments'.[17] Crowley realised that to prevent this he would have to pay regular wages. But the local supply of money was not enough for an organisation of such scale. In 1700, in a desperate attempt to find copper coins, he instructed a servant that the next time he went to Newcastle, to 'goeth to all the retail shops in his way' and to offer 4d., 6d., or 8d. premium on each pound's worth of copper he could buy.[18]

To resolve this problem, as early as 1699, he decided to issue what he termed current bills to be issued as a form of cash payment for wages and other things. The current bills were issued on printed forms from books with counterfoils like those of the Banks of England and Scotland: both bill and counterfoil were to bear 'numbers and other characters'. From the outset, Crowley resolved that 'they may be vallued in all places better than money'. He followed the Bank of England's practice and resolved 'not to give out any of the Current Bills till money be first laid by and secured for the punctual payment of them … in Specie and not by Bank or Goldsmith notes'. The bills could be cashed either at the works in County Durham or at his London offices. It seems clear that they were issued for particular amounts rather than round figures like Scottish notes. Although none of these notes have survived, nor have any accounts concerning them, the company minutes suggest they were successful and worked much like informal notes of hand. Johnathan Swift wrote later of these bills that:

> In the several towns and villages where he dealt, and many miles round, he gave notes, instead of money, from twopence to twenty shillings, which passed current in all shops and markets, as well as in houses, where meat or drink was sold.[19]

15 M. W. Flinn (ed.), *The Law Book of the Crowley Ironworks* (Durham, 1952), pp. xix, xxv–xxvi.

16 Ibid., pp. 133–9.

17 Ibid., pp. 66, 71, 128, 139–42.

18 Ibid., pp. 50–6. In addition to prevent borrowing because of poverty, he set up his own poor relief system (p. 154ff.).

19 M. W. Flinn, *Men of Iron: The Crowleys in the Early Iron Industry* (Edinburgh, 1962), pp. 178–82.

Crowley's example shows that, although it is their provision of fixed investment capital that has attracted most of the attention of historians, one of the main purposes behind the establishment of industrial banks was to provide small circulating notes and drafts for the payment of wages. By the mid-century, industrial banks were being set up in increasing numbers in places such as Birmingham, Cornwall (for mining), Durham, and Manchester, many of which issued small notes of values of £1 or as low as 10, 5, or even 2½ shillings.[20] One Newcastle cobbler even issued a note for two pence![21] Such payments were most common for paying wages in textile manufacturing areas. In Lancashire, banks circulated bills and bank drafts as currency rather than issuing notes.[22]

The use of the majority of such notes, however, was set up in the banker's favour, as they required that the bearer bring change in silver for a guinea if their notes were of a smaller value. This was done as a result of the shortage of small change, and also allowed the banks to issue a lot of small notes beyond what they could meet in payments from their cash reserves. According to Adam Smith, this was the main weakness of the early banking system in Scotland and England:

> Where the issuing of bank notes for such very small sums is allowed and commonly practiced, many mean people are both enabled and encouraged to become bankers. A person whose promissory note for five pounds, or even for twenty shillings, would be rejected by every body, will get it to be received without scruple when it is issued for so small a sum as a sixpence. But the frequent bankruptcies to which such beggarly bankers must be liable, may occasion a very considerable inconveniency, and sometimes even a very great calamity to many poor people who had received their notes in payment.[23]

As a result of this subjection of 'the poorer sort of manufacturers, Artificers, Labourers ... to great extortion and abuse', a bill was passed in 1777 preventing the issuing of notes below £5 in value, which lasted until the gold suspension period beginning in 1797.[24] After that date, employers had to rely on a large increase in the production of private copper and lead tokens.[25]

[20] Pressnell, *County Banking*, pp. 143, 16–18.
[21] George Unwin, *Samuel Oldknow and the Arkwrights: The Industrial Revolution at Stockport and Marple*, 2nd ed. (Manchester, 1968), p. 179.
[22] Pressnell, *County Banking*, p. 19.
[23] Adam Smith, *An Inquiry into the Nature and Causes of the Wealth of Nations*, ed. R. H. Campbell, A. S. Skinner, and W. B. Todd (Oxford, 1976), I , pp. 323, 292ff. Hereafter WN.
[24] Pressnell, *County Banking*, pp. 16, 144.
[25] George Selgin, *Good Money: Birmingham Button Makers, the Royal Mint, and the Beginnings of Modern Coinage, 1775–1821* (Ann Arbor, 2008), pp. 120ff.

Smith's example shows that there were limits to the amount of paper currency a local economy could absorb when the workforce was large compared to the local population. The early factory owner, and friend and associate of Richard Arkwright, Samuel Oldknow of Stockport, was already employing over 450 weavers in 1786, and many spinners. His first factory, built in Mellor, was finished in 1790 and created work for 2,000 people. To deal with such a large workforce, he paid his workers partially in receipts of paper money. Despite this system, Oldknow still provided houses, milk, coals, meat, and beds, the cost of which was deducted from the wages before they were paid to save having to issue too many notes.[26] He also had connections with a firm of bankers in Derby who supplied him with cash in order to help pay wages in cash when his workers needed it.

The Fiscal Monetary State

The need for some amount of ready money to circulate together with paper notes when large workforces were employed meant that many early industrialists became revenue collectors to obtain such cash. There was a continual rise in the size of the national debt because of the cost of warfare. By 1720 it stood at £50 million, and after the war of the Austrian Succession £76 million. This then rose to £131 million in 1763 and £245 million by 1783.[27] Since the security of all this borrowing was based on future taxes raised to pay for the interest on the debt, taxation was continuous and heavy by European standards. By 1705, over £5 million was being collected every year on average, which had risen to £6 million by the 1730s and over £8 million by the 1760s.[28] As John Brewer has shown, this was largely achieved through increasing taxation of consumption through the excise tax. By 1708 there were 50 collectors, 199 supervisors, and 1,810 local gaugers involved in the county administration of the excise tax. This number grew to over 3,000 by 1763.[29] There were also collections of the land tax every year, although because Parliament was largely composed of landowners the amount collected did not rise so steeply over time compared to the excise. There were about fifty receivers-general for the land tax, together with numerous deputy-receivers and sub-distributors and parish

[26] Unwin, *Samuel Oldknow*, pp. 42–50. 70–1.
[27] John Brewer, *The Sinews of Power: War, Money and the English State, 1688–1783* (London, 1994), pp. 174.
[28] Patrick K. O'Brien, 'The Political Economy of British Taxation, 1660–1815', *The Economic History Review* 41, no. 1 (1988), p. 3.
[29] Brewer, *Sinews of Power*, pp. 96–7, 104–5.

collectors.[30] Finally, customs duty collected amounted to £500,000–1,000,000 each year before 1750.

Since returning all of these small payments to London every year would have been so cumbersome as to be almost impossible, in order for the fiscal state to grow it needed to tap into the system of inland bill remittance to London as much as possible by using tradesmen as regional receivers of local collection. In this way, the value of taxes could be returned to London as bills of exchange, which could then be discounted with suppliers to the Army, Navy and Royal Court, or with London tradesmen acting as bankers.[31] The advantage of such a system was that coins and small local bills collected as taxes could be kept within the local community and recirculated much faster.[32] John Child, who was the receiver for Wiltshire in the early eighteenth century, for instance, was the brother of Sir Francis Child, who was a prominent London banker at the time.[33]

Industrialists such as clothiers were just as important. Thomas Marsden (discussed in Chapter 3) of Bolton and Nathaniel Mollineux of West Houghton, who were engaged in the fustian trade, were both 'returners of revenue' in the late seventeenth century. Joseph Berwick, a Worcester draper, was receiver-general of the land tax for the county for several years before he formally entered banking in 1781, after many years of informally remitting bills to London. In 1780, the first report of the Revenue Inquiry listed at least six receivers-general of the land tax who can be identified as bankers, and a further six who were to enter banking within the next dozen years.[34]

In order to obtain the specie he needed to pay his weavers in the 1710s, the mercer Joseph Symson of Kendal (examined in Chapter 3) formed a close relationship with the collectors of the excise for Kendal and Thirsk, and three successive holders of this post made deposits of their collection with him, which he then remitted to London by bill. He placed orders with weavers, who because of high demand were able to demand ready money instead of credit when selling their work.[35] He was friends with the Westmoreland tax commissioner, Alan Chambre, Sir Richard

[30] Pressnell, *County Banking*, p. 57.

[31] Aaron Graham, 'Military Contractors and the Money Markets, 1700–15', in Aaron Graham and Patrick Walsh (eds.), *The British Fiscal-Military States, 1660–c.1783* (Abingdon, 2016), pp. 83–112.

[32] Pressnell, *County Banking*, pp. 56, 62.

[33] Temin and Voth, *Prometheus Shackled*, 68ff.

[34] Pressnell, *County Banking*, pp. 60–1.

[35] S. D. Smith, *The Letter Book of Joseph Symson of Kendal 1711–1720* (London, 2001). Letter 86 clearly refers to weavers seeking the highest price through competition between cloth purchasers. See also pp. 41, 45, 60, 134, 501.

Sandford (master of the Mint), and William Ashurst, who were all in positions to appoint excise receivers.[36] Symson remitted a total of £1,108 of excise collections in bills of exchange drawn on London directly, and more could have been discounted locally.[37] This figure represents 6.4 per cent of his bills to London, which suggests it could have been quite easily absorbed by the London market.

As noted above, Symson needed specie because the local weavers had the ability to demand immediate payment for their work. Although Symson never mentioned making any payments directly to weavers themselves, he clearly used his position to become a local de facto banker – collecting local payments in coin and converting their value into bills of exchange.

In a less economically developed region it could be more difficult to find enough businesses to facilitate the movement of tax receipts to London. This can be gleaned from the correspondence of Sir James Lowther, the great early eighteenth-century Cumbrian coal merchant responsible for the development of Whitehaven. Rural Cumberland remained one of the poorest areas of England in the eighteenth century, and as a result there was a competition between the various tax receivers there and Lowther to find enough discounters for their bills in London. In the 1730s, for instance, some collectors were sent to Manchester and Leeds to see what remittances could be had there. Lowther used his wealth and power to place clients of his as collectors and pressured them to use the more traditional drovers to remit the tax money to London, thus avoiding the Whitehaven market, with unfortunate results for two of them who went bankrupt. It was not until the north-east to France tobacco re-export trade opened up in the 1740s that the pool of remittance opportunities was expanded sufficiently in London to enable both tax and business bills from Whitehaven to be drawn on London through commercial markets.[38]

Thomas Turner, the Sussex shopkeeper, was also the local sub-collector of the land and window tax from 1760 to 1766, and before this he did the accounts for the then-collectors gratis in anticipation of some mutual favours, although he complained that the collectors did not even pay for the paper they used.[39] The following passage shows how coins were collected:

[36] Ibid., pp. lxvii–lxix. [37] Ibid., p. cxxviii.

[38] J. V. Beckett, *Coal and Tobacco: The Lowthers and the Economic Development of West Cumberland, 1660–1760* (Cambridge, 1981), pp. 115–18.

[39] David Vaisey (ed.), *The Diary of Thomas Turner* (Oxford, 1985), pp. 10, 45, 47. Hereafter, Turner, *Diary*.

Fri. 5 June [1761] … In the forenoon delivered to Tho. Durrant the following cash in order for him to carry to Maresfield to pay the general receiver of the land tax, viz., 6 thirty-six-shilling pieces, 4 moidores, 83 guineas, 4 eighteen-shilling pieces, 2 nine-shilling pieces, 2 half do., 9 shillings, 25 half guineas, [Total] £121 i7s. bd. I also gave him besides 8 half-guineas and 1 guinea to exchange if any of the money should be refused.[40]

The process by which a retailer or clothier transitioned from being a tradesman to a full-time banker can be explored in detail for a slightly later period by examining the diary of James Oakes, a Sussex yarn maker and wholesaler residing in Bury St. Edmunds, who subsequently developed into a country banker. He joined the existing company of his Uncle Orbell Ray as an apprentice, and later became partner before inheriting the whole firm in 1768. In 1767 the company had a capital value of about £20,000 and an annual net profit of over £1,650.[41] Of this income, £400 and £575 were taken out by Orbell Ray and Oakes, respectively. Since no comparable records survive after this date, we cannot know how much income Oakes made on his own after his partner died a year later, but it would have been around £1,000. By the 1790s his business consisted of buying largely long-staple Lincolnshire wool from various markets and Stourbridge fair. He had it sorted, scoured, and combed in his own specially built premises in Bury. At a later date he also built workmen's cottages for thirty of his woolcombers. But the reason why he needed ready money was to pay an enormous number of spinners. By 1790 he was employing around 50 combers who would have provided enough wool to employ at least 1,500 spinners spread throughout the county. Oakes hired agents to deliver his wool, collect yarn, and pay wages.[42]

His ability to pay so many people was helped by the fact that he was appointed receiver-general of the land tax for the Western Division of Suffolk in 1787. Before this the position had been held for thirty-four years by Thomas Fenn, a local bay maker who also eventually branched into banking. Oakes' comments in his diary make clear how useful being a collector was for someone employing so many workers. To obtain the position he spent a lot of effort helping his patron, the Duke of Grafton, with local electioneering. The receivership was a strenuous job that first required a bond of £21,000 signed by sureties.[43] It required travelling throughout the division to receive money from the local collectors, who were not supposed to travel more than 10 miles because of the amount of

[40] Ibid., p. 226.
[41] Jane Fiske (ed.), *The Oakes Diaries: Business, Politics and the Family in Bury St. Edmunds 1778–1827* (Stowmarket, 1990), I, pp. 4–5, 17, 42.
[42] Ibid., pp. 27–34. [43] Ibid., pp. 55–60.

cash they were carrying, as there was no allowance for loss. The balancing of the accounts was also a very stressful business that needed to be completed under time pressure. He reported that on one occasion he only took a few hours off to attend his daughter's wedding, and on another had only what he described as a 'scrambling dinner'. These instances, given the normal parameters of contemporary sociability, are quite strikingly 'modern' in prioritising bureaucratic efficiency over sociability.[44] On journeys back to Bury, Oakes sometimes carried several thousand pounds and hired an armed guard to go with him. He would then submit payment to the Treasury in the form of inland bills. This provided him with very large amounts of cash. In October 1797 he reported he had collected £11,000 from 110 parishes in just three months (there are 517 parishes in all of Suffolk).[45]

Regular tax collection and the bureaucratic organisation of the excise tax in the eighteenth century helped putting-out cloth masters obtain cash for wages either by collecting taxes themselves, like Oakes, or buying parcels of coins from those who did.[46] There are other examples of clothmakers who also became bankers, such as the Gurneys, with whom Oakes had some contact, and the Quaker Thomas Fox of Wellington, who also drew on the stocks of cash collected by receivers.[47] The combination of tax collection and involvement with industry was then one means by which industrial wages might be paid, and the lack of cash in the eighteenth century would have been partially alleviated by the regularisation of yearly tax collection. If there had not been such regular coin collection, it is difficult to imagine how it might have been done privately in such an organised way. It also depended on a well-developed clearing market in London, where collection and spending could be matched through bill discounting. Taxation thus provided liquidity for wage payments even if much came out of the pockets of the poor through duties.

The Professionalisation of Local Banking

The number of individuals and partners who began to deal exclusively in what today we would call financial services and to call themselves bankers multiplied rapidly after *c.*1750. As noted earlier, by 1784 there were at least 119 banks in England, which had risen to about 230 in 1793 and 366 in 1799, together with 51 banks in Scotland by this date.[48] In 1809,

[44] Ibid., p. 58. [45] Ibid., p. 357. [46] Ibid., p. 55ff.
[47] Hubert C. Fox, *Quaker Homespun: The Life of Thomas Fox of Wellington, Serge Maker and Banker, 1747–1821* (London, 1958).
[48] Pressnell, *County Banking*, pp. 6–11, 44.

the first year of official statistics on the number of banks, there were 755 listed in England and Wales. The great majority of these were founded outside the capital.[49] Although there is no way of knowing just how much of an initial expansion this represented, as opposed to a replacement of activity previously undertaken by quasi-banker tradesmen, it undoubtedly represents a very rapid professionalisation, with 10–15 new banks being created each year. Unfortunately, surviving accounting records of note issuance can only be found in any detail after 1790. These show that it was still common for early country banks to issue notes for specific amounts of money on a personal basis. Indirect records indicate that notes for rounded amounts were being issued to pay workers, but they do not seem to have become the normal practice until after the turn of the century.[50]

It is difficult to know what value the note issue was for the country banks in the late eighteenth century. The only figure we have comes from 1808 to 1809, when £14.5 million of notes were stamped for duty, although Pressnell estimates there may have been as many as £18 million in circulation for various reasons.[51] If this was the case in 1793, when the number of banks was only one-third of the number in 1809, perhaps the note circulation was around £6 million. Of this total it is probable that notes of £1 or less formed around 40–50 per cent of circulation, but the estimates are very broad.[52] Although local notes would have circulated more rapidly, this number is small compared to roughly contemporaneous accounts of the circulation of bills of exchange. In a pamphlet published in 1812, a Liverpool banker made an estimate for the period after 1793. He claimed that, based on the annual drawings of inland bills worth £1 billion and foreign bills worth £200 million at an average usance of 2–3 months, there was a daily circulation of £160–250 million worth of bills of exchange, compared to what he estimated to be about £40–50 million in Bank of England and local bank notes.[53]

Adam Smith on Capital, Banking, and Currency

One person who was certainly aware of the importance of this great rise in banking services and financial liquidity was Adam Smith. I have written elsewhere of how the *Wealth of Nations* was as much an attempt to

[49] Joslin, 'London Private Bankers', pp. 172–3.

[50] For instance, Hammond & Company, or the Canterbury Bank, issued smaller notes in the value of 10s. 6d., £1 1s. in the 1790s. Lloyds Bank records, GB 386 A/53/60/6/2; Pressnell, *County Banking*, pp. 140–4.

[51] Note the discussion of Pressnell that this was the only year where all previous notes had been destroyed, so all were new, but it is still probably an underestimate because bankers kept some in reserve and some were not stamped. Pressnell, *County Banking*, pp. 145–6.

[52] Pressnell, *County Banking*, pp. 147–9.

[53] Ibid., p. 170ff.

systemise the importance of financial capital as it was about the division of labour and free marketing.[54] Like John Law before him, Smith was concerned to establish how paper credit could be used to provide a more efficient form of circulating capital within a nation through the use of banks:

> Money … may be compared to the highroads of a country, which bear neither corn nor grass themselves but circulate all the corn and grass in the country. If we could find any way to save the ground taken up by highways, we would encrease considerably the quantity of commodities and have more to carry to the market … Hence the beneficial effects of the erection of banks and paper credit. It is easy to shew that the erection of banks is of advantage to the commerce of a country.[55]

In his earlier *Lectures on Jurisprudence* he made a very interesting comparison of why Scottish banking succeeded, while John Law's scheme to expand the paper currency in France failed. The reason for this, he argued, was that Law continued to believe that public opulence consisted of money, and that 'the value of money is arbitrary, founded on the common consent of mankind' rather than on productivity.[56] It was this belief that allowed the inflation of Law's currency and the spectacular collapse of the French economy.[57] In contrast, the Scottish banks lent to local merchants and manufacturers who borrowed money to invest and also to pay wages that could be used to consume more. In this way, the money supply was linked to the cycle of production and consumption that it was meant to support.[58] Smith also stressed the importance of local trust, which was absent in Law's national currency:

> When the people of any particular country have such confidence in the fortune, probity, and prudence of a particular banker, as to believe that he is always ready to pay upon demand such of his promissory notes as are likely to be at any time presented to him; those notes come to have the same currency as gold and silver money, from the confidence that such money can at any time be had for them.[59]

Smith was also influenced by his friend David Hume, who wrote a substantial amount on the nature of money.[60] Hume believed the value

[54] Craig Muldrew, 'From Commonwealth to Public Opulence: The Redefinition of Wealth and Government in Early Modern Britain', in John Walter, Steve Hindle, and Alexandra Shepard (eds.), *Remaking English Society: Social History and Social Change in Early Modern Society* (Woodbridge, 2013), pp. 317–40; Craig Muldrew, 'Self-Control and Savings: Adam Smith and the Creation of Modern Capital', in Simon Middleton and James Shaw (eds.), *Market Ethics and Practices, c.1300–1850* (London, 2018), pp. 63–86.

[55] Adam Smith, *Lectures on Jurisprudence*, ed. R. L. Meek, D. D. Raphael, and P. G. Stein (Oxford, 1978), p. 504 (hereafter LJ); WN, pp. 323–44.

[56] LJ, p. 519. [57] Ibid., pp. 512, 515–21. [58] Ibid., p. 508. [59] WN, p. 292.

[60] Richard Cantillon, *Essay on the Nature of Commerce in General*, ed. Anthony Brewer (New Brunswick, 2001), pp. 120–30; Anne-Robert Turgot, *The Formation and Distribution of Wealth*, ed. Kenneth Jupp (London, 1999), pp. 42–3.

of money to be the result of a social agreement and was therefore ultimately fictitious.[61] He believed 'the advantage of paper-credit and banks to be superior to their disadvantages'. But Hume, as a sceptic, retained a Lockean anxiety that the value of paper money was dangerously susceptible to erosion of confidence, and as a result supported a policy of legal convertibility to gold or silver rather than the Scottish practice of relying on trust and land titles.[62]

In contrast, Smith, in the *Lectures on Jurisprudence* and in the earlier drafts of the *Wealth of Nations*, believed such problems of excessive risk could be minimised by having small amounts in a multitude of institutions, which would be in competition with each other to attract custom by being prudent.[63] However, when the *Wealth of Nations* was almost ready for publication, the Ayr Bank failed in 1772 (see 'Scotland' in Chapter 9), causing Smith to revise his discussion. In order to remedy the problem of over-issuance of currency, he suggested that no banknotes should be issued below £5, even though he realised this would reduce potential additional consumption by 'perhaps, little more than half the quantity of goods, is as much considered'.[64] But even more significant was his advocacy of regulation to prevent the over-issuance of paper credit even though it was a violation of natural liberty:

> those exertions of the natural liberty of a few individuals, which might endanger the security of the whole society, are, and ought to be, restrained by the laws of all governments.[65]

But Smith was not only interested in the institutional formation of capital. He was, of course, also a moral philosopher, and in both the *Theory of Moral Sentiments* and the *Wealth of Nations* he wrote about the values discussed in Chapters 5 and 6 of self-love, happiness, and interest. In his first book, Smith built on the theories of Francis Hutcheson, Hume, and Adam Ferguson to provide a socio-psychological argument as to why beneficial behaviour was more natural than potentially untrustworthy behaviour motivated by selfish and antisocial behaviour.[66] Most importantly, for our purposes, he followed Frances Hutcheson in placing less emphasis on the role of self-love as a cause of benevolence.[67]

61 Carl Wennerlind, '"An Artificial Virtue and the Oil of Commerce": A Synthetic View of Hume's Theory of Money', in Carl Wennerlind and Margaret Schabas (eds.), *David Hume's Political Economy* (Abingdon, 2008), pp. 108–9.

62 Ibid., pp. 109–10. 63 LJ, p. 504. 64 WN, p. 323. 65 WN, p. 324.

66 Jerome Schneewind, *The Invention of Autonomy: A History of Modern Moral Philosophy* (Cambridge, 1998), pp. 330–1, 349–53.

67 Francis Hutcheson, *An Inquiry into the Original of Our Ideas of Beauty and Virtue*, ed. Wolfgang Leidhold (Indianapolis, 2004), pp. 86–9, 91, 93, 96, 103–9, 122–9; Nicholas Phillipson, *Adam Smith: An Enlightened Life* (London, 2010), p. 52.

Smith followed Hutcheson's belief in the superiority of benevolent feelings to self-love; however, he thought that Hutcheson placed too much reliance on the deity for a moral sense. He wished to develop a more universal ethics that could be based solely on psychology. To do this he used the concept of interest, arguing that we have an interest in promoting our own happiness by seeking the *approbation* of others on the basis of benevolent actions. But, unlike the earlier thinkers discussed in Chapter 6, he chose *not* to equate self-love with interest, but rather acknowledged how our passions lead us to think our own small discomforts are more important to us than much greater suffering of others according to our need for self-preservation.

To overcome this, while still stressing the moral autonomy of the self, Smith put much more emphasis on the role of what he termed 'self-command' within a person as central to both virtue and happiness. He claimed there were what he termed the amiable and respectable virtues. The first involved the 'indulgent humanity' of sympathetic hearts, while the latter were the 'virtues of self-denial, of self-government, of that command of the passions which subjects all the movements of our nature to what our own dignity and honour, and the propriety of our own conduct require'. For this, what he termed the impartial spectator was crucial:

> When our passive feelings are almost always so sordid and so selfish, how comes it that our active principles should often be so generous and so noble? … what is it which prompts the generous, upon all occasions, and the mean upon many, to sacrifice their own interests to the greater interests of others? … it is not that feeble spark of benevolence which Nature has lighted up in the human heart, that is thus capable of counteracting the strongest impulses of self-love. It is a stronger power … It is reason, principle, conscience, the inhabitant of the breast, the man within, the great judge and arbiter of our conduct. It is he who, whenever we are about to act so as to affect the happiness of others, calls to us, with a voice capable of astonishing the most presumptuous of our passions, that we are but one of the multitude, in no respect better than any other in it.[68]

This led humanity 'to feel much for others and little for ourselves', and Smith claimed, 'to restrain our selfish and to indulge our benevolent affections, constitutes the perfection of human nature'.[69]

Smith also criticised Hutcheson on this account, claiming that his system did not sufficiently explain how approbation of the inferior virtues of prudence, vigilance, circumspection, temperance, constancy, and

[68] Adam Smith, *The Theory of Moral Sentiments*, ed. D. D. Raphael and A. L. Macfie (Oxford, 1976), pp. 137, 262.
[69] Ibid., pp. 23–5.

firmness could arise. It was in such cases that self-love or self-interest could also be valuable:

> The habits of oeconomy, industry, discretion, attention, and application of thought, are generally supposed to be cultivated from self-interested motives, and at the same time are apprehended to be very praise-worthy qualities, which deserve the esteem and approbation of every body. The mixture of a selfish motive, it is true, seems often to sully the beauty of those actions which ought to arise from a benevolent affection. The cause of this, however is not that self-love can never be the motive of a virtuous action, but that the benevolent principle appears in this particular case to want its due degree of strength …
>
> … Carelessness and want of oeconomy are universally disapproved of, not, however, as proceeding from a want of benevolence, but from a want of the proper attention to the objects of self-interest.[70]

But, for Smith, all of these and other virtues obtained their lustre from self-command.[71] This practice of self-command was vital for saving. The internal spectator looks at a person's self-command with a wonder and admiration when he abstains 'from present pleasure in order to secure greater pleasure to come'. From this arises the passion of present esteem, which is the motivation for the 'practice of frugality, industry, and application, though directed to no other purpose than the acquisition of fortune'.[72] He repeated this again in a section he added in 1790, after writing the *Wealth of Nations*, where he claimed that the man who through the 'steadiness of his industry and frugality', with an eye on future 'ease and enjoyment', 'is naturally contented with his situation, which by continual, though small accumulations, is growing better and better every day'.[73]

The interest of others as well as the self was also crucial. As stated in the first sentences of the *Theory of Moral Sentiments*: 'How selfish soever man may be supposed, there are evidently some principles in his nature, which interest him in the fortune of others, and render their happiness necessary to him.' Here interest plays a crucial role in the social working of sympathy. To be happy ourselves, we need others to be happy, and to have them regard our actions as conducive to their happiness:

> When the happiness or misery of others depends in any respect upon our conduct, we dare not, as self-love might suggest to us, prefer the interest of one to that of many.[74]

It was a central contention of the *Theory of Moral Sentiments* that this interest was more powerful than negative passions, and was not

[70] Ibid., p. 304. [71] Ibid., pp. 113, 137, 241. [72] Ibid., pp. 189–90.
[73] Ibid., p. 215. [74] Ibid., pp. 166, 235–6. Also see pp. 64, 138, 241, 245, 310.

competitive.[75] In the economic discourse of the *Wealth of Nations* this aspect of interest was not abandoned for the interest of the marketplace except in a constrained area of action.[76] Much more important was the passion of desiring to better oneself through saving, which was motivated by the idea of self-command.[77]

Although his claims about self-love and self-interest motivating market activity in the *Wealth of Nations* have become much more famous, he did not describe them as behaviour deserving approbation. They only had a utility function. Indeed, the 1766 notes on his *Lectures on Jurisprudence* claimed that he said 'the principle in the mind which prompts to truck, barter, and exchange, th'o it is the great foundation of arts, commerce, and the division of labour, yet it is not marked with any thing amiable'. In fact, they were 'mean' and held in 'contempt', but the reason they were so strongly implanted by nature was so they would have no occasion for additional force to engage men's actions.[78] Similarly, his use of self-love in the *Wealth of Nations* was not positive, but designed to show how a society of strangers could be dependent on one another: 'where a man stands at all times in need of the co-operation and assistance of great multitudes, while his whole life is scarce sufficient to gain the friendship of a few persons'.[79] As a result, the marketplace worked through interest in bargaining and exchange, while saving, in contrast, worked through benevolence.

It was probably for this reason that he stressed saving as a means of creating capital rather than liquidity creation, as earlier writers such as Law had done. Whereas they had advocated creating a circulating currency based on the security of land, Smith argued that this could be achieved through the savings of individuals – including the wage labourers themselves – invested in productive activity. He did not discuss mortgaging very much, although he did provide an example in which he argued that savings would be much more profitably invested in commerce or industry than a plot of land, unless the aim was agricultural improvement.[80] This was probably related to his desire to stress the value of labour and industry as vital to a modern economy based on the division of labour and financial liquidity. But it was also because his aim was to describe an economic system that could describe how wealth was created, as well as turned into circulating capital, which could be used for both consumption and investment.

[75] Ibid., pp. 10, 34, 50, 237. [76] Muldrew, 'Self-Control and Savings', p. 70.
[77] Pierre Force, *Self-Interest before Adam Smith: A Genealogy of Economic Science* (Cambridge, 2003), pp. 124–5.
[78] LJ, p. 527. [79] WN, I, pp. 26–7. [80] WN, I, ch. IV, 19.

As I've argued elsewhere, the savings of the successful poor who earned enough to have probate accounts made for them went up in the eighteenth century. But it is very difficult to know if this was the case for the great majority, for whom we have no records.[81] However, we know from the work of Ann Kussmaul that farm servants' wages were mostly used to build up savings to marry and start households when they finished service. Using Wrigley and Scofield's estimates of the age structure of the English population and Kussmaul's data, we can make a rough estimation of what the value of these savings might have been in the first half of the eighteenth century. Most young people entered service from age 11 onwards, but did not always earn a wage in their first year. It is more difficult to estimate when service ended, but since the average age of marriage was around twenty-seven for men and twenty-five for women in the 1720s and 1730s, we could use twenty-four as a possible end age for service estimates.[82] This gives us a period of twelve years of potential savings. Of course, some young people served less than this and some longer, while many others ended service but were able to continue saving by working in the cloth industry, which was expanding at this time.[83]

If we use the population estimates for 1731, then about 24 per cent (1,299,437 individuals) of the population was aged 12–24.[84] But of course wealthier farmers did not need to send their children out as servants, and families in trade sent their sons out as apprentices, which would have had different patterns of saving, so perhaps this population figure could be reduced by 20 per cent to account for wealthier households where the saving was done by the parents and not the young adults, giving us a figure of 1,039,550. Using wages recorded at Spalding Lincolnshire hiring fairs between 1767 and 1785, Kussmaul estimated that the average amount that both sexes could save in a year if they saved half of their wages was £4 10s., and £6 if they saved two-thirds.[85] If we assume that all young people between these ages were saving these amounts

[81] Craig Muldrew, 'From Credit to Savings? An Examination of Debt and Credit in Relation to Increasing Consumption in England, c.1650 to 1770', *Quaderni Storici* 137 (2011), pp. 401–9; Craig Muldrew, 'Little to Leave: Labourers' Goods and the Probate Process in Early Modern England', in Margareth Lanzinger, Janine Maegraith, Siglinde Clementi, Ellinor Forster, and Christian Hagen (eds.), *Negotiations of Gender and Property through Legal Regimes (14th–19th Century): Stipulating, Litigating, Mediating* (Leiden, 2021), pp. 311–44.

[82] Ann Kussmaul, *Servants in Husbandry in Early Modern England* (Cambridge, 1981), pp. 70–2, 79–80; E. A. Wrigley, R. S. Davies, J. E. Oeppen, and R. S. Schofield, *English Population History from Family Reconstitution, 1580–1837* (Cambridge, 1997) p. 134.

[83] Muldrew, 'Credit to Savings', pp. 404–7.

[84] Wrigley *et al.*, *Population History from Family Reconstitution,* pp. 614–15.

[85] Kussmaul, *Servants in Husbandry*, pp. 81–2.

each year for twelve years, we get maximum figures of £56,135,679 and £74,847,572. In addition to this we know that 'friendly societies' were increasing in number in the eighteenth century. These were organisations that enabled workers to collectively save a small amount each week for sickness or old age. They were generally organised by alehouse keepers, whereby members would contribute a few pence or a shilling a week out of their wages to a common box.[86] In 1801, Sir Frederick Eden estimated that friendly societies had 648,000 members. Even if each only saved £2 each a year, on average, over the course of ten years this would represent £12,960,000.[87] Thus, it is certainly the case that the working poor were saving considerable amounts, justifying Smith's emphasis. However, these savings were not as large as the capital raised on the security of mortgage or bond by those wealthier individuals who had money to lend, which Smith paid little attention to. Money lent on mortgage was, of course, a type of saving of wealth generated from the profit of some other economic endeavour, but it was not the savings of poorer people.

It used to be questioned how the author of the *Theory of Moral Sentiments*, which stressed benevolence over self-love, could have gone on to stress the self-interest of selling in the market in the *Wealth of Nations*. But, as we have seen here, it is actually a solution to understanding Smith and his economic theory properly. A Smithian 'capitalism' was one most definitely based on individual virtue, not simple accumulation. Although Smith never used the term capitalism, which was not coined until the nineteenth century, in the introduction to the *Wealth of Nations* he described the purpose of the first two books to be the improvement in the productive powers of labour and the nature of the 'capital stock' needed to turn this into exchangeable wealth. In this sense it was a system in which capital played a transformative role.

However, it was not a capitalism based primarily on the profit-seeking nature of exchange. This was the motivation to truck and barter, but not to save. Neither was it a capitalism of a supposedly moral-free mathematical risk assessment and a self-regulating society of selfish rewards. For Smith, this would always be open to manipulation by the corrupting interest of powerful wealthy individuals. Smith's capitalism was a transformation of the older morality of public credit as reputation for paying back one's debts to one of saving and betterment, in which an internalised moral system worked together with an institutional financial system based around ethical individuals.

[86] Penelope Ismay, *Trust Among Strangers: Friendly Societies in Modern Britain* (Cambridge, 2018), pp. 85–118.
[87] Ibid., p. 71.

How, then, did Smith's name become so associated with market individualism? Certainly he was critical of regulation, and especially so of the English Corn Laws that he thought inhibited agricultural innovation by controlling prices during bad harvests rather than supporting purchasing power. He also stressed that economic liberty created new innovations and wealth as far as was possible. However, in order for this effort to be turned into wealth in the form of capital, he saw his project as one of moral self-regulation more than government regulation. He was also better known for the labour theory of value than for economic liberty in the period after his death.[88]

Jeremy Bentham, in his utilitarian philosophy first published in 1780, has a better claim to be seen as the theorist with whom modern economic individualism originated. He attacked customary communitarian justice (which he saw as injustice) and argued that moral choice, including economic motivation, had to be reduced to only an individual basis. In order to establish a convincing moral basis to criticise the acceptance of customary law, and to decide how to establish the justice of legislation, he made the individual's pleasure or pain the means of judgement, not community standards:

> The community is a fictitious *body*, composed of the individual persons who are considered as constituting as it were its members. The interest of the community then is, what? – the sum of the interests of the several members who compose it. It is in vain to talk of the interest of the community, without understanding what is the interest of the individual. A thing is said to promote the interest, or to be for the interest, of an individual, when it tends to add to the sum total of his pleasures: or, what comes to the same thing, to diminish the sum total of his pains.[89]

Bentham went on to advocate that it would be ethical for people to act out of benevolence, but he did not believe there was any moral rationale to force someone to act morally if they did not want to:

> the only interests which a man at all times and upon all occasions is sure to find adequate motives for consulting, are his own. Notwithstanding this, there are no occasions in which a man has not some motives for consulting the happiness of other men.[90]

For instance, he disagreed with those who thought the poor should not be helped, and he believed people were free to act in charitable ways, but to compel someone to part with their wealth if they did not want to help

[88] Muldrew, 'From Commonwealth to Public Opulence', pp. 329–39; G. Stedman Jones, *An End to Poverty? A Historical Debate* (London, 2004), pp. 3–5, 36–41.
[89] Jeremy Bentham, *An Introduction to the Principles of Morals and Legislation* (Oxford, [1823] 1907), p. 3; chs. I.5–I.6.
[90] Ibid., pp. 312–13; chs. XVII.8–XVII.9.

the poor had to be decided on the basis of a calculus of individual happiness.[91] Political or legal compulsion had no moral validity. Such an ideology became very important in creating the legal decisions that would lead to the doctrine of freedom of contract and free trade.

The literature on Bentham is huge and one must be cautious, but there is certainly a relationship here between William Hutton's ideas written in the same decade about personal responsibility and class ethics, or the move from a communal legal regime of contractual enforcement through litigation to one based on the protection of capital as property. This is quite different to Smith's more egalitarian belief in industry and frugality, which he did not link to property in general, and seems to have thought that small holdings best promoted these habits, not large estates.[92]

Bentham's line of argument was taken up by critics of redistribution who thought the poor should be able to save more. Bentham went on to write extensively about the Poor Law, and because of his philosophy he believed it was necessary to convince potential rate payers rather than to coerce them. He also believed that the labour of the poor could be rightfully claimed by those taxed.[93] This was no longer a political economy of Smith's interest of the many, but of self-government and private property that would develop in opposition to early British socialism.[94]

Bentham's individualism was eventually taken up by Ludwig von Mises to oppose Marxism in the 1920s. Of course, there is a huge history to be told of what happened to ideas of individualism between these two periods, but for the purposes of the ethical/institutional developments traced in this book, Smith's moral capitalism of the self-interested and, at the same time, benevolent individual who bargains and saves for the good of himself or herself better describes people's motivation. By doing so, such individuals created capital, and thus increased the wealth of society. Smith was very critical of what he saw as the self-interest of merchants who used monopoly powers to keep prices high, and believed that free competition would create a more level playing field. However, he does not seem to have foreseen the great power that accumulated capital would give people, allowing them to avoid being moral, even when their capital was accumulated competitively.

[91] Ibid., pp. 3, 312–14. [92] Smith, WN, IV, ch. 19.
[93] Jeremy Bentham, 'Essays on the Subject of the Poor Laws' in Michael Quinn (ed.), *The Collected Works of Jeremy Bentham: Writings on the Poor Laws* (Oxford, 2001), I, pp. 8–38.
[94] Gregory Claeys, *Machinery, Money, and the Millennium: From Moral Economy to Socialism, 1815–1860* (Princeton, 1987).

Conclusion

Adam Smith's political economy of what we might call emotional capital formation is a natural ending point for this book. It sums up how the pamphlet debate arguing for economic growth caused by currency creation that began in the seventeenth century eventually achieved fruition. In the 1650s, authors like Samuel Hartlib or William Potter saw a country in which increased population growth had led to unemployment and increasing poverty. Their proposed solution was to increase employment in industry by first increasing agricultural production and then using the increase to employ extra bodies in industrial production. But they realised that this could not be done within the confines of the informal oral credit system that had developed in England up until that time. Too often employers were unable to find enough currency to pay workers outside of agriculture, where they could be paid in kind. As a result, the poor had to purchase goods on credit, often at higher prices because they were not trusted, while periods of unemployment could lead to them not being able to purchase enough to keep themselves properly fed. Thus, it was proposed that some form of paper currency was needed to overcome this problem by essentially increasing liquidity.

In economic terms the debate was not very sophisticated, especially in the lack of consideration of the potential inflationary effect of monetary creation; however, most theorists were very clear on one point – they believed that an increase in the money supply in a form that could be used to pay wages would kickstart economic growth. Growth was not being held back by lack of investment or technology, but by the lack of an adequate means of payment. Almost all industrial production at this time was small-scale and took place in households. However, in those larger-scale enterprises such as mining and shipbuilding there is evidence of significant technological innovation in the seventeenth century. Both coastal and merchant ships became larger and were more efficiently sailed by fewer men.[1] The

[1] Ralph Davis, *The Rise of the English Shipping Industry* (Newton Abbot, 1962), pp. 44–80.

technology of digging and draining deeper mines was continually expanding and led to the development of the steam engine in 1712.[2] Along the River Tyne, horse- and gravity-powered railways were developed to move coal to the coastal ships, and much capital was invested in fen drainage schemes.[3] In small-scale household production the spinning and weaving of new draperies occurred in the 1630s and the stocking knitting frame, a technological innovation of great sophistication, was invented as early as 1589. In the period before the 1680s there was enough existing capital in the form of bonds or account transfers for such investments, but not enough circulating capital to employ people and allow a wider range of the population to buy new goods.[4]

If there is one thing that deserves to be stressed above anything else in this book, it is the importance of such liquidity creation to economic growth. The main problem, which all of those pamphleteers who proposed various forms of paper credit currency in the late seventeenth century grappled with, was one of trust; how could the personal character-based trust, on which private oral credit had relied, be recreated in a system using anonymous paper money? The obvious answer was to base it on some kind of collateral, and three main sorts were proposed: land, government revenue, and stocks of goods. Land, for most writers, was the most obvious source of security since it was immobile and its value changed only slowly over time. Tax revenue had long been associated with banking in other countries, but was vulnerable to government overspending. Many proposals also suggested using goods as collateral, but such proposals were unsuccessful because of goods' easy mobility.

The preoccupation of modern economics literature in linking credit and microfinance to investment-based growth has seriously neglected the equally important question of how macroeconomics can be used to understand the need to pay wages and to provide consumers, especially poorer consumers, with the purchasing power to maintain demand for any goods that investment might be able to produce. In England in the eighteenth century, mortgages were used to solve this problem by creating capital that local landowners could use to pay for both goods and for wages, with paper notes of hand. This freed up a vast amount of capital. Certainly mortgaging could provide capital for agrarian improvement

[2] John Hatcher, *The History of the British Coal Industry before 1700* (Oxford, 1984), pp. 257–64.

[3] H. C. Darby, *The Draining of the Fens*, 2nd ed. (Cambridge, 1956), pp. 39–48.

[4] This is not to say that there were no difficulties in raising capital for very large projects where returns to the investment were slow to materialise, as discussed in Koji Yamamoto, *Taming Capitalism before its Triumph: Public Service, Distrust, and 'Projecting' in Early Modern England* (Oxford, 2018), pp. 156–73.

and later investment in canals and industry, but mostly it acted as a basis for currency creation laid on top of the very different interpersonal credit system that had previously developed based on personal trust.[5]

Most histories of what has come to be known as the financial revolution, however, have focused on the successful use of tax revenue to create forms of capital and paper instruments of government debt used primarily by wealthy merchants and tradesmen in London. Certainly the creation of the Bank of England and the issuance of Exchequer bills and stocks in other companies such as the East India Company or South Sea Company created many millions of pounds worth of transferable paper instruments (Table 2.1). But most of these were issues for very large values of £100 or more, so while they turned out to be a very good means of saving capital and earning interest, they were not very useful as circulating currency. It has been a major contention of this book that the concept of the financial revolution needs to be expanded beyond London. This is not intended to in any way criticise these excellent histories, but to suggest that, while the conversion of government debt into paper loans was certainly significant, it was actually land that provided more capital through mortgaging in the rest of England and through the Bank of Scotland, Royal Bank of Scotland, and land banks in the Thirteen Colonies.

However, we have no means of knowing how much of this borrowing was used to create paper money as opposed to being saved or used for expenditure. For the latter half of the eighteenth century, valiant attempts have been made to make estimates of the money supply in Britain using country bank note issues to measure what effect its size might have had on economic growth.[6] But for England before 1760 this is completely impossible because of the local nature of notes. However, we do know that the trade in internal bills of exchange was very large, and must have been supported by local notes.

We also know that litigation over problematic credit declined precipitously in the early eighteenth century from a situation where it had been socially normative before. This was because the possession of capital provided a pool of financial value that could be used to meet future obligations, whereas a positive balance on a debit–credit ledger was only an obligation that needed to be redeemed from someone else in the

[5] Dan Bogart, 'Turnpike Trusts and Property Income: New Evidence on the Effects of Transport Improvements and Legislation in Eighteenth-Century England', *Economic History Review* 62, no. 1 (2009), pp. 128–52.

[6] These are discussed in Paul Kosmetatos, *The 1772–73 British Credit Crisis* (Basingstoke, 2018), pp. 70–125.

future. By reducing the number of times obligations were not met, this would have had the beneficial economic effect of lowering the transaction costs of credit. Since most informal credit took the form of sales credit without interest, this meant that, in general, prices had to be set higher to factor in the risk of defaults. Logically, then, if more paper credit was used to pay debts, prices might have come down if profits went up. Indeed, in the period 1660–1770 prices did indeed fall slightly for agricultural products and quite significantly for industrial goods before 1750.[7] But other factors, such as low population growth and increasing production of goods, were also present, and we have no way of measuring how often paper was used in comparison to credit. Thus, any effects of lower transaction costs are difficult to measure without a constant series of cost and retail prices.

If it is impossible to quantify the effect of liquidity creation on economic growth and industrialisation, what we can say for certain is that there was an extensive public debate that argued that the creation of credit currency would lead to more industrial employment, and that this indeed happened in the period after *c.*1680 – in the cloth industry, in Birmingham and Sheffield metal manufacture, in Midlands pottery, in London glass-making, iron production, and much else. Thus, to some extent this explanation chimes with the quantity theory of money put forward by Friedman and Schwartz in their *Monetary History of the United States 1867–1960*, that economic activity is correlated to the supply of money.[8] However, I do not see money as an unproblematic lubricant created as the economy needs it. This book has argued the exact opposite – that creating a means of exchange that is liquid, reliable, and trusted is one of the most difficult economic institutions to get right because it involves creating trust over long distances with little knowledge of the source of the trust. Also, the financial revolution is often looked at through the prism of modern banking institutions and seeing what looks most like them – that is, the Bank of England. Here I have tried to see how things developed first out of problems of informal credit and ideas to solve them. This investigation has shown that what was important was not top-down institutional creation, but evolutionary flexibility and adaption.

Much more widespread trust in the honesty of accurate bookkeeping and the writing of paper instruments needed to develop to augment – but

[7] Mark Overton, 'Prices from Probate Inventories', in Tom Arkell, Nesta Evans, and Nigel Goose (eds.), *Until Death Do Us Part: Understanding and Interpreting the Probate Records of Early Modern England* (Oxford, 2000), p. 140.

[8] Milton Friedman and A. J. Schwartz, *A Monetary History of the United States 1867–1960* (Princeton, 1963).

certainly not replace – individual promise-keeping. But perhaps more than anything else it was also a change in morals that permitted trust to be transferred to the evolving institutional landscape, especially through the concept of interest. This was not in any way a modern narcissistic concept of self-interest, but a matrix of socially interested individuals acting out of innate self-love, deeply tied to the Christian religion. Individual happiness, as a condition of self-love, was also stressed as a motivation for saving and spending on consumption goods. This was, though, more individualistic than the previous credit system, which had so much mutual interdependence in chains of credit, since it allowed wealth to be constructed out of much more private interest-earning capital invested in bonds and mortgages. It also allowed liquidity to become more impersonal where the circulation of paper credit was used to replace oral sales credit, although in England outside of London this still remained bound by local knowledge.

At the same time a more Puritan sense of self-denial survived, especially among non-conformists, in the form of a Lockean type of guilt at misbehaviour. This was not a denial of enjoyment through overconsumption to prevent losing one's credit, but was rather more strategically aimed at that which might harm the common interest, such as cheating or corruption. We saw this in the guilt John Cannon felt when he first tried unsuccessfully to correct a mistake in his Excise accounts, and later in his anxiety that his accounting had a reputation for accuracy, or in the propriety of the directors of the Bank of Scotland, or the strict rules of behaviour enforced by the English Excise Tax Office.[9] This was needed to create capital that was safely organised by trusted individuals. The credible commitment thesis stressed that it was Parliamentary oversight that made government debt safe from misuse by a wilful absolute monarch. But the tax collection agencies, not just for the excise tax but the land tax and customs too, had to be trusted to the extent that most of the money collected would be used by the state for the purposes for which it was collected. There has also been a great deal of argument about the political and social means by which people came to believe that the government would continue to honour their debt, but in simple economic terms the system of national liquidity together with economic growth meant that the government could spend more than ever before and not need to worry that its debt could not be absorbed by the economy.

Where banks were created, as in Scotland, the directors also had to be trusted not to over-issue currency based on the value of land. In England

[9] John Brewer, *The Sinews of Power: War, Money and the English State, 1688–1783* (London, 1994), pp. 101–14.

this was done privately and often led to landowners over-leveraging the value of their estates, and the law gave lenders the right to foreclose in such cases. But for most borrowers the fear of such a possibility kept their borrowing within the means of their property. Unfortunately there is no way of measuring the degree to which over-leveraging might have been a problem, since the system was designed to keep this private unless there was a need to go to court.

This story also points towards a somewhat different interpretation of the relationship between slavery and economic growth in the eighteenth century. As was noted in Chapter 1, merchant capital in London and then Liverpool was vital to investment in the ships and forts needed for the trade.[10] But the investment of profits generated by the trade within England was only one part of a broader development of capital which used – but was not driven by – mercantile credit, whether from the slave trade or other overseas commerce. The ever-increasing widespread demand for sugar (as well as tea imported from China), though, probably could not have been so successfully developed had it not been for the development of paper bills and notes. By the 1780s, at the latest, almost all labouring families were reportedly drinking sugared tea, and national consumption has been estimated at 25–30 lb per person.[11] In the 1790s Sir Frederick Eden reported many families spending a shilling per week on tea, sugar, and butter – the equivalent of £2 12s. per year. Thus, while merchant capital was certainly created in significant amounts through the triangular Atlantic trade, its development was fundamentally based on popular consumption, made possible by increased liquidity.

Also of great importance in terms of capital formation was the fact that after 1710, through consumption taxes, poorer families contributed the bulk of tax revenue through excise and customs, which rose from about £5 million at that date to £14 million in 1785. By 1788 the customs on tea, sugar, and tobacco formed 13.7 per cent of public revenue; the excise on beer and malt 23.8 per cent; rum and gin 10.3 per cent; and salt and coal 6.74 per cent. This made a total of 54.5 per cent. In comparison, the land and window taxes, which fell more heavily on wealthier households, accounted for only 17.56 per cent.[12] As a result, investment in government debt was actually dependent on poorer families being able to afford to buy goods of which the price had been

[10] Joseph E. Inikori, *Africans and the Industrial Revolution in England: A Study in International Trade and Economic Development* (Cambridge, 2002), pp. 314–61.

[11] Elizabeth Boody Schumpeter, *English Overseas Trade Statistics 1697–1808* (Oxford, 1960), p. 57.

[12] Patrick K. O'Brien, 'The Political Economy of British Taxation, 1660–1815', *The Economic History Review* 41, no. 1 (1988), pp. 3, 11.

increased to pay excise and customs tax to support the national debt. Thus, popular consumption, supported by the liquidity of capital through the fiscal system described in Chapter 10, probably had a more widespread effect on the use of capital in Britain than that accumulated by those merchants who dealt in enslaved people, or who traded in the sugar and tobacco that was part of that consumption.[13]

It has also been a contention of this book that this rise in wealth was not just an English phenomenon, but that currency creation in Scotland and the American Colonies promoted an *Atlantic world* of increased consumption and production. But what about the rest of the world? Was early modern capital global? In terms of the spread of local paper currency, we know almost nothing apart from what has been mentioned here about France, Naples, and Genoa. Where there was reciprocal overseas trade, bills of exchange were used. When this happened we can say that there was capital accumulation. However, trade that lacked any form of reciprocal exchange of goods or services whose value could be cancelled against each other could not be financed through bills of exchange or other forms of credit over any long-term period. Such trade could only be done through colonial occupation or the use of gold and silver. By far the greatest trade of this sort was that between Europe and East Asia, which was continually growing in size over the course of the late seventeenth and eighteenth centuries. The major goods in this trade were all Asian – spices, silks, cotton cloth, and porcelain. Asian countries had no desire for European woollen cloth and little for any other European products, so markets were not created. Some historians have postulated that it was the European exploitation of precious metals from the Americas that led to the evolution of a metal/goods-based trade. However, given that much of the trade in spices was taken over first by Portuguese and then Dutch colonial exploitation, and that later the British introduced land taxes in India to help pay for their trade imbalances, this cannot be a complete explanation.[14]

[13] In addition, at least after 1760, some of the wages used to purchase sugar and tobacco were earned in the making of manufactured goods exported to the American Colonies, pointing to the importance of a wider system of Atlantic trade and consumption based on American bank currency as well as British paper notes, which was much wider than just merchant accumulation. For a summary of this position see, David Richardson, 'The Slave Trade, Sugar, and British Economic Growth, 1748–1776', *The Journal of Interdisciplinary History* 17, no. 4 (1987), pp. 739–69; Maxine Berg and Patricia Hudson, *Slavery, Capitalism and the Industrial Revolution* (Cambridge, 2023), chs. 6–7.

[14] Javier Cuenca Esteban, 'India's Contribution to the British Balance of Payments, 1757–1812', *Explorations in Economic History* 44, no. 1 (2007), pp. 154–76; Latika Chaudhary, Bishnupriya Gupta, Tirthankar Roy, and Anand V. Swamy (eds.), *A New Economic History of Colonial India* (London, 2015), pp. 101–2, 108.

Whatever the reason for this imbalance, it meant that silver, and to a lesser extent gold, were drained out of Europe during the seventeenth and eighteenth centuries. The monetary historian Akinobu Kuroda has argued that this led to a major change in the way payments worked in the world economy. While Europe increasingly began to rely on the types of credit this book has discussed, Asia – especially its largest economy, China – was able to achieve economic growth using metallic currencies.[15] It was for this reason that silver, which had hitherto not been of great importance in China as a currency, began to be used more often. Previously, copper coinage in the form of the *wen* coin was the most important coin used in China. During the Song dynasty (960–1279) and its successors the Yuan (1279–1368) and Ming (1369–1644), state-issued paper currency was widely and successfully used. However, under the Yuan it eventually depreciated in value and subsequent attempts to reintroduce it during the Ming dynasty were unsuccessful. When paper lost its value, the Chinese state tried to replace it with further issues of bronze and copper coins.

Copper coinage, modelled on the original Chinese *wen*, also formed the basis of most Asian currency regimes apart from Japan. Copper was much more viable in Asia than in Europe, both because governments took a greater interest in providing and regulating it as a currency, and – as Kuroda has argued – because there was a greater social bifurcation between local markets and long-distance trade, both within Asia and between Asia and Europe.[16] This was because copper coins never had enough value to be used extensively in long-distance trade, where silver was necessary. As a result of trade with Europe, silver flowed from the mines in South America to Asia. In total the world stock of silver increased from 35,000 tons in 1500 to 168,000 tons in 1800.[17] Of this, it is probable that China absorbed between one-third and half of the new production, and India and the Ottoman Empire also received a considerable percentage to pay for European purchases of textiles and other commodities.[18]

Although most Indian states used types of gold, silver, and copper coinage, Indian merchants had also long been using an instrument much

[15] Akinobu Kuroda, *A Global History of Money* (London, 2020), pp. 119–28.

[16] Ibid., pp. 23–32.

[17] Andre Gunder Frank, *ReORIENT: Global Economy in the Asian Age* (Berkeley, 1998), pp. 143–5.

[18] Ibid., pp. 147–8; Om Prakash, *European Commercial Enterprise in Pre-colonial India: New Cambridge History of India II* (Cambridge, 1998), pp. 157–60; Jan Lucassen, 'Deep Monetisation: The Case of the Netherlands 1200–1940', *Tijdschrift Voor Sociale en Economische Geschiedenis* 11, no. 3 (2014), pp. 78–9.

like a bill of exchange, called a *hundi*, for trade within the subcontinent and throughout the Indian Ocean and into East Asia. Like a European bill of exchange, the *hundi*'s value was supported by personal networks, often involving kin and tightly knit merchant communities.[19] However, because even fewer records survive of these businesses than for European merchants, it is difficult to piece together any detail about the extent of their usage.[20] Within the Indian Ocean trade there were long-standing trade routes where such things as ivory, gold, wheat, and fruit were exported east to Africa and the Red Sea, while cotton cloth, spices, cowries, silks, and rice were exported into the subcontinent. On the other side of India, similar goods were traded to Indonesia, the Philippines, Japan, and Canton for silks, porcelain, spices, and copper. Where Indian merchants had outposts, *hundi*s could be used, but silver seems to have been dominant in this trade.[21]

In contrast to Asia, the societies of Sub-Saharan Africa never became a part of the gold and silver international monetary system. Instead the continent used a multiplicity of different forms of currency. These took the form of copper manillas (bracelets), iron bars, various textiles, glass beads, salt, and various other objects.[22] The most important and well-known currency was the cowrie shell, which came from the Indian Ocean, and the Maldives in particular. As a result, European purchases of enslaved people had to be done using these commodities. A great deal of cowries were collected by European and Asian trading companies in order that they could be used to purchase slaves for the Atlantic trade; possibly 26,000,000 lb or ten billion shells were used in this way.[23] Indian cotton textiles, which had traditionally entered Africa through the Indian Ocean trade, also became an important form of payment for the enslaved in the Atlantic trading system once European companies such as the East India Company and the United East India Company (*Vereenigde Oostindische Compagnie*) began importing calicos from India

[19] Prakash, *European Commercial Enterprise*, pp. 161–3; Marina Martin, 'A South Asian Mercantile Model of Exchange', in Keith Hart (ed.), *Money in a Human Economy* (New York, 2017), pp. 209–28.

[20] Kirti N. Chaudhuri, *Asia before Europe: Economy and Civilisation of the Indian Ocean from the Rise of Islam to 1750* (Cambridge, 1990), pp. 182–9.

[21] Ibid., pp. 182–202, 210, 214–17; Kuroda, *Global History*, pp. 88–90.

[22] Jane Guyer and Karin Pallaver, 'Money and Currency in African History', in Thomas Spear (ed.), *Oxford Research Encyclopaedia of African History* (New York, 2018), pp. 3–5; Marion Johnson, 'The Cowrie Currencies of West Africa Part I', *Journal of African History* 11, no. 1 (2012), pp. 17–49; Philip D. Curtin, 'Africa and the Wider Monetary World', in J. F. Richards (ed.), *Precious Metals in the Later Medieval and Early Modern Worlds* (Durham, NC, 1983), pp. 231–68.

[23] Frank, *ReORIENT*, pp. 135–7.

to Europe. These were bought in London and other European ports by slave trading voyages to purchase slaves.

Another important commodity used by Europeans to purchase African slaves for the same trade were copper and iron bars. These could be used as a form of currency in bar form, but could also be melted down to make tools, weapons, and pots. Both metals were mined and smelted in Africa in sophisticated ways, but in the early modern period European iron production advanced with the introduction of water-powered blast furnaces. This meant that European slave traders were able to supply much larger amounts of iron with the result that iron bars became an important commodity traded in exchange for slaves.[24] There is also a debate that the growth of the Atlantic slave trade was at least partially driven by African traders' desire to obtain cowries, cloth, and iron for liquidity.[25] There is evidence that increased supply led to inflation as records show that iron and copper bars became less valuable over time.[26] While informal credit certainly played a role in the purchase of the enslaved from African traders, the current literature does not indicate that accounts and bills of exchange did.[27] As in the case of Virginia, it was possible to manage a quite sophisticated economy using informal credit and commodity currencies. The bills of exchange that drove the expansion of the Liverpool capital market were used in the trade between Britan and the colonies, not in the African trade itself.[28]

To sum up, we can say that, while in most of Europe, India, and the Ottoman Empire paper instruments in the form of bills of exchange and other forms of paper drafts on families acting as exchange bankers existed among merchants, most local exchange involved the use of copper and silver coins.[29] I think we can agree with the conclusions of Kuroda: in economies in which there was a strong preference for monetary cash settlements – in both large and small transactions – over the use of credit,

[24] Chris Evans and Göran Rydén, '"Voyage Iron": An Atlantic Slave Trade Currency, its European Origins, and West African Impact', *Past and Present* 239, no. 1 (2018), pp. 45–52.

[25] Paul Lovejoy, *Transformations in Slavery: A History of Slavery in Africa* (Cambridge, 2009), pp. 105–7.

[26] Toby Green, 'Africa and the Price Revolution: Currency Imports and Socioeconomic Change in West and West-Central Africa during the Seventeenth Century', *The Journal of African History* 57, no. 1 (2016), pp. 1–24.

[27] David Richardson, 'Background to Annexation: Anglo-African Credit Relations in the Bight of Biafra, 1700–1891', in Olivier Pétré-Grenouilleau (ed.), *From Slave Trade to Empire: Europe and the Colonisation of Black Africa, 1780s–1880s* (London, 2004), pp. 47–68.

[28] Kenneth Morgan. 'Remittance Procedures in the Eighteenth-Century British Slave Trade', *Business History Review* 79(4) (2005), pp. 715–749.

[29] Japan was something of an exception. Kuroda, *Global History*, pp. 133–5, 141–4.

conditions were not present to 'endogenously lead to the establishment of long term capital markets'.[30] Thus, where the state provided small-scale copper coinage, it might be possible to have capital markets in merchant- and state-backed forms of credit in a Braudelian sense, but these would remain separate from local society. But, in terms of local small-scale capital formation through savings and the use of paper currency, we still have little evidence outside of the study presented in this book to make even speculative conclusions.

Returning to Britain, eventually capital accumulation led to the creation of new class relations, with an elite middle class who justified their possession of financial capital as a type of property resulting from savings and good financial management. This study has emphasised that societies that want to have economic stability need a system of morality that can convince people that it is good to be honest, and that this goodness is rewarded socially, as Smith suggested, or alternatively reinforced through religious practices and beliefs. But, whereas Smith emphasised the frugality and honest savings of small labourers and artisans over merchant capital, ironically the accumulation of the types of capital he so brilliantly described led to the poor being denounced as incapable of such financial acumen and savings. For William Hutton, this was axiomatic of the workers in Birmingham, and even for those sympathetic to the plight of the poor later in the eighteenth century, such as Sir Frederick Eden, the drinking of sugared tea and eating too much meat was criticised as a wasteful luxury. This idea of property also changed the concept of forgiveness of the debts of the unfortunate poor, to a situation whereby such loss was seen as the inevitable result of a lack of proper foresight. By the nineteenth century planning for the future through saving was seen not only as a way to insure oneself against loss, but also as a sign of good character.[31] As liquidity and saving became more common, forgiveness became less necessary, and debt much more chastised as a moral failing. In keeping with this trend, the law of contract also became more strict and less equitable, and imprisonment increased. The slogan 'liberty and property' became the self-defining term for the middle class elite.

The shift from the old communal regulatory regime, which stressed equality before the law, to one based on the securing of property rights in mortgaged land, annuities, bonds, or shares was also a shift to a much

[30] Ibid., p. 138.

[31] Margot C. Finn, *The Character of Credit: Personal Debt in English Culture, 1740–1914* (Cambridge, 2003), pp. 18–20.

more class-based system. This did, however, provide the security that meant that local small-scale credit could be turned into a form of paper currency that was trusted within small areas. This held an advantage for poor wage earners who could then become less dependent on oral trust or household goods, of which they had little. But, most importantly, it meant that anxiety about financial loss and downward mobility that was so prevalent when personal credit dominated was no longer such a worry for those with extensive amounts of capital. It meant that the profit-seeking aspect of market behaviour could be justified, not just in terms of useful commerce, but now in the service of capital formation for its own sake, while being morally justified by the act of 'prudent saving'. Charity and hospitality were certainly still seen as virtuous behaviours, but, as Jeremy Bentham stressed, they were no longer obligations needed to maintain the bonds of the social order, but were now simply a personal choice. Such order was increasingly being created by the institutions of capital rather than mutual obligation. But still, the prioritising of the motivation of personal gain as the sole motivational ethic behind capital formation was some way into the future. The institutions of capital formation were still young enough that the ethical stress on honesty in financial accounting and probity in the personal accounting of income and expenditure were considered socially necessary. Pure self-interested maximisation was simply not intellectually viable, as I hope I have shown here.

Epilogue: The Phantom of Liberty

Many of the modern ideas of capitalism are not Smithian. The real intellectual source of modern capitalism should be sought in Jeremy Bentham's focus on the ethical utility of the happiness of isolated selves, of which society was only ever an aggregate. Bentham was more concerned with the compulsive force of 'irrational' customary laws, but this eventually paved the way for the marginal revolution and the development of what we might tentatively term the 'systemised autonomy' of individual economic actors aggregated into trends. The family tree of *Homo economicus* can be traced back directly to Bentham through the Austrian School of Economics' emphasis on individual rational decision-making as the basis for efficient economic organisation.[32] A genealogy leading forward from Smith would imply that autonomy is an illusion, as

[32] Craig Muldrew, 'Politics and Economics of Markets', in Roberto Scazzieri and Ivano Cardinale (eds.), *The Palgrave Handbook of Political Economy* (London, 2018), pp. 93–5, 126–8.

interdependence exists as much as it ever did, but is now managed by economists, engineers, and other technicians using aggregate mathematical data, more than individuals themselves. I will conclude by arguing that the justification for my project is to show, by returning to its origins, that the autonomous value that lies at the heart of modern capital is an illusion. Capitalism *is* a social system, and freedom does not exist without an obligation to maintain the value that lies at its heart. The difference between it and socialism comes down to the question about the acceptable degree of economic equality or inequality, not between community or autonomy. From a moral perspective, capital, in this interpretation, is more of a good thing than bad, and its defenders have a point that it is an enabling factor that allows created wealth to be used in ways that were impossible before. This can be used to reduce pain and poverty. But it also permits the accumulation of profits, which can be used to create power for a small number to enrich themselves, but also to exploit, enslave, subjugate, and kill to maintain that power. Capital itself does not determine a moral choice.

Capital began as a socially embedded 'thing' created and maintained by institutions consisting of social structures as much as individual assumptions. It was fundamentally not individualistic, and pure competition was damaging to the maintenance of capital. This probably sounds as if I am completely trying to turn what we assume about capital on its head by saying capital is communitarian. But this is not quite the case, because it is also maintained by a fundamental concentration of wealth in the hands of those who make the capital. This is the foundation of modern inequality, but it also supports a sort of free-riding individualism based on accumulated wealth that no longer feels it necessary to support the foundations of that wealth. Instead, it takes wealth to be simply created by private individual entrepreneurialism, which is valorised above prudence. Thus, in ending, we can go back to the point made in the Introduction of why it is important to dissect the meaning of capitalism as a term. It is because this is the only way we can reinstate the value of capital as an extremely useful social creation, while rejecting the reification of the self-made individual for what it is – a free-riding illusion. It is a class ideology masked as a saving grace. A *deus ex machina* with magical pulleys, a tautology whose only ancestors are the ghosts of self-made selves that never were.

It is ironic, and in our age possibly tragic, that capitalism is almost everywhere linked to hyper-individualism, when it is actually the most fragile of collective endeavours. Capital in this sense is the 'phantom of liberty', a phrase I have taken from Luis Buñuel's wonderful surrealist film on bourgeoise defence of social convention. As some critics have pointed out, the phantom is a reference to the 'spectre' in the *Communist Manifesto*, but Buñuel's satire was also always directed against the inability of the bourgeoisie, as a class, to see beyond its own self-important social horizons, and I would argue that the conditions of modern capitalism are also an absurdity that we continue to perpetuate if we think of freedom without obligation. The most ardent supporters of capitalism celebrate its ability to support individualist risk-taking innovation. But it is very much a cooperative freedom – innovators motivated primarily by profit need to be regulated to avoid the economically and socially damaging effects of fraud, exploitation, pollution, monopoly, and so on. The maintenance of any wealth that individuals create exists within a matrix of politics, law, norms of politeness, and group ethics that give value to a chimera that strangers have come to accept all over the world. But, as Wolfgang Streeck has pointed out in his recent series of essays critiquing contemporary capitalism, there is a contradiction within capitalism between the social relations underpinning the security of capital and the desire to make greater profits through risk and competition.[33] In short, if creative destruction blows up the foundations, it will destroy the whole edifice.

[33] Wolfgang Streeck, *How Will Capitalism End? Essays on a Failing System* (London, 2016), pp. 28–37.

Select Bibliography

Manuscript Sources

Bank of Scotland Archives

NRAS 945/1/94/1-3 General ledgers 1696–1716.
NRAS 945/1/5/3 Minute book 1696–1725.
NRAS 945/1/ 5/4 Minute book 1725–1742.
NRAS 945/1/11/1 Index to minutes 1696–1808.
NRAS 945/1/248/1 Record of torn twenty shilling notes 1704–1713.
NRAS/945/1/248/13 Record of torn notes 1730–1757.
NRAS/945/1/248/14 Record of torn notes 1748–1766.
NRAS 945/1/134/1A, 1B Treasurer's cash book A and B, 1696–1704.
NRAS 954/1/93/1 Journal 1696.

Bodleian Library, Oxford

MS Locke c.1 Lovelace Collection, ledgers of accounts, 1671–1704.
MS Locke F.1–10 Locke's journals, 1675–1704.

Bristol Archives

Z33 04413, 04414, 04753, 04754 Bristol Court of Conscience, court action books, 1692, 1729–1745.

Dorset History Centre

PE-WM/GN/5/1-6 Queen Elizabeth's Free Grammar School in Wimborne Minster, bills receipts and other accounts, 1573–1752.
DC-LR/G9/11-120 Lyme Regis Bourgh, Bills and Receipts, 1661–1780.
DC/SYB/F/1/1/2 Bundle of accounts, Bills, receipts of William Swetnam, 1629.

Essex Record Office

D/DBa A30-101 Barrington Family of Hatfield Broad Oak, bills and receipts, 1626–1690.

Hampshire Archives

5M50/1054 Bundle of bills and vouchers of Thomas Puckridge for the Southwick Estate, March 1736–February 1737.
5M50/2110-2125 Day books of Thomas Puckridge containing accounts of receipts and expenses, 1701–1733.
44M69/E7/41, 52 Estate and personal accounts of Capt. Thomas Jervoise, 1616–1693, bundles of bills, receipts and accounts, 1654–1689.
44M69/E8/7/3-115 Estate and Personal Accounts of Thomas Jervoise III, 1667–1743, bundles of bills and receipts, 1687–1740s.

Hertfordshire Archives

DE/R/F75/1 Family and business papers and correspondence of the Radcliffe Family of Hitchin Priory, receipts and bills, 1732–1733.

Kent Archives Centre

Fa/FV17-195 Faversham Borough Records, bills, receipts and vouchers, 1622–1770.

Lancashire Archives

DDHCL/15/1/3-4 Ashenton of Downham, steward's records, accounts 1738–1744.
DDHCL/15/2/1-4 Ashenton of Downham, steward's records, vouchers, 1671–1743.

Leeds University Archives

Marriner 184 Day book, 1771

Liverpool Record Office

920, PLU 9 Diary and account books of John Plumbe: 1725, 1727, 1729, 1732, 1736, 1737, 1739, 1740, 1748, 1750, 1756, 1757
920 PLU 6 Account book of John Plumbe 1697–1720.

London Metropolitan Archives

CLC/313/I/B/032/MS 25575 Saint Paul's Cathedral: dean and chapter, accounts, vouchers, bills and receipts relating to building work at the cathedral and to the rebuilding of the cathedral after the Great Fire.
CLC/313/I/B/012/MS 2548, Saint Paul's Cathedral: dean and chapter, acquittance books, containing signed receipts for sums of money paid (mainly to craftsmen and suppliers) in connection with rebuilding work at the cathedral.
MDR1 Register of memorials, Middlesex deeds register, 1709–.
CLA/038/02/001-002 London Court of Requests, ledger books.

National Archives

PRO, PRIS 10/157 Prisoners committed and discharged: Fleet Prison, 1697–1702.

Norfolk Record Office

NRO, KLC/C25/1-34 King's Lynn Guildhall court books, 1590–1690.

North Yorkshire Record Office

ZQH/9 Chaytor family letters.

Post Office Archives

Post 2 /1-104 Receiver general's cash books, 1677–1809.
Post 3/1-33 Accountant general's annual accounts, 1678–1938.
Post 94/1-11 Sub-series, accounts, 1667–1677.

Royal Bank of Scotland Archives

RB/252 Record of cancelled banknotes, 1742–7154.
RB/175/1 Issues of bank notes 1728–1735.

Sheffield City Archives

LD1156/1/3 Bills of John Brown for the Thomas Hollis Charity Hospital, 1730–1731.

Somerset Archives

DD/S/BT/14 Butleigh court papers, 1447–1928, Box 14.
DD/S/BT/2/20 Butleigh court papers, 1447–1928, Box 2, draft assignment of mortgage term in meadow in Butmore, Baltonsborough, 1723.
DD/S/BT/8/7/16 Butleigh court papers, 1447–1928, Box 8, mortgage of land in Southmoor, Henly and Darksham, Butleigh, 1731.
DD/S/BT/8/7/18 Butleigh court papers, 1447–1928, Box 8, assignment of mortgage of lands in Southmoor, Henly and Darksham, Butleigh, 1738.
DD/SAS/1193/4 John Cannon's memoirs (herein Cannon, *Chronicles*).

West Yorkshire Archives Service

Bradford STST/3/1–90 Stott-Stanhope of Eccleshill Park, family and estate records, financial papers, accounts, bills and receipts.
Bradford SpSt/5/4/3/1-68 Spencer Stanhope of Horsforth, family and estate records, financial, bills and receipts.
Calderdale, KMA/727 Armytage Family of Kirklees Hall, Clifton-Cum-Hartshead, cash book 1743–1747.

Calderdale, KMA/732 Armytage Family of Kirklees Hall, Clifton-Cum-Hartshead, vouchers.
Calderdale, HAS/327 Ledger of John Howarth.
Halifax, HAS 759 John Howard bill book.

Published Documents

Ashcroft, M. Y. (ed.), *The Papers of Sir William Chaytor of Croft 1639–1721* (Northallerton, 1984).
Broad, John (ed.), *Bishop Wake's Summary of Visitation Returns from the Diocese of Lincoln, 1705–1715* (Oxford, 2012).
Cholmeley, Richard, *The Memorandum Book of Richard Cholmeley of Brandsby 1602–1623* (Northallerton, 1988).
Fiske, Jane (ed.), *The Oakes Diaries: Business, Politics and the Family in Bury St. Edmunds 1778–1827, vols. I–II* (Martlesham, 1990).
Flinn, M. W. (ed.), *The Law Book of the Crowley Ironworks* (Durham, 1952),
Hey, David (ed.), *Yorkshire West Riding Hearth Tax Assessment Lady Day 1672* (London, 2007).
Hitchcock, Tim, Shoemaker, Robert, Emsley, Clive, *et al.*, *The Old Bailey Proceedings Online, 1674–1913*, version 7.0 (2012). www.oldbaileyonline.org.
Latham, Robert and Mathews, William (eds.), *The Diary of Samuel Pepys*, vols. I–X (London, 1970–1983).
Lloyd, Thomas, J. M. (ed.), *The Autobiography of Richard Baxter, Being the Reliquiae Baxterianae* (London, 1925).
Mathews, William (ed.), *The Diary of Dudley Ryder 1715–1716* (London, 1939).
Money, John (ed.), *The Chronicles of John Cannon Excise Officer and Writing Master, vols. I–II* (Oxford, 2010).
Riden, Philip (ed.), *George Sitwell's Letterbook, 1662–66* (Chesterfield, 1985).
Roseveare, Henry, *Markets and Merchants of the Late Seventeenth Century: The Marescoe–David Letters 1668–1680* (Oxford, 1987).
Smith, S. D. (ed.), *The Industrious Tradesman: The Letter Book of Joseph Symson of Kendal, 1711–1720* (London, 2001).
Steckley, George F. (ed.), *The Letters of John Paige, London Merchant, 1648–1658* (London, 1984).
Vaisey, David (ed.), *The Diary of Thomas Turner* (Oxford, 1985).

Printed Primary Sources

A Description of the Office of Credit by the Use of Which None Can Possibly Sustain Loss, But Every Man May Certainly Receive Great Gain and Wealth (London, 1665).
Aquinas, *Sumna Theologica*, Christian Classics online edition. www.ccel.org/ccel/aquinas/summa.html.
Aristotle, *Nicomachean Ethics*, trans. Robert C. Bartlett and Susan D. Collins (Chicago, 2011).
Ashley Cooper, Anthony, Third Earl of Shaftesbury, *Characteristics of Men, Manners, Opinions, Times*, ed. Lawrence Klein (Cambridge, 1999).

Baillie, Robert, *Satan the Leader in Chief to All Who Resist the Reparation of Sion: As It Was Cleared in a Sermon to the Honourable House of Commons at Their Late Solemn Fast, Febr. 28. 1643* (London, 1643).

Baxter, Richard, *A Christian Directory or a Sum of Protestant Theologie, and Cases of Conscience* (London, 1673).

A Treatise of Self-Denyall (London, 1660).

Richard Baxter's Confession of His Faith, Especially Concerning the Interest of Repentance and Sincere Obedience to Christ, in Our Justification & Salvation (London, 1655).

The Saints Everlasting Rest (London, 1650).

Bentham, Jeremy, *Introduction to the Principles of Morals and Legislation*, printed in Mary Warnock (ed.), *Utilitarianism* (London, 1962).

Butler, Joseph, *The Works of Joseph Butler Containing the Analogy of Religion and Sixteen Celebrated Sermons* (London, 1867).

Cantillon, Richard, *Essai sur la nature du commerce en general* (Paris, 2011).

Essay on the Nature of Trade in General, ed. Henry Higgs (London, 1959).

Cary, John, *A Discourse on Trade* (London, 1745).

Chamberlain, Hugh, *A Brief Account of the Intended Bank of England* (London, 1694).

Childe, Josiah, *Discourse about Trade* (London, 1690), reprinted in McCulloch, *Early English Tracts on Commerce* (Cambridge, 1954).

Cicero, *On Duties*, ed. M. T. Griffin and E. M. Atkins (Cambridge, 1991).

Cumberland, Richard, *A Treatise of the Laws of Nature*, trans. John Maxwell (1727), ed. Jon Parkin (Indianapolis, 2005).

Davenant, Charles, *Discourses on the Public Revenues*, printed in Sir Charles Whitworth (ed.), The Political and Commercial Works of That Celebrated Writer Charles Davenant (London, 1771).

Dawes, William, *Self-Love the Great Cause of Bad Times: A Sermon Preached before the Society of the Mystery of the Goldsmiths* (London, 1701).

Defoe, Daniel, *Robinson Crusoe*, ed. John Richetti (London, 2001).

The Complete English Tradesman (London, 1745) reprinted by Burt Franklin, New York, 1970, vols. I–II.

Descartes, Rene, *Discourse on Method*, trans. F. E. Sutcliffe (Harmondsworth, 1968).

Durham, James, *Heaven Upon Earth in the Serene Tranquillity and Calm Composure, in the Sweet Peace and Solid Joy of a Good Conscience Sprinkled with the Blood of Jesus* (Edinburgh, 1685).

Franklin, Benjamin, *A Modest Inquiry into the Nature and Necessity of a Paper Currency* (Philadelphia, 1729).

Godfrey, Michael, *A Short Account of the Bank of England* (London, 1695).

Gough, Richard, *The History of Myddle*, ed. D. Hey (Harmondsworth, 1981).

Guthrie, William, *The Christian's Great Interest: in Two Parts* (London, 1705).

Haslam, D. G. and Morton, C., *Post Office Notices Extracted from the London Gazette 1660–1800* (London, 1989).

Howard, John, *The State of the Prisons in England and Wales: With Preliminary Observations and an Account of Some Foreign Prisons* (Cambridge, 2013).

Hutton, William, *Courts of Requests: Their Nature, Utility, and Powers Described, with a Variety of Cases, Determined in That of Birmingham* (Birmingham, 1787).

The Life of William Hutton (Studley, 1998).
Kelly, Patrick Hyde, *Locke on Money, vols I–II* (Oxford, 1991).
King, Gregory, *Natural and Political Observations and Conclusions upon the State and Condition of England*, printed in George F. Barnett (ed.), Two Tracts by Gregory King (Baltimore, 1936).
Lackington, James, *The Memoirs of the Forty-five First Years of the Life of James Lackington* (London, 1794).
Law, John, *Money and Trade Considered with a Proposal for Supplying the Nation with Money* (Edinburgh, 1705).
Locke, John, *An Essay Concerning Human Understanding*, ed. Roger Woolhouse (Harmondsworth, 1997).
Essays on the Law of Nature (1663–4), in M. Goldie (ed.), *Locke: Political Essays* (Cambridge, 1997), pp. 79–133.
Some Thoughts Concerning Education, ed. John Yolton and Jean Yolton (Oxford, 1989).
Two Treatises of Government, ed. Peter Laslett (New York, 1963).
L. R., *A Proposal for Supplying His Majesty with Twelve Hundred Thousand Pounds by Mending the Coin, and Yet Preserve the Ancient Standard of the Kingdom* (London, 1695).
Malynes, Gerald de, *Consuetudo vel lex Mercatoria* (London, 1622).
Mandeville, Bernard, *The Fable of the Bees,* ed. F. B. Kaye (Oxford (1924).
Mill, John Stuart, *Utilitarianism*, printed in Mary Warnock (ed.), Utilitarianism (London, 1962).
Mun, Thomas, *England's Treasure by Forraign Trade* (London, 1664), reprinted in J. R. McCulloch, *Early English Tracts on Commerce* (Cambridge, 1954).
Nicholas, Sander, *A Briefe Treatise of Usurie, Made by Nicolas Sander D. of Diuinitie* (Leuven, 1568).
Parker, Henry, *Of a Free Trade: a Discourse Seriously Recommending to Our Nation the Wonderful Benefits of Trade* (London, 1648).
Perkins, William, *A Golden Chaine: or The Description of Theologie Containing the Order of the Causes of Salvation and Damnation, According to Gods Word* (Cambridge, 1600).
Plutarch, *Moralia*, trans. W. C. Helmbold (London, 1939).
Potter, William, *The Key of Wealth or A New Way for Improving of Trade* (London, 1650).
Reasons against a Registry of Lands (London, 1678).
Reasons for a Registry (London, 1678).
Rushworth, William *The Dialogues of William Richworth or The Judgment of Common Sense in the Choise of Religion* (London, 1640).
Scarlet, John, *Stile of Exchanges* (London, 1684).
Smith, Adam, *An Inquiry into the Nature and Causes of the Wealth of Nations, vols. I–II,* ed. R. H. Campbell, A. S. Skinner, and W. B. Todd (Oxford, 1976).
Lectures on Jurisprudence, ed. R. L. Meek, D. D. Raphael, and P. G. Stein (Oxford, 1978).
The Theory of Moral Sentiments, ed. D. D. Raphael and A. L. Macfie (Oxford, 1976).
Smith, John, *Select Discourses* (London, 1660).

Steuart, Sir James, *An Inquiry into the Principles of Political Economy being an Essay on the Science of Domestic Policy in Free Nations* (London, 1767).
Stillingfleet, Edward, *Fifty Sermons Preached upon Several Occasions by Edward Stillingfleet, Late Lord Bishop of Worcester* (London, 1707).
Tillotson, John, *Of Sincerity and Constancy in the Faith and Profession of the True Religion, in Several Sermons* (London, 1695).
Sermons Preach'd Upon Several Occasions by His Grace John Lord Arch-Bishop of Canterbury, vol. I (London, 1694).
Tucker, Josiah, *The Elements of Commerce and Theory of Taxes* (Bristol, 1755).
Turgot, Anne-Robert, *Réflexions sur la Formation et la Distribution des Richesses* (Paris, 1766).
The Formation and Distribution of Wealth, ed. Kenneth Jupp (London, 1999).
Wheeler, John, *Treatise on Commerce* (London, 1601).
Whichcote, Benjamin, *Select Sermons of Dr. Whichcot in Two Parts* (London, 1698).
Wootton, David (ed.), *John Locke, Political Writings* (Harmondsworth, 1993).
Wright, Thomas, *The Passions of the Minde in Generall* (London, 1604).

Newspapers

Daily Courant, London, Tuesday, 3 January 1721, Issue 5991.
Newcastle Courant, 7 May 1737.
The Spectator, 12 March 1711, Issue 10.

Secondary Works

Anderson, B. L., 'Money and the Structure of Credit in the Eighteenth Century', *Business History*, 12 (1970), pp. 85–101.
'Provincial Aspects of the Financial Revolution of the Eighteenth Century', *Business History* 11 (1960), pp. 11–22.
'The Attorney and the Early Capital Market in Lancashire', in F. Crouzet (ed.), *Capital Formation and the Industrial Revolution* (London, 1972), pp. 223–55.
Arkell, Tom, 'The Probate Process', in Tom Arkell, Nesta Evans, and Nigel Goose (eds.), *Until Death Do Us Part: Understanding and Interpreting the Probate Records of Early Modern England* (Oxford , 2000), pp. 3–37.
Beckert, Sven, *Empire of Cotton: A New History of Global Capitalism* (London 2016).
Bogart, Dan, 'Turnpike Trusts and Property Income: New Evidence on the Effects of Transport Improvements and Legislation in Eighteenth-Century England.' *Economic History Review* 62, no. 1 (2009), pp. 128–52.
Brace, Laura, *The Idea of Property in Seventeenth-Century England: Tithes and the Individual* (Manchester, 1998).
Braudel, Fernand, *Civilization and Capitalism, 15th–18th Century* (London, 1982).

Brewer, John, *The Sinews of Power: War, Money and the English State, 1688–1783* (London, 1994).

Briggs, Chris, 'Mortgages and the English Peasantry c.1250–c.1350', in Chris Briggs and C. J. Zuijderduijn (eds.), *Land and Credit: Mortgages in the Medieval and Early Modern European Countryside* (London, 2018), pp. 17–80.

Broadberry, Steven, Campbell, Bruce, Klein, Alexander, *et al.*, *British Economic Growth, 1270–1870* (Cambridge, 2015).

Brock, Leslie V., *The Currency of the American Colonies, 1700–1764: A Study in Colonial Finance and Imperial Relations* (New York, 1975).

Brooke, Christopher, *Philosophic Pride: Stoicism and Political Thought from Lipsius to Rousseau* (Princeton, 2012).

Brooks, C. W., 'Interpersonal Conflict and Social Tension: Civil Litigation in England, 1640–1830', *Lawyers, Litigation and English Society since 1450* (London, 1998), pp. 27–62.

Law, Politics and Society in Early Modern England (Cambridge, 2008).

'Litigation and Society in England, 1200–1830', in *Lawyers, Litigation and English Society Since 1450* (London, 1998), pp. 63–128.

Pettyfoggers and Vipers of the Commonwealth: The 'Lower Branch' of the Legal Profession in Early Modern England (Cambridge, 1986).

Buchan, James, *John Law: A Scottish Adventurer of the Eighteenth Century* (London, 2018).

Callaway, Dave and Murphy, Jonathan, *Paper Money of Scotland, vol. I* (Sutton, 2018).

Campbell-Smith, Duncan, *Masters of the Post: The Authorized History of the Royal Mail* (London, 2011).

Carswell, John, *The South Sea Bubble* (Stroud, 1993).

Challis, C. D. (ed.), *A New History of the Royal Mint* (Cambridge, 1992).

Checkland, S. G., *Scottish Banking: A History, 1695–1973* (London, 1975).

Chiapello, Eve, 'Accounting and the Birth of the Notion of Capitalism', *Critical Perspectives on Accounting* 18 (2007), pp. 276–93.

Clapham, John, *The Bank of England: A History, Vol. 1 1694–1797* (Cambridge, 1944).

Coffman, D'Maris, Leonard, Adrian, and, Neal, Larry (eds.), *Questioning Credible Commitment: Perspectives on the Rise of Financial Capitalism* (Cambridge, 2013).

Costabile, Lilia and Eduardo, Nappi, 'The public banks of Naples between Financial Innovation and Crisis', in Lilia Costabile, and Larry Neal (eds.), *Financial Innovation and Resilience: The Outstanding Achievements of the Public Banks of Naples (1462–1808)* (London, 2018), pp. 17–53.

Cullen, L. M. and Smout, T. C. (eds.), *Comparative Aspects of Scottish and Irish Economic and Social History, 1600–1900* (Edinburgh, 1977).

Davies, K. G., 'Joint-Stock Investment in the Later Seventeenth Century', *Economic History Review* 2nd ser., 4 (1952), pp. 283–301.

de Roover, Raymond, *Money, Banking and Credit in Medieval Bruges: Italian Merchant-Bankers, Lombards and Money-changers: A Study in the Origins of Banking* (Cambridge, MA, 1948).

The Rise and Decline of the Medici Bank, 1397–1494 (Cambridge, MA, 1963).

de Vries, Jan and van der Woude, Ad, *The First Modern Economy: Success, Failure, and Perseverance of the Dutch Economy, 1500–1815* (Cambridge, 1997).

Dermineur, Elise M., 'Rethinking Debt: The Evolution of Private Credit Markets in Preindustrial France', *Social Science History* 42, no. 2 (2018), pp. 317–42.

(ed.) *Women and Credit in Pre-industrial Europe* (Turnhout, 2018).

Desan, Christine, *Making Money: Coin, Currency, and the Coming of Capitalism* (Oxford, 2014).

Dickson, P. G. M., *The Financial Revolution in England 1688–1756* (London, 1967).

Dunn, John, '"Bright Enough for All Our Purposes": John Locke's Conception of a Civilized Society', *Notes and Records of the Royal Society of London* 43 (1989), pp. 133–53.

Earle, Peter, *The Making of the English Middle Class* (London, 1989).

Elias, Norbert, *The Civilizing Process: The History of Manners and State Formation and Civilization* (Oxford, 1994).

Erickson, Amy Louise, 'Coverture and Capitalism.' *History Workshop Journal* 59, no. 1 (2005), pp. 1–16.

Women and Property in Early Modern England (London, 1993).

Feavearyear, A. E., *The Pound Sterling: A History of English Money* (Oxford, 1931).

Finn, Margot C., *The Character of Credit: Personal Debt in English Culture, 1740–1914* (Cambridge, 2003).

'Women, Consumption and Coverture in England, c. 1760–1860', *The Historical Journal* 39, no. 3 (1996), pp. 703–22.

Flinn, M. W., *Men of Iron: The Crowleys in the Early Iron Industry* (Edinburgh, 1962).

French, Henry, *The Middle Sort of People in Provincial England 1600–1750* (Oxford, 2007).

French, Henry and Hoyle, R. W., 'The Land Market of a Pennine Manor: Slaidburn, 1650–1780', *Continuity and Change* 14, no. 3 (1999), pp. 349–83.

Gayton, Juliet, 'Mortgages Raised by Rural English Copyhold', in Chris Briggs and C. J. Zuijderduijn (eds.), *Land and Credit: Mortgages in the Medieval and Early Modern European Countryside* (London, 2018) pp. 47–80.

Gelderbolm, Oscar and Jonker, Just, 'Enter the Ghost: Cashless Payments in the Early Modern Low Countries, 1500–1800', in R. J. van der Spek and Bas van Leeuwen (eds.), *Currency and Crisis: In Search of Trust, 2000 BC to AD 2000* (London, 2018), pp. 224–47.

Glaisyer, Natasha, 'Calculating Credibility: Print Culture, Trust and Economic Figures in Early Eighteenth-century England' *The Economic History Review* 60, no. 4 (2007), pp. 685–711.

Goldberg, Dror, 'The Massachusetts Paper Money of 1690', *The Journal of Economic History* 69, no. 4 (2009), pp. 1092–106.

Goldie, Mark, 'Middle Way Religion', in Mark Goldie (ed.), *The Entering Book of Roger Morrice: Roger Morrice and the Puritan Whigs* (Woodbridge, 2007).

Goldthwaite, Richard A., *The Economy of Renaissance Florence* (Baltimore, 2009).

Grassby, Richard, *The Business Community of Seventeenth Century England* (Cambridge, 1995).

Grubb, Farley, 'Creating Maryland's Paper Money Economy, 1720–1740: The Confluence of Political Constituencies, Economic Forces, Transatlantic Markets, and Law', *Journal of Early American History* 2019, no. 1 (2019), pp. 34–58.

'Is Paper Money Just Paper Money? Experimentation and Variation in the Paper Monies Issued by the American Colonies from 1690–1775', *Research in Economic History* 32 (2016), pp. 147–224.

Hatcher, John, *The History of the British Coal Industry before 1700* (Oxford, 1984).

Hindle, Steve, *On the Parish? The Micro-Politics of Poor Relief in Rural England, c. 1550–1750* (Oxford, 2004).

The State and Social Change in Early Modern England, c.1550–1640 (Basingstoke, 2002).

Hirschman, Albert O., *The Passions and the Interests: Political Arguments for Capitalism before its Triumph* (Princeton, 1977).

Hoffman, Philip, Postel-Vinay, Gilles, and Rosenthal, Jean-Laurent, *Priceless Markets: The Political Economy of Credit in Paris, 1660–1870* (Chicago, 2000).

Hont, Istvan, *Jealousy of Trade: International Competition and the Nation-State in Historical Perspective* (Harvard, 2005).

Hoppit, Julian, 'Compulsion, Compensation and Property Rights in Britain, 1688–1833', *Past and Present.* 210, no. 1 (2011), pp. 93–128.

Risk and Failure in English Business 1700–1800 (Cambridge, 1987).

Horsefield, J. Keith, *British Monetary Experiments, 1650–1710* (London, 1960).

Horwitz, Morton J., *The Transformation of American Law, 1780–1860* (Cambridge, MA, 1977).

Hoyle, R. W. (ed.), *Custom, Improvement and the Landscape in Early Modern Britain* (Farnham, 2011).

Hudson, Pat, *The Genesis of Industrial Capital: A Study of the West Riding Wool Textile Industry c.1750–1850* (Cambridge, 1986).

Hunt, Edwin S., *The Medieval Super-Companies: A Study of Peruzzi Company of Florence* (Cambridge, 1994).

Hunt, Margaret R., *The Middling Sort: Commerce, Gender, and the Family in England 1680–1780* (Berkeley, 1996).

Hutchison, T. W., *Before Adam Smith: The Emergence of Political Economy, 1662–1776* (Oxford, 1988).

James, Susan, *Passion and Action: The Emotions in Seventeenth-Century Philosophy* (Oxford, 1997).

John, Styles, '"Our traitorous moneymakers": The Yorkshire Coiners and the Law, 1760–83', in John Brewer and John Styles (eds.), *An Ungovernable People: The English and Their Law in the Seventeenth and Eighteenth Centuries* (New Brunswick, 1980), ch. 5.

Jones, Norman, *God and the Moneylenders: Usury and the Law in Early Modern England* (Oxford, 1989).

Joslin, D. M., 'London Private Bankers, 1720–1785', *The Economic History Review* 7, no. 2 (1954), pp. 167–86.

Kadane, Matthew, *The Watchful Clothier: The Life of an Eighteenth Century Protestant Capitalist* (New Haven, 2013).

Keibek, Sebastian, 'From Probate Inventories to Households: Correcting the Probate Record for Wealth Bias'. Cambridge working paper 28 (2017).

Kerridge, Eric, *Trade and Banking in Early Modern England* (Manchester, 1988).
Klein, Lawrence E., *Shaftesbury and the Culture of Politeness: Moral Discourse and Cultural Politeness in Early Eighteenth-Century England* (Cambridge, 1994).
Kosmetatos, Paul, *The 1772–73 British Credit Crisis* (London, 2018).
Kuroda, Akinobu, *A Global History of Money* (London, 2020).
Kussmaul, Ann, *Servants in Husbandry in Early Modern England* (Cambridge, 1981).
Lemire, Beverly, *The Business of Everyday Life: Gender, Practice and Social Politics in England, c.1600–1900* (Manchester, 2005).
Levine, David and Wrightson, Keith, *The Making of an Industrial Society: Whickham, 1560–1765* (Oxford, 1991).
Li, Ming-Hsun, *The Great Recoinage of 1696 to 1699* (London, 1963).
Macleod, Christine, 'The 1690s Patents Boom: Invention or Stock-Jobbing?', *The Economic History Review* 39, no. 4 (1986), pp. 549–71.
Maegraith, Janine, and Muldrew, Craig, 'Consumption and Material Life', in Hamish Scott (ed.), *Oxford Handbook of Early Modern European History, vol. I* (Oxford, 2015), pp. 369–97.
Marshall, Gordon, *Presbyteries and Profits: Calvinism and the Development of Capitalism in Scotland, 1560–1707* (Edinburgh, 1992).
Marshall, Richard K., *The Local Merchants of Prato: Small Entrepreneurs in the Late Medieval Economy* (Baltimore, 1999).
Mayhew, Nicholas, *Sterling: The History of a Currency* (New York, 2000).
McCusker, John and Menard, Russell R, *The Economy of British America, 1607–1789* (Chapel Hill, 1985).
McGowen, Randall, 'From Pillory to Gallows: The Punishment of Forgery in the Age of the Financial Revolution', *Past & Present* 165 (1999), pp. 107–40.
Meiksins Wood, Ellen, *Origin of Capitalism* (Cambridge, 2016).
Miles, M., '"Eminent Practitioners": The New Visage of Country Attorneys c.1750–1800', in G. R. Rubin and David Sugarman (eds.), *Law, Economy and Society, 1750–1914: Essays in the History of English Law* (Abingdon, 1984), pp. 470–503.
'The Money Market in the Early Industrial Revolution: The Evidence from Two West Riding Attorneys, c.1750–1800', *Business History* 23 (1981), pp. 127–46.
McCusker, John J. and Menard, Russell R., *The Economy of British America, 1607–1789* (Durham,. NC, 1991).
Muldrew, Craig, 'Afterward: Mortgages as Mediation between Kin and Capital', in Chris Briggs and C. J. Zuijderduijn (eds.), *Land and Credit: Mortgages in the Medieval and Early Modern European Countryside* (London, 2018), pp. 309–26.
'"Blunderers and Blotters of the Law"? The Rise of Conveyancing in the Eighteenth Century and Long Term Socio-Legal Change', in Michael Lobban, Joanne Begiato, and Adrian Green (eds.), *Law, Lawyers and Litigants in Early Modern English Society: Essays in Memory of Christopher W. Brooks* (Cambridge, 2019), pp. 229–53.
'Class and Credit: Social Identity, Wealth and the Life Course in Early Modern England', in Henry French and Jonathan Barry (eds.), *Identity and Agency in England, 1500–1800* (London, 2004), pp. 158–72.

Food, Energy and the Creation of Industriousness: Work and Material Culture in Agrarian England, 1550–1780 (Cambridge, 2011).

'From a "Light Cloak" to the "Iron Cage": An Essay on Historical Changes in the Relationship between Community and Individualism', in Alexandra Shepard and Philip Withington (eds.), *Communities in Early Modern England* (Manchester, 2000), pp. 156–77.

'From Commonwealth to Public Opulence: The Redefinition of Wealth and Government in Early Modern Britain', in John Walter, Steve Hindle, and Alexandra Shepard (eds.), *Remaking English Society: Social History and Social Change in Early Modern Society* (Woodbridge, 2013), pp. 317–40.

'From Credit to Savings? An Examination of Debt and Credit in Relation to Increasing Consumption in England, c.1650 to 1770', *Quaderni Storici* 137 (2011), pp. 391–414.

'Happiness and the Theology of the Self in Late Seventeenth Century England', in Michael Braddick and Joanna Innes (eds.), *Suffering and Happiness in England 1550–1850* (Oxford, 2017), pp. 65–86.

'"Hard food for Midas", Cash and Its Social Value in Early Modern England', *Past and Present* 170 (2001), pp. 78–120.

'Little to Leave: Labourers' Goods and the Probate Process in Early Modern England', in Margareth Lanzinger, Christina Maegraith, Siglinde Clementi, Ellinor Forster, and Christian Hagen (eds.), *Negotiations of Gender and Property through Legal Regimes (14th–19th Century): Stipulating, Litigating, Mediating* (Brill, 2021), pp. 311–44.

'Money and the Everyday', in Christine Desan (ed.), *A Cultural History of Money in the Age of Enlightenment* (Bloomsbury, 2019), pp. 95–120.

'Politics and Economics of Markets', in Roberto Scazzieri and Ivano Cardinale (eds.), *The Palgrave Handbook of Political Economy* (London, 2018), pp. 91–132.

'Self-Control and Savings: Adam Smith and the Creation of Modern Capital', in Simon Middleton and James Shaw (eds.), *Market Ethics and Practices, c.1300–1850* (Routledge, 2018), pp. 63–86.

'Self-Love and the Transformation of Obligation to Self-Control in Early Modern British Society', in Laura Kolb and George Oppitz-Trotman (eds.), *Early Modern Debts 1550–1700* (London, 2020), pp. 353–401.

'The Culture of Reconciliation: Community and the Settlement of Economic Disputes in Early Modern England', *Historical Journal* 39, no. 4 (1996), pp. 915–42.

The Economy of Obligation: The Culture of Credit and Social Relations in Early Modern England (London, 1998).

'The Emergence of the "Middle Sort" of People', in Keith Wrightson (ed.), *A Social History of England, c.1500–c.1750* (Cambridge, 2016), pp. 290–309.

'The Social Acceptance of Paper Credit as Currency in Eighteenth Century England: A Case Study of Glastonbury *c.*1720–1742', in Marcella Lorenzini, Cinzia Lorandini, D'Maris Coffman (eds.), *Financing in Europe: Evolution, Coexistence and Complementarity of Lending Practices from the Middle Ages to Modern Times* (London, 2018), pp. 133–59.

Munro, Neil, *The History of the Royal Bank of Scotland, 1727–1927* (Edinburgh, 1928).

Murphy, Anne L., *The Origins of English Financial Markets: Investment and Speculation before the South Sea Bubble* (Cambridge, 2012).

Murphy, Antoin E., *John Law: Economic Theorist and Policy-Maker* (Oxford, 1997).

Neal, Larry, *The Rise of Financial Capitalism: International Capital Markets in the Age of Reason* (Cambridge, 1993).

Nettels, Curtis P., *The Money Supply of the American Colonies before 1720* (Madison, 1934).

North, Douglass C. and Weingast, Barry R., 'Constitutions and Commitment: The Evolution of Institutions Governing Public Choice in Seventeenth-Century England', *The Journal of Economic History* 49, no. 4 (1989), pp. 803–32.

O'Brien, Patrick K., 'The Political Economy of British Taxation, 1660–1815', *The Economic History Review* 41, no. 1 (1988), pp. 1–32.

Parkin, Jon, *Science, Religion, and Natural Law: Richard Cumberland's De legibus naturae* (Woodbridge, 1999).

Paul, Helen J., *The South Sea Bubble: An Economic History of its Origins and Consequences* (London, 2011).

Paul, Tawny, *The Poverty of Disaster: Debt and Insecurity in Eighteenth-Century Britain* (Cambridge, 2019).

Phillipson, Nicholas, *Adam Smith: An Enlightened Life* (London, 2010).

Piketty, Thomas, *Capital in the Twenty-First Century* (Harvard, 2014).

Poovey, Mary, *A History of the Modern Fact: Problems of Knowledge in the Sciences of Wealth and Society* (Chicago, 1998).

Reinert, Sophus A., *Translating Empire: Emulation and the Origins of Political Economy* (Cambridge, MA, 2011).

Rogers, James Steven, *Early History of the Law of Bills and Notes* (Cambridge, 2009).

Rubini, Dennis, 'Politics and the Battle for the Banks, 1688–1697', *The English Historical Review* 85, no. 337 (1970), pp. 693–714.

Saville, Richard, *Bank of Scotland: A History, 1695–1995* (Edinburgh, 1996).

Schneewind, Jerome, *The Invention of Autonomy: A History of Modern Moral Philosophy* (Cambridge, 1998).

Schweitzer, Mary, *Custom and Contract: Household, Government, and the Economy in Colonial Pennsylvania* (New York, 1987).

Scott, W. R., *The Constitution and Finance of English, Scottish and Irish Joint-Stock Companies to 1720. Vols 1–3* (Cambridge, 1912).

Shepard, Alexandra, *Accounting for Oneself: Worth, Status, and the Social Order in Early Modern England* (Oxford, 2015).

Slack, Paul, *Poverty and Policy in Tudor and Stuart England* (London, 1985).

The Invention of Improvement: Information and Material Progress in Seventeenth-Century England (Oxford, 2015).

Smail, John, *The Origins of Middle-Class Culture: Halifax, Yorkshire, 1660–1780* (Ithaca, 1994).

Sombart, Werner, *Der moderne Kapitalismus (Historisch-systematische Darstellung des gesamteuropäischen Wirtschaftslebens von seinen Anfängen bis zur Gegenwart), vols 1–3*. (München, 1928).

Spellman, W. M., *The Latitudinarians and the Church of England, 1660–1700* (Athens, GA, 1993).

Spufford, Peter, 'From Antwerp and Amsterdam to London: The Decline of Financial Centres in Europe', *De Economist (Netherlands)* 154, no. 2 (2006), pp. 143–75.

Supple, Barry, *Commercial Crisis and Change in England, 1600–1642: A Study in the Instability of a Mercantile Economy* (Cambridge, 1959).

Tawney, R. H., *Religion and the Rise of Capitalism* (Harmondsworth, 1926).

Temin, Peter and Voth, Hans-Joachim, *Prometheus Shackled: Goldsmith Banks and England's Financial Revolution after 1700* (New York, 2012).

Tracy, James D., *A Financial Revolution in the Habsburg Netherlands: Renten and Renteniers in the County of Holland, 1515–1565* (Berkeley 1985).

Tuck, Richard *Philosophy and Government 1572–1651* (Cambridge, 1993).

Tully, James, *A Discourse on Property, John Locke and His Adversaries* (Cambridge, 1980).

Unwin, George, *Samuel Oldknow and the Arkwrights: The Industrial Revolution at Stockport and Marple*, 2nd ed, (Manchester, 1968).

Wakelam, Alexander, *Credit and Debt in Eighteenth Century England: An Economic History of Debtors' Prisons* (London, 2020).

Wallerstein, Immanuel, *World-Systems Analysis: An Introduction* (Durham, 2004).

Wedd, Imogen, 'Mortgages and the Kentish Yeoman in the Seventeenth Century', in Chris Briggs and C. J. Zuijderduijn (eds.), *Land and Credit: Mortgages in the Medieval and Early Modern European Countryside* (London, 2018), pp. 81–116.

Wennerlind, Carl, *Casualties of Credit: The English Financial Revolution, 1620–1720* (Cambridge, MA, 2011).

Whyman, Susan, *The Useful Knowledge of William Hutton: Culture and Industry in Eighteenth-Century Birmingham* (Oxford, 2018).

Williams, Eric, *Capitalism and Slavery* (London, 2022).

Wrightson, Keith, *English Society 1580–1680*, 2nd ed. (London, 1993).

'"Sorts of people" in Tudor and Stuart England', in Jonathan Barry and C. W. Brooks (eds.), *The Middling Sort of People: Culture, Society and Politics in England, 1550–1800* (London, 1994), pp. 28–51.

Wrigley, E. A., 'Urban Growth and Agricultural Change: England and the Continent in the Early Modern Period' in *People, Cities and Wealth* (Chichester, 1988), pp. 133–56.

Wrigley, E. A., Davies, R. S., Oeppen, J. E., and Schofield, R. S., *English Population History from Family Reconstitution 1580–1837* (Cambridge, 1997).

Yamamoto, Koji, *Taming Capitalism before its Triumph: Public Service, Distrust, and 'Projecting' in Early Modern England* (Oxford, 2018).

Yamey, B. S., 'The Historical Significance of Double-Entry Bookkeeping: Some Non-Sombartian Claims', *Accounting, Business & Financial History* 15, no. 1 (2005), pp. 77–88.

Zuijderduijn, C. J. and Briggs, Chris (eds.), *Land and Credit: Mortgages in the Medieval and Early Modern European Countryside* (London, 2018).

PhD Theses

Barker, Joseph, 'Geographical Variation in Patterns of Landholding and Agrarian Social Relations *c.* 1800' (PhD Thesis, Cambridge University, 2007).

Ben Or, Idit, 'Non-governmental Monies in Early Modern England: A Social, Political and Material Culture Analysis' (PhD Thesis, Hebrew University of Jerusalem, 2021).

Danna, Raffaele, 'The Spread of Hindu-Arabic Numerals in the European Tradition of Practical Arithmetic: A Socio-Economic Perspective (13th–16th Centuries)' (PhD Thesis, Cambridge University, 2020).

Digby, Ali, 'Political Economy, the Labour Theory of Value, & the Chartist Movement' (PhD Thesis, Cambridge University, 2017).

McCurdy, Hank, 'Social Incidence and Economic Significance of the Growth of Transferable Paper Instruments in Seventeenth Century England' (PhD Thesis, Cambridge University, 2007).

Index